EU ENLARGEMENT

THE CONSTITUTIONAL IMPACT AT EU AND NATIONAL LEVEL

ASSER INSTITUTE COLLOQUIUM ON EUROPEAN LAW
SESSION XXX – SEPTEMBER 2000

organized in co-operation with

The Constitutional and Legal Policy Institute (COLPI)
Budapest – Hungary

T.M.C. ASSER INSTITUUT
The Hague

EU ENLARGEMENT

The Constitutional Impact at EU and National Level

edited by

Alfred E. Kellermann
T.M.C. Asser Instituut, The Hague

Jaap W. de Zwaan
Erasmus Universiteit, Rotterdam

Jenö Czuczai
European Law Academy, Budapest

T•M•C•Asser Press
The Hague

Published by T.M.C.ASSER PRESS
P.O.Box 16163, 2500 BD The Hague, The Netherlands

Sold and distributed in North, Central and South America
by Kluwer Law International,
101, Philip Drive, Norwell MA 02061

In all other countries, sold and distributed
by Kluwer Law International, Distribution Centre,
P.O.Box 322, 3300 AH Dordrecht, The Netherlands

ISBN 90-6704-132-7

T.M.C. Asser Instituut - Institute for Private and Public International Law, International Commercial Arbitration and European Law
Institute Address: R.J. Schimmelpennincklaan 20-22, The Hague, The Netherlands; P.O. Box 30461, 2500 GL The Hague, The Netherlands; Tel.: (31-70)3420300; Fax: (31-70)3420359; URL: www.asser.nl
The T.M.C. Asser Institute was founded in 1965 by the Dutch universities which offer courses in international law in order to promote education and research in the fields of law in which the Institute specialises: private international law, public international law including the law of international organisations, international commercial arbitration and the law of the European Union. The Institute discharges this task by organising educational programmes, by the establishment and management of documentary compilations and by undertaking academic research, in some cases in cooperation with international organsations and academic institutions, as well as by the dissemination of information deriving therefrom and by the publication of monographs and series. The Institute organises *Asser College Europe*, a project in cooperation with East and Central European countries whereby research and educational projects are organised and implemented.

Constitutional and Legal Policy Institute - Budapest, Hungary
Institute Address: Nador utca 11, H-1051 Budapest, Hungary; Tel. (36-1)3273102; URL: www.osi.hu/colpi; e-mail: colpi@osi.hu
The Constitutional and Legal Policy Institute (COLPI) is the legal institute of the Open Society Institute network, closely affiliated with the Central European University in Budapest. It aims to support legal reform in all countries of Central and Eastern Europe, including all former Soviet republics and Mongolia. Its main activities are related to legal education, and the protection of human rights, rule of law, and democracy. Special attention is being paid to issues of criminal justice and the judiciary. COLPI's activities are not only aimed at research, but it undertakes, in particular, large operational support programmes in cooperation with local Soros foundations in the various countries.

FOREWORD

The subject of this Conference concerns the impact the enlargement of the European Union has on the constitutional provisions of both levels of European administration, the national and the European level.

This subject is the more attractive because the 'constitutional' impact of enlargement is an essential element in the context of the 'rule of law' as one of the general principles of the Union.[1] Here a relationship does exist with objectives such as a good and transparent system of governance, a democratic legislative process, an independent judiciary and an adequate system of legal protection.

As to the national level, the implications membership of the Union has for the constitutional texts of the (candidate) member States have a connection with the fundamental characteristics of Community law such as priority of European law (over national law), direct applicability and direct effect. These principles reflect the interest in ensuring that European law, once applied in the national context by the public authorities or the judiciary, is made fully effective, for the benefit not only of the public authorities but also of the ordinary citizen.

As to the European level, since the Asser Conference was held in December 2000 an agreement has been reached about the terms of the Treaty of Nice. The final outcome of this so-called Intergovernmental Conference 2000, which aimed at providing for an adequate preparation of the working of the institutions in the perspective of the enlargement of the European Union, has been commented upon as a modest step in the process of European Integration.

The IGC 2000 has also called for a new Intergovernmental Conference to be held in the year 2004. As subjects to be discussed in that conference have been selected:[2]

- the establishment and monitoring of a more precise delimitation of competences between the European Union and the member States, reflecting the principle of subsidiarity;
- the status of the Charter of Fundamental Rights of the European Union proclaimed in Nice, in accordance with the conclusions of the European Council in Cologne;
- a simplification of the Treaties with a view to making them clearer and better understood without changing their meaning;
- the role of national parliaments in the European architecture.

---

[1] Art. 6(1) EU.

[2] See the Declaration on the Future of the Union to be included in the Final Act of the Conference.

Whereas the Asser Conference focused on both levels of government, the national and the Union level, the IGC 2004 will mainly deal with the European level of government.

During our Conference the proposal was made that the Conference should be kept intact as a platform enabling experts from the present and the candidate States to discuss themes of a common interest. The IGC 2000 also has stressed the interest of a public debate to be held between all interested circles: politics, public authorities, academic world and interest groups, about the fundamental themes to be debated in the year 2004.

These new developments in the context of the IGC 2000 thus represent an extra impetus to maintain our Conference as a permanent network of expertise.

JAAP W. DE ZWAAN
Chairman of the Conference

ACKNOWLEDGEMENTS

The T.M.C. Asser Instituut gratefully acknowledges the generous support it received in the organization and/or financing of the Conference 'The Constitutional Impact of Enlargement at EU and National level', held 20-24 September 2000 in The Hague and the publication of its proceedings, from the following Institutions and Organizations:

The Constitutional Legal Policy Institute (COLPI), Budapest

The European Commission, Brussels

The European Parliament, Strasbourg / Brussels

The Ministry of Foreign Affairs of The Netherlands, The Hague

The Ministry of Justice of The Netherlands, The Hague

The Ministry of Economic Affairs of The Netherlands, The Hague

The Ministry of the Interior and Kingdom Relations of the Netherlands,
The Hague

The Municipality of The Hague

Central Bank of the Netherlands, Amsterdam

Berenschot International Solutions, Utrecht

Clifford Chance, Amsterdam / London

VSB Fonds, The Hague

Royal Netherlands Academy of Arts and Sciences (KNAW), Amsterdam

the Members of the Editorial Board, who edited the contents with
scholarly expertise and dedication

and

the former colleagues of the T.M.C. Asser Instituut
(Mieke Eijdenberg, Tony Wade)
and Asser Press (Marjolijn Bastiaans) for the practical support
and technical realization of this book.

SUMMARY TABLE OF CONTENTS

SESSION II
The National Level: Impact on Constitutions and Courts of EU Member States

SESSION III
National Level : Impact on the Constitutions and Courts of the Candidate Countries

Annexes

DETAILED TABLE OF CONTENTS

SESSION III
National Level : Impact on the Constitutions and Courts of the Candidate Countries

The Mediterranean Countries Malta, Cyprus and Turkey

SESSION IV
IGC and Future Perspectives for the European Architecture

FINAL SESSION
Practical Implementation of the Challenges of Accession

ABBREVIATIONS

AJCL	American Journal of Comparative Law
AJIL	American Journal of International Law
All ER	All England Law Reports
AP	Accession Parnership
BGBl.	Bundesgesetzblatt
Bull EC	Bulletin of the European Commission
BverfG	Bundesverfassungsgericht
CEECs	Central and Eastern European Countries
CFDT	Confédération Française Démocratique du Travail
CFI	Court of First Instance
CFSP	Common Foreign and Security Policy
Charter	Charter of Fundamental Rights
CIS	Commonwealth of Independent States
CLJ	Cambridge Law Journal
CLR	Columbia Law Journal
CMLR	Common Market Law Reports
CMLRev.	Common Market Law Review
COLPI	Constitutional Legal Policy Institute
COM	Commission Document
COSAC	Conference of European Affairs Committees in the National Parliaments of the member States
CSCE	Conference on Security and Cooperation in Europe
Dalloz Jur.	Dalloz Jurisprudence
DR	Decisions and Reports
EA	Europe Agreement
EAEC	European Atomic Energy Community
EAGGF	European Agricultural Guidance and Guaranty Fund
EC	European Community
ECA	European Communities Act
ECB	European Central Bank
ECEC	Estonian Constitutional Expert Commission
ECHR	European Convention on Human Rights
ECtHR	European Court of Human Rights
ECJ	European Court of Justice
ECR	European Court Reports
ECSC	European Coal and Steel Community
ECSC	European Conference on Security Cooperation
ECT	European Community Treaty (also TEU)
EEA Agreement	European Economic Area Agreement
EEC	European Economic Community
EFTA	European Free Trade Association
EJIL	European Journal of International Law
ELRev.	European Law Review
EMS	European Monetary System
EMU	European Monetary Union
EP	European Parliament
ERDF	European Regional Development Fund
ERM	Exchange Rate Mechanism

ESCB	European System of Central Banks
ESCU	European Conference on Security Cooperation
ESF	European Social Fund
EU	European Union
EUI	European University Institute, Florence
Euratom	European Atomic Energy Community
Eur. Court HR	European Court of Human Rights
Europol	European Police Cooperation
FIDE	Fédération Internationale pour le Droit Européen
FIFG	Financial Instrument for Fisheries Guidance
FRG	Federal Republic of Germany
GATT	General Agreement on Tariffs and Trade
GDR	German Democratic Republic
ICAO	International Civil Aviation Organization
ICJ	International Court of Justice
ICLQ	International Comparative Law Quaterly
IG	Instrument of Government
IGC	Intergovernmental Conference
IJEL	Irish Journal of European Law
ILO	International Labour Organization
ILM	International Legal Materials
ILRM	Irish Law Reports Monthtly
IR	International Relations
JCMS	Journal of Common Market Studies
LGDJ	Librairie Générale de Droit et de Jurisprudence
LQR	Law Quaterly Review
MEP	Member of the European Parliament
MP	Members of Parliament
NATO	North Atlantic Treaty Organization
NGO	Non-Governmental Organization
NIS	Newly Independent States
NPAA	National Programmes for the Adoption of the Acquis
NQHR	Netherlands Quaterly of Human Rights
nyr	not yet reported
OGH	Oberster Gerichtshof
OJ	Official Journal of the European Community
ONP Directive	Open Network Provision Directive
OSCE	Organisation de la Sécurité et de la Coopération en Europe
PCA	Partnership and Cooperation Agreements
QMV	Qualified Majority Voting
TEC	Treaty of the European Community
TEU	Treaty on European Union
TRNC	Turkish Republic of Northern Cyprus
VAT	Value Added Tax
VfGH	Verfassungsgerichtshof
VwGH	Verwaltungsgerichtshof
WIPO	World Intellectual Property Organisation
Yale L.J.	Yale Law Journal
YEL	Yearbook of European Law
ZaöRV	Zeitschrift für ausländisches öffentliches Recht und Völkerrecht

REPORT ON THE CONFERENCE

Alfred E. Kellermann*

CONTENTS

OPENING SPEECH BY L.W. GORMLEY[1]

It is with great pleasure that I welcome participants to the 30th session of the Asser Institute Colloquium on European Law, once again in this magnificent setting at Scheveningen: The Hague on the Sea.

The subject of our deliberations: institutional and constitutional aspects of enlargement raises a number of key issues for the future direction of the European Union itself, as well as major questions for the constitutional order of the candidate countries; it is that second aspect which is dealt with here. The Copenhagen criteria[2] rightly place political and legal aspects at the head of the requirements which the candidate countries must meet. These aspects: stability of institutions guaranteeing democracy, the rule of law, human rights and respect for and protection of minorities, are now also clearly anchored in the Treaty on European Union, albeit in broader terms.[3]

In such broader terms they serve as touchstones not merely for candidate countries but also for conduct of the existing member States. In the light of the

* General Secretary T.M.C. Asser Instituut, The Hague; Senior Lecturer and Consultant in the Law of the European Union.

[1] Barrister; Professor of European Law & Jean Monnet Professor, Rijksuniversiteit Groningen. (Jean Monnet Centre of Excellence); Chairman of the T.M.C. Asser Institute Committee for European Law.

[2] Bull. EC 6-1993 point I.13.

[3] Art. 6(1) TEU.

A.E. Kellermann et al. (Eds.), EU Enlargement: The Constitutional Impact at EU and National Level

not infrequently significant success of extremist parties in some of the present member States, the respect for and protection of minorities is of particular importance in assessing conformity with the broad west-European consensus as to tolerance in modern society. A society which is at ease with itself and its component parts is more likely to be a tolerant society. Yet in many areas of Europe (both within the European Union and outside) central problems arise from the perception of uncertainty as to identity, and in many regions the much-voiced anguish caused by the apparent lack of a clear feeling of belonging. Globalisation, and even regionalisation at anything more than the neighbourhood level, have awakened these emotions: the reaction to a feeling of no longer being in control of one's destiny is to seek someone else to blame. In such conditions, intolerance breeds, and the phenomenon of the enemy within is created to shoulder the blame along with the alleged external enemy.

Enlargement of the European Union may well serve to provide a framework within which the feeling of belonging and the sense of identity achieve new dimensions, for the existing member States and their citizens on the one hand, and for the candidate countries and their citizens on the other. That will only come about, however, with a sea-change in the appreciation of the Union in the eyes of its citizens. Central to that sea-change will be a shift in legislative power from the Council to the European Parliament, the seeds of which have already been sown in the systematic improvement of Parliament's voice at every substantive amendment of the Community and Union Treaties. In other words, the peoples of the Union must feel that it has something more to offer them than simply the creation of yet another layer of the political class: unrepresentative, uncontrollable and concerned with its self-perpetuation and its own importance. What is perceived to be lacking are visions and strategies to ensure the well-being of the Union's citizens and its other residents, and inclusive measures designed to bring an end to social, economic and political exclusion. Enlargement may in fact prove to be the catalyst for a complete reanalysis of the role of the member States in the decision-making process, as the present institutional structure becomes ever more unwieldy and inappropriate. In Union-level decision-making circles, however, there is no clear policy consensus: achieving the balance between the cultures of North and South, East and West, and between the interests of the larger member States and those of the smaller member States, is proving an elusive target. Legal structures not only shape and give form to political concepts, they may also serve as models for architectural inspiration. The need for stable institutions guaranteeing democracy is in the first instance addressed to the candidate countries, but it is a need which should not be forgotten at the Union level itself. If the present structure of the Union is an interim phase in its development, it will have to be seen to be democratic and to command the confidence of its citizens before the peoples of candidate countries can really be expected to exchange their present situation for membership of a Union committed to further integration. The need for change and adaptation is therefore not confined to the national level: it indubitably forms the greatest challenge for the political class at the level of the Union itself.

Within the Union the rule of law itself is a principle which can be used to develop confidence in the minds of citizens in the future European architecture. That itself will demand another sea-change a complete revision of the attitude of the political class to law and legal institutions. Many politicians, particularly those in regional or local assembles, seem to have difficulty in accepting the *acquis communautaire*: concepts such as the uniformity of application of Community legislation, the duty to cooperate, and the obligation to conform to a set of rules once those have been agreed are not infrequently under attack. Thus calls for regional authorities not to be bound by Community measures when they have not participated in the adoption of those measures ignore the essential place of the duties set out in Article 10 EC in ensuring the effectiveness of Community law and the ability of those upon whom it confers rights to benefit therefrom.[4] The low value which some politicians and administrations in the present member States place on compliance with legal instruments (evidenced by the constant stream of infringement proceedings and the increasing recourse to national courts by individuals seeking to establish or use their rights or to obtain damages for loss suffered) does not send a convincing message about respect for the rule of law to politicians in the candidate countries.

Another aspect central to respect for the rule of law is confidence in the proper functioning of the judiciary, particularly in its willingness to take on politicians and the administration. Even in some member States the awareness of the impact of Community law is still developing surprisingly slowly, and there is still a clear need not merely for information multiplication, but for steps to facilitate the appreciation of Community law as an integral and dynamic element within each member State's legal order. Sometimes Community law is perceived as being in this world but not of it, and in certain judicial circles in some member States there is still an astonishing degree of ignorance about its effects. In relation to the candidate countries there may well be problems in effecting the transformation from the judicial culture of the past in order to ensure that judges take full account of the requirements of the Community legal order. Given that national judiciaries in the member States have not infrequently had major problems copping with the impact of Community law, it will be scarcely surprising if there are not still a few hitches in the early years following enlargement. That said, though, the process of training the judiciary and the civil service in the candidate countries is

---

[4] No matter how appealing such sentiments are to regional politicians seeking to increase their influence, they remain wholly alien to the fundamental concepts of the Community as developed in the case-law of the Court of Justice. Even the FIDE Conference at Helsinki was unfortunately not immune from people seeking to promote such sentiments. While the regional sensitivities on which such sentiments are based may be politically understandable, they would undoubtedly lead the Community ship straight onto the rocks.

proceeding apace, and the new entrants in the next enlargements will in fact be the best-prepared of any new entrants to the Community or the Union.

To a certain extent enlargement issues are often seen as mechanical: the *acquis communautaire* must be taken on board; what can be negotiated is flexibility in terms of transitional periods, assistance in restructuring to meet Community requirements, and little more. The essential changes in the national systems of the candidate countries are discussed in the various papers presented at this conference, in conjunction with experiences of member States which have acceded on earlier enlargements. Yet, as I have tried to highlight, enlargement will bring with it a whole series of challenges, and it is in the discussion of these challenges, as well as in the mastery of more technical detail, that the mutual understanding and exchange of experiences which this conference promotes is at its most useful.

Parallel to the challenges of enlargement, the whole architecture of the Union will have to be rethought. The absence of political consensus about the future direction of the Union means that the prediction that those entering the edifice which the Union represents may well have to wear hard hats for some time to come[5] shows no sign of becoming inaccurate. It is to be hoped that the papers presented here will contribute in a stimulating manner to the debate, and that they may assist the builders in their task, as well as encourage improvement in architectural design.

I. REASONS TO HOLD THE CONFERENCE

The Conference on 'The Constitutional Impact of Enlargement at EU and National Level', held in The Hague on 20-23 September 2000 was the 30th session of the Colloquium on European Law of the T.M.C. Asser Institute, an interuniversity institute founded in 1965 by eight law faculties of the Dutch universities in the field of public international law, private international law, European law and commercial arbitration.

The Asser conferences are characterized by the quality of the legal debates between lawyers and academics that focus on both theoretical and practical viewpoints. These academic debates stimulate brainstorming, as everybody is free to present his own ideas and give his own personal viewpoint.

More than threehundred participants (eighty from the candidate countries) attended this successful conference. The rapporteurs and speakers were representatives from the European institutions (European Commission, European Parliament, European Court of Justice) and representatives of the Governments of the Netherlands and some candidate countries and many representatives of national

[5] Gormley in O'Keeffe & Twomey (ed.), *Legal Issues of the Amsterdam Treaty* (Oxford, 1999) p. 57 at p. 70.

civil, administrative and constitutional courts. Finally, professors and research fellows from universities in Europe, Canada and the United States attended the conference, together with nearly all the law faculties of the Dutch universities.

The first reason to hold a conference on the impact of Enlargement at National Level, was that the EU candidate countries may learn from the experiences and problems which the EU member States have encountered in adapting their constitution or constitutional principles to the legal obligations taken under the EC Treaty since 1958. The candidate countries are obliged in the process of accession (Europe agreements, Agenda 2000) to harmonize and adapt their national legislation and therefore also, as far as necessary, their national constitutions and constitutional practice.

In organizing a conference to analyze the constitutional impact of enlargement at national level there were a number of factors to consider. For example, the accession criteria as formulated by the European Council of Copenhagen in June 1993.

> 'Membership requires that the candidate country has achieved stability of institutions guaranteeing democracy, the rule of law, fundamental rights and respect for and protection of minorities.'

These topics are generally in most states regulated by and protected by the national constitution or national constitutional laws. Therefore, we have to analyze the relevant national constitutional provisions guaranteeing democracy, the rule of law, human rights and protection of minorities. Analyzing the national provisions is, however, not enough. It is also necessary to assess how the democracy works in practice and to evaluate constitutional practice: to what extent are the various rights and freedoms exercised?

Another important reason is that, in parallel with the accession negotiations, one should also keep in mind the constitutional requirements to be met before new Members can join the EU. *In the first place* the accession treaties will need to be ratified by the existing and future member States according to their constitutional requirements. In order to ratify the accession treaties and to accord direct effect and supremacy to EC law, it may be necessary in some candidate countries to adapt their national constitutions and incorporate provisions concerning the transfer of sovereign or state powers to an international organization such as the EU.

In the second place a condition for accession is that the national constitutions of the candidate countries have to comply with the *acquis communautaire* not only in theory but also in practice. The European Court of Justice may, for example, have propounded the theory of supremacy of Community law and repeatedly emphasized its requirements, but its practical application in the EU member States is, however, ultimately dependent on the internal acceptance by the national courts of the member States. A different attitude has further been developed by the national courts between the application of primary or secondary community law. For non-member States, like the candidate countries, it is clear that the legal effect of these community constitutional principles always depend on the nature and content of their national constitutional provisions and practice and the way it is interpreted by the national judiciary and influenced by national traditions.

The second reason to hold this Conference was to contribute to the legal debate on the drawing up of a Draft Charter of Fundamental Rights of the European Union. This Charter will raise many legal questions concerning its relationship to and impact on other international charters and national constitutions and its impact on Enlargement.

The last but certainly not the least reason to hold this conference was to discuss the Institutional Reform of the EU, a necessity in view of enlargement (IGC) as well as the other 'Constitutional Issues' on the Agenda of the European Council to be held in December 2000 in Nice.

II. INTERNATIONAL LAW IN THE NETHERLANDS

International law merits special attention in the Netherlands. One example of this special notice is the above-mentioned foundation of an interuniversity institute for international law such as the T.M.C. Asser Institute. Since the fall of the Berlin Wall, the Asser College Europe programme, with the financial support of the Netherlands Ministry of Foreign Affairs, has offered postgraduate courses in International Trade and Business Law for postgraduate lawyers from Central and Eastern Europe in The Hague, 'the legal capital of the world' as it has been termed by Boutros Gali.

One of the Copenhagen criteria for accession is, inter alia,. respect for the rule of law. The rule of law is not only European law. Therefore, it is considered that for accession it is also necessary to improve the knowledge of the lawyers, civil servants and judges of the candidate countries in other fields such as public international law, private international law and international trade law as well as public and private national law. Thanks to these post-graduate training programmes many lawyers of Central and Eastern Europe have deepened their knowledge of EU law, international trade law, business law, international arbitration and private international law. Since 1994 more than threehundred scholarships have been awarded within the framework of Asser College Europe to young talented individuals, some of whom are currently engaged in accession negotiations.

As a preparation for accession we are currently offering courses in The Hague as well as in the candidate countries for civil servants, lawyers, judges, (staff) members of parliament (present at this conference were Slovenian, Latvian and Czech members) from many candidate countries in the framework of several Phare projects.

The Netherlands Ministry of Justice is emphasizing the importance of cooperation with the candidate countries and is therefore providing technical assistance in the various fields of law to the countries of Central and Eastern Europe, which gave rise to the realisation of a Phare Project on 'The Reinforcement of the Rule of Law' within the framework of the European Union.

It is worth mentioning that in her Throne Speech on Tuesday 19 September 2000 for the Opening of the Plenary Session of the Dutch Parliament, the Queen of the Netherlands, Beatrix referred implicitly to some of the topics of this conference where Her Majesty said:

> 'Our Constitution has built-in and permanent values. It is also a dynamic document where essential changes in society find their place. The Government is committed that a number of issues are to be incorporated into the Constitution, especially the corrective referendum.
> Europe is no longer foreign territory. Europe is our future where we will find our future opportunities. In the dynamic process of European cooperation far-reaching steps have been made.
> The enlargement with Central and Eastern European countries is a historic task.
> It offers economic opportunities for the candidate-states and the current member States and also [firmly] anchors democracy and stability on our own continent. The thorough preparation for its membership requires hard work for the new countries. The Netherlands supports them in this effort.'

The study of international law always merits special notice in the Netherlands, the country of Hugo Grotius. [6] The evolution of the thinking of Grotius is well known. In *Mare Liberum* he rejects the idea that any part of the sea can be exclusive property and therefore fishing remains free and open to all. This way of thinking may have inspired the principle of equal access by all Community fishermen to the territorial waters and fishing zones of all member States which was a major obstacle on the road to enlargement in 1973. Unlike the original member States the United Kingdom had an old tradition of fishing zones reserved for coastal fishermen.

Other examples of the attention drawn to international law in the Netherlands are Article 90 of the Dutch Constitution: 'The Government promotes the development of the international legal order' and the following passages of the Speech given on behalf of the Minister of the Interior and Kingdom Relations at the Conference on 21 September 2000 (See infra, Article Jit Peters for the full text):

---

[6] See, International Law and The Grotian Heritage, A commemorative colloquium held at The Hague on 8 April 1983 on the fourth centenary of the birth of Hugo Grotius, edited and published by the T.M.C. Asser Instituut, 1985. International Law in the Netherlands, edited by H.F. van Panhuys, et. al., Three Volumes, published by T.M.C. Asser Instituut , Sijthoff & Noordhoff – Oceana , 1978 and following years.

'The Dutch constitution
As far back as the early 1950s, a debate took place in the Netherlands on the question of whether to incorporate provisions in the Constitution that would make it possible to give direct effect to rules of international law and judgments handed down by international courts. The point at issue was not really whether direct effect should be possible or indeed permissible in the existing system, but whether the Constitution should say so in so many words.
...
The Dutch Constitution can therefore prohibit judicial review of the constitutionality of Acts of Parliament or treaties (which have been ratified by the legislature either explicitly or tacitly) on the one hand and on the other not only permit but even order that Acts of Parliament and indeed the Constitution itself be reviewed in the light of international law and if necessary be declared inapplicable.'

III. MAIN CONFERENCE QUESTIONS AS DISCUSSED IN THE OFFICIAL SPEECHES

The speakers, rapporteurs, panel members and participants were invited to discuss and answer the main Conference questions in their written papers and contributions to the debate at the conference. The answers may be found in the respective final contributions of the authors to this book.

In the following I have selected some passages of only the official speeches, as far as they could be considered as dealing with the main Conference questions. The selected passages are preceded by the relevant questions. The selected speeches are from M. Gunter Verheugen, the EU Commissioner for Enlargement, M. Richard Corbett, MEP, M. A.H. Korthals, the Dutch Minister of Justice, M. Dick Benschop, the Dutch State Secretary for Foreign Affairs and Jit Peters on behalf of the Dutch Minister of the Interior and Kingdom Relations.

QUESTIONS CONCERNING EU LEVEL

EU Constitutional Order/IGC

1. *What are your suggestions for further development of the Constitutional Order of the Union in the perspective of enlargement, for example: Will the Pillar structure be maintained (intergovernmental cooperation) with the introduction of more or less Community working methods, or is it feasible to further improve the 'constitutional character' of the EU (communautarization)?*
2. *What are your suggestions for EU institutional reform? How to adapt the institutions to make a success of enlargement?*

• Gunter Verheugen in his Dinner Speech

'My view is that the IGC agenda is necessary and sufficient for enlargement. Three of the core IGC items may be known, somewhat misleadingly, as the "Amsterdam leftovers", but they are by no means minor matters. They are politically sensitive issues, which were left over, precisely because they were so difficult to handle.

What we are talking about here is whether in a EU of twenty-eight or more members, each member State should continue to have one Commissioner, with two Commissioners reserved for each of the larger member States. Personally, in the interest of efficiency I would opt for a smaller Commission, which can retain its dynamism when this situation arises, but on this as well as on all IGC matters the decision of course rests with the member States.

Another question is whether the present system of voting in the Council, which is deliberately tilted against bigger countries, can remain as it is in a future Union dominated by small or medium-sized members? My view is that the current imbalance should not be left to deteriorate any further. Adjustments should therefore be made so a country's voting power in the Council will more closely correspond to the size of its population.

Finally, there is the question whether, with an additional thirteen or more potential vetoes in the Council, we can afford to continue having unanimity in important areas of EU decision-making? I am an advocate of a generous extension of qualified majority voting because otherwise the risk of a stalemate in EU affairs will be too great. Not because I believe that the new member States will be less integration-friendly than the existing ones, but because statistically the increase in numbers will inevitably make consensus much harder to achieve.

The increase in numbers also poses the question whether the existing Treaty arrangements for closer co-operation between a limited number of member States should be strengthened. I would be in favour of making closer co-operation more flexible, as long as three conditions are met: closer co-operation must stay within the institutional framework of the Treaties, it must not go against existing Community policies, and participation must be open to all member States able and willing to join. If these conditions are met, closer co-operation will not weaken the EU. It will promote further integration, by allowing some pioneer member State to make the first steps ahead in new areas, whilst others can join later, at their own pace. (...)

If a new IGC were to be launched, it should not be a condition for enlargement. There is a big difference between the present and a possible new IGC: the Amsterdam leftovers and the rest of the Nice agenda concern issues intrinsically linked to the efficient functioning of the EU after enlargement. The post-Nice agenda is different: the wider institutional debate is legitimate in its own right, and the applicant countries should have the opportunity to participate and express their views.'

- Richard Corbett in his Dinner Speech

'I shall mention the IGC issues only briefly, as they have been covered by Commissioner Verheugen. First, the size of the Commission. At this stage, two alternatives are on the table: one Commissioner per member State or a fixed figure. The first alternative has the advantage that every member State can feel that it is present in the Commission (although Commissioners do not have the task of representing their own country, they do bring a knowledge of that country with them) but the disadvantage is the Commission appearing intergovernmental and remaining somewhat oversized. The second alternative is opposed by those who fear that they would not have a representative in the Commission – although it would inevitably be tied to an equitable rotation system. Indeed, Commissioner Barnier said that it is not a question about whether every country should have a Commissioner: the only issue is whether they should all have one at the same time!

Which ever solution is chosen, the President of the Commission must have a stronger role. In this regard, it is essential to put in the treaty the right, secured by President Prodi in practice, for the President to be able to dismiss individual Commissioners – a power sadly lacking in the last Commission.

Regarding the weighting of the votes in the Council and the importance of extending qualified majority voting, I have little to add to what Commissioner Verheugen said. Suffice to say that I think it essential that QMV be extended to appointments as well: imagine what would happen if unanimity is still required to appoint the president of the central bank, but there is gridlock while the euro falls still further on international exchanges!'

- Dick Benschop in his Opening Speech

'So what will be the "constitutional impact of enlargement at EU level"? What constitutions – including unwritten ones – have in common is that they contain fundamental rules for the actions of the state; the government has to observe certain formal requirements and procedures. Constitutions determine the powers of the legislature, the executive and the judiciary. They determine the relationships between the central, local and regional authorities. Last but not least, constitutions enshrine fundamental rights: classical human rights, the rights of citizenship, and often social and economic rights as well.

Given this definition, it seems to me irrefutable that the European Union possesses a constitutional order.

I scarcely need to summarise the features of the EC and EU Treaties to remind you of how much they resemble a European constitution. Nonetheless, certain elements are absent or poorly developed. Fundamental rights, in particular, occupy as yet a humble place in the Treaties. Nor is their cohesiveness all it could be. Some have even spoken of "a Europe of bits and pieces".

It is therefore imperative, as I have said, for us to reach agreement in the IGC about vigorous reforms of the institutions. This is essential in the short term. In the longer term we shall have to consider further measures. For the Netherlands, the most important criteria are conserving, and where possible improving, the effectiveness, legitimacy and unity of the Union.'

EU Charter of Fundamental Rights

3. *What is your opinion on the drafting of a Charter of Fundamental Rights of the European Union (Annex IV of the Presidency Conclusions of 3-4 June 1999 Cologne)? What will be the legal effect, and impact, for the national constitutions? What will be the relationship with the European Convention for the Protection of Human Rights, European Social Charter and the Community Charter of the Fundamental Rights of Workers?*

- Gunter Verheugen in his Dinner Speech

'It looks more and more certain, however, that the debate on the future of Europe will not be limited to the Nice agenda. In fact, it has already been broadened to cover the Charter of Fundamental Human Rights. It is expected that a draft Charter will be adopted by the Convention in September with a view to its submission to the European Council at Biarritz in October. I cannot but stress how important it will be to have the Draft Charter endorsed by all the member States. It should enhance the legitimacy of the Union and should bring it closer to its citizens for whom fundamental rights matter a great deal.

In addition to the Charter, the institutional debate looks increasingly likely to focus in the future on topics such as the re-organisation of the Treaties, the division of responsibilities between the Commission and the member States or even a European Constitution or the final destination of the European project.

These are fundamental questions on the future of Europe, which seem to fall outside the scope of the current IGC. In a joint Article in today's FAZ, Chancellor Schröder and PM Giulano Amato called for a new IGC to deal with these issues, whose launching should be decided already at Nice (...)'.

- A.H. Korthals in his Dinner Speech

'The most politically advanced expression of concern for the Rule of Law is the draft Charter on fundamental rights of the European Union, which is unfortunately faced with resolving a number of drawbacks.

Firstly, I think that the concurrence of this Charter and the European Convention for the Protection of Human Rights and Fundamental Freedoms of the Council of Europe can pose an obstacle: for citizens, for the member States and, last but not least, for the administration of justice. The long term practical and political complications cannot be underestimated.

Secondly, I anticipate that granting social rights at European level will have an unintentional impact on national legislation. This may give rise to social, financial and legal consequences that will place the equilibrium of rights and duties under pressure.

Thirdly, I refer to the complex relationship between the national courts and legislation. The interaction between European and national areas of law will also increase as the duties of the European Court of Justice grow'.

- Dick Benschop in his Opening Speech

'Simultaneously with the IGC, work is under way on a Charter of Fundamental Rights. At Nice a draft version should be ready. The unique character of this project is clear from the composition of the "Convention" working on the draft. The Netherlands wants the Charter to be broad in scope – that is to say, to constitute a complete and modern definition of fundamental rights. This formulation must reflect the texts of existing international instruments, such as the European Convention for the Protection of Human Rights and Fundamental Freedoms – the ECHR – in order to rule out, if at all possible, differences in interpretation. The Netherlands also favours the accession of the European Community and – if possible – the European Union, to the ECHR.

Once the text has been agreed, we must decide on the Charter's place within the corpus of European law. There is no point in having an eloquent text without any binding force. Of course, this is easier said than done. Many problems will be raised and discussed at this conference. I hope that solutions will also be forthcoming, so that this great political aspiration may come to fruition.

In the next few years, we must tackle the incorporation of the Charter of Fundamental Rights into European law. The revision of the Treaties – a topic on which the European University Institute in Florence has already done some hard thinking – is another important theme that will have to be addressed in the near future. In this context, a debate about the relationship between the powers of the Union and those of the member States will be unavoidable'.

QUESTIONS CONCERNING NATIONAL LEVEL

National constitutions candidate countries

1. *Would your constitution require amendment for the ratification of the EU Treaty, EC Treaty, Euratom Treaty? If yes, please address the procedures concerning amendment.*
2. *If your constitution has to be amended for accession to the EU, what practical problems can be envisaged? Which procedures for amendment are to be followed?*

National constitutions candidate countries and EU member States

3. *Which specific national constitutional provisions are in your opinion contrary to and contradicting the acquis?*

• Gunter Verheugen in his Dinner Speech
'In parallel to the accession negotiations, one should also keep in mind the constitutional requirements to be met before new Members can join the EU.

As you know the constitutional implications of enlargement are manifold. At the national level, the accession treaties will need to be ratified by the existing and future member States according to their own constitutional requirements. As the contributions to this Conference demonstrate there is also another side of the coin that is often forgotten: any constitutional changes or other constitutional implications in the candidate countries themselves which will be necessary to meet the obligations of EU membership. These issues are indeed very important; the earlier we know exactly what will be needed, the more time will be gained later when the applicants are about to cross the threshold of membership.'

Role of national courts

4. *Do the courts in your country accept the principle of direct effect and supremacy of international law obligations, such as Community law, and do the courts accept a different attitude for primary or secondary community law and on which principles is their reasoning based (Community law, constitutional law or international law)?*
5. *Do the courts in your country recognize a rule of interpretation, whereby national law must be interpreted in conformity with international obligations (principle of indirect effect)?*
6. *Could you mention and comment on some interesting cases of your Supreme Court and/or Constitutional Court dealing with such problems?*
7. *If a Community measure is inconsistent with prior international commitments of your State, do your national courts give priority to the prior international* commitments?

• Jit Peters on behalf of the Dutch Minister of the Interior and Kingdom Relations in his Speech
'Since the middle of the nineteenth century, the Dutch legal system has allowed for rules and case law developed under international law to have direct effect in the Netherlands. Under the Mannheim Convention, the Central Commission for the Navigation of the Rhine enjoyed both regulatory and quasi-judicial powers. The Act of 18 June 1869 explicitly stated that Dutch judicial bodies should take account of decisions by the Rhine Navigation Commission in their own judgments. Rules laid down by the Commission therefore had immediate effect in

Dutch law. In short, it was possible even under the 19th-century Constitution for law from an international source to take direct effect, but the legislature still felt it necessary explicitly to incorporate this piece of international law into the Dutch system. Direct effect was apparently not a matter of course.

It was in fact the prospect that internationalisation and "supranationalisation" would take off in a big way that caused those responsible for drafting the new Dutch Constitution to state unambiguously in Article 92 that legislative, executive and judicial powers could be conferred on international institutions by treaty and in Article 93 that provisions of law from supranational sources would have direct effect provided they were "binding on all persons by virtue of their contents". In other words, no further action by the national legislative authorities was required.

The Netherlands went still further, by providing in Article 94 that statutory regulations in force within the Kingdom, regardless of whether they had been introduced before or after the creation of a supranational authority, would be inapplicable if they were incompatible with provisions of treaties that were binding on all or with resolutions by international institutions. The reasoning behind this was that once the Netherlands had given an undertaking at international level, it would not take it back unilaterally by subsequently introducing incompatible domestic legislation. This meant that the landmark decision by the European Court of Justice in the *Van Gend en Loos* case, establishing the supremacy of European law over the national law of the member States, did not hit the Netherlands like a bolt from the blue.'

IV. SUMMARY REPORT OF INTERVENTIONS AND OBSERVATIONS MADE DURING THE CONFERENCE SESSIONS

The following interventions, observations and remarks made during the respective Conference sessions have summarized and reported in this Paragraph rather than being included in a final conference paper.

Session I

Walter Van Gerven[7] addresses three points which were raised in Professor Weiler's speech:

a. Judicial architecture
b. Legitimacy and the need to formalise the constitution
c. Rules for Code of Conduct

[7] Walter van Gerven, former Advocate-General at the European Court of Justice and a former member of the Committee of Independent Experts

Ad a. Specialisation of judges and setting up of a Constitutional Court
The speaker emphazised the advantages of having specialised chambers in the ECJ (see also his contribution on the 'Role and Structure of the European Judiciary' at the 1995 Conference of the Asser Institute; also in ELR, 1996, p. 211). Such chambers would handle issues in certain complex areas of Community law, such as social security, taxation, conflict of laws. (...) One of the larger chambers could specialize in constitutional matters. That is a better solution in the speaker's view than to set up a special constitutional court for the Community. To assist such specialized chambers it would be useful to set up, within the Court's research department, specialized units as well.

The speaker also emphazised the need to maintain the function of Advocate-General at the ECJ. Their opinions are indeed an important factor to enhance the transparency of the Court's case law. Once the judgment is rendered in a case the AG's opinion fulfills the same role as a concurring opinion when it is followed, and as a dissenting opinion when it is not followed.

Ad b. EU Constitution
Whether the EU should have a written constitution depends on which part of the constitution we are talking of: basic rights, establishment and organisation of institutions and the institutional balance between them, or which governmental form the Community or Union should take.

As for the first, there should be a written catalogue of basic rights including the economic and social rights which are characteristic for an economically integrated Community.

These rules must be binding: if they are not, it might be better to leave it to the ECJ to develop them, as in the past. If the catalogue of rights were not to be made binding, there should at least be an obligation for the Community Courts to take it as guidance in interpreting Community law. Moreover, those Courts should be encouraged to enlarge the possibility for individual applicants to lodge complaints with the court for violation of basic rights by attaching a broader interpretation, in Article 230, paragraph 4, EC, to the words 'individually and directly' concerned.

Regarding the second part there is already a comprehensive set of rules and case law on the organisation of, and the balance between, the institutions. It may be too early to undertake a redrafting of these rules. However, it is certainly worth the effort to make them more coherent and less complicated.

As for the third part relating to the governmental form the Community should take it is certainly too early to draft those rules (other than in the form of a discussion paper), since there is no clear vision yet on which form the Community (let alone the Union) should take (a presidential system or a 'purely' parliamentary system; the speaker's own preference goes to an elected president). There is, however, one issue which, according to the speaker, needs urgent attention (and which risks being neglected because of the ongoing enlargement negotiations), as follows.

Ad c. Rules for Code of Conduct

That issue concerns the drafting of rules (not necessarily hard law) concerning the standards which members of the institutions, and particularly the Commissioners, should observe in carrying out their duties and the responsibility and political sanctions they can incur if they do not observe the rules. In other words, standards in public life must be elaborated and laid down in rules of conduct under the guidance of, and to be monitored by, an independent committee. Indeed, in the absence of a democratically elected legislature in the Community (only one component of the legislature is directly elected: the Parliament, and it has limited powers only), it is crucial to enhance the democratic credibility and legitimacy of the other components through the adoption of such standards (which must also apply to the Parliament if it wishes to assume the task of controlling the observance of such rules by the Commission). Such standards should concern, and flesh out, the duties of integrity, accountability and political responsibility of all those holding high office. These matters have been dealt with extensively in Chapter 7 of the second report of the Independent Experts' Committee which was submitted to Parliament on 10 September 1999. (See more particularly Recommendations 74-87 reproduced in the beginning of the report). That chapter deals more specifically, amongst many other matters, with the collective and individual responsibility of members of the Commission, whereby it is proposed that collective responsibility should remain a matter for the Parliament to decide, whilst individual responsibility is a matter for the President of the Commission (see further Recommendation 86).

Answering a question regarding the internal constitutional order, Mr. Van Gerven stated that there should be a right of censure against Commissioners by the European Parliament and a power of the President to dismiss a Commissioner.

Stefan Griller added to the comment made by van Gerven that this is a departure from Community law in which the European Commission is a collegiate body and the decision-making is collegiate. That principle protects Commissioners against political pressures; since there is often tremendous pressure on a Commissioner, he wonders whether this is the right way to go and might it not be better to have a right of censure by the European Parliament instead, which is a less politically charged way of dealing with problems.

According to van Gerven collective responsibility is now and should remain a matter for the European Parliament to determine. Where the individual responsibility of a Member of the Commission is concerned, it is first for the President to address the issue, eventually after Parliament has passed a motion of dissatisfaction against a particular Commissioner. However, in deciding to act or not to act, the President engages his/her own political responsibility and will have to account for it before Parliament.

- Henry G. Schermers on the role of the EU Charter

The link between the European Convention of Human Rights ('ECHR') and the Charter of Fundamental Rights (further 'Charter') does not change. We can look at this relation from a legal angle as well as from a political angle.

As to the legal use of the Charter; the Charter does add new rights – *the social rights and the right to scientific research* (Art.13). According to Article 13 scientific research shall be free of constraints. (...) The incorporation of this right into the draft charter contradicts recent developments in scientific research especially in connection with cloning, when there have been heated discussions whether to restrict the freedom of research or to allow the maximum of it. As to the use of the Charter in practice the ECJ has to accept the Charter as comprising general principles of law. All acts contrary to the principles of law will be void, so if a codification of human rights is made then the ECJ will not be able to ignore it. It is then irrelevant whether the Charter is formally binding or not.

The Charter has political relevance for the Community. The Community displays itself to the world as the defender of human rights. Respect for human rights is one of the criteria for awarding development aid to the developing countries. It can be 'politically difficult' to require each country to have strong protection of human rights when the European Union does not want to be bound itself. Having a Charter will help promote the political role of the Union in the world. The Charter might produce rather a doubtful legal effect for European citizens if they cannot invoke it directly against their own governments or the Community. There has been consensus that one of the aims of the Charter is to 'bring the Union closer to the people of Europe' by guaranteeing rights. That requires that the people get some access to the Charter.

The candidate countries are parties to the ECHR and need now also to ratify the Charter. Therefore, the Charter does make their entrance more complicated.

The separation of jurisdictions between Luxembourg (ECJ) and Strasbourg (European Court of Human Rights: ECHR) is not entirely possible and could not prevent possible clashes between the two jurisdictions. When an illegal act of a member State executing Union law occurs, both ECHR and Charter are applicable. Both courts in Luxembourg and in Strasbourg are competent. (...) The clash is undesirable for the reason that it makes the procedure very lengthy. The individual who first complains to the national courts, then (via a preliminary request) to the ECJ and subsequently, when the national remedies are exhausted, to the European Court of Human Rights, may be discouraged by the ineffectiveness of the justice.

- Joseph Weiler, Harvard Law School, European University Institute Florence

Enhanced cooperation

Mr Joseph Weiler provided a personal view of the issue of enhanced co-operation. He continues to view enhanced co-operation with suspicion, He asked the question why some states should hold back other states that want to go ahead. He expressed a degree of uncertainty about this issue. The essential part of his answer was his interpretation of the principle of majority voting as the principle that prevents a minority from blocking the majority. To the states this principle means that they have to live with a certain discipline, which is also the essence of democracy.

Mr. Weiler presents another dimension of the principle – majoritarianism, e.g., without qualified majority voting (QMV) the states cannot go ahead, because going ahead and leaving behind those who disagree would violate the principle of solidarity. The current state of the art expresses the balance accomplished through compromise between QMV, unanimity, etc. It is 'conceptually troublesome' that there is QMV which means that the states have to abide by the decisions of the majority but, on the other hand, there are situations when they ask the Community to 'let them do what they like'. Weiler puts the emphasis on the balance.

Representation of the regions

Mr. Weiler finds the representation of the regions and the problems of non-participation of these regions in the government to be a sobering example of the lack of democratic accountability at the EU level.

According to Weiler accountability and representation are the basic principles through which the rule of law can be sustained; if they cannot be observed then we can no longer speak about democracy.

Weiler senses that there are many deficiencies in Europe yet to be confronted. He asserts that there is no area of national sovereignty that could be excluded from reach by the Community.

The far more critical element seems to be the division of the competences between the Community and the member States. In his answer Mr. Weiler proposed to establish a *'Constitutional Council'* – a body that would consult each legislative proposal a priori before it entered into force. The Council would be presided by the President of the European Court of Justice (ECJ) and be composed of the constitutional judges of the member States. This composition would enhance the legitimacy of the Community and diffuse the constitutional challenge issued by the '*Bundesverfassungshof*' and other national constitutional courts of Europe.

Session II

To a question from Eppo Jansen why the introduction of the Euro as a single currency was never mentioned in relation to the limitation of the country's sovereignty and eventual constitutional complications, Alan Dashwood answered that the decision to join the Monetary Union is one of the greatest importance. This fact was recognized by two (France, Germany) of the six constitutions of the original member States.

The constitutions of the other countries did not even mention it, even though there were many discussions. The question, however, is whether the old provisions dealing with the transfer of powers are sufficient for joining the economic and monetary union. Governments and Parliaments were quite pragmatic in the end stating that it is sufficient. This conservative attitude of the officials in the member States of the Union is rather disappointing.

The joining of the monetary union should, however, not be a constitutional problem for the UK from this point of view. As soon as Parliament decides to join the single currency and so instructs the courts and other authorities, any constitutional problems will be overcome. That is, perhaps, one of the advantages of having an unwritten constitution. It is one of the principles of the common law that once you commit yourself to the EU, then you need to stick to it in good faith.

Are there problems in four of the original countries with the supremacy of the EC Treaty over national constitutions? Bruno de Witte answered that this is more a theoretical than a practical problem. Conflicts between those two are very rare, almost non-existent. However, theoretically, it is an issue. It is very difficult for constitutional courts created by the national constitutions to accept that the constitution as the supreme authority has been replaced by an international treaty. The Dutch constitution has solved this by saying that the courts are not allowed to question the constitutionality of treaties, thus guaranteeing the supremacy of EC law.

On a question whether Membership of the EU involves particular rules and principles of national constitutional law which the candidate countries should adopt on the model of the present member States, Bruno de Witte answered that the original Six member States did not have to face the present constitutional challenges because they created the law and their constitutions are therefore not an example of the best European model that should be copied.

Session III

• Marc Maresceau on Europe Agreements, Agenda 2000 and Accession Partnership

The Europe Agreements were proposed by the European Commission in 1990 to CEECs to accompany the political and economic transition in these countries. The problems were raised from the start – the EC saw EAs as alternatives to accession while CEECs saw them as instruments towards the accession: a kind of bilateral pre-accession agreement, so there was an essential difference in the approach between EC and CEECs which is still present. By 1996 10 Europe Agreements (EA) had been signed.

As a political remark it may be said that through the proliferation of EAs we have created a comprehensive network of legal and political relations between Central and Eastern Europe and the EU. But note must be taken of a new dividing line being introduced in Europe – the countries of the former USSR and Russia (except the Baltic States) are excluded.

The Russian dimension becomes more important as the negotiations are proceeding. Verheugen said enlargement should bring stability in Europe – in Maresceau's opinion this is not true!

The most important chapter is that on trade; we have already achieved much in establishing the free trade area for the associated countries are the second most important trading partner of the EU. An interesting point to mention is that the surpluses are created on the side of the EU not on the side of the associated countries.

The last point to be mentioned is the human dimension – provisions on movement of persons, and right of establishment. These issues are coming before the Court of Justice. There is a question whether the right of establishment implies a right of movement: in other words, can the Polish *establish* themselves in a member State and at the same time *move* to a member State. Movement of persons is as a matter of fact not especially treated in the Europe Agreements, only the movement of workers.

Agenda 2000

On 15 July 1997 the Commission published Agenda 2000, which laid out the strategic approach by the Commission on enlargement, and which included differentiation among candidates. The Commission made a clear linkage between enlargement and the need for institutional reform.

Marc Maresceau expressed criticism on the actions of the Commission. The external effects of the enlargement were not seriously considered and had been under-estimated. The examples to quote are Turkey and Russia.

One must also gain the impression that the Commission did not browse through all the volumes of the position documents submitted by each negotiating party. The opinions of the Commission on the applications of the ten countries were published on the same day as Agenda 2000. The Commission decided to select five candidates for the *first wave and excluded five others*. This opinion was endorsed by the Luxembourg Council in December of 1997 but the Council suggested to start the process with *all* ten countries plus Cyprus, which was a more intelligent decision.

The accession process included an Enhanced Pre-Accession strategy based on Accession Partnerships which set out the legal, political and economic priorities of each country concerned which were individually considered. There is a need for enhanced pre-accession aid since the CEECs have difficulties financing the accession process.

Regarding the negotiations, 30 chapters were opened. The easy ones were quickly opened and rather quickly closed, which means negotiations are over for rather a large number of chapters. There are sensitive chapters that raise problems – for instance movement of persons: there is growing awareness of this issue on the part of the member States. Austria published its position paper on movement of persons, where it requested transitional periods to be granted and Germany is heading in the same direction.

The obligations of Schengen and visa requirements should be discussed at this conference as well. The candidates have different visa requirements from those applied by EU member States – they are in fact more open than EU members. For instance, Poland and Hungary have no visa requirements for EU members, which do apply visa requirements. The CEECs align police requirements with the requirements in the EU, and the result is that they have to close tougher external borders with Ukraine. We have to be careful so that enlargement does not make new dividing lines in Europe. In this manner, we are not making a big contribution to peace and security.

• Maciej Mataczynski, University of Poznan on transfer or delegation of sovereign powers

Mataczynski commented on the wording of the provisions of the national constitutions concerning the possibility of the transfer of the sovereign powers of the Candidate State to the European Community.[8] As was already mentioned in the presentation given by Professor Janusz Justynski, Article 90 sec. 1 of the Polish Constitution of 2 April 1997 authorizes the Parliament to delegate, by virtue of an international agreement, to an international organization or international institution the competence of the State in relation to certain matters. The Polish Constitution does not specifically name the international organization that, should the conditions laid down in Article 90 sec. 2 of the Polish Constitution be fulfilled, would receive the aforementioned competence. Is this a good solution? Does it not water down the transfer clause? With an ever globalizing world, the transfer of certain elements of State competence occurs in the case of many international agreements. A good example is the discussion on the ratification by Poland of the statute of the international criminal court. Some experts and politicians argued that, as this matter concerns the transfer of jurisdictional competence of Polish courts to the international tribunal, the extraordinary procedure as prescribed in Article 90 sec. 2 should apply.[9]

[8] I would not like to engage in the discussion whether one should name it 'transfer' or 'delegation' of the sovereign powers, as such controversy has emerged during the conference. It is noteworthy that one of the speakers has pointed out that delegation means the temporal and controlled transfer of a certain scope of powers to a lower authority, and that this was obviously not what the ECJ has meant by saying that '*States have limited their sovereign rights, albeit within limited fields.*'

[9] Presently the Polish Ministry of Justice prepares the request for the adoption by the Council of Ministers of the governmental proposal of the project of the law authorising the President of the Republic of Poland to ratify the statute. This means that in this case Polish authorities apply the regular procedure for the ratification of international agreements as prescribed by Article 89 sec. 1 of Polish Constitution, rather than an extraordinary one. Representatives of the Ministry of Justice, Ministry of Foreign Affairs and Legislative Council of the Prime Minister have unanimously accepted this solution.

Naturally there were sound reasons why the Polish *pouvoir constituant* has decided to adopt the aforementioned solution. Politically speaking, there were many advantages of such 'neutrality' of constitutional provisions. In the fierce political campaign before the national constitutional referendum, the Eurosceptical opposition could no longer vindicate the argument that the adoption of the constitution means the loss of Polish sovereignty to European Union. Nevertheless, this reasoning has at least partly failed. The argument on the loss of sovereignty was raised anyway. Additionally, the opposition challenged the elasticity of the open-clause.

He concluded his intervention by stressing the relevance of the answer we give to the question whether the transfer clauses in the constitutions of Applicant States should specifically name the European Community as an international organization authorized to exercise those transferred powers. From the political point of view (and by 'political' in this context he understand something that goes down to the very foundations of each and every 'polity', the expression of its historical and future direction rather than short term, opinion poll inspired gestures) transfer of the sovereign competence of the State is not an everyday thing. It is a fundamental societal choice. Therefore, it can not just be left open to the parliamentary majority, however large and qualified.[10] It is not *any* international organization that Poland wishes to transfer part of its sovereign competencies to. It is the very concrete European Community aiming to create an ever closer union among the peoples of Europe. And popular critics of the discussed provisions have raised this argument.

Taking the opportunity of this intervention he would like to make a short clarification. Contrary to what was raised by one of the speakers, there is no general ban on the acquisition of immovable property by foreigners in Poland. According to Article 1 sec. 1 of the law of 24 March 1920 on the acquisition of immovable property by foreigners (OJ 1996, No. 54, item 254 with further amendments), such acquisition is allowed subject to consent by the Minister of Internal Affairs. Such consents are granted in the overwhelming majority of applications.

Session IV

- Pieter van Nuffel on IGC

Pieter van Nuffel's intervention focused on the question whether the Intergovernmental Conference (IGC) brings constitutional changes.

After having stressed the terminology issue raised by granting the Treaties a 'constitutional' status, his finding is a paradox. On the one hand, from a formal point of view, van Nuffel thinks that the IGC does address constitutional issues

[10] It should be stressed that the majority required for exercising such a transfer according to Article 90 of the Polish Constitution is higher than the one required for amending the constitution itself!

such as the possibility to grant new competence or powers to the institutions. However, these changes are not brought about by treaties of accession but by modification of the Treaties. On the other hand, from a substantial point of view, the IGC does not discuss the real future architecture of the EU, nor does it discuss the reorganisation of the Treaties. These two topics, including the status of the future EU Charter on Fundamental Rights are 'post Nice agenda' issues.

On the contrary, the IGC concentrates on the questions necessary for permitting enlargement. In fact, the purpose is to maintain the necessary *status quo*, keeping as much as possible the current framework despite enlargement. Therefore, the IGC does not deal with constitutional changes.

- Frank Vibert on ideas for the Agenda of the IGC

Frank Vibert focused on the following question: why is there so much difficulty on agreeing on the agenda, given that the issues are not new? Apart from political reasons, Vibert suggested another explanation: beneath the surface, there is an emphasis on a more fundamental debate between three perspectives.
1st perspective: let us focus on what works and what will work in the future;
2nd perspective: let us improve the existing structure;
3rd perspective: let us improve the current structures but in the light of more fundamental changes which aim at a constitutionally orientated structure.

In the first perspective, some member States put the emphasis on flexibility and differentiation for this leads to closer co-operation, a shift to soft legislation, bilateral initiatives or member State co-operation/working groups to supplement the Commission.

The danger with this perspective is twofold:
- it can bring inconsistencies
- it is not transparent since no one really know what is going on.

This leads to a move towards stronger constitutional structures.

Vibert presents a list of items, such as a monetary constitution. However, as no agreement can be found yet, there is a need for transition mechanisms such as treaty simplification/codification, closer co-operation between some member States, but these transitory vehicles do not seem to work properly.

This difficult situation leads one to think that there are no easy shortcuts to a constitutional future. Some obstacles are linked to the fact that:
- there are no agreements on principles of good government in the EU, contrary to the USA at the time of the founding fathers.
- there are functions of government in the Union (the Union is a regulatory state) which will lead to a different range of functions undertaken by the member States.

In general, with regard to the IGC, one should be careful in respect of the way chosen to prepare the IGC, in particular in respect of the method. In this sense, it should not be shaped as the EU Charter leading to 'moral law' made by specialists which may not be close to the Union's citizens.

The 2004 IGC could be the time for constitutional reform if the method is rightly prepared and if there is a success in Nice.

• Francis Jacobs on IGC and the ECJ

Francis Jacobs focused on the institutional consequences of enlargement on the European Court of Justice (ECJ). These consequences would be twofold: composition (1) and functions (2).

In respect of (1), although it would be desirable to limit the number of judges, it is not probably feasible. There will therefore still be one Judge per member State. However, it would be necessary to keep the plenary court limited to eleven judges. As regards Advocates-General it seems that their number would be maintained identically as now (at eight). However, this means that they should not give an opinion in every case (see Ole Due report).

As far as (2) is concerned, Francis Jacobs stressed that some categories of preliminary rulings would probably be transferred to the CFI. If it is left open which ones, a solution at Treaty level would be to open the prohibition entailed in the EC Treaty, coming to a practical solution afterwards. A right of appeal to the ECJ should not be automatic. With increased powers, the CFI would need more judges. Six new judges should be appointed.

Concerning direct actions, the Courts should be empowered to create specialised chambers (staff cases, trade mark law). In this context, appeal would be possible to the CFI. Consequently, the CFI would no longer keep its current name but which one? this is another question. Finally, another aspect relates to the rules of procedure of the Court which should be modified at QMV and no longer at unanimity by the Council.

• Attila Harmathy on IGC and candidate countries

Attila Harmathy stressed that this Conference was an occasion for candidate States to express their views on the IGC which they are not allowed to do in the current system. His short contribution was devoted to asking questions in relation to the title of the conference. For instance, are constitutional problems of the EU really caused by the enlargement? If not, does the enlargement constitute an additional impact on the constitutional problems of the EU? What is the real basis for constitutional problems? He stressed the difficulties for candidate countries to approximate their legislation to the EU 'moving target', especially when human rights are concerned.

• Michiel Patijn devoted his intervention to three remarks concerning the IGC

– the IGC agenda concerns the 'left overs' of Amsterdam;

– it is not called upon to resolve the constitutional problems of the EC/EU; it does not, for instance, tackle the issue of a possible European Union Security Council for crisis management in the second pillar.

– any enlarged EC will have problems which cannot be solved only by changing the Treaties.

• Bruno de Witte on the text of the Robert Schuman Centre in Florence and IGC

Bruno de Witte focused his attention on the restructuring of the Treaties, a terminology that he prefers to 'reorganisation'. He explained the work undertaken by the Robert Schuman centre of the EUI at the request of the EC Commission.

The purposes of the work were:
1) visibility;
2) link with possible greater flexibility for revision of the Treaty by distinguishing provisions of a more fundamental nature than the others;
3) the text could serve as a constitution for the EU (this latter point was, however, not spelt by the Commission itself).

The text is a selection of ninety articles. It has given some insight into the limits of such an exercise. Indeed, for instance, it clearly appears that the Commission's functions cannot be exactly grasped through this text. As regards discrimination also, the text reveals that it should be applicable at EC and EU level, but is it really the case in practice? Does this principle have the same scope in both Treaties? This shows, that the text would not be ready for adoption if it were on the agenda of the IGC (which is not the case). It gives the Governments a possible text to work upon in the future.

De Witte stressed that a (more important) second report on reforming the Treaty revision procedures has been undertaken for the Commission but has not yet been disclosed. It addresses issues such as the role of the European Parliament and the role of the national parliaments (consulted during the process of accession or after?) and also the question of unanimity which can be seen as a rule of paradox, since it would also enable States to move back from further integration.

Session V

• Leonard Besselink on the EU Charter and level of protection

Besselink first maked a brief remark to the answer of Professor Lenaerts to a previous question, where he suggested that the level of protection to be provided by the Charter (and the ECJ) should not fall below what is common to the constitutional traditions of the member States; everything would fall apart if the ECJ should comply with the individual standards of the various member States. He respectfully disagreed. As Besselink had pointed out in an article in the Common Market Law Review in 1998, things would not fall apart if the Court were to apply the best national standard as a European standard in relevant cases, or it could alternatively respect a particular national conception of fundamental rights as some EU analogue to the margin of appreciation doctrine of the Strasbourg Court. This would upgrade the protection of fundamental rights throughout the Union.

The question related to the material scope of Article 6(2) TEU. In his view there is one respect – apart those mentioned in the very interesting presentation of Professor Lenaerts – in which it is more limited than under standard ECJ case law, and that deserves attention. It concerns the fact that reference is made only to one human rights treaty, the ECHR, whereas in the case law the ECJ includes also all the other human rights treaties to which member States are a party. Notably that concerns the UN Convention on Civil and Political Rights, which contains an important provision which is absent in the ECHR: Article 27 on the protection of minorities. This provision does not only contain a prohibition of discrimination but also a positive duty to respect their identities, which other duties evolve. If the narrower formulation of Article 6(2) TEU can be understood as a political signal towards the ECJ not to be too strident in its approach to fundamental rights protection, as Professor Lenaerts has suggested here and on other occasions, does that also apply to this?

Another point he wished to put forward is his great difficulty in giving such a broad meaning to the word 'implementation' as Professor Lenaerts gave it in a previous answer, so as to include such cases as were at hand in the *Familia Press Verlag* case before the ECJ (case C-368/95 of 1997). Here the member State was not implementing EC law at all – that is giving positive effect to an EC measure – but the question was whether an existent 'autonomous' member State law infringed on the free movement of goods and could be justified under the 'rule of reason' (i.e., exclusively within the context of negative integration).

Finally, as to the *Emesa* order issue: the European Court of Human Rights should clarify its case law as to the question whether it depends on his institutional affiliation whether an Advocate-General's opinion is to be considered a statement on which parties should have a right to respond, or whether this is also the case irrespective of whether the Advocate-General is a member of the public prosecution or any other state or public institution.

His question aims at the problem of the relationship between the Charter, the ECHR and national bills of rights; the Charter does include rights that are not in the ECHR but are protected by member States. In fact the Charter was initiated merely because member States, especially Germany, had a problem with the extent of the protection provided by the ECJ. In fact, its Constitution (Art. 23) requires at the EU level an amount of protection which is equivalent to the protection provided by the German Constitution. Is the possibility of a gap between the Charter and national constitutions much more important than that between the ECHR and the Charter? Does this problem hinder the dialogue between the ECJ applying the Charter and national courts applying the national bills?

V. PRELIMINARY CONFERENCE FINDINGS AND FOLLOW-UP

1) **Preliminary Conference findings**

The Secretary of State for Foreign Affairs of The Netherlands, Dick Benschop, who is a Member of the Reflection Group, declared in his opening speech to the Conference that he will distribute the Preliminary Conference findings, suggestions and results to the members of the IGC.

Therefore, Preliminary Conference findings (See infra) were drafted by the author of this conference report in cooperation with Jaap de Zwaan, Jeno Czuczai and Francis Jacobs. In more detail, however, many points and original thoughts are reflected in their respective final papers for the conference.

On 17 November 2000 these Conference findings were sent to Minister Benschop, accompanied by the Conference Reader and a Special Post-Conference Reader, for distribution among the Members of the Reflection Group. Allthough not all the preliminary findings, results and conclusions are of direct interest for the coming IGC Agenda, it was considered that they may be of sufficient interest to be included in the Agenda of the IGC after Nice.

2) **Project Proposal**

During and after the Conference (See Summing-up by De Zwaan) it was further considered to continue the network of participants to this conference. A proposal was published in the Conference Reader for a multi-country project for the development of some European models of constitutions. These European models of constitutions could be helpful for the candidate countries for the adaptation of their constitutions and as a comparative study in a multi-country research project of their constitutions, could make the texts more transparant (See Conference Finding Point No. 9).

The project would further, by the training of judges, prosecutors and lawyers in the candidate countries in the field of European law, improve the awareness of the national judiciary of their role as Community courts. This is a necessity for the following reasons.

The European Commission requires that the candidate countries on being a Member should apply and give priority to Community law in their national legal orders. For the European Commission it does not in theory matter what the Constitution looks alike, as long as Community law is applied in the national legal order of the member States with priority and as long as primacy, direct effect and direct applicability of Community law are applied by the national courts. At the Conference, however, it was stated that it matters how the Constitution looks for both political and psychological reasons and with reference to the 'European deficit' of some national constitutions.

To reach this result in the candidate countries not only the text of the constitutions are relevant and important, but especially the interpretation of the constitution ('living constitutions') by the national (constitutional) courts (See Conference Finding Point No. 8).

At the conference most candidate countries expressed their wish to participate in such a multi-country project. It was suggested that from every country three persons would participate. A representative of the judiciary (Judge of the Constitutional court for example), a representative of Government or parliament, and a representative of legal science (Professor of constitutional/or and European law). A side-effect of their participation would be that their skills and knowledge of European and comparative constitutional law would be enlarged.

English texts of the national constitutions of the thirteen candidate countries, and relevant documents and literature, may be found on the Asser website (**www.asser.nl/impact** (see documents)).

What are the advantages of this project?
The candidate countries may learn from the discussions in such a multi-country project from each other's experiences with the adaptation of their national constitutions for EU accession and thus do not have to re-invent the wheel!

The aim of the suggested project proposal is to raise the awareness of politicians, judges, experts and the general public in the candidate countries for the constitutional problems of accession, legal protection and the rule of law. The Copenhagen accession criteria refer explicitly to democracy, the rule of law, human rights and the protection of minorities, topics which are generally regulated by the national constitution or constitutional provisions.

For an assessment of how these principles work in practice and to evaluate whether the respective rights are also exercised in practice, an analysis of the national constitutional provisions and practice is necessary.

Practice has shown further that for accession there is a growing need to adapt the national constitutions and constitutional laws for the following reasons.
a) For some constitutions this adaptation is necessary in order to be able to ratify the Treaty of the European Union. The constitutions of the candidate countries may not form an obstacle for the accession of the candidate countries to an international organization, as the EU, for example, is considered.
b) In some smaller candidate countries, who have regained their independence since 1991, there are political and psychological objections against, for example, the transfer of sovereignty.
c) In some national constitutions the way in which the texts deal with the European integration process is rather poor and not transparent ('European deficit'). In its comparative approach, the project would support the efforts of the applicant countries in order to guarantee a more or less uniform legal language and terminology concerning EU topics and would stimulate the applicant countries to draft better constitutional texts.

d) There are many national constitutional provisions which are contrary to and contradict the *acquis.*

An example of the problems of the transfer of sovereignty is the English text of Article 90(1) of the Polish Constitution which speaks about *delegation* of the competence of the organs of a State authority to an international organization, whereas it was observed at the conference that it should be *transfer* of the competence to an international organization. The meaning of *delegation* in constitutional law is limited to transfer of powers to a *lower* institution or organization. The transfer of sovereign or state powers to the European institutions is *permanent* according to Community law, and it is not possible to draw these powers back, as is suggested by the use of the term delegation.

3) **Political Impact of the Conference in the Netherlands**

The Dutch Minister of the Interior and Kingdom Relations in his speech on 21 September 2000 stated:

> 'The EU is referred to in everyday language as "the fourth tier of government" (namely the tier above municipal, provincial and central government in the Netherlands). This shows in fact that we scarcely regard the European Union as being of a different order, so to speak, from our national legal order.
> But after nearly half a century of European integration, words like Europe, the European Union or the European Community cannot be found in our Constitution, despite the fact that everyone living in this country is confronted with European legislation and its consequences on a daily basis.'

In Point No. 9 of the Conference Findings it was stated that the Netherlands Constitution does not refer at all to the EU and EC Treaty.

In the Senate of the Netherlands (Session 2000-2001, No. 37. 26200VI no. 65 on 10 October 2000 a Motion was proposed by Jurgens c.s. (Hirsch Ballin, Kohnstamm, De Wolff) requesting the government to add to the planned Amendment of the Dutch Constitution in 2002 a Proposal which recognizes the membership of the Netherlands of the European Union etc. (...)

4) **Publication of the Conference Proceedings**

This book contains the respective answers and references to the main conference questions. The answers were given and statements made by the speakers and other high qualified legal authors in their final reports for these Conference Proceedings.

Respecting the principle of subsidiarity, the final reports and contributions are not uniform but their drafting is influenced by everybody's personal opinion and the various national experiences and problems. The order of the authors is chronological, according to the same order in which they were requested to speak in the Conference Sessions.

In order to improve the understanding of the constitutional impact of enlargement at EU level for those who consult this book, we have not only annexed the preliminary Conference Findings but also the most recent documents and texts concerning the European Council in Nice, the Nice Treaty and the Charter on Fundamental Rights.

We hope that this publication will be useful as basic material for our next international conference which will be held in 2003 to make suggestions for the constitutional reform of IGC 2004.

The Hague, 23 February 2001

Annex

Preliminary Conference Findings, Results and Conclusions

1. It is in the interest of an enlarged EU to increase the effectiveness of its legal order. To achieve security, democracy and effectiveness of the rule of law, it is necessary to have an effective and transparent administration, an independent judiciary and an adequate system of legal protection at EU and national level. National constitutions and the national courts interpreting these constitutions play an important role for the legal protection of the citizens of the European Union and the candidate countries.

2. The Enlargement must also address broader geo-political questions and focus on the improvement of the cooperation and partnership with non-candidate countries situated at the new borders such as Ukraine and Russia. Enlargement should not create new obstacles between the EU and the Common wealth of Independent States (CIS) countries.

3. The EU Charter of Fundamental Rights appears as a whole to be well drafted and politically balanced. The Charter does add *new rights* – the social rights and right to scientific research (Art. 13) as well as new principles – good governance (Art. 40) and is therefore more tailor-made for the EU. The Charter has *political relevance* for the EU. Certainly, as a *legal* instrument, it needs refinement, e.g., in order to make clear which are the restrictions that may apply to the rights of the Charter. The Charter might produce a rather doubtful *legal* effect for the European citizen, if they cannot invoke it directly against their own governments or the EU.

   The candidate countries should be involved in the drafting of the final text of the Charter, which would not form a new obligation for accession if the Charter were to reflect the constitutional traditions of the candidate countries. The opponents of the Charter proposed that the EU must again investigate whether accession to the European Convention on Human Rights, under the changed political environment since the Treaty of Amsterdam, would not be possible and feasible.

The opponents further mentioned the absence of a human rights policy of the Community with the possibility to monitor, investigate, regulate and prosecute for violations of human rights. They finally referred to the many texts which already deal with human rights protection such as the EC Treaty, Article 12 (ex Art. 6) and Article 13 (ex Art. 6a); the EU Treaty, Article 6 (ex Art. F) and 7 (ex Art. F.1); the European Convention on Human Rights; the UN Treaties as well as the national constitutions of the EU member States and candidate countries.

4. The IGC 2000, the Treaty of Nice and the reform of the EC's institutions with a view to its enlargement, were debated from the short term and long term viewpoint.

For the short term the IGC is considered to be not more than a starter, whereas the main course is still lacking.

Attention has been paid especially to solutions for the reorganization of the *European Court of Justice.*

In order to diminish the workload of the ECJ it has been suggested to train the judges of the national courts in order to improve the quality of the requests for a preliminary ruling; that the Court of First Instance will have more jurisdiction over direct actions, including those filed by institutions and member States; and will also have jurisdiction over certain specific categories of preliminary references; and, finally, to establish specialized chambers within the Court of First Instance.

5. However, in the IGC 2000 progress should be made and agreement reached to pass over to more qualified majority voting (QMV) for a large number of articles for which unanimity is now required. The consequence of more QMV is not a new transfer of sovereignty from the State to the EC institutions or what was called at the conference the transfer of 'the exercise of certain state powers'. More QMV may be contrasted with the transfer of sovereignty, for which in some countries in such case a national referendum might be regarded as necessary (virtually nowhere it is actually a constitutional requirement).

The procedures for *reinforced co-operation or closer co-operation* need more flexible arrangements. However, the core conditions should be maintained.

The reorganisation of the *European Commission* as a result of the Report of the Committee of Independent Experts has been considered to have a constitutional impact.

Regarding the number of Commissioners, one national Member per member State is not a must in an EU after enlargement. This would seriously affect the Commission's capability to act efficiently as a college, thereby weakening its position in the institutional architecture of the Union.

A Commission composed of a limited number of Commissioners, irrespective of the number of member States, would be a better guarantee to maintain its efficiency.

As concerns the weighting of votes in the *Council* three options were put forward: simple re-weighting, double majority and the introduction of a new key related to concrete economic criteria such as financial contribution. However, comparative studies, for example concerning the situation in the US, have shown that the number of votes to be cast in the Senate has no relationship at all with the above criteria. Every State is equally represented in the Senate.

6. In many candidate countries accession to the EU will most likely contribute to the constitutional modernization of the country. The lack of political consensus blocked constitutional reform but the accession will most likely give an impetus to fundamental changes in this respect. This will concern especially the implications of their Membership for the national constitutional provisions concerning the following topics:
A) the principle of the transfer of the exercise of certain state powers to the EU (deriving from national state sovereignty)
B) supremacy, primacy or priority of community law
C) direct applicability
D) direct effect
E) specific provisions from the EU and EC Treaties (European citizenship, voting rights, etc.)
F) specific provisions in national constitutions which contradict the *acquis communautaire* such as the acquisition of land by non-residents.
A country-by-country approach reveals the fact that various approaches do exist and that constitutional changes are dependent on the respective national legal order.

7. The aim of the screening process is to help the countries concerned to increase their understanding of the rules that underpin the EU and identify more clearly which issues they need to address as they adopt and implement the *acquis communautaire*. The relevant sectors are identified but not the constitutional *acquis*. A chapter on the constitutional *acquis* should be added and included. A post-screening meeting should be held for the candidate countries aimed at helping them to understand what the constitutional requirements of the accession process are about.

8. The constitutional aspects are especially important in the pre-accession period. The national constitutions of the candidate countries determine the legal consequences of the rule of law in the national legal order: legal protection, direct applicability, direct effect and supremacy, primacy or priority of community law. They determine the capability to enforce Community law in the national legal order in the pre-accession period. To reach a satisfactory system of legal protection not only the texts of the constitutions are decisive but also the interpretations given by the national courts when interpreting the constitutions and constitutional laws ('*living constitutions*'). These constitutional aspects as well as an adequate legal protection have to be adjusted and regulated before accession.
In the *Progress Reports* from the European Commission one can not find directives or suggestions to adapt national constitutions as the European Commission considers national constitutions as belonging to the people and falling within the national sovereignty of the states. There are, further, so many different constitutional traditions in Central and Eastern Europe, that the European Commission cannot establish in advance whether one country's Constitution permits accession without the prior amendment to the Constitution or not.

9. In order to help the candidate countries with the constitutional problems for their accession it was suggested as a follow-up of the conference, to initiate a project in which European models for national constitutions could be developed and further to

improve by training the awareness of the national judiciary of their role as Community judges. This project would be useful not only for the candidate countries, but also for the EU member States as there does exist in some countries a 'European deficit' of the constitutional provisions.

For example, the Netherlands Constitution does not refer at all to the EU and EC Treaties. From a political and legal point of view it is an odd situation that the text of the Constitution contains many trivial rules but fails to acknowledge one of the central constitutional realities of the country, namely, its membership of the European Union, with all the legal consequences deriving therefrom.

Most representatives of the applicant countries expressed the hope that they would be involved in this project, in which three persons per country could take part – a representative of the judiciary (for example, a member of the national Constitutional Court), a representative of the Government or Parliament and an academic.

10. The need for a reform of the structures of the Treaties and the suggested texts of the European University Institute in Florence in this respect were welcomed for the Agenda of the IGC after Nice. The first stage would consist in restructuring the Treaties. The second stage would be aimed at the adoption of a Treaty containing all the characteristics of a real European Constitution. The Draft Charter of Fundamental Rights could be integrated in this Constitution.

The Project Proposal on the preparation and adaptation of the national constitutions of the candidate countries mentioned under 9. could contribute to an adaptation or revision of the national constitutional texts, in which national constitutional legislators will fully reflect the true importance of the European integration process. Perhaps the development of such European models for national constitutions could also contribute to the development of a European Constitution.

The procedure for the drafting of the Charter of Fundamental Rights by the sixty-two Members of the Convention was evaluated as a very useful experiment, which procedure could be also be used for the drafting of a European Constitution.

SESSION I
The European Architecture
(Constitutional Order and Charter of Fundamental Rights)

EUROPE 2000 – THE CONSTITUTIONAL AGENDA AN OUTLINE

Joseph Weiler *

DOES EUROPE NEED A CONSTITUTION?

In substance Europe's legal order is in many senses constitutional – especially in that it demands a constitutional discipline and loyalty in the legal requirements it makes vis-à-vis member State branches of government: vis-à-vis legislatures it insists on supremacy, vis-à-vis courts it insists on direct effect and vis-à-vis governments it abolishes reciprocity, counter measures, the principal artifacts of State responsibility, namely, the classical pacific instruments of government in international relations. Europe already enjoys judicial protection of human rights, the ECJ gives decisions and rulings of a constitutional nature when necessary, and even subsidiarity and the issue of competences, a key element in all federal systems, is considered in Europe to be justiciable – though how effective this would be is another matter. In some senses it has a common law constitution, unwritten but addressing all the issues which more formal constitutions address.

The Question then has to be refined: Does Europe need a formalization of its constitutional order?

Recently there has been a revival of the drive for a formal constitution. The rationale for this drive may be located in the following five reasons.

1. Europe may have a constitutional legal order but the problem is that it does not have traditional constitutional legitimation – its constitutional order has not been approved in a manner which gives it the kind of legitimacy that is commensurate with the discipline it demands and especially the kind of autonomous authority to transcend Statal authority. What is needed, it is argued, is a process which will define the European peoples as a p*ouvoir constituent* and then a formal constitutional adoption process.

2. A second dimension to the question 'Does Europe Need a Constitution' is the argument that asserts the non-functionability of the Treaties as a constitution. The

* Harvard Law School, European University Institute Florence.

A.E. Kellermann et al. (Eds.), EU Enlargement: The Constitutional Impact at EU and National Level

Treaties are far too long and detailed and undifferentiated. Trivial stuff, by the mere fact that it is part of the Treaty, is given constitutional status and the important, truly constitutional norms are submerged and do not get the prominence they deserve. One result is to make the process of constitutional amendment bog down with detail instead of focus on truly structural stuff.

3. A third dimension to the question 'Does Europe Need a Constitution' is the question of the Court: does Europe need a Constitutional Court in the way it exists in many of the European countries. This has become especially acute in the light of the well-known 'rebellion' of national high courts in the last decade.

4. A fourth argument for a constitution concerns the introduction of a formal bill or catalogue of rights instead of the common law, unwritten system now prevailing. The Charter exercise, now underway, is considered as an important element of such a constitution, though formally the eventual status of the Charter is yet to be decided.

5. The final dimension concerns the issue of limiting the competences of the Union. Only a constitution, it is argued, can effectively anchor the jurisdiction of the Union in a binding way.

DOES EUROPE *REALLY* NEED A CONSTITUTION?

Allow me now to express some skepticism about each of these five elements. My overall view is that the European constitutional architecture is in urgent need of repair in various aspects, but that a formal process of adopting a constitution is not only pragmatically not feasible but might even be conceptually undesirable.

I will take each of the five points in turn.

Constitutional legitimation

At some level the final product, a European Constitution adopted through some process articulating a European constituent power composed of the European peoples will resolve many of the problems now facing European constitutionalism, especially its authority vis-à-vis member State constitutionalisms. If the objective is to open up the debate to a truly democratic, non-court and non-elite led constitutional discourse, than the need can be fully justified. But if the object is to increase the stability of the European order (and that is how it is typically presented) than the process might be counterproductive and yield the opposite: a decrease in stability. There are many aspects of European constitutionalism which, in common law fashion, have become conventional and accepted by the players involved but which, I suspect, if thrown again into the public arena will re-ignite old fires and stoke old debates. Marriage counselling and frank debate between spouses often leads to divorce. The British *detto* let sleeping dogs lie may well be wise counsel in this situation.

But beyond this pragmatic speculation on the effect of a constitutional process on the stability of the European constitutional order I harbour a more principled and conceptual doubt.

A formal constitution would rob Europe of its most important constitutional innovation: the principle of constitutional tolerance.

Instead of the current anchoring of constitutional discipline in the voluntary acceptance by constitutional organs in the member States, with Europe being a primus inter pares, it would introduce a formal hierarchy equal to that found in federal states, thus removing Europe's very special originality.[1]

The non-functionability of the Treaties

I entirely agree with this critique of the current constitutional architecture. But the remedy does not require the adoption of a European constitution. It is perfectly possible from a legal point of view and feasible from a political point of view to engage in a redactive process, undertaken already by a team led by Yves Meny of the Robert Schumann Centre at the European University Institute in Florence, which would reduce the Treaties to their essential constitutional nature and transform the non-constitutional provisions into normal measures of Community law. This would be a very valuable exercise, but it does not require a new constitution.

The judicial architecture

The European judicial branch is composed of two limbs. We should, rightly, speak of the European *Courts* of Justice – not the ECJ and the Tribunal of First Instance, but those two courts coupled with member State courts.

The judicial malaise of Europe can be summarized in the following proposition:

We ask too much of the European Court and the Tribunal and we ask too little of national courts.

It has become apparent to all, even the Court itself, that the current architecture of European courts will become functionally intolerable and symbolically retrograde in a Community of, say, twenty-six. But the problem is not simply one of a well-

[1] For full discussion see 'Mancini v. Weiler: Europe – The Case for Statehood ... And the Case Against: An Exchange'. Harvard Jean Monnet Working Paper No. 6/98 (also Vol. 4 European Law Journal (1998)).

functioning system which may be strained by a new heavy burden – the premise of most Court reform including the admirable new Due Report. The problem is also inherent, i.e., an architecture that served the Community well in its foundation and consolidation phases but which would merit rethinking and reform even if the Community were not to enlarge.

I want to begin by raising three issues which are considered by some as taboo in the debate on the future judicial architecture: The tasks of the Court, the qualifications of the Judges and the nature of the judicial conversation between the European Court and national courts.

My theses here are simple:

a. The Court cannot effectively discharge its duty given its present tasks and present composition. This is not just a question of work load, a problem which is widely acknowledged. It is also a question of competences and credibility.

b. The style of judicial decisions is outmoded, does not reflect the dialogical nature of European constitutionalism, and is not a basis for confidence building European constitutional relations between the European Court and its national constitutional counterparts.

Any discussion of the judicial architecture must start with the preliminary reference procedure, one of the most remarkable and successful dimensions of the European legal order and European constitutionalism.

Its success means, however, that:

Barring the very few cases of 'inappropriate' references, the ECJ is obliged to deal with a growing number of references – the equivalence of almost *all* cases pending before national courts going to the national constitutional court before they can be disposed of at first instance.

It also means that the ECJ has to answer questions on all aspects of European law: one day a most specialized issue of agricultural law, the next day a complex issue of product liability and, increasingly, other aspects of private law and on day three, address, most critically, profound issues of constitutional law which engage the highest courts and the deepest legal values of the member States.

Couple these two features together and the trajectory becomes one of implosion.

One issue is that of workload. The issue is not simply the delays which the heavy load on both Court and Tribunal create – justice delayed is justice denied. It is, and this is usually only whispered, an issue of quality of justice. With the prompting of a former Member of the Court we tried in my Harvard Seminar to construct the schedule of a judge at the ECJ. Approximate as our calculations must have been, we concluded that between meetings and deliberations and actual hearings the workload is such that judges have very little time to think deeply about many of the cases – especially those for which they are not the Reporting Judge – which they eventually have to decide. This has various consequences, one of which concerns the role of Legal Secretaries. In the United States the question of the appropriate role and influence of judicial clerks has been discussed intensely. I believe that similar questions may be legitimately raised about the role and influence of Legal Secretaries at the ECJ. This is not meant in any way to impugn the integrity of the process but simply to bring arithmetic to bear on the problem. The year has so many days, the day has so many hours, the Court has so many judges, the judges have so many cases (indeed many) – time to think, to reflect, to deliberate is the most scarce resource of the Institution. Justice delayed is justice denied, but so is hurried justice, scantily deliberated justice, justice in which Legal Secretaries write and judges merely approve. The fault is not that of the Court. We ask too much of it.

The success of the preliminary reference also makes us forget the fact that in this procedure, the ECJ is both court of first and last instance – in principle a very unsatisfactory situation in itself, constituting indeed a violation of a fundamental principle of justice. This fact alone would call at least for the most careful and deliberative process in each and every case – since there is no appeal – but this is exactly what we do not allow the Court to do because of the heavy burden we place on it.

But the matter does not end simply with workload and time burden. Strangely, even paradoxically, the ECJ concept follows more the Anglo-American model of a plenary court supposedly competent in all areas of law rather than the Continental model of specialized courts – as we find in different ways in Germany, Italy, France, Greece and other countries. There is the general issue of specialization and the most delicate one is the functioning of the ECJ when it sits as the Constitutional Court of the Union.[2] One of the peculiarities of the European system is that its most decisive constitutional issues depend, as a matter of legal realism, on a relationship of trust, confidence and credibility between the European Court and its national counterparts. The European Court can pronounce on the supremacy of Community law, or on the Frankovich principle of member State liability all it wants, so to speak. These doctrines become effective only when accepted and practised by national courts under the guidance of the highest courts in each member State.

It is no secret that the 1990s saw a certain erosion in the relationship. The German 'Maastricht Decision' in which the German Constitutional Court declared, in defiance of established case law of the ECJ, that national authorities may disregard European law measures if they fall outside the competences of the Community as understood by German State organs, is notorious. Less well-known areas show a number of decisions by other high courts in various member States that display similar defiance. The Italian Constitutional Court declared that it did not

[2] In some respects, every time it is called upon to interpret the Treaty it could be said to be sitting as the Constitutional Court since the Treaty is the Union's constitution. I mean, instead, when it sits on matters that would be considered of a constitutional nature in the legal cultures of most member States.

regard itself in most cases that come before it as a Court or Tribunal in the sense of Article 177 (now 234) and, thus, outside the duty to make preliminary references. Troubling decisions have come out of Denmark, Belgium and Greece. And the Banana saga before the German Court continues to cast a shadow.

It does not surprise me that there is a certain credibility issue. The members of the ECJ are jurists of the highest quality. But only a few of them are constitutionalists. When European law and the European Court demand subordination even of the most important constitutional principles of a member State (such as the protection of fundamental human rights) to European law, it is critical that such decision emanate from a tribunal which is capable, *and seen to be capable,* of comprehending the constitutional sensibilities of the member State at issue and communicating that comprehension to its national counterparts. Without this we can only expect more 'Maastricht decisions'. The same can also be said, of course, regarding decisions of the Court on complex economic matters such as intellectual property, competition and the like. I focus on the constitutional dimension because it is politically the most sensitive and it touches often on legal values that go to the very identity of the member States. The position of the European Court is different from that of the Supreme Court of the United States and even of the House of Lords. Its relationship with, and dependence on, national courts is far more delicate and sensitive.

In thinking about the future of European law, consideration must be given to whether finally the European Court system should become European (rather than Anglo-American) and see the establishment of specialized jurisdictions, among them a European Constitutional Court composed of judges whose qualifications and expertise would be mostly in this field.

Whereas in relation to the architecture I think the model should be less Anglo-American and more Continental, as regards the style of judgments, I think the Court should abandon the cryptic, Cartesian style which still characterizes many of its decisions and move to the more discursive, analytic and conversational style associated more with the common law world – though practised by others as well, notably the German Constitutional court. As noted above, especially in its Constitutional jurisprudence, it is crucial that the Court display in its judgments that national sensibilities were fully considered and taken into account. And it must amply explain and reason its decisions if they are to be not only authoritarian but also authoritative.[3] The Cartesian style with its pretense of logical legal reasoning and inevitability of results[4] is not conducive to a good conversation with national courts. In the same vein I would argue for the introduction of sepa-

---

[3] See J. Vining, The Authoritative and the Authoritarian (Chicago: University of Chicago Press, 1986).

[4] Cf. Lasser, 'Judicial (Self-)Portraits: Judicial Discourse in the French Legal System', 104 Yale L.J. 1325 (1995).

rate and dissenting opinions. One of the virtues of separate and dissenting opinions is that they force the majority opinion to be reasoned in an altogether more profound and communicative fashion. The dissent often produces the paradoxical effect of legitimating the majority because it becomes evident that alternative views were considered even if ultimately rejected. As a precondition for these changes in the style of ECJ decisions the member States in the next IGC would have finally to eliminate a continuous affront to the integrity of the European legal system, namely, the renewability provisions for sitting judges on the Court. The European Parliament has proposed, twice, in its input to two successive IGCs that judges on the ECJ be appointed to one non-renewable term of office, thus removing any appearance of dependence on a member State. (Whilst we are at it, the same should be true also for Commissioners who are meant to be independent ...). The refusal of the member States to accede to that request is simply unacceptable. Once this elementary anomaly is corrected, the conditions for dissents and separate opinions would be open.

The new architecture should also address issues at the national level. The main recommendation here is to encourage a more proactive style of relationship between the national courts and their European counterparts.

National courts must be encouraged to move away from the model that to be a good European Court is to make preliminary references to the European Court of Justice and to say Amen to the pronouncements of the Court.

To be a good European Court is to engage the European Court of Justice in a continuous conversation where it is not only the parties and the Commission which inform the sensibility of the European Courts but also the judicial branch of the national judiciary. Right now we have two models: lower courts (with some notable exceptions like the formidable Finanzgericht of Hamburg) simply frame questions for the European Court and follow the rulings. By contrast, some of the most august higher courts regard themselves as the custodians of national constitutional values, the gatekeepers whose task is to make sure that core values of the national polity are not compromised by European norms. They do not regard themselves as part of a European constitutional conversation whose object would be to both shape European constitutional values and re-shape national ones.

The technology of a new style of conversation should encourage member State courts at all levels not simply to ask the question but to propose what they think ought to be the correct ruling and, most importantly, inform the European Court in the reference itself of the constitutional and other concerns that the national legal order has when referring the question to the European Court of Justice.

Human Rights

The vows were taken in Cologne, the tie consummated in Tampere and birth is planned for Nice. The proposed European Charter of Human Rights is now under way in characteristic Euro-fashion, by a slightly bloated body composed of representatives of the Governments of the member States, of the Parliaments of the member States, of the European Parliament and of the Commission. Work appears to be on schedule.[5]

But does Europe really need it? Will it actually enhance the protection of fundamental human rights in the Union? After all, the citizens of Europe appear to 'suffer' from a surfeit rather than a deficit of judicial protection of their fundamental rights protected as they are by national constitutions and national courts, by the safety net provided by the European Convention of Human Rights and by the European Court of Justice which at least since 1969 has purported to guarantee that Community measures violating fundamental human rights that form part of the common constitutional tradition of the member States are unacceptable and would be struck down.

So why a new Charter at all? There is much promise in the exercise but also serious problems and risks and it is those that I wish briefly to highlight in this editorial.

Most important in the eyes of the Charter promoters is the issue of perception and identity. Ever since Maastricht, the political legitimacy of the European construct has been a live issue; the advent of EMU with its barely accountable European Central Bank has added fuel to a perception of a Europe concerned more with markets than with people. It may be true that the European Court guarantees legal protection against human rights abuses, but who is aware of this?

A Charter, its supporters say, will render visible and prominent that which until now was known only to dusty lawyers. Additionally, the Charter, as an important symbol, will counterbalance the Euro and become part of the iconography of European integration and contribute both to the identity of and identification with Europe.

These are weighty considerations but they are, too, part of a risky strategy which may backfire. The final status of the Charter, a controversial issue, was left to be decided by the IGC. It is known that some prominent member States are opposed to enshrining it in the Treaties or giving it any other binding legal character. Such an outcome will produce the opposite effect – a symbol of European impotence and refusal to takes rights seriously. From no perception we will have moved to a negative perception.

---

[5] One must celebrate the appointment of representatives of both member State governments and national Parliaments and also the relative transparency of the process. The official website http://db.consilium.eu.int/df/default.asp?lang=en is mostly useful and is a good source for the official line on the Charter as well as source documents.

Clarity is a second justification often invoked to justify the exercise. The current system of looking to the common constitutional traditions and to the ECHR as a source for the rights protected in the Union is, it is argued, unsatisfactory and should be replaced by a formal document listing such rights. But would clarity actually be added?

First, much of the Charter will be drafted in the magisterial language characteristic of our constitutional traditions: Human Dignity is Inviolable, etc. There is much to be said for this tradition, but clarity is not one of them.

Second, by drafting a list, we will be jettisoning one of the truly original features of the current constitutional architecture in the field of human rights – the ability to use the legal system of each of the member States as an organic and living laboratory of human rights protection which then, case by case, can be adapted and adopted for the needs of the Union by the European Court in dialogue with its national counterparts. A Charter may not thwart that process, but it runs the risk of inducing a more inward looking jurisprudence and chilling the constitutional dialogue.

Drafting a new Charter, it is said, would give the chance of introducing much needed innovation to our constitutional norms which are shaped by aging constitutions and international treaties. Issues such as bio-technology, genetic engineering, privacy in the age of the internet, sexual identity and, most importantly, political rights empowering the individual could be dealt with afresh, placing the Charter at the avant-garde of European constitutionalism.

But what if the Charter sticks, as the current draft at least in part illustrates, to the rusty and trusty formulae of yesteryear around which constitutional consensus already exists and thus avoids innovation – not an unlikely outcome given a body composed of representatives of governments and parliaments from fifteen different countries operating on the principle of consensus. This outcome would not merely consecrate the status quo. It could be regressive: each time an innovative concept were to be argued before the European Court, it would be pointed out that a proposal to that effect was considered in the drafting of the Charter and failed. It would be much harder for the Court to crystallize a Community right when such was considered and rejected by a political constituent assembly. One can already see, in for example the definition of the scope of human rights protection, how the current process has cut down on the status quo.

There is something very troubling that in this exercise of constitutional drafting de facto ultimate say is given to the executive branches of the member States in the context of the IGC.

Finally, if the purpose of the Charter is to enhance the protection of fundamental rights in the Union, the most troubling aspect of this entire exercise is the fact that it serves as a subterfuge, an alibi, for not doing that which is truly necessary.

The real problem of the Community is the absence of a *human rights policy* with everything this entails: A Commissioner, a Directorate General, a budget and a horizontal action plan for making those rights already granted by the Treaties and judicially protected by the various levels of European Courts effective. Much of the human rights story, and its abuse, takes place far from the august halls of courts. Most of those whose rights are violated have neither knowledge or means to seek judicial vindication. The Union does not need more rights on its lists, or more lists of rights. What is mostly needed are programmes and agencies to make rights real, not simply negative interdictions which courts can enforce.

The best way to drive the point home is to think of competition policy. Imagine our Community with an Article 85 and 86 (currently 81 and 82) interdicting restrictive practices and abuse of dominant position, but not having a Commissioner and a DG4 to monitor, investigate, regulate and prosecute. That is exactly the situation with human rights. For the most part the appropriate norms are in place. If violations were to reach the Court, the judicial reaction would be equally appropriate. But would there be any chance effectively to combat anti-trust violations without a DG4? Do we have any chance in the human rights field, without having a similar institutional set up?

One reason we do not have a policy is because the Court, in its wisdom, announced in Opinion 2/94 that protection of human rights is not one of the policy objectives of the Community and thus cannot be a subject for a proactive policy.

Far more important than any Charter for the effective vindication of human rights would be a simple Treaty amendment which made the active protection of human rights within the sphere of application of Community law one of the policies of the Community alongside other policies and objectives in Article 3 and a commitment to take all measures to give teeth to such a policy expeditiously.[6]

Would it not be nice if the current stealth IGC surprised us all and in addition to the Charter also amended Article 3 and formally announced the establishment of a Human Rights policy?

Competences

The final issue relates to the competences of the Union and Community. In one of its most celebrated cases in the early 1960s the European Court of Justice described the Community as a '... new legal order for the benefit of which the States have limited their sovereign rights, albeit in limited fields'. There is a widespread anxiety that these fields are limited no more. Indeed, not long ago a prominent

[6] For a fully fledge discussion of the need and content of such a policy, see Philip Alston and J.H.H. Weiler, 'An "Ever Closer Union" in Need of a Human Rights Policy: The European Union and Human Rights', Harvard Jean Monnet Working Paper 1/99 www.law.harvard.edu/programs/JeanMonnet/

European scholar and judge wrote that there '... simply is no nucleus of sovereignty that the member States can invoke, as such, against the Community'.[7]

The problem of competences is, in part, one of perception. The perception has set in that the boundaries which were meant to circumscribe the areas in which the Community could operate have been irretrievably breached. Few perceptions have been more detrimental to the legitimacy of the Community in the eyes of its citizens. And not only its citizens. Governments and even courts, for example the German Constitutional Court, have rebelled against the Community constitutional order because, in part, of a profound dissatisfaction on this very issue. One cannot afford to sweep this issue under the carpet. The crisis is already there. The main problem, then, is not one of moving the boundary lines but of restoring faith in the inviolability of the boundaries between Community and member State competences.

Comparative analysis of federal systems demonstrates that any attempt to formulate constitutional boundaries which will be impervious to centralized transgression is doomed. The problem rests in the fact that historically, centralized courts charged with policing constitutional boundaries have either identified with an expansionist ideology or have abdicated such control to the political process. By contrast, in those few instances where the central adjudicatory body did not itself become an agent of transgressing boundaries, the boundaries were maintained.

Any proposal which envisages the creation of a new institution is doomed in the eyes of some. And yet I propose the creation of a Constitutional Council for the Community, modeled in some ways on its French namesake. The Constitutional Council would have jurisdiction only over issues of competences (including subsidiarity) and would, like its French cousin, decide cases submitted to it after a law was adopted but before coming into force. It could be seized by any Commission, Council, any member State or by the European Parliament acting on a majority of its Members. I think that serious consideration should be given to allowing member State Parliaments to bring cases before the Constitutional Council.

The composition of the Council is the key to its legitimacy. Its President would be the President of the European Court of Justice and its Members would be sitting members of the constitutional courts or their equivalents in the member States. Within the European Constitutional Council no single member State would have a veto power. All its decisions would be by majority.

The composition of the European Constitutional Council would, I believe, help restore confidence in the ability to have effective policing of the boundaries

---

[7] Lenaerts, 'Constitutionalism and the Many Faces of Federalism', 38 A. J.Com. L 205 (1990) at p. 220. The Court, too, has modified its rhetoric: in its more recent Opinion 1/91 it refers to the member States as having limited their sovereign rights '... in ever wider fields.' Opinion 1/91, [1991] ECR 6079, Recital 21.

as well as underscore that the question of competences is fundamentally also one of national constitutional norms but still subject to a binding and uniform solution by a Union institution

I know that this proposal might be taken as an assault on the integrity of the European Court of Justice. That attitude would, in my view, be mistaken. The question of competences has become so politicized that the European Court of Justice should welcome having this hot potato removed from its plate by an *ex ante* decision of that other body with a jurisdiction limited to that preliminary issue. Yes, there is potential for conflict of jurisprudence and all the rest – but nothing that competent drafting cannot deal with.

DRAFTING A CHARTER OF FUNDAMENTAL RIGHTS OF THE EUROPEAN UNION

Henry G. Schermers *

1. IS THE COMMUNITY BOUND BY THE CONVENTION?

Is the European Union already bound by the human rights codified in the European Convention on Human Rights? When on 18 April 1951 the European Community for Coal and Steel was established the Convention was not yet in force but when in March 1957 the EEC and EURATOM Treaties were signed five of the six signatory states were parties to the Convention. Only France ratified the Convention at a later date (3 May 1974). Five states had restricted the powers of their governments. Could they transfer unrestrictive powers to a new Community?

Especially in Germany the submission that the European Communities would not be bound by human rights raised problems. The first chapter of the German Federal Constitution enumerates the most important human rights. Subsequently, in Article 79 the Constitution provided that the basic principles laid down in these articles may not be amended. It was obvious that the powers of the German Federal Government were restricted by the human rights enumerated in the Constitution and that the German Government had no authority to create an international organisation which would not be bound by the same fundamental rights. According to many German lawyers the classical rule that nobody can transfer more powers than he has means that all powers of the European Communities are restricted by the same fundamental human rights that restrict the powers of the German Government.

Although the academic discussion on this problem was almost entirely German, the problem existed for most other member States as well. There were good reasons to presume that the Community was necessarily bound by the same human rights which limited the powers of the member States. However, there was no legal relationship between the European Communities and the institutions of the European Convention on Human Rights. If ever the European Court of Human Rights were to decide that the Community had to pay damages or had to

* Professor of Law, Leyden University. Former member of the European Commission of Human Rights.

A.E. Kellermann et al. (Eds.), EU Enlargement: The Constitutional Impact at EU and National Level

change its legislation, how could such a judgment be enforced if the Community was not legally bound?

The question then arose what one could do if the Community took a decision in violation of the Convention. Because of the procedure for decision-making it is unlikely that the Community will ever make regulations or directives contrary to the Convention. But an individual decision contrary to the Convention could be possible.

In July 1978 the first case against the Community came before the European Commission of Human Rights. It had to decide on application 8030/77 of the Confédération Française Démocratique du Travail (CFDT). The case was brought against the European Communities and alternatively against their member States jointly and against each of the member States separately (at that time Belgium, Denmark, France, Germany, Ireland, Italy, Luxembourg, the Netherlands, U.K.).

Article 18 of the ECSC Treaty provided:

> 'A Consultative Committee shall be attached to the High Authority. It shall consist of not less than 60 and not more than 84 members and shall comprise equal number of producers, of workers and of consumers and dealers. The members of the Consultative Committee shall be appointed by the Council. In the case of the producers and workers, the Council shall designate representative organisations among which it shall allocate the seats to be filled. Each organisation shall be required to draw up a list containing twice as many names as there are seats allotted to it. Appointment shall be made from this list.'

CFDT sent two names for one of the posts allocated to the workers' organisations of France.

CFDT was the second largest workers' organisation in France and also the second largest organisation of workers in the coal and steel industry. Three smaller French organisations were represented in the Consultative Committee but representation of CFDT was systematically refused.

CFDT had no possibility to bring this situation before the Court of Justice of the European Communities. It complained in Strasbourg under Articles 11, 13 and 14 of the Convention.

The European Commission of Human Rights held:

> '2. The Commission would first like to point out that the applicant is complaining of the act of an organ of the Communities, i.e., the Council of the European Communities, relating to the composition of another organ of the Communities, i.e., the Consultative Committee to the High Authority. This is an act whose effects concern the internal organisation of the European Communities who under Article 6 of the ECSC Treaty, Article 210 of the EEC Treaty and Article 184 of the EAEC Treaty have their own legal personality and are represented by their own institutions, each acting within the ambit of their powers.

On the alleged responsibility of the European Communities itself

3. In so far as the application is directed against the European Communities as such the Commission points out that the European Communities are not a Contracting Party to the European Convention on Human Rights (Art. 66 of the Convention). To this extent the consideration of the applicant's complaint lies outside the Commission's jurisdiction *ratione personae.*

On the alleged responsibility of the member States of the European Communities jointly

4. In so far as the application is directed against "the member States jointly", the Commission finds that the applicant has not defined what it means by this. On this point the Commission considers that the application is in fact directed against the Council of the European Communities. It follows that a consideration of the applicant's complaints, in this case also, lies outside the Commission's jurisdiction ratione personae.

On the alleged responsibility of the member States of the European Communities severally

5. In so far as the application is directed against each of the member States of the European Communities who are at the same time Contracting Parties to the Convention the question might be raised whether the act complained of, which was carried out by an organ of the European Communities, can involve the responsibility of the 9 member States of the European Communities under the Convention.

6. Whatever the answer to this question the Commission points out that as far as France is concerned a consideration of the application lies outside its jurisdiction *ratione personae* as France has not so far recognised the right of individual petition under Article 25 of the Convention.

7. As regards the eight other member States of the European Communities, the Commission considers that an examination of the applicant's complaints is also outside its jurisdiction *ratione personae* since these States by taking part in the decision of the Council of the European Communities had not in the circumstances of the instant case exercised their "jurisdiction" within the meaning of Article 1 of the Convention.

For these reasons the Commission

DECLARES THE APPLICATION INADMISSIBLE.[1]

After this case all complaints against the Community have been declared inadmissible for the reason that the Community was not bound by the Convention.

[1] CFDT Case, no. 8030/77, Decision of 10 July 1978, 13 DR 231, at pp. 239, 240.

2. ARE THE MEMBER STATES LIABLE FOR INFRINGEMENTS BY THE COMMUNITY?

Germany was bound by the Convention when it concluded the EEC Treaty. It could be submitted, therefore, that Germany had not been able to transfer unrestricted powers to the Community and that Germany remained responsible for any violations of the Convention by the Community. This issue finally came before the European Commission of Human Rights.

In December 1979 the Commission of the European Communities imposed a fine of 1,450,000 European Units of Account (DM 3,596,667) on the firm M & Co for having violated Article 85(1) of the EC Treaty (now Art. 81).

M & Co challenged the fine before the Court of Justice of the European Communities (ECJ). They claimed that they had not had a fair trial for, inter alia, the following reasons:

a. that the EC Commission acted both as a prosecuting and decision-making authority;
b. that they had not been informed about all charges which were determined in the EC Commission's decision;
c. that the EC Commission had not made available for examination all documents on which it later based its decision;
d. that the observations of the Advisory Committee (on Restrictive Practices and Monopolies) had not been communicated to them.

The ECJ reduced the fine to 400,000 Units of Account (DM 992,892) but it did not annul the decision of the Commission.

Execution of judgments of the ECJ is through the national authorities. M & Co brought an action against the execution before the German courts. In January 1985 the Federal Constitutional Court dismissed the constitutional complaint against the Federal Minister of Justice issuing a writ of execution and in April 1987 the same court rejected a complaint against the execution of this writ.

Subsequently, M & Co brought this case before the European Commission of Human Rights.

The Commission was faced with a dilemma. On the one hand, the rights enumerated in the Convention should be protected and it should not be tolerated that the States, parties to the Convention could 'contract out' of their obligations by transferring unrestricted powers to others.

On the other hand, it was hard to accept that the member States of the Communities would be obliged to check the legality of Community acts before executing them. This would conflict with the very idea of supranationality. The unchallengeable priority of Community law has been achieved over a period of time and with great effort of many people involved. In *Costa-ENEL*, the ECJ held:

> 'By creating a Community of unlimited duration, having its own institutions, its own personality, its own legal capacity and capacity of representation on the international plane and, more particularly, real powers stemming from a limitation of sovereignty or a transfer of powers from the States to the Community, the member States have limited their sovereign rights, albeit within limited fields, and have thus created a body of law which binds both their nationals and themselves.
>
> It follows from all these observations that the law stemming from the Treaty, an independent source of law, could not, because of its special and original nature, be overriden by domestic legal provisions, however framed, without being deprived of its character as Community law and without the legal basis of the Community itself being called into question.
>
> The transfer by the States from their domestic legal system to the Community legal system of the rights and obligations arising under the Treaty carries with it a permanent limitation of their sovereign rights, against which a subsequent unilateral act incompatible with the concept of the Community cannot prevail.'[2]

Several members of the European Commission of Human Rights had specialized in European Community law for many years. They had followed and supported the development towards full priority of Community law over national law. They had encouraged national judiciaries to accept the priority of Community law and they had observed that the national judiciaries indeed accepted that priority. By doing so the national supreme courts in fact 'ratified' that priority on behalf of their states.[3]

Article 1 of the Statute of the Council of Europe provides that the aim of the Council is to achieve greater unity between its Members. The preamble of the Convention confirms this aim. Taking this into account it must be understandable that several members of the Commission were reluctant to accept that Germany should verify the legality of a Community decision before executing it. Such requirement would seriously harm the priority of Community law as many future applicants would then – rightly or wrongly – oblige national courts to decide on the legality of Community acts by challenging that legality.

Finally, in its decision on the admissibility of M & Co's claim, the Commission tried to find a reasonable balance between all interests, holding:

> 'The Commission first recalls that it is in fact not competent *ratione personae* to examine proceedings before or decisions of organs of the European Communities, the latter not being a Party to the European Convention on Human Rights (see No. 8030/77, *CFDT* v. *European Communities*, Dec. 10.7.78, DR 13 p. 231; No 13539/88, *D.* v. *European Communities*, Dec. 19.1.89). This does not mean, however, that by granting executory power to a judgment of the European Court of Justice the competent German authorities acted quasi as Community organs and are to that extent beyond the

[2] *Costa-ENEL* case (6/64) 15 July 1964 [1964] ECR 585, at 593, 594.

[3] Matthias Herdegen at a conference in Malmö in August 1999.

scope of control exercised by the Convention organs. Under Article 1 of the Convention the member States are responsible for all acts and omissions of their domestic organs allegedly violating the Convention regardless of whether the act or omission in question is a consequence of domestic law or regulations or of the necessity to comply with international obligations (cf., *mutatis mutandis*, No. 6231/73, *Ilse Hess* v. *the United Kingdom*, Dec. 28.5.75, DR 2, p. 72 (74)).
The question therefore is whether by giving effect to a judgment reached in proceedings that allegedly violated Article 6 the Federal Republic of Germany incurred responsibility under the Convention on account of the fact that these proceedings against a German company were possible only because the Federal Republic has transferred its powers in this sphere to the European Communities.
For the purpose of the examination of this question it can be assumed that the anti-trust proceedings in question would fall under Article 6 had they been conducted by German and not by European judicial authorities (cf., Eur. Court H.R., Öztürk judgment of 21 Feb. 1984, Series A no. 73, pp. 17-22, paras. 46-56; No. 11598/85, Dec. 11.7.89, DR 61, p. 125).
It has next to be observed that the Convention does not prohibit a member State from transferring powers to international organisations. Nonetheless, the Commission recalls that "if a State contracts treaty obligations and subsequently concludes another international agreement which disables it from performing its obligations under the first treaty it will be answerable for any resulting breach of its obligations under the earlier treaty" (cf., No. 235/56, Dec. 10.6.58, Yearbook 2, p. 256 (300)). The Commission considers that a transfer of powers does not necessarily exclude a State's responsibility under the Convention with regard to the exercise of the transferred powers. Otherwise the guarantees of the Convention could want only be limited or excluded and thus be deprived of their peremptory character. The object and purpose of the Convention as an instrument for the protection of individual human beings requires that its provisions be interpreted and applied so as to make its safeguards practical and effective (cf., Eur. Court H.R., Soering judgment of 7 July 1989, Series A no. 161, p. 34, para. 87). Therefore the transfer of powers to an international organisation is not incompatible with the Convention provided that within that organisation fundamental rights will receive an equivalent protection.
The Commission notes that the legal system of the European Communities not only secures fundamental rights but also provides for control of their observance. It is true that the constituent treaties of the European Communities did not contain a catalogue of such rights. However, the Parliament, the Council and the Commission of the European Communities have stressed in a joint declaration of 5 April 1977 that they attach prime importance to the protection of fundamental rights, as derived in particular from the Constitution of the member States and the European Convention for the Protection of Human Rights and Fundamental Freedoms. They pledged that, in the exercise of their powers and in pursuance of the aims of the European Communities, they would respect and continue to respect these human rights (Official Journal of the European Communities, XX, 1977, Information and Notices, No. C 103/I). In addition the Court of Justice of the European Communities has developed a case-law according to which it is called upon to control Community acts on the basis of fundamental rights, including those enshrined in the European Convention on Human Rights. In accordance with this reasoning the Court of Justice underlined in the present case that the right to a fair

hearing is a fundamental principle of Community law. It stated that Community law contained all criteria which are prerequisites not only to examine but, if necessary, to remedy the applicant company's complaint that its right to a fair hearing was violated (see p. 76 of the judgment). However, it came to the conclusion that this complaint was unfounded.
The Commission has also taken into consideration that it would be contrary to the very idea of transferring powers to an international organisation to hold the member States responsible for examining, in each individual case before issuing a writ of execution for a judgment of the European Court of Justice, whether Article 6 of the Convention was respected in the underlying proceedings.
It follows that the application is incompatible with the provisions of the Convention *ratione materiae* and must be rejected in accordance with Article 27 para. 2 of the Convention.

For these reasons, the Commission

DECLARES THE APPLICATION INADMISSIBLE.'[4]

Four years later Mrs Matthews brought a case for Community violation of human rights against the United Kingdom. As a citizen of Gibraltar she had not been permitted to participate in the voting for the European Parliament. As Article 3 of the First Protocol to the Convention gives a right to participate in elections for the legislature she claimed that the UK had violated her fundamental right by not providing a possibility for her to participate in the voting. It was disputed whether the European Parliament was part of the legislature. If it was not, Article 3 of the First Protocol to the Convention would not at all be applicable. Furthermore, the case differed from M & Co because the exclusion of Gibraltar from the voting for the European Parliament was laid down in a treaty text and therefore not subject to any control by the ECJ. Unlike the previous cases the Commission declared this case admissible (though it did not find a violation of the Convention) which meant that it could be brought before the European Court of Human Rights. This Court found in its new composition that the United Kingdom had breached Article 3 of Protocol 1. The Court did not refer to M & Co and it is not clear whether it confirmed the Commission's reasoning that Community member States would not have been liable if there had been sufficient judicial control by the Community itself.

3. FURTHER DEVELOPMENTS

For the sake of the supremacy of Community law one may hope that the Court will follow M & Co, for the sake of human rights protection this may be differ-

[4] M & Co case, no. 13258/87, Decision of 9 Feb. 1990, 64 DR 138, at pp. 144-146.

ent. If M & Co is followed, judgment of the conformity of supranational rules with the requirements of the Convention is left to the judiciary of the supranational organisation. In practice, this will usually be the Community. In practice, the member States will be liable only if the organisation exercises no judicial control itself. If M & Co is not followed any infringement committed by the Community can be attributed to the member States, because they empowered the Community. In order to fulfil their obligations under the Convention all member States would then be obliged to verify whether a Community act is in conformity with the Convention before it can be executed. If after such verification any doubt would remain all affected individuals could then bring an application against any member State (or against all member States at the same time, or each against a different member State) and the member State would have to explain and defend the Community act in Strasbourg. This would create great practical problems and may finally force the Community to accede to the European Convention. After adherance to the Convention cases could be brought against the Community itself which would enable the Community to defend itself in Strasbourg.

4. THE CHARTER

Would the addition of a Charter of Human Rights to the Treaty of the Union offer a solution? Clearly, the answer must be: 'No'. A charter of human rights in the Treaty of the Union would perform the same role as a chapter on human rights in any national constitution. It would contain rights which individuals must exhaust before they are permitted to bring a complaint to the European Court of Human Rights. But the Charter could not replace the Convention. Even if the Charter would be literally the same as the European Convention on Human Rights the interpretation of the provisions by the ECJ could diverge from the interpretation by the European Court of Human Rights. Therefore, individual applicants would continue to attack in Strasbourg member States for acts committed by the Community. However interesting a charter of human rights may be for the citizens of the Union, it will not solve any future conflict with the European Convention on Human Rights.

The right to bring a complaint to the Strasbourg Court, which is guaranteed by the Convention, cannot be taken away without the agreement of all 41 Convention states. The Charter will offer valuable protection against infringements of human rights by Community institutions. At the moment this protection is offered by the Court of Justice, but it is not guaranteed by the text of any Treaty. With respect to the protection of human rights by the member States it can offer no more than duplication.

If the citizens of the Union could invoke the Charter before the ECJ against any infringement of fundamental rights, be it by the Community or by a member

State, then also the individual could subsequently bring his case to the European Court of Human Rights.

In the event of a violation by a member State this would lead to further delays in a field where cases already take too long. Imagine, how a case would develop:

A citizen is of the opinion that his state infringed one of the human rights guaranteed by both the Charter and the Convention. Wishing to bring his case before the Human Rights Court he starts exhausting domestic remedies. Then at first or second instance the national court postpones its decision for requesting a preliminary ruling of the ECJ about the conformity with the Charter. After some two years the ECJ rules. If it finds a violation the case may be finished somehow. But usually it will not find a violation (in Strasbourg some 95% of the complaints brought do not lead to a finding of a violation). The national court will rule accordingly and the applicant will go on exhausting domestic remedies. Finally, his case will come before the European Court of Human Rights, which will decide the question, unless it will apply Article 35 para. 2b of the Convention which provides that the Court shall not deal with any individual application that has already been submitted to another procedure of international investigation. However, it may be doubted whether the internal procedures of European Union qualify as international investigations by which investigations by a human rights body were probably meant and not investigations by the highest court of a particular legal order. In any case the proceedings will lead to further delay. As cases already take too much time this seems undesirable.

In practice, this scenario may be rare. The Charter will not apply to purely domestic matters of the member States. Acts of member States can be challenged under the Charter before the ECJ only when they are in execution of Community rules. We may hope that this will reduce the number of acts challengeable under domestic law of a member State as well as under the Community Charter, as well as under the Convention, because in practice these possibilities may accumulate.

There remain the cases against the Community. There will be little change. At present violation of human rights will be a ground for annulment of a Community act. The ECJ applies fundamental human rights as general principles of law. Acceptance of the Charter will offer a clearer and more binding foundation to the existing case-law, but there is no clear indication that it will change that case-law.

In its report of 16 May 2000 the Select Committee on the European Union of the House of Lords in the UK concluded that the potential significance of the Charter, both politically and legally, is very great. Certainly this is true for the political significance. Propagating the protection of human rights throughout the world without oneself being formally bound by them weakens the position of the Union. Whether the Charter will be legally important will depend on its final content. In as far as it will add human rights to those accepted by the ECJ it may indeed be important.

The Select Committee also concluded that accession to the Convention is 'the crucial step' in filling the gap in the protection of fundamental rights currently lacking within the Union. This is a remarkable conclusion as in their previous reports[5] the Select Committee advised against such accession. We hope that this new conclusion may lead to UK support for the Union becoming a party to the European Convention on Human Rights.

[5] House of Lords, Select Committee on the European Union *Human Rights*, 71st Report 1979-80 HL Paper 362; and ibid., *Human Rights Re-examined*, 3rd Report 1992-93, HL Paper 10.

ON HUMAN RIGHTS AND THE IDEA OF A EUROPEAN CHARTER OF FUNDAMENTAL RIGHTS

Roger Errera *

Starting from the present situation relating to fundamental rights in the EU and some of the criticism it has been subjected to, I shall try to discuss some of the issues raised by the idea of a European Human Rights Charter. I have been guided by two ideas: the recognition of what has been so far achived in the field of human rights in the EC/EU; and, secondly, the necessity, in view of the importance of the issue, to be clear about what one wants to do, and its consequences.

1. THE PRESENT SITUATION OF FUNDAMENTAL RIGHTS IN EC LAW

There is, to-day, an 'acquis communautaire' relating to fundamental rights. Some of them are contained in the Treaty itself. I will not discuss them here. For the rest, I will discuss briefly three points:

1. This 'acquis' has one author: the ECJ. A few words on its method are in order;
2. I will then comment on the contents of such an acquis;
3. And then on its scope.

1) The ECJ and its method:
The main architect has been, and is, the ECJ. There is no need to repeat here the different stages of its growth and the external context of this dupt, e.g., the attitudes of domestic constitutional courts (Germany, Italy).

The main tool[1] has been that of the general principles of (Community) law.[2] Such a technique is familiar to other courts (e.g., the ICJ or the French Conseil d'Etat). As to the source of such fundamental rights, the ECJ has been increasingly using either written instruments: the ECHR, other human rights treaties ratified by the member States and the common constitutional traditions of the mem-

* Member of the Council of State, Paris.

[1] Well before Maastricht or Amsterdam or the Single Act.

[2] E.g., the UN Covenants: *Dzodzi* (1990); *Solvay* (1989); *Johnston* (1994); *Bergemann* (1988) and The European Social Charter: *Blaizot* (1988); *Defrenne* (1978); *Speybrouk* (1992).

A.E. Kellermann et al. (Eds.), EU Enlargement: The Constitutional Impact at EU and National Level

ber States. The Maastricht and Amsterdam treaties contain a timely and partial codification of such a method.

The Court has always underlined that its dicta relating to fundamental rights were always to be seen and interpreted in the context of the objectives and of the structures of the EC.

One of the consequences is the following: while borrowing extensively from the case law of the ECHR the ECJ has always maintained its autonomy as to the interpretation of both the convention and the case law.

2) The result is an impressive one:

a) A complete enumeration of all the fundamental rights recognized, i.e., created by the Court and belonging to such a corpus would take too long. I will quote some of them:

- the right to domestic judicial review whenever a right conferred by EC law is at stake: *Johnston* (1985) quoting articles 6 and 13 ECHR
- freedom of expression: *ERT* (1991)
- non-retroactivity in criminal law: *Kent Kirk* (1984), *Landeweyck* (1980)
- freedom of association: *Rutili* (1975)
- property, and free exercise of economic and professional activities: *Nold* (1974), *Hauer* (1979)
- the right to a fair trial within a resonable delay, see *Baustahlgewebe* (1998)
- Non-discrimination on religious grounds, *Prajs* (1976)
- protection of family life: *Commission* v. *Germany* (1989)

b) In addition to these rights, the case law of the ECJ has affirmed a set of very important legal principles:

- legal certainty
- Vertrauensschütz ('protection de la confiance légitime')
- Non bis in idem.[3]

3) As to the scope of these fundamental rights, they apply not only to all EC decisions, but also to domestic decisions whenever they relate to an area covered by EC law: See *Wachauf* (1989); *ERT* (1991). If this condition is not fulfilled, the court tacks jurisdiction, as shown in *Kremzow*.

2. THE DEFECTS OF THE PRESENT SYSTEM

Although it has achieved a number of remarkable and valuable results, the present system may suffer from a number of defects. It is not, it has been suggested, as complete and as clear as it should be.

[3] This list is not a closed one. New developments in the case law may add other rights or principles. This is an open-ended operation.

I shall make five remarks.

1) There is no complete enumeration of fundamental rights in the Treaty.

2) There are real limitations[4] on the role of the Luxembourg Court:
a) the referral procedure is a slow one, and depends exclusively on national courts;
b) the Treaty limits direct action before the ECJ (Art. 230);
c) the jurisdiction of the Court is limited by the Amsterdam Treaty in relation to titles IV and VI of the Treaty.

3) While it is true that the ECJ increasingly quotes[5], uses and applies the ECHR, it does so through the notion of general principles of Community law. It is thus free to interpret the Convention, which is not incorporated, as such, into EC law.[6] Hence there is the risk and the reality of divergences between the Luxembourg and Strasbourg Courts.
The examples are well known, and there is no need to describe them fully here. Their importance should not be over stressed. See, e.g.:
- on the scope of Article 8, as to searches in the premises of companies:
  according to the ECHR, Article 8 applies: *Niemetz* (Dec. 12, 1992). *Chappell* (March 3, 1989).
  according to the ECJ, it does not: *Hoechst* (Sept. 21, 1989) (see also CFI, *LVM*, 1999).
  - on the role of the Advocate general, see *Emesa Sugar* (February 4, 2000),
  - on the procedure of administrative penalties (right to silence and to absence of self-incrimination), see ECJ, *Orkem* (1989) and ECHR, *Funke* (1993) and *Murray* (1996).
- on the scope of Article 10, see:
  - ECHR, *Open Door* v. *Ireland* (October 29, 1992),
  - ECJ, *Grogan* (October 4, 1991), showing an absence of convergence.

4) While the contribution of the ECJ to the affirmation of fundamental rights as part of EC law is fully recognized, the present situation lacks legal certainty and needs clarification.

5) The Amsterdam Treaty has increased the jurisdiction of both the EC and the EU (immigration, asylum – for the EC: title IV) (title VI for the EU).
What will be done in these areas may affect fundamental rights. But the Amsterdam Treaty limits the jurisdiction of the ECJ in these very areas.

---

[4] Procedural and jurisdictional ones.
[5] Since *Rutili* (1975).
[6] The ECHR has no jurisdiction over EC acts.

3. THE REMEDIES: A CHARTER? WHY, AND WHAT FOR?

1. Proposals other than a Charter?
a) Accession of the EC to the ECHR
It is not on the agenda of the IGC. It never was. Such an accession would need a revision of both treaties, by 41 and 15 states respectively. The length and very outcome of such an exercise are highly unpredictable. It would, in the professed opinion of its proponents, lead to the subordination of the ECJ to the ECHR, i.e., the end of the autonomy of the EC legal system, all this for a very marginal benefit.
b) Institutional reforms in the EC or EU:
- a Human Rights Directorate
- a Human Rights Commissioner
- a Human Rights Chamber in the ECJ
- Monitoring mechanisms in EC countries.

2) The Charter and beyond[7]
A) A charter: what for?
There are indeed many answers to such a simple – and vital – question:
a) According to the conclusions of the Cologne Council of June 1999 the aim is to affirm the exceptional importance of human rights and their scope in a manner that can be seen and understood by the citizens of the Union. What these citizens will do with such a charter and how they might use it is not to be found in the Cologne communiqué.
b) Other people think that the affirmation and existence of such a charter might be one of the elements in the process of constitutionalization of the EU, and is seen as a valuable objective.
c) Other people would like such a charter to be, one day, incorporated into the treaties and thus become part of EC law, and invoked before the ECJ or the CFI.
Other aims may exist. One must be clear about them, and be able to choose between symbols and realities or, at least, to distinguish between them. The EU citizen, in the name of which all this is supposedly done, is entitled to this.

B) Let us go further.
If such a charter has full legal value, i.e., is incorporated into the treaties, what about its contents?
– If the contents are, in fact, that of the ECHR, I see little interest in such an operation: the divergences between Strasbourg and Luxembourg will not disappear. Since, in view of the ECJ's case law and of the Amsterdam Treaty, the substance

[7] I am one of those who attach great weight to the Cologne Council initiative, and to the work of the Convention, under the chairmanship of Pr Herzog. It is the first initiative of that sort. I am certain that it will have major consequences, both legal and political.

of the ECHR is, more or less, de facto incorporated into EC law, why go to such trouble?

– If the contents are the ECHR as it stands to-day, plus new clauses relating to areas not covered by it (and not by EC law to-day), will this replace Article 6.2 of the EU Treaty? Will the ECJ be forbidden to use general principles of law or common constitutional traditions?

This might lead to a regression, not a progress.

We shall probably have, at the Nice Council, a political declaration. But its future status must be watched with care.

C) Finally what I believe is this:

1. Respect for human rights is a condition of the legality of the EC's acts. They are a vital dimension of EC law. They are not, in general, unless the Treaty says so, among the Community's objects, or objectives.

2. The differences of approach between the ECJ and the ECHR, leading at times to divergences are not only inevitable, they are fully legitimate. When it decides a case, including those with a human rights dimension, the ECJ does so by taking into account, as it is bound to, the structures and objectives of the Community. This applies both to the substance of the rights and to the scope of their possible limitation. This is indeed the justification of the necessary autonomy of the ECJ in the interpretation of the ECHR or of other treaties.

D) To try to create a perfect legal system without any gaps or inconsistencies is a rather vain exercise.

Both courts do have exchanges and contacts. They are aware of each other's existence, case law, and problems. Both of them know that, not far from them, there are governments[8], and constitutional courts.[9]

The *Matthews* case has shown the extent to which the ECHR is prepared to review domestic decisions taken to implement EC law, albeit a treaty.

Enlightened pragmatism, gradual process and useful dialogue have, to this day, produced better results than the full application of logic and procustean geometry, what Professor Weiler has aptly called the 'politics of image', the 'policy of evasion', that is, the exact reverse of 'taking rights seriously'.

---

[8] 'Die Herren des Vertrages', to quote the German Constitutional Court decision of 1993.

[9] If the authority and primacy of the ECJ is weakened, they will surely take note, and draw the consequences.

THE EU CHARTER OF FUNDAMENTAL RIGHTS: A BUILDING BLOCK FOR THE EUROPEAN CONSTITUTIONAL ORDER

Ernst M.H. Hirsch Ballin*

The work on the Draft Charter of Fundamental Rights of the European Union has been completed. After intense discussions on previous drafts and hundreds of amendments, the 62 members of the Convention met for the last time on October 3, 2000 in Brussels and reached consensus – notwithstanding individual comments on some of the articles – that the draft was ready for presentation to the European Council. In December 2000, the Charter was proclaimed as a leading document for European cooperation. The member States are still divided on the question of whether or not in the future the Charter will be a part of the Treaties. Answering this question will probably take several years. For myself as well for the other Dutch members of the Convention, an important point since the beginning of the work has been, and will be also in the future, the relationship with the European Convention for the Protection of Human Rights and Fundamental Freedoms.

Both Houses of the Dutch Parliament have expressed their view that the European Union and the European Community should accede to the European Convention. There are simply no sound arguments against. All the current member States and possible future member States of the Union are bound by the European Convention and, according to the case law of the Strasbourg Court of Human Rights, the contracting parties are bound by the Convention also in the application of EU law.

The work on the Charter can be viewed as an escape from the question that could have been on the table of the intergovernmental conference, i.e., the approval of clauses in the European Treaties allowing accession to the European Convention on Human Rights. Apparently some politicians, even in the highest ranks, tend to be frightened by the legal discipline and judicial powers. These politicians may not really feel reassured, but they should understand that there is simply no escape from judicial review. According to well-established case law and Article 6 of the Treaty on European Union, the Luxembourg Court, along with the national judiciaries, already has the obligation to examine the conformity

* Senator and Professor of International Law, Tilburg University.

A.E. Kellermann et al. (Eds.), EU Enlargement: The Constitutional Impact at EU and National Level

of European decisions with the rights and freedoms under the European Convention. What is at stake, however, is that we should not have different interpretations of these fundamental rights by the Courts in Strasbourg and Luxembourg, respectively. In the long run, we cannot do without a coordination mechanism between the Luxembourg and Strasbourg Courts, based on the acknowledgement that the unity of doctrine in EC law has its proper place in Luxemburg, and interpretation of fundamental rights in Strasbourg. The Charter aims at minimizing the risks through using identical phrasing for rights that are the same in both documents.

Maybe we could have done without a Charter of Fundamental Rights of the European Union if the European Council had managed to apply for EU and EC membership of the European Convention. In my opinion, the approval of a Charter would nevertheless constitute a favourable development that could pave the way for a plain acceptance of the European Convention. Hopefully, it will make politicians realise that having two uncoordinated spheres of jurisdiction is in nobody's interest.

Beside this rather pragmatic argument in favour of the Charter, I see another, more fundamental, reason to support the likely outcome of our work. In my opinion, the Charter will have the chance to contribute in a significant manner to the constitutional development of the European Union.

A few months ago, leading German and French politicians came up with ideas on a European constitution. Their approach was not a mere repetition of older proposals for a hierarchical, state-like European structure. The emphasis has shifted to forms of effective cooperation between the EU, member States, and other entities, based upon a well-balanced distribution of powers. Fundamental rights can contribute to a reliable distribution of powers, for two reasons. One reason is simply that they put limits on the exercise of powers; the other reason is that they help to identify the scope of EU competencies.

A European Constitution will not be built in a day. Apart from the political impossibility, this would be very uncharacteristic of the development of European cooperation to date. In the light of the history of European cooperation in the second half of the past century, a constitutional development by subject is much more likely to take place. As a matter of fact, such a development started long ago with the birth of separate European institutions, including the equivalent of a constitutional court. It seems likely to me that the proclamation of a Charter of Fundamental Rights will be the first and maybe decisive moment in the phased genesis of a European Constitution.

If the Charter were a mere reproduction of the European Convention, its significance would be limited to closing the gap with the protection of fundamental rights in the member States. It is beyond doubt important: it puts the brake on possible attempts on the part of European authorities to meddle in the personal responsibilities of citizens and entities in civil society. But there is more. The Charter will also stand for rights and legal principles that reflect the very nature of the European Union and a vision on its future: rights concerning citizenship of the Union and economic and social rights. Therefore, I expect that the Convention will promote the constitutional development of the EU.

From the outset, the European Communities were conceived as a legal system and thus essentially more than a free trade association. This view on European cooperation is markedly different from the free trade orientation that has prevailed world-wide since the last decade of the 20th century. The unregulated global economy lacks a legal framework that protects vulnerable interests like those of working children and the environment.

The latest draft of the Charter includes chapters on citizenship, equality, and solidarity. I have supported this broad view on fundamental rights in the EU. Thus, the Charter will bring more than a restatement of the rights ensuing from the citizenship of the European Union and some well-known elements of the European Social Charter. It will also deal with new issues in the sphere of fundamental rights like the physical and mental integrity of the person in the fields of medicine and biology, the protection of personal data, the integration of persons with disabilities, and everyone's right to reconcile their family and professional lives. In doing so, the Charter will contribute to an understanding of the foundations on which an emerging European Constitution will be built. In my contribution to the final discussions, I proposed to add a clear recognition of the cultural, religious, ethnic, and linguistic diversity in Europe; the Union shall respect this diversity. The result of our work will hopefully contribute to the constitution of Europe in the sense that the Charter will clarify the foundations of existing and future cooperation.

Finally, I would like to draw your attention to the significance of the right to an effective remedy and the right of access to the courts in the European Convention. That is, however, more suitable for individual rights than for social and economic rights. In my opinion, it is very appropriate that a Charter that includes economic and social rights will also include a right to good administration as the basic condition for the realisation of such rights. The EU expresses itself as a union and a legal order committed to human dignity in its political, cultural, economic, and social dimensions. The very first article of the draft Charter will convey the core message: 'The dignity of the person must be respected and protected. The EU's foundations are different from that of a utilitarian security alliance and go beyond that of an economic "commonwealth".'

My conclusion can be summarised in three points:

1. The Charter appears to be, as a whole, well drafted and politically balanced. Certainly, as a legal instrument, it needs some improvement, e.g., in order to be precise on the restrictions that may apply to the rights of the Charter. Subject to this condition, it can help to bridge the gap between the ECHR system of protection of human rights and the method applied by the Court of Justice of the EC.

2. The completion of the Charter removes some arguments against adhesion to the ECHR.
3. The Charter identifies the EU as a public law structure with a constitution. Its character is expressed in the decision to include economic, social, and cultural rights.

THE IMPACT OF THE EU CHARTER OF FUNDAMENTAL RIGHTS ON THE CADIDATE COUNTRIES

Evgeni Tanchev *

I wish to touch three points:

1. THE IMPACT OF THE CHARTER ON THE APPLICANT COUNTRIES

It will alter the sphere of adapting the constitution of the applicants. It will increase the rights in the catalogue of the national constitutions. Constitutions of all of the Central and East European countries that are now applying for full EU membership were reactive to the past and have reduced some of the economic and social rights. Economic difficulties in the transition have contributed further the insufficient protection of social and economic rights. Adapting the national constitutions to the EU Charter of Fundamental Rights in the applicant countries will lead to the incorporation of the second and third generation of rights in the text of the national constitutions and the entrenchment of rights will be a guarantee to the economic and cultural freedom of Europeans in Central and Eastern Europe.

The protection mechanism of the Charter will differ from that of the ECHR especially due to the effect of EC law. The Charter will have direct horizontal effect while the ECHR has no such effect. It protects citizens' *political rights* against the national government and in some cases citizens against encroachment on their fundamental rights by private parties – both physical and legal persons – through the construct of the so-called 'drittwirkung'.

There might be some negative effects due to the overlapping jurisdictions of the ECJ and ECHR even if the scope of the protection of the EU Charter is reserved for EU legislation in conflict with and impacting the constitutional safeguards of the rights of the citizens of the EU.

It is dubious at least that the different standards and procedures introduced by the ECJ and ECHR for the protection of fundamental rights will bring about a better protection of human rights.

Where EU citizens opt for protection through the ECJ the EU Fundamental Charter might have a negative effect on the Council of Europe as well by reserv-

* Professor, Sofia University, Bulgaria.

A.E. Kellermann et al. (Eds.), EU Enlargement: The Constitutional Impact at EU and National Level

ing the field of application of ECHR protection to the citizens against the national governments in the non-EU member States.

The effect of the EU Charter might be instrumental in promoting the so-called 'enhanced cooperation', which is but another formulation of integration at different speeds, variable geometry or centre of gravity, which will lead to a difference in the integration process thereby creating different degrees of integrated membership and different types of acquis communautaire.

2. SIGNIFICANCE OF THE EU CHARTER FOR THE CONSTITUTION OF THE UNION BEFORE THE ENLARGEMENT

Reform is crucial for the future of the EU. The scope of the reform can be questioned: 'minimum' reform will be as dangerous as 'maximum' reform. It will create difficulties, even governmental crises. The middle grounds should combine the gradual communautarization of the second and third pillar into the first pillar leading in this way to the transformation of functionalism to a federal union or a political confederation, which will not follow any of the existing patterns previously or presently witnessed by human civilization. The EU Charter is a further step in the transformation of the status of Europe from statelessness and stateness. At a certain moment there will a Constitution of Europe which will be adopted and the Charter is an important brick in the building of such future written constitution of the EU. From modern history we know that statehood has not always begun with constitutions but Charters, Declarations and Bills of Rights have precede and facilitate the drafting of written constitutions for many reasons and certainly because they require less consensus on the structuring of the institutional design.

3. RELEVANCE OF EC POLICY IN THE FIELD OF HUMAN RIGHTS

I completely agree with Weiler's view that if the Charter is of little use if it does not contain an obligatory list of rights. He supports his argument with the observation that the Founding Fathers of the US Constitution declined to include a bill of rights in the US Constitution for the reason that if they did not enumerate all the rights then they did not protect human rights at all.

INSTITUTIONAL AND CONSTITUTIONAL CHALLENGES FOR THE EUROPEAN UNION – SOME REFLECTIONS IN THE LIGHT OF THE TREATY OF NICE

Jan Wouters*

I. INTRODUCTION

These are paradoxical times. On the one hand, the EU integration process has recently been given fresh impetus by the Intergovernmental Conference ('IGC') which resulted in the Treaty of Nice,[1] the EU Charter of Fundamental Rights solemnly proclaimed by the Council, the European Parliament and the Commission on 7 December 2000 in Nice,[2] the development of a Common European Security and Defence Policy and, not least, the introduction of the euro. The debate on the EU's finality has gained new momentum with speeches by prominent politicians such as Minister Joschka Fischer,[3] President Jacques Chirac[4] and Prime Minister Tony Blair[5] and will without doubt intensify in the course of the 'deeper and wider debate about the future of the European Union' called for by the 'Declaration on the Future of the Union' attached to the Nice Treaty.[6]

On the other hand, one cannot fail to notice some tendencies that, to say the least, do not go in the direction of European integration as it was originally conceived by the founding fathers of the Communities. There is a clear revival, possibly more forceful than ever before, of intergovernmentalism in the EU. Lord Douglas Hurd has a point when he observes that since the Maastricht Treaty, Europe has moved forward on an intergovernmental basis: 'In the last nine years it

* Professor of International Law and the Law of International Organizations, Leuven University; *Of Counsel*, de Bandt, van Hecke, Lagae & Loesch – Linklaters & Alliance.

[1] Treaty of Nice amending the Treaty on European Union, the Treaties establishing the European Communities and certain related Acts (OJ, 2001, C 80).

[2] Charter of Fundamental Rights of the European Union (OJ, C 364, 1). See also Presidency Conclusions Nice European Council Meeting 7, 8 and 9 December 2000, SN 400/00 EN, point 2.

[3] J. Fischer, *From Confederacy to Federation – Thoughts on the Finality of European Integration*, Speech at the Humboldt University in Berlin, 12 May 2000 (http://www.auswaertiges-amt.de/6 archiv/é/r/r000512b.htm).

[4] *Discours prononcé par Monsieur Jacques Chirac Président de la République française devant le Bundestag*, Berlin, 27 June 2000.

[5] Prime Minister Tony Blair's Speech to the Polish Stock Exchange, Warsaw, 6 October 2000.

[6] 23rd Declaration attached to the Nice Treaty's Final Act.

A.E. Kellermann et al. (Eds.), EU Enlargement: The Constitutional Impact at EU and National Level

is the Council of Ministers that has gained ground and the Commission that has retreated'.[7] Recent events, such as the imposition of 'bilateral' diplomatic sanctions by fourteen national governments on Austria because of the presence of a far-right party in its government, even show a tendency to act intergovernmentally outside the EU's institutional framework.[8] Even if this scenario may not be repeated because of the preventive mechanism laid down in the new Article 7(1) EU, it cannot be denied that 'networking between governments' has become fashionable. This is strongly tied to the increasingly important role of the European Council. From economic and social policy coordination to defence matters, the European Council has never before been so wide-ranging in its activities and so dominant vis-à-vis the EU's institutions. The Commission, for its part, seems to have been increasingly weakened due to arguments over mismanagement, internal reforms, lack of vision and poor communication, while the Court of Justice is becoming ever more flooded with cases. Are the EU's institutions becoming dinosaurs endangered by their size and cumbersome procedures while national governments settle matters *inter se*?

In the light of these developments, it is remarkable to see how the EU's governments managed to stick to a rather narrow institutional agenda at the 2000 IGC, confined essentially to the size of the Commission, the size of the majority needed for qualified majority voting in the Council, weighting of votes in the Council and making the machinery for closer cooperation more flexible. True, the Nice Treaty which came out of this is broader in its scope since it also changes various nuts and bolts of the other EU institutions and bodies – not least the Court of Justice. Still, the overall perspective at the IGC was limited, as stated in the preamble to the Nice Treaty, to 'preparing the institutions of the Union to function in an enlarged Union';[9] or, in the words of the aforementioned Declaration on the future of the Union, the Nice Treaty 'opens the way for enlargement of the Union', and with its ratification the EU 'will have completed the institutional changes necessary for the accession of the new member States'.[10] The contrast with the (emphatically long-term or personal) constitutional visions expressed by Joschka Fischer and Jacques Chirac could hardly be starker.

---

[7] D. Hurd, 'Europe's dream need not be a nightmare', *Financial Times*, 18 August 2000.

[8] The shunning of the EU institutions even went so far that the three personalities who had to report on the Austrian government's commitment to the common European values, were appointed by the President of the European Court of Human Rights, rather than by the President of the EU's Court of Justice. Could some secret amusement about this fact be read into the final words of the statement by the President of the European Court of Human Rights of 29 June 2000: 'I am naturally aware that this task has been entrusted to me in recognition of the independent and impartial character as a judicial institution of the Court over which I have the honour to preside'?

[9] Second recital to the Preamble.

[10] Point 2 of the Declaration.

The present contribution does not aim to provide a commentary on the Nice Treaty.[11] Rather, it seeks to raise the question whether, between the Nice Treaty's minimalist institutionalism, on the one hand, and the bold constitutionalism professed by the aforementioned leaders on the other, it would not have been preferable to adopt a middle-of-the-road approach, in which the need for greater efficiency would have been reconciled and considered together with the need for increased legitimacy of the EU's institutions (II), and in which more concrete steps would be taken to strengthen the EU as a true constitutional legal order (III). As happens so often, a number of issues ('leftovers') has been deferred to the next IGC, which is planned for 2004; this should be the occasion to bring constitution-building to the fore (IV).

II. ENHANCING THE EU'S EFFICIENCY *AND* LEGITIMACY: A MISSED OPPORTUNITY

What was to be feared, in the light of the IGC's restricted agenda, has in fact materialized: if anything, the institutional reforms put forward by the Nice Treaty remain limited to the efficiency of the EU's institutions solely with a view to enlargement. They hardly[12] extend to ways in which the *legitimacy* of the EU's institutions can be reinforced. The Treaty itself does not even hint at legitimacy, even though this concern had been obliquely raised in the Presidency Conclusions of the Feira European Council (19-20 June 2000), where reference was made to 'Treaty changes which will ensure that the Union continues to have properly functioning, efficient *and legitimate* institutions after enlargement'.[13]

---

[11] At the time of writing, the first commentaries have been published. See, inter alia, R. Barents, 'Some Observations on the Treaty of Nice', *Maastricht Journal of European and Comparative Law* (2001), forthcoming; J. Cloos, 'Nice: une étape obligée', *Revue du Marché commun et de l'Union européenne* (2001), pp. 5-10; F. Dehousse, 'Nice: un traité trop petit pour une Europe trop grande', *Journal des tribunaux* (2001), p. 13; J. De Zwaan, 'Het Verdrag van Nice. Een bescheiden stap in het proces van Europese integratie', *Sociaal-Economische Wetgeving* (2001), pp. 42-52; J.-V. Louis, 'Le Traité de Nice', *Journal des tribunaux. Droit européen* (2001), pp. 25-34; M. Petite, 'Nice, traité existentiel, non essentiel', *Revue du Droit de l'Union européenne* (2000/4), pp. 887-903; D. Vignes, 'Nice une vue apaisée. Réponse à deux questions', *Revue du Marché commun et de l'Union européenne* (2001), pp. 81-83; X.A. Yataganas, *The Treaty of Nice. The Sharing of Power and the Institutional Balance in the European Union – A Continental Perspective* (Cambridge, Harvard Jean Monnet Working Paper, 01/01).

[12] As a fortunate exception, one may mention the change which the Nice Treaty brings to Article 263 EC, with regard to the composition of the Committee of the Regions. The old text generally provides that the Committee consists of 'representatives of regional and local bodies'; the new text will provide that the Committee consists of 'representatives of regional and local bodies who either hold a regional or local authority electoral mandate or are politically accountable to an elected assembly'. This change definitely enhances the legitimacy of the Committee of the Regions and will hopefully enable the Committee to strengthen its institutional profile and position.

[13] Presidency Conclusions Santa Maria da Feira European Council, 19 and 20 June 2000, SN 200/00, EN, point 3 (emphasis added).

The Declaration on the future of the Union makes clear that the legitimacy concern has in essence been passed on to the 'post-Nice' debate, where the Conference recognizes 'the need to improve and to monitor the democratic legitimacy and transparency of the Union and its institutions, in order to bring them closer to the citizens of the member States'.[14]

In truth, the legitimacy debate is long overdue. Regardless of the prospect of enlargement, the EU's institutions today are in desperate need of increased legitimacy. In the wake of the resignation of the Santer Commission, the recurrent reports concerning poor control and mismanagement of Community programmes and the ongoing equivocal support for the EU expressed by national political leaders, the credibility and legitimacy of the EU's institutions in the eyes of Europe's citizens has sunk to record depths. The historically low turnout at the 1999 European Parliament elections (in the Netherlands, for example, fewer than 30%, half of what it was in 1979) confirms a tendency towards apathy, if not hostility, by the electorate vis-à-vis the EU and its institutions.[15]

It is submitted that only a reform of the institutions that, apart from their efficient functioning, enhances their democratic character and introduces better checks and balances and greater openness, can safeguard the EU's future. Obviously, not all aspects of these problems necessitate Treaty changes:[16] some can be dealt with by means of secondary legislation, others even by means of purely internal measures or codes of conduct.[17] Still, it would be wise to undertake the exercise globally, simultaneously and in a coherent manner for all EU institutions, bodies and organs taken together, instead of the rather fragmented approach

[14] Point 6 of the Declaration.

[15] See the interesting analysis of the EU institutions' legitimacy deficit by Ph. de Schoutheete, *The Case for Europe. Unity, Diversity and Democracy in the European Union* (Lynne Rienner, 2000), pp. 53-56.

[16] I will not dwell here on ways to improve efficiency for each and every institution without Treaty changes. For the *Commission*, this exercise should in any event take account of the valuable recommendations contained in the two reports of the Committee of Independent Experts: Committee of Independent Experts, *First Report on Allegations regarding Fraud, Mismanagement and Nepotism in the European Commission*, 15 March 1999; Id., *Second Report on Reform of the Commission. Analysis of current practice and proposals for tackling mismanagement, irregularities and fraud*, 10 September 1999 (DOC EN\DV\381\381230EN.doc). The *Council* meanwhile has, as is known, taken some concrete steps to improve its functioning (see the new Rules of Procedure of the Council as adopted by Council Decision 2000/396/EC, ECCS, Euratom of 5 June 2000 (OJ, 2000, L 149, 21); see also the Communication from the Council – Follow-up of the Helsinki Council Conclusions on 10 and 11 December 1999 – Council formations (OJ, 2000, C 174, 1)). Likewise, some modest improvements have been adopted for the Court in the latest revision of the latter's rules of procedure (amendments to the Rules of Procedure of the Court of Justice of 16 May 2000 (OJ, 2000, L 122/43)).

[17] The merits of codes of conduct have been rightly stressed by the Committee of Independent Experts in its *Second Report on Reform of the Commission* (supra, previous note), point 7.7.1: 'An advantage of codes of conduct is that they give guidance by way of flexible rules, which are however as concrete as possible. Without imposing legally binding obligations, they may exert a high degree of moral persuasion because of their widely accepted ethical content.'

which currently is followed by the Commission, the Council and the Court, respectively. That is an important guideline which should be kept in mind throughout the 'post-Nice' process and the IGC announced for 2004.

Let us, in this respect, try to contribute to the 'post-Nice' debate by briefly focusing on some ways to improve the legitimacy of institutions.

The very first thing to do in order to improve the institutions' legitimacy is to stick to the conditions for appointment laid down in the Treaties and to secure more democratic control in this respect. An important case in point is the appointment of Judges and Advocates-General to the Court of Justice. The qualifications required by Article 223 EC (independence beyond doubt, eligibility for the highest judicial offices in the country concerned or to be a jurisconsult of recognised competence) are, to say the least, not always fulfilled in practice. At present, one can hardly speak of 'peer pressure' among governments in the appointment process. Stronger guarantees for independence and competence of the Court's Members are an absolute prerequisite for a Union which claims to be 'founded on the principles of (...) the rule of law'.[18] Why not link the scrutiny of the observance of the aforementioned requirements to a stronger democratic component in the appointment procedure by giving an advisory role to the European Parliament?[19] In addition, as indicated in the paper by J.H.H. Weiler,[20] something needs to be done in relation to the Members' six-year term of office and the renewability thereof. It would be preferable by far for the Court's Members' independence to make their term a non-renewable one of twelve years, as proposed in the *Due Report,*[21] or to have a longer but renewable term of nine years, as in the case of the International Court of Justice.[22]

Speaking of enhancing the Court's legitimacy, one may also make the link with greater openness and accountability in the Court's decision-making process. It is submitted that the peoples of Europe are entitled to know what the Court's judges stand for. The least that could be done in this regard is to indicate, as the International Court of Justice has done since 1978, the number and names of the

---

[18] Article 6(1) EU.

[19] Compare the European Parliament's powers in the case of the appointment of Members of the Court of Auditors (Art. 247(3) EC) and of Members of the Executive Board of the European Central Bank (Art. 112(2)(b) EC).

[20] J.H.H. Weiler, 'Europe 2000 – The Constitutional Agenda', p. 3.

[21] *Rapport du groupe de réflexion sur l'avenir du système juridictionnel des Communautés européennes*, January 2000, p. 51. This proposal has been made before, after the example of the German *Bundesverfassungsgericht*, inter alia, by the European Movement (see the first report of its Committee for Institutional Affairs of 28-29 April 1995, p. 14) and the Bertelsmann Foundation (W. Weidenfeld (ed.), *Europe '96. Reforming the European Union*, Bertelsmann Foundation 1994, 38).

[22] See Article 13(1) Statute of the International Court of Justice. Until recently, this was also the case for the European Court of Human Rights, but since the entry into force of Protocol No. 11, the Court's Judges have a renewable term of six years.

judges who formed the majority.[23] J.H.H. Weiler also argues convincingly in favour of the introduction of separate and dissenting opinions of the Court. I would support that suggestion, both with a view to supplementing the Court's often tersely reasoned judgments with alternative opinions presumably written in a more lively style, and with a view to making the judges more accountable. This may seem contradictory: does not the confidentiality of the Court's deliberations and of the various views defended therein best protect the judges' independence vis-à-vis the member States, in particular their own State?[24] The point is that confidentiality of deliberations – which as such is fully compatible with a system of separate or dissenting opinions – should not become a cover for a climate of secretiveness,[25] in which judges hide their own thoughts and positions. Rather than pushing judges to bow to political pressure from their member State of origin, a system of separate and dissenting opinions would impose responsibility on them by inducing them to make their actual opinion publicly known. It is also submitted that, in the current stage of European integration, introducing this system would not endanger the 'uniform application of Community law' but would rather act as a stimulus for the Court's responsiveness to the often complicated constitutional and societal problems of the EU member States. The overall result would be a stronger legitimation of the Court's case law and, hopefully, a richer style of reasoning.

If this system were to be introduced, the question arises as to what should be done with the function of Advocate-General at the Court.[26] In fact, this question may already be raised after the Nice Treaty. This treaty changes Article 222 EC in a sense which makes clear that Advocates-General will not longer be asked to make submissions in all cases before the Court.[27] Even though the Nice Treaty gives an important task to the First Advocate-General (when he considers that there is a serious risk of the unity or consistency of Community law being af-

[23] See A. Eyffinger, *La Cour internationale de justice 1946-1996* (Kluwer Law International, 1999), p. 143. See, with regard to the 1978 change to the Court's Rules, *The International Court of Justice* (ICJ, 1996, 4th edn.), pp. 20 and 70.

[24] See e.g., H.G. Schermers, *Inleiding tot het internationale institutionele recht* (Kluwer, 1985, 2nd edn.), p. 107, para. 327.

[25] See, very accurately, as applied to the Commission, the Committee of Independent Experts in its *Second Report on Reform of the Commission*, point 7.6.3: 'Secretiveness means a lack of openness in matters where no real justification for confidentiality exists. Confidentiality must be the exception, not the rule. Openness is (...) a question of mentalities and attitudes, arising from the basic principle that the public has a right to know how public institutions use the power and resources entrusted to them.'

[26] See, for suggestions in order to revalorize the role of the Advocate-General, W. van Gerven, 'The role and structure of the European judiciary now and in the future', in J.A. Winter and Others (eds.), *Reforming the Treaty on European Union – The Legal Debate* (Kluwer Law International, 1996), pp. 221, 234-235.

[27] The Advocate-General will only have to make reasoned submissions 'on cases which, in accordance with the Statute of the Court of Justice, require his involvement'.

fected by a decision of the Court of First Instance in an appellate case against a judicial panel or in preliminary proceedings, he may propose that the Court review that decision[28]), the question may be asked whether eight Advocates-General will be necessary under the new system.[29]

Legitimacy and accountability should also be improved at the level of other institutions. In spite of the precedent created by the resignation of the Santer Commission on 15 March 1999 and all the internal reform projects that have been launched by the Prodi Commission in the meantime, the mechanisms for calling Members of the Commission to account are still much too laborious. The commitment allegedly made by each Member of the current Commission vis-à-vis Mr. Prodi to resign, should the latter ask him or her to do so,[30] is seen as a valuable step in this direction. It is a welcome development that the Nice Treaty – following the suggestions of the Commission,[31] the Parliament[32] and the *Dehaene Report*[33] – has codified this into the EC Treaty, albeit that a Member must only resign if the President so requests after obtaining the approval of the College.[34] Nevertheless, it could be argued that, if the President is for one reason or another – e.g., political pressure from a member State – not willing or able to exercise this power, it should be made possible for the European Parliament to take action vis-à-vis the Commissioner concerned, for example by giving the Parliament (and not only the Commission and the Council, as is presently the case) the power under Article 216 EC to apply to the Court of Justice in order to obtain the compulsory retirement of that Member for the reasons mentioned in that Article.[35] Since this would only be an extension of an institutional mechanism

[28] Article 62 of the new Statute of the Court of Justice.

[29] It may be noted that the new Article 224 EC allows the Statute of the Court to provide that the Court of First Instance be assisted by Advocates-General. The new Statute of the Court of Justice which the Nice Treaty attaches to the EU Treaty, the EC Treaty and the EAEC Treaty, does not yet provide for this. Article 49 of the new Statute only stipulates that the members of the Court of First Instance may be called upon to perform the task of an Advocate-General. It thereby incorporates Article 2(3) of Decision 88/591/ECSC, EEC, Euratom. As is known, the Court of First Instance has not made us of this possibility for many years.

[30] See the speech of President-Elect Prodi before the European Parliament on 21 July 1999, *Bulletin of the EU*, 7/8-1999, point 2.2.1.

[31] See the Communication of the Commission's President and Commissioner Barnier of 10 November 1999, I.5, and the Commission's IGC Opinion, *Adapting the Institutions to Make a Success of Enlargement*, 26 January 2000, p. 11.

[32] Resolution of 18 November 1999 on the preparation of the reform of the Treaties and the next Intergovernmental Conference, *Bulletin Quotidien Europe*, Doc. No 2163, 26 November 1999, point 25.

[33] R. Von Weiszäcker, J.-L. Dehaene and D. Simon, *The Institutional Consequences of Enlargement. Report for the European Commission*, Brussels, 18 October 1999, 2.2.1 *in fine*.

[34] New Article 217(4) EC.

[35] I.e., that the Member of the Commission concerned no longer fulfils the conditions required for the performance of his duties or that he has been guilty of serious misconduct.

which is currently available, it is hard to claim that it would run counter to the principle of collegiate responsibility.

Some reflections may be added here concerning the position of the President of the European Commission. The Nice Treaty continues the development started by the Amsterdam Treaty by considerably reinforcing the President's position.[36] The latter (i) decides on the Commission's internal organisation, (ii) structures and allocates the responsibilities incumbent upon the Commission, (iii) may reshuffle the allocation of those responsibilities during the Commission's term of office, (iv) may devolve certain duties to his colleagues while retaining authority,[37] (v) appoints vice-presidents after obtaining the College's approval and (vi) can request a Member to resign after obtaining the College's approval.[38] One could observe that, with these changes, the Commission is clearly evolving towards a presidential regime. In terms of efficacy, this is probably a desirable and even necessary development, especially since the Nice Treaty opens up the prospect of a Commission of up to 27 Members.[39] But the question arises whether this increase in powers should not be countered by stricter checks and balances. If the European Parliament is given the power under Article 216 EC that has been proposed above, this concern may already be partly appeased. But there may be cases where the conditions for using this procedure are not met[40] and where it is nevertheless clear that there is a serious dysfunction problem involving the President. It may be necessary to make a special proviso for this hypothesis by amending the censure procedure of the European Parliament as laid down in Article 201 EC.

The legitimacy of the EU's institutions also depends strongly on their degree of openness towards European citizens. Although it is true that openness is not primarily a question of legal texts or codes of conduct but rather a question of mentalities and attitudes,[41] for an entity with such far-reaching and encompassing

---

[36] Except for one point, namely, the new Article 214(2) EC, where it is added that the list of other persons whom the Council intends to appoint as Members of the Commission, has to be drawn up 'in accordance with the proposals made by each member State'. The importance of this clause is somewhat downplayed by M. Petite (supra, n. 12, at p. 893), who observes that this formula 'vise uniquement à faire en sorte que le Conseil ne puisse pas désigner comme membre de la Commission une personnalité qui n'aurait pas été proposée par le gouvernement de l'Etat membre dont elle a la nationalité.'

[37] The new Article 217(2) *in fine* EC provides that 'the Members of the Commission shall carry out the duties devolved upon them by the President under his authority'. Compare the German version ('die ihnen vom Präsidenten übertragenen Aufgaben').

[38] New Article 217 EC.

[39] See Article 4 of the Protocol on the enlargement of the European Union, which the Nice Treaty attaches to the EU Treaty and the Treaties establishing the European Communities.

[40] The procedure of Article 216 EC can only be applied if the Member of the Commission in question 'no longer fulfils the conditions required for the performance of his duties or if he has been guilty of serious misconduct'.

[41] See Committee of Independent Experts, *Second Report on the Reform of the Commission*, point 7.6.3.

powers as the EU,[42] guarantees of openness are needed at the constitutional level. Admittedly, the Amsterdam Treaty has introduced the Union's express commitment to an administration operating 'as openly as possible',[43] and this was further defined in the new Article 255 EC regarding the right of access of citizens (and legal persons) to documents of the Parliament, the Council and the Commission. But this right is made subject to general principles which for the time being still need to be defined[44] and can still suffer at the hands of exceptions in the Rules of Procedure of the respective institutions.[45] No doubt a still stronger constitutional commitment to openness should be given in the Treaties, such as an extension of the right of access to documents to include *all* the EU's institutions, bodies and agencies, and a further limitation of possible exceptions to this right. An important constitutional role is reserved to the Court of Justice and the Court of First Instance in this respect. Whereas the Court of Justice has shown itself sympathetic to a progressive constitutionalization of the right of access to EU documents in *Netherlands* v. *Council*,[46] the Court of First Instance has become a real frontrunner in this matter over the last decade.[47] This case law constitutes an in-

---

[42] I will not enter here into the debate whether the EU as such has international legal personality. Let me just observe that this issue may be looked at afresh in the light of the new Article 24(6) EU, pursuant to which agreements concluded by the Council under the second Pillar 'shall be binding on the institutions of the Union'. Compare, under the old Article 24 EU, K. Lenaerts and P. Van Nuffel, *Constitutional Law of the European Union* (Sweet & Maxwell, 1999, ed. by R. Bray), p. 612, para. 16-003.

[43] Article 1, second para., EU.

[44] This will need to be done before 1 May 2001, as Article 255(2) EC requires the measure to be adopted within two years after the entry into force of the Amsterdam Treaty. See the Commission's proposal for a Regulation of the European Parliament and of the Council regarding public access to European Parliament, Council and Commission documents (OJ, 2000, C 177, 70). On 16 November 2000, after voting a considerable number of amendments, the Parliament referred the issue back to committee to enable further discussions with Commission and Council with a view to securing a compromise that would contain much more limited grounds for possible exceptions. The Parliament is also opposed to the new Council code which denies access to certain defence-related documents, adopted on 14 August 2000 (see Council Decision 2000/527/EC amending Decision 93/731/EC on public access to Council documents and Council Decision 2000/23/EC on the improvement of information on the Council's legislative activities and the public register of Council documents, OJ, 2000, L 212, 9 and Decision of the Secretary-General of the Council/High Representative for the Common Foreign and Security Policy of 27 July 2000 on measures for the protection of classified information applicable to the General Secretariat of the Council, OJ, 2000, C 239, 1). The Netherlands has started annulment proceedings against this Decision: pending Case C-369/00, *Netherlands* v. *Council* (OJ, 2000, C 316, 19). A bit later, the European Parliament started annulment proceedings as well: pending Case C-387/00, *European Parliament* v. *Council* (OJ, 2000, C 355, 15).

[45] Article 255(1) EC, with reference to paras. 2 and 3. See the justified criticism and proposed restrictive interpretation of this provision by R. Bieber, 'Reformen der Institutionen und Verfahren – Amsterdam kein Meisterstück', *Integration* (1997), p. 236, at p. 238.

[46] Case C-58/94 *Netherlands* v. *Council* [1996] ECR I-2169, paras. 34-36.

[47] See, inter alia, Case T-194/94 *Carvel and Guardian Newspapers* v. *Council* [1994] ECR II-2765; Case T-105/95 *WWF UK* v. *Commission* [1997] ECR II-313; Case T-124/96 *Interporc Im- und Export GmbH* v. *Commission* [1998] ECR II-231; T-83/96 *Van der Wal* v. *Commission* [1998]

teresting illustration of the interaction between the common constitutional heritage of the member States, on the one hand, and the EU's evolving constitutional framework, on the other.[48] The European Ombudsman's actions against Commission and Council secrecy also play an important role in this regard.[49]

Finally, the legitimacy of the EU institutions would be improved by enhancing their democratic status. In the work of the IGC which led to the Nice Treaty, far too little attention has been paid to this point, apart from the debate on extension of the list of cases in which the co-decision procedure applies, the outcome of which is, in any event, relatively modest.[50] It is, admittedly, not an easy point: improving the democratic nature of the institutions raises intricate questions, not only regarding the procedure for the appointment or election of their members, but also concerning their closeness to Europe's citizens, their representativeness and, again, their accountability in terms of 'checks and balances'.

Rapprochement with the citizens, in other words bridging the wide gap between the EU and its citizens, will not be achieved through Treaty amendments. Neither can it be expected that drafting solemn new texts such as a 'Millennium Declaration'[51] or even a Charter of Fundamental Rights (the legal value of which is in any event still very much an open question[52]) will contribute much. Rather, European and national politicians will need to invest more seriously in explaining the EU and its policies to their citizens and engaging in an interactive dialogue with them. Closeness to the citizen cannot be viewed completely separately from its geographical dimension:[53] in a Union of 25 to 30 States, there will be a

---

ECR II-545 (set aside by the Court of Justice in Joined Cases C-174/98 and C-189/98 P *Netherlands and Van der Wal* v. *Commission* [2000] ECR I-1); Case T-174/95 *Tidningen Journalisten, Svenska Journalistförbundets Tidning* v. *Council* [1998] ECR II-2289; Case T-188/97 *Rothmans International* v. *Commission* [1999] ECR II-2463; Case T-14/98 *Hautala* v. *Council* [1999] ECR II-2489; Case T-92/98 *Interporc Im- und Export* v. *Commission* [1999] ECR II-3521; Judgment of 6 April 2000 in Case T-188/98 *Kuijer* v. *Council*, not yet published in the ECR; Judgment of 13 September 2000 in Case T-20/99 *Denkavit* v. *Commission*, not yet published in the ECR; and Judgment of 12 October 2000 in Case T-123/99 *JT's Corporation* v. *Commission*, not yet published in the ECR.

[48] See J. Wouters, 'National Constitutions and the European Union', 27 *Legal Issues of Economic Integration* (2000), p. 25, at pp. 50-51.

[49] See recently the Ombudsman's two draft recommendations of 13 March 2001 in which he asks the Council to reconsider the application of Statewatch (a UK body fighting for openness and transparency) for access to certain documents.

[50] Only in seven cases in which the Nice Treaty has replaced unanimity by qualified majority voting in the Council has the co-decision procedure been rendered applicable (see Arts. 13(2), 63(1), 63(2)(a), 65, 157(3), 159, third para. and 191 EC).

[51] See the Millenium Declaration of the Helsinki European Council of 10 and 11 December 1999, *Bulletin of the EU* 12-1999, pp. 15-16.

[52] See on this issue B. de Witte, 'The Legal Status of the Charter: Vital Question or Non-Issue?', paper presented at the workshop 'The Charter of Fundamental Rights of the European Union' held at the Ius Commune Conference at Leuven University on 23 November 2000 and forthcoming in *Maastricht Journal of European and Comparative Law* (2001).

[53] Although it is obviously wrong to question for instance the democratic legitimacy of the European Parliament by considering it too distant to represent the electorate validly: this argument has been rightly refuted by Ph. de Schoutheete, *The Case for Europe*, p. 53.

strongly-felt need for a greater presence of Europe in every member State; for the citizens of Central and Eastern Europe especially, Brussels, Luxembourg and Strasbourg may be far too remote. This is not a plea for a relocation of the seats of institutions; rather, it expresses a concern that needs to be taken seriously in order to safeguard the continuing acceptance of the EU, especially by young democracies with fragile market economies which can be heavily affected by EU decisions. It may be a plea for 'multilevel governance', to which we will return below (infra, IV).

Representativeness remains an important concern for an entity such as the EU, in which the multitude of organs is each presumed to represent a proper interest (or a multitude of interests).[54] For the European Parliament, the reallocation of seats in the perspective of enlargement has been made by the Nice Treaty[55] with the maximum number of seats set at 732.[56] That may be a relief, but the representativeness of the Parliament's members cannot be dissociated from the need for a more uniform procedure for parliamentary elections. Although the Amsterdam Treaty has brought this prospect closer and the Parliament has come up with proposals,[57] a decision has still not been reached in the Council. Representativeness also becomes a very important problem whenever the power to adopt rules is delegated, either to a particular institution (for example, the Commission on the basis of Art. 86 EC) or a specialized agency (of which the EU currently knows not less than twelve[58]), or to non-governmental actors, such as European employer

---

[54] See K. Lenaerts and E. de Smijter, 'The question of democratic representation: on the democratic representation through the European Parliament, the Council, the Committee of the Regions, the Economic and Social Committee and the National Parliaments', in *Reforming the Treaty on European Union – The Legal Debate*, pp. 173-197.

[55] See Declaration No. 20 'on the enlargement of the European Union'. There is an unjustifiably unequal treatment in the current text of Belgium, Greece and Portugal, on the one hand (22 seats each), and the Czech Republic and Hungary on the other hand (20 seats each), in spite of the similar population size (around 10 million).

[56] New Article 189, para. 2, EC.

[57] See new Article 190(4), first para., EC; new Article 21(4), first para., ECSC Treaty; new Article 108(4), first para., Euratom Treaty. On 15 July 1998, the European Parliament drew up a proposal based on the system of proportionate representation, following the report of 2 June 1998 of G. Anastossopoulos: see resolution A4-0212/98 on a draft electoral procedure incorporating common principles for the election of Members of the European Parliament (OJ, 1998, C 292, 66).

[58] They are listed, together with short descriptions, at http://europa.eu.int/en/agencies.html. These agencies are: the European Centre for the Development of Vocational Training (Cedefop), the European Centre for the Improvement of Living and Working Conditions, the European Agency for Cooperation, the European Environmental Agency, the European Training Foundation, the European Monitoring Centre for Drugs and Drug Addiction, the European Agency for the Evaluation of Medicinal Products, the European Office for Harmonisation in the Internal Market (Trademarks and Designs), the European Agency for Health and Safety at Work, the Community Plant Variety Office, the Translation Centre for Bodies of the European Union and the European Monitoring Centre on Racism and Xenophobia.

and employee representatives where European collective agreements are concluded.[59]

III. STRENGTHENING THE CONSTITUTIONAL LEGAL ORDER OF THE EU

The current emphasis on the EU's commitment to human rights through the drawing up of a Charter of Fundamental Rights somewhat obscures the need for further efforts to strengthen two other foundations of the Union that are stated in Article 6(1) EU, namely, democracy and the rule of law. On both counts, there is indeed a need for quite some improvement before the EU can be considered as embodying a full-fledged constitutional legal order.

In the first place, there is a need to improve the democratic legitimation of certain Community acts and nearly all EU acts. As is known, under the EC Treaty, the co-decision procedure, especially since the Treaty of Amsterdam, best stands the test of democratic legitimation. For matters in which the unanimity rule still applies in the Council, democratic legitimation should be provided at the national level through ministerial accountability to the parliamentary assemblies concerned – even though reality teaches that this has become something of a myth.[60] However, there are still a number of instances of Community decision-making in which the input of the European Parliament is poor and in which the Council nevertheless takes decisions by a qualified majority. The legislation on agriculture and common commercial policy provide two important (and vast) illustrations of this.[61] It is remarkable to see how increasing the role of the European Parliament in these fields was not on the agenda of the IGC which led to the Nice Treaty. The Nice Treaty, besides, creates new cases of democratic deficit when it introduces qualified majority voting in the Council in a number of cases without correspondingly introducing co-decision or even a right to be consulted for the European Parliament. Thus, the Parliament will not even need to be consulted on monetary law provisions for the euro zone,[62] on the negotiation and conclusion of agreements in the fields of trade in services and the commercial aspects of intel-

[59] See in this regard the important judgment of the Court of First Instance in Case T-135/96 *UEAPME* [1998] ECR II-2335.

[60] See e.g., R.H. Lauwaars and C.W.A. Timmermans, *Europees recht in kort bestek* (Tjeenk Willink, 1999), p. 67.

[61] It seems rather illusory to expect that the democratic deficit in these sectors could be remedied by the Amsterdam Treaty's Protocol 'on the role of national Parliaments in the European Union'.

[62] New Article 123(4) EC. Under the original Article 123(4) (ex Art. 109l(4)) the Parliament did not need to be consulted either. Still, when the Council adopted Regulation (EC) No. 974/98 of 3 May 1998 on the introduction of the euro (OJ, 19998, L 139, 1), the opinion of the Parliament had been asked (OJ, 1996, C 380, 50).

lectual property;[63] the Parliament will only have to be consulted on economic, financial and technical cooperation measures with third countries[64] and on the adoption of financial regulations and rules on the responsibility of financial controllers.[65]

Matters are worse for the Second Pillar (i.e., the Common Foreign and Security Policy), where there is no significant role for the European Parliament, nor for national parliaments.[66] As is known, things have to some extent improved for the Third Pillar (i.e., police and judicial cooperation in criminal matters), since the Amsterdam Treaty has given the European Parliament a consultative role. But for such sensitive subjects as those dealt with in the Third Pillar, stronger democratic legitimation is needed, especially when qualified majority voting is progressively introduced (as is, after Amsterdam, already the case for certain implementing decisions).

Last but not least, there is the need to further strengthen the Union's 'rule of law' foundations. If one accepts, together with the Court of Justice, that a system based on the rule of law presupposes the putting in place of 'a complete system of legal remedies and procedures' at EU level, in which neither the EU's institutions nor its member States can avoid a review of the legality of their actions under the EU's constitution,[67] it is clear that this goal has not yet been attained. Even within the context of the Community treaties, the present system should be complemented in at least two important respects. The first is a relaxation of the conditions under which individuals may directly appeal to the Court of First Instance against a Community act affecting their fundamental rights. The case law of the European courts relating to the conditions for admissibility of Article 230, fourth paragraph, EC still remains too strict in this regard.[68] Surely it is possible for the case law to become somewhat more flexible on this point, but amending the aforementioned provision specifically for this purpose would be preferable by far.[69] Secondly, the problematic curtailing of the Court's competences in relation

[63] New Article 133(5) EC, with the important restrictions in its second, third and fourth paragraphs and without prejudice to the new Article 133(6) EC.

[64] New Article 181a EC.

[65] Amended Article 279 EC. Qualified-majority voting in the Council will only start here as from 1 January 2007.

[66] Title V of the EU Treaty is not even mentioned in the Amsterdam Treaty's Protocol 'on the role of national parliaments in the European Union'.

[67] See especially Case 294/83 *Les Verts* v. *Parliament* [1986] ECR 1339, para. 23; Case C-2/88 IMM Zwartveld [1990] ECR I-3365, para. 16.

[68] See very recently Court of First Instance, Judgment of 27 June 2000 in Joined Cases T-172/98, T-175/98 and T-177/98 *Salamander and Others* v. *European Parliament and Council*, not yet published in the ECR, paras. 74-75.

[69] See recently B. de Witte, 'The Past and Future Role of the European Court of Justice in the Protection of Human Rights', in Ph. Alston (ed.), *The EU and Human Rights*, (OUP, 1999), p. 859, at pp. 875-877 and 892-893; N. Reich, 'Zur Notwendigkeit einer Europäischen Grundrechtsbeschwerde', *Zeitschrift für Rechtspolitik* (2000), pp. 375-378.

to the EC Treaty's Title on 'Visas, asylum, immigration and other policies related to the movement of persons' should be reversed as quickly as possible. In particular the preclusion of any competence for the Court with regard to measures on the crossing of internal borders or with regard to measures 'relating to the maintenance of law and order and the safeguarding of internal security'[70] raises serious questions as to the effectiveness of the EU's legal protection system under this Title.[71] Matters are, however, still more problematic under the Second and Third Pillars. How can the complete exclusion of jurisdiction of the Court under the Second Pillar be justified in a Union which is based on the rule of law? The situation under the Third Pillar is only slightly better: although the Court has been afforded certain powers, there is neither a provision for a direct appeal by individuals nor a compulsory preliminary rulings mechanism. If constitutional issues should arise with regard to decisions, framework decisions or agreements adopted under this Title – which seems inevitable – it is exclusively the national courts that would be able to provide effective legal protection.

IV. TOWARDS THE NEXT IGC: TRUE CONSTITUTION-BUILDING?

With the ink on the signatures of the Nice Treaty barely dry, the 'post-Nice' debate has taken off. In the Declaration on the future of the Union, the Conference called for 'a deeper and wider debate about the future of the European Union', to be launched in 2001 by the Swedish and Belgian Presidencies through wide-ranging discussions with all interested parties. Following a report at the Göteborg European Council in June 2001, this should result in a declaration of Laeken/ Brussels containing 'appropriate initiatives for the continuation of this process' at the European Council summit in December 2001. This process, so the Declaration specifies:

> 'should address, inter alia, the following questions:
> - how to establish and monitor a more precise delimitation of powers between the European Union and the member States, reflecting the principle of subsidiarity;
> - the status of the Charter of Fundamental Rights of the European Union, proclaimed in Nice, in accordance with the conclusions of the European Council in Cologne;[72]

---

[70] Article 68(2) EC.

[71] R. Barents and L.J. Brinkhorst, *Grondlijnen van Europees Recht* (Tjeenk Willink, 1999), p. 559, consider this exception, which was inserted under French pressure at a very late stage of the intergovernmental conference leading to the Amsterdam Treaty, to be scandalous. On p. 569, the authors wonder whether the similar preclusion of the Court's competence by Article 35(5) EU, within the context of the Third Pillar, is compatible with the European Convention on Human Rights.

[72] What the latter condition means is not entirely clear. Possibly it is a reference to the statement, at the end of the Decision of the Cologne European Council of 3-4 June 1999 on the drawing up of a Charter of fundamental rights, that, after the Charter's proclamation, 'it will (...) have to be considered

- a simplification of the Treaties with a view to making them clearer and better understood without changing their meaning;
- the role of national parliaments in the European architecture.'

These 'leftovers of Nice' are, as the Declaration indicates, not exhaustive but merely illustrative. The question may also be raised whether they are the most relevant and urgent issues, leaving apart the legal status of the Fundamental Rights Charter. Some critical observations can be made in this regard.

First of all, the question of a more precise delimitation of powers between the EU and its member States is a highly controversial matter. It is known that the German government pushed hard for this item under pressure from the German *Länder*, which insist on a clearer demarcation of competences (*Kompetenzabgrenzung*). The theme is a Pandora's box since, undoubtedly, some member States would hope to use it in order to strengthen the EU's competences, but most others may well want to seize the occasion to strip the EU of certain competences. Too strict a delimitation of competences would fly in the face of the dynamic nature of the European integration process. This dynamism has been rendered possible through a step-by-step approach based on a Treaty method which assigns objectives to the EC/EU, confers powers upon them and specifies the tools of action and limitations in the relevant Treaty chapter. By the same token, one should not overlook the delimitating function of existing provisions such as Article 5 EC. Above all, in many fields of activity in which the EU intervenes, the interwovenness of decision-making and implementing levels (international, Community, national, regional) is such that, purely from the point of view of efficiency, it is almost absurd to delineate spheres of competence rigidly.

The question may be raised whether, instead of focusing on delimitation of powers, the post-Nice debate would not do better to look at ways to establish smoother and more loyal cooperation between the different political levels within the EU and, if necessary, develop further institutional arrangements for this purpose. Rather than strictly demarcating spheres of competence, the EU should be further developed as a multi-level governance system in which, depending on each policy sphere, tasks and – even more so – responsibilities are attributed to

whether and, if so, how the Charter should be integrated into the treaties' (*Bulletin of the EU*, 6-1999, pp. 35-36). It may be noticed that there is a remarkable textual difference between the Dutch version, on the one hand, and other language versions like the English, French and Italian, on the other, of the Decision. In the Dutch version, the Decision contains the statement, at the end of the first paragraph of the Decision: 'The Charter must serve as a guiding principle for the Union in the accomplishment of its tasks and must make it easier for citizens to enforce their fundamental rights before the court' (*'Het handvest moet de Unie tot leidraad dienen bij de uitvoering van haar taken en het de burgers gemakkelijker maken hun grondrechten voor de rechter af te dwingen'*). In the third paragraph of the Dutch version of the Decision, it is added in the mission statement of the Convention that it should also establish a draft of the 'possible necessary complementary provisions on the enforcement of fundamental rights'; this part of the sentence does not appear either in the other languages mentioned above.

different layers and in which the different players are linked together by efficient arrangements while preserving a sufficient degree of autonomy.[73]

As far as the simplification of the Treaties is concerned, some scepticism may be justified as well. The question remains not only one of methodology but also of scope. The methodology proposed by the *Dehaene report*, consisting of a division between a basic treaty and a separate treaty with more technical provisions, in which the former would be subject to amendment through an IGC and unanimity whereas the latter could be changed by a special majority, seems tempting. Yet it does not seem warranted from the outset to assume that this really leads to more simplicity. Multiple cross-references and caveats (in the style of 'as specified in Article X of Treaty Y' or 'without prejudice to Article X of Treaty Y') may well obscure the final result or, on closer inspection, make the 'simpler' presentation deceptive. The challenge, it is submitted, lies not so much in simplifying the Treaties but in *merging* them into a fully coherent basic Treaty, divided into logically coherent titles. Coherence would mean, for instance, that all aspects of foreign policy of the EU – whether belonging, for instance, to CFSP, common commercial policy or development policy – are dealt with in one and the same title. This is not a plea for a fully-fledged communitarization of CFSP, nor for weakening the *acquis communautaire* in other areas. The respective roles of the institutions and decision-making mechanisms may remain different but the areas of EU activity should be more clearly grouped.

It is, moreover, wrong in my view to concentrate simplification efforts on Treaty texts alone. Equally important, if not more important, should be an effort at structural simplification by streamlining the Union and the Communities and their working methods and tools of action. Does it make sense to continue to distinguish between the EU and the three – from mid-2002 onwards, two – Communities? Is it sensible to distinguish between directives under the EC Treaty and 'framework decisions' in the Third Pillar? If greater clarity and simplicity is being sought, efforts should likewise concentrate on simplifying the institutional identity of the EU. This need for simplification, in the sense of more unification, obviously also applies to the differences in judicial protection mechanisms under the Union's first and third pillars.

---

[73] On Europe as a multi-level governance system, see in particular F. Scharpf, *Governing in Europe. Effective and Democratic?* (Oxford University Press, 1999), and the important conclusions of this author at pp. 184-204. See also A. Benz and B. Eberlein, *Regions in European Governance: The Logic of Multi-Level Interaction* (EUI Working Paper RSC No 98/31); T.A. Börzel and T. Risse, *Who is Afraid of a European Federation? How to Constitutionalize a Multi-Level Governance System* (Harvard Jean Monnet Working Paper No 7/00); B. Kohler-Koch, *Europe in Search of Legitimate Governance* (ARENA Working Papers 99/27); B. Kohler-Koch and M. Knodt, *Multi-Level Governance: The Joy of Theorizing and the Anguish of Empirical Research* (ECPR Workshop on 'Regional Integration and Multi-Level Governance', Bern, 27 February-4 March 1997); G. Marks, L. Hooghe and K. Blank, 'European Integration from the 1980s: State-centric versus Multi-Level Governance', *Journal of Common Market Studies* (1996), pp. 341-378.

Finally, as far as the role of national parliaments in the European architecture is concerned, some caution also seems to be required. Clearly, a large degree of involvement of national parliaments with the functioning of the Union seems desirable, as this helps to reduce the democratic deficit and to foster a European policy. The Amsterdam Treaty has already given an impetus in this regard with the Protocol on the role of national Parliaments in the European Union. Still, stronger involvement of national parliaments in the EU process should not go hand in hand with a weakening of the role of the European Parliament, which has been rightly described by the European Court of Human Rights in its *Matthews* judgment as 'that part of the European Community structure which best reflects concerns as to "effective political democracy".'[74] It is submitted that, as the institution in which the 'peoples of the States brought together in the Community'[75] are represented, the European Parliament deserves priority treatment, in that its role as a fully-fledged co-legislator in matters where acts of a legislative nature are adopted should be guaranteed throughout all spheres of action of the EU.

In particular, the idea of a two-chamber system for the European Parliament, in which a second chamber would consist of representatives of national parliaments but without touching the status of the Council of Ministers, should be fiercely resisted. This would weaken the position of the present Parliament and make the already unwieldy legislative procedures of the EU even more cumbersome. If the idea of a two-chambers Parliament is to be further explored, it seems more fruitful to turn the Council of Ministers into a second chamber – which is, in a way, already the case under the co-decision procedure – and work towards a system in which the first chamber (i.e., the original European Parliament) is directly elected and represents the peoples of Europe whereas the second chamber would consist of delegates of national and/or subnational governments. Meanwhile, what really matters, in our view, is that the European Parliament and national parliaments should develop cooperation with each other that is as fruitful and effective as possible as part of a truly European parliamentary culture, through regular exchanges and discussion fora, including obviously the Conference of European Affairs Committees (COSAC).[76]

The foregoing reflections make clear that the agenda for the 2004 IGC should, in my view, not be limited to the four themes mentioned in the Declaration on the future of the Union. The true challenge ahead of us is to give the EU a fully-fledged constitutional order which stands in coherent interrelation with the national constitutional orders of its member States. At the level of the EU's basic treaties (preferably: treaty), this necessitates further elaborated institutional checks and balances, a stronger constitutional commitment to openness, more in-

---

[74] European Court of Human Rights, *Case of Matthews* v. *The United Kingdom*, 18 February 1999 (Application No. 24833/94), *Reports of Judgments and Decisions*, 1999-II, para. 52.

[75] So the expression of Article 189 EC.

[76] Protocol on the role of national parliaments in the European Union, points 4-7.

volvement of the European Parliament in certain policy fields and a further increase in the Court's jurisdiction. Almost none of these issues were addressed during the IGC which led to the Nice Treaty and it is not very promising that they do not (yet) form part of the agenda of the 2004 IGC. All of this may be seen as yet another illustration that the EU's constitution-makers are focusing too strongly on the EU's political architecture, and not strongly enough on its *constitutional* architecture. But, in the long run, it is those Treaty changes, together with the other changes suggested above, which will lay the foundations for a sustainable constitutional order and for a successfully enlarged Union.

SESSION II
The National Level: Impact on Constitutions and Courts of EU Member States

THE DUTCH CONSTITUTION AND DUTCH CONSTITUTIONAL VALUES

Speech given on behalf of the Minister of the Interior and Kingdom Relations at the symposium on the constitutional impact of enlargement at EU and national level
The Kurhaus, 21 September 2000

Jit Peters*

Ladies and Gentlemen,

It was a great honour for the Minister of the Interior and Kingdom Relations to be invited by the T.M.C. Asser Institute to open this session of the symposium on the constitutional impact of enlargement at EU and national level. However, under the constitution of the Netherlands the Minister has a prior commitment at this time: he and the rest of the government are engaged in the debate on the budget for 2001 in the Lower House of the Dutch Parliament. He has asked me to convey to you his best wishes for a successful conference, and to speak on his behalf on the impact of European integration on the Dutch constitutional system.

I shall begin by taking you back in time to 1953, when our Constitution was amended to include provisions making it possible for supranational sources of law to take effect in the Dutch legal system. This undoubtedly facilitated the incorporation of European law into the Dutch legal order. I shall go on to discuss some of the effects European legal rules have since had on the Dutch legal system, and the problems we have encountered as a result. In conclusion, I shall examine certain constitutional values which are very close to our hearts here in the Netherlands. These are values which we believe should retain their importance even after the further integration of the legal systems of Europe.

THE DUTCH CONSTITUTION

As far back as the early 1950s, a debate took place in the Netherlands on the question of whether to incorporate provisions in the Constitution that would

* Deputy-Director General, on behalf of the Minister of the Interior and Kingdom relations of the Netherlands.

A.E. Kellermann et al. (Eds.), EU Enlargement: The Constitutional Impact at EU and National Level

make it possible to give direct effect to rules of international law and judgments handed down by international courts. The point at issue was not really whether direct effect should be possible or indeed permissible in the existing system, but whether the Constitution should say so in so many words.

Since the middle of the nineteenth century, the Dutch legal system has allowed for rules and case law developed under international law to have direct effect in the Netherlands. Under the Mannheim Convention, the Central Commission for the Navigation of the Rhine enjoyed both regulatory and quasi-judicial powers. The Act of 18 June 1869 explicitly stated that Dutch judicial bodies should take account of decisions by the Rhine Navigation Commission in their own judgments. Rules laid down by the Commission therefore had immediate effect in Dutch law. In short, it was possible even under the 19th Century Constitution for law from an international source to take direct effect, but the legislature still felt it necessary explicitly to incorporate this piece of international law into the Dutch system. Direct effect was apparently not a matter of course.

In the years after the Second World War it became clear that internationalisation was the order of the day in both politics and law. Alongside purely intergovernmental bodies, such as the Rhine Navigation Commission, in which the Netherlands was represented as a sovereign State, the post-war period witnessed the emergence of supranational forums with the power under treaties to lay down their own rules.

The obvious example was the United Nations Security Council, which – under the UN Charter – has been able to take decisions at various important moments which are binding on all the UN member States, even though only some of them have a seat in the Security Council and hence a voice in the decision.

In 1950, the Van Schaik Constitutional Commission was appointed in the Netherlands, with instructions to prepare the ground for a thorough revision of the Constitution to bring it into line with the post-war world. The Commission dealt with all manner of subjects which are not relevant here. It also recommended the inclusion of new provisions in the Constitution concerning the relationship between law originating from supranational sources and the Dutch legal system.

The Van Schaik Commission's report shows that the Netherlands foresaw the creation of supranational institutions other than the United Nations, institutions that could be granted more far-reaching powers. The new order was heralded by the Treaty on the European Defence Community and the Treaty on the European Coal and Steel Community (ECSC). The European Convention for the Protection of Human Rights and Fundamental Freedoms and the Treaties which set up the European Economic Community and Euratom soon followed.

It was to be expected that the European treaties would themselves contain provisions – as the ECSC Treaty did – from which individuals and companies in the member States could, and should, derive rights, even if only the right to ensure that supranational executive organs would be guided in their relations with those same individuals and companies by the provisions of the Treaties.

It was, in fact, the prospect that internationalisation and 'supranationalisation' would take off in a big way that caused those responsible for drafting the new Dutch Constitution to state unambiguously in Article 92 that legislative, executive and judicial powers could be conferred on international institutions by treaty and in Article 93 that provisions of law from supranational sources would have direct effect provided they were 'binding on all persons by virtue of their contents'. In other words, no further action by the national legislative authorities was required.

The Netherlands went still further, by providing in Article 94 that statutory regulations in force within the Kingdom, regardless of whether they had been introduced before or after the creation of a supranational authority, would be inapplicable if they were incompatible with provisions of treaties that were binding on all or with resolutions by international institutions. The reasoning behind this was that once the Netherlands had given an undertaking at international level, it would not take it back unilaterally by subsequently introducing incompatible domestic legislation. This meant that the landmark decision by the European Court of Justice in the *Van Gend en Loos case*, establishing the supremacy of European law over the national law of the member States, did not hit the Netherlands like a bolt from the blue.

Yet another amendment was introduced in 1953 to help open up the Dutch constitutional system to international law. Since then, the Dutch Constitution has stated that any provisions of a treaty that conflict with the Constitution may only be ratified if there is a two-thirds majority in favour in both Houses of Parliament. At first sight this might seem like an additional obstacle. But closer inspection reveals that this is not the case. An amendment to the Dutch Constitution involves two stages: first both Houses have to pass it by a simple majority; then an election is held and both Houses of the newly elected Parliament have to pass the amendment by a two-thirds majority. In fact, strange as it may seem, the procedure for amending the Constitution is more complicated than that for introducing a treaty that conflicts with the Constitution. In the case of a treaty, a two-thirds majority in both Houses on one occasion is sufficient, and there is no need to dissolve Parliament and hold a general election. The Dutch Constitution can, therefore, prohibit judicial review of the constitutionality of Acts of Parliament or treaties (which have been ratified by the legislature either explicitly or tacitly), on the one hand, and, on the other, not only permit but even order that Acts of Parliament and indeed the Constitution itself be reviewed in the light of international law and if necessary be declared inapplicable.

THE IMPACT OF THE EU ACQUIS ON THE NETHERLANDS

This system – open to the influence of international and supranational sources of law as it is – came into being with the 1953 constitutional amendments. Since then, there have been a number of minor amendments and a general revision of the Constitution in 1983, but, apart from an occasional detail, no changes have been made to the provisions on the direct effect of international or supranational law. It seems as if the constitutional debate was brought to such a successful conclusion in 1953 that it has never had to be reopened, despite the great advances made by Europe since that time.

The EU is referred to in everyday language as 'the fourth tier of government' (namely, the tier above municipal, provincial and central government in the Netherlands). This shows in fact that we scarcely regard the European Union as being of a different order, so to speak, from our national legal order.

But after nearly half a century of European integration, words like Europe, the European Union or the European Community cannot be found in our Constitution, despite the fact that everyone living in this country is confronted with European legislation and its consequences on a daily basis.

Even the microphone which conveys my words to you can only stand here because it carries the EU's seal of approval, the 'CE mark'.

Leaving aside that example, estimates of the volume of European legislation in the Netherlands vary: some say it affects 40 per cent of all legislation in force in this country, others go as far as 70 per cent. For historical reasons – the Netherlands is one of the six founder members of the European Union – we might assume that after walking side by side for nearly half a century the Dutch constitutional system and 'Europe' would have learned to keep in step. And generally speaking they have: the Netherlands comes out fairly well if we measure the number of formal disputes over how EU legislation is applied in the Netherlands.

Nevertheless, I do have some observations to make on one area where the Netherlands is still wrestling with the European order. Things do not always proceed smoothly when it comes to implementation, and especially prompt implementation, of legislation emerging from Brussels. The most notorious example is the European Court of Justice judgment in the *Securitel* case, which revealed that the Netherlands had been unaware of the notification directive under which Brussels should have been notified of all manner of technical regulations before they could take effect. Although the incident was relatively unimportant in itself, it had far-reaching political repercussions, and a large-scale operation had to be mounted to remedy the omissions of the past.

Not only have we sometimes been unaware of the existence or the applicability of EU rules, we have also had problems with the speed of implementation required by Brussels. Such speed is difficult to reconcile with the Dutch tradition of great care in the drafting of legislation, the perfect example of the polder model. This is a process which often involves not only the Council of State, the government and both Houses of Parliament, but also various advisory bodies and interest groups. The Dutch government spent a very long time pondering how to expedite implementation. This resulted in a number of organisational measures, including three-monthly progress reports in the Cabinet on the implementation of

EU directives, and frequent reports to Parliament. To an ever greater extent, too, implementation may now take place via royal decrees and ministerial orders rather than the time-consuming procedure of passing Acts of Parliament. It is even possible, under very strict conditions, for implementation through secondary legislation to derogate from the statutory provisions. To ensure that the Netherlands can continue to fulfil its obligations relating to implementation, the question of tacit parliamentary approval of implementation legislation is currently under discussion. However, this would require an amendment to the Constitution, and for the present the government, the Council of State and the Lower House all agree that fulfilling obligations to the Community should not mean that national parliaments are completely sidelined.

The example of the rules on notification shows that even after nearly half a century we have still not come to terms with the fact that Brussels sets rules and that we sometimes overlook them in our day-to-day work. It also shows that our national legislation still cannot quite keep up with Brussels' regulatory output – and it is falling behind still further since the EU began to make itself felt in an ever wider range of areas – because our national democratic procedures require more time and are still too precious for us to ignore.

DUTCH CONSTITUTIONAL VALUES

This brings me to my observations on democracy in the EU, or rather the democratic deficit still afflicting the EU, and our attitude to this in the Netherlands.

The first direct election to the European Parliament in 1979 put an end to the existence of double mandates. No longer are the members of the EP also members of the Dutch Parliament. Since then, national political parties have held regular talks with like-minded parties in the EP, but there is still hardly any provision for structured consultation between the Dutch Parliament and the elected Dutch representatives in Brussels and Strasbourg. To date, the Lower House has once welcomed Dutch MEPs to an official meeting at which the MEPs were permitted to speak. But a direct exchange of views between MEPs and the members of the Dutch government who put forward positions and reach compromises in the Council of the European Union in Brussels is out of the question for constitutional reasons. You see, members of the Dutch government are accountable to the Dutch Parliament and its members and to nobody else. In fact the experts are by no means agreed on whether it is constitutionally permissible for MEPs to address a meeting of the Dutch Lower House.

In this connection, there is no rule at European level comparable to the one that governs the constitutional relationship between government and Parliament in the Netherlands. This means that so far decision-making in the Council of the European Union and the European Council has taken place behind closed doors, subject to little or no parliamentary scrutiny.

I here refer to Article 68 of the Dutch Constitution:

> 'Ministers and State Secretaries shall provide, orally or in writing, the Houses either separately or in joint session with any information requested by one or more members, provided that such information does not conflict with the interests of the State.'

The obligation to provide information takes precedence over everything else: a member of the government may refuse to provide information only if by doing so he or she might damage the interests of the state. Confidentiality to protect the privacy of individuals or the commercial or industrial interests of companies is in principle not an argument for denying information to members of parliament. At most, it is an argument for providing information to MPs subject to the restrictions of confidentiality.

Europe, at present, does not go nearly as far. A debate is currently under way as to whether the European Parliament and its members should be entitled to receive information that is not in the public domain, and if so, under what conditions. In other words, MEPs have a much more limited right to information, and one that does not measure up to Dutch standards. We believe that the right in principle of a representative assembly to know everything is the fundamental advantage that Parliament enjoys over individual citizens, and it is this right that enables parliamentarians to do what they are there to do, namely, to oversee the executive. If MPs were only entitled to receive information already in the public domain, they would have not the slightest advantage over any newspaper or even interested members of the public.

So here we have a very important constitutional principle: members of parliament should, in theory, be able to know everything, for otherwise they cannot scrutinise the executive as they are supposed to.

And what about the media? Not to mention the citizens (or *citoyens* as French constitutional law has it), who are not only consumers of but also stakeholders in the government of the state. In our view they should be able to obtain as much information as they can. Freedom of information is thus the fundamental principle. Although it is only twenty years or so since the Netherlands introduced legislation providing for public access to government information, the idea that such access is an essential prerequisite of democracy dates back to J.R. Thorbecke, the man who drafted the country's first really democratic constitution in 1848:

> 'Openness sheds light, secrecy creates darkness. The public consideration of matters of public importance will awaken interest and inquiry and lead to knowledge and competence. Secrecy evokes mistrust and arms discontent or unrest with dangerous weapons against the government.'

In our view, the way in which the EU's institutions operate still reflects too little of this traditional Dutch principle. By Dutch standards we are forced to depend too much on unofficial sources of information acting as whistle-blowers. And it is perhaps no coincidence that the Brussels official who recently did such groundbreaking – and certainly sensational – work was a Dutchman.

At the moment, the EU is discussing European legislation on freedom of information deriving from Brussels, Luxembourg and Strasbourg. As I said a moment ago, the Netherlands believes that the right of a parliament and its members to have access to all information (limited only by the interests of the state) is one thing, while the right of every citizen to be denied access to as little information as possible (unless it would cause disproportionate damage to the freedom or opportunities of another, as with personal privacy or industrial secrets) is a principle of at least equal importance.

It seems as if the Europe of the fifteen does not yet agree on this point. The differences are clear from the terms used: while one country talks of public access to government information, another legislates on official secrets. The subject being regulated is the same, but the differences in terminology go beyond semantics.

I would like to conclude by discussing another speciality of the Netherlands. It may not be peculiar to this country, but it is something very dear to our hearts.

The Dutch constitutional tradition is one of autonomous municipalities and provinces. Municipal autonomy dates back to the town charters and manorial rights of the Middle Ages, and continued on throughout the time of the Republic because the towns enjoyed so much economic power. In fact, the Dutch Republic was no more than a loose federation of seven provinces, instituted by the Union of Utrecht in 1579, much looser than the federal states of the twentieth century. And following the French occupation, the Congress of Vienna forged these provinces and towns into what we call a devolved unitary state: a state which until 1830, or 1839 by our way of thinking, also embraced the southern Netherlands. Municipal – and provincial – autonomy is still a highly important principle, which was enshrined in even stronger form in the 1992 revision of the Municipalities Act. Ever since the foundation of the Kingdom, the government in The Hague, in line with centuries-old custom, has always been extremely reluctant to correct a municipal authority or to bring it to book. And if this does happen – on average twice a year, spread over some six hundred municipalities – it is surrounded by plenty of legal safeguards for the municipalities and their executives. This is the background to the current debate as to how far The Hague can go to oversee and even correct municipal and provincial authorities in their implementation of legislation emanating from Brussels.

A case such as the penalty payment recently imposed on Greece because the local authorities in Crete had failed to take sufficient measures against the dumping of waste would pose problems in the Netherlands too. To hold central government liable for the penalty payment would be impossible, nor would it be effective in such a case, but simply to charge the penalty payment to the 'guilty' municipality or province would be extremely controversial in the Dutch system, however justified it might appear at first sight. The fact is that no provision at all has been made for cases of this kind in the Netherlands.

However, the fact that since the 1950s the Netherlands has acceded to the entire series of European treaties means that we must find a modus vivendi for such cases. Article 10 of the EC Treaty enjoins the member States to ensure fulfilment of the obligations arising out of the treaty. This is what the Netherlands signed up to in 1953 and – as I said earlier – for better or for worse.

CONCLUSION

Individuals perceive themselves in the first place as citizens of a nation state, and they will continue to do so. We should always bear this in mind by respecting national values like freedom of information, the protection of fundamental rights and the devolution of powers.

On the other hand, individual citizens should be more closely involved in European decision-making, for example through referendums and perhaps in the future through the direct election of the President of the European Commission.

Thank you.

CONSTITUTIONAL ASPECTS OF EUROPEAN UNION MEMBERSHIP IN THE ORIGINAL SIX MEMBER STATES: MODEL SOLUTIONS FOR THE APPLICANT COUNTRIES?

Bruno de Witte*

INTRODUCTION

The leading principle of negotiations on accession to the European Union is that of the wholesale acceptance of the *acquis de l'Union* by the candidate country. A quite separate question is whether there is also an *acquis constitutionnel* to be accepted by the candidate state: does membership of the European Union involve the adoption of particular rules and principles of *national constitutional law* on the model of the constitutions of the present member States? I will contribute to answering this question by looking at the constitutional law of six out of the fifteen present member States of the EU, namely the founding states that set up the European Communities in the 1950s (hereafter, 'the Six'). These six states are being lumped together within one single chapter of this book, whereas most of the other member States are treated in separate individual papers. The justification for this different treatment must be that the Six, unlike the later members, were able to mould the European Communities in accordance with their own preferences and in compliance with their national constitutional rules and principles, and did not have to face accession to an existing institutional system. In this respect, the constitutional experience of the Six is less obviously relevant for the present candidate countries than the experience of the nine member States that joined later.

This being said, the governing elite of the Six often think of their countries as prominent artisans of the European integration process and, perhaps, as models to which the applicant states should look, rather than to the more recent members whose European credentials are less firmly established. With respect to the theme of the conference, one might imagine that the manner in which the constitutions of the Six have dealt with 'Europe' would set a particularly meaningful example for the new applicants. This, however, is hardly the case. It is true that the Six have a long common constitutional history, in the sense that they have been exposed to the same constitutional challenges, first in the founding period of the

* Professor of European Law (EUI, Florence). On leave from the University of Maastricht.

A.E. Kellermann et al. (Eds.), EU Enlargement: The Constitutional Impact at EU and National Level

Communities, and then in all the subsequent phases of the European integration process. Yet, as will be argued in the following pages, the constitutional responses they gave to these common challenges have been far from homogeneous. There is simply no 'common constitutional model' of the Six in respect of European integration; they can therefore not, as a group, provide a role model for the constitutional actors in Central and Eastern Europe, Cyprus and Malta. The constitutional approach adopted by *single* countries among the Six may provide constitutional inspiration, but not more than the experience of any other of the present member States of the European Union.

In the following pages, I will first take a chronological approach to the subject and distinguish three broad phases:

- *Phase 1*, from 1946 to 1964, is a period in which the Six were still on their own. It started with the adoption of the Constitution of the Fourth Republic in France, the first post-war constitution providing for the limitation of sovereignty in favour of international organisations, and ended with the judgement of the European Court of Justice in *Costa* v. *ENEL* that raised new constitutional issues which the Six had not clearly identified when setting up the Communities.
- *Phase 2,* from 1964 to 1992, is a long period without any spectacular transformations of the EC legal system, during which the national courts in the Six (rather than the constitutional legislators) developed constitutional doctrines allowing them to enforce EC law at the domestic level in accordance with the mandate thrust upon them by the ECJ in *Costa* v. *ENEL* and subsequent judgements.
- *Phase 3*, which leads from 1992 to the present, is marked by new efforts, in some of the Six at least, to adapt the constitutional texts to the changing reality of European integration. This new period started with the constitutional debates on the ratification of the Maastricht Treaty, which set in motion a brief period of constitutional ferment.

After this short chronological analysis, the second part of the paper will identify three issues relating to membership of the European Union, for which there is not yet a clear solution in the constitutional law of most of the Six countries. By pointing out these outstanding problems, I want to show that the candidate countries are not faced with a simple and unambiguous *acquis constitutionnel*, which they should absorb in the same uncritical way as they absorb the *acquis communautaire*; in reality, the national constitutional systems of the member States old and new are still struggling to come to terms with the unprecedented and elusive phenomenon of European integration.

I. THREE PHASES IN THE CONSTITUTIONAL ADAPTATION TO MEMBERSHIP

I.1 Phase One (1946-1964): The Limitation of Sovereignty Clauses as the Basis for Membership of the Communities

The European Coal and Steel Community was created in 1951 as an international organisation based on a treaty between the Six. Whereas this treaty was an ordinary international agreement in formal terms, it was far from ordinary in its content. A major, and at the time startling, innovation of the 'Schuman Plan', a major contrast with earlier pre-war and post-war cooperation projects, was that sovereign states should agree to surrender their powers over their coal and steel industries to a supranational body, the High Authority. By signing the European Coal and Steel Treaty, as it emerged from the Schuman Plan through negotiations in 1950, the governments of the Six agreed to relinquish national control over these two sectors of the economy and to allow the supranational High Authority to exercise autonomous 'state' powers in their stead.

The way for this international innovation had been paved by the unprecedented openness to international cooperation displayed by the new post-war constitutions of the three largest participants in the ECSC project. In France, Italy and Germany, the post-war restoration of democracy had been accompanied by the express constitutional recognition of the fact that effective international cooperation was necessary in order to prevent new wars and to avoid the excesses caused by unbridled State sovereignty. Each of these three new constitutions contained a provision permitting limitations of sovereignty or transfer of sovereign powers to international institutions. All three provisions are still a part of the constitutional law of these countries today.

In *France*, paragraph 15 of the preamble of the Constitution of the Fourth Republic adopted in 1946[1] stated that 'subject to reciprocity, France consents to limitations of sovereignty necessary for the realisation and the defence of peace.'[2] Article 11 of the Italian Constitution of 1948 declares in strikingly similar terms that 'Italy may consent, on equal terms with other States, to limitations of sovereignty necessary to establish an order ensuring peace and justice among nations, and it will favour international organisations which have that aim.'[3] Article 24(1)

---

[1] Although the 1946 Constitution is no longer in force, its preamble is incorporated by reference in the first paragraph of the preamble of the present Constitution of 1958. Both preambles are part of the '*bloc constitutionnel*' which is binding law for all French authorities (see Th. Renoux & M. de Villiers, *Code constitutionnel* (Paris: Litec, 1994) at p. 9).

[2] 'Sous réserve de réciprocité, la France consent aux limitations de souveraineté nécessaires à l'organisation et à la défense de la paix.'

[3] 'L'Italia ... consente, in condizioni di parità con gli altri Stati, alle limitazioni di sovranità necessarie ad un ordinamento che assicuri la pace e la giustizia fra le Nazioni; promuove e favorisce le organizzazioni internazionali rivolte a tale scopo'.

of the German Basic Law of 1949 expresses the same intention in active, rather than passive, wording: 'The Federation may by legislation transfer sovereign powers to international institutions'.[4]

The function of each of these provisions was to facilitate the approval and entry into force of treaties for which otherwise a prior constitutional revision would have been needed. Indeed, derogation from the constitutional allocation of State powers can normally be made only by means of a revision of the constitution; the limitations of sovereignty clauses were meant to allow such derogation by the simple signature and approval of an international treaty. Whereas Article 24(1) of the German Basic Law is quite open-ended, the French and Italian provisions contain some conditions; the question of constitutional interpretation that unavoidably arose in France and Italy was to define which international treaties were covered by these clauses, and which were not, either because their purpose was not among the ones mentioned by the constitution, or because they contained limitations going beyond what was 'necessary' for the sake of international cooperation. In the Italian Parliament, for instance, it was argued that membership of the ECSC would require a prior constitutional revision, but that position was overruled. Again, in 1957, the parliamentary opposition argued that the Rome Treaties could not be approved, in accordance with Article 11, by a simple majority vote, because they entailed a constitutional revolution.[5] Also, some authors took the view that Article 11 did not even cover economic cooperation treaties such as the ECSC or the EEC Treaty.[6] Similar discussions took place in the French Parliament. In the end, though, all three countries approved both the ECSC Treaty and the Treaties of Rome (EEC and EAEC) on the basis of the 'limitation of sovereignty' clause, and without making amendments to the text of their constitutions.

The model set in the post-war years by the three leading member States was imitated by the Netherlands and Luxembourg some years later, at a time when these countries had already joined the ECSC (but not yet the EEC). The Netherlands adopted a constitutional amendment in 1953 (Article 67 of the Constitution, now renumbered as Article 92) allowing for the attribution of legislative, executive and judicial powers to international organisations, and Luxembourg did the same in 1956 (Article 49bis).[7] The sixth member, Belgium, acted only much later. In that country, constitutional lawyers had expressed misgivings about the legality of joining the ECSC first, the EEC and Euratom later, in the absence of any constitutional clause authorising the transfer of powers to international

---

[4] 'Der Bund kann durch Gesetz Hoheitsrechte auf zwischenstaatliche Einrichtungen übertragen¢.

[5] See, with further references, M. Mazziotti, 'Appunti sulla sentenza della Corte costituzionale riguardante la legge istitutiva dell' ENEL', *Giurisprudenza Costituzionale* (1964).

[6] See e.g., L. Ferrari Bravo, 'L'issue de l'affaire Costa c. ENEL devant le Conciliatore de Milan', *Cahiers de droit européen* (1966) p. 200, at pp. 207-208.

[7] 'L'exercice d'attributions réservées par la Constitution aux pouvoirs législatif, exécutif et judiciaire peut être temporairement dévolu par traité à des institutions de droit international.'

organisations,[8] but it took until 1970, in the context of a much broader revision of the Belgian Constitution, before such an enabling provision was finally inscribed in the Constitution. An Article 25bis was enacted (today renumbered as Article 34) stating that 'the exercise of delimited powers can be attributed by treaty or by law to institutions of public international law'.[9] It is striking that none of the three Benelux countries made express reference to the European Communities when they amended their constitutions, although the EC were undoubtedly the prime example the constitutional legislators had in mind when making the amendments.

I.2 Phase Two (1964-1992): The Constitutional Reception of the Primacy Doctrine

One of the main challenges for all member States' constitutional systems has been how to accommodate the primacy doctrine of the European Court of Justice and the exacting demands it makes on the national courts. There is a clear distinction to be made, in this respect, between the Six, for whom the *Costa* v. *Enel* judgment of 1964 may have come as an unexpected surprise, and the states joining the EC at a time when primacy was a firmly established and widely publicized characteristic of the Community legal order for which they could (if necessary) make constitutional preparations.

Among the Six, the *Costa* judgment required no special efforts from the courts in the Netherlands and Luxembourg, where the supremacy of international treaty provisions over national legislation was accepted prior to the entry into force of the EEC Treaty, either on the basis of a clear constitutional rule (in the Netherlands)[10] or on the basis of the case law of the supreme court (in Luxembourg). In Belgium, the courts reacted promptly and loyally to the European Court's mandate. The 1971 judgment of the Belgian *Cour de Cassation* in the *Franco-Suisse*

---

[8] These misgivings expressed in legal writing did not affect the attitude of Belgian courts. At the time, the Acts authorising membership of the European Communities were, like all other acts of parliament, immune from judicial review.

[9] In French: 'L'exercice de pouvoirs déterminés peut être attribué par un traité ou par une loi à des institutions de droit international public.' For an analysis of the reform and a description of the preceding constitutional debate, see J.V. Louis, 'L'article 25 bis de la Constitution belge', *Revue du marché commun* (1970) p. 410.

[10] Article 94 of the Dutch Constitution (as renumbered in 1983): 'Legislation in force within the Kingdom shall not apply if this application is incompatible with provisions of agreements which are binding on anyone and which have been entered into either before or after the enactment of such legislation.'

To a large extent, the ECJ doctrines of the supremacy and direct effect of EC law were anticipated by Dutch constitutional law, and they were therefore easily received by Dutch courts; see, on this process of interaction between Dutch constitutional law and EC law, M. Claes and B. de Witte, 'Report on the Netherlands', in A.-M. Slaughter, A. Stone Sweet and J.H.H. Weiler, eds., *The European Court & National Courts – Doctrine and Jurisprudence* (Oxford, Hart Publishing 1998) p. 171.

Le Ski case is a model of what national courts can achieve in the absence of clear constitutional guidelines. Although the Belgian Constitution was silent on the matter of the domestic effect of international or European law, the supreme court adopted the principle of primacy as it had been formulated in *Costa,* and based it on the nature of international law and (*a fortiori*) of EC law. The other Belgian courts soon followed the same line.[11]

In France, on the contrary, despite the existence of a constitutional provision (Article 55) clearly recognising the priority of international treaties even over later French laws, the courts were surprisingly slow to accept that this constitutional provision could actually be used as a conflict rule in real cases and controversies. The *Cour de Cassation*, taking the lead for the 'ordinary' court system, decided to cross the Rubicon in the 1975 *Cafés Jacques Vabre* judgment. The *Conseil d'Etat* (and the administrative courts subject to its authority) followed suit much later, with the *Nicolo* decision in 1989, after what must have been a very painful revision of established truths. One may note that one of the arguments used by the *Commissaire* Frydman, when advising the *Conseil* in *Nicolò* to change its views on the primacy of EC law, was that the supreme courts of surrounding countries (even those with ingrained dualist traditions) had long recognized this primacy.[12]

The countries to which Frydman referred were, obviously, Italy and Germany. In both countries, the duty imposed by *Costa* to give precedence to Community law over any conflicting national norm went well beyond what the mainstream constitutional doctrine of the 1960s could accept as regards the domestic force of international treaty law. Yet, by emphasizing the distinction between EEC law and 'ordinary' international law, the European Court had encouraged the German and Italian courts to find a specific solution ensuring the primacy of Community law without necessarily extending this primacy to other international treaties (unlike what happened in the four other countries). Indeed, the Italian Constitutional Court (the ECJ's indirect interlocutor in *Costa* v. *ENEL*) started off on a 'long march'[13] during which it gradually came to recognize the supremacy of Community law over national legislation, on the basis of the EC law's special nature that

---

[11] For a synthetic view of the evolution before and after *Le Ski*, see H. Bribosia, 'Report on Belgium', in Slaughter et al., op. cit. n. 10, at pp. 10-21.

[12] On the evolution and present situation in France, see J. Rideau, *Droit institutionnel de l'Union et des Communautés européennes*, 3rd. edn. (Paris, LGDJ, 1999) at p. 998 et seq. (and further references to an abundant literature on p. 969).

[13] This expression is used to describe the sequence of Constitutional Court judgments from 1964 to the present by G. Greco, 'Rapporti tra ordinamento comunitario e nazionale', in M. Chiti and G. Greco, eds., *Trattato di diritto amministrativo europeo* (Milano, Giuffrè 1997) p. 399, at p. 401. For an English language analysis of the evolution in the Italian Constitutional Court's case law on the domestic effect of EC law, see M. Cartabia, 'The Italian Constitutional Court and the Relationship Between the Italian Legal System and the European Union', in Slaughter et al., op. cit. n. 10, at p. 133 (as well as the contribution by F. Ruggeri Laderchi in the same volume).

distinguishes it from other international treaties; a similar evolution has taken place, much more rapidly and smoothly, in Germany. In Italy, Article 11 of the Constitution, the limitation of sovereignty clause, became the constitutional peg on which to hang the primacy of Community law, or, to quote another frequently used metaphor, the instrument piercing the barrier of dualism and allowing Community law to have 'full compulsory efficacy' within the Italian legal order. The underlying reasoning may be spelled out as follows: one of the 'limitations of sovereignty' allowed by the terms of Article 11 is that the Parliament accepted, when ratifying the EEC Treaty, that its statutes would no longer be enforceable by the Italian courts when found to be incompatible with Community obligations. In the interpretation of Article 24 of the German Constitution adopted by the Constitutional Court since the late 1960s, that article has come to play almost exactly the same role as Article 11 of the Italian Constitution. Article 24's explicit and primary function was to allow for membership of international organisations with incisive powers such as those of the European Communities; but its implicit and secondary function has become to serve as the constitutional 'bridge' allowing Community law to enter the German legal order carrying its flags of supremacy and direct effect.

By the early 1990s, therefore, the necessary adjustments of constitutional doctrine allowing for the primacy of EC law over national acts of parliament had been accomplished in all six countries. Yet, this primacy of EC law was not expressly inscribed in any of the six constitutions; the France and the Netherlands had a written rule, but dating from the 1950s and applying to international treaties in general, whereas the four other constitutions remained entirely silent on the important question of the domestic effect of EC law.

I.3 Phase Three (1992-2000): The Constitutional Reaction to Maastricht, and beyond

The Single European Act (1986) did not leave any traces in the constitutions of the Six, but the signing of the Treaty on European Union (1992) set in motion a constitutional amendment process in two countries. In Germany, the amendments were made on the Government's and Parliament's initiative, and received the reserved blessing of the Constitutional Court in its famous *Maastricht* judgement; in France, the *Conseil Constitutionnel* first identified three points on which the new Treaty was incompatible with the existing constitutional text, and the constitution was then amended so as to remove the inconsistency.[14] In both countries,

---

[14] There is a very rich literature on the French and German constitutional reforms post-Maastricht, and on the related judgments of their constitutional courts. For a comparative analysis of the French and German judgments on the Treaty of Maastricht (with many references to the literature in both countries), see C. Grewe and A. Weber, 'Le Traité de l'Union devant les juridictions constitutionnelles', IX-1993 *Annuaire international de justice constitutionnelle* (1995) p. 11.

this resulted in constitutional provisions that explicitly recognise the existence of the European Union[15] whereas, as indicated before, the ECSC and the EEC had not been mentioned in any of the six Constitutions. Article 23 of the German Basic Law, which now applies alongside the general international cooperation clause of Article 24, gives express support to the creation of the European Union and entrenches the participation rights of the *Länder* in the European integration process; it also entrenches substantive conditions for participation of Germany in the European integration process.[16] Articles 88-1 to 88-4 of the French Constitution, while giving specific constitutional approval to the clauses of the Maastricht Treaty which the *Conseil Constitutionnel* had found to be contrary to the constitution as it stood, also refer in general terms, and for the first time, to the existence of the EC and EU.

Belgium and Luxembourg, on the other hand, showed a considerable amount of constitutional 'pragmatism'. Although the article of the Maastricht Treaty granting to European Union citizens a right to vote in local elections was in clear contrast with provisions of their constitutions reserving the right to vote to the country's own nationals, both countries' governments and parliaments decided that the Treaty could be ratified without prior revision of the constitution, and that there would be time to adapt it later, in time for the next local elections. This attitude was criticised by legal authors as it undoubtedly trivialises the legal standing of the Constitution.[17]

Nor were the constitutions modified in Italy and the Netherlands. On the question of the right to vote for EU citizens, there was (unlike in the four other countries) no substantive conflict of norms requiring constitutional correction; indeed, the Netherlands had long recognised the right to vote to *all* resident foreigners at local elections. Nevertheless, several legal writers both in the Netherlands and in Italy argued that the Maastricht Treaty contained such far-reaching provisions,

---

[15] The central provisions are:
– Article 88-1 French Constitution: 'La République participe aux Communautés européennes et à l'Union européenne, constituées d'Etats qui ont choisi librement, en vertu des traités qui les ont instituées, d'exercer en commun certaines de leurs compétences.'
– Article 23(1) German Basic Law: 'Zur Verwirklichung eines Vereinten Europas wirkt die Bundesrepublik Deutschland bei der Entwicklung der Europäischen Union mit, die demokratischen, rechtsstaatlichen, sozialen und föderativen Grundsätzen und dem Grundsatz der Subsidiarität verpflichtet ist und einen diesem Grundgesetz im wesentlichen vergleichbaren Grundrechtsschutz gewährleistet.(...)'.
(The following paragraphs of Article 23 organise the participation of the *Länder* in European Union affairs).

[16] For a detailed recent analysis of the many faces of Article 23 of the German Basic Law, see C.D. Classen, 'Artikel 23', in H. von Mangoldt, F. Klein, C. Starck, eds., *Das Bonner Grundgesetz*, Vol. 2, 4th edn. (2000) p. 426.

[17] See, for instance, F. Delpérée, 'La Belgique et l'Europe', *Revue française de droit constitutionnel* (1992) p. 643; and K. Rimanque and J.Wouters, 'De betekenis van de Grondwet voor de Europese rechtsorde', *Preadviezen van de vereniging voor de vergelijkende studie van het recht van België en Nederland* (Deventer, Tjeenk Willink 1998) at pp. 43-46.

particularly in the monetary field, that constitutional amendments were required.[18] In both countries, these views were quietly ignored by government and the parliament, approval of the Maastricht Treaty was given in accordance with the ordinary rules for the approval of treaties, and the existing text of the constitution was left untouched. The broad 'limitation of sovereignty' clauses were, once again, considered to be capacious enough to deal with this new advance in the European integration process.

The post-Maastricht phase of constitutional reform was thus limited to two countries only, and was short-lived. When, some years later, the Treaty of Amsterdam was adopted, the prevailing attitude was, again, that of minimising the constitutional implications of this further deepening of the integration process. This Treaty led to a small constitutional amendment in only one of the Six countries, namely France, where, after a decision of the *Conseil Constitutionnel* finding the new immigration powers of the EC to be incompatible with existing constitutional law, a special clause was added to the Constitution in order to cure this incompatibility.[19]

II. THE CONSTITUTIONAL ASPECTS OF EU MEMBERSHIP: SOME UNRESOLVED PROBLEMS

II.1 The European Deficit of National Constitutional Texts

The way in which the constitutional texts of the Six deal with the European integration process is rather disappointing, particularly in view of the political support which their governments and parliaments (and, indeed, their populations) have constantly given to that process. Until 1992, when the French and German constitutions were modified in the wake of the adoption of the Treaty on European Union, none of the six constitutions contained language referring, in express terms, to the European integration process. During the whole existence of the European Communities before Maastricht (that is, forty years altogether), only two constitutional amendments were made which, though not mentioning the EC ex-

[18] For Italy, see the arguments by M. Luciani, 'La Constitution italienne et les obstacles à l'intégration européenne', *Revue française de droit constitutionnel* (1992) p. 663; for the Netherlands, see the summary description of the debate in A. Kellermann, 'Ratification Processes of the Treaty on European Union – The Netherlands', *ELRev.* (1993) p. 242.

[19] For an English language comment on the French constitutional response to the Treaty of Amsterdam, see S. Boyron, 'The French Constitution and the Treaty of Amsterdam: A Lesson in European Integration', *Maastricht Journal of European and Comparative Law* (1999) p. 169. There was also some limited discussion in the German literature on the constitutional legality of ratification of the Amsterdam Treaty (see mainly, M. Pechstein, 'Amsterdamer Vertrag und Grundgesetz', *Die Öffentliche Verwaltung* (1998) p. 569) but the government made no move to amend the Basic Law which remained as it stood after Maastricht.

plicitly, were clearly made with a view to the EC: the 1953 revision of the Dutch Constitution and the 1970 amendment of the Belgian Constitution.

Even today, there is not a single hint in the Dutch and Italian Constitutions to the fact that the country is a member State of the European Union; the constitutional basis for membership, and for the application of EC law, is still to be found in old provisions dating from the late 40s and early 50s.[20] A few years ago, Italy came close to inserting new provisions in its Constitution dealing with the European integration process. The provisions were part of a general draft for the revision of the Constitution, and failed to be enacted because the political agreement on the whole draft collapsed in the summer of 1998.[21] In the Netherlands, the fact that the general constitutional framework does not put any obstacles in the way of the European integration process is taken as a justification for leaving things as they are, although some writers occasionally point to the odd situation that the text of the Constitution contains many rather trivial rules but fails to acknowledge one of the central constitutional realities of the country, namely its membership of the European Union, with all the legal consequences deriving therefrom.

II.2 Constitutional Limits to the Primacy of European Law

In the view of the European Court of Justice, any directly effective rule of EC law should prevail over any conflicting rule of national law whatever its rank in the domestic hierarchy of norms. However, this 'absolute supremacy' even over national constitutional rules is not easily accepted by the courts in the member States, including the courts of a number of the founding member States.[22]

The Italian Constitutional Court has consistently held, ever since its *Frontini* judgment of 1973, that EC law may derogate from 'ordinary' rules of constitutional law, but not from certain fundamental principles or inalienable rights of

[20] In Belgium, the constitutional silence has been broken in 1993 when, on the occasion of the general federal reform of the country, provisions were included on the participation of the Regions and Communities in European affairs. However, membership of the European Union, as such, is not mentioned in the text of the Constitution.

[21] For a detailed analysis of the draft articles on the European Union (written at the time their enactment seemed still probable), see F. Sorrentino, 'La partecipazione dell'Italia all'Unione europea', *Rivista italiana di diritto pubblico comunitario* (1998) p. 891; and C. Curti Gialdino, 'Revisione costituzionale ed Unione europea. Prime osservazioni sul progetto della commissione parlamentare per le riforme costituzionali', *Scritti in onore di Giuseppe Federico Mancini*, Vol. II (Milano, Giuffrè, 1998) p. 125. See also, for a more normative analysis, A. La Pergola, 'Quale *Europa-Artikel* per l'Italia?', in ibid., p. 537.

[22] For a nutshell comparative view of the 'constitutional reservations' to the recognition of the full supremacy of EC law, see B. de Witte, 'Direct Effect, Supremacy and the Nature of the Legal Order', in P. Craig and G. de Búrca, eds., *The Evolution of EU Law* (Oxford, OUP 1999) p. 177, at pp.199-205. For a stimulating doctrinal contribution to the question of control of EU law in the light of (national) constitutional law, see J. Wouters, 'National Constitutions and the European Union', 27 *Legal Issues of Economic Integration* (2000) p. 25, at pp. 72-90.

persons. The latter are, in Italian legal parlance, 'counter-limits' (*controlimiti*) to the limitations of sovereignty allowed by Article 11 of the Constitution: when *State* institutions exercise sovereign powers, they must respect the fundamental values and principles of the Constitution, and these values and principles must continue to be respected when state powers are attributed to the *European* institutions. In its *Fragd* ruling of 1989, the Italian Court went so far as to state that it could control the consistency of *individual* rules of EC law with the fundamental principles of the Italian Constitution, particularly (but not only) in the field of human rights.[23] The Court has not actually used this review power so far, but it is clear that there is no place, in this scheme of thought, for the recognition of an absolute primacy of Community law.

German constitutional case law presents a similar, and better-known, picture. The German Constitutional Court held, in its *Solange-I* and *Solange-II* judgments of 1974 and 1986, with express reference to the doctrine of its Italian counterpart, that Article 24 of the *Grundgesetz* 'does not confer a power to surrender by way of ceding sovereign rights to international institutions the identity of the prevailing constitutional order of the Federal Republic by breaking into its basic framework, that is, into the structure that makes it up'.[24] One important part of this constitutional identity is respect for fundamental rights. On this point, the *Solange-II* judgment specified that the Constitutional Court would refrain from controlling whether individual EC acts respected fundamental rights (this being a matter left to the ECJ), but that it could control whether the general regime of fundamental rights protection in the EC continued to be equivalent to the German constitutional standard. In its recent judgment of 7 June 2000, the Court confirmed this position.[25]

The 'constitutional identity' referred to in *Solange-II* is broader than the fundamental rights question. Article 23 of the Basic Law, adopted in 1992 (that is, after *Solange-II)* has spelled this out by requiring the European Union to respect 'democratic, rule-of-law, social and federal principles as well as the principle of subsidiarity', and the Constitutional Court added to this, in the *Maastricht* judgment of 1993, that it would control whether the EU institutions remain within the

---

[23] Judgment of 21 April 1989, n. 232, in *Rivista italiana di diritto pubblico comunitario* (1991) p. 138, with note by V. Angiolini; see the English language comment by G. Gaja, 'New Developments in a Continuing Story: The Relationship between EEC Law and Italian Law', *CMLRev.* (1990) p. 83. On the Court's doctrine of 'counterlimits', see M. Cartabia, *Principi inviolabili e integrazione europea* (Milano, Giuffrè 1995), pp. 95-138, and the synthesis by M. Cartabia and J.H.H. Weiler, *L'Italia in Europa. Profili istituzionali e costituzionali* (Bologna, Il Mulino 2000) at pp. 167-173.

[24] Judgment of 22 October 1986 (*Solange-II*), passage as translated in (1987) 3 *CMLR* p. 225, at p.257.

[25] *BverfG*, 2 BvL 1/97 of 7 June 2000, in *Europäische Zeitschrift für Wirtschaftsrecht* (2000) p. 702 (with a case note by F.C. Mayer, 'Grundrechtsschutz gegen europäische Rechtsakte durch das BverfG: Zur Verfassungsmäßigkeit der Bananenmarktordnung', at p. 685).

limits of their attributed powers. The exact significance of this 1993 judgment has been the object of considerable controversy in Germany and abroad; the judgment has also been attacked by many scholars,[26] but so far the abstract hypothesis of an *ultra vires* act of the EU has not materialized in the Karlsruhe case law.[27]

Thus, the constitutional clauses about limitation of sovereignty have been given a closely similar interpretation by the Italian and German Constitutional courts in the context of European integration. These clauses have been used in a double capacity. On the one hand, they allow for the smooth integration of EC law into the national legal system, discarding dualist doctrine for the exclusive benefit of EC law and ensuring the direct effect and primacy of EC law in all 'normal' situations (see section I.2 above). On the other hand, the sovereignty clauses allow the constitutional courts of these two countries to protect what they consider to be the core of the constitution against EU encroachments.

The position in French law is not fundamentally different. Although the *Conseil Constitutionnel* does not directly control the constitutionality of EC legislative acts, the ordinary and administrative courts still consider the Constitution as the highest norm, and will not enforce the primacy of international treaty law (including EU law) when such enforcement would run counter to a constitutional norm.[28] Even in Belgium, the exemplary attitude of the *Cour de Cassation* in *Le Ski* is now overshadowed by the ambiguous position adopted by the *Cour d'Arbitrage*, the quasi-constitutional court created in 1980, which declared itself competent to review the constitutionality of international treaties even after their

[26] Most significantly by three former German judges at the ECJ: U. Everling, 'The Maastricht Judgment of the German Federal Constitutional Court and its Significance for the Development of the European Union', *Yearbook of European Law* (1994) 1; M. Zuleeg, 'The European Constitution under Constitutional Constraints: The German Scenario', *ELRev.* (1997) p. 19; G. Hirsch, 'Europäischer Gerichtshof und Bundesverfassungsgericht: Kooperation oder Konfrontation?', *Neue Juristische Wochenschrift* (1996) p. 2457.

[27] The question of constitutional review of ultra vires acts of the European Union is treated in full detail by F.C. Mayer, *Kompetenzüberschreitung und Letztentscheidung* (München, Verlag C.H. Beck 2000); see particularly, for the position in German law, pp. 88-137; in other member States, pp. 138-259.

[28] Conseil d'Etat (Ass.), judgment of 30 October 1998, '*Sarran et Levacher et autres*', in *Revue du droit public (*1999) p. 946. Among the many comments on this judgment, see J.F. Flauss, ibid., p. 919; J. Dehaussy, 'La Constitution, les traités et les lois: à propos de la nouvelle jurisprudence du Conseil d'Etat sur les traités', *Journal du droit international* (1999) p. 675; C. Richards, '*Sarran et Levacher*: ranking legal norms in the French Republic', *ELRev.* (2000) p. 192. The same position (priority of the Constitution over international treaties) was adopted by the Cour de Cassation in its recent *Fraisse* judgment: Cass. Ass. 2 juin 2000, in *Revue du droit public* (2000) p. 1050, with comment by X. Prétot, 'La Cour de Cassation, la Constitution et les traités – a propos de l'arrêt de l'assemblée plénière du 2 juin 2000', ibid., p. 1037. For some general reflections on the relation between EC law and French constitutional law, see F. Chaltiel, 'Droit constitutionnel et droit communautaire', *Revue trimestrielle de droit européen* (1999) p. 395.

entry into force although it has never, as yet, exercised this power in relation to EC law.[29]

The cause of all these reservations against an absolute primacy of EC law is the fact that constitutional courts, quite understandably, cannot accept that any source of law might prevail over the national constitution itself, which after all is the source of their own existence. If the constitution is seen as the basis for recognizing the primacy of Community law, then absolute primacy of the type postulated by the European Court in *Internationale Handelsgesellschaft* is only possible by way of an 'auto-limitation' clause in the constitution. The Netherlands offers a solitary example of such a clause. Article 120 of the Dutch Constitution expressly prohibits national courts from reviewing the constitutionality of treaty provisions and of decisions of international organizations, and thereby ensures the absolute supremacy of treaties once they have been properly ratified. Accordingly, the Dutch courts have never hinted at the existence of constitutional limits to the enforcement of EC law.

II.3 The Tension between Constitutional Traditions and the Reality of European Integration

In post-1945 Western Europe, a doctrinal compromise emerged, which was common to the Six (with the possible exception of the more internationalist position in the Netherlands) between the traditional concept of state sovereignty and the new needs of international cooperation and European integration. This common conceptual approach may be summarised as follows. Sovereignty continues to reside in the people and is to be exercised primarily by the institutions of the state.[30] This exercise of sovereign powers may be dispersed horizontally, among the central institutions of the state (the legislative, the executive and the judiciary), but there is no conceptual obstacle against its vertical dispersion, allowing sub-national institutions (such as the *Länder* in Germany and the Regions and Communities in Belgium) to participate in the exercise of sovereign powers. Similarly, thanks to the post-war constitutional innovations, the exercise of State powers may henceforth be attributed to international institutions such as the European Community. As a result, action in the framework of the European institutions 'somehow appears as another mode for the member States to assume their own

[29] See Y. Lejeune and Ph. Brouwers, 'La Cour d'Arbitrage face au contrôle de la constitutionnalité des traités', *Journal des Tribunaux* (1992) p. 671; Rimanque and Wouters, op. cit. n. 17, pp. 30-43.

[30] See Article 3 of the French Constitution: 'La souveraineté nationale *appartient* au peuple qui l'*exerce* par ses représentants et par la voie du référendum...' (emphasis added), and Article 1, second sentence, of the Italian Constitution: 'La sovranità *appartiene* al popolo, che la *esercita* nelle forme e nei limiti della Costituzione' (emphasis added).

sovereignty, not any longer through autonomous, but through common decision-making.'[31]

The constitutional connection between the (old) principle of popular sovereignty and the (new) attribution of powers to international organisations is particularly clearly illustrated by the Belgian Constitution. Its Article 25 (now renumbered as Article 33) enunciates, since 1831, the principle of sovereignty in the following terms: 'All powers proceed from the Nation. They are exercised in the manner laid down by the Constitution'.[32] In 1970, in order to suppress constitutional misgivings about the fact that State powers had been attributed to the European Communities (see above), a new Article 25bis (now Article 34) was inserted immediately after Article 25, stating that '[t]he exercise of delimited powers can be attributed by treaty or by law to institutions of public international law.' The place of this amendment in the text of the Belgian Constitution, just after the sovereignty clause, shows that the attribution of powers to international organisations, such as the European Communities, was (and is) seen as a *qualification* of the principle of sovereignty. The restricted nature of this qualification is denoted by the fact that only the *exercise* of powers can be transferred to the international institution (which implies that they can return to the institutions of the State upon termination of the treaty or some other event in the future) and that the powers should be *delimited* (which presumably means that a substantial number of powers should remain at the national level). The idea that European integration is nothing but the common exercise of sovereign powers of the nations is also clearly expressed in Article 88-1 of the French Constitution. It continues to command widespread support among constitutional authors in Germany,[33] France and Italy.

From this perspective of the *joint exercise of sovereignty,* the institutions of the European Union are, as it were, acting on behalf of the various sovereign peoples of the member States. Yet, and this has remained firmly established in constitutional doctrine, nothing has changed in the basic rule that *sovereignty itself continues to reside in the people* and may therefore not be *alienated.* This compromise allowed all member States, at least at the time of accession to the European Communities, the precarious preservation of the traditional unitary concept of sovereignty while at the same time allowing for the incipient 'integration of sovereignties'[34] imposed by post-war political developments in Europe.

---

[31] K. Lenaerts, 'Constitutionalism and the Many Faces of Federalism', 38 *AJCL* (1990) p. 205, at pp. 231.

[32] In the French version of the Constitution: 'Tous les pouvoirs émanent de la Nation. Ils sont exercés de la manière établie par la Constitution.¢

[33] See particularly the views of the former Constitutional Court Judge Paul Kirchhof, 'Der Deutsche Staat im Prozess der europäischen Integration', in *Handbuch des Staatsrechts der Bundesrepublik Deutschland,* Vol. VII (1992) p. 855.

[34] This expression was used, in the first line of his course at the Hague Academy, by P. De Visscher, 'Les tendances internationales des constitutions modernes', 80 *Recueil des Cours* (1952-II) p. 511.

But the European integration has moved on. Has it not become an artificial contrivance to explain the operation of the European Union institutions as the 'common exercise of State sovereignty', when we know that important decision-making powers are exercised by the Commission and the European Parliament, who operate independently from the states, and that the Council itself increasingly decides by qualified majority, so that a particular state can be outvoted? Should not the constitutions of the original Six member States take the lead and develop a more realistic account of the interaction between the European Union and the national institutions? If a further deepening of European integration occurs, for which support is particularly strong among the political elite of the Six, then a number of national constitutional obstacles will have to be tackled. Perhaps the time will then come for a complete revision of the national constitutions, in which the constitutional legislators will finally recognise and describe the true importance of the European integration progress in the 'living constitutions' of the member States. In this respect, the situation in the Six may, after all, not be so different from that of the candidate countries which are also faced with the question whether their constitutions, despite their recent origin, may need to be changed so as to facilitate adaptation to the European Union legal order.

THE BRITISH WAY: THE COHABITING WITH COMMUNITY LAW

Alan Dashwood*

The United Kingdom may have had a sometimes stormy political relationship with the European Union, but it has integrated smoothly into the Union's legal order. The constitutional machinery which has carried forward this process of integration is found in the European Communities Act 1972 ('the ECA'), and more particularly in three short provisions of its section 2. In the first part of this paper, I recall the rationale behind, and the content of, those provisions. In the second part, I consider the practical operation of the machinery in section 2 of the ECA, and the implications of this for the general theory of the modern UK constitution.

1. THE MACHINERY OF THE ECA

The relevant provisions of the ECA constitute a very British solution to a specifically British problem.

The problem is well known. On the one hand, the new legal order established by the Community Treaties is characterised by its primacy over the law of the member States and the direct effect of a whole range of the provisions contained within it; in adhering to such an order, the member States have limited their sovereign rights in ever wider fields.[1] On the other hand, the ultimate principle of the legal order of the United Kingdom is the sovereignty of Parliament. The statutes Parliament enacts prevail over all other forms of law, and it is the duty of the courts to obey them. The traditional view is that Parliament's powers are, in principle, unlimited and illimitable. The only thing Parliament cannot do is to bind itself for the future: any attempt to do so would be futile, since the courts must always give effect to the latest expression of Parliamentary will.[2]

At the time of the ECA, the most distinguished proponent of the traditional, and dominant, view of Parliamentary sovereignty was Professor (now Sir Will-

* Professor of European Law and Director of the Centre of European Legal Studies, University of Cambridge; formerly, Director in the Legal Service of the Council of the European Union.

[1] Opinion 1/91, *EEA Agreement* [1991] ECR 6079, at para. 21.

[2] See Wade, 'The Basis of Legal Sovereignty' [1955] CLJ 172; Turpin, *British Government and the Constitution*, 4th ed. (Butterworths 1999), pp. 22 et seq.

A.E. Kellermann et al. (Eds.), EU Enlargement: The Constitutional Impact at EU and National Level

iam) Wade. There was also a so-called 'new view', championed by writers such as Heuston[3] and Marshall[4], according to which it was possible for Parliament to bind itself to legislate in a certain manner or form (say, by a two-third majority, rather than the customary simple majority) for specified purposes; that rule would then have to be observed, until it was changed in the prescribed way. However, the proponents of the new view would not admit the possibility of Parliament's limiting its substantive competence.[5] How, then, on either view, could the proper functioning of the Community legal order be guaranteed in the United Kingdom?

A solution not open to the draftsman of the ECA, because too flatly contradictory to the principle of Parliamentary Sovereignty, was the straightforward transfer to the Community institutions of supreme legislative competence in the matters in which they are authorised by the Treaties to act. The solution chosen was for Parliament itself to issue an instruction that Community law be given effect in the United Kingdom, and to reinforce this with a strong rule of construction requiring other statutes to be interpreted accordingly, and a requirement that, in determining questions of Community law, our courts apply the principles laid down by the Court of Justice.

The main instruction is contained in section 2(1) of the ECA, which provides:

> 'All such rights, powers, liabilities, obligations and restrictions from time to time created or arising by or under the Treaties, and all such remedies and procedures from time to time provided for by or under the Treaties, as in accordance with the Treaties are without further enactment to be given legal effect or used in the United Kingdom shall be recognised and available in law, and be enforced, allowed and followed accordingly; and the expression "enforceable Community right" and similar expressions shall be read as referring to one to which this subsection applies'.

That provision achieves a great deal with very few words. It directs that the legal consequences flowing from the Treaties, which the latter themselves require to be produced automatically in the United Kingdom, by virtue merely of their existence within the Community order, shall be so produced. The rights etc. to which the subsection relates are to be recognised and available in law, while retaining their Community character: this is not a marriage of legal systems but a co-habitation within the same British house. The whole stock of directly applicable and directly effective Community law was thus placed at the disposal of the courts of the United Kingdom, alongside the common law and statutes. The subsection applies, moreover, to all Community rights etc. 'from time to time created or aris-

---

[3] Heuston, *Essays in Constitutional Law*, 2nd ed. (Stevens 1964).

[4] Marshall, *Constitutional Theory* (OUP 1971).

[5] For an elegant exposition of the two views of sovereignty, see Craig, 'Sovereignty of the United Kingdom Parliament after Factortame' (1991) 11 YBEL 221.

ing'; in other words, to those subsisting at the time of accession and those which have come into existence subsequently.

The second relevant provision of the ECA is tucked away in section 2(4). It consists of the wording: '... any enactment passed or to be passed, other than one contained in this Part of this Act, shall be construed and have effect subject to the foregoing provisions of this section ...'. Parliament is here saying, in effect, that all existing and future statutes are to be so read, and to have such legal force, as not to derogate from the earlier provisions of section 2, and especially subsection (1). At the very least, solid protection is thereby given against the implied qualification or repeal of Community provisions applicable in the United Kingdom pursuant to the subsection.

The third provision deserving mention is section 3(1), which states:

> 'For the purposes of all legal proceedings any questions as to the meaning or effect of any of the Treaties, or as to the validity, meaning or effect of any Community instrument, shall be treated as a question of law (and, if not referred to the European Court, be for determination as such in accordance with the principles laid down by any relevant decision of the European Court)'.

The part of the subsection not in brackets is designed to exclude, in the case of Community law, the normal rule of our system that questions of foreign law are dealt with as questions of fact, thus having to be provided by expert evidence. That such a provision was thought necessary is a further indication that Community law is being accommodated with, but has not been assimilated into, domestic law.

For present purposes, however, the part of the subsection in brackets is of greater interest. Domestic courts are told that, if they do not refer a question of Community law to the Court of Justice, they must determine it in accordance with the principles laid down by any relevant decision of the latter. The case law that English and Scottish judges are required to accept as authoritative and binding on them, includes those fundamental rulings of the Court defining the relationship between the Community and the national orders. They are thus under instructions to give effect in the United Kingdom to the view that Community law takes of that relationship.

I call the solution comprised in the three provisions I have discussed a 'British' one, because effect is loyally given to Community law in the United Kingdom, through the loyal obedience of the courts to the will of Parliament expressed in the ECA.

2. THE ECA AND THE MODERN CONSTITUTION

The subtly designed machinery of the ECA has been successful in ensuring that the Community order functions in the United Kingdom in the manner required by the Treaties. There have been no rebellions by the higher courts in this country, like that of the Conseil d'Etat of France in the *Cohn Bendit* case[6], on the controversial issue of the direct effect of directives. Nor has there been recourse to reasoning like that of the Bundesverfassungsgericht in *Brunner*[7], that a national court may refuse to enforce a measure it believes to have been adopted (e.g., under Article 308 EC) in excess of the Community's conferred powers. Such reasoning would, indeed, be precluded for courts in the United Kingdom, if the Court of Justice had found the measure in question to be valid: Parliament itself requires, pursuant to section 3(1), that they accept the Court's authority to decide what counts as Community law, and to define the outer limits of the Community order.

The acid test of the ECA machinery is provided by a case like *Factortame*, where the situation before the court is precisely the one a statute has been enacted in order to regulate, in a sense that conflicts with a relevant Community provision of earlier date: the machinery will be seen to be effective, if it secures the disapplication of the statute in favour of the earlier Community provision. The Merchant Shipping Act 1988, in issue in *Factortame*[8], was specifically designed to prevent the re-registration of fishing vessels belonging to Spanish and other no-British owners, whose rights of establishment under the EC Treaty were found by the Court of Justice to have been thereby violated. Since that finding was unhesitatingly accepted by the English courts, the test was passed with flying colours. I should make clear that there was evidently no intention, on the part of the United Kingdom authorities, in securing the passage of the 1988 Act, deliberately to flout Community law: as they were to reveal at a later stage in the litigation, they acted on the best legal advice that the contemplated measure was lawful.

As to the implications for constitutional theory of the operation of the machinery provided by the ECA, there are, broadly, two views to be considered. I call these (without any claim to originality), respectively, the 'construction' and the 'self-limitation' views.[9]

According to the construction view, the effect of the machinery is to create an unusually powerful rule of interpretation, but nothing more than that. The various relevant provisions of section 2 of the ECA are sufficient to raise a presumption that Parliament, whenever it legislates, intends to act in conformity with Community law. The presumption may, however, be displaced by express language. As Lord Denning put it in *Macarthys* v. *Smith:*

---

[6] [1979] Dalloz Jur. 155.

[7] [1994] CMLR 57.

[8] The relevant *Factortame* proceedings were those on the substantive issue of violation of the EC Treaty.

[9] See Wade, 'Sovereignty-Revolution or Evolution', (1996) 112 LQR 568.

> 'If the time should come when our Parliament deliberately passes an Act with the intention of repudiating the Treaty or any provision in it or intentionally of acting inconsistently with it and says so in express terms then I should have thought that it would be the duty of our courts to follow the statute of our Parliament. I do not however envisage any such situation ...'.[10]

Even the construction view represents an evolution of constitutional theory, since it recognises that Parliament can prevent the doctrine of implied repeal from operating.[11] The doctrine has traditionally been regarded as an incident of continuing sovereignty. It means that a statute will automatically repeal any existing rules that it contradicts (including ones contained in earlier statutes), without it being necessary for an express statement of an intention to repeal.

The position of Parliament as the supreme legislator of the United Kingdom is formally preserved, by acknowledging the possibility of express derogation from the ECA. Until recently, like Lord Denning in *Macarthys* v. *Smith*, I had regarded that possibility as purely theoretical. However, there are proposals in the draft manifesto recently published by the Conservative Party ('Believing in Britain') which make me less confident that there may not in the future be an occasion when something of the kind is attempted.

The self-limitation view is more radical. It is based on a passage from the speech of Lord Bridge in *Factortame (No. 2)*, which it is necessary to cite at length:

> 'Some public comments on the decision of the Court of Justice, affirming the jurisdiction of the courts of the member States to override national legislation if necessary to enable interim relief to be granted to protection of rights under Community law, have suggested that this was a novel and dangerous invasion by a Community institution of the sovereignty of the United Kingdom Parliament. But such comments are based on a misconception. If the supremacy within the European Community of Community law over the national law of member States was not always inherent in the EEC Treaty it was certainly well established in the jurisprudence of the Court of Justice long before the United Kingdom joined the Community. Thus, whatever limitation of its sovereignty Parliament accepted when it enacted the European Communities Act 1972 was entirely voluntary. Under the terms of the 1972 Act it has always been clear that it was the duty of a United Kingdom court, when delivering final judgment, to override any rule of national law found to be in conflict with any directly enforceable rule of Community law. Similarly, when decisions of the Court of Justice have exposed areas of United Kingdom statute law which failed to implement Council directives, Parliament has always loyally accepted the obligation to make appropriate and prompt amendments. Thus there is nothing in any way novel in according supremacy to rules of Community law in areas to which they apply and to insist that, in the protection of rights under Community law, national courts must not be prohibited by rules of na-

---

[10] [1979] 3 All ER 325.

[11] Craig, op. cit., at p. 251.

tional law from granting interim relief in appropriate cases is no more than a logical recognition of that supremacy'.[12]

As Sir William Wade has pointed out[13], there is nothing in that passage to suggest that Lord Bridge considered the issue as one of the statutory interpretation. The thrust of the reasoning is that, by passing the ECA, Parliament limited its sovereign powers, to some extent at least; and it did so voluntarily, because the primacy of Community law over national law was perfectly familiar at the time of the United Kingdom's accession. The missing step in the reasoning, but one it may be justifiable to supply, is that Parliament's act of self-limitation is effective in law to the extent necessary to enable the Community order, with all of its known characteristics, to function within the United Kingdom.[14]

If that is what Lord Bridge meant, it does contrast strikingly with the traditional view of Parliamentary sovereignty. Parliament must be taken to have renounced, for as long as the United Kingdom remains a member of the European Union, any power to legislate contrary to Community law; a statute purporting to do so would not have to be obeyed by the domestic courts. The limitation would be lifted only if the United Kingdom quit the Union.

My colleague, Trevor Allan, has pointed out that the requirement of judicial obedience to statutes is a principle of common law, and that accordingly 'its nature and scope are matters of reason, governed by our understanding of the constitution as a whole'.[15] He goes on to argue that the notion of democratic legitimacy, which might be thought to underlie the principle, may well place constraints on the powers of Parliament (for instance, protecting certain individual rights, which are connected with the idea of citizenship in a free society, against legislative encroachment). In similar vein, Sir John Laws, who is quoted by Allan, has written: 'the doctrine of Parliamentary sovereignty cannot be vouched by Parliamentary legislation; a higher-order law confers it, and must of necessity limit it'.[16]

Lord Bridge's reasoning in *Factortame* exemplifies that new understanding of the principle of Parliamentary sovereignty. Craig has described the basis of the reasoning as 'contractarian',[17] and I agree. The limitation of Parliament's su-

---

[12] [1991] AC 603, at p. 658.

[13] Op. cit. [1996] 112 LQR at pp. 572 to 572.

[14] *Cf. Factortame (No. 1)*, where Lord Bridge spoke of section 2(4) of the ECA as having 'precisely the same effect as if a section were incorporated in Part II of the Act of 1988 which in terms enacted that the provisions with respect to registration of British fishing vessels were to be without prejudice to the directly enforceable Community rights of nationals of any member State of the EEC': [1990] 2 AC 85, at p. 140. There is no indication in that passage that Lord Bridge considered the effect of section 2(4) could be neutralised by express statutory language.

[15] See Allan, 'Parliamentary Sovereignty: Law, Politics and Revolution', (1997) 113 LQR, 443, at p. 449.

[16] See, 'Law and Democracy', (1995) PL 72, at p. 87.

[17] Op. cit., p. 249.

preme legislative power was an element in the bargain the United Kingdom made when it acceded to the Communities. Good faith demands that the bargain be kept; and it would be incompatible with the nature of Parliamentary sovereignty, as a common law principle, to cause it to be broken.

The 'self-limitation' view of the impact of the ECA, as here explained, has the great authority of Lord Bridge behind it, but it was not endorsed by the other members of the House of Lords in *Factortame (2)*. Whether that view, or the less adventurous 'construction' view, prevails, only time will tell. However, it is clear that European Union membership has been a major factor in the reassessment which is taking place of the ultimate principle of the British constitution.

IRELAND AND THE EUROPEAN UNION: CONSTITUTIONAL LAW AND PRACTICE

Gerard Hogan*

1. THE IRISH CONSTITUTION AND THE EUROPEAN UNION AND EUROPEAN COMMUNITY

Ireland is governed by a written Constitution which was adopted by referendum in 1937. From a lawyer's perspective the Constitution largely follows the American model inasmuch as the Constitution seeks to protect individual rights and the courts are given express (and extensive) powers of judicial review of legislation. The structures of government, on the other hand, largely follow the United Kingdom model: the Irish Constitution follows the system of parliamentary democracy with arrangements for a fused legislative and executive system. The Constitution carefully enshrines the principle of the separation of powers and the courts have frequently invalidated legislation which is found to infringe this principle.

The Constitution is, moreover, a rigid one: it can only be amended by means of a Bill to amend the Constitution which is passed by both Houses of the Oireachtas (Parliament) and which is subsequently approved by a majority of voters at a referendum. The Constitution also carefully protects the sovereignty of the Irish State, a factor which, of course, assumed (and still assumes) enormous importance in the context of Ireland's original accession to the European Economic Community (as it then was) in 1973.[1]

As we shall presently see, there have been four separate constitutional amendments dealing with Ireland's membership of the European Community/European Union. As we shall see, the Government and the Oireachtas have been constitutionally obliged on each of these occasions to go back to the Irish public to obtain its approval before further sovereignty and competence can be transferred to the European Union.

* Law School, Trinity College, Dublin.

[1] Whelan, 'National Sovereignty in the European Union' in T. Murphy and P.M. Twomey, eds., *Ireland's Evolving Constitution, 1937-1997* (Oxford, Hart Publishing 1998).

A.E. Kellermann et al. (Eds.), EU Enlargement: The Constitutional Impact at EU and National Level

2. THE 1972 AMENDMENT

Along with the United Kingdom and Denmark, Ireland was in the first wave of new countries to accede to the European Economic Community (as it then was) in January 1973. Following a referendum in June 1972, the original Article 29.4.3[2] was added to s 4 of Article 29 by the Third Amendment of the Constitution Act 1972.[3] Article 29 of the Constitution deals with international relations and Article 29.6 confirms that Ireland is a dualist State:

> 'No international agreement shall be part of the domestic law of the State save as may be determined by the Oireachtas.'

In the light of this, legislation was necessary to make the European Community treaties part of the domestic law of the State. However, for reasons which we will presently examine, it was not sufficient merely to enact legislation for this purpose, but a constitutional amendment was also necessary. The structure and format of these constitutional amendment are of interest.

The first limb of Article 29.4.3 permitted Ireland to join the European Coal and Steel Community; the European Atomic Energy Community and the European Economic Community. The second sentence provided that:

> 'No provision of this Constitution invalidates laws enacted, acts done or measures adopted by the State which are necessitated by the obligations of membership of [the European Union or of] the Communities or prevents laws enacted, acts done or measures adopted by the European [Union or by the] Communities or by institutions thereof or by bodies competent under the Treaties establishing the Communities, from having the force of law in the State.'[4]

It will be seen that this amendment was very broad and gave a large measure of constitutional immunity to Community laws, measures and acts. An amendment of this kind was necessary to avoid manifest conflict between the Constitution

[2] The original Article 29.4.3 of the Constitution contained two elements: the permission to join the Community (sometimes described in Irish constitutional law as 'the licence') and the immunity 'necessity obligations' clause. The importance of this clause is described below, but it suffices for the present purposes to say that this clause has now been separated out and is now contained (since the coming into force of the Treaty of Amsterdam and the 18th Amendment of the Constitution Act 1998) in Article 29.4.7.

[3] The referendum to make this amendment was used, in the political sense, as the issue on which the people voted for or against joining the Communities 1,041,890 votes were cast in favour of the amendment, 211,891 against: the 'yes' vote was thus 82.4% of the total.

[4] This is now numbered as Article 29.4.7 since the coming into force of the Treaty of Amsterdam. The words in brackets were added by the Eleventh Amendment of the Constitution Act 1992 (providing for accession to the Maastricht Treaty) and the present Article 29.4.7 was numbered as Article 29.4.5 between 1993 (the date of the coming into force of the Maastricht Treaty) and the 1999 (the date of the coming into force of the Treaty of Amsterdam).

and Community law. This, for example, the statement contained in Article 15.2.1 of the Constitution that the Oireachtas has exclusive law-making powers is plainly inconsistent with the provisions of the Treaty conferring law-making powers on the Community.[5]

Likewise, Article 34 provides that the judicial power of the State may (limited exceptions aside) be exercised only by the judiciary. In the absence of an immunity clause such as Article 29.4.7, the purported exercise of judicial power by the Court of Justice and (since 1988) the Court of First Instance would have been unconstitutional.

It will, however, also be noted that Article 29.4.7 only protected acts done, measures adopted etc. which were 'necessitated' by the obligations of Community law. This suggested that the constitutional immunity would only extend to those measures whose adoption was legally obligated as a matter of Community law. This issue was to come very much to the fore in a number of important constitutional cases and in the debate concerning the 18th Amendment of the Constitution Act dealing with the Amsterdam Treaty.

3. THE CROTTY CASE AND THE SINGLE EUROPEAN ACT

In 1986-1987 the limits of the scope of the licence contained in Article 29.4.3 and the immunity contained in Article 29.4.7 were demonstrated in the celebrated case of *Crotty* v. *An Taoiseach.*[6] In this case the plaintiff, a private citizen, successfully prevented the State from ratifying the Single European Act in the absence of a referendum. The Supreme Court[7], speaking by Finlay C.J. in *Crotty's* case, said that the first sentence of (the original) Article 29.4.3 must be construed as:

> 'an authorisation given to the State not only to join the Communities as they stood in 1973, but also to join in amendments of the Treaties so long as such amendments do

[5] As the Supreme Court said in *Crotty* v. *An Taoiseach* [1987] IR 713, 769:

'The capacity of the Council to take decisions with legislative effect is a diminution of the sovereignty of member States, including Ireland, and was one of the reasons why the Third Amendment to the Constitution was necessary.'

[6] [1987] IR 713; [1987] ILRM 400. See generally, Hogan, 'The Supreme Court and the Single European Act' (1987) 22 *Irish Jurist* p. 55; St. Bradley, 'The Referendum on the Single European Act' (1987) 12 *ELRev.* p. 301; J. Casey, '*Crotty* v *An Taoiseach*: A Comparative Perspective' in J. O'Reilly, ed., *Human Rights and Constitutional Law: Essays in Honour of Brian Walsh* (Dublin, The Round Hall Press 1992) and Temple Lang, 'The Irish Court Case which delayed the Single European Act' 24 (1987) *CMLRev.* p. 709.

[7] For further analysis of the inter-relationship between the Constitution and European Community law, see Collins and O'Reilly, 'The Application of Community Law in Ireland, 1973-1989' 27 (1990) *CMLRev.* p. 315; Reid, *The Impact of Community Law on the Irish Constitution* (Dublin, 1990).

> not alter the essential scope or objectives of the Communities ... To hold that the first sentence of Article 29.4.3 does not authorise any form of amendment to the Treaties after 1973 without a further amendment of the Constitution would be too narrow a construction; to construe it as an open-ended authority to agree, without further amendment of the Constitution, to any amendment of the treaties would be too broad.'[8]

While the Preamble and Article 30 of the Single Act made it clear that European political union' between the member States was a 'possible ultimate objective', Finlay C.J. said that there was no doubt but that if that aim were ever realised:

> 'it would constitute an alteration in the essential scope and objectives of the Communities to which Ireland could not agree without an amendment of the Constitution.'[9]

As Article 313 (ex Art. 247) of the Treaty of Rome provides that any amendment shall enter into force 'after being ratified by all the member States in accordance with their respective constitutional requirements', domestic legislation giving effect to such amendments could not be said to be 'necessitated' by the obligations of membership.

It does not follow, however, that every such amendment would be unconstitutional without the protection of (what is now) Article 29.4.7. In *Crotty's* case, the constitutionality of the European Communities (Amendment) Act 1986 (which gives effect to the various amendments of the Treaty of Rome contained in Title II of the Single European Act) was upheld by the Supreme Court, despite the fact that it was not a 'necessitated' provision. The Court found that the creation of a new court of first instance attached to the European Court of Justice was not an infringement of the judicial power contained in Article 34.1 of the Constitution since it did not affect 'in any material way the extent to which the judicial power has already been ceded to the European Court'.

But Title III of the Single European Act (which provided for European Political Co-operation) was found to be unconstitutional without the immunity conferred by Article 29.4.7, as it interfered the power of the Government contained in Article 29.4 to conduct foreign affairs. The Supreme Court also indicated that amendments to the treaties which had the effect of altering the essential scope or objectives of the Communities would fall outside the terms of the licence in Article 29.4.3 and would be unconstitutional. It had also been argued that the changes proposed in Title II such as qualified majority voting to allow for the approximation of laws concerning the provision of services, the working environment, health and safety of workers; co-operation on economic and monetary policy; and the new powers given to the Community to deal with the environ-

---

[8] [1987] IR at 767.
[9] Ibid., 771.

ment went beyond the original objectives of the Communities. This argument was rejected:

> 'In many instances the Treaty of Rome provided a requirement that a decision on a particular topic should be unanimous, but would after the expiry of a particular stage or of the transitional period require only a qualified majority. The Community was thus a developing organism with diverse and changing methods for making decisions and an inbuilt and clearly expressed objective of expansion and progress, both in terms of the number of its member States and in terms of the mechanics to be used in the achievement of its agreed objectives Having regard to these considerations, it is the opinion of the Court that neither the proposed changes from unanimity to qualified majority, nor the identification of topics which, while now separately stated, are within the original aims and objectives of the EEC, bring these proposed amendments outside the scope of the authorisation contained in Article 29.4.3.'[10]

Following the judgment of the Supreme Court in *Crotty* v. *An Taoiseach*[11], the Tenth Amendment of the Constitution Act 1987[12] allowed the State to ratify the Single European Act.

4. THE 1992 (MAASTRICHT) AMENDMENT

In the wake of the *Crotty* case, it was plain that a constitutional amendment would be necessary to enable the State to ratify the far-reaching amendments effected by the Maastricht Treaty. Sub-sections 4,5 and 6 of Article 29 were added by the Eleventh Amendment of the Constitution Act 1992[13] which allowed the State to ratify the Maastricht Treaty on European Union and the Luxembourg Agreement on Community Patents.[14]

5. CONSTITUTIONAL IMMUNITY ONLY EXTENDS TO MEASURES 'NECESSITATED'

This question arose in *Crotty's* case in the context of whether ratification of the Single European Act was 'necessitated' by the obligations of Community mem-

[10] Ibid., 769-770.

[11] [1987] IR 713; [1987] ILRM 400.

[12] The 10th amendment was carried by 755,423 votes to 324,977: the 'yes' vote was just short of 70% in favour.

[13] The 11th Amendment was carried by 1,001,076 votes to 448,655: the 'yes' vote was approximately 68.7%. See generally, Murphy, 'Maastricht: Implementation in Ireland' 19 (1994) *ELRev.* p. 94.

[14] As there was no legal obligation on the State to ratify this particular Convention and given that it appeared to trench, to some degree, at least, on the powers of the Irish courts, it was apparently concluded that a specific constitutional amendment was necessary to enable this to be done.

bership. If it was so necessitated, Article 29.4.7 would have conferred on it an immunity against constitutional attack. But the Supreme Court took the view that, as Article 33(1) of the Single Act provided that it would only come into force once all member States had ratified it 'in accordance with their respective constitutional requirements', ratification by the State was not a *legal* obligation of membership, i.e., this presupposed that each member State had a discretion in the matter.

The extent to which individual Acts of the Oireachtas, delegated legislation, administrative acts etc. which implement European Community legislation or measures can be said to be 'necessitated' by Article 29.4.7 has been considered in a series of recent cases in the wake of the *Crotty* decision. The problem arises where the EC legislation or measure itself confers a discretion on the member States: can the exercise of such discretion be said to be so necessitated? In *Lawlor* v. *Minister for Agriculture*[15] the plaintiffs challenged the provisions of the European Communities (Milk Levy) Regulations, 1985 insofar as they gave retroactive effect to the provisions of Commission Regulation (EEC) No. 1371/84 which itself established the milk quota regime throughout the Community. In effect, the plaintiff claimed that the decision of this State to apply the EC Regulations retroactively[16] interfered with his property rights[17] and was thus an unjust attack on those rights, contrary to Article 40.3. Murphy J. was of the view that even if the Irish regulations infringed the plaintiff's property rights, he concluded that the 'apparent infringement would fall within the exception provided by Article 29.4.3' , since it seemed to him that:

> 'the word "necessitated" in that sub-section could not be limited in its construction to laws, acts or measures all of which are required in all of their parts to be enacted, done or adopted by the obligations of membership of the Community. It seems to me that the word necessitated in this context must extend to an include acts or measures which are consequent upon membership of the Community and are in general fulfillment of the obligations of such membership and even where there may be a choice of degree of discretion vested in the State as to the particular manner in which it would meet the general spirit of its obligations of membership.'[18]

Quite apart from the fact that this seems an unusually broad interpretation of the word 'necessitated', it is also one which seems inconsistent with the reasoning in *Crotty's* case. If one were to apply this test then the Single Act would have been

---

[15] 1 [1990] IR 356.

[16] Article 5 of the EC Regulations allowed member States a discretion as to whether to apply the milk quota regime retroactively to transfers taking place after 1 January 1983.

[17] Since the (Irish) regulations applied retroactively back to January 1983, they affected the sale of part of the plaintiff's farm in November and thus had the effect of depriving the plaintiff of part of his (very valuable) milk quota for the farm.

[18] 1 [1990] IR at 377.

regarded by the Supreme Court as enjoying constitutional immunity under Article 29.4.3 as it was clearly a measure 'consequent upon membership of the Community.'[19]

In the subsequent decision of *Greene* v. *Minister for Agriculture*[20] Murphy J. seemed to acknowledge this fact. Here the plaintiffs challenged the constitutionality of the decision of the Minister to impose off-farm income limits in respect of certain headage payments for farmers in disadvantaged areas[21] and it seemed plain that this scheme would be found to violate the guarantee in respect of the protection of the family contained in Article 41[22] of the Constitution unless the ministerial decision could be said to enjoy constitutional immunity under Article 29.4.7. Murphy J. found that the directive in question conferred an 'almost unqualified discretion' with regard to the imposition of conditions by member States with regard to headage payments and, qualifying somewhat the *Lawlor* test, he observed that:

> 'There must be a point at which the discretion exercised by the State or the national authority is so far-reaching or so detached from the result to be achieved by the directive that it cannot be said to have been "necessitated" by it ... It does seem to me that the word "necessitated" as used in Article 29.4.3 involves questions of degrees of necessity or at least limits as to discretion. In the present case ... that the particular provisions introduced by the defendants with regard to the income of the farmer or his spouse could not be said to have been necessitated by the obligations of the State as a member of the Communities.'[23]

Shorn of the constitutional immunity, Murphy J. proceeded to invalidate the schemes as being contrary to Article 41.[24]

---

[19] It may be queried whether this analysis is consistent with the legislative history of Article 29.4.3. The Third Amendment of the Constitution Bill, 1971 originally employed the formula 'consequent on the obligations of membership', but was amended during its passage through the Oireachtas, precisely because it was desired to retain constitutional control over all measures which were not legally required by the obligations of Community membership: see 258 *Dáil Debates* at Col. 402 and Hogan, 'The Supreme Court and the Single European Act' 22 (1987) *Irish Jurist* p. 55, at pp. 59-62.

[20] 2 [1990] IR 17; [1990] ILRM 364.

[21] The Ministerial scheme allowed farmers whose farm income was below a certain maximum figure to obtain headage payments, but the income of spouses was not taken into account in calculating this income limit. This in turn meant that married couples were effectively penalised vis-à-vis unmarried couples living together.

[22] Having regard to the decisions of the Supreme Court in *Murphy* v. *Attorney General* [1982] IR 241 and *Muckley* v. *Ireland* [1985] IR 472.

[23] 2 [1990] IR at 25.

[24] See also *Condon* v. *Minister for Agriculture* [1993] IJEL p. 151 (a case concerning the method of implementation of a ministerial discretion under a Community regulation) Lynch J. said that insofar as the details of the implementation of the Regulation was reasonable, it was 'necessitated' by Community obligations. If, however, it was determined that:

This entire question was, however, considered by the Supreme Court in *Meagher* v. *Minister for Agriculture & Food*.[25] In this case the Minister had promulgated a statutory instrument under the provisions of the European Communities Act 1972 giving effect to various Directives prohibiting the use of growth promoters in cattle. The Minister's order purported to extend the time period within which them any prosecution could be taken from six months to two years, although it must be stressed that the Directive was entirely silent on the question of the time period within any such prosecution might be taken. Although the Minister's order expressly purported to amend earlier statute law which confined the time limit within which such prosecutions must be commenced to six months and even though such a course of action would ordinarily be constitutionally prohibited[26], it was argued that this aspect of the ministerial order was nonetheless 'necessitated' within the meaning of Article 29.4.7 in that a longer time period was objectively necessary to facilitate the prosecution of these offences.[27]

Although the Supreme Court accepted that Article 249 EC (ex Art. 189) permitted member States a choice as to the form and methods it would adopt in transposing Directives in domestic law, it nonetheless held that this method of transposing Directives by means of ministerial order was 'necessitated' for the purposes of Article 29.4.7:

> 'The Court is satisfied that, having regard to the number of Community laws, acts done and measures adopted which either have to be facilitated in their direct application to the law of the State or have to be implemented by appropriate action into the law of the State, the obligation of membership would necessitate facilitating of these activities, in some instances, at least, and possibly in a great majority of instances, by the making of ministerial regulation rather than legislation of the Oireachtas.'[28]

In this case, the Court concluded that the extension of the time limit for prosecutions from six months to two years was so 'necessitated' on the ground that the Minister responsible for the transposition of the Directive had considered this to be necessary for the effective prosecution of Community law. This reasoning is generally considered to be not satisfactory:

> 'the details of implementation were unreasonable or unfair, then they could hardly be said to necessitated by the obligations of Community membership and they would be open to constitutional challenge.'

This test seems questionable, inasmuch as it appears to conflate a test of reasonableness with that of legal necessity for the purposes of Article 29.4.7.

[25] 1 [1994] IR 329.

[26] Since Article 15.2.1 reserves to the Oireachtas the exclusive right to make and to amend legislation.

[27] There was evidence that by reason of the waiting lists for 'sophisticated analytical procedures' in the State forensic laboratory necessary in prosecutions of this kind, the statutory time period for prosecution would not otherwise be met.

[28] Ibid., 352.

> 'The crucial word [in Article 29.4.7] is, obviously, "necessitated". In its overall context – especially the phrase "obligations of membership" – this conveys the idea of something imperatively required, or made mandatory, by such membership. It would not appear sufficient that Community membership makes what has been done "convenient" or "desirable".'[29]

The Court nevertheless indicated that in certain situations implementation would require the enactment of legislation by the Oireachtas[30] and that this flexible interpretation of 'necessitated' does not nonetheless give the Government a carte blanche in the manner in which they transpose Directives into domestic law.

6. THE 1998 (AMSTERDAM) AMENDMENT

While it was generally accepted that the Supreme Court had given a very broad interpretation in *Meagher* of what was 'necessitated' by the obligations of Community law, even this interpretation would not be sufficiently flexible to deal with the 'variable geometry' introduced by the Treaty of Amsterdam. It was accordingly recognised that the traditional 'necessitated obligations' formula would no longer suffice in circumstances where member States were increasingly empowered to take decisions which resulted from a voluntary act on their part.

Accordingly, an entirely new provision, Article 29.4.6, enables the State to exercise certain options and discretions contained in the Treaty of Amsterdam, provided the prior consent of both Houses of the Oireachtas is obtained:

> 'The State may exercise the options or discretions provided by or under Articles 1.11, 2.5 and 2.15 of the [Amsterdam] Treaty and the second and fourth Protocols set out in the said Treaty but any such exercise shall be subject to the prior approval of both Houses of the Oireachtas.'

6.1 **Article 1.11**

Article 1.11 replaced the former Title VI of the Maastricht Treaty with a new Title VI dealing with provisions on police and judicial cooperation in criminal

---

[29] Casey, *Constitutional Law in Ireland* (Dublin, 2000) at 211. See also Travers, 'The Constitutionality of the Implementation of EC Directives into Irish Law' 88 (1994) *Gazette of the Incorporated Law Society of Ireland* p. 99; Hogan, 'The Implementation of European Union Law in Ireland: the *Meagher* case and the Democratic Deficit' 2 (1994) *Irish Journal of European Law* p. 190; Hogan and Whelan, Ireland and the European Union (London, 1995) at pp. 51-67.

[30] As Denham J. put it in her concurring judgment (1 [1994] IR at 213):

> 'If the Directive left to the national authority matters of principle or policy to be determined then the 'choice' of the Minister would require legislation by the Oireachtas. But where ... the situation is that principles and policies were determined in the directive, then legislation in a delegated form, by regulation, is a valid choice.'

matters. Article 34 (ex Art. K.6) enables the Council to adopt framework decisions 'for the purpose of approximation of the laws and regulations of the member States' and to 'establish Conventions which it shall recommend to the member States for adoption in accordance with their respective constitutional requirements.'

6.2 **Article 2.5**

Article 2.5 inserted a new Article 11 (ex Art. 5A) in the EC Treaty. This is a general provision allowing a group of member States to develop closer co-operation between themselves under the First Pillar under certain conditions.

6.3 **Article 2.15**

Article 2.15 inserts a new Title IV (ex Title IIIa) in the EC Treaty. This deals with visas, asylum, immigration and other policies relating to free movement of persons.

7. SECOND AND FOURTH PROTOCOLS

The Second Protocol deals with the integration of the Schengen *acquis* into the framework of the European Union and the Fourth Protocol deals with the special position of both the United Kingdom and Ireland in respect of the Schengen Agreement.

The question of what constitutes an 'option or discretion' for this purpose remains to be judicially explored, but this phrase is designed to provide constitutional immunity for certain voluntary acts taken by Ireland pursuant to these provisions of the Treaty of Amsterdam. Thus, for example, Article 35 of the Treaty of European Union (ex Art. K.7)[31] enables the Court of Justice to give preliminary rulings on the validity and interpretation of framework decisions and on the interpretation of any conventions established under Title VI, but the jurisdiction of the Court under this provision is, in a sense, voluntary, as Article 35.2 provides that:

> 'By a declaration made at the time of signature of the Treaty of Amsterdam or at any time thereafter, any member State shall be able to accept the jurisdiction of the Court of Justice to give preliminary rulings as specified in Article 35.1.'

The net effect of the 'options and discretions' clause, therefore, is that Ireland could validly exercise the option to accede to the jurisdiction of the Court of Jus-

[31] As inserted by Article 1.11 of the Treaty of Amsterdam.

tice in respect of such framework decisions and conventions, provided, of course, the prior approval of the Houses of the Oireachtas had been obtained. Likewise, since Article 34(d) TEU (ex Art. K.6) provides that the Council may 'establish conventions which it shall recommend to the member States for adoption in accordance with their respective constitutional requirements', it is plain that in the case of Ireland, these constitutional requirements – namely, Article 29.4.6 – require at a minimum that any such convention be approved by both Houses of the Oireachtas.

8. SUPREMACY OF COMMUNITY LAW

Save for one isolated and inconclusive instance dealing with abortion[32], the Irish courts have unhesitatingly acknowledged the supremacy of Community law.[33] In addition, the case law shows that the Irish courts have adopted *Marleasing* principles to ensure that national law is interpreted in a manner compatible with Community law, even where this may mean that some occasional violence is done to national legislation.

A good example of this principle is supplied by the judgment of Keane J. in *Murphy* v. *Bord Telecom Éireann*.[34] In this case the issue was whether the Anti-

[32] There was a hint of rebellion on the part of Walsh J. in *Society for the Protection of Unborn Children (Ire.) Ltd.* v. *Grogan* [1989] IR 713, where the plaintiff had been granted an interlocutory injunction prohibiting the dissemination by university students of information regarding abortion services in the United Kingdom. The case was referred to the Court of Justice under Article 234 EC and the Court held (Case C-159/90, [1991] ECR 4685) that although the provision of abortion services might constitute a 'service' for the purposes of the EC Treaty, in the absence of a commercial link between the defendants students and the British clinics, the defendants could not invoke the freedom to provides services conferred by the Treaty in this instance. In the interval, the law was changed by the 14th Amendment of the Constitution Act 1992 (which allowed the provision of such information under certain specified conditions) and the injunctions were finally discharged by the Supreme Court: *Society for the Protection of Unborn Children (Ire.) Ltd.* v. *Grogan (No. 5)* 4 [1998] IR 343. However, the Court clearly indicated that even in this most sensitive of areas, it regarded itself as absolutely bound by any decision of the Court of Justice.

[33] *Crotty* v. *An Taoiseach* [1987] IR 713; *Meagher* v. *Minister for Agriculture and Food* 1 [1994] IR 319; *Nathan* v. *Bailey Gibson Ltd.* 2 [1998] IR 162; *Society for the Protection of Unborn Children (Ire.) Ltd.* v. *Grogan (No. 5)* 4 [1998] IR 343. See generally Henchy, 'The Irish Constitution and the EEC' 1 (1977) *DULJ* p. 20; Walsh, 'Reflections on the effects of membership of the European Communities and Irish law' in Capotorti eds. '*Du droit international au droit de l'integration: Liber amicorum Pierre Pescatore* (Nomos, 1987); Collins and O'Reilly, 'The Application of Community Law in Ireland, 1979-1989' 27 (1990) *CMLRev.* p. 215; Reid, *The Impact of Community Law on the Irish Constitution* (Dublin, 1990); Temple Lang, 'The Widening Scope of Constitutional Law' in Curtin and O'Keeffe eds., *Constitutional Adjudication in European Community and National Law* (Butterworths, 1992); Gallagher, 'The Constitution and the Community' 2 (1993) *Irish Journal of European Law* p. 129 and O'Leary, 'The Reciprocal Relationship between Irish Constitutional Law and the Law of the European Communities' in Murphy and Twomey eds., *Ireland's Evolving Constitution, 1937-1997* (Hart Publishing, 1998).

[34] [1988] ILRM 53.

Discrimination (Pay) Act 1974 applied to a situation where female workers performed work of greater value than that performed by their male colleagues, but where they were actually paid less. Keane J. initially ruled[35] that the 1974 Act did not provide a remedy in this situation, but the Court of Justice ruled following a reference that such a result would be incompatible with the equal pay provisions of Article 141 (ex Art. 119) of the Treaty of Rome.[36] When the matter came back again before Keane J. he noted that:

> 'The interpretation of [the 1974 Act] in accordance with the canons of construction normally applied in the Irish courts has in the present case yielded a result which is in conflict with Article [141] as interpreted by the Court of Justice. Where such a conflict exists, national law must yield primacy to Community law. The exclusive role of the making of laws assigned to the Oireachtas by Article 15 of the Constitution has been expressly modified by Article [29.4.7] so as to enable Community law to have the force of law in the State. Where such a conflict arises, the national law is, accordingly, inapplicable.'[37]

In other words, the Irish courts were now required to interpret the 1974 Act in the manner required by Article 141 (ex Art. 119) (as interpreted by the Court of Justice), even if this meant departing from an earlier judicial ruling authoritatively interpreting the 1974 Act in a different fashion.

This point was also made by the Supreme Court in *Nathan* v. *Bailey Gibson Ltd.*[38], a case where a female employee claimed that she had suffered indirect discrimination by being denied a particular promotion opportunity by reason of the operation of a 'closed shop' with particular trade unions of which she was not a member. Applying *Marleasing*-type reasoning, Hamilton C.J. observed that it was well established that:

> '... national or domestic courts in interpreting a provision of national law designed to implement the provisions of a directive, should interpret their national law in the light of the wording and the purpose of the directive in order to achieve the result envisaged by the directive.'[39]

It followed that the Court was under an obligation 'as far as possible' to interpret the Anti-Discrimination (Pay) Act 1974:

> 'in the light of the wording and purpose of the directive in order to achieve the result pursued by the directive, viz., establishing that there shall be no discrimination on

---

[35] *Murphy* v. *Bord Telecom Éireann (No 1)* [1986] ILRM 483.
[36] Case 157/86 [1988] ECR 673.
[37] [1989] ILRM 53, at 59.
[38] 2 [1998] IR 162.
[39] Ibid., 174.

grounds of sex either directly or indirectly by reference in particular to marital or family status.'[40]

9. RESOLUTION OF POTENTIAL CONFLICTS BETWEEN THE CONSTITUTION AND COMMUNITY LAW

The potential for conflict between the precepts of Community law on the one hand and the Constitution on the other is a real one which may yet present difficulties for the Irish courts. The conventional view is, of course, that where there is a conflict between the provisions of the Constitution and Community law itself, the latter takes precedence. This is not only the view of the Court of Justice[41], but has also been emphatically endorsed by both the High Court[42] and the Supreme Court.[43]

Interestingly, however, there have been some hints that the national courts may be reluctant to yield total supremacy in the area of fundamental rights. Thus, in *Society for the Protection of Unborn Children (Ire.) Ltd.* v. *Grogan*[44] the defendants argued that the provisions of the anti-abortion provisions of Article 40.3.3 of the Constitution had been *pro tanto* qualified by the provisions of the Treaty of Rome dealing with the right to supply services. Walsh J., for one, clearly reserved to this proposition:

> 'It was sought to be argued in the present case that the effect of [Article 29.4.7] ... is to qualify all rights, including fundamental rights, guaranteed by the Constitution. Any answer to the reference from the Court of Justice will have to be considered in the light of our own constitutional provisions. In the last analysis only this Court can decide finally what are the effects of the interaction of [Article 40.3.3] and [Article 29.4.5].'[45]

For reasons already explained, these remarks must be regarded as isolated ones and entirely confined to an area of great sensitivity and would not nowadays be

---

[40] Ibid., 175.

[41] See, e.g., Case 26/62 *Van Gend en Loos* v. *Nederlandse Administratie der Belastingen* [1963] ECR 1; (Case 106/77)(*Simmenthal* [1978] ECR 629; (Op.1/91) *Re Draft Treaty on the European Economic Area* [1991] ECR I-6079. As the Court observed in the *Draft Treaty* opinion:

> 'The EEC Treaty, albeit concluded in the form of an international agreement, none the less constitutes the constitutional charter of a Community based on the rule of law ... The essential characteristics of the Community legal order which has thus been established are in particular its primacy over the law of the member States and the direct effect of a whole range of provisions which are applicable to their nationals and to the member States themselves.'

[42] *Murphy* v. *Bord Telecom Eireann* [1989] ILRM 63; *Lawlor* v. *Minister for Agriculture* 1 [1990] IR 356; *Society for the Protection of Unborn Children (Ire.) Ltd.* v. *Grogan (No. 3)* 1 [1993] CMLR 197.

[43] *Campus Oil Ltd.* v. *Minister for Industry and Energy* [1983] IR 82.

[44] [1989] IR 753.

[45] Ibid., 768-769.

followed.[46] These remarks nevertheless echo a wider debate which has taken place in other Community countries (such as Germany[47] and Italy[48]), namely, whether the primacy of Community law extends even to cases where that law appears to infringe fundamental rights. While these concerns remain among some members of the judiciary of individual member States, the emerging jurisprudence of the Court of Justice which stresses the protection of fundamental rights having regard to national Constitutions[49] and the European Convention of Human Rights[50] means that such future 'rebellions' are unlikely. This point is underscored by Article 6(2) of the Treaty on European Union which declares that:

> 'The Union shall respect fundamental rights, as guaranteed by the European Convention for the Protection of Human Rights and Fundamental Freedom ... and as they result from the constitutional traditions common to the member States, as general principles of Community law.'

This brings us next to the issue of whether the draft Chart of Fundamental Rights is either necessary or even desirable.

---

[46] *Society for the Protection of Unborn Children (Ire.) Ltd.* v. *Grogan* 4 [1998] IR 343.

[47] The German Constitutional Court originally took the view that it reserved the right to question the validity of Community measures which appeared to conflict with fundamental principles of German constitutional law: see *Internationale Handelsgesellschaft* 2 [1974] CMLR p. 540. This decision was, however, qualified by two subsequent rulings of the Constitutional Court: see *Wunsche Handelsgesellschaft* 3 [1987] CMLR p. 225 and *Re Brunner* 1 [1994] CMLR p. 97.

[48] The Italian Constitutional Court has twice hinted that it may review Community measures 'in the unlikely event' that they 'conflict with fundamental principles of the constitutional order or with the inalienable rights of the human being.' In such circumstances, it reserved the right to hold those Community acts to have exceeded the scope of the limitations of the transfer of Italian sovereignty to the Community institutions provided for by Article 11 of the Italian Constitution (a provision broadly comparable to Article 29.4.7 of the Irish Constitution): see *Frontini* v. *Ministero delle Finanze* [1973] Giur. Cost. p. 2041 and *Spa Granital* v. *Amministrazione finanziaria* [1984] Giur. Cost. p. 1098 and, more generally, La Pergola and del Duca. 'Community Law, International Law and the Italian Constitution' 79 (1985) *AJIL*, p. 598.

[49] See, e.g., (Case 4/73) *J. Nold KG* v. *Commission* [1974] ECR 491 ('the Court cannot allow measures which are incompatible with fundamental rights recognised and guaranteed by the Constitution of those States'); (Case 44/79) *Hauer* v. *Rheinland-Pfalz* [1979] ECR 3727; (Case 63/83) *R.* v. *Kirk* [1984] ECR 2689.

[50] See, e.g., (Case 85/87) *Dow Benelux* v. *Commission* [1989] ECR 3137 (Article 8 of ECHR can be invoked in Community law to protect private dwellings of natural persons); (Case 5/88) *Wachauf* v. *Germany* [1989] ECR 2609 (implementation by member States of Community law must 'as far as possible' comply with the requirements of the European Convention of Human Rights); Case C-250/89 *Elliniki Radiophonia Tileorassi* [1991] ECR 1-2925 (exercise by national authorities of discretionary powers under Treaty of Rome have to be assessed in the light of European Convention of Human Rights).

10. THE CONSTITUTION AND THE DRAFT CHARTER OF FUNDAMENTAL RIGHTS OF THE EUROPEAN UNION

Following the declarations of the European Council at Cologne and Tampere in June and December respectively of 1999, a draft charter of fundamental rights of the European Union is now ready for consideration at the Nice summit. At present, it remains unclear whether the Charter will be given legal status and made justiciable in courts of law or whether the Charter will simply be a political declaration. As far as Ireland is concerned, the legal nature and scope of this Charter will present considerable constitutional issues.

While it is true that Article 6.2 of the Treaty of European Union commits the Union to respecting the European Convention of Human Rights and as they result from the constitutional traditions common to the member States, the Charter involves a far more ambitious project than anything hitherto undertaken. Chapter I (Dignity); Chapter II (Freedoms); Chapter III (Equality); Chapter V (Citizens' Rights) and Chapter VI (Justice) broadly reflect traditional civil and political rights and to that extent largely mirror (although in some instances with important substantive and linguistic differences) the provisions of the European Convention of Human Rights. However, there are some draft provisions which are entirely new: thus, for example, the draft Articles 24, 25 and 26 (dealing respectively with the rights of the child, elderly and the disabled) have no counterpart in the ECHR. Many (but not all) of these rights are, in any event, already well-established in Irish domestic constitutional jurisprudence. Chapter IV (Solidarity) deals with socio-economic rights. These rights find no real counterpart in the ECHR or, for that matter, with the exception of the provisions of Article 42 (dealing with education) in the Irish Constitution. Chapter VII (General Provisions) is of critical importance inasmuch as it seeks to lay down parameters concerning the scope of application of the Charter. It also seeks to create a general limitation clause which enables legislators to impose limitations on the scope and exercise of the Charter rights subject to key principles such as proportionality. Again, such general limiting clauses may be found in Articles 40-44 of the Irish Constitution and also in the ECHR.

11. THE SCOPE OF THE CHARTER

With the exception of the question of whether the Charter is to have legal status, the most important single question relates to the scope of the Charter and the extent to which it applies to member States such as Ireland. The draft Article 51.1 provides that:

> 'The provisions of this Charter are addressed to the institutions and bodies of the Union with due regard to the principle of subsidiarity and to the member States only

> when they are implementing Union law. They shall therefore respect the rights, observe the principles and promote the application thereof in accordance with their respective powers.'

Many may find the terms of Article 51 somewhat puzzling, especially having regard to the type of rights protected under the Charter. The objective of this vital clause is, of course, clear, since in essence, Article 51 seeks to confine the scope of the Charter to both the institutions of the Union (e.g., the Commission) and to member States so far as they implement Union law. Such a restriction is, of course, a perfectly understandable one. Were such a restriction not in place, it would effectively create a European Constitution which, to all intents and purposes, would largely supersede analogous provisions in national Constitutions and it would also vest the Court of Justice with very considerable new powers.

12. SOME DIFFICULTIES WITH THE SCOPE OF THE RIGHTS CONFERRED BY THE CHARTER

Against this background, the level of protection for particular rights may prove to be more illusory than real. This is perhaps, best illustrated by a series of examples.

Article 9 of the draft Charter provides that:

> 'The right to marry and the right to found a family shall be guaranteed in accordance with the national laws governing the exercise of these rights.'

Neither the Union or the Community has any present competence whatever in family law matters.[51] Nor can one readily think of any possible set of circumstances in which the implementation by a member State of Community law could possibly involve such a right. The right protected, on the other hand, is a valuable right which enjoys protection under our own Constitution and which has been the subject of important litigation in this State.[52] It seems curious that such a right is effectively emptied of substance, simply because the so-called horizontal clause of Article 51.1 so confines its application to circumstances which are never likely to (and, perhaps, could never) arise in practice.

A similar point could be made in respect of many of the traditional civil and political rights sought to be protected by the Charter, including, for example, Ar-

[51] Leaving aside the Brussels II Convention dealing with the recognition of foreign divorces and the enforcement of ancillary relief orders.

[52] See, e.g., *Murray* v. *Ireland* [1985] IR 532. This case concerned the rights of married prisons to procreate. It is just possible that a similar issue might arise in the case of a prisoner detained following conviction for an domestic offence created in order to give effect to the provisions of EU legislation, assuming that this amounted to an 'implementation measure' by the State for the purposes of Article 51

ticle 2.2 (abolition of the death penalty) or Article 14 (the right to education, including 'the possibility to receive free compulsory education'). Having regard to Article 51.1 a member State would be free under the terms of the Charter to retain the death penalty for, say, murder, treason or genocide, the language of Article 2.2 notwithstanding. All that Article 2.2. really means is that either the EU could not prescribe the death penalty in respect of offences created pursuant to EU legislation[53] or (possibly) that member States could not prescribe such a penalty in respect of offences created by domestic legislation which sought to give effect to Community law.

Article 14.2 seems also rendered largely meaningless by virtue of the horizontal provisions of Article 51. Leaving aside the decidedly awkward language of the draft (whereby the right is expressed to be 'the possibility to receive free compulsory education'), such education is presently a matter for each member State and neither the Union nor the Community have any competence in this regard. Again, if for example, a member State wished to impose charges for primary education, one of the paradoxes of the Charter is that, apparently, they would be entirely free to do so, since (a) they are not an institution of the Union or (b) in so doing, they would not be implementing Community law.

The same might apply to many of the proposed socio-economic rights. The draft Article 35, for example, provides that:

> 'Everyone has the right of access to preventive health care and the right to benefit from medical treatment under the conditions established by national laws and practices. A high level of human health protection shall be ensured in the definition and implementation of all Union policies and activities.'

Yet it is hard to see how the first sentence of this provision could ever be effective in practice. Medical treatment is governed to all intents and purposes exclusively by national law and practices. While it is true that certain EU legislation indirectly has had implications for health care (such as harmonisation of standards for pharmaceutical products) it is not easy to see how, having regard to Article 51.1, this right to health care could ever be applied to a member State. Article 35 by definition only confers a right to health care under 'the conditions established by national law and practices.' Yet Article 51 confines the scope of the Charter so as to apply to member States when they are *implementing* Union law.

The effect of this legal paradox appears to be that the first sentence of Article 35 – with the apparently comprehensive promise of an enforceable right to universal health care – is entirely stripped of its meaning. The right in question is made dependent on national law and practices. Having regard to Article 51.1, the

[53] And since it is up to the member States to prescribe through domestic legislation the penalties in respect of offences the creation of which was ultimately mandated by Council Regulations or Directives, this seems rather meaningless.

right could *never* be invoked against member States, since the Charter confines its application to circumstances where member States are implementing Union law. But by the definition in Article 35 the right of access to health care is made dependent on national law and practice, so that we find we are in circumstances where the Charter – again by definition – could never apply.

As is apparent from what has just been stated, the extent to which member States are bound by the 'implementation' provision of Article 51 is also unclear. Obviously, member States would be bound by the Charter insofar as they, e.g., sought to transpose a Directive into national law or inasmuch as they exercised a discretionary power conferred by EU legislation. But this is, to some extent, already the position at present, inasmuch as the member States are bound to respect the general principles of Community law (including fundamental human rights) in transposing EU legislation into national law or in exercising a discretion conferred by Community law: see the judgment of the Court of Justice in Case C-260/89 *Elliniki Radiophonia Tileorassi.*[54] (Of course, one key difference is that the Charter recognises as fundamental certain rights not hitherto so regarded by either national Constitutions or the ECHR.) Perhaps the difficulties involved in the 'implementation' provision might be illustrated by the following example:

A farmer is suspected of having committed offences under the Animal Remedies Act 1993, which legislation, inter alia, transposed certain EC Directives with growth promoters into domestic law. He is arrested by the police, but it happens that this arrest is unlawful. Can he rely on Article 6 of the Charter (which guarantees personal liberty) in these circumstances? The answer must be probably not, since it seems hard to characterise the actions of the police in this example as amounting to an implementation measure by Ireland for the purposes of Article 51. But if Article 6 cannot be invoked at this most basic level, the utility and value of the Charter may be questioned.[55] On the other hand, if it could be so characterised, then many actions of this State could be so regarded and the Charter would then apply to a whole range of powers and functions exercised by national authorities.

---

[54] [1991] ECR I-2925.

[55] Cf. the difficulties which this characterisation issue presented the Court of Justice in Case C-299/95 *Kremzow* v. *Austria* [1997] ECR I-2629. Here an Austrian judge had been found guilty of murder, but this conviction was found to contravene Article 6 ECHR by the European Court of Human Rights. The former judge then sued the Austrian state for damages in respect of his imprisonment, claiming that he had been deprived of his right of free movement as an EC national. The Court of Justice was able to hold that the case fell outside the scope of EC law on the ground that a 'purely hypothetical prospect of exercising that right does not establish a sufficient connection with Community law to justify the application of Community provisions.' Of course, Kremzow's right of free movement remained hypothetical precisely because he was imprisoned at the time. But it is easy to vary the facts in a way in which the underlying issues in *Kremzow* present enormous problems of characterisation.

13. WOULD RATIFICATION OF THE CHARTER REQUIRE A REFERENDUM?

On the assumption that the Charter sought to confer legal rights and to be justiciable in the courts, then it is very hard to see how the Irish Government could safely proceed to adopt the draft Charter in the absence of a referendum. This is especially so given that, as we have already seen, the present Charter now clearly goes far beyond the existing level of the (unwritten) 'general principles of law common to the constitutions of all member States' and the ECHR itself. It could not accordingly be said that the Charter merely reduces to writing existing 'unenumerated' rights already recognised by the European Court and whose protection is already envisaged by Article 6.2 TEU. If the Charter had been confined to expressly enumerating all the rights presently deemed fundamental by the ECHR and by national constitutions, there would be force to the argument that it would in substance be going no further than the present Article 6.2 TEU. However, there seems little doubt but that the present version of the Charter does far beyond the ambit of Article 6.2 in the recognition of rights and, hence, one compelling argument against the necessity for a referendum is thereby undermined.

It is also pertinent to observe that there is at present no Treaty basis for this Charter. It is true that the draft Article 51.2 provides that:

> 'This Charter does not establish any new power or task for the Community or for the Union or modify powers and tasks defined by the Treaties.'

But this statement merely concerns the substantive limits of Community law and does not take from the fact that a new Treaty basis will be have to be found to give the Charter meaningful legal status (assuming it is not be a merely political declaration). One assumes, therefore, that in those circumstances the IGC will propose the appropriate Treaty amendment to accommodate the Charter.

Against this background and judged by the yardstick of the *Crotty* case[56] dealing with the Single European Act it would be very difficult (if not well nigh impossible) to say that this Charter was (a) within the scope and contemplation of the existing Treaties and (b) that it was 'necessitated' by the obligations of Community law for the purposes of Article 29.4.7 of the Constitution. In view of *Crotty* one would have to be able to answer both (a) and (b) affirmatively before concluding that no amendment was necessary. In these circumstances, the inevitable conclusion is reached that the Charter could only be adopted by Ireland following a referendum.

If, on the other hand, the Charter was simply a political declaration and was made expressly non-justiciable then it is seems unlikely that a referendum would

[56] [1987] IR 713.

be legally necessary. If the Charter is simply a political declaration, then it probably will obviously have little implications for member States, beyond being an important addition to what is sometimes termed 'soft law', i.e., political instruments to which the courts sometimes have recourse in bolstering legal argument and conclusions. Thus, for example, the Court of Justice would presumably refer to the Charter in order to support its conclusion that a particular right mentioned therein formed part of the general principles of Community law which the institutions and the member States were obliged to respect for the purposes of Article 6(2) of Treaty on European Union. It may be noted that a similar 'soft law' declaration was adopted by the European Parliament in 1977 and although it has sometimes been alluded to in passing by the European Court, rather less is heard these days of this Declaration. Of course, this Charter is altogether more elaborate and comprehensive and it may be that even if it is given purely political status that much more will be made of it by the Court of Justice. While the potential for de facto enforcement is there in such circumstances and parts of the Charter might be tacitly given quasi-legal or Treaty series by the Court of Justice, it seems unlikely that the Court would employ the Charter in such circumstances radically to enhance the status of that document or to create a new jurisdiction for itself.

THE DANISH CONSTITUTIONAL ORDER

Henning Koch*

1. THE STATE OF THE CONSTITUTION (SECT. 20 & SECT. 88 CONSTITUTIONAL ACT)

The ordinary procedure for amending the Danish constitution is an extremely laborious – and risky – enterprise.

A bill shall be passed unamended by two successive sessions of Parliament with an intermediate election. After its final passage and within 6 months the bill must then be submitted to the population for approval or rejection by direct voting. If a majority of the electors taking part in the referendum, constituting at least 40 per cent of the electorate, has voted in favour of the Bill and it subsequently receives the Royal Assent, the Bill will form an integral part of the Constitutional Act (Sect. 88). This version of popular participation makes the formation of a new Constitution conditional upon a minimum of activity on the part of the voters, since a high proportion of 'stay-at-home voters' will block any change.

With this conservative and preservative procedure Denmark was ready to meet a new epoch in international relations after the Second World War. But in 1953 the Constitution was amended in order to simplify the enrolment of Denmark into a supranational organisation by adding to the constitutional Act a specific procedure of quasi-amendment.

The first subsection of the new provision (Sect. 20) runs as follows:

> 'Powers vested in the authorities of the Realm under this Constitution Act may, by statute and to a specified extent, be delegated to international authorities set up by mutual agreement with other states for the promotion of international rules of law and cooperation'.

The inspirational model was the establishment of the European Coal and Steel Community (1952).

In the published travaux préparatoires of the 1953 constitution, which is still in force, it says:

* Professor of Constitutional Law, LL.D., at the University of Copenhagen.

A.E. Kellermann et al. (Eds.), EU Enlargement: The Constitutional Impact at EU and National Level

> 'In the last few years the trend of developments is towards an increased international co-operation even in spheres, where the powers conferred on the international organisations are of a nature hitherto regarded as part of the sovereignty of each individual state. ... According to the present constitution Denmark will not be authorized to accede to such treaties. It would be advisable, if Denmark too through its constitution were to open the way for surrendering sovereignty to such international organisations serving to encourage an international legal system and collaboration'.

The sensitive word sovereignty was thus not trumpeted forth in the Constitution itself, but as is evident from the proposition, the intention was to render possible a self-created restriction on the competences normally vested in the national powers – e.g., the legislative, the executive and the judicial powers – without amending the constitution. Sect. 20 Constitutional Act was a special provision designed for Danish membership of supranational organisations, not of international organisations like the United Nations.

The Accession Act (see below) refers to the *exercise of powers:* a more accurate expression. In the travaux préparatoires to the Constitution the actual word 'sovereignty' is specifically mentioned in connection with verbs like: 'surrender', 'renounce' or 'cede', whereas the terminology 'transfer' or 'confer on' is used when concluding that the transferred powers can always be withdrawn, through an Act of Parliament adopted by way of only a simple majority. The re-establishment of the original separation of powers in the national setting requires no particular procedure. The wording of the constitution itself is therefore 'delegate'. Linguistically, on the one hand, it makes no sense to be authorized to withdraw renounced powers, but on the other hand the word: 'delegate' contains legal connotations of the transferring of powers from a superior to an inferior level or system.

This form of entrusting parts of the jurisdiction to a collective body does not equal a fundamental amendment of the constitution, following the ordinary amendment procedure in Sect. 88, since the power delegation in question is per definition temporarily, or rather: valid until further notice.

In order to avoid needless and futile political discussions it seems wise to state explicitly in the constitution that the powers may be withdrawn, through whatever procedure is required.

According to Sect. 20(2) Constitutional Act any such transfer of powers should be enacted through an Act of Accession adopted by a majority of 5/6 of the members of the Parliament.

In other words, the decision was thought to be primarily in the hands of the representative democracy. Only if this qualified majority could not be obtained was the Bill, as adopted by a simple majority, to be submitted to a decisive referendum, i.e., if the government still wanted to pursue the matter. In this case a majority of the electors, here constituting not less than 30 per cent of all persons entitled to vote, is needed in order to reject the Bill. This is the opposite situation of the validity test of an ordinary amendment, since the Bill will be valid unless it is actively disapproved of by a majority. Abstainers therefore – be it unknowingly – promote change.

It is noteworthy, to say the least, that this exclusive and explicit legal authority has never been enforced as it was intended with respect to the 5 Danish bills of accession containing a transfer of powers to the European Community/European Union (1972, 1992, 1993, 1998, 2000). This is due to the fact that already in 1971 – prior to introducing the first accession bill – a formal agreement was reached between the government and Parliament, whereby, irrespective of the actual votes cast in the Parliament, a decisive referendum would have to be held in any case.

By an interpretation of the Constitution that came close to an interpretation contra legem, a constitutional convention was thus invented, in effect stating that a referendum would take place whenever amendments to the European Treaties were made indicating any further transfer of sovereignty (only in 1986 a consultative referendum was initiated, since the Single European Act was not seen to contain rules implying or prescribing a transfer of powers). This convention has been upheld in connection with every accession act by all governments and parliaments up to the present.

The creative interpretation of the Constitution has been explicitly restated ('irrespective of obtaining a majority of 5/6') in the travaux préparatoires of the recent Bill of Accession of May 2nd 2000 with regard to Denmark joining the third phase of the Economic and Monetary Union. The 6th referendum on matters concerning the European Community/European Union including the above consultative referendum took place on September 28th 2000. 53% of the voters participating voted No, and only 47% said Yes to removing the special Danish reservation to the introduction of the euro according to the Maastricht Treaty, a reservation that was instituted by the Edinburgh Agreement of 1992.

For almost 30 years then the Danish government and Parliament have deliberately abstained from making use of a clear authority to engage in further European development without holding referenda.

This persistent and invariable practice could be understood as expressing a (revised) constitutional conviction that, in order to secure the genesis of a legitimate European demos, the Danish demos – i.e., seen from a Danish perspective at least – unconditionnally must participate autonomously and directly in all decisions concerning the development of the European Union. The creation of this convention should as a minimum be seen as the Danish version of the fulfilment of the ambition of 'eine lebendige Demokratie', to use the phraseology of the German Maastricht Case (1993)[1], thus displaying the diversity of the concepts of democracy as a constitutional validity parameter.

---

[1] Entscheidungen des Bundesverfassungsgerichts, Vol. 89 (Tübingen, J.C.B. Mohr (Paul Siebeck) 1994) p. 186.

2. DIRECT EFFECT AND SUPREMACY OF EC LAW

The original Act of Accession from 1972, which is still in force, describes the accession by way of a bulk reference to the relevant treaties. The same technique has been used in the later accession acts.

The key provision (paragraph 2) simply states that the powers vested in the authorities of the Danish constitution 'may be exercised by the EC institutions to the extent prescribed in the undermentioned treaties'. The following provision (para. 3) then declares the EC law to be 'directly applicable' as far as authorized by Community law. This general statement today covers Article 2 (former B) paragraph 1, item 5 introduced in the Treaty of The European Union (Maastricht): 'The Union shall set itself the following objectives: ... to maintain in full the acquis communautaire ...', which in principle confers validity on the (already displayed) judicial activism by the EC court. The national provisions referred to consequently include in Danish law the court's decisions to give direct effect to directives under certain conditions.

No Danish constitutional provision seems to be contrary to the acquis, unless the future judges of the court in their ingenious interpretations overstep the borders of the separation of powers in the Danish constitution (cf. Sect. 3) e.g., by turning themselves into legislators, or by applying Article 6 paragraph 2 (cf. Art. 46(d)) of the Treaty of the European Union (Maastricht) which violates the domestic provisions concerning human rights.

However the aforesaid review does not solve the crucial – and intricate – problem of the supremacy of the Community law. Neither the Constitution nor the accession acts give any answers to this question.

The fact that the European Community in its own self-knowledge was superior and therefore could claim supremacy in case of a divergence between EC law and national law was known and recognized during the parliamentary debates in 1972 concerning the first accession bill, but it was not – and could not be – stated in the law.

3. THE PRINCIPLE OF INDIRECT EFFECT

In this situation it seems convenient to fall back on the domestic principles of a (modified) dualistic system with respect to incorporation of international law in order to help solving a concrete legal dispute. The Constitution contains no express provisions with regard to the effect of international law on domestic law.

According to Danish constitutional law possible contradictions between the two legal systems are to be decided on the basis of one of three unwritten rules.

The rule of interpretation dictates that if there is any doubt about the interpretation of a domestic provision, the courts should prefer the interpretation that will best comply with international law. The subject of the interpretation is the domestic text in the comparison with the international text. It is the legal exercise of *completing* the national text.

The rule of presumption prescribes that in the event of divergence between a recent piece of legislation and a treaty of older standing the conflict should be resolved by applying the domestic rule in a manner that brings the former into conformity with the treaty, unless it is a clearly expressed intention behind the legislation to violate international law. This rule does not presuppose any questions raised about the correct interpretation of the domestic provision. The primary object of the interpretation, therefore, is the intent of the legislator. The legal exercise consists in *correcting* the national text.

The administrative authorities is the primary target group of the so-called rule of instruction. It says that the executive should exercise their discretionary powers in such a way that administrative acts, whether specific decisions or general regulations, conform to international obligations.

It is a fair question to raise whether these three rules represent a full understanding of the principles of Danish law regulating the incorporation of international law.

In constitutional theory it has been maintained that the present state of things in Denmark can be described most appropriately as 'a practical monism', indicating that international law constitutes a source of law even as part of domestic law and that national courts may apply international law without explicit authority.

Such a position could be legitimized by a renewed and dynamic interpretation of Sect. 64 of the Constitution. It opens with the following expression: 'In the performance of their duties the judges shall be governed solely by the law'. Although the last word has never been interpreted as restricted only to statute law, thus including general principles of law, it has not yet in practice been seen as the instrument for incorporation of international law.

Obviously a resort to the ordinary principles of interpretation in order to resolve conflicts between domestic law and Community law does not make allowance for the sui generis status of the European Community.[2]

4. SUI GENERIS? – THE CONTRAST BETWEEN THE USUAL AND THE UNUSUAL STATE

By the judgment of April 6th 1998 the Danish Supreme Court took a clear stance in the professional (and political debate) that had run for almost 30 years. It was a case of abstract judicial review and was the first of its kind in Denmark.[3]

---

[2] Ole Due, Danish Preliminary References' in David O'Keeffe, ed., *'Judicial Review in European Union Law' – Liber Amicorum in Honour of Lord Slynn of Hadley* (The Hague, Kluwer Law International 2000) pp. 363-375.

[3] Fredrik Thomas, 'Das *Maastricht*-Urteil des dänischen Obersten Gerichtshofs vom 6. April 1998', 58 *ZaöRV* (1998) pp. 879-906. Sten Harck and Henrik Palmer Olsen, 'Decision Concerning

The court has admitted 12 citizens the right to present a case about the constitutionality of the ratification of the Maastricht Treaty, irrespective of any concrete and actual interest (locus standi).

No provision in the Danish constitution provides the Supreme Court with authority to exercise constitutional review.

The court ruled on questions about the required specificity of the transferred powers, the kompetenz-kompetenz issue, the practice concerning Article 235 (now Art. 308), judicial activism by the EC court, the precedence of EC law and the problems regarding democratic control of the EU by Danish political authorities.

The decision runs as follows, *inter alia:*

'The Act of Accession delegates powers to the EC to the extent laid down in the EC Treaty ... The EC Treaty is based on a principle of conferred powers, cf. Article 3b(1) and Article 4(1) of the Treaty. The institutions of the Community may act only within such limits for the operation of the Community as appear from the provisions of the Treaty, and within these limits the institutions may only exercise such powers as have been conferred upon them by or pursuant to the Treaty.

The principle of conferred powers thus implies a restriction on the powers of the institutions which is in keeping with the demand for specification in Sect. 20 of the Constitution. The Supreme Court finds that the specific rules of authority in the EC Treaty meet this demand.

... However, ... the appellants specifically claimed that the general provision of authority in Article 235 of the EC Treaty enables the incorporation of new areas of responsibility under the powers of the EC to an extent which implies that the demand for specification in Sect. 20 of the Danish Constitution has not been observed. ...

It appears from the wording of Article 235 that the fact that action by the Community is considered necessary in order to attain one of the objectives of the Community does not in itself constitute sufficient background for applying the provision. It is a further condition that the intended action is "in the course of the operation of the common market". This – compared with Article 2 under which the tasks of the Community shall be promoted "by establishing a common market and an economic and monetary union and through implementation of common policies or action as stated in Articles 3 and 3a" – is to be understood so that the intended action shall lie within the scope of the operation of the common market that appears from the other provisions of the Treaty, including in particular Part Three on the policy of the Community and the listing in Articles 3 and 3a of the individual fields of operation. This interpretation is in accordance with the Government's memo of 21st January 1997, to the Parliament's European Committee (...) and is confirmed by opinion 2/94 of 28th March 1996 of the European Court of Justice in plenary session, (...) where it is stated in paragraphs 29 and 30 (ECR 1996-I, page 1788):

The Maastricht Treaty', 93 *AJIL* (1999) pp. 209-214. Ole Due, 'The Danish Ratification of The Maastricht Treaty before The Danish Supreme Court', Marianne Dony, ed., '*Mélanges en Hommage à Michel Waelbroeck*', *Études de Droit Européen et International* (Bruxelles, Bruylant 1999) pp. 313-331. Hjalte Rasmussen: 'Confrontation or Peaceful Co-existence? On The Danish Supreme Court's Maastricht Ratification Judgment' in O'Keeffe, op. cit. n. 2, at pp. 377-390.

"29. Article 235 is designed to fill the gap where no specific provisions of the Treaty confer on the Community institutions express or implied powers to act, if such powers appear none the less to be necessary to enable the Community to carry out its functions with a view to attaining one of the objectives laid down by the Treaty.
30. That provision, being an integral part of an institutional system based on the principle of conferred powers, cannot serve as a basis for widening the scope of Community powers beyond the general framework created by the provisions of the Treaty as a whole and, in particular, by those that define the tasks and the activities of the Community. On any view, Article 235 cannot be used as a basis for the adoption of provisions whose effect would, in substance, be to amend the Treaty without following the procedure which it provides for that purpose".

The stated interpretation of Article 235 must be taken as the basis even though, prior to the amendment of the Treaty, the provision may have been applied on the basis of a wider interpretation.

A legislative act which does not go any further than to confer powers to issue legislative acts or decide upon other measures in accordance with the interpretation of Article 235 ... does not constitute a violation of the demand for specification in Sect. 20 of the Constitution.

Any adoption pursuant to Article 235 must be unanimous. Therefore the Government may prevent the provision from being applied to any adoption which is beyond the stated scope for Denmark's delegation of powers to the EC. The Government cannot assist in the adoption of bills which fall outside this scope and therefore presuppose additional transfer of sovereignty. On the background of the objective which Article 235 is intended to support it is unavoidable that the precise delimitation of the scope of application of the provision may give rise to doubts. In view thereof it is considered that the Act of Accession grants the Government a not insignificant margin. ...

Any question on the validity of an act of law or another action passed in pursuance of Article 235 may therefore be brought before the EC Court of Justice, and in that event the Court of Justice shall ensure that the scope of the operation of the Community is observed.

The fact that the detailed determination of the powers vested in the institutions of the community may give rise to doubts, and that the jurisdiction to give rulings concerning the interpretation of such questions is transferred to the EC Court of Justice cannot in itself be regarded as incompatible with the requirement for specification in Sect. 20 of the Constitution.

The fact that the EC Court of Justice in its interpretation of the Treaty also attaches importance to factors of interpretation other than the wording of the provisions, including the objectives of the Treaty, is not in violation of the assumptions on which the Act of Accession was based, nor is it in itself incompatible with the demand for specification in Sect. 20(1) of the Constitution. The same applies to the law-making activities of the EC Court of Justice within the scope of the Treaty.

... The appellants have pleaded that the jurisdiction of the EC Court of Justice under the Treaty, held against the principle of precedence for EC law, implies that Danish courts of law are prevented from enforcing the limits for the transfer of sovereignty which has taken place by the Act of Accession and that this must be taken into consideration when assessing if the demand for specification in Sect. 20(1) of the Constitution has been observed.

By adopting the Act of Accession it has been recognised that the power to test the validity and legality of EC acts of law lies with EC Court of Justice. This implies that Danish courts of law cannot hold that an EC act is inapplicable in Denmark without the question of its compatibility with the Treaty having been tried by the EC Court of Justice, and that Danish courts of law can generally base their decision on decisions by the Court of Justice on such questions being within the limits of the surrender of sovereignty. However, the Supreme Court finds that it follows from the demand for specification in Sect. 20(1) of the Constitution, held against the Danish courts's access to test the constitutionality of acts, that the courts of law cannot be deprived of their right to try questions as to whether an EC act of law exceeds the limits for the surrender of sovereignty made by the Act of Accession. Therefore, Danish courts must rule that an EC act is inapplicable in Denmark if the extraordinary situation should arise that with the required certainty it can be established that an EC act which has been upheld by the EC Court of Justice is based on an application of the Treaty which lies beyond the surrender of sovereignty according to the Act of Accession. Similar interpretations apply with regard to community-law rules and legal principles which are based on the practice of the EC Court of Justice.

... On the background mentioned, the Supreme Court finds that neither the additional powers that have been delegated to the Council in pursuance of Article 235 of the EC Treaty, nor the law-making activities of the Court of Justice can be regarded as incompatible with the demand for specification in Sect. 20(1) of the Constitution.

... With regard to the question whether transfer of sovereignty in accordance with the Act of Accession is of such a nature that it is in violation of the assumption of the Constitution of a democratic system of government, it is noted that any delegation of part of the Parliament's legislative powers to an international organisation will involve a certain encroachment on the Danish democratic system of government. This has been taken into consideration when drawing up the rigorous requirements for adoption under Sect. 20(2). In so far as concerns the EC Treaty, legislative powers have been transferred primarily to the Council, in which the Danish Government – answering to the Parliament – can exercise its influence. It is reasonable to assume that the Parliament has been entrusted to consider whether participation by the Government in the EC cooperation should be conditional upon any additional democratic control. Nor does the Supreme Court in this respect find any basis for holding the Act of Accession unconstitutional' (translation by the Danish Ministry of Foreign Affairs).

By way of the quoted reasoning the Danish Supreme Court affirmed the judgment of the High Court of Justice dismissing the plaintiff's claims.

THE SPANISH CONSTITUTIONAL ORDER

Gregorio Garzón Clariana*

INTRODUCTION

The Spanish Constitution of 1978 was drafted bearing in mind the prospect of Spain's participation in the process of European integration.[1] The Constituent Assembly took special account of the possible accession of Spain to the European Communities and the constitutional experiences of the member States which had already acceded. Finally, in 1986, at the time of accession, these circumstances, together with the fact that in the 1980s Community case law on the primacy and direct effect of Community law was already well-established, favoured an adaptation of the Spanish constitutional system to the Community legal system in conditions similar to those prevailing in other member States.

Article 93 of the Spanish Constitution is the key provision since it authorises the transfer of powers to international organisations. Article 95 is also relevant since it addresses the possibility that international treaties may be unconstitutional. However, in the Spanish legal system, the entire body of constitutional legislation ('bloque constitucional') includes the so-called 'organic laws' provided for in the Constitution, some of which also have significant effects on European integration and which were not clearly foreseen at the time of their adoption.

The constitutional framework is, therefore, more complex than appears at first sight. With that in mind, the author had already foreseen soon after the accession of Spain that two different types of difficulties or, so to speak, complexities,

* The Jurisconsult of the European Parliament, Professor of Law
The opinions expressed by the author are exclusively personal and do not reflect the position of the institution which he has the honour to serve.

[1] In fact, more generally, as Pérez Royo says 'the Spanish Constitution of 1978 is a very late product of the consolidation cycle of democratic constitutionalism in Europe and, therefore, benefits from the European experience in this field. The problems which would have to be faced were known in detail, the methods of solving them were also known and had been proven, and the social and economic conditions for applying such methods to those problems were more than satisfied. In those circumstances, the truth is that it would have been odd if we had drawn up a Constitution which needed revision a few years later'; *Curso de Derecho Constitucional,* 4th edition, Marcial Pons, Madrid, 1997, p. 709.

A.E. Kellermann et al. (Eds.), EU Enlargement: The Constitutional Impact at EU and National Level

could arise: in the first place, the judicial guarantee of the primacy of Community law; and secondly, in view of the complex territorial organisation of Spain which derives from the Constitution the distribution of powers between the central institutions of the State and the 'Self-governing Communities'.[2] This forecast has been amply confirmed by subsequent case law and practice.

I. THE CONSTITUTIONAL FRAMEWORK

Article 93 of the Spanish Constitution is the 'legal constitutional base'[3] of Spain's accession to the European Communities. Its final draft is worded as follows:

> 'Authorisation may be granted by an organic act for concluding treaties by which the exercise of powers derived from the Constitution shall be transferred to an international organisation or institution. It is incumbent on the Cortes Generales [Parliament] or the Government, as the case may be, to ensure compliance with these treaties and with resolutions originating in the international and supranational organisations to which such powers have been so transferred.'

Article 93 went through different drafting stages:

a) Article 6(3) of the preliminary draft text of the Constitution[4] mentions the vesting of powers derived from the Constitution in institutions governed by international law *under a system of parity.*
b) Article 86 of the draft text[5] maintains the need for parity which, nevertheless, disappears at the stage of consideration by the constitutional committee of the Senate.[6]

With the removal of the condition of parity, the final wording of Article 93 of the Spanish Constitution is in keeping with the situation established by the Community legal order.[7]

In this way, Article 93 allowed, without major disputes, the transfer of State powers to the European Communities. However, the provision itself specifies that the transfer concerns the *exercise* of sovereign powers and not sovereign power

---

[2] See G. Garzón Clariana, *España en las Comunidades Europeas: algunas cuestiones jurídicas, Anuario Hispano-Luso-Americano de Derecho Internacional,* Vol. 8, 1997.

[3] Term is used by A. Mangas, *Derecho comunitario europeo y derecho español.* 2nd edition. Madrid, 1987, p. 21.

[4] Official Gazette of 5 January 1978.

[5] Official Gazette of 17 April 1978.

[6] Official Gazette of 6 April 1978.

[7] See for the same view Pérez Tremp, *Derecho constitucional,* Vol. I, 2nd edition, Tirant lo Blanch, Valencia, 1994, p. 107.

itself, which still belongs to the Spanish nation, as is clear from Article 1(2) of the Spanish Constitution.[8] This was later confirmed by the Constitutional Court in its declaration of 1 July 1992 in which it stated that '*By virtue of Article 93, the Cortes Generales may transfer or assign the exercise of powers derived from the Constitution but may not decide upon the Constitution itself ...*'[9]

This transfer of powers is effected *by means of an organic law*, that is, by a qualified majority, although a relatively small one, even smaller than that required by other constitutions. The reason for this is that Article 93 was drafted with Spain's integration in the EEC in mind, which was unanimously supported by all political parties. The final wording of Article 93 substantially reduces the 3/5ths majority provided for in the initial draft. This has been criticised by scholars who believe that, given the importance of the commitment which was entered into, and taking into account the fact that Article 93 could be used for other purposes of integration for which such broad political support could not be assured, it would had been preferable if the legislature had kept the 3/5ths majority.[10]

Organic Law 10/1985 of 2 August 1985 authorising the accession of Spain to the European Communities was adopted on the basis of Article 93 of the Constitution. It contains a short preamble and a single article which authorises the ratification of the Accession Treaty. *Spain's accession to the EEC did not require a constitutional reform* since *the Constitution had already provided for a specific mechanism for integration in a supranational organisation.*

However, it was necessary to amend the Constitution after some changes were made to the Community Treaties. This illustrates both the limitations of Article 93 and the legal consequences of Article 95 in respect to the constitutional review of international treaties as interpreted by the Constitutional Court.

Article 95 of the Spanish Constitution enables *a preliminary as well as a subsequent* review of international treaties to be carried out. It provides as follows:

> '1. The provisions of any international treaty containing stipulations contrary to the Constitution shall require prior constitutional amendment.
> 2. The Government or either House may request the Constitutional Court to declare whether or not there is an inconsistency.'

Article 95 expressly establishes only a system for *reviewing the constitutionality of treaties before they are concluded by Spain.* The Government and the Houses of Parliament are empowered to seek a prior declaration of constitutionality from the Constitutional Court. However, Parliamentary minorities are not empowered to do so.

---

[8] Article 1(2) of the Spanish Constitution: '*National sovereignty is vested in the Spanish people, from whom all state powers emanate.*'

[9] Declaration of the Constitutional Court of 10 July 1992, Official Gazette No. 177, Supplement of 24 July 1992. F.J. 4.8.

[10] See A. Mangas Martín, *Derecho comunitario europeo y Derecho español,* Madrid, 1986.

As regards the nature of the declaration of unconstitutionality, although the decision of the Constitutional Court under Article 95 cannot be considered to be a 'judgment' as it is not delivered in a contentious case, it is not merely an opinion. It is a binding judicial decision and, as such, it takes effects *erga omnes* (Declaration of the Constitutional Court of 1 July 1992 in Case 1236/92 regarding Article 8 B(1) of the Treaty on European Union; right to stand as a candidate in municipal elections).

If the Constitutional Court declares a treaty provision to be incompatible with the Constitution, '*the immediate and direct executive effect is to be the reform of the Constitution prior to the adoption of the treaty*' (see the above declaration). In the event of incompatibility, there are three possible solutions: a) renegotiate the treaty in order to remedy the problems that have arisen; b) reform the Constitution; c) refuse to sign the treaty.

The text of the Constitution provides explicitly for the prior review of treaties but does not expressly say that they can be the subject of a subsequent action on grounds of unconstitutionality, that is, once they have been ratified. However, the provisions relating to actions on grounds of unconstitutionality refer in general terms to proceedings against 'laws and legislation having the force of law', which includes international treaties, as was later expressly specified by the Organic Law on the Constitutional Court.

Hence there are two possibilities: the action on grounds of unconstitutionality (which may be brought by the Prime Minister, the Ombudsman ('Defensor del Pueblo'), 50 members of Congress or 50 Senators and the Self-governing Communities if the treaty in question affects their area of self-government), and the issue of unconstitutionality raised by a court or tribunal.

Another factor which has to be borne in mind in the context of Spain's participation in the process of European integration is the territorial organisation of the State. Part VIII of the Spanish Constitution defines the form in which Spain is organised as a state composed of Self-governing Communities. The shaping of Spain as a State of Self-governing Communities meant *recognition* of the Spanish historical and social reality. It is precisely to this historical nuance that Professor Sánchez Agesta refers when he says that 'the new structure that is at present established in Spain is not so much an act of intent as an *acceptance of its history*'.[11]

To translate such history into legal provisions was no easy feat, all the more so bearing in mind the specific historical moment in which the Constitution was drafted and the efforts to reach a consensus which a peaceful transition to democracy required. The system of Self-governing Communities constitutes one of the greatest achievements of the Spanish Constitution (and probably one of the factors which has most contributed to the subsequent development and definitive es-

[11] See L. Sánchez Agesta, p. 391.

tablishment of the young Spanish democracy) but it is not free from complications. Sure enough, the Spanish Constitution of 1978 establishes a system which respects the unity of the nation, the identity of the State in the institutional order and the unity of the Spanish internal market. The relevant constitutional provisions are too numerous to be listed here. This aspect does not seem to raise any difficulties from the point of view of European integration.

The problem, however, lies in the fact that the various Self-governing Communities are very different in terms of population, size, economic strength and historical and cultural identity. Admittedly, this diversity was already acknowledged in Article 2 of the Constitution which distinguishes between '*nationalities*' and '*regions*' in establishing the right to self-government. In legal terms, the consequence is that the Constitution itself establishes certain 'models' of Self-governing Communities with sharp differences in the level of empowerment. Furthermore, given the fact that each Self-governing Community has its own statute of devolution, approved by the Spanish Parliament, which takes into account the wishes and priorities of each territory, diversity is even greater. The final result is a complex system for the allocation of powers, as can be seen from the (relatively ample) case law of the Constitutional Court, in order to resolve conflicts between the central authorities of the State and the Self-governing Communities. Naturally this complexity has a direct impact on the question of who is empowered to enforce Community law.

II. PRIMACY OF COMMUNITY LAW

From the point of view of the Spanish constitutional system, Community law raises two sets of questions: first, the hierarchy in rank between Community law and the Constitution; and secondly, the judicial guarantee of primacy, that is, which court is competent to guarantee the primacy of Community law. The two questions are intimately related in the case law of the Spanish Constitutional Court, as can be seen from some selected cases:

The 'infraconstitutional' rank of Community law.

Judgment No. 28/1991 of 14 February 1991: action on grounds of unconstitutionality by the Basque Parliament. Elections to the European Parliament. Single constituency. Incompatibility of mandate.

The action lodged by the Basque Parliament claimed that the Organic Law on the general electoral system, which makes it incompatible to hold office simultaneously as a member of the European Parliament and as a member of the Basque Parliament, was contrary to Council Decision 76/787 (European Electoral Act), and therefore contrary to Actions 93 and 96(1) of the Spanish Constitution.

The Basque Parliament contended that a provision of national law cannot derogate from a provision of Community law which authorises a dual mandate, and added that Article 93 of the Constitution entrusts the Government and the Cortes Generales with the task of ensuring compliance with Community law.

The Court rejected the view that a breach of a Community provision entails a breach of Articles 93 and 96(1) of the Spanish Constitution (that is to say, incompatibility between a Community provision and a national provision does not lead to a problem of unconstitutionality) and accordingly held that it had no jurisdiction to decide on the compatibility of national law with Community law:

> 'The possible breach of European Community legislation by national or regional laws or provisions adopted subsequently *does not mean that there is a constitutional dispute but only* a conflict of infraconstitutional provisions that must be resolved in the exercise of ordinary jurisdiction'.

Judgment No. 64/1991 of 22 March 1991: application for relief to the Constitutional Court (*recursos de amparo*) against various decisions of the Secretariat General for Fisheries regarding the system of allocation of fishing quotas for access for Spanish fishing vessels to fisheries in NEFAC, and against the judgments of the National High Court *(Audiencia Nacional)* and the Supreme Court.

> '... it is not for the Constitutional Court to review the question whether the activities of the public authorities are consistent with European Community law. Such review is a matter for the ordinary courts in their task of applying Community law and, where appropriate, for the Court of Justice of the European Communities by means of an action for failure to fulfil an obligation. ... It is therefore a question of an infraconstitutional nature and for that reason is excluded from the scope of applications for relief as well as from that of all other constitutional proceedings ..., any such conflicts must be dealt with in contentious proceedings under administrative law.'

The Constitutional Court went on to state that

> 'in matters brought before the ordinary courts, influenced where appropriate by the Court of Justice of the European Communities, the Constitutional Court cannot intervene in any way through the issue of unconstitutionality that could eventually be raised given that, since the object of the proceedings is solely to verify whether a national provision is consistent with a provision of European Community law, the primacy of Community law requires that only those courts should be called upon to ensure its direct effect, as the Court of Justice of the European Communities held in its judgment of 9 March 1978 in *Simmenthal*'.

It is clear, therefore, that the Constitutional Court discusses the 'infraconstitutional status' of Community law on the basis, among other things, of the requirements derived from its *primacy.* This line of reasoning may seem paradoxical, but it can be explained inasmuch as it reflects the purpose of this case law, that is to say, to afford the most effective judicial guarantee of primacy as possible. A consequence of this is that such case law should be commented on not only from the point of view of the legal principles involved but also from the point of view of its practical impact.

These judgments obviously raise a question of principle since they are not easy to reconcile with the case law of the Court of Justice of the European Communities on the *absolute* primacy of Community law, even over the Constitutions of the member States.

This point of view has been underlined by legal scholars in Spain. For example, according to A. Mangas: 'the Constitutional Court has made an unnecessary statement, which has no legal base and is contrary to Spain's legal commitments'. The legal result pursued by Article 93 of the Constitution, which provides for the transfer of the exercise of powers to supranational institutions, is the acceptance of Community law 'with its own requirements, including its absolute primacy'. 'Community provisions are not infraconstitutional. Nor should they be dramatically qualified as supraconstitutional (...) Community law has an "extra or metaconstitutional" status'.[12]

However, this aspect should not be dramatised. In practice, it is hard to see how a Constitutional Court could take the opposite view, that is, uphold the supremacy of Community law over the Constitution which it is meant to enforce. As is shown by the case law of other member States, there is a sort of *legal conundrum* in the notion that a State founded on democracy and national sovereignty could ever accept the supremacy of other rules over its own Constitution. The real problem is not this, but the risk that, in practice, Constitutional Courts might wrongly apply provisions of Community law because they are deemed to be contrary to the Constitution.

There is at least one potential risk in Spain, as is shown by the need to reform the Constitution in order to adapt it to the amendment of the Community Treaties where incompatibilities arise between the former and the latter, as witnessed by the reform of the 1978 Constitution after the Maastricht Treaty of 1992.

It should be pointed out that the reform of the 1978 Constitution as a consequence of the entry into force of the Maastricht Treaty has been the only one effected in the Spanish Constitution until now.

The relevant texts are as follows:

Art. 8B(1) of the Maastricht Treaty:

> 'Every citizen of the Union residing in a member State of which he is not a national shall have the right to vote and to stand as a candidate at municipal elections in the member State in which he resides under the same conditions as nationals of that State.'

---

[12] *La Constitución y la ley ante el Derecho comunitario-comentario a la sentencia del Tribunal Constitucional 28/1991* Revista de Instituciones Europeas, Vol. 18 no. 2 May-August 1991.

Article 13(2) of the Constitution provides:

> 'Only Spanish nationals shall be entitled to the rights recognised in Article 23, except in cases which may be established by treaty or by law concerning the right to vote in municipal elections, and subject to the principle of reciprocity.'

The Government used the mechanism for a prior review of constitutionality in Article 95 for the first time and asked the Constitutional Court whether there was an inconsistency between those two provisions and, if so, whether it could be resolved through the mechanism established in Article 93 or if the Constitution had to be reformed.

The Constitutional Court declared that it had to *examine compatibility* not only with Article 13(2), as the Government asked, but *with 'the whole' of the Constitution.* The Court examined compatibility with Articles 23 (right of citizens to participate in public affairs) and 1(2) (national sovereignty is vested in the Spanish people) and concluded that: a) there is an *inconsistency only with Article 13(2)* and b) *that inconsistency cannot be resolved by means of Article 93.* The latter is not an alternative to Article 95 or to Article 167 (mechanism for constitutional reform). Article 93 provides for the transfer of the exercise of powers to international organisations and permitted the accession of Spain to the European Communities. The question here, however, is not the transfer of powers but simply the fact of conferring on non-nationals certain rights which Article 13(2) denies them. *It is not a question of transferring powers but of conferring personal rights. In order to do so it is necessary to amend Article 13(2).*

That provision was amended on 27 August 1992 by means of the Article 167 procedure (without a referendum) with the backing of all the political parties. Article 13(2) now reads 'the right to vote and to stand in municipal elections'. The right to stand as a candidate in municipal elections was extended to all foreign nationals, not only to citizens of member States.

There is another potential risk: the possibility that, unlike the Constitutional Court, the ordinary courts and especially the Supreme Court may consider that inconsistencies between national provisions and Community provisions in fact raise a question of constitutionality and not of legality, which could also lead to a negative conflict of jurisdiction leaving the primacy of Community law without effective judicial protection in Spain.

The danger of this kind of *table tennis* between the Constitutional Court and the Supreme Court was anticipated by this author in his above-mentioned paper of 1987, which was probably considered at the time by some as a simple academic *diversion* unlikely to be confirmed by events. However, judicial decisions in the 1990s have shown that the danger was real.

The fact is that the Supreme Court has declared unequivocally, for example in its judgment of 24 April 1990 *(Confederación Interprofesional Lechera española),*[13] that incompatibilities between provisions of Community law and Spanish legal provisions adopted subsequently raise a question of unconstitutionality *by reason of the Spanish legislature's lack of competence.* Fortunately, the Supreme Court has generally considered that Spanish courts should, in such cases, not apply the Spanish provision without having to raise a question of unconstitutionality in proceedings before the Constitutional Court. However, there is at least one well-known *obiter dictum* according to which, in such cases, the Supreme Court should declare that it *lacks jurisdiction.*[14]

III. A STATE OF SELF-GOVERNING COMMUNITIES

The complex territorial structure of the State established by the 1978 Constitution has been implemented in legal and practical terms since the entry into force of the statutes of devolution approved thereafter (over a period of years) by the various Self-governing Communities.

This feature, which is specific to the existing Spanish constitutional system, has an indirect, albeit in practice decisive, influence on the observance of the provisions of Community law in Spain.

It would be rash to attempt to summarise here the features of a system which is complex by nature and where, furthermore, the case law of the Constitutional Court dealing with conflicts of jurisdiction between the central authorities of the State and the different authorities of the Self-governing Communities is abundant. Only a few ideas can be considered here in broad outline.

In this context, the State of Self-governing Communities established in Spain generates two broad sets of constitutional issues: first, who has jurisdiction to apply Community law in Spain (the State or the Self-governing Communities); and secondly, what can the central authorities of the State do to ensure fulfilment of the obligations which rest on the State by virtue of the Community Treaties in the event of the failure to apply or resulting from the incorrect application of the rules of Community law by a Self-governing Community when the latter, and not the central authorities of the State, is competent to adopt the implementing measures required by such rules.

As for the constitutional provisions applicable to the distribution of powers between the State, on the one hand, and each Self-governing Community, on the other, for the application of Community law, there are considerable variations between the statutes of devolution of the different nationalities and regions in at least three respects: a) the power to apply international treaties; b) the matters which fall within the jurisdiction of each Self-governing Community and c) the

---

[13] Text available in NOTICIAS/C.E.E., 1990, p. 149.

[14] Cf. P. Pérez Tremps: *Constitución española y Communidad europea,* Madrid, 1994, pp. 145-146.

type of measures, whether legislative or merely administrative, by virtue of which powers are conferred on every Self-governing Community in matters within its jurisdiction, whether on an exclusive basis or jointly with the State.

Moreover, these variables (together with the fact that Community legislation in some areas is often brought into being by a series of legal acts with distinct legal bases in the Treaties) have a 'salami effect' in that, in one and the same Self-governing Community, the distribution of powers in order to implement a Community policy may be of a certain complexity. This was clearly reflected, almost from the beginning, in the case law of the Constitutional Court, for example, in its judgment concerning the powers of the Basque country in regard to consumer protection.[15]

On the other hand, the uneven practical capabilities of the public administrations of the different Self-governing Communities in following up and implementing Community law provisions in their respective fields of jurisdiction helps to explain certain breaches of Community law, identified by the European Court of Justice, which occurred despite the generally *European-minded* approach of these Communities. By way of illustration, mention may be made of the following judgments:

1. Judgment of the Court of Justice of 28.05.98 in Case C-298/97: Directive 91/157/EEC on batteries and accumulators containing certain dangerous substances

Article 6 of Directive 91/157/EEC obliges member States to draw up programmes in order to achieve the objectives laid down in the directive (reduction of the heavy-metal content of batteries and accumulators; promotion of marketing of batteries and accumulators containing smaller quantities of dangerous substances; etc.). Spain stated that the directive had been transposed into Spanish law by a royal decree which incorporates the provisions of Article 6 of the directive and specifies that the Self-governing Communities are responsible for giving effect to the programmes in question.

The Court stated that

> 'according to settled case law, a member State may not plead provisions, practices or circumstances existing in its internal legal system in order to justify a failure to comply with the obligations and time-limits laid down in a directive'.

[15] Cf. G. Garzón Clariana, *La protección de los consumidores en el Derecho Comunitario europeo y las competencias de las Comunidades Autónomas, Asociación Española para el Estudio del Derecho Europeo: La integración de España en las Comunidades Europeas y las competencias de las Comunidades Autónomas,* Barcelona, Generalitat de Catalunya, 1985.

2. Judgment of the Court of Justice of 1.10.98 in Case C-71/97: Directive on protection of waters against pollution caused by nitrates from agricultural sources

The Court declared that by failing to designate the zones considered to be vulnerable and to notify the Commission of those designations and by failing to establish the codes of good agricultural practice for the Self-governing Communities other than Andalucía, Cantabria, Madrid, Murcia, Navarre and Valencia, Spain had failed to fulfil its obligations under Articles 3 and 4 of Directive 91/676 on protection of waters against pollution caused by nitrates from agricultural sources.

In its defence, Spain alleged that the delay in implementing the directive was due, on the one hand, to technical difficulties involved in its implementation and, on the other, to the fact that the State and the Self-governing Communities have concurrent powers in the fields covered by the directive.

The arguments relating to the concurrent powers were not accepted by the Court. It pointed out that according to settled case law, a State may not plead provisions and practices or circumstances existing in its internal legal system in order to justify a failure to comply with the obligations and time-limits laid down in a directive.

3. Judgment of the Court of Justice of 13.04.00 in Case C-274/98: Directive on protection of waters against pollution caused by nitrates from agricultural sources

In this case, the Court declared that by not establishing the action programmes referred to in Article 5 of the directive in question, the Kingdom of Spain had failed to fulfil its obligation under the directive.

In their defence, the Spanish authorities explained that the obligation laid down by the directive to designate vulnerable zones lies on the autonomous regions, since the applicable royal decree provides that they are responsible for such designations.

The Court recalled that it

> 'has consistently held that member States cannot rely on provisions, practices or circumstances in their own legal orders to justify failure to comply with the obligations and time-limits laid down by a directive'.

The Court added that

> 'neither the division of powers as between the State and the autonomous regions nor the obligation to comply with directions given in the national legislation transposing the directive into national law can serve to justify failure to comply with the obligations imposed by the directive'.

There is no doubt that judgments like the ones cited above underline the importance of the machinery available in order to allow the intervention of the State or the application of the provisions adopted by its central authorities in cases of failure to apply or incorrect application of Community law provisions by a particular Self-governing Community.

It must be said in this respect, however, that Article 93 of the Constitution does not seem to constitute a sound legal base empowering the State to intervene by means of specific procedures which differ from the more general mechanisms for intervention provided for in Part VIII of the Constitution or which result from the repercussions of other constitutional provisions (for example, on the powers of the Constitutional Court or of the Council of State). However, many of these mechanisms are not really suited to ensuring compliance with Community law or else their price in political terms is too high (this is especially the case of State intervention in authoritarian form which is possible under Article 155 of the Constitution).

For this reason, the author suggested some years ago that the possibilities offered by Article 149(1)(iii) of the Constitution should be explored. This provision lays down that 'international relations' fall in any event within the exclusive jurisdiction of the State. The basic idea was obviously to seek inspiration from the experience gained in Italy on the basis of a constitutional provision which was practically identical.[16] But in its most recent case law the Constitutional Court has adopted a fairly strict interpretation of Article 149(1)(iii) and has, consequently, raised new questions as to whether this approach is legally viable.[17]

It is not surprising that in this situation the different public authorities involved have set in motion informal procedures to ensure sound cooperation. There is even a series of agreements signed in the 1990s by the Sectoral Conference for European Community affairs, composed of senior officials from the Ministry for Public Administration, the State Secretariat for the European Communities and the State Secretariat for local government, on behalf of the central government, and of the councillors of the Self-governing Communities designated by their presidents. This Conference, which met for the first time on 16 March 1989, has produced some interesting agreements which may be summarised as follows:[18]

The first agreement deals with the action to be taken in the case of an infringement attributable to an act or omission on the part of a Self-governing Commu-

---

[16] Cf. G. Garzón Clariana, et al., *La ejecución del Derecho comunitario europeo en España y las competencias de las Comunidades autónomas, Institut d'Estudis Autonómics: La aplicación del Derecho comunitario europeo por organismos subestatales,* Barcelona, Generalitat de Catalunya, 1986 (this text exists in Spanish and Catalan versions).

[17] See Judgment of 26 May 1994 in Case 165/94 on the decree of the Basque Government with respect to relations with the European Communities and the Council of Europe.

[18] Cf. e.g., A. López Castillo, '*Creación y aplicación del Derecho comunitario europeo y Comunidades Autónomas*'. REDC, May-August, no. 35, 1992, p. 125.

nity, distinguishing between proceedings before the Commission and those before the Court of Justice of the European Communities.

In the case of proceedings before the Commission, the purpose is to coordinate action by the Self-governing Communities and the State. The State Secretariat for the European Communities is responsible for transmitting to the Self-governing Communities the complaints, letters of formal notice, reasoned opinions, etc. which it receives from the Commission, with a view to coordinating their replies, so as to forward the final answer to the Commission.

With regard to proceedings before the Court of Justice, the Self-governing Communities may, in the case of an infringement of Community law resulting from an act or omission attributable to them, cooperate in the adoption of the position to be taken by the Kingdom of Spain before the Court.

The second agreement defines the procedure to be followed in order to fulfil the obligation under Community law to notify State aids to the Commission, where such aids are granted by the Self-governing Communities themselves.

This approach is not, therefore, strictly limited to the internal application of the provisions of Community law. However, it would seem to be a fairly positive feature, so far as compliance with such provisions is concerned, in the light of the 1999 Commission's report on monitoring the application of Community law. In that report the Commission emphasizes, in the chapter on the environment, that:

> 'The causes of the delays in transposing directives are the same as those highlighted in previous reports – internal institutional and administrative structures of the member States, transposal techniques, specific difficulties in particularly sensitive areas (chemicals, biotechnology), and possible lack of coordination between representatives of the member States who negotiate the directives and the bodies in the member States which will be responsible for implementing them.'[19]

CONCLUDING REMARKS

It might perhaps seem inappropriate to draw general conclusions from the Spanish constitutional order in a colloquium designed to make readily available the experience cumulated in all the present member States of the European Union. But developments in Spain call for two remarks that could be useful for States candidates for accession.

First, the need to amend the Spanish Constitution in 1992, to adapt it to the Maastricht Treaty, shows that political consensus on European integration, or a 'monistic' tradition regarding the incorporation of international law, are not in themselves a guarantee that adaptation to changing Community law will not re-

---

[19] XVIth Report on monitoring the application of Community law (COM(1999)301 final), 09/07/1999.

quire amending the Constitution. If one wants to avoid such a risk – which can even imply having recourse to cumbersome and costly referendum procedures – then the key factor is careful drafting of the constitutional provisions on Community law.

Secondly, ensuring the primacy and direct effect of Community law depends not only on the provisions in the Constitution specifically designed to facilitate accession to the Union, but also on the general context of the Constitution. More specifically, providing for a Constitutional Court, or self-governing territories, can certainly have an impact on the smooth operation of Community law – although not necessarily a *negative* one. As both Spanish case law and practice illustrate, the co-existence of a Constitutional Court and a Supreme Court can be a potential source of conflicts of jurisdiction, but this is not in itself an obstacle to the efficient implementation of Community law.[20] Similarly, a complex territorial organisation can result in legal disputes over who has the power to apply Community law at the domestic level. But the practical consequences should not be overdramatized, inter alia, because legal complexities can also be partly overcome by pragmatic procedures.

In the final analysis, one should always bear in mind that public institutions have a life of their own. The text of the Constitution should be such as to facilitate, to the maximum extent, the implementation and enforcement of Community law, but this is not just a task for Constitutional drafters. It is work for many people everyday.

[20] Cf. Hinojosa Martínez and Segura Serrano, *La aplicación judicial del Derecho comunitario en España en 1999, Revista de Derecho comunitario europeo*, 8 (2000), pp. 565 et seq.

THE ADAPTATION OF THE PORTUGUESE CONSTITUTIONAL ORDER TO COMMUNITY LAW

Rui Manuel Moura Ramos*

1. The relationship between Community law and constitutional law in Portugal has been characterized by the progressive adaptation of the Portuguese constitution and constitutional practice to the needs and development of the Community system. Such adaptation had begun even before Portuguese accession to the European Communities, as evidenced by the four revisions that the Portuguese 1976 constitution has undergone to date (1982, 1989, 1992 and 1997)[1], Portuguese legal writings and courts' practice (mainly, that of the constitutional court).

A) THE INITIAL 1976 CONSTITUTION AND ITS REVISIONS

2. In so far as the Constitution is concerned, we can even say that such adaptation began even before Portugal's accession to the European Communities took place (1st January 1986). In fact, the Portuguese Constitution of 2 April 1976 (which established the Portuguese Second Republic), did not envisage either accession to supranational organizations (as is the case with the European Communities) nor the effects of the acts of such organizations in domestic law. That situation has even led some commentators to the conclusion that, at that stage, accession to supranational organizations was not admitted by the constitutional order in view of the fact that the transfer of sovereignty rights implied by such an accession was not foreseen and thus not allowed.[2]

* Professor, Law Faculty, University of Coimbra, Judge, European Court of First Instance, Luxembourg

[1] For the effect and contents of these revision procedures in general see mainly Jorge Miranda, *Manual de Direito Constitucional*, vol. I, 6th edition, Coimbra, 1997, Coimbra Editora, pp. 374-403 and Gomes Canotilho-Vital Moreira, *Constituição da República Portuguesa Anotada,* 3rd revised edition, Coimbra, 1993, Coimbra Editora, pp. 19-27 (although this last commentary does not deal with the 1997 revision).

[2] See Gomes Canotilho-Vital Moreira, *Constituição da República Portuguesa Anotada*, Coimbra, 1978, Coimbra Editora, p. 45, note VI to Article 8 and Vital Moreira 'Revisão constitucional e princípios fundamentais', in *Constituição e revisão constitucional*, Lisboa, 1980, Editorial Caminho, p. 75. In the sense that accession to the EEC did not require the revision of the constitutional fundamental principles but would imply a *praxis* that would preclude or put in jeopardy the

Meanwhile, this situation has been overtaken by the subsequent development of Portuguese constitutional law.

3. The first revision of the Constitution took place in 1982[3], prior to Portuguese accession but after the beginning of the negotiations that led to it (1978). Mention must be made of the fact that some provisions that were clearly incompatible with Community rules have been abrogated.[4] But the essential step on the path of adaptation to the future accession was the insertion of a provision [Article 8(3)] with the aim of allowing the automatic integration of secondary legislation produced by international organizations with Portuguese law[5,6]. According to the new rule 'legislation emanating from the competent bodies of international organizations to which Portugal is a party is directly in force in the internal order, as long as such is found expressly established in the respective constitutive treaties'. Although the contents of the provision dealt with all secondary legislation of international organizations there was no doubt that it was mainly focused on Community law and it was generally underlined that its purpose was to permit the application of Community law in the Portuguese legal order along the lines set up

goal fixed in Article 2 of the Constitution (transition to socialism), see Macaísta Malheiros, 'Adesão ao M. C. e a Revisão Constitucional', in 6 *Fronteira* (April-June 1979), pp. 15-21 and Vital Moreira, 'A Constituição económica e a revisão constitucional', in *Constituição e revisão constitucional,* loc. cit., pp. 121-123.

Considering, on the contrary, that the initial Portuguese Constitution of 1976 was substantially incompatible with the spirit of the Rome Treaty, see Fausto de Quadros, 'Problemas políticos e constitucionais do alargamento da Comunidade Europeia', in 2 *Política Externa: Estudos e documentos* (1978), pp. 33-42. On this subject, in general and with great detail, see Maria Isabel Jalles, 'Implicações jurídico-constitucionais da adesão de Portugal às Comunidades Europeias. Alguns aspectos', in 116 *Cadernos de Ciência e Técnica Fiscal*, Lisboa, 1980, Centro de Estudos Fiscais da Direcção-Geral das Contribuições e Impostos-Ministério das Finanças, and Mota de Campos, *A ordem constitucional portuguesa e o direito comunitário*, Braga, 1981, Editora Pax.

[3] Constitutional Law no. 1/82, 30 September 1982.

[4] That was the case of Article 38(4) which reserved ownership of periodical and non-periodical publications to non-profit-making legal persons and to editorial and journalist companies or individuals of Portuguese nationality. By allowing discrimination based on nationality, the rule was in direct contradiction with the right of establishment, as provided for by Article 52 of EEC Treaty.

[5] Prior to Constitutional Law no. 1/82, Article 8 of the Constitution dealt only with the integration of general international law [stating in Article 8(1) that the norms and the principles of general or common international law are an integral part of Portuguese law] and of conventional international law [prescribing in Article 8(2) that the norms belonging to international conventions duly ratified or approved enter into force in the internal legal order after their official publication and as long as they internationally bind the Portuguese State].

[6] As to the fact that Article 8(3) goes beyond the integration of EEC law, and referring also to the secondary legislation of other international organizations (for example UN law), see Moura Ramos, 'Portugal', in *The integration of international and European Community law into the national legal order. A study of the practice in Europe* (edited by Pierre Michel Eisemann), The Hague, 1996, Kluwer Law International, pp. 461-494 (particularly pp. 482-486) and Paulo Canelas de Castro, 'Portugal's world outlook in the Constitution of 1976', in 71 *Boletim da Faculdade de Direito da Universidade de Coimbra*, (1995), pp. 469-543 (particularly pp. 535-538).

by Community law and jurisprudence. With the adoption of this rule, the constitutional will, in the sense of the possibility of the accession to the European Communities, was therefore clarified.

4. Despite the adoption of this provision, there were certain problems that remained unsolved[7], partly because of the restrictive formulation of Article 8(3) that just foresaw the direct applicability of regulations. However, the second constitutional revision[8] removed the word 'expressly' from Article 8(3), thereby allowing a wider implementation of Community acts in the Portuguese legal order, and reaffirmed strongly Portugal's commitment to the European Communities. A new provision in Article 7(5) provides that 'Portugal pledges itself to the reinforcement of the European identity and in the strengthening of action by the European States in favour of peace, economic progress and justice in the relations between peoples' and one of the European institutions, the European Parliament, was expressly mentioned in Articles 136(b) and 139(3)(c) when the Constitution dealt with its election.

5. But although these revisions were mainly focused on the rethinking of the governmental system and on the elimination of the ideological references put forward during the revolutionary period in the first case, and on the reform of the organization of the economy in the second one[9], the third revision process[10] was devoted solely to the implications of some of the Communities' choices: those made by the 1992 Maastricht Treaty.[11] The main change is the constitutionalization of the European Union, made in Article 7(6) where the conditions of the participation of Portugal in such an institution are laid down. According to this provision, 'Portugal may, in conditions of reciprocity, and with respect to the principle of subsidiarity and bearing in mind the fulfilment of the principle of economic and social cohesion, agree to a common exercise of necessary powers in the construction of a European Union'.[12] Besides this essential aspect, it is also

[7] On this topic see, in particular, António Vitorino, *A adesão de Portugal às Comunidades Europeias. A problemática da aplicabilidade directa e do primado do direito comunitário face ao nosso ordenamento jurídico*, Lisboa, 1984, Cognitio.

[8] Constitutional Law no. 1/89, 8 July 1989.

[9] Besides op. cit., supra note 1, see Vital Moreira, 'A segunda revisão constitucional', in 7 *Revista de Direito Público* (1990), pp. 9-24 and Maria Manuel Leitão Marques, 'A Constituição Económica depois da segunda revisão constitucional', in 9 *Revista de Direito Público* (1991), pp. 9-33.

[10] Constitutional Law no. 1/92, 25 November 1992.

[11] For an overview hereof in Portuguese legal writings see *A União Europeia*, Coimbra, 1994, Faculdade de Direito – Curso de Estudos Europeus. And for the contents of the revision see mainly Jorge Miranda, 'O Tratado de Maastricht e a Constituição Portuguesa', in *A União Europeia na Encruzilhada*, Coimbra, 1996, Almedina, pp. 45-62.

[12] Lucas Pires *(Introdução ao direito constitucional europeu*, Coimbra, 1997, Almedina, pp. 106-107) sees in this the recognition of a situation where sovereignty (as well as citizenship) has been shared between two legal orders (the domestic and the Community ones).

provided in a new Article 15(5) that 'the law can still attribute, in conditions of reciprocity, the right to elect and to be elected as a member of the European Parliament, to the citizens of the member States of the European Union residing in Portugal', thus giving effect to the new EC Treaty rules on European citizenship [Articles 8 to 8-E, in particular 8-A)].[13] In the framework of the realization of the Economic and Monetary Union, the revision eliminated the exclusive right of the Bank of Portugal to issue currency and to define the main goals of the finance and monetary system (now provided for in the EC Treaty).[14]

Finally, the functions of the Portuguese Parliament (Assembly of the Republic) in the decision-making process within the European Union have been reinforced, Articles 166(f) and 200(i) recognizing its competence to 'follow and enhance, according to the law, the participation of Portugal in the process of the construction of the European Union and, to that end, requiring the Government to present to the Assembly the relevant information'.[15]

6. The impact of the last constitutional revision[16] was less than that of the previous one[17], even if it stressed one of its main ideas, the strengthening of the role of the national Parliaments in European construction. With respect to this purpose, two provisions deserve mention. The first [Article 164(p)] reserves to the absolute competence of the Assembly of the Republic the system for appointing members of the bodies of the European Union (with the exception of the Commission). And the second [Article 161(n)] provides that one of the powers of the Assembly of the Republic is to deliver its opinion, according to law, on those matters pending a decision in European Union bodies that fall within its reserved legislative competence. Besides this general clause which echoes and clarifies the former Article 166 (now 163(f)), Article 112(9) states that the 'transposition of

---

[13] On this question see Moura Ramos, 'Maastricht e os direitos do cidadão europeu', in *A União Europeia* (loc. cit., supra, note 11, pp. 93-129).

[14] Article 105 reads now: 'Bank of Portugal, as the national central bank, collaborates in the definition and execution of monetary and financial policies and issues currency, according to law'.

[15] On this subject and underlining the legal development see Moura Ramos, 'O Parlamento português no processo de criação da União Europeia' in 13/14 *Legislação. Cadernos de Ciência de Legislação* (April-December 1995), pp. 179-189 and João Miranda, *O papel da Assembleia da República na construção europeia,* Coimbra, 2000, Coimbra Editora.

[16] Constitutional Law no. 1/97, 20 September 1997.

[17] For comments on this topic, see mainly Alexandre Sousa Pinheiro-Mário João Brito Fernandes, *Comentário à IV Revisão constitucional*, Lisboa, 1999, AAFDL, António de Araújo, *A revisão constitucional de 1997. Um ensaio de história político-constitucional*, Coimbra, 1999, Coimbra Editora, and Jorge Bacelar de Gouveia, 'A quarta revisão da constituição portuguesa', *in Estudos de Direito Público*, v. I, Lisboa, 2000, Principia, pp. 81-100.

For the debate that took place in Portugal before this revision and which concerned also the possibility of a referendum on Portuguese membership of the European Union, see Lucas Pires, *Portugal e o Futuro da União Europeia. Sobre a revisão dos Tratados em 1996*, Lisboa, 1995, Difusão Cultural, and the various contributions gathered *in A Revisão do Tratado da União Europeia,* Coimbra, 1996, Livraria Almedina.

Community directives to the domestic legal order shall be in the form of Laws or Decree-Laws, as necessary', a provision that excludes the intervention of the autonomous regions in the framework of transposition[18] but seems also to put an excessive burden on the bodies fulfilling the legislative function.[19] This reduction in the importance of the regional units is in a certain way compensated for by the rules of Article 227(1)(v) and (x) that recognize, among the powers of these units, the power to 'deliver their opinion, on their own initiative or after consultation by the sovereign bodies, (...), in matters relating to their specific interest, on the definition of the positions of the Portuguese State in the framework of the process of European construction' and to 'participate in the process of European construction by being represented in the respective regional institutions and in the delegations participating in the Community decision-making process where matters relating to their specific interest are at stake'.[20]

7. We can thus conclude that Portuguese constitutional law has, by its evolution and revision procedures, adapted itself to the European Treaties and their development. One can mention the elimination of discrepancies and the accommodation to the case-law of the European legal system and to the evolution of the Community competence. This adaptation, meanwhile, has not meant that some questionable options, such as those contained in the last (1997) constitutional revision, have not been taken.

B) THE PORTUGUESE LEGAL OPINION ON THE COMMUNITY LEGAL ORDER

8. The approach taken by Portuguese legal writings concerning the Community legal order is also characterized by the same openness we have noticed in the constitutional evolution. The special nature of the Community system, as well as its autonomy, is largely recognized mainly with regard to the provisions of Articles 7(6) and 8(3). The primacy of Community rules over Portuguese legal solu-

[18] For the previous situation on this particular point, see Moura Ramos, 'The Case of Portugal', in *National Administrative procedures for the preparation and the implementation of Community decisions* (ed. Spyros A. Pappas), Maastricht, 1995, European Institute of Public Administration, pp. 441-452.

[19] For the situation in force before this change, see Marcelo Rebelo de Sousa, 'A transposição das directivas comunitárias para a ordem jurídica nacional', in 4/5 *Legislação. Cadernos de Ciência de legislação*, (1992), pp. 69-94. And for a discussion of the subject, with reference to the recent changes, see Margarida Afonso, 'Community directives: effects, efficiency, justiciability. The Portuguese case' in 5 *Temas de Integração* (1998), pp. 111-152.

[20] Maintaining that these powers were already contained in the previous constitutional law (since the 1989 revision) and in secondary legislation, cf. Moura Ramos, 'Le droit de la coopération décentralisée au Portugal' in *Le Droit appliqué à la coopération interrégionale en Europe*, Paris, 1995, LGDJ, pp. 149-168.

tions at a non-constitutional level is indisputably accepted as well as other interpretations laid down by the Court of Justice in its case-law, such as the direct effect of directives, and has also been recognized by the courts.[21] A lack of consensus exists, however, regarding the relationship between Community law and constitutional law, the majority of legal opinion favouring a position of non-supremacy of the former over the latter[22], notwithstanding a growing number of views in the opposite sense.[23]

Such a discussion does not seem to create a conflict with Community principles, since it is possible to accommodate the application of the provisions of the two legal systems, by seeking to interpret the constitution according to Community law[24], and by using the preliminary reference mechanism, adopted by the Portuguese Constitutional Court, when faced with the assessment of the degree of conformity of the basic principles of Portuguese constitutional law with Community provisions.[25] Furthermore, the practice of a restrained intervention of the Court of Justice[26] and of the Portuguese Constitutional Court[27] seems to facilitate the prevention of confrontational attitudes.[28]

---

[21] See Moura Ramos 'Relações entre a ordem interna e o direito internacional e comunitário', in *Da Comunidade Internacional e do seu Direito. Estudos de Direito Internacional Público e de Relações Internacionais*, Coimbra, 1996, Coimbra Editora, pp. 265-281 (pp. 274-279).

[22] See, for instance, Gomes Canotilho-Vital Moreira (op. cit. note 1), Mota Campos, *As relações da ordem jurídica portuguesa com o direito internacional e o direito comunitário à luz da revisão constitucional de 1982,* Lisboa, 1985, Instituto Superior de Ciências Sociais e Políticas (even if it supports *de iuri condendo* the opposite solution) and Jorge Miranda, 'La constitution portugaise et le traité de Maastricht', in 12 *Revue française de droit constitutionnel* (1992), p. 679 et seq.

Recently, Gomes Canotilho ('Da Constituição dirigente ao direito comunitário dirigente', *in Colectânea de Estudos de Homenagem a Francisco Lucas Pires*, Universidade Autónoma de Lisboa, pp. 143-153) has underlined the role of Article 10 EC Treaty as revealing the binding character for the member States of the duties deriving from the Treaty and stressed the nature of the Community treaties as *directive international treaties.*

[23] See Gonçalves Pereira-Fausto de Quadros, *Manual de Direito Internacional Público*, 3rd edition, Coimbra, 1993, Almedina, and also Baptista Machado, *Introdução ao direito e ao discurso legitimador*, Coimbra, 1983, Almedina, who argues for a position of equality between constitutional and Community law, underlining, however, that the latter could not undermine the fundamental rights recognized by the Constitution.

[24] Moura Ramos (op. cit. note 21, at p. 276) and Canelas de Castro (op. cit. note 6, at p. 517).

[25] To this effect Cardoso da Costa, 'O Tribunal constitucional português e o Tribunal de Justiça das Comunidades Europeias', *in Ab uno ad omnes. 75 Anos da Coimbra Editora*, Coimbra, 1998, Coimbra Editora, pp. 1363-1380, at p. 1376.

[26] To this effect Carlos Botelho Moniz-Paulo Moura Pinheiro, 'As relações da ordem jurídica portuguesa com a ordem jurídica comunitária. Algumas reflexões', in 4/5 *Legislação. Cadernos da ciência da legislação* (April-December 1992), pp. 121-144, at p. 139.

[27] One must underline that the question of non-conformity of Portuguese ordinary legislation with Community law can be dealt with solely by the ordinary courts, without the intervention of the Constitutional Court. See Nuno Piçarra, 'Note to the Mecanarte Decision (C-348/89, of 27 July 1991) of the Court of Justice' in *Colectânea anotada de Jurisprudência Comunitária (os casos Portugueses)*, 10 *Divulgação do Direito Comunitário*, (1992), pp. 39-50 and Cardoso da Costa (op. cit. note 24, pp. 1369-1373).

[28] Conflicts are also considered as rather uncommon by some authors. See Carlos Botelho Moniz, 'A Constituição da República Portuguesa e a participação de Portugal na União Europeia', in *Juris*

C) THE PORTUGUESE CASE LAW AND COMMUNITY LAW

9. The above conclusions seem to be confirmed by Portuguese case law, both from the ordinary and from the superior courts, as well as from the constitutional court.

I would just underline that the direct effect of directives was recognized immediately after the Portuguese accession by a decision of the Court of Appeals *(Tribunal da Relação)* of Coimbra[29] and that the primacy of Community law was also acknowledged by the Portuguese Supreme Court *(Supremo Tribunal de Justiça)*, again in a case where a directive (Directive 64/22) was involved.[30]

However, greater importance must be attached to some decisions of the Constitutional Court. Besides having recognized the direct effect of regulations, stressing also that their modalities of implementation fall within the realm of domestic constitutional law[31], this court affirmed its readiness to use the preliminary reference mechanism[32], by considering itself a court or tribunal within the mean-

---

et De Jure. Nos vinte anos da Faculdade de Direito da Universidade Católica Portuguesa-Porto, 1998, Universidade Católica Portuguesa-Porto, pp. 1225-1247 and Manuel Proença de Carvalho, 'A Constituição Portuguesa e as normas comunitárias: polémica e "mentiras piedosas" ', in *Estudos em Homenagem ao Banco de Portugal. 150. Aniversário (1846-1996)*, Lisboa, 1998, Banco de Portugal, pp. 251-260.

[29] See the decision of 30 July 1986, in 360 *Boletim do Ministério da Justiça* (1986), p. 307 et seq.

[30] See the decision of 19 December 1991, in 412 *Boletim do Ministério da Justiça* (1991), p. 229 et seq.

[31] Decision no. 184/89 (case no. 201/86), of 1 February 1989 (*in Diário da República*, I Série, no. 57, 9 March 1989, pp. 1044-1062.

The position taken by the Portuguese Constitutional Court is along the lines of that of the Austrian Constitutional Court, which by decision of 10 March 1999 made a preliminary reference to the Court of Justice [see Alina Lengauer 'Duties of National Authorities and National Courts resulting from Article 10 EC Treaty (National Report Austria), in *The duties of co-operation of national authorities and courts and the community institutions under Article 10 EC*, XIX FIDE Congress, I, pp. 19-34, at p. 23] and of the Belgian Court of Arbitration, which had already done so on 19 February 1997, leading to the Decision of 16 July 1998 in Case C-93/97 (see Amarylis Verhoeven, 'The application in Belgium of the duties of loyalty and co-operation', ibid., pp. 35-62, at p. 58-59). It is well known that other constitutional courts have taken a different stand. While the German *Bundesverfassungsgericht* has until now been silent on the matter, the Italian *Corte Costituzionale* does not consider itself a 'court or tribunal' within the meaning of Article 234 EC (formerly Article 177) (see, on the evolution of this position, Claudio Di Turi, 'Ancora sul rapporto tra giurisdizione nazionali e corte comunitaria in tema di rinvio pregiudiziali ex art. 177 del Trattato di Roma', *Diritto comunitario e degli scambi internazionali*, 1997, pp. 165-174) and the Spanish Constitutional Court refuses for its part to put a preliminary question on the ground that such a mechanism only has a role to play in the judicial application of Community law – a task belonging according to its view to the ordinary courts and not to the Constitutional Court (see, on this point, Diego Linan Nogueras-Manuel Lopez Escudero, 'Loyauté constitutionnelle et loyauté communautaire en droit espagnol', in *The duties of co-operation of national authorities and courts and the community institutions under Article 10 EC,* loc. cit, pp. 283-322, pp. 310-311).

[32] Decision no. 163/90 (case no. 154/89), of 23 May 1990 (in *Diário da República*, II Série, no. 240, 18 October 1991, pp. 10430-10433). Relying on this decision, it has been considered that the

ing of Article 234 (ex 177) of the EC Treaty and excluded questions of compatibility of ordinary Portuguese law with Community law from the scope of its purview. For this purpose, it limited the concept of unconstitutionality to cases of breach of a constitutional provision or principle by a provision of secondary legislation, thus removing from consideration situations where fundamental law is infringed on the ground of a breach of an infraconstitutional norm (incidental unconstitutionality).[33]

These judgments seem to provide confirmation of the optimistic conclusion that we have mentioned above and which is shared by other Portuguese scholars.[34]

10. The adoption of a Charter of Fundamental Rights of the European Union (as proposed by the Cologne European Council) will not change substantially the pattern presently presented. In my view this Charter should specify citizens' fundamental rights that the Union is nowadays already bound to respect under Article 6(2) of the Treaty on European Union. The enumeration to be established should not lose touch with the common constitutional traditions of the member States as currently provided for, and must take into consideration these domestic traditions, as well as other international or Community instruments, such as the European Convention for the Protection of Human Rights, the European Social Charter and the Community Charter of the Fundamental Rights of Workers. As I see it, the new Charter should be binding on the Union, and it should influence the member States' national constitutions to an equal extent by establishing a *common core* concerning the fundamental rights that a politically organized society must safeguard in an integration process.

11. In the light of the foregoing considerations, it does not seem that the alternative between communitarization and maintenance of a structure of intergovernmental cooperation would be a crucial one. The essential would be that in the

---

conflicts between Portuguese constitutional law and Community law seem could be solved. See Cruz Vilaça-Pais Antunes-Nuno Piçarra, 'Droit constitutionnel et droit communautaire. Le cas portugais', in *Rivista di Diritto Europeo*, 1991, pp. 301-310, Maria Luísa Duarte, 'O Tratado da União Europeia e a garantia da Constituição (Notas de uma reflexão crítica)', in *Estudos em Memória do Professor Doutor João de Castro Mendes*, Lisboa [no date], Lex, pp. 605-715, and Canelas de Castro (op. cit. note 6, p. 519).

For a case where the answer to the question referred for a preliminary ruling was subsequently taken into account, see decision no. 414/99 (case no. 940/98) of 29 June 1999 (in *Diário da República*, II Série, no. 61, 13 March 2000, pp. 4841-4842).

[33] See decisions nos. 326/98 (case no. 25/97) of 5 May 1998, in *Diário da República*, II Série, no. 160, 14 July 1998, pp. 9745-9747, 621/98, (case no. 320/97) of 3 November 1998, in *Diário da República*, II Série, no. 65, 18 March 1999, pp. 4035-4036, 570/98 (case no. 233/96), of 7 October 1998, in *Diário da República*, II Série, no. 276, 26 November 1999, pp. 17872-17876.

[34] Besides those cited supra, note 32 see also Cardoso da Costa (op. cit. note 25) and Carlos Botelho Moniz (op. cit. note 28).

framework of the enlargement process, both the ability to adapt state structures to the needs of the integration process and restrained behaviour on the part of the Union bodies regarding national special features and identities[35] should be maintained.

[35]Also underlining such attitudes in the past see Lucas Pires, '"Competência das competências": competente mas sem competências?', 130 *Revista de Legislação e de Jurisprudência* (1997-1998), pp. 354-359, at pp. 356-357.

THE EUROPEAN UNION AND THE GREEK CONSTITUTIONAL ORDER

Kostas Chryssogonos*

1. NATIONAL CONSTITUTION

The Greek Constitution of 1975 addresses the problem of the relationship between international and national law, as well as matters related to the accession of Greece to the European Communities, in its Art. 28.[1]

As far as international law in general is concerned one could hardly classify the Greek legal system as either monistic or dualistic. It is rather a mixture of both, since 'generally recognized rules of international law' (mainly international customary law, as well as general legal principles recognized by the international community) form a part of internal law directly, without any transformation, whereas international conventions need to be transformed through a statute. Both those sources of law have superior validity in comparison to ordinary statutes or normative acts, but they do not prevail over the constitution itself.[2]

The accession to the European Economic Community back in 1979 (effective as of January 1, 1981) was based upon paragraphs II and/or III of Article 28, which were meant to serve for that purpose,[3] although no specific reference to the

---

* Professor of Constitutional Law, University of Thessaloniki.

[1] 'I. Generally recognised rules of international law, as well as international conventions after they have been sanctioned by law and after they enter into force according to each one's terms, form an integral part of internal Greek law and prevail over any contrary provision of law.

II. To serve an important national interest and to promote co-operation with other States, competences provided for in the Constitution may be recognised by treaty or agreement to agencies of international organisations. A majority of three-fifths of the total number of members of Parliament is required for the approval of the Act which sanctions the treaty or agreement.

III. Greece may freely proceed, by virtue of an Act passed by the votes of the absolute majority of the total number of Members of Parliament, to limitations on the exercise of national sovereignty, insofar as this is dictated by an important national interest, does not infringe human rights and the foundations of democratic government and is effected on the basis of the principle of equality and on the condition of reciprocity'.

[2] See Ph. Spyropoulos, Constitutional Law in Hellas, The Hague-Athens 1995, p. 38.

[3] See D. Evrigenis, Legal and constitutional implications of Greek accession to the European Communities,CMLRev. 1980, p.157 et seq. (p. 160),Th. Antoniou, Europäische Integration und griechische Verfassung, Frankfurt a.M. 1985, p. 5 et seq.

A.E. Kellermann et al. (Eds.), EU Enlargement: The Constitutional Impact at EU and National Level

European integration can be found there. However there is a confusion between the procedural and material prerequisites of those two paragraphs: paragraph II seems to be setting higher procedural but lower material demands in comparison to paragraph III. As a consequence it has been argued that the constitutional foundation of the Greek accession was the composition of both paragraphs. In other words, a 3/5 parliamentary majority was needed together with the existence of a compelling national interest, the non-infringement of human rights and foundations of democratic government, as well as respect for the principles of equality and reciprocity.[4] It should be noted that Law No. 945/1979, which sanctioned the European Communities Treaties, as well as Law No. 2077/1992, which sanctioned the Maastricht Treaty, were affirmatively voted by a 3/5 majority of the Parliament.

There is no doubt whatsoever concerning the prevalence of both primary and secondary community laws over conflicting Greek laws and normative acts, either prior or later. It is less clear which is the reason for this prevalence: it could be found either in Article 28 of the Constitution or in the nature of European law, which must be applied unvaryingly in all member States, because otherwise its existence would be jeopardized.[5] If the reason for the superiority of European law is Article 28, then it is most likely that European norms do not prevail over conflicting constitutional norms,[6] although some legal scholars tend to accept that Article 28 institutes a special, latent revisionary procedure, parallel to that foreseen in Article 110 of the Greek Constitution, and that therefore European law supercedes even the Constitution itself.[7] If, on the other hand, the reason for the superiority is the nature of European law, then no distinction could be drawn between constitutional and other norms and European law has to prevail over all of them.[8] An intermediate theoretical position is that European law may not, in any case, exceed the material limits within which a transfer of competences has taken place according to Article 28 II and III of the Constitution (non-infringement of human rights and foundations of democratic government, etc.)[9].

There are no obvious contradictions between the European Union, European Community and Euratom Treaties, on the one hand, and the Greek Constitution

[4] See A. Fatouros, International law in the new Greek Constitution, AJIL 1976, p. 492 et seq. (pp. 499-500), D. Tsatsos, Constitutional Law, vol. A, 4th edn. Athens-Komotini 1994, p. 360 (in Greek).

[5] ECJ 6/64, *Costa* v. *ENEL*, Rec. 1964, p. 1141.

[6] See E. Venizelos, Lectures on Constitutional Law, I, Thessaloniki 1991, p. 161 (in Greek).

[7] See G. Papadimitriou, Europäische Integration und nationales Verfassungsrecht in Griechenland, in: U. Battis/D. Tsatsos/D. Stefanou, Europäische Intergration und nationales Verfassungsrecht, Baden-Baden 1995, p. 149 et seq. (p. 155 et seq.), J. Iliopoulou-Straga, Greek Constitutional Law and European integration, Athens-Komotini 1996, p. 37 et seq. (in Greek).

[8] See P. Stagose/E. Sahpekidou, European Communities Law, Thessaloniki 1994, pp. 156-158 (in Greek).

[9] See A. Manitakis, The limits of Community competence and their constitutional evaluation, 'To Syntagma' (Law Review) 1984, p. 472 et seq. (pp. 495-496).

on the other, although there is an ongoing discussion in Greek legal theory about possible discrepancies between them[10]. Therefore no constitutional amendment was considered to be required prior to the ratification of the Maastricht Treaty through Law No. 2077/1992.

It should also be mentioned that a major amendment proposal, which could result in changing almost half of the Articles of the Constitution, is now under discussion in Parliament. According to Article 110 the need for revision of the Constitution shall be confirmed by a resolution of Parliament adopted by a special majority. Subsequently, the next Parliament shall decide definitively, also by a special majority, on the provisions to be revised. The need to revise, among others, Article 28 II-III has been confirmed by a resolution of the previous Parliament, which was dissolved in March 2000. The Parliament which was elected in the general elections of April 2000 will decide within its current session (until June 2001) on the final wording of Article 28. The aim of the revision is to add an interpretative clause to Article 28 II-III, in order to make it easier for Greece to participate in the process of European integration, under observance of the safeguards already foreseen in Article 28 II-III.[11]

2. ROLE OF COURTS

Greek courts have rarely confronted the problem of the hierarchical relationship between European law and the national constitution. In some cases it is obvious that the Greek court is deliberately trying to avoid addressing the issue by denying the existence of a divergence between EU law and the constitution. For example, a Division of the Council of State (supreme administrative court) considered that the Constitution prevails over EC law. It therefore concluded that, since Article 16 paragraph V of the Constitution foresees that education at university level in Greece shall be provided exclusively by Greek public institutions, a bachelors degree obtained at a French University on the ground of studies which have partially taken place on Greek soil cannot be recognized even if this would violate EC law.[12] However, the Division transferred the whole case, because of its major importance, to the Plenum of the Council of State, which evaded the issue of hierarchy between the Constitution and EC law, by holding that non-recognition of the university degree in question did not contravene EC law.[13]

In other cases, where the conformity of national norms below the constitutional level (such as statutes, presidential decrees, etc.) to EC law was questioned, Greek courts readily admitted that EC law, either primary or secondary, is to be

[10] See, e.g., Iliopoulou-Straga, op. cit., p. 56 et seq.
[11] See E. Venizelos, The revision of the Constitution, Athens-Komotini 1998, p. 276 (in Greek).
[12] Council of State 2809/1997, 'To Syntagma' 1998, p. 943 et seq.
[13] Council of State 3457/1998, 'To Syntagma' 1998, p. 961 et seq.

given precedence over the national norms. However, this conclusion was not based on the nature of European law, but on Article 28 of the Greek Constitution. Furthermore, no specific reference to any paragraph of Article 28 was made. It is therefore hard to distinguish whether Community law is regarded as a subsystem of international treaty law, according to paragraph I of Article 28, which ranks between the constitution and common statutes, or whether its prevalence over national norms that contradict it is a consequence of the transfer of competences to community agencies, according to paragraph II.

More specifically, the Council of State[14] and the Areopag (supreme civil and penal court)[15] accept that, after the accession of Greece to the European Communities, according to Article 28 EC law forms an integral part of the internal Greek legal order and prevails over any law contradicting it. Both supreme courts have stated further that EC law has direct effect in the Greek legal order and that the abolition of internal laws contradicting it is not a prerequisite for its validity, since it prevails anyway over those laws. The Council of State[16] as well as the Areopag[17] have also held that EC directives may become directly effective and binding on the state, if the national lawmaker has not converted them into internal law within the limits provided by them and if the content of the directive is clear and precise enough. However, such an unconverted directive is effective only vertically (against the state) and not horizontally (between private parties).[18]

It should be mentioned here that no Constitutional Court exists in Greece and therefore the judicial review of the constitutionality of laws and/or their conformity to European and international law is allowed to every court. The result of a judgment of non-conformity is, in principle, that the law will not be applied in concreto, although formally it still remains valid, since case law precedents are principally not binding. As far as regulatory acts of the executive branch are concerned, their validity (including conformity to European law) can be directly challenged before the Council of State (Art. 95 Ia of the Constitution). However, the omission to convert an EC directive into Greek law may not be challenged in such a direct way before the Council of State, because its implementation could take place either through a parliamentary statute or through a regulatory act of the executive.[19]

As far as the interpretation of national provisions is concerned, there seems to be no explicit reference to any rule whereby these provisions should be interpreted in conformity with international or, more specifically, with EC law obligations. However, such an interpretation has actually been practiced sometimes. For example, concerning the meaning of the term 'public service', to which only

[14] See Council of State Decision 2152/1986, 'To Syntagma' (Law Review) 1986, p. 452 et seq.
[15] See Aeropag 1008/1993, 'Elliniki Dikaiosyni' (Law Review) 1994, p. 355 et seq.
[16] Council of State 3493/1995, 'Armenopoulos' (Law Review) 1996, p. 100 et seq.
[17] Aeropag 23/1998, 'To Syntagma' 1998, p. 1141 et seq.
[18] Aeropag 23/1998 (see fn. 17).
[19] Council of State 2070/1999, 'Nomiko Vima' (Law Review) 2000, p. 361 et seq.

Greek citizens have access according to Article 4 paragraph IV of the Constitution, the Council of State seems to have adapted the constitutional interpretation,[20] in order to avoid any collision with Article 48 of the EC Treaty, as it has been interpreted by ECJ.[21]

There is also no answer to be found in Greek case law concerning the matter of priority where a Community measure is inconsistent with the international commitments of Greece, either prior or subsequent to it.

3. ROLE OF GOVERNMENT AND ADMINISTRATION

It is difficult to pass a general judgment on the extent to which the Greek Government and administrative authorities are implementing the acquis communautaire in practice, because the matter of implementation is often complicated and because the acquis now penetrates a huge variety of issues. Greek authorities seem in most cases to be willing faithfully to implement the acquis, in part due to the fact that the overall political climate in the country is favorable to Greek participation in the European integration process. The visibly positive results of the membership of the EC over the last two decades have led both major political forces (the New Democracy Party and the Socialist Party, which was eurosceptic in the early 1980s), as well as public opinion for its most part, to a pro-European attitude. Therefore, the political conditions for the implementation of community obligations do exist in most cases. Sometimes, however, administrative malfunctions and/or the resistance of strong pressure groups have led to long delays and to condemnations at the ECJ.

The case of Directive 89/48/EEC is fairly representative. This directive, which provides for a general system of recognition of third-level education degrees certifying professional training of at least three years, has not been fully implemented in Greek law, mainly because of the strong resistance of the Technical Chamber of Greece (TEE). Members of the TEE are engineers having obtained a university degree on the ground of studies which regularly take five years. They are vehemently opposing the recognition of significant professional rights to engineers who have obtained a technical education degree on the ground of studies which regularly take three and a half or four years. The inability of the authorities to solve this critical situation has already led to one condemnation at the ECJ.[22]

In another case, Greece was found to be in breach of its obligations arising from Article 4 and 6 of Directive 75/442/EEC and from Article 5 and 12 of Directive 78/319/EEC, because the way of disposing of garbage in the area of Chania, Crete, was not in conformity with the demands arising from these direc-

[20] Council of State, Decree elaboration 380/1996, 'To Syntagma' 1996, p. 1069 et seq.
[21] ECJ C-290/94, *Commission* v. *Greece*, Decision of 2.7.1996.
[22] ECJ C-365/93, *Commission* v. *Greece*, Decision of 23.3.1995.

tives.[23] Nevertheless, the reactions of local populations against placing the necessary installations near their villages caused a further delay of several years in achieving compliance with these directives is concerned. The result was a second condemnation in the same case through the ECJ,[24] which was accompanied by a 20,000 euros per day fine, for as long as non-compliance continues.

4. CONCLUDING REMARKS

As an overall conclusion one could remark that the Greek constitutional order has adapted in a rather satisfying way to the demands of EC law, despite problems arising in particular issues.

However, there is a good chance that Greece could be found more often to be in breach of EC law if private persons were permitted to challenge the conformity of internal laws to EC law before the ECJ, even after exhausting domestic remedies. Of course, this could probably be the case not only for Greece, but also for many other member States. So far the European Convention on Human Rights, which opens up the possibility of individual application to the European Court of Human Rights (Art. 34f) as a last resort against violations of conventional rights by its member States, seems to be setting a fairly good example of a relatively effective implementation of transnational rules.

In contrast, Article 227 (ex-Art. 170) and 228 (ex-Art. 171) of the EC Treaty give direct access to the ECJ, as far as breaches of community law by member States are concerned, only to the Commission and to the other member States. Indirect access to the ECJ is permitted to individuals by Article 234 (ex-Art. 177), since allegations of breaches of EC law before national courts may lead them to submit a preliminary question to the ECJ, concerning the interpretation of the community rules. However, it is up to the national court to judge whether such an interpretation is necessary or not. It seems that sometimes Greek courts tend to dismiss allegations of non-conformity of national norms to EC law, without considering it necessary to submit a preliminary question to the ECJ, even though it is likely that the ECJ could interpret the community provisions coming into question in a different way.[25] The failure of some national courts, even of last resort, to make references to the ECJ, in cases in which they ought to, is of course not only a Greek problem. On the contrary, the theory of the 'act clair', which is of French origin,[26] has been repeatedly applied by various national courts,[27] potentially undermining the primacy of community law. Therefore, one could seek for solutions rather at EU than at national level.

[23] ECJ C-45/91, *Commission* v. *Greece*, Decision of 7.4.1992.

[24] ECJ C-387/97, *Commission* v. *Greece*, Decision of 4.7.2000.

[25] See, for example, Council of State 4674/1998, 'To Syntagma' 1999, p.106 et seq.

[26] See J. Boulouis, Droit institutionnel de l'Union européenne, 5th ed. Paris 1995, pp. 302-303.

[27] See, for example, A. Arnull, The European Union and its Court of Justice, Oxford 1999, p. 68, Boulouis, op. cit., p. 300.

INTRODUCTION TO THE PROBLEMS IN THE AUSTRIAN, THE FINNISH AND SWEDISH CONSTITUTIONAL ORDER

Stefan Griller*

I. INTRODUCTION

The purpose of this contribution is to give an introduction into the most fundamental constitutional aspects of EU membership in Austria, Finland and Sweden. The emphasis is on the opening up of the national legal systems for EU and EC law, especially the transfer of powers including the supremacy of Community law. Some remarks are devoted to the participatory rights of national parliaments in Community law-making, and to the fate of neutrality, even if the latter is of specific *constitutional* relevance only in Austria. Excluded are further fundamental issues such as the constitutional conditions for and practice of the implementation of directives, or constitutional aspects of state liability in cases of a breach of Community law; excluded also are provisions of a more complementary nature irrespective of their importance, such as constitutional amendments concerning the elections to the European Parliament.

II. AUSTRIA

A. A Fundamental Change of the Austrian Constitutional System

As a constitutional prerequisite of EU membership, the Austrian constitution had to be totally amended. 'Total revision' (*Gesamtänderung*) in this context is meant as a terminus technicus: a total revision of the Austrian constitution requires not only, like every constitutional law, a 2/3 majority in parliament, but also a positive vote in a referendum.[1] Such a procedure has to take place whenever one of

---

* Professor Research Institute for European Affairs, Wirtschaftsuniversität Wien.

[1] Article 44 para. 3 B-VG (Bundes-Verfassungsgesetz = Federal-Constitutional Law).

The Austrian constitution is, generally speaking, a rather flexible legal instrument. There is no 'eternity clause', meaning that, at least in principle, every change can be introduced, provided that the procedure for constitutional amendments is observed. [This prevailing view has recently be challenged by *Pernthaler*, Der Verfassungskern, Vienna 1998.] A 2/3 majority vote in parliament (the National Council/Nationalrat) is necessary as well as the explicit designation of the provision as a constitutional law. A referendum has only to take place if 1/3 of the members of Parliament so wish.

A.E. Kellermann et al. (Eds.), EU Enlargement: The Constitutional Impact at EU and National Level

the fundamental principles of the constitution is to be amended or abandoned. These principles are democracy, the rule of law, the separation of powers, the liberal principle enshrined in the guarantee of fundamental rights and freedoms, and the federal and the republican organisation of the state.

There was widespread consent that EU membership would bring about a fundamental change to several of these principles, at least that of democracy, separation of powers and the rule of law.[2]

Against this background, the Austrian Parliament passed a bill, which was the subject of a referendum before its entry into force and before the signing of the Treaty of Accession. The referendum took place in June 1994 and produced a vast majority of more the 66% of positive votes.

The result of this procedure, the Constitutional Act on Austria's Accession to the EU[3] (the so-called EU Accession Act) in its most important Articles reads as follows[4]:

Only in cases of a total revision is a referendum mandatory. Amendments of the constitutional legal order also need not necessarily be incorporated into the core constitutional act, the Bundes-Verfassungsgesetz (Federal Constitutional Act), but can instead also be done by leges fugitivae. This is a similarity to the situation in Finland (see below in the text near n. 67).

[2] Compare for the following, e.g., *Griller*, 'Verfassungsfragen der österreichischen EU-Mitgliedschaft', *Zeitschrift für Rechtsvergleichung und Europarecht* 1995, pp. 89-115; *Griller*, Individueller Rechtsschutz und Gemeinschaftsrecht, in *Aicher/Holoubek/Korinek* (Hrsg), Gemeinschaftsrecht und Wirtschaftsrecht, Vienna 2000, pp. 27-157; *Öhlinger*, Verfassungsfragen einer Mitgliedschaft zur Europäischen Union (1999); *Öhlinger/Potacs*, Gemeinschaftsrecht und nationales Recht, Vienna 1998; *Schäffer*, Österreichischer Landesbericht, in *Schwarze* (ed), Die Entstehung einer europäischen Verfassungsordnung, Baden-Baden 2000, pp. 339-387; all with further references.

For contributions in English compare *Seidl-Hohenveldern*, Constitutional Problems Involved in Austria's Accession to the EU, CMLRev. 1995, pp. 727-741; *Lengauer*, First Experiences with EU-membership – the Case of Austria, in *Kandžija* et al. (eds.), Economic System of European Union and Adjustment of the Republic of Croatia, Lovran 1999, pp. 539-551.

For a general survey on the Austrian legal system in English compare *Hausmaninger*, The Austrian Legal System, Vienna 2000; on the legal effects of EU membership, pp. 92-99.

[3] Bundesverfassungsgesetz über den Beitritt Österreichs zur Europäischen Union, BGBl (Federal Law Gazette) 1994/744.

[4] Translation by the author. The complete original version of this brief law is as follows:
'Bundesverfassungsgesetz über den Beitritt Österreichs zur Europäischen Union
Auf Grund des Ergebnisses der Volksabstimmung wird kundgemacht:
Artikel I
Mit Zustimmung des Bundesvolkes zu diesem Bundesverfassungsgesetz werden die bundesverfassungsgesetzlich zuständigen Organe ermächtigt, den Staatsvertrag über den Beitritt Österreichs zur Europäischen Union entsprechend dem am 12. April 1994 von der Beitrittskonferenz festgelegten Verhandlungsergebnis abzuschließen.
Artikel II
Der Staatsvertrag über den Beitritt Österreichs zur Europäischen Union darf nur mit Genehmigung des Nationalrates und der Zustimmung des Bundesrates hiezu abgeschlossen werden. Diese Beschlüsse bedürfen jeweils der Anwesenheit von mindestens der Hälfte der Mitglieder und einer Mehrheit von zwei Dritteln der abgegebenen Stimmen.
Artikel III
Mit der Vollziehung dieses Bundesverfassungsgesetzes ist die Bundesregierung betraut.'

> Article I: With the approval of the Austrian people to this Constitutional Law the competent organs under the federal constitution are authorized to conclude the Treaty on Austria's Accession to the EU according to the results of the accession conference agreed upon on April 12, 1994.
> Article II: The Treaty on Austria's accession to the EU may only be concluded with the approval of the *Nationalrat* [National Council] and the *Bundesrat* [Federal Council]. These decisions require the presence of at least half of the respective members and a two-thirds majority of the votes cast.

It was contended that this text hides more than it reveals. This is certainly true insofar as it did not make clear that the referendum (the 'approval of the Austrian people') was mandatory and why this was the case.

However this may be, the legal effects of this authorization of the total revision of the Austrian Constitution by concluding the Treaty of Accession[5] may be summarized as follows:

- Austria's accession to the EU was enacted on the basis of a specific constitutional law of the highest possible rank within the Austrian legal order.
- The authorization for this step was deliberately narrow: it covered only the conclusion of the Treaty of Accession according to the results of the accession conference in April 1994. Any later alterations of the drafted text would have been excluded from approval and ratification. Furthermore, the authorization does not cover later amendments of the EU legal order, especially not those agreed upon during intergovernmental conferences.[6]
- The EU Accession Act only implicitly – by referring to the Draft Treaty of Accession and the Act of Accession which included, inter alia, the obligation to accept the *acquis communautaire* – tackled the crucial issue of the relation between EC (and EU) law and Austrian law.[7] As will be discussed further, this leaves several core aspects open to controversy.

An important and direct consequence of this way into the EU is that every future amendment of the Treaties is difficult to judge in terms of its constitutional ratification requirements. In particular, every approval and subsequent ratification of such amendments without constitutional majorities would be risky. An allegation to have violated the constitution would be very likely. Consequently, in the case of the Amsterdam Treaty, the government again decided to propose the approval and the ratification of the Treaty on the basis of a special Constitutional Act. By contrast to the Accession Treaty, this Constitutional Act was (rightly) not treated as a total revision of the constitution. But like the EU Accession Act it necessi-

---

[5] It is submitted that the changes were not brought about directly by the EU Accession Act, but by the conclusion of the Treaty of Accession on the grounds of the EU Accession Act.

[6] Article 46 (ex Art. N) TEU.

[7] On these issues, nothing can be found either in the flanking constitutional measures adopted to ease the transition to EU membership (see below n. 12).

tated a qualified approval of the Treaty – this time, the Amsterdam Treaty – by the Austrian Parliament. The approval by the *Nationalrat* [National Council] and the *Bundesrat* [Federal Council] required the presence of at least half of the respective members and a two-thirds majority of the votes[8], which is the majority usually required for amendments of the Constitution.

As a consequence, it might be said that the Austrian way into the EU appears to be unique among all EU members.[9] This is so since the accession happened on the grounds of a constitutional law of the highest possible rank. As we shall see, this prevented several obstacles to proper implementation of Community law in Austria which occurred in other countries. A certain similarity, however, seems to exist with regard to the traditional Irish way[10] to enact a specific constitutional law for each amendment of the basic Treaties.

Austria's Accession to the EU did not only entail the most fundamental change to the constitutional order since 1918, the starting point of the continuous development of the Austrian constitutional order;[11] the Austrian parliament also passed flanking constitutional measures, mainly providing for the participation of Austrian organs in EU decision-making (including the CFSP), for the election of Austrian members to the European Parliament, and for the appointment of members to the European Commission, the ECJ and the CFI, the Court of auditors, the board of the European Investment Bank, the Economic and Social Committee, and the Committee of the Regions.[12] A delicate issue is the fate of Austria's permanent neutrality. Only the first and the last mentioned issue shall be explained further.[13]

---

[8] Article I Bundesverfassungsgesetz über den Abschluß des Vertrages von Amsterdam (Constitutional Act on the conclusion of the Amsterdam Treaty), BGBl (Federal Law Gazette) I 1998/76.

[9] The Austrian Chancellery could rely on a comparative study on the constitutional foundations of membership in the then 12 EC member States, which was undertaken as a part of the preparations for membership – see *Griller/Maislinger/Reindl*, Fundamentale Rechtsgrundlagen einer EG-Mitgliedschaft. Verfassungsfragen der Übernahme von EG-Recht in den bisherigen Mitgliedstaaten in vergleichender Sicht, Vienna 1991. It might be concluded that at least in parts the specific steps taken were a deliberate departure from the previous examples.

[10] An important difference is of course the rank of the authorizing provision.

[11] Naturally, this means with the exception of the nazi government from 1938-1945. After 1945, the constitutional order was 'reset' to the state of the law in 1933 (before the constitutional amendments which led to the so-called 'Ständestaat').

[12] Articles 23a-23f B-VG. Compare, e.g., *Grabenwarter*, 'Änderungen der österreichischen Bundesverfassung aus Anlaß des Beitritts zur Europäischen Union', *Zeitschrift für ausländisches öffentliches Recht und Völkerrecht* 1995, pp. 166-190; *Holzinger*, Die Auswirkungen der österreichischen EU-Mitglietschaft auf das österreichische Verfassungsrecht, Journal für Rechtspolitik 1996, pp. 160-192.

[13] See below II.C. and II.D.

B. Consequences for the Relation Between EC Law and Austrian Law

1. *Unconditional Membership*

Unlike other EU members, Austria in the course of its accession procedure, did not adopt any constitutional reservations regarding EU membership. By contrast, the reasons attached to the draft EU Accession Act make abundantly clear that the intention was to accept unconditionally the principles developed by the ECJ governing the relation between EC law and national law. It was explicitly stated that the EU Accession Act should guarantee the opening up of the Austrian legal order for the legal order of the EU according to its specific requirements, especially including supremacy and direct effect.[14]

Thus, the prevailing view is that the EU Accession Act does not, like, e.g., Article 23 of the German Basic Law, include any *specific constitutional* reservation regarding the implementation and enforcement of primary or secondary EC law.[15] Provided EC (and EU) law is within the boundaries of the 'results of the accession conference' of 1994, every alteration of the Austrian legal system was accepted in advance. There might be a – more theoretical – possibility to question the legality of EC or EU law in cases of apparent and severe *ultra vires acts*, but not one founded on the violation of *constitutional* principles.[16]

However, the 'Austrian way' also provoked a debate on further consequences which might be of general interest, and which might also influence future case law, if that did not already happen tacitly. A first possible interpretation of the reported constitutional changes is that the Austrian constitution was opened up for the incorporation of EC and EU law, and that this includes amendments of the traditional rules governing the relationship of municipal law and international law. These alterations, however, would be limited by the need for the proper fulfilment of the membership duties to abide by EC and EU law. These alterations would therefore not go further than what is necessary to reach that goal.[17] Consequently, the Treaty of Accession would have to be considered as a Treaty transformed into the Austrian legal order, the legal effects of which are not determined by the traditional constitutional rules for international Treaties, but by the

---

[14] See 1546 BlgNR (attachments to the minutes of the National Council) XVIII. GP (legislative period), p. 4.

[15] E.g., *Griller* (n. 2) Verfassungsfragen p. 99 et seq.; *Öhlinger* (n. 2) p. 180 et seq.

[16] This is not to say that thereby constitutional principles could not be 'protected' indirectly (because of a lack of competence of the Communities, e.g., to dissolve the Austrian Parliament).

The issue in the above text is also to be distinguished from eventual changes of primary law by subsequent treaties like the Amsterdam or the Nice Treaty. The conclusion of such treaties will, as was explained above, nearly always trigger the necessity of further constitutional steps.

[17] Argued in *Griller*, Der Stufenbau der österreichischen Rechtsordnung nach dem EU-Beitritt, Journal für Rechtspolitik 2000, p. 273 (p. 278 et seq.).

jurisprudence of the ECJ. Secondary EC law would form a part of Austrian law, its legal effects to a large extent also being determined by EC law.

An alternative view is that Austria's accession to the EU is, in terms of the consequences for the legal system, to be treated as the accession to a federal state.[18] Consequently, the Accession Treaty is to be seen as both an international Treaty and similar to the founding act of a federal state. Consequently, there cannot be any 'transformation' of the Accession Treaty – and, consequently, of the *acquis communautaire* and future EC legislation – into the Austrian legal order. Moreover, the legal effects of Community law in Austria are in no way influenced by (modified) principles on the relationship between municipal and international law, but solely by the 'autonomous' legal order of the EC and EU respectively.

A third reading put forward in the debate is that EC law and national law are two distinct legal systems, to be treated in the sense of a dualist understanding.[19] EC law and national law are founded in two completely separated legal grounds ('Geltungsgründe'), and not by one common legal fundament. Also this position arrives at a complete alteration of the legal situation. The conclusion to be drawn is that EC law is not 'part of the law of the land' in Austria. Due to the dualist construction, EC law forms a legal order of its own. Also according to this view the Treaty of Accession has not been transformed into the Austrian legal order, which would be the same for the *acquis communautaire* and presumably also for future secondary legislation. However, it is hard to see how to resolve possible conflicts between EC law and national law on the ground of this 'dualist approach', except if the EU Accession Act could be read as incorporating the 'second', the EU legal order, into the Austrian legal system.

At first sight, all this might appear as a purely academic debate. However, it can be argued that the consequences of EU membership especially for the functions of the system of judicial protection enshrined in the Austrian constitution – to be discussed below – are dependent on the underlying theoretical approach.

2. *Supremacy and Openness to Judicial Enforcement of EC Law in the Judiciary*

Supremacy of Community law was quickly and undisputedly accepted by all three of the Highest Courts in Austria – the Supreme Court (*Oberster Gerichtshof* – OGH), mainly competent for issues of private law and penal law, the Constitutional Court (*Verfassungsgerichtshof* – VfGH), inter alia, competent for the constitutional scrutiny of law of a general nature (be it statutory law passed by parliament or ordinances issued by the executive) as well as for the scrutiny of indi-

---

[18] Argued in *Öhlinger* (n. 2) p. 194, p. 201 et seq.

[19] Argued in *Funk*, Rechtserzeugung heute – Rechtserzeugung im 21. Jahrhundert, in *Holoubek/Lienbacher* (eds.), Rechtspolitik der Zukunft – Zukunft der Rechtspolitik (1999) p. 45 (p. 49 et seq.).

vidual acts for alleged violations of the constitution, and the Administrative Court (*Verwaltungsgerichtshof* – VwGH), mainly competent to deal with complaints against administrative decisions addressed to individuals ('Bescheide').[20] However, it is still very interesting to contemplate on the scope of the principle and the consequences for the courts.

A recent case[21] concerns indirect conflicts between EC law and Austrian law in the field of legal protection. The Constitutional Court did not hesitate to set aside a *constitutional* law provision which restricted access to the Administrative Court in Austria. The Constitutional Court considered whether the Austrian law on telecommunications ('TKG') was compatible with the pertinent Community law, in particular the so-called Open-Network-Provision Directive (ONP Directive).[22] Article 5a para. 3 of that Directive requires member States to ensure that suitable mechanisms exist at national level under which a party affected by a decision of the national regulatory authority has a right of appeal to a body independent of the parties involved. In Austrian law, this body is the Telekom-Control-Kommission. In terms of the Austrian legal system, this is not a court (*Gericht*) but a board (*Kollegialbehörde*), that is, an executive body entrusted with judicial functions under the Federal Constitution. It is thus (very likely) a tribunal within the meaning of Article 6 ECHR and a court or tribunal within the meaning of Article 234 TEC. A special provision of the Constitution (Art. 133 no. 4 B-VG) excludes appeals before the Administrative Court whenever such a board decides a matter at last instance.[23] Recognising that Article 5a of the ONP Directive has direct effect, the Verfassungsgerichtshof held that primacy of Community law over national law requires that Article 133 no. 4 B-VG, which is the only obstacle to such an appeal, should be set aside in this case.

As a result, appeal to the Administrative Court (VwGH) appeared possible. However, the VwGH quite obviously was not convinced by the interpretation given by the Constitutional Court.[24] When the matter was brought before the VwGH,[25] this court sought a preliminary ruling by the ECJ aiming to clarify whether Article 5a ONP Directive really had to be interpreted to the end that the Telekom-Control-Kommission itself has to be excluded as the required indepen-

---

[20] Compare only the first judgments in this respect: VfGH 26 Nov. 1996, B 2955/95; VfGH 12 April 1997, G 400/96 (VfSlg 14.805/1997); VwGH 23 Oct. 1995, 95/10/0081; VwGH 25 June 1996, 96/09/0088; OGH 14 Sept. 1995, 8 Ob S 37/95. See also *Öhlinger/Potacs* (n.2) p. 84 et seq.

[21] VfGH, B 1625/98, 1999-02-24.

[22] Dir 90/387/EEC as amended by Dir 97/51/EC.

[23] Such an appeal to the VwGH is only admissible if explicitly stated by the ordinary law regulating the matter in question. However, this was not so in our case.

[24] In fact, it can hardly be said that the interpretation given by the VfGH was beyond reasonable doubt. Therefore one could have assumed an obligation of the VfGH itself under Article 234 TEC to bring the matter before the ECJ. The VwGH in its reference to the ECJ rightly pointed to Case C-54/96, *Dorsch Consult*, [1997] ECR, I-4961, paras. 40 et seq., which raises doubts regarding the position of the VfGH.

[25] VwGH, Zl 99/03/0071, 1999-11-24; see the pending case C-462/99, *Connect Austria*.

dent appellate body and if so, whether the directive was, on this point, unconditional and precise enough to supersede the mentioned constitutional provision excluding an appeal to the VwGH.

In the case at issue, there is an obvious controversy between the two courts of public law on the interpretation of the directive at issue, and the better arguments might be on the side of the VwGH. But the judgment of the VfGH provides evidence for the far-reaching openness of Austrian courts to give way for the efficient application of EC law. In this regard, and instead of going more into the analysis of the case law, it might be instructive to point to the table at the end of this paper which shows that in 1999 Austria was second to none even in terms of *absolute* figures concerning requests for preliminary rulings of the ECJ, already during the years before remarkably high numbers were registered. In the meantime, all three of the Highest Courts – including the Constitutional Court[26] – have sought preliminary rulings by the ECJ.

However, it is already more difficult to explain why this is so. I would suggest that is it a combination of, first, the *unconditional* constitutional basis of EU membership, second, a sound preparation of EU membership which included the introduction of specific procedural rules for the opening of preliminary ruling procedures not only in ordinary courts but also for tribunals and for the courts of public law, third, a remarkable effort in the field of post-graduate education aiming at lawyers and civil servants to make them familiar with issues of EC law, and fourth, a result of the rich variety of courts and tribunals within the federal constitutional system which all come in touch with issues of European Integration.

3. *Constitutional Review as a Means to Enforce EC Law?*

(1) A controversial issue is whether a violation of EC law could at the same time also be qualified as a violation of the Austrian constitution. This would open the existing competence of the Constitutional Court to measure Austrian law by constitutional provisions also for the enforcement of EC law. The arguments in favour of such a position are that, on the grounds of the EU Accession Act, there is a *constitutional* duty to abide by EC law, or that EC law is to be regarded as 'material' constitutional law insofar as it has always to be taken into consideration when a new act is to be adopted, and at least partly also that the Community principle of equivalent judicial protection for EC law requires the application of a remedy which is open for complaints on alleged violations of the constitution.[27]

---

[26] VfGH, B 2251/97, B 2594/97, 1999-03-10 (VfSlg 15.450/1999). The case concers a state aid matter. Some critics would add that this happened after a four year period of hesitation.

[27] For a discussion of the issue see *Griller*, in *Aicher/Holoubek/Korinek* (n. 2), p. 127 et seq. The prevailing view in literature is critical to such suggestions and supports the position of the Constitutional Court – e.g., *Öhlinger/Potacs* (n. 2) p. 152 et seq.; compare also two literary contributions of

However, the Constitutional Court rejected that view.[28] It declared that in its view a violation of EC law is, under Austrian law, equal to a violation not of constitutional, but of 'ordinary' legislation.[29] Consequently, the protection against violations of EC law is, according to the VfGH, not a matter for this court, but a matter of the Administrative Court, which is in principle competent to prevent all sorts of violation of the law by the executive. And in fact, within its competence, the VwGH follows this view.

(2) Another judgment by the Austrian *Verfassungsgerichtshof* (VfGH)[30] considered the relationship between the principle of the primacy of Community law and the functions of the *Verfassungsgerichtshof* regarding the constitutional review of national legislation in the national legal order. The issue was whether a possible conflict of national law with superseding EC law could be an obstacle for the VfGH to declare that law null and void on the ground of violation of the constitution (not on the ground of violation of EC law!). The problem occurred since the admissibility of a respective complaint is dependent on an alleged violation of the constitution by eventual 'application' of the respective law. But if the primacy of Community law prevents the application of the law, would that not mean that any procedure on the violation of the constitution is to be declared inadmissible as long as the compatibility of the law with EC law is not established?

The core aspect of the judgment is that such constitutional scrutiny is only inadmissible if the application of the law in question is completely inconceivable ('denkunmöglich'). As long as the contention that there is no superseding EC law is fairly reasonable there is also no hindrance for the court to fulfil its duty of constitutional review.[31]

The case concerned the *Burgenländische Tourismus-Förderungsgesetz* (Promotion of Tourism Act in the Province of Burgenland) 1992, providing for a tax to promote tourism in Burgenland on the basis of the net yield 'within the meaning of the VAT Act (*Umsatzsteuergesetz*)'. In similar cases in Styria, the Tyrol

---

sitting judges of the Constitutional Court (VfGH): *Holzinger*, Zu den Auswirkungen der österreichischen EU-Mitgliedschaft auf das Rechtsschutzsystem der Bundesverfassung, in *Haller* et al. (eds.), Staat und Recht. Winkler-FS, Vienna 1997, p. 351 (at p. 357); *Korinek*, Die Bedeutung des Gemeinschaftsrechts für das verfassungsgerichtliche Verfahren, in *Holoubek/Lang* (Hrsg) Das verfassungsgerichtliche Verfahren in Steuersachen, Vienna 1998, p. 31 et seq.

[28] VfSlg (Constitutional Court Reports) 14.886/1997: '... ein Verstoß gegen Gemeinschaftsrecht [ist] aus der Sicht des Verfassungsgerichtshofes der Verletzung einfachgesetzlicher Vorschriften gleichzuhalten ..., die wahrzunehmen der Verwaltungsgerichtshof berufen ist ...'.

[29] Obviously this position has a strong affinity to that of the a) Spanish Constitutional Court; compare Judgment No. 28/1991 of 14 February 1991, and Judgment No. 64/1991 of 22 March 1991, and the contribution of *Garzón Clariana* in this volume; and b) the Portuguese Constitutional Court; starting with decision No 326/98 (case.E 25/97) of 5 May 1998, in Diário da República, II Série, n.E 160, 14 July 1998, pp. 9745-9747, and the contribution of *Moura Ramos* in this volume.

[30] VfGH, G 2/97, 1998-06-24 (VfSlg 15.215/1998).

[31] For a discussion of the judgment see *Griller*, in *Aicher/Holoubek/Korinek* (n. 2), p. 138 et seq.

and Carinthia, the *Verwaltungsgerichtshof* (VwGH) had sought preliminary rulings from the Court of Justice on the question whether Article 33 para. 1 of the Sixth VAT Directive precluded such taxes, i.e., whether this was a form of VAT or not.[32] The VfGH did not refer the question to the ECJ but reviewed the statute *for constitutionality* in relation to the domestic legal order. Its justification for proceeding in this fashion was that there was no possible conflict between its decision whether or not to annul the statute and the fact that the effect of the primacy of Community law was that legislation conflicting with Community law was automatically disallowed. The VfGH declared that where it did not annul a statute for incompatibility with the Austrian Constitution, it was for the highest Austrian court exercising public-law jurisdiction to clarify the question of compatibility with Community law (seeking a preliminary ruling in appropriate cases).[33]

In the instant case, the VfGH held that it had to annul a phrase of the scrutinized law as inconsistent with the *constitutional* principle of equality, since applying the phrase would render net yields not only in Burgenland but throughout the country subject to the tax to promote tourism.

As a consequence of the position that constitutional scrutiny is only admissible as long as the applicability of the law is not completely unconceivable ('denkunmöglich'), the VfGH, in a later case, terminated a procedure aiming at the annulment of a statutory law for the reason that its inapplicability was obvious.[34] The court noted that after the complaint against a decision of an administrative body had been filed with the VfGH, a judgment of the ECJ had made it sufficiently clear that the law at issue – concerning a differentiation between full-time and part-time employees in the pharmaceutical sector regarding financial claims – violated the equal pay principle under EC law.[35] Supremacy of EC law thus required the law in the present case to be set aside. Consequently, the precondition for the constitutional scrutiny was missing, which led to the termination of the procedure.

The starting point of the procedure had been a complaint against an administrative decision which actually had applied the Austrian law. Since that law was,

---

[32] The ECJ in Joined Cases C-338/97, C-344/97 and C-390/97, *Erna Pelzl and Others*, [1999] ECR I-3319 could not find a violation of Community law: 'The Sixth Council Directive (77/388/EEC) of 17 May 1977 on the harmonisation of the laws of the member States relating to turnover taxes – Common system of value added tax: uniform basis of assessment, and in particular Article 33 thereof, does not preclude a charge of the kind introduced by the Steiermärkische Tourismusgesetz, the Tiroler Tourismusgesetz and the Kärntner Fremdenverkehrsabgabegesetz, which is payable by traders in a federal Land who have an economic interest in tourism, which is calculated, in principle, on the basis of annual turnover and from which input tax is not deductible.'

[33] At that stage, eventual primacy and direct effect would lead to an obligation to disallow the Austrian law.

[34] VfGH G 57/98, 1998-11-12 (VfSlg 15.368/1998).

[35] Article 119 (now Art. 141) ECT. The VfGH referred to Case C-243/95, *Hill Stapleton*, [1998] ECR, I-3739.

according to the VfGH, inapplicable, this rendered the administrative decision illegal, simply for the reason that the required legal fundament in an Act of Parliament was missing. The Court stated – after having terminated the constitutional scrutiny of the inapplicable law, and coming back to the orginal complaint against the administrative decision – that the decision violated the fundamental right to private property, since it severely curtailed this right without a proper legal basis.[36]

C. Participatory Rights of Parliament

In an effort to mitigate the repercussions of EU membership on the constitutional principle of democracy, an effort was made to foster parliamentary influence as well as regional and local influence for the conduct of Austria's representatives in the EU. The primary target of these efforts were the ministers as members of the Council of the European Union. Without going into detail it might be said that the most important rules concern participatory rights of the Austrian provinces and of the *Nationalrat* [National Council], the peoples chamber of the Austrian Parliament. Included is not only a right to be informed on developments at EU and EC level, but also a right to issue opinions which are binding on the government.[37]

The federal government is obliged to inform the provinces (*die Länder*) on all projects of the European Union which affect the autonomous sphere of the *Länder*. The *Länder* (and also representative bodies of local entities) have the right to express opinions in these matters. In the case of the *Länder*, such opinions are binding on the federal government provided that they reach a 'uniform' opinion.[38] This is only the case if a majority of the 9 *Länder* votes for such an opinion and no one makes use of its veto right. The federal government may only depart from a uniform opinion for compelling reasons of foreign and integration policy. In practice this procedure is of minor importance.

The second and in practice more important possibility is that the *Nationalrat* [National Council] adopts an opinion on projects of the European Union. Such

[36] VfGH B 3073/96, 1999-03-05 (VfSlg 15.448/1999).

[37] For this – in Austria at the time of accession politically very sensitive issue (the solution being said to have been the price of the then opposition parties for their consent to EU membership, which was needed to achieve the required 2/3 majority in parliament) – see e.g., *Fischer*, Die Demokratisierung der EU aus der Sicht des österreichischen Parlaments, in *Leicht* (ed.), Regierungskonferenz 1996. Wohin steuert die EU? (1996) pp. 167-178; *Morass*, Österreich im Entscheidungsprozess der Europäischen Union, in *Tàlos/Falkner* (ed.), EU-Mitglied Österreich, Vienna 1996, pp. 32-49; *Öhlinger*, Die Mitwirkung des Nationalrates, des Bundesrates und der Länder an der Entstehung von sekundärem Gemeinschaftsrecht, in *Griller/Rill* (ed.), Verfassungsrechtliche Grundfragen der EU-Mitgliedschaft, Vienna 1997, pp. 1-20, *Schäffer*, Österreichs Beteiligung an der Willensbildung in der Europäischen Union, insbesondere an der europäischen Rechtsetzung, Zeitschrift für öffentliches Recht 1996, pp. 3-73.

[38] Article 23d para. 2 B-VG (Federal-Constitutional Law).

opinions are binding on the Austrian representative in the Council if it concerns matters to be transformed by federal law or aiming at the enactment of directly effective measures which would otherwise be a matter of federal legislation.[39] Again a departure from such an opinion is only allowed for compelling reasons of foreign and integration policy. Furthermore, the minister has to consult the National Council before such departure takes place. Should the measure of the European Union entail an alteration of federal constitutional law, a departure from the opinion is only allowed if the National Council does not object within due time.[40]

In practice and after some difficulties at the beginning, this procedure leads to a regular information of the *Länder* and the Parliament on issues of European integration. In fact there is a problem that those instances have to deal with a huge amount of material. Binding opinions are rather the exception.

D. **Permanent Neutrality**

1. *Neutrality under the TEU?*

It is still a disputed issue whether or not neutrality is compatible with EU membership. The dispute concerns Austria, which prior to EU membership was considered a *permanently* neutral country, as well as Finland, Sweden and Ireland, which were deemed to conduct a consistent policy of neutrality.[41] It shall only be summarized briefly here why good reasons strike for the position that neutrality in both variants is incompatible with EU membership.[42] This is necessary fully to understand the ambiguous constitutional developments in Austria during the first years of EU membership. Regarding the situation in Sweden and Finland it is argued that the development is even less visible than in Austria, for the simple reason that neutrality is not enshrined in the constitutions of these countries.[43] However, as for the substance, the 'fading out' of the status of neutrality, the situation is much alike.

---

[39] Article 23e para. 2 B-VG. It shall only be mentioned here that a related right exists under Article 23e para. 6 B-VG for the *Bundesrat* [Federal Council], the chamber consisting of representatives of the parliaments of the Austrian provinces (*Länder*), providing for the participiation of the *Länder* in the law-making procedure at the federal level, which is an essential element of the federal principle of the Austrian Constitution. However, the right to issue a binding opinion is restricted to cases where a project of the European Union would have to be transposed by a constitutional act requiring the consent of the *Bundesrat*; the practical relevance of that constellation is dubious.

[40] Article 23e para. 3 B-VG.

[41] That could also be characterized as a policy of non-alliance aiming at neutrality in the case of war between others.

[42] For a more detailed discussion compare *Griller/Droutsas/Falkner/Forgó/Nentwich*, The Treaty of Amsterdam (2000) pp. 431-440. For a 'Swedish perspective' compare *Lysén*, Some Views on Neutrality and Membership of the European Communties: The Case of Sweden, CMLRev. 1992, pp. 229-255.

[43] This is also the reason why there is no special sub-chapter for Finland and Sweden on the issue of neutrality in this paper.

The legal rules of neutrality as enshrined in international law include several duties for a neutral state: duties of abstention, especially the prohibition on participating in a war between other states; duties of prevention, e.g., concerning the passage of foreign troops and territorial overflights; and duties of equal treatment, especially concerning eventual restrictions on trade in war materials, and – a controversial issue – eventual restrictions on trade in goods other than war materials, the latter being subject to scrutiny not under a strict equal treatment requirement, but under the prohibition to intervene in a war (e.g., by unilateral embargo measures). Permanently neutral States,[44] such as Austria, have to respect, in addition, the so-called pre-effects ('Vorwirkungen') of neutrality, i.e., they are required, even in times of peace, to work towards preventing their potential involvement in future wars. For example, according to its Neutrality Act, Austria must not join military alliances, nor must it allow the establishment of military bases on its territory.

Membership of the EU and EC has, for some time, been regarded as being inconsistent with neutrality by Europe's neutral States. In the 1950s and 1960s, all neutral EFTA countries (four of them now being EU members, plus Switzerland) saw neutrality as a major obstacle to EEC membership. However, it has always been controversial whether neutrality and EC, and later, EU membership, are reconcilable.[45] The crucial issue is whether the provisions on CFSP, and the corresponding provisions in the TEC, authorise member States to remain neutral in the case of a conflict between third States or between a member of the Union or the Union itself and a third State. As a matter of principle, it appears reasonable, at first sight, to answer this question in the affirmative. There are three reasons in favour of this view. First, there is the principle of unanimity,[46] which renders possible the blocking of decisions inconsistent with neutrality. Second, according to the TEU, '[t]he policy of the Union ... shall not prejudice the specific character of the security and defence policy of certain member States'.[47] This clause, said to be inserted in the Maastricht Treaty on the request of Ireland, aims to create a shield for neutrality. Third, one could have recourse to the safeguard clauses embodied in the TEC,[48] e.g., in a case where embargo measures are implemented by secondary EC law.

---

[44] These are states that are bound, under international law, to remain neutral in cases of future wars between subjects of international law.

[45] The dramatic shift in the political debate becomes abundantly clear in *Harden* (ed.), Neutral States and the European Communities (1994), in the contributions by *Calvocoressi* p. 144 et seq., *Freymond* p. 1 et seq., *Huldt* p. 104 et seq., *Jankowitsch/Porias* p. 35 et seq., *Lipponen* p. 63 et seq.

[46] Article 23 TEU.

[47] Article 17 para. 1 subpara. 4 TEU. The text continues as follows: '... and shall respect the obligations of certain member States, which see their common defence realised in the North Atlantic Treaty Organisation (NATO), under the North Atlantic Treaty and be compatible with the common security and defence policy established within that framework'.

[48] Articles 296 and 297 TEC (Arts. 223 and 224 TECold).

However, while political evaluation of each case, including an eventual veto, is certainly in line with the Treaties, the same does not seem to be true with regard to a *general reservation* on grounds of neutrality (or on other grounds). Mutual solidarity and the absence of reservations, as foreseen by the TEU,[49] appear to render impossible a *general* reservation, based on whatever national policy principles, in the field of CFSP. With regard to Finland, Sweden and Austria, a Joint Declaration contained in the Final Act to the Accession Treaty[50] makes this principle abundantly clear. Declaration No. 1 on Common Foreign and Security Policy, which – according to Article 31 para. 2 lit b of the Vienna Convention on the Law of Treaties – is relevant for the interpretation of the TEU, states, inter alia, that the Union and the EFTA States

> 'agree that the new member States will, from the time of their accession, be ready and able to participate fully and actively in the Common Foreign and Security Policy as defined in the Treaty on European Union; the new member States will, on accession, take on in their entirety and without reservation all the objectives of the Treaty, the provisions of Title V thereof, and the declarations attached to it'.

Systematic blocking of *all* measures inconsistent with neutrality (especially of unilateral embargo measures against belligerent States), as well as insisting, *without exception*, on being exempted from such measures or not having to participate, certainly cannot be regarded as 'participat[ing] fully' in the CFSP, nor as 'tak[ing] on in their entirety and without reservation' the provisions of Title V of the TEU. Certainly there is no obligation to participate in every, or not to block any, action that is irreconcilable with neutrality. It is only systematic obstruction of the adoption of measures, for the sole reason that they are inconsistent with neutrality, which has to be regarded as prohibited.

At the time of EU accession, the resulting effects on neutrality could be seen as affecting economic duties of neutrality only.[51] The new status of the European neutrals after Maastricht could be described, therefore, as one of mere *military or differential neutrality*.

The Amsterdam Treaty, by paving the way for the so-called Petersberg tasks,[52] introduces a major military dimension into the CFSP. Thus, the obligation relating to solidarity discussed above now covers a wider range of measures. These issues go even more to the substance of the law of neutrality than the modification of economic obligations. It is the *general* obligation to stay neutral in a situation of war that is the essential element of neutrality. And it is this aspect that has been discarded, not only in the context of economic sanctions, but also, quite

---

[49] Article 11 para. 2 TEU.

[50] 1994 OJ (C 241) 21 as amended by 1995 OJ (L 1) 1.

[51] And it should be reminded that such duties were disputed as a part of the law on neutrality, at least as regards goods other than war materials. That made the issue less spectacular.

[52] Article 17 para. 2 TEU.

generally, within CFSP and especially within the framework of the Petersberg tasks. Systematic blockage of such measures for the sole reason of neutrality – which would be the duty of a neutral state – would be, as noted, illegal.

As a consequence and summing up it is submitted that both the concept of permanent neutrality and a constant neutrality policy are inconsistent with EU membership. Finland and Sweden seem to have adapted their policy accordingly.[53]

2. *The Constitutional Developments in Austria*

Austria's Permanent Neutrality is – or better, as argued here: has been – an obligation by virtue of a special constitutional law enacted in 1955.[54] Austria has explicitly amended its constitution – but not the Neutrality Act (!) – twice with regard to CFSP matters: first, in the course of EU accession, and, second, during the ratification procedure relating to the Amsterdam Treaty. The Constitution now explicitly allows for Austria's participation not only in economic sanctions against third countries, but also in Petersberg actions. After the second amendment, the crucial passage of the relevant Article of the constitution[55] now reads as follows[56]:

---

[53] As an example of remarkable clarity in this respect, compare the speech of *Pertti Torstila*, Director General for Political Affairs, Finnish Ministry of Foreign Affairs, EU and NATO, delivered in Helsinki 31 March 2000 (available at http://formin.finland.fi/english/): 'Since its accession to the European Union in 1995, Finland had no longer regarded itself as a neutral country. For us – in a union with common foreign and security policy – there are no neutrals; militarily non-allied yes, but no neutrals. One should not forget that "the Petersberg tasks" were included in the Amsterdam Treaty at a joint Finnish-Swedish initiative.'

Swedish comments on the recent changes appear to be more cautious – compare, e.g., 'The Renewal of Sweden's Defence: Phase 2. Unofficial shortened version of the Government Defence Bill 1996/97:4 passed by Parliament on 20 November and 13 December 1996', at p. 8 (available at http://forsvar.regeringen.se/propositionermm/propositioner/pdf/p9697_4c.pdf): 'Sweden's non-participation in military alliances with the aim of making it possible for our country to be neutral in the event of a war in our vicinity remains unchanged.' But compare also *Lysen* (n. 42) who arrived at similar results as in the above text already in 1992.

[54] Bundesverfassungsgesetz vom 26. Oktober 1955 über die Neutralität Österreichs (Constitutional Act of 26 October 1955 on Austria's Neutrality), BGBl (Austrian Federal Law Gazette) 1955/211.

The following remarks concentrate on the constitutional law aspects and leave aside the equally delicate issue of an eventual modification of Austria's obligation under international law to stay neutral.

[55] Article 23f para. 1 Federal Constitutional Law (Bundesverfassungsgesetz), as amended by the Constitutional Act, BGBl (Federal Law Gazette) I 1998/83.

[56] Translation by the author. The original version is as follows: 'Österreich wirkt an der Gemeinsamen Außen- und Sicherheitspolitik der Europäischen Union auf Grund des Titels V des Vertrages über die Europäische Union in der Fassung des Vertrages von Amsterdam mit. Dies schließt die Mitwirkung an Aufgaben gemäß Art. 17 Abs. 2 dieses Vertrages sowie an Maßnahmen ein, mit denen die Wirtschaftsbeziehungen zu einem oder mehreren dritten Ländern ausgesetzt, eingeschränkt oder vollständig eingestellt werden. Beschlüsse des Europäischen Rates zu einer

> 'Austria takes part in the Common Foreign and Security Policy of the European Union enshrined in title V of the Treaty on European Union as amended by the Treaty of Amsterdam. This includes taking part in tasks according to Article 17 para. 2 of this Treaty and in measures which interrupt or reduce, in part or completely, economic relations with one or more third countries. Decisions of the European Council regarding a common defence of the European Union and regarding the integration of the Western European Union into the European Union require a decision of the *Nationalrat* [National Council] and of the *Bundesrat* [Federal Council], at least half of the respective members being present and a two-thirds majority of the votes cast, and an explicit designation as constitutional law.'

The first two sentences have to be regarded as a derogation from the constitutional commitment to permanent neutrality. However, and mainly for political reasons, explicitly amending the Constitutional Act on Austria's neutrality was avoided.[57] Consequently, the legal situation lacks clarity. Furthermore, there are still some remainders of neutrality to be found. Above all, the unchanged parts of the Neutrality Act in connection with the amendments mentioned do not authorise departures from neutrality commitments *except* in the framework of CFSP, i.e., not in other cases. Moreover, the establishment of a common defence, and consequently membership of a military alliance, remain prohibited. Yet, one decisive aspect has been abandoned, i.e., the principle of non-intervention in a war, which has hitherto been a core aspect of neutrality. The 'rest' is not enough, therefore, to be considered as permanent neutrality.

The summarising conclusion is that EU membership and permanent neutrality, as well as a constant policy of neutrality, are not compatible. The 'European

---

gemeinsamen Verteidigung der Europäischen Union sowie zu einer Integration der Westeuropäischen Union in die Europäische Union bedürfen der Beschlussfassung des Nationalrates und des Bundesrates *in sinngemäßer Anwendung des Art. 44 Abs. 1 und 2*' – the passage in italics meaning what is circumscribed in the above text after the end of the quotation.

[57] Permanent neutrality had been a hotly debated issue in the years before accession. As late as 1994 the Austrian government and the competent Parliamentary Committee in the debate on the Draft EU Accession Act claimed that Austria could accede to the EU without amending or deleting the Neutrality Act [1600 BlgNR XVIII. GP, 12 (1600 supplement to the minutes of the Nationalrat, 18th legislative period, at p. 12)]. However, the same document (at p. 13) provides proof that the repercussions on permanent neutrality were clearly detected, when the Committee stated that eventual participation in economic sanctions could be incompatible with Austrian law, and should therefore be authorized by a specific constitutional foundation which would not touch upon the 'core features' *('Kernbestand')* of Austrian neutrality. That could only be interpreted as the intention to enact a material derogation of the Neutrality Act without changing the wording of that Act, which was later realized by the insertion of Article 23f B-VG.

A similar ambiguous attitude was chosen when that Article was changed in order to accommodate the changes to come by the Amsterdam Treaty [which can be inferred from the Parliamentary debate: StenProt der 130. Sitzung des NR, 20. GP (Minutes of the 130th session of the Nationalrat, 20th legislative period)].

Even today there is still no clear statement of the Austrian government acknowledging that development, although it is obvious from the mentioned parliamentary debates on the constitutional amendments that the legal implications for Austria's neutrality were clearly recognized.

Neutrals', including Austria, are well aware of this fact,[58] and have been prepared to participate in the Common Foreign and Security Policy in the spirit of mutual solidarity and without general reservation.

III. FINLAND

A. The Conclusion of the Accession Treaty and the Implementation Act

The Finnish constitution was completely revised in 1999.[59] Accession to the EU in 1995 was based on the former version of the constitutional legal order. As for the substance, however, the new order did not change the relevant constitutional set of rules governing Finland's EU membership.[60]

At the time of accession the Finnish Constitution consisted of several constitutional acts,[61] most important of which were the Constitution Act (of 1919) and the Parliament Act (of 1928). International agreements were to be concluded by the President. Important international agreements such as the Accession Treaty to the EU had also to be approved by Parliament, in the form of a resolution. Simple majority was at that time sufficient.[62]

However, due to the dualist tradition of the Constitution, the conclusion of an international Treaty alone would not produce any legal effect internally. Thus it was (and also today still is) also necessary to incorporate the agreement into an internal act. Usually the agreement is simply attached to that act – a decree or an

[58] Even if their political reasoning is not always consistent, and public statements far from being precise.

[59] The Constitution of Finland (731/1999) was adopted on 11 June 1999. The English version can be found at http://www.eduskunta.fi/. At the same address a survey on the Finnish legal system as well as an introduction to the background of the constitutional reform is given: *Nousiainen*, The Finnish System of Government: From a Mixed Constitution to Parliamentarism. According to *Nousiainen*, the constitutional reform had several objectives: '(1) the codification of the constitutional laws of Finland, (2) the uniformisation and modernisation of the normative structures, or a sort of "periodic maintenance" of the Constitution, and (3) the revision of the current arrangements for the separation of powers. At all stages, it was carefully emphasised that the aim is not to intervene into the foundations of the political system of Finland, but instead the matter is of a limited reform, building exactly on the continuity of the old traditions.'

[60] Compare for the following especially *Aalto*, Accession of Finland to the European Union: First Remarks, ELRev. 1995, pp. 618-628; *B. Cottier*, Finlande, in: *l'Institut Suisse de droit compare* (ed.), Conséquences institutionelles d'une adhèsion à l'Union européenne, Zürich 1999, pp. 231-241; *Jääskinen*, The Application of Community Law in Finland: 1995-1998, CMLRev. 1999, pp. 407-441; *Pohjolainen*, National constitutional law and European integration, in 17th FIDE Congress, Vol. I, National constitutional law vis-à-vis European integration, Berlin 1996, pp. 399-426; *Rosas*, Finland's Accession to the European Union: Constitutional Aspects, European Public Law 1995, pp. 166-170.

[61] That has been changed under the new constitution which repealed, among others, the Parliament Act of 1928.

[62] See Aalto (n. 60) p. 619.

act of parliament – without changing its original wording, which appears to bring the procedure near to that of general transformation.[63]

As for the necessary act to be adopted in the special case of EU membership, the Accession Treaty was considered to derogate fundamentally from the Constitution.[64] The impingement on Finland's sovereignty and also the transfer of powers to supranational bodies was of specific importance. This was done in an ex ante scrutiny of the Accession Treaty by the Constitutional Law Committee of Parliament,[65] which is in charge of the supervision of the constitutionality of proposals and other matters.[66]

The Finnish constitution allows for constitutional *leges fugitivae*, that is derogations from the constitution which need not be incorporated formally into the text of the constitution.[67] In the case of international agreements, this can be done by a two-thirds majority of the votes cast in Parliament.[68] In the case of the Accession Treaty this possibility was used in order to adopt the EU Act.[69]

Consequently, there was no formal change to the wording of the Finnish constitution involved in the ratification and incorporation procedure. The fundamental change to the Finnish legal system apparently has to be understood by the

---

[63] Some authors call that a 'de facto monism' – see *Rosas* (n. 60) p. 167. The issue shall not be gone into more deeply here. However, it may be said that the incorporation technique of international law into the national legal order is not decisive for its monist or dualist character. Rather is it the eventual change of the legal foundation of the incorporated provisions.

[64] See especially *Aalto* (n. 60) p. 620 et seq.; *Rosas* (n. 60) p. 167 et seq.

[65] Constitutional Law Committee of Parliament, PeVL 14/1994 vp, p. 92.

[66] Now Section 74 of the New Constitution. The Constitutional Law Committee shall issue statements on the constitutionality of legislative proposals and other matters brought for its consideration, as well as on their relation to international human rights treaties. [There is no Constitutional Court in Finland.]

[67] Apparently this is still possible to a certain extent under Section 73 para. 1 of the new Constitution. This provisions allows for 'the enactment of a limited derogation of the Constitution'. Regarding such leges fugitivae, the situation is similar to that in Austria: compare above n. 1.

[68] Article 69 para. 1 of the then Parliament Act. This was upheld by Section 95 para. 2 of the new Constitution, which reads as follows: 'A Government bill for the bringing into force of an international obligation is considered in accordance with the ordinary legislative procedure pertaining to an Act. However, if the proposal concerns the Constitution or a change to the national territory, the Parliament shall adopt it, without leaving it in abeyance, by a decision supported by at least two thirds of the votes cast.'

By contrast, according to Section 73 of the new Constitution – corresponding to Article 67 of the Parliament Act in force at the time of the decision on EU membership – amendments or derogations of the Constitution by internal law 'shall in the second reading be left in abeyance, by a majority of the votes cast, until the first parliamentary session following parliamentary elections. The proposal shall then ... be adopted without material alterations in one reading in a plenary session by a decision supported by at least two thirds of the votes cast. However, the proposal may be declared urgent by a decision that has been supported by at least five sixths of the votes cast. In this event, the proposal is not left in abeyance and it can be adopted by a decision supported by at least two thirds of the votes cast.'

[69] No. 1540/1994. In addition a consultative referendum was organized in October 1994. It produced 57% of Yes-votes.

meaning of the EU Act itself.[70] This Act is very short and contains only three sections. It states Finland's EU membership and provides for the internal legal force of primary and secondary EC and EU law under the conditions laid down by the *acquis communautaire.*

The same technique was used for the incorporation of the Amsterdam Treaty. The Committee of Constitutional Law in this case was of the opinion that this was necessary because of the additional transfer of powers by the communitarization of parts of the third pillar, other new competences, but also the explicit possibility to conclude agreements with third parties in the field of the CFSP.[71]

The new Finnish constitution which entered into force on 1 March 2000 – and consequently was neither applicable on the occasion of Finland's EU accession nor on the conclusion of the Amsterdam Treaty, but will be of relevance for future developments like the conclusion of the Nice Treaty – includes a Chapter 8 on 'International Relations'. This Chapter implicitly acknowledges Finland's EU membership by regulating the participatory rights of parliament in EU matters. However, it does not draw on the membership status itself or on any question of the relation between Finnish law and European Union law. Apparently, it did not change the original and specific foundation of EU membership, especially also not the dualist approach of the constitution. There is still the categorical difference between the acceptance of an international obligation and its bringing into force within the internal legal order.[72] But it should be mentioned that according to the new Section 94 para. 2 an international obligation concerning the Constitution now is also to be approved – not only incorporated – by at least two thirds of the votes cast (and no longer by simple majority). Furthermore, Section 94 para. 3 now stipulates that '(a)n international obligation shall not endanger the democratic foundations of the Constitution'. This might be read as a pertaining condition of EU membership, which might in the future give rise to discussion. Its applicability in the case of EU membership as developed before its entering into force remains uncertain.

B. Consequences for the Relationship Between EC Law and Finnish Law

The consequences of the Finnish way into the EU for the specific features of Community law – primacy and direct effect – are far-reaching. The opening up of

[70] A specific constitutional provision on the transfer of powers was not only considered unnecessary, but also questionable. This was so for the mentioned Article 69 Parliament Act, which allowed for derogations from the constitution with regard to international agreement but presumably did not allow for the wording of the constitution to be changed. That would have to be done by the specific procedure foreseen for such amendments; compare *Aalto* (n. 60) p. 623.

[71] Opinion of 27 March 1998, PeVL 10/1998 vp.

[72] Section 94 and 95 of the new Constitution.

the Finnish legal order was done using a procedure generally considered as allowing 'exceptions'[73] from the Constitution, or, as it is metaphorically called, on the basis of the 'hole theory'[74] meaning that the contents of the exception from the Constitution are to be found in the provisions authorized by this procedure. In the case of EU membership this implies not only an exemption from constitutional law boundaries for the whole *acquis communautaire* as accepted at the time of accession, but also for future secondary law enacted on the grounds of the accepted *acquis*.[75] Consequently, according to this 'hole theory' as applied by the Constitutional Law Committee of the Finnish Parliament, 'Parliament can legislate within the framework of the obligations deriving from Community law with a simple majority as the constitutional impediment has already been removed by the adoption of the *EU Act* as an exception to the Constitution, even if the Community obligation would materially conflict with the Constitution'.[76] Eventual limits to that exception might thus arise primarily whenever the competence of the Union or the Communities to legislate is disputed.

Illustrative in this context is the case of entering into the third stage of EMU. The Committee of Constitutional Law of the Parliament not only accepted the large margin of discretion for the Council, but also the prerogative of the ECJ to determine the legality of such a decision.[77] The Committee also found the loss of the decision-making powers of the Bank of Finland covered.[78] It extended that reasoning even to Community measures based on Article 308 (ex-Art. 235) ECT.[79] By contrast, the Committee was of the opinion that, at the time of accession, Finland did not accept any definitive obligation to participate in the Exchange Rate Mechanism.[80] It did so despite the fact that participation in the ERM was one of the so-called convergence criteria which had to be fulfilled as a prerequisite to enter into the third stage of EMU. As a consequence of the

[73] *Aalto* (n. 60) p. 620; *Rosas* (n. 60) p.168.

[74] *Jääskinen* (n. 60) p. 408, p. 411.

[75] Some experts criticized this as a violation of the constitution. They contended that fundamental changes of the core elements of the constitution effecting sovereignty, democracy, representativity, rule of law, primacy of the constitution and fundamental rights, have to be done by the 'normal' procedure for the amendment of the constitution by constitutional law (compare above n. 68) – see especially *Jyränki*, Euroopan unioni ja Suomen valtiosääntö, XXIX Suomalaisen Lakimiesyhdistyksen vuosikirja 1996 (with a summary in German language).

[76] *Jääskinen* (n. 60) p. 411 – see also at 411 et seq. regarding the subsequent practice of the Constitutional Law Committee based on this theoretical approach.

This theory leaves ample room for discussion on the relationship between Finnish law and Community law which seems to resemble the problems raised in Austria (equally on the grounds of a constitutional provision – in the case of Austria a EU specific provision – introducing an exception from traditional constitutional restraints); compare the above text after n. 17.

[77] Opinion of 11 June 1997, PeVL 18/1997 vp. This is clearly in contrast to the Maastricht decision of the German Constitutional Court, BVerfGE 89, p. 155 (p. 187 et seq.).

[78] Opinion of 11 March 1998, PeVL 7/1998 vp.

[79] Opinion of 14 June 1996, PeVL 3/1996 vp.

[80] Opinion of 19 April 1996, PeVL 7/1996 vp.

Committee's opinion, the legislative procedure applicable to the accession to the ERM was not 'covered' by the EU Act.

There was also a case where a proposal for a regulation was deemed unconstitutional on the ground that it included a provision for officials of *other member States* to participate in inspections in Finland.[81] The Committee made a difference between such inspection rights of Community institutions (which are covered) and of member States' officials. The final version of the regulation made this right subject to the permission of the other member State involved which resolved the matter for Finland. But the example illustrates eventual future conflicts between the constitution and EC measures. The conclusion might be that the Committee considered the Draft Regulation *ultra vires*. It is not easy to argue how else its position could be reconciled with the 'hole theory', since there is no *a priori* reason in sight why the exception from the constitution could not include the right of the Community to confer inspection rights on officials of other member States. It is also obvious that there might arise a tension with regard to the prerogative of the ECJ to determine the legality of secondary legislation as accepted by the Committee.[82] To this extent the situation resembles that in other member States.[83] An eventual conflict between such ex-ante review and finally enacted secondary Community law would trigger the need for an amendment of the Constitution. Should that not be done, Finnish courts might need to judge on the secondary legislation with a view to an eventual 'evident conflict with the Constitution.'[84] Such conflict might lie in the transgression of the exception granted by the EU Act.

The every-day experience of the Finnish courts shows that the issue of an eventual conflict between the 'constitutional authorization' of EU membership and supremacy of EC law is of a rather theoretical nature. However, it can be added that precedence over *constitutional* law in the above-mentioned sense of

[81] Opinion of 14 June 1996, PeVL 3/1996 vp – compare *Jääskinen* (n. 60) p. 412 et seq.

[82] See above n.77.

[83] As for Austria, compare above near n. 16.

[84] Section 106 of the Constitution. However, the provision appears to be applicable by analogy only, since secondary Community law might, strictu sensu, not come under the term 'Act' in Section 106. Should the analogy be denied, the situation would be even more complicated. On the one hand, it could be argued that the EU Act as exception rule does not apply, which would render secondary legislation inapplicable irrespective of the gravity of the mistake. On the other hand, it could be argued that the EU Act would not empower the courts to scrutinize the legality of secondary legislation; eventual consequences would then to be drawn by parliament. [The issue might be of relevance also in the absence of an opinion of the Constitutional Law Committee.]

According to the acceptance of the prerogatives of the ECJ as mentioned above (n. 77), the Finnish court would in any case certainly first have to refer the matter to the ECJ under Article 234 ECT. The materialisation of a conflict would thus require an ultra vires act of the Communities together with an ultra vires act of the ECJ upholding the illegal secondary legislation. This makes the matter highly theoretical, as has recently become apparent in Germany in a decision of the German Constitutional Court (rectifying speculations during the years after the *Maastricht* judgment); see BVerfG, 2 BvR 1210/98, 17 February 2000.

the limits of the 'hole theory' so far has not been tested. But apart from that, ample case law is proving that the Finnish courts rapidly accepted primacy and direct effect according to the case law of the ECJ.[85] The first case was decided in 1996 when the Supreme Administrative Court (*Korkein hallinto-oikeus*) ruled that Finnish authorities had to set aside the Finnish VAT Act (an Act of Parliament) which was found to be in conflict with the VAT directive which provided for more far-reaching tax deduction rights of the citizens.[86] The Administrative Court expressly referred to the principles expressed in the case law of the ECJ.

To give only one more example: in a recent case the Supreme Administrative Court[87] held that the national regulations on parallel imports of medicines were incompatible with the Community principle of free movement of goods. According to the Court, the National Agency for Medicines (*Lääkelaitos*) could not refuse a parallel importer authorisation to sell medicines on the grounds that he used a different size of packaging from the approved importer.

This development is all the more remarkable against the background that originally Finnish courts were not empowered to measure Finnish law by the provisions of the constitution.[88] This has changed under the new Constitution. Now there is, similarly to the situation in Sweden, the power of the courts to 'give primacy to the provision in the Constitution' over an Act of Parliament whenever the application of that Act would be in 'evident conflict' with the Constitution.[89] Consequently, even today the right to 'review' the legality of Acts of Parliament under EC law exceeds that under constitutional law.[90]

C. **Participatory Rights of Parliament**

Section 96 of the Finnish Constitution provides for the 'Participation of the Parliament in the national preparation of European Union matters.'[91] According to this provision, Parliament considers those proposals for acts, agreements and other measures which are to be decided in the European Union and which otherwise, according to the Constitution, would fall within the competence of the Parliament. The Government shall, for the determination of the position of the Parliament, communicate a proposal to the Parliament. The proposal is considered in

---

[85] Compare especially *Jääskinen* (n. 60) p. 416 et seq.

[86] Supreme Administrative Court, 31 Dec. 1996, KHO 1996 B 577; See *Jääskinen* (n. 60) p. 416 et seq.

[87] Korkein hallinto-oikeus, 10 September 1999, No. 1789/3/98 2461.

[88] See *Pohjolainen* (n. 60) p. 417.

[89] Section 106 of the new Constitution.

[90] The situation is similar in Sweden. In Austria, by contrast, courts in doubt over the constitutionality of Acts of Parliament have the right to bring the matter before the Constitutional Court.

[91] A similar provision governs the participation in CFSP matters (Sect. 97). Compare for the following especially *Jääskinen* (n. 60) pp. 413-416; *Jääskinen/Kivisaari*, Parliamentary Scrutiny of European Union Affairs in Finland, in *Wiberg* (ed.), Trying to Make Democracy Work – The Nordic Parliaments and the European Union, Södertälje 1997, pp. 29-47.

the Grand Committee and ordinarily in one or more of the other Committees that issue statements to the Grand Committee.[92] However, a proposal pertaining to foreign and security policy is considered by the Foreign Affairs Committee. Where necessary, the Grand Committee or the Foreign Affairs Committee may issue to the Government a statement on the proposal. In addition, the Speaker's Council may decide that the matter be taken up for debate in plenary session, 'during which, however, no decision is made by the Parliament'. Thus, apparently the consultation mechanism cannot produce strictly binding results for the government. However, the effectiveness of the system is guaranteed by the constitutional principle of accountability of each minister before the Parliament.[93]

IV. SWEDEN

A. The Amendment of the Swedish Constitution

The Swedish Constitution consists of four fundamental laws: the Act of Succession (1810), the Freedom of the Press Act (1949), the Instrument of Government (1974) and the Freedom of Expression Act (1991).[94] Any amendment of these laws requires two decisions of the *Riksdag* of identical wording. The second decision may not be taken until elections for the *Riksdag* have been held following the first decision, and the newly-elected *Riksdag* has been convened. On the request of at least one third of the members of the *Riksdag* a decisive referendum is to be held simultaneously with the election for the *Riksdag*.[95]

The most important element of the Swedish Constitution, the *Instrument of Government* (*Regeringsformen* – hereinafter: IG) was amended as a preparation for EU membership.[96]

Chapter 10 IG on the 'Relations with other States' includes Article 5 which provides – already in its version prior to the preparation for EU membership – for

[92] The Government shall also provide the appropriate Committees with information deriving from the consideration of the matter in the European Union. The Grand Committee or the Foreign Affairs Committee shall also be informed of the position of the Government on the matter.

[93] Section 60 para. 2 of the new Constitution.

[94] See http://www.riksdagen.se/arbetar/grondbok_en/index.htm. Further quotations are primarily taken from this source. It shall be noted, however, that this version of the IG's wording (in English) differs in several important points from that included in the book cited at n. 96. Most important are the differences mentioned below in nn. 99 and 100.

[95] Chapter 8, Article 15 IG. In the case of a referendum, the Bill shall be deemed to be rejected, if the majority of those taking part in the referendum vote against the proposal, and if the number of voters exceeds half the number of those who registered valid votes in the election.

[96] Compare for the following especially *Bernitz*, Swedish Report, in *Schwarze* (ed.), Die Entstehung einer europäischen Verfassungsordnung, Baden-Baden 2000, pp. 389-459; *B. Cottier*, Suède, in: l'Institut Suisse de droit comparé (ed.), Conséquences institutionelles d'une adhèsion à l'Union européenne, Zürich 1999, pp. 243-261; *Holmberg/Stjernquist*, Introduction, in *Sveriges riksdag* (ed.), The Constitution of Sweden, Stockholm 2000, pp. 9-62; *Lysén*, National constitutional

the transfer of powers to international organizations. According to that article, any right of decision-making may be entrusted, to a limited extent, to an international organization for peaceful cooperation of which Sweden is a member or is to become a member or to an international court of law. However, no right of decision-making relating to matters concerning the enactment, amendment, or repeal of a fundamental law, of the Parliament Act or of the Act concerning elections for the Parliament, or which regards a limitation of any of the rights and freedoms guaranteed by the IG may be delegated.[97]

These provisions were considered to be insufficient as a sound basis for Sweden's EU membership.[98] Consequently, a new first paragraph was inserted in 1994 into Article 5 specifically dealing with the accession to the EU. It reads as follows:

> 'The *Riksdag* may entrust the right of decision-making[99] to the European communities so long as these provide protection for rights and freedoms corresponding to the protection provided under this Instrument of Government and the European Convention for the Protection of Human Rights and Fundamental Freedoms. The *Riksdag* authorises such delegation[100] in a decision which has the support of at least three

---

law and European integration, in 17th FIDE Congress, Vol. I, National constitutional law vis-à-vis European integration, Berlin 1996, pp. 427-439.

Bernitz as well as *Holmberg/Stjernquist* also provide a general survey on the Swedish legal system.

[97] The provisions relating to the enactment of fundamental laws shall apply in respect of any decision concerning such delegation. If time does not permit a decision in accordance with such provisions, the *Riksdag* may approve a delegation of the right of decision-making by a majority of no fewer than five sixths of those present and voting and no fewer than three fourths of the total membership of the *Riksdag*.

[98] The prevailing view was that these provisions could not accommodate the actual needs, despite the fact that they had been drafted – some thirty years ago – with a view to an eventual accession to the then European Communites. The conditions of an a priori 'limited extent' of an eventual transfer of powers as well as the exclusion of any limitation of fundamental rights was considered to preclude the use of the provision for an accession to the EU as it stood at the beginning of the 90s – compare *Bernitz* (n. 96) p. 424 et seq.; *Holmberg/Stjernquist* (n. 96) p. 39.

[99] This is the version taken from the website of the *Riksdag* (see above n. 94). The version in the book edited by the *Riksdag* (above n. 96) is: 'The *Riksdag* may transfer a right of decision-making ...'. For the original version compare the following footnote.

[100] This is the version taken from the website of the *Riksdag* (see above n. 94). The version in the book edited by the *Riksdag* (above n. 96) is: 'The *Riksdag* shall authorise such transfer ...'.

It goes without saying that this is an important difference. While the term 'delegation' might insinuate that the delegated power is bound to respect all limits valid for the delegating authority, that might be different for a 'transfer' of powers in certain areas.

The Swedish text uses the word 'överlåtelse' which might rather point in the direction of the book version. The original wording of the paragraph is as follows:

'Riksdagen kan överlåta beslutanderätt till Europeiska gemenskaperna så länge som dessa har ett fri- och rättighetsskydd motsvarande det som ges i denna regeringsform och i den europeiska konventionen angående skydd för de mänskliga rättigheterna och de grundläggande friheterna. Riksdagen beslutar om sådan överlåtelse genom beslut, varom minst tre fjärdedelar av de röstande förenar sig. Riksdagens beslut kan också fattas i den ordning som gäller för stiftande av grundlag.'

fourths of those present and voting. The *Riksdag* may also take such a decision in the manner prescribed for the adoption of a fundamental law.'[101]

When Parliament gave its assent to the accession Treaty on 14 December 1994 based on this provision, it also passed a second measure: The *Act on the Accession to the EU*,[102] which was mainly aimed at incorporating EC law into the Swedish legal order. This was done against the background of the dualist tradition of the Swedish legal system. The Accession Act enumerates the most important basic treaties and instruments of the EU. The Act on Accession also produces a sort of a doubling of the constitutional authorization to transfer decision-making powers to the EU: it allows for the EC to take decisions with legal force in Sweden to the extent and with the effects which follow from the Treaties and other instruments listed in that law.[103]

During the ratification process of the Amsterdam Treaty it became apparent that the drafting of Chapter 10 Article 5 IG, which allows for the transfer of powers to the 'European Communities', being at the same time silent on the European Union, was very narrow.[104] However, the government decided to leave the IG untouched, arguing that even after the Amsterdam Treaty the cooperation within the third pillar remained purely intergovernmental.[105] Consequently, the Instrument of Government remained unchanged. By contrast, the Act of Accession had to be amended in order to insert the Amsterdam Treaty as a source of primary law determining the transfer of powers.

---

[101] A transitional provision – attached to the Instrument of Government – on the enactment of the Amendment Act (SFS 1994:1375) states: 'If the *Riksdag* has approved an agreement on Swedish accession to the European Union following the holding of a referendum on the matter throughout the whole of the country, the *Riksdag* shall be entitled to entrust to the European Communities rights of decision-taking resulting from such accession without applying the qualified majority rules set out in Chapter 10, Article 5. The *Riksdag* shall also be entitled to approve the incorporation into Swedish law of the Communities' rules at the time of accession in the same manner as applies to the delegation of rights of decision-making.'

The referendum on EU accession which took place in November 1994 was of a consultative nature and not mandatory. It produced 52.3% yes-votes of the votes cast.

[102] Lag med anledning av Sveriges anslutning till Europeiska unionen (SFS 1994:1500).

[103] It is not quite clear which *additional* legal effects might flow from this part of the Act on Accession to the EU, given that the authorization to transfer decision-making powers is already included in 10:5 IG, and given that this authorization presumably also covers the specific Community features of supremacy and direct effect. Since Parliament's approval of the Accession Treaty was based on this constitutional authorization, it was argued that the enactment of the Accession Act had been superfluous; compare on the subject *Lysén* (n. 96) p. 432 et seq.

[104] Compare for the following especially *Bernitz* (n. 96) p. 431 et seq.; *Cottier* (n. 96) p. 250 et seq.

[105] The implication seems to be that Chapter 10 Article 5 para. 1 IG does not apply to the EU. The consequence might be that para. 2 is to be applied.

B. Consequences for the Relationship Between EC Law and Swedish Law

1. *The Limits to Supremacy of EC Law in Sweden*

As mentioned above, according to Chapter 10 Article 5 paragraph 1 IG, the Swedish Parliament may transfer decision-making powers to the European Communities 'as long as they provide for the protection of fundamental rights and freedoms equivalent to that guaranteed by this instrument and the European Convention on Human Rights'.

The passage cited was inspired by the German Basic law, especially by Article 23, and mirrors the requirement of a comparable level of fundamental rights protection not only as a prerequisite but as a continuing condition for membership. Consequently, similar questions as to eventual reservations of the courts regarding supremacy and direct effect might arise as in Germany.

Up to the present this seems to be regarded as only a rather theoretical possibility in Sweden, certainly while courts appear to accept the prevalence of EC law in general.[106] However, experience from other member States reveals that such a 'theoretical possibility' might gain actual importance very quickly.[107] Against this background the ambiguity of the Constitutional situation is rather delicate. It has to be noted that an eventual (limited) derogation from fundamental rights and freedom is mentioned only with regard to the IG itself and the ECHR. It has been concluded that the more detailed rights as enshrined in the Freedom of the Press Act and the Fundamental Law on Freedom of Expression, including the right to 'free access to official documents',[108] might not be protected by Chapter 10 Article 5 IG.[109] Derogations from those rights would thus be less problematical, as regards the supremacy of Community law. However, taking the preparatory works into account, the contrary appears to be more plau-

[106] In its first case involving a conflict between EC law and national law (RR 1997:65) the Supreme Administrative Court held that the prohibition of an appeal against a decision of the Department of Agriculture was in conflict with the general principles of Community law which had to prevail – compare as for the details *Bernitz* (n. 96) p. 447 et seq. The case led to an amendment of the relevant procedural laws in Sweden.

For another example that the issue is thoroughly scrutinized even in cases where it is not obvious, see Case C-319/97, *Kortas*, [1999] ECR, I-3143.

Bernitz (n. 96) p. 456 stresses that during the first five years of EU membership 'there have been no court cases or other events which have brought the Swedish "solange" provision into a current issue.'

[107] It shall suffice here to mention the recent judgment of the German Constitutional Court regarding the constitutionality of the EC banana market order (2 BvL 1/97, 7 June 2000 = EuZW 2000, 702); and the (finally failed) motion in Austria to block the step into the third stage of the EMU by a negative referendum (see *Griller*, Blockademöglichkeiten gegen die Einführung des Euro?, Journal für Rechtspolitik 1997, pp. 221-233).

[108] Article 2 Freedom of the Press Act.

[109] *Cottier* (n. 96) p. 249.

sible.[110] The Parliamentary Constitutional Committee,[111] among others, stressed the limits of the constitutional authorization to 'delegate' powers and the fundamental importance of the freedom of opinion, which entails public access to official documents.[112] Thus, the conclusion would be that eventual derogations from the Freedom of the Press Act and the Freedom of Expression Act, but also from the fundamental rules concerning the governing of the State,[113] could not take effect without the prior amendment of the Swedish constitution.[114] This implies a serious reservation against the principle of supremacy.

Equally remarkable is the legal reasoning which was given by the Parliamentary Constitutional Committee: it is the differentiation between the delegation of powers according to 10:5 IG and the procedural requirements for formal amendments of the constitution according to 8:15 IG. As a consequence, eventual derogations from the Swedish constitution would have to be implemented by constitutional law, thus putting an obstacle to Community law taking precedence over conflicting Swedish constitutional law. This is remarkable insofar as opening up the national *constitutional* order for the supremacy of future Community law can be understood as a specific form of an anticipated amendment of the constitution,[115] the specificity being that law – and even constitutional law – conflicting with directly applicable Community law would not be deleted but is instead no

[110] Compare *Bernitz* (n. 96) p. 420 et seq.; *Holmberg/Stjernquist* (n. 96) p. 40 et seq.

[111] According to Article 4 Riksdag Act, the Committee on the Constitution, among others, shall prepare matters concerning the fundamental laws. The supplementary provision in Article 4.6.1. makes clear that this includes to 'prepare matters concerning legislation in the fields of constitutional and general administrative law'.

[112] 1993/94:KU 21, Grundlagsändringar inför ett svenskt medlemskap I Europeiska unionen.

[113] It shall only be noted here that this notion is ambiguous due to the fact that membership of the EU inevitably entails important changes to the fundamental rules concerning the governing of the State, not least the system of law-making including supremacy of Community law. On the other hand, there is certainly an area of governing the state which is excluded from Community competences (such as the rules to elect the *Riksdag* and to enact Swedish law). This means that also the notion of 'fundamental rules concerning the governing of the State' might give rise to disputes.

[114] It shall be mentioned that the position referred to in the above text partly implies a specific protection also with regard to Chapter 2 IG (despite the wording of Chapter 10 Art. 5 IG). This is so since Chapter 2 includes the 'freedom of information' (Art. 13), that is the 'freedom to procure and receive information and otherwise acquaint oneself with the utterances of others'. Insofar as the Freedom of the Press Act and the Law on Freedom of Expression cover specific aspects of the freedom of information, they might be seen as leges speciales.

It should also be noted that the Freedom of the Press Act actually was modified on the occasion of the EU accession. Chapter 1 Article 9 No. 2 now allows for bans on commercial advertising 'in accordance with obligations pursuant to accession to the European Communities'; and Chapter 5 Article 1 now provides that the owner of a periodical may not only be a Swedish citizen or a Swedish legal person, but also 'a foreign national or foreign legal person', subject to a specific act of law (which might still include sort of a discrimination). See for these provisions *Bernitz* (n. 96) p. 441 et seq.

[115] To use another terminology (taken from 10:5 IG): a delegation or a transfer of the power to amend the constitution.

longer applicable within the scope of Community law.[116] This view appears to be rejected by the above-mentioned differentiation between the delegation of powers and the amendment of the constitution. If this is so, then it could endanger primacy not only for the 'excluded' parts of the constitution, especially the Freedom of the Press and the Freedom of Expression Act, but in especially those fundamental rights provided for in Chapter 2 IG. However, it would be an exaggeration to interpret the Constitutional Committee in such manner. Such an interpretation would undermine the core objection to opening the Swedish legal order, including, at least in principle, constitutional provisions, for European Community law. Thus, it has to be concluded that supremacy is accepted with the exception of those rights enshrined in the Freedom of the Press and the Freedom of Expression Act, and with the exception of the fundamental rules concerning the governing of the state.[117]

2. *Access to Documents and Positive Discrimination as Examples*

(1) That access to official documents was a delicate issue for Sweden from the outset is obvious from the unilateral declarations attached to the Act of Accession.[118] A reconfirmation followed immediately after Sweden's accession to the EU. Already at the beginning of 1995, the *Svenska Journalistförbundet* (the Swedish Journalists' Union) tested the way in which the Swedish authorities applied Swedish citizens' right of access to information in respect of documents relating to European Union activities. It contacted 46 Swedish authorities, among whom were the Swedish Ministry of Justice and the national Police Authority (*Rikspolisstyrelsen*), seeking access to a number of Council documents relating to the setting up of the European Police Office (Europol), including eight documents held by the national Police Authority and 12 held by the Ministry of Justice. In response to its requests the applicant was granted access to 18 of the 20 documents requested. It was refused access by the Ministry of Justice to two documents on the ground that they concerned the negotiating positions of the Netherlands and German Governments. The *Svenska Journalistförbundet* also contacted the Council to get access to the same 20 documents. The Council

[116] The duty of the member State to *explicitly* adjust its legal order accordingly is to be distinguished.

[117] See also *Bernitz* (n. 96) p. 423.

[118] See OJ 1994 C 241, p. 397. Declaration No. 47 by Sweden reads as follows: 'Open government and, in particular, public access to official records as well as the constitutional protection afforded to those who give information to the media are and remain fundamental principles which form part of Sweden's constitutional, political and cultural heritage.'

The member States 'answered' by a unilateral declaration stating: 'The present member States of the European Union take note of the unilateral Declaration of Sweden concerning openness and transparency. They take it for granted that, as a member of the European Union, Sweden will fully comply with Community law in this respect.'

granted access first to only two, and finally to four of these documents, and refused access to the remaining 16. The reasons given for that negative decision were that in the Council's view

> 'access to those documents cannot be granted because their release could be harmful to the public interest (public security) and because they relate to the Council's proceedings, including the positions taken by the members of the Council, and are therefore covered by the duty of confidentiality'.[119]

Access to the Council's documents is governed by Council Decision 93/731/EC on public access to Council documents.[120] This decision establishes the principle of access of the public to Council documents, and specifies exceptions to that principle.

> 'Access to a Council document shall not be granted where its disclosure could undermine:
> – the protection of the public interest (public security, international relations, monetary stability, court proceedings, inspections and investigations),
> – the protection of the individual and of privacy,
> – the protection of commercial and industrial secrecy,
> – the protection of the Community's financial interests,
> – the protection of confidentiality as requested by the natural or legal person who supplied any of the information contained in the document or as required by the legislation of the member State which supplied any of that information.'[121]

Article 4(2) of the Decision opens an additional matter by adding that '[a]ccess to a Council document may be refused in order to protect the confidentiality of the Council's proceedings'.

For the purpose of this analysis, it is not necessary to go into the details of the CFI's judgment. Suffice it to sketch the main aspect (insufficient reasoning of the Council) which decided the CFI to annul the Council decision denying access to the documents.

According to the Court, the Council is, regarding the first category of *mandatory exceptions*

> 'obliged to consider in respect of each requested document whether, in the light of the information available to it, disclosure is in fact likely to undermine one of the facets of public interest protected'.[122]

---

[119] Case T-174/95, *Svenska Journalistförbundet,* [1998] ECR, II-2289, para. 18.
[120] OJ 1993 L 340, p. 43, as amended by OJ 1996 L 325, p. 19.
[121] Article 4(1) Decision 93/731/EC.
[122] Case T-174/95, *Svenska Journalistförbundet,* [1998] ECR, II-2289, para. 112.

Things are different with regard to the second category, the so-called *discretionary exception.*

> 'By way of contrast, the wording of the second category, drafted in enabling terms, provides that the Council may also refuse access in order to protect the confidentiality of its proceedings ... It follows that the Council enjoys a margin of discretion which enables it, if need be, to refuse access to documents which touch upon its deliberations. It must, nevertheless, exercise this discretion by striking a genuine balance between, on the one hand, the interest of the citizen in obtaining access to the documents and, on the other, any interest of its own in maintaining the confidentiality of its deliberations ...'[123]

The Council might also rely jointly on an exception derived from the first category and one relating to the second category in order to refuse to grant access to documents.

The statement of reasons for a decision refusing access to a document must, according to the Court, contain '– at least for each category of documents concerned – the particular reasons' for which the Council considers that disclosure of the requested documents comes within the scope of one of the exceptions provided for in Decision 93/731.[124] This had not happened in the case at issue.

Under these circumstances the ruling of the Court offers no answer to the question whether the Council was, as to the merits, mistaken in refusing access in all the sixteen cases.[125] It should be noted that this implies the issue of whether the disclosure by the Swedish authorities had been illegal. The Council explicitly contended in the proceedings before the CFI that the release of the documents in question by the Swedish authorities to the applicant constituted a breach of Community law, since no decision had been taken to authorise such a disclosure.[126] The Swedish government objected by arguing that there 'is no implied Community rule based on a common legal tradition whereby only the author of a document may decide whether a document is to be released or not'.[127]

However, if provisions to secure secrecy in the Council are to make sense at all, the question might not be whether there is a common legal tradition of the kind referred to by the Swedish government, but rather whether supremacy of Community law requires the setting aside of conflicting national provisions, even fundamental rights, and even those granting access to the documents in question. If the representatives of the member States in the Council could grant such access

---

[123] Case T-174/95, *Svenska Journalistförbundet,* [1998] ECR, II-2289, para. 113.

[124] Case T-174/95, *Svenska Journalistförbundet,* [1998] ECR, II-2289, para. 117.

[125] It is also far from clear whether the new Art. 255 ECT, inserted by the Treaty of Amsterdam and guaranteeing a right of access to European Parliament, Council and Commission documents will tilt the balance remarkably in the direction of enhanced access to documents.

[126] Case T-174/95, *Svenska Journalistförbundet,* [1998] ECR, II-2289, para. 56.

[127] Case T-174/95, *Svenska Journalistförbundet,* [1998] ECR, II-2289, para. 61.

irrespective of the Council rules of procedure, this might amount to the reduction of those rules' binding force to the Council as such, not including its members – the result being somewhat absurd by exempting the major addressees from the application of the secrecy rules. By contrast, if those rules are binding on the members, they might not ignore their Community duty of secrecy by referring to conflicting national law. Against this background, the relationship of the Community rules on secrecy and the Swedish constitutional 'right to procure information on any subject whatsoever',[128] and the right to 'free access to official documents',[129] becomes crucial.

According to the Swedish constitution, this right may be restricted – subject to specification in a special act of law – only if restriction is necessary having regard to certain aspects of public interest, such as the security of the Realm or the prevention or prosecution of crime.[130] It is not very difficult in general, if not even in the case at issue, to imagine such a conflict between the Community rules eager to provide for secrecy, and the Swedish constitution with its tradition of far-reaching access to documents.[131]

On the grounds of Chapter 10 Article 5 IG such a conflict is not easy to resolve. Most likely is that the Swedish right to access to documents would prevail, given that 10:5 IG does not allow for derogations from that right without a specific amendment of the constitution.

(2) Another example of some actual importance might be the issue of gender equality. It touches at the same time on eventual conflicts between a constitutional permission and a Community law prohibition.[132]

---

[128] Chapter 2, Article 2 Fundamental Law on Freedom of Expression.

[129] Chapter 2, Article 1 Freedom of the Press Act.

[130] Chapter 2, Article 2 Freedom of the Press Act.

[131] See also *Bernitz* (n. 96) p. 439 et seq.; *Cottier* (n. 96) p. 253 et seq.; *Österdahl*, CMLRev. 1999, p. 1059 (especially at p. 1074 et seq.).

However, it should also be said that Chapter 2 Article 2 No. 1 of the Freedom of the Press Act allows for restrictions having regard to the relations of the Realm 'with another state or international organisation'. Arguably the issue raised in the above text might come under this clause. The matter shall not be gone into more deeply – suffice it to say that that 2:1:1 Freedom of the Press Act requires that any restriction of the right of access to official documents to be 'scrupulously specified in the provisions of a special act of law'. The Secrecy Act, which is to be seen as such an act of law, provides that secrecy 'shall apply to any information concerning Sweden's relations to another state, or otherwise concerning another state, an international organisation ..., if it can be assumed that disclosure of the information would disturb Sweden's international relations or would otherwise cause damage to the country.'

[132] Which leads, by definition, to a 'one-sided conflict of norms': making use of the permission leads to a violation of the prohibition, while complying with the prohibition is no violation of the permission. Consequently, precedence of Community law would require one to disapply the permission as well as the provisions enacted on the grounds of the permission.

In *Abrahamsson*,[133] the ECJ stated that Article 2(1) and (4) of Directive 76/207/EEC[134] and Article 141 IV ECT[135]

> 'preclude national legislation under which a candidate for a public post who belongs to the under-represented sex and possesses sufficient qualifications for that post must be chosen in preference to a candidate of the opposite sex who would otherwise have been appointed, where this is necessary to secure the appointment of a candidate of the under-represented sex and the difference between the respective merits of the candidates is not so great as to give rise to a breach of the requirement of objectivity in making appointments'.[136]

At stake was a Swedish regulation[137] which, for a limited number of 30 posts of university professors, and in an effort to push forward towards a fairer allocation of teaching posts between the sexes, called for a rather far-reaching form of 'positive discrimination'.

> 'A candidate belonging to an under-represented sex who possesses sufficient qualifications ... must be granted preference over a candidate of the opposite sex who would otherwise have been chosen (positive discrimination) where it proves necessary to do so in order for a candidate of the under-represented sex to be appointed ... Positive discrimination must, however, not be applied where the difference between the candidates' qualifications is so great that such application would give rise to a breach of the requirement of objectivity in the making of appointments.'[138]

The ECJ first reconfirmed its earlier jurisprudence allowing for 'positive and negative criteria to be taken into account which, although formulated in terms which are neutral as regards sex and thus capable of benefiting men too, in gen-

---

[133] Case C-407/98, *Abrahamsson*, 6 July 2000, not yet reported.

[134] Council Directive 76/207/EEC of 9 February 1976 on the implementation of the principle of equal treatment for men and women as regards access to employment, vocational training and promotion, and working conditions, OJ 1976 L 39, p. 40.

Article 2(1) reads: 'For the purposes of the following provisions, the principle of equal treatment shall mean that there shall be no discrimination whatsoever on grounds of sex either directly or indirectly by reference in particular to marital or family status.' Article 3(4) reads: 'This Directive shall be without prejudice to measures to promote equal opportunity for men and women, in particular by removing existing inequalities which affect women's opportunities in the areas referred to in Article 1(1).'

[135] As amended by the Amsterdam Treaty: 'With a view to ensuring full equality in practice between men and women in working life, the principle of equal treatment shall not prevent any member State from maintaining or adopting measures providing for specific advantages in order to make it easier for the under-represented sex to pursue a vocational activity or to prevent or compensate for disadvantages in professional careers.'

[136] Case C-407/98, *Abrahamsson*, 6 July 2000, not yet reported, para. 56.

[137] The Förordningen (1995:936) om vissa anställningar som professor och forskarassistent vilka inrättas i jämställdhetssyfte (Swedish Regulation concerning certain professors' and research assistants' posts created with a view to promoting equality, 1995:936).

[138] Article 3 Regulation 1995:936.

eral favour women'.[139] But the Court also emphasised that the application of such criteria 'must be transparent and amenable to review in order to obviate any arbitrary assessment of the qualifications of candidates',[140] and he found that requirement violated in the Swedish case.

At first glance the issue does not involve constitutional aspects. The provision which was found to be in conflict with Community law was a regulation enacted by the government. However, the ECJ also mentions that the reference in the regulation to the 'requirement of objectivity', limiting the authorization for 'positive discrimination', was included in the regulation

> 'in deference to Article 9 of Chapter 11 of the Swedish Constitution, according to which, for the purpose of appointments to State posts, only objective criteria are to be taken into account, such as merits (length of previous periods of service) and abilities (aptitude for the post, evidenced by theoretical and practical training and previous experience)'.[141]

What the Court did not mention, though, is Chapter 2 Article 16 IG, which reads as follows:

> 'No Act of law or other statutory instrument may entail the discrimination of any citizen on grounds of sex, unless the relevant provision forms part of efforts to bring about equality between men and women or relates to compulsory military service or any corresponding compulsory national service.'

Let us – if only for the sake of argument – assume that, taken altogether, the Swedish constitution would allow for the enactment of the regulation cited. Supremacy of Community law would then make that authorization inapplicable.[142] Given that the constitutional provision involved is included in Chapter 2 of the Instrument of Government, supremacy in this case is covered by Chapter 10 Article 5 IG.

C. Participatory Rights of Parliament

Also in Sweden the decrease in power of the national parliament caused by EU membership should to a certain extent be counterbalanced by the insertion of provisions into the constitution reinforcing parliamentary influence on the govern-

---

[139] Case C-407/98, *Abrahamsson*, 6 July 2000, not yet reported, para. 47.

[140] Case C-407/98, *Abrahamsson*, 6 July 2000, not yet reported, para. 49.

[141] Case C-407/98, *Abrahamsson*, 6 July 2000, not yet reported, para. 15.

Compare Chapter 11, Article 9, para. 1, sentence 2 IG: 'When making appointments to posts within the State administration attention shall be directed only to objective factors such as merit and competence.'

[142] Assuming that nothing is preventing the direct effect of the Community law provisions involved.

ment, especially in European matters.[143] According to Chapter 10 Article 4 *Riksdag* Act[144] the *Riksdag* appoint 'an Advisory Committee on European Union Affairs (the EU Advisory Committee) ... for the purpose of conferring with the Government on European Union matters'. The Advisory Committee consists of seventeen members coming from all the political parties in the *Riksdag*. More detailed supplementary provisions ensure that the Committee is furnished with sufficient information by the government, and that consultation takes place if the Committee so wishes.

There is no explicit right of the Advisory Committee or the *Riksdag* itself to issue binding instructions which would determine the conduct of the minister in the EU Council, e.g., during the negotiations for the enactment of secondary legislation. However, the risk of not cooperating with the Committee is always a no confidence motion,[145] which might lead to a discharge of the minister.

In practice, the Advisory Committee deals with issues which are taken up in the Council of the EU and in the European Council. It is also consulted concerning Sweden's position in intergovernmental conferences for the revision of the Treaties.

V. CONCLUDING REMARKS

Three previous rounds of enlargement and more than five years to prepare for EU membership could not guide Austria, Finland and Sweden safely so as to avoid very familiar controversies and deficiencies in the constitutional preparation of their accession. The three countries continued with the 'common tradition' of the founding members as well as previously acceding countries to act on the grounds of the respective traditional doctrine and practice. By contrast, a transparent and comprehensive constitutional act revealing the fundamental changes which were at stake was not a primary concern. Against this background it is no surprise that the constitutional steps taken in order to pave the way into the European Union differ remarkably (also) between Austria, Finland and Sweden. Austria had to totally revise its constitution, which was done by a specific Constitutional Act of Parliament subject to a mandatory referendum. Sweden amended its Instrument of Government by inserting an authorization of EU membership, but deliberately inserted a far-reaching reservation against unlimited supremacy of Community

---

[143] See for the following *Bernitz* (n. 96) p. 437 et seq.; *Cottier* (n. 96) p. 258 et seq.

[144] The Riksdag Act is not constitutional law, but it comes '(i)mmediately below the level of fundamental law' [*Holmberg/Stjernquist* (n. 96) p. 32]; 8:16 IG that amendments to the Riksdag Act may be done either in the same way as amendments to the constitution (with the exclusion of the option of a binding referendum) or by a single decision taken by three fourths of those voting. Supplementary provisions, however, may be enacted by the same majorities as ordinary law.

[145] Chapter 6 Article 5 IG.

law in Sweden. Finland did not formally change the wording of its constitution but adopted the Implementation Act by 'constitutional majority'.

As a consequence it has to be said that taking the constitutional adaptations in Austria, Finland and Sweden as a model for future enlargements cannot be recommended. By contrast, the new member States might serve, like the old ones, as examples for the candidate countries of which mistakes should and could be avoided.

All three of the new member States seem to cope well with the specific Community law features of primacy and direct effect, even if none of the new legal texts deals expressly with these issues. However, specific difficulties became apparent in Austria with its system of a centralized constitutional review including an exclusive right of the Constitutional Court to review the constitutionality of Acts of Parliament. First, the Constitutional Court decided not to open the system for the protection of EC law, but confined it for remedies against violations of constitutional law. Second, such constitutional review is deemed available even in cases where the compatibility of the Act under scrutiny with EC law is dubious. Thus, for the purpose of the review procedure an eventual duty to disapply that Act regarding a specific case is discarded.

Measured by the number of references, Austria's courts appear to be the most open for the application of the new law and the system of coherent implementation. This is true not only when compared to Finland and Sweden, but also when compared to other EU member State courts.[146]

Member State	Year									
	1990	1991	1992	1993	1994	1995	1996	1997	1998	1999
Belgium	17	17	16	22	19	14	30	19	12	13
Denmark	5	2	3	7	4	8	4	7	7	3
Germany	34	50	62	57	44	51	66	46	49	49
Greece	2	2	1	5	-	10	4	2	5	3
Spain	6	4	5	7	13	10	6	9	55	4
France	21	24	15	22	36	43	24	10	16	17
Ireland	4	1	-	1	2	3	-	1	3	2
Italy	25	18	22	24	46	58	70	50	39	43
Luxembourg	4	2	1	1	1	2	2	3	2	4
Netherlands	9	17	18	43	13	19	10	24	21	23
Austria						2	6	35	16	56
Portugal	2	3	1	3	1	5	6	2	7	7
Finland						–	3	6	2	4
Sweden						6	4	7	6	5
United Kingdom	12	13	15	12	24	20	21	18	24	22
Total	**142**	**186**	**162**	**204**	**203**	**251**	**256**	**239**	**264**	**255**

146 The table is taken from the XVII Report on monitoring the application of Community law, COM(2000)92 final, Vol. VI (Annex VI), p. 13.

It might also be instructive to mention the openness of *final instances* to start a preliminary ruling procedure showing that even in absolute figures Austria was second only to Germany in 1998 and to Germany and the Netherlands in 1999– compare the Commission Report, p. 14.

THE CONSTITUTIONAL IMPACT OF THE FORTHCOMING ENLARGEMENT OF THE EU: WHAT CAN BE LEARNT FROM THE EXPERIENCE OF THE EXISTING MEMBER STATES?

Francis G. Jacobs*

On the basis of the reports presented to this conference on the constitutional impact of enlargement, my task is to summarise the lessons to be learnt from the experience of the existing member States.

It is necessary for this purpose to attempt an overview of the constitutional solutions adopted in the existing member States. This is a hazardous exercise since, although it has been possible to draw on the reports from experts reporting the position in nearly all the member States, any summary of the experience at second hand is inevitably derivative and will seem, given the restraints of space, superficial. It must be hoped that these disadvantages will be partly offset by the provision of an overall survey which may highlight the lessons to be learnt from the experience of the existing member States.

The survey looks first at the founding member States and then at the successive enlargements.

1. THE FOUNDING MEMBER STATES: BELGIUM, FRANCE, GERMANY, ITALY, LUXEMBOURG, THE NETHERLANDS

When the EEC Treaty was drawn up in 1957, few constitutional difficulties were foreseen, or indeed foreseeable.

The Treaty itself contained few precise clues of the constitutional issues it would raise. It was, of course, widely recognised that the establishment of the new Community, even more than the ECSC before it, was a great step in international organisation and in the transfer of sovereign powers. But the EEC was less explicitly 'supranational' than the ECSC. And there were few provisions of an explicitly constitutional character.

The Treaty did, it is true, set up institutions with legislative powers; but any specific terms spelling out the implications of this novel feature seem to have

* Advocate-General of the Court of Justice of the European Commission, Luxembourg.

A.E. Kellermann et al. (Eds.), EU Enlargement: The Constitutional Impact at EU and National Level

been avoided. The legislative instruments were given the unexciting denominations 'regulations' and 'directives'. Although the Treaty stated that regulations were to be binding in their entirety and directly applicable in all member States, the notions of direct effect and primacy of Community law were not even suggested by the Treaty. And regulations were to be adopted only in certain limited sectors, such as agriculture, free movement of workers and social security, and competition. Other sectors were to be subject to the less constricting 'directives', which were binding only as to the result to be achieved, but left the choice of form and method to the member States. Except for delegated or secondary measures, which could be adopted by the Commission, all regulations and directives were to be adopted by the Council, composed of representatives of member State governments, and in most cases acting unanimously.

Moreover, although the Treaty provided for a Court of Justice of permanent and automatic, non-optional jurisdiction, it could not be anticipated how the Treaty would come to be interpreted by the Court. The key notions of direct effect and primacy were set out by the judgments of the Court only in 1963 (*Van Gend en Loos*) and 1964 (*Costa* v. *ENEL*). It is clear that if *Van Gend en Loos* had been decided the other way (as it might very well have been) then the Community would have developed very differently.

With the benefit of hindsight it is easy to see that the Community as it developed was very different from the Community as it was founded in 1957.

It is therefore perhaps not surprising that the founding member States did not find it necessary to make radical amendments to their constitutions on setting up the EEC.

As Professor de Witte has pointed out[1], in France, Italy and Germany the post-war restoration of democracy had been accompanied by express constitutional recognition of the fact that effective international cooperation was necessary in order to prevent new wars and to avoid the excesses caused by unbridled State sovereignty. Each of these three new constitutions contained a provision permitting limitations of sovereignty or transfer of sovereign powers to international institutions.

In France, paragraph 15 of the preamble of the Constitution of the Fourth Republic adopted in 1946 stated that 'subject to reciprocity, France consents to limitations of sovereignty necessary for the realisation and the defence of peace'. Article 11 of the Italian Constitution of 1948 declares in strikingly similar terms that 'Italy may consent, on equal terms with other States, to limitations of sovereignty necessary to establish an order ensuring peace and justice among nations, and it will favour international organisations which have that aim'. Article 24(1) of the German Basic Law of 1949 expresses the same intention in active, rather than passive, wording: 'The Federation may by legislation transfer sovereign powers to international institutions'.

---

[1] See the report by Bruno de Witte, above, p. 65

All three constitutional provisions are still in force today.

In all three countries, notwithstanding controversy about the adequacy of these provisions, both the ECSC Treaty and the later Treaties of Rome (EEC and Euratom) were approved without further constitutional amendment.

The model set by France, Italy and Germany was followed some years later by the Netherlands (in 1953), Luxembourg (in 1956) and Belgium (not until 1970). The same model was followed in that, even after the ECSC and the later Communities were founded, the constitutional amendments were in entirely general terms and made no reference to the Communities. Thus the Belgian amendment states that 'the exercise of delimited powers can be attributed by treaty or by law to institutions of public international law'.

Despite, on the one hand, the reticence of these constitutional amendments and, on the other hand, the emerging constitutional innovations of the EEC, the courts of the founding member States succeeded in giving effect to Community law and in recognising, in particular, the notions of direct effect and primacy.

As is again pointed out by Professor de Witte, the assertion by the ECJ of the primacy of Community law caused less difficulty in the Netherlands and Luxembourg than in the other founding member States: the supremacy of treaties over national legislation was accepted prior to the EEC Treaty, either by a constitutional provision (the Netherlands) or by the case law of the supreme court (Luxembourg). In Belgium, France, Germany and Italy, by contrast, the primacy of Community law was recognised only after substantial difficulties were overcome.

Nevertheless, by the early 1990's and the incidence of the Maastricht Treaty (which itself required further constitutional amendments in several member States), it could be said that the necessary adjustments of constitutional doctrine allowing for the primacy of EC law over national legislation had been accomplished in all the founding member States. Yet, as Professor de Witte points out, this primacy of EC law was not expressly inscribed in any of the six constitutions; France and the Netherlands had a written rule, but one dating from the 1950's and applying to treaties in general, whereas the four other constitutions remained entirely silent on the central question of the domestic effect of EC law.

As already mentioned, the Treaty on European Union, which entered into force on 1 November 1993, resulted in significant constitutional amendments in several member States.

2. THE FIRST ENLARGEMENT (1973): DENMARK, IRELAND AND THE UNITED KINGDOM

The States joining the Communities in 1973 were in a different position from the founding member States. The primacy of Community law, and the consequent impact on national sovereignty, albeit within limited fields, were now well known, and it was therefore possible to make both political and constitutional arrangements. In some cases and in some respects, however, a minimalist solution was adopted. The three new States responded to the challenge in very different ways.

In Denmark, where amendments to the constitution are difficult to attain, reliance was placed on a 1953 amendment (Section 20) similar to the very general provisions contained in the constitutions of several of the founding member States, according to which: 'Powers vested in the authorities of the Realm under this Constitution Act may, by statute and to a specified extent, be delegated to international authorities set up by mutual agreement with other States for the promotion of international rules of law and cooperation'. Thus, it was not considered necessary or desirable (or perhaps feasible) to introduce a specific amendment to make provision for accession to the Communities or to recognise the primacy of Community law.

In Ireland, by contrast, a very specific amendment was made to the Constitution in 1972 to provide a basis for Irish membership of the Community:

> 'The State may become a member of the [ECSC, EEC and Euratom]. No provision of this Constitution invalidates laws enacted, acts done or measures adopted by the State necessitated by the obligations of membership of the Communities or prevents laws enacted, acts done or measures adopted by the Communities, or institutions thereof, from having the force of law in the State.'

That amendment, which was followed by the European Communities Act of 1972, seemed well designed to allow for the constitutional and legal requirements of membership and it is not therefore surprising to learn that it has been considered as a possible model by at least one of the applicant countries.

In the United Kingdom, in the absence of a formal constitution, only an enabling Act of Parliament could be used; and because of the principle of Parliamentary sovereignty, which implied that no Parliament could bind its successor, it seemed impossible to provide for the primacy of Community law in relation to a subsequent Act of Parliament. In the result the European Communities Act 1972, recognised as an ingenious feat of draughtsmanship, made compendious provision for the reception of Community law in the United Kingdom but could do no more, in respect of primacy, than, first, to include a somewhat obscurely worded sub-section (Section 2(4)) apparently designed to ensure such primacy in so far as was possible; and secondly, to make binding on United Kingdom courts (by Section 3(1)) the case law of the ECJ, including not only its decisions but also 'the principles laid down by' the ECJ, which could be taken to include the principles of direct effect and primacy.

That the Act did have the effect of ensuring the primacy of Community law over subsequent United Kingdom legislation was recognised unequivocally by the House of Lords, sitting as the highest United Kingdom Court, in the *Factortame* litigation.

3. THE SECOND ENLARGEMENT (1981): GREECE

It is agreed that the relevant provision of the Greek constitution (of 1975) is Article 28, which reads as follows:

> '1. Generally recognised rules of international law, as well as international conventions after they have been sanctioned by law and after they enter into force according to their respective terms, form an integral part of internal Greek law and prevail over any contrary provision of law.
> 2. To serve an important national interest and to promote co-operation with other States, competences provided for in the Constitution may be recognised by treaty or agreement to agencies of international organisations. A majority of three-fifths of the total number of members of Parliament is required for the enactment of the law which sanctions the treaty or agreement.
> 3. Greece may freely proceed by law passed by the absolute majority of the total number of members of Parliament to limitations of the exercise of national sovereignty, insofar as this is dictated by an important national interest, does not infringe human rights and the foundations of democratic government and is effected on the basis of the principle of equality and under the condition of reciprocity.'

There is however disagreement over whether accession to the Community was based upon the second or third paragraph of the Article, or on both paragraphs. The voting requirements of both paragraphs were fulfilled. It is suggested that there is in any event no doubt concerning the prevalence of Community law over conflicting Greek law, whether prior or subsequent.

4. THE THIRD ENLARGEMENT (1986): SPAIN AND PORTUGAL

In Spain, Article 93 of the Constitution is regarded as providing the basis for Spain's accession to the Communities. It provides as follows:

> 'Authorisation may be granted by an organic act for concluding treaties by which the exercise of powers derived from the Constitution shall be transferred to an international organisation or institution. It is incumbent on the Cortes Generales [Parliament] or the Government, as the case may be, to ensure compliance with these treaties and with resolutions originating in the international and supranational organisations to which such powers have been so transferred.'

It is also of interest to note the view of the Spanish Constitutional Court, as recorded in the Spanish report[2], to the effect that conflicts between Community law and Spanish law are not a matter for the Constitutional Court. That view could

---

[2] See the report by Gregorio Garzón Clariana, above, p. 117

result in a position consistent with the position taken by the ECJ, notably in the *Simmenthal* case, that it is for the ordinary courts to give effect to Community rights and to set aside, where necessary, any conflicting provisions of national law, and that such conflicts should not be reserved to a constitutional court or to any other special procedure which would prevent the ordinary courts from giving immediate effect to Community law.

In Portugal, successive amendments to the Constitution in 1982, 1989 and (to take account of the Treaty on European Union) 1992 provided the foundations for the adaptation of the Portuguese legal order to the European Treaties. As in Spain, the possible non-conformity of Portuguese legislation with Community law is dealt with by the ordinary courts, without the intervention of the Constitutional Court.

5. THE FOURTH ENLARGEMENT (1995): AUSTRIA, FINLAND AND SWEDEN

Austria, almost uniquely, adopted a constitutional law expressly and specifically providing for accession to the European Union. That law did not however directly regulate the relationship between Community law and national law. The Austrian Constitutional Court has taken the position that a violation of Community rights is not a violation of constitutional rights. As with Spain and Portugal, therefore, the outcome should be that it is open to the ordinary courts to set aside provisions of national law which conflict with Community law.

In Finland, we are informed that the Constitution permits derogations which need not be formally incorporated in the text of the Constitution: in the case of treaties, such derogations can be approved by a two-thirds majority of the votes cast in Parliament. In the case of the Treaty of Accession, that was done after a scrutiny of the Treaty by the Constitutional Law Committee of Parliament. The Implementation Act, which was adopted under the above procedure, contains the necessary substantive provisions, which are very brief: the Act states Finland's membership of the EU and provides for EC and EU law to have the force of law in Finland under the conditions laid down by the *acquis communautaire*.

In Sweden, in contrast, the Constitution was amended to provide for accession to the EU: more precisely, one provision of part of the Constitution, the 'Instrument of Government' (*Regeringsformen*) – the characteristic provision dealing with transfer of powers to international organisations – was amended to provide that the Swedish Parliament may transfer decision-making powers to the EC 'as long as they provide for protection of fundamental rights and freedoms equivalent to that guaranteed by this instrument and by the European Convention on Human Rights'.

5.1 Typology of constitutional amendments

Three broad categories of constitutional amendment can be identified; briefly:
(1) General provisions allowing for the transfer of certain powers to international organisations;
(2) General provisions allowing for the transfer of powers but directed specifically to the EC or EU;
(3) Specific amendments, for example removing special rights for nationals: e.g., the ownership or publishing of journals in Portugal, or, following the Treaty on European Union, conferring on citizens of the Union the right to vote in municipal elections.

All three categories can give rise to difficulties. To put the matter again very briefly:
(1) General provisions framed in terms of international organisations at large are unlikely to recognise the specific character of the EC/EU or to make adequate provision for key doctrines such as the direct effect and primacy of EC law.
(2) General provisions directed specifically to the EC/EU may, if appropriately framed, make it easier to resolve the above difficulties but will not typically be able to overcome crucial difficulties: in particular, will it be for the ECJ or for the member State's constitutional court to resolve the question of the scope of the powers transferred.
(3) Specific amendments may be adequate to deal with such conflicts between constitutional provisions and Community provisions as have already been identified, but will be unable to resolve conflicts which materialise subsequently.

5.2 Typology of potential conflicts

The above brief analysis suggests that it may be helpful to outline the main categories of potential conflict between national constitutions and European law.

(1) A first case concerns the exercise by the European institutions of transferred powers: where, under the constitution, powers have been transferred to the EC/EU, who is to adjudicate on whether powers have been exercised going beyond the scope of those transferred? From a European perspective it may seem inherently anomalous that such adjudication should be left to the national courts of each of the member States. However, the perspective of the national courts, and particularly that of a national constitutional court, may be different. The dilemma seems intractable. The following sub-category may however provide some reassurance that solutions are nonetheless possible.
(2) A sub-category is the case where it is alleged that the exercise of powers by the EC/EU conflicts with fundamental rights protected by the constitution. This is the most debated aspect of the subject, and is of great interest from a doctrinal

point of view, perhaps because at a theoretical level it is one of those wonderful problems which admit of no possible solution. No doubt a constitution cannot provide, explicitly or implicitly, that powers may be exercised by an international body even where they infringe fundamental rights protected by the constitution. In practice, however, the ECJ itself has sought to overcome this difficulty by developing its own case law requiring the Community to observe fundamental rights recognised by the national constitutions; and this case law is now also enshrined in the Treaty. This solution has hitherto been broadly acceptable in the legal systems of the member States, and it does indeed seem the only practical solution. Since what is in issue is the validity of a Community measure, it does not seem sensible to leave the decision to each national system.[3]

(3) A third category is the more general case where the constitution does not make adequate provision for the primacy of Community law. As is shown by the national reports, these difficulties have generally been overcome (if sometimes only after periods of uncertainty) by the national courts themselves, which have progressively recognised that the primacy of Community law, even if not explicitly provided for by the national constitution, is inherent in the very nature of the Community system. Nonetheless such a pragmatic solution cannot, once again, provide any guarantee that difficulties will not recur.

(4) A fourth category is that of specific constitutional provisions which transpired to be in conflict with the Treaty as interpreted by the ECJ. For example, constitutional provisions in several member States reserving posts in the public service to a State's own nationals have been found to conflict with the Treaty provisions on the free movement of workers and on freedom of establishment as interpreted by the ECJ.

Such specific conflicts cannot always be readily resolved by constitutional amendment: the amendment procedures may (as for example in Denmark) be extremely laborious. An alternative solution may be found in other ways: interpreting the constitutional provision in the light of the more general provisions designed to give effect to Community law; or, if that is not possible, a 'sympathetic' interpretation of the specific provision – so that, in the example taken above, 'public service' is interpreted as restrictively in the Constitution as it is by the ECJ in the Treaty. Such interpretations may be encouraged by the realisation that specific provisions of this kind are not inherently of a constitutional nature: the restriction of posts in the public service to a State's nationals is not a matter

[3] It seems to me that the German Constitutional Court rightly recognised this reality long ago, when it held that, so long as the protection of fundamental rights was in general adequately ensured by Community law, it would not seek to review on this ground the validity of a particular Community measure. The subsequent judgment of the German Constitutional Court in the Maastricht Treaty case does not seem to have changed that basic position. Indeed it has been reaffirmed in the Court's recent judgment in the bananas case.

universally regulated at the constitutional level; it may be regulated at the level of ordinary legislation, over which Community law can more easily be held to prevail.

6. CONCLUSIONS

At a constitutional level, our first conclusion may be that difficulties are of two different orders. In some member States, constitutional provisions were not sufficiently adapted to facilitate the full effect of Community law. In some cases, this was the result of difficulties posed by the national constitution itself. The United Kingdom provides a rather extreme example.

The difficulties were exacerbated where, as happened in some member States on accession, the constitutional requirements of membership were not properly confronted, and the necessary conclusions were not drawn.

It is true that many of the difficulties have been overcome, in a very remarkable way, by judicial ingenuity, by constructive dialogue between the ECJ and national courts, and perhaps above all by a creative and pragmatic approach of the national supreme courts. But this does not seem a wholly satisfactory recipe for the future.

In the first place, there are, as we have seen, continuing problems in the existing member States. Several national supreme courts still hesitate to recognise unconditionally the primacy of Community law, and find no adequate basis in the national constitution to do so. The situation therefore remains precarious.

Secondly, if solutions to conflicts have largely proved possible to date (in a relatively favourable legal and judicial climate) there can be no guarantee that this will continue. The path of further constitutional amendment after accession may not always be available. It is impossible to foresee where constitutional difficulties may arise. Many of the applicant States are newly independent, with independence provisions firmly rooted in their constitutions, and with constitutional courts standing guard over them. As integration progresses, the need for clear constitutional provision for accession becomes increasingly indispensable. In the context of enlargement, it would seem paradoxical if close attention is paid to the detailed transposition of the entire corpus of Community legislation by the candidate States, while little interest is shown in the constitutional provisions needed to make them effective.

Indeed it could be said that it is not only constitutionally and legally necessary to make in advance the constitutional changes entailed by accession; it is also socially and politically to confront the constitutional implications of membership of the EU before, not after accession. It seems in the interests of all sides that that undoubtedly difficult task should be undertaken, and properly carried out.

SESSION III
National Level : Impact on the Constitutions and Courts of the Candidate Countries

The Mediterranean Countries Malta, Cyprus and Turkey

The Central and Eastern European Countries

EUROPE AGREEMENTS IN THE LIGHT OF SOVEREIGNTY AND LEGITIMACY: THE CASE OF ESTONIA

Anneli Albi*

While it is usually the EU membership that is regarded as encroachment on state's sovereignty, this paper suggests that also the pre-EU-accession adaptations such as harmonising law under the Europe Agreement to the acquis communautaire, law of foreign states in the formation of which CEECs have no participation, signify a subordination of state independent decision-making powers to the EU and should therefore require either authorising constitutional amendment or a rather open modern approach to sovereignty. This is particularly the case of Estonia, whose constitution, as a reflection of country's oppressive history, protects sovereignty exceptionally strictly through several safeguards. The main positions of this paper could, in principle, apply also to several other CEE countries, depending on the level of constitutional protection of sovereignty in their constitutions.

INTRODUCTION

The writings on harmonising CEE candidate countries' law, policy and institutional structures to the EU requirements usually describe abundantly the harmonisation procedures, while there is rarely discussion on, for instance, the economic cost of harmonisation or the suitability of applying EU models to the CEE transformation countries. Amongst other issues, it is surprising that the CEECs, many of which strictly protect sovereignty in their constitutions after the 50-year USSR domination, have not raised constitutional problems in regard to harmonising law to the EC *acquis*, which is a foreign law in the formation of which CEECs have no participation.

This paper suggests that the harmonisation under the Europe Agreements as well as other European adaptations such as institutional reorganisations, accession negotiations, expenditure of state budget for this end, signify a fundamental

* Researcher at the European University Institute, Florence (Italy).

A.E. Kellermann et al. (Eds.), EU Enlargement: The Constitutional Impact at EU and National Level

subordination of state independent decision-making powers to the EU and should therefore require either *authorising constitutional amendment* or *a rather modern open approach to sovereignty*. The article contemplates the constitutionality of harmonisation and other European adaptations in the example of Estonia, but its main positions could, in principle, apply to several other CEECs, depending on the degree of sovereignty protection in their constitutions.

1. PROTECTION OF SOVEREIGNTY IN THE CONSTITUTION

Prompted by an oppressive history, the Estonian Constitution, similarly to its Baltic counterparts, very strictly protects the country's sovereignty through several safeguards. As set forth in Article 1, the Constitution makes an elaborate distinction between three closely interrelated notions: (a) independence (*iseseisvus*), (b) sovereignty (*sõltumatus*) and (c) popular sovereignty, declaring them timeless and inalienable.

> Art 1. Estonia is an *independent and sovereign* democratic republic, *wherein the supreme power of the state is vested in the people.*
> Art 1(2). The independence and sovereignty of Estonia are *timeless and inalienable* [emphasis added].[1]

These provisions cannot be amended except by means of a referendum (Art. 162). Further, the Constitution does not provide direct clauses on international cooperation, although generally recognised norms and principles of international law are an inseparable part of the Estonian legal order (Art. 3) and Parliament is to ratify, inter alia, treaties with which Estonia joins international organisations (Art. 120). Similar exceptionally strict constitutional safeguards on sovereignty are present also in the constitutions of Latvia and Lithuania, which perhaps renders the three Baltic constitutions a distinct group.

Beside these manifold safeguard clauses on sovereignty, the austerity of the sovereignty requirement is reinforced by applying to it an interpretation provided by the inter-war Estonian Republic's (1918-1940) constitutional lawyer A.-T. Kliimann.[2] His interpretation has recently been used by the Estonian Constitutional Expert Commission [ECEC] in documents prepared as a basis for further discussion on constitutional amendments.[3] In this interpretation, 'independence'

---

[1] Constitution of the Republic of Estonia. Estonian Translation and Legislative Support Center, 1996, 1. Internet: http://www.rk.ee/rkogu/eng/epseng

[2] Kliimann, A.-T., Eesti iseseisvuse areng [Development of Estonia's Independence], Õigus 1935/ 2, pp. 49-50.

[3] Põhiseaduse 1. Peatükk 'Üldsätted' [1 Chapter of the Constitution 'General Provisions']. In: Eesti Vabariigi Põhiseaduse Ekspertiisikomisjoni Lõpparuanne. [Final Report of the Constitutional Expert Commission of the Estonian Republic], ptk 3.2. Internet: http://www.just.ee/pohiseadus/

implies the prohibition against a state becoming part of another state or federation (generally known as external sovereignty), while 'sovereignty' means non-subordination of law-giving to a foreign power (internal sovereignty). The ECEC adds to the sovereignty concept theoretically a more contemporary content, noting that obligations undertaken by international treaties are part of contemporary sovereignty, with the exception that this would not apply to situations where *a state subjects itself by mutual agreement to unilateral domination of the other party.*[4] In applying Article 1 to concrete cases such as the constitutional implications of EU membership, the ECEC adheres strongly to the definitions provided by Kliimann and emphasises the value of state this has been known since the wave of formation of nation-states, underlining the importance of thinking in the sovereign nation-state paradigm. As the author has learned from unofficial discussions with some constitutional lawyers of Latvia and Lithuania, their legal scholarship uses similarly to Estonia the 'traditional' understanding of sovereignty as suggested in the writings of the inter-war republics' authors.

In the light of the above austere constitutional safeguards on sovereignty, reinforced by the inter-war period of the 'traditional' interpretation of sovereignty, Estonia's ongoing pre-EU-accession adaptations raise the issue of their constitutionality. The unilateral harmonisation of Estonian law to a foreign law under the Europe Agreement, institutional reorganisations, appropriations of the state budget for this end and other EU adaptations are likely to trespass on the inflexible constitutional limits set for the governmental institutions.[5] The following chapters, after insight into the European adaptations process, suggest that it requires either a constitutional authorisation by referendum or a modern rather open interpretation of state sovereignty.

2yldsatted.htm; Võimalik liitumine Euroopa Liiduga ja selle õiguslik tähendus Eesti riigiõiguse seisukohalt. Põhiseaduse juriidilise ekspertkomisjoni aruanne. [Potential Accession to the European Union and its Legal Consequences from the point of view of Estonian Constitutional Law. The Report of the Constitutional Expert Commission]. Manuscript, 1998, pp. 3-5. Internet: http://www.just.ee/juridica2.html

[4] Põhiseaduse 1. Peatükk 'Üldsätted'..., supra, ptk 3.2.

[5] The question of constitutionality of Government activities in respect of EU accession was recently also offically addressed to Estonian officials by the leader of the Eurosceptic Party, K. Kulbok. He makes the issue more complex by making reference, allegedly for philological purposes, to § 62 of the Criminal Code, according to which activity against Estonia's independence and sovereignty is sanctioned by imprisonment. He has also mentioned in publicity a possibility of launching a case for constitutional review of Estonia's EU integration documents. Communication in public e-mail list ut.juura.vestlus@lists.ut.ee, 21.03.2000, 14.06.2000, 12.06.2000, 10.05.2000.

2. HARMONISATION AND OTHER EUROPEAN ADAPTATIONS IN THE LIGHT OF SOVEREIGNTY

2.1 Unilateral harmonisation under the Europe Agreement

Under the Europe Association Agreement [EA], concluded in 1995 and effective since 1998, Estonia has undertaken an extensive unilateral harmonisation of its law to a foreign legal system, in the formation of which the country has no participation. Read together with the White Paper, Accession Partnerships and other EU documents on accession principles, the harmonisation covers wide areas, extending from the internal market to the state's core functions, such as foreign and monetary policy, touching even upon areas over which the EU lacks competence in regard of its present member States. The Europe Agreement sets forth harmonisation obligation and priority fields in Articles 68 and 69:

> Article 68:
> The Parties recognise that *an important condition for Estonia's economic integration into the Community is the approximation of Estonia's existing and future legislation to that of the Community*. Estonia shall endeavour to ensure that its legislation will be gradually made compatible with that of the Community.

> Article 69:
> *The approximation of laws shall extend to the following areas in particular*: customs law, company law, banking law, company accounts and taxation, intellectual property, financial services, rules on competition, protection of health and life of humans, animals and plants, protection of workers including health and safety at work, consumer protection, indirect taxation, technical rules and standards, nuclear law and regulation, transport, telecommunications, environment, public procurement, statistics and product liability. Within these areas rapid progress in the approximation of laws should in particular be made in the fields of the internal market, competition, protection of workers, environmental protection, consumer protection, financial services and technical rules and standards.

While these articles set forth only the priority areas, in view of the Copenhagen criteria for accession,[6] the candidate state is to bring its legislation into accordance with approximately 80,000 pages of the *acquis communautaire,* including the Treaties, secondary legislation, ECJ case law, soft law and international agreements. Further, differently from the previous enlargements, the obligatory *acquis* in the context of CEECs takes a remarkably wider scope. According to the European Commission Agenda 2000[7] and a Council of Ministers' document on

---

[6] Bull EC 6-1993, pt I.13.

[7] Agenda 2000, Vol. I, 15 July 1997, Part 2: The Challenge of Enlargement. Internet: http://www.europa.eu.int/comm/enlargement/agenda 2000/strong/21.htm.

accession principles,[8] the harmonisation covers also institutional structures and the long term values and goals which the EU is currently developing, such as the Common Foreign and Security Policy, Monetary Union and Justice and Home Affairs. It thus covers even policy areas which have not been adopted by all the member States (Schengen, EMU), while the Accession Partnerships add also areas beyond the EU domestic competences (judicial reform, prison conditions, social security system reform, pension reform, civil service reform, etc).[9] The strategy for harmonisation in the internal market areas with a set of concrete measures to be implemented is provided by the European Commission in the White Paper.[10] The Accession Partnerships,[11] issued by the European Commission since 1998, set the harmonisation deadlines and provide for European Commission supervision on meeting the *acquis* demands.

Beside the comprehensiveness of the legislative harmonisation fields, the harmonisation obligation, as has been pointed out in regard to the experience of the EC-EFTA relations, may in soft form also cover the policy areas and judicial and administrative implementation.[12] This is even recommendable, for instance in order to ensure the uniform interpretation of the Europe Agreement provisions in the EU and Estonia as well as between candidate states themselves.[13] However, as the Hungarian Constitutional Court has recently appropriately stated in its Europe Agreement case,[14] interpretation based on application criteria of EU law would require constitutional authorisation. This judgment makes one wonder how much more compellingly the *harmonisation* to foreign law would need constitutional authorisation.

Estonia, for its part, has declared in the Government Activity Plan of 1996 that '[t]he legal policy for joining the EU forms part of the legal policy of the Estonian state,'[15] which in the explanation of H. Pisuke, the Head of the International Law Department of the Ministry of Justice

---

[8] 2078th Council meeting General Affairs, Brussels, 30/31 March 1998 (ref PRES/98/96).

[9] Grabbe, H., A Partnership for Accession? The Implications of EU Conditionality for the Central and East European Applicants. European University Institute, Robert Schuman Center, Working Paper No. 99/12.20 et seq.

[10] White Paper: Preparation of the Associated Countries of Central and Eastern Europe for Integration into the Internal Market of the Union. COM(95) 163 final.

[11] Accession Partnership – Estonia – March, 1998. Internet: http://www.europa.eu.int/comm.enlargement/estonia/ac part 03 98/index

[12] See discussion in Evans, A., Voluntary Harmonization in Integration between the European Community and Eastern Europe. In: ELRev., 1997, Vol. 22, pp. 207-208.

[13] R. Maruste, the former President of the Supreme Court in a dissenting opinion, and L. Meri, the President of the Republic in constitutional review proceedings have stressed that as a part of Estonia's legal-political obligation to approximate Estonia's law under the EA, the Estonian legislative acts in judicial proceedings also should be assessed in the light of EU law, including ECJ judgments. See resp. Estonian National Court, 3-4-1-4-98, R. Maruste eriarvamus [dissenting opinion], 27.05.1998, and Dec 1. 3-4-1-96. Available in English: http://www.nc.ee/english/

[14] Hungarian Constitutional Court, Decision 30/1998. (VI 25) AB, *Magyar Közlöny*. Available in German: http://www.mkab.hu/Dec/deu/30-1998.htm

[15] Government Activity Plan for Joining the European Union. June 1996, Tallinn.

> '... has the ultimate goal of conformity of the Estonian legal system with the *acquis communautaire in all its areas*. The Estonian legal policy is based on the assumption that *the whole legal system* must be harmonised with the requirements of EC law [emphasis added]'.[16]

In practice, the creation of the Estonian legal system after the re-establishment of the Republic's independence has proceeded largely from the EU law; all the draft legislation has to undergo substantial control on compatibility with EU law by the European Law Division of the Ministry of Justice.[17] If EU law has been involved in a composition of a legal act, reference to the concrete EC directives and their publication data is made in the preamble to the act, which has been condemned by the Legal Department of the Office of the *Riigikogu* for the reason that it is a reference to legislation of the law of foreign states.[18] In order to facilitate the harmonisation work for the officials, the Ministry of Justice has issued a special Methodology on approximation of Estonian law to EC law.[19]

Besides the comprehensive harmonisation, Pisuke states furthermore that as a legal consequence of the political decision expressed by the Government in the Accession Application (28 November 1995), the *EC law is in principle already now superior for Estonia*:

> 'The main legal consequence for Estonia in joining the EU is that Estonia must recognise, in principle, the supremacy of the *acquis communautaire* over the Estonian legal system and that Estonia must apply its whole state regulatory mechanism to the approximation of the legal system to the *acquis communautaire*'.[20]

It is not clear from the article whether Mr Pisuke represents his own opinion or the official position of Estonia's legal policy, but since this statement is almost literally found also in other sources,[21] it seems to be a generally recognised position. Although the supremacy of EC law is not legally binding until the status of membership is achieved, the above statement represents indeed the *de facto* situation where Estonia has to proceed in its legislation from the EC law in view of its membership goal.

Harmonisation in the case of the CEECs has been qualified as 'voluntary harmonisation', since it differs from the EU Member States' harmonisation obli-

---

[16] Pisuke, H., Estonia and the European Union: European Integration in Estonia. In: Juridica International 1996. Law Review of University of Tartu, AS Juura, 1996, pp. 2-5, Internet: http://www.juridica.ut.ee/Juridica/International/1996/n-1/inco.htm3.

[17] See further Laffranque, J., Influence of European Community Law on Estonian Law and, in particular, Law-Making. In Juridica International IV, 1999, p. 88 et seq.

[18] Laffranque, J., supra, p. 90.

[19] See for overview in English Laffranque, J., supra, p. 88 et seq.

[20] Pisuke, 1996, supra, p. 2.

[21] In Tanning, L., Rahvusvaheline ja Euroopa Liidu majandus [International and European Union Economy]. Tallinn, 1999, p. 291.

gation,[22] and differently from the EEA Agreement the harmonisation in the EA is proposed as a 'voluntary legislative programme' with no enforcement procedures but national control mechanisms.[23] However, from the candidate states' side, all of whose priority is the goal of EU accession, harmonisation is an obligation. This appears when reading the EA together with the candidate states' Accession Applications and the accession criteria formulated in the above-mentioned EU documents such as the Copenhagen criteria, the Council of Ministers' document on accession principles, the White Paper and Accession Partnerships. While the two first-mentioned declare full harmonisation a precondition for accession, the implementation of the White Paper and Accession Partnership form the basis for evaluating the candidate country's readiness for accession in the European Commission annual Opinions. Non-compliance with these documents would mean postponement or denial of EU membership as well, as under the Accession Partnership, suspension of financial assistance.

In addition, whether or not harmonisation is ultimately a legal obligation, it is, together with other European adaptations, a serious subordination of state independent decision-making power and requires, in the light of the internal strict constitutional protection of sovereignty, a constitutional authorisation.

2.2 No participation in the formation of the rules, minimum bargaining room in negotiations

The harmonisation obligation is furthermore difficult to reconcile with the sovereignty requirements considering that Estonia has no participation in the formation of the *acquis* which it has to take over, until the eventual future membership has taken place in the undetermined future. Moreover, the *acquis* has to be taken over with minimum bargaining and minimum consideration of Estonia's and other CEECs special circumstances.

Differently from the EEA Agreement, the present harmonising candidate states have no participation even in regard to new draft EC legislation.[24] Apart from the 'Structured Relationship' talk-shop of CEE Heads of States and Ministers in the framework of the European Council since 1994, as well as the European Conference which replaced it in 1998, the only institutionalised means to participate in law-making which has an impact on the CEECs are infrequent cases in the EU comitology system, where the third state experts may be invited to pertinent meetings.[25]

---

[22] Evans, supra, p. 202.

[23] See Maresceau, M., Montaguti, E., The Relations between the European Union and Eastern Europe: A Legal Appraisal. In: CMLR, 1995, No. 6, p. 1336.

[24] See on EEA Evans, A., The integration of the European Community and Third States in Europe. Oxford: Clarendon Press, 1996, supra, p. 257 et seq.

[25] See Evans, A., European Union Decision-Making, Third States and Comitology. ICLQ, 1998, Vol. 47, p. 267 et seq.

The CEECs have had only a marginal say also in regard to the contents of the Europe Agreements and the other discussed EU policy instruments.[26] It has been suggested that the mechanic adoption of the EC legal rules, designed for economies of rather different stages of development and containing anomalies deriving from the specific political contexts of their adoption time, does not take into account the interests and economic, political and legal situation of the CEECs, particularly in the light of their severe structural economic problems.[27] In rather simplified terms, the priority measure for the CEECs to reduce the gap of living standard with the EU countries is high economic growth, which they have so far achieved due to a competitive advantage of low cost production factors, while imposition of EU social, environmental and technical standards ends this competitive advantage. Thus, for instance, several commentators have suggested that, in the environmental and social spheres, the CEECs should not carry out the harmonisation until shortly before the accession,[28] that CEE economies should be allowed substantial derogations in terms of production conditions, while the products themselves would have to meet the Single Market standards.[29]

Further, the EU competences in regard of CEECs are exercised without justifying and restraining principles such as subsidiarity, proportionality and competence, with little involvement of restraining institutions, such as the EU Council, European Parliament, national parliaments, and ECJ.[30] A conclusion in H. Grabbe's words:

> 'There is a paradox in EU-CEE relations: *applicants are treated like member States in the extent of their obligations under the APs, but as applicant they have no rights and little say in determining the substance of relations, leaving the EU as a hegemonic actor* [emphasis added].'[31]

The *accession negotiations* offer no major change in this 'asymmetric power relation'. The Council of Ministers has confirmed that the full harmonisation with strictly limited transition opportunities forms a principle for future accessions.[32]

---

[26] Sedelmeier, U., The European Union's Association Policy towards Central and Eastern Europe: Political and Economic Rationales in Conflict. (1994) Brighton, Sussex European Institute, cited in Grabbe, supra, p. 34.

[27] Evans, 1997, supra, p. 201 et seq.; Nello, S., Smith, K.E., The European Union and Central and Eastern Europe. The Implications of Enlargement in Stages. Ashgate: Aldershot 1998, p. 18, with reference to Smith, A., Holmes, P., Sedelmeier, U., Smith, E., Wallace, H. Young, A., The European Union and Central and Eastern Europe: Pre-Accession Strategies. Brighton: Sussex European Institute 1996; Grabbe, H., Hughes, K., Eastward Enlargement of the European Union. London, The Royal Institute of International Affairs, 1998, p. 37.

[28] Nello, Smith, supra, p. 18, with reference to Smith et al., supra.

[29] Grabbe, Hughes, 1998, supra, p. 36, with reference to Smith et al., supra.

[30] Grabbe, supra, p. 24.

[31] Grabbe, supra, p. 24.

[32] 2078th Council meeting General Affairs, Brussels, 30/31 March 1998 (ref PRES/98/96).

Earlier accessions of countries economically and politically more comparable to CEECs – Greece, Spain and Portugal – were allowed considerable compromises. The consolidation of democracy in these countries was expected to take place after EU membership, and also long transition periods were allowed so as to aid economic development: more than a decade for some trade policy issues, agriculture, 5-7 years for abolition of customs duties and adjustment of monopoly, etc.[33]

However, in regard to CEECs, several EU statements indicate that the room for bargaining is much more limited, although the need for specific conditions is, considering their economic situation, comparable to the cases of Portugal and Greece. According to Agenda 2000 and other sources, most of the *acquis* for CEECs is non-negotiable, which in the Commission officials' statements means 99%.[34] In comparison with earlier accessions, it has been made clear that CEECs are not to seek derogations, and no long transition periods are allowed; for instance, generally most 5 years instead of 17, in well-defined spheres.[35] The negotiations also have a limited role considering that whether the candidate countries meet the conditions is judged by the Commission under the Accession Partnerships, rather than through the official accession negotiations running in parallel.[36]

2.3 No EU legal obligation to accept membership

The unilaterality of the Europe Agreement, under which Estonia engages itself for extensive and irreversible harmonisation, institutional reorganisations, remarkable public expenditure, etc., is all the more imposing as the EU has for its part no legal obligation to accept the membership of Estonia or the other candidate countries. The Preamble of the Europe Agreement declares that, '[r]ecognising the fact that Estonia's ultimate objective is to become a member of the European Union ... [the association aims to] help Estonia to achieve this objective.' This objective of Estonia's accession is formulated rather vaguely so as not to express the EU promise of future membership: membership is recognised as *Estonia's* ultimate objective rather than as a mutual goal, as is also the case with the other EAs.[37] The negotiating history of the first EA states, Poland, Hungary and the Czech Republic, shows that the EU was rather reluctant to make any reference to accession in the Agreements and even this vague formulation is the result of the candidate states' strong lobbying.[38] For instance, the Polish State Secretary insisted on a reference to accession, declaring that, considering that Po-

[33] See Grabbe, supra, p. 23; Grabbe, Hughes, supra, p. 59.

[34] Grabbe, supra, p. 23.

[35] E.g., Grabbe, supra, p. 22 et seq. Also Radio Free Europe news e-mail list, RFE/RL NEWSLINE Vol. 4, No. 56, Part II, 20 March 2000.

[36] Grabbe, supra, p. 23.

[37] Maresceau, Montaguti, 1995, supra, p. 1332.

[38] Van Ham, P., The EC, Eastern Europe and Unity. Discord, Collaboration and Integration since 1949. London: Pinter, 1993, p. 198.

land has abolished the barriers but the EU remains closed to half of Poland's exports, there is no government in the world which would submit such a one-sided agreement to its parliament for ratification.[39]

From the political aspect, however, one could invoke the Copenhagen European Council Summit declaring the Associated countries' membership to be a common goal, setting forth the accession preconditions and making a more substantial commitment to enlargement.[40] On the other hand, the Copenhagen criteria are formulated rather broadly and allow a considerable degree of subjectivity.[41] The example of the accession of Greece shows that the country may achieve membership rather for political reasons, considering that in economic terms Greece, with its structure of agriculture and weak industrial base, was economically hardly ready for accession.[42]

Thus, the harmonisation remuneration is a hope to accede, not the promise of accession by the EU.[43] On the political level, one may rely on the eventual fulfilment of the broadly formulated Copenhagen criteria, but these do not set forth a fixed timetable and the enlargement does not only depend on the applicant states' efforts, but also on the EU inner institutional reform.

2.4 General imbalance of Europe Agreement obligations

The Europe Agreement is also generally unbalanced in regard to the rights and obligations of the parties[44] – beside the unilateral harmonisation and having no say in the rules, the Agreement is often said to be disadvantageous also in economic terms. It opens Estonia's market, whereas EU markets remain closed by customs duties, minimum prices, quotas and the possibility to apply safeguard measures to most products where Estonia has a competitive advantage. Estonia, for its part, may for political reasons not use these trade barriers, since this would give a potential sign of unreadiness for accession. Further, since the EU accession deprives Estonia from the Free Trade Agreement with Ukraine and the Baltic States, the only countries with which Estonia has a positive trade balance,[45] the Estonian economy, rather than being helped to prepare for the EU membership

[39] Cited in Van Ham, supra, p. 198.

[40] Bull EC 6-1993, pt I.13.

[41] See more Nello, Smith, supra, p. 20 et seq.

[42] See Van Ham, supra, p. 196.

[43] Kennedy, D., Webb, D.E., The Limits of Integration: Eastern Europe and the European Communities. CMLR, 1993, Vol. 32, p. 1117.

[44] See more Raba, K., The Balance between Rights and Duties in the Europe Agreement between Estonia and EU, paper forthcoming in Gothenburg University Anthology of Symposium on Europe Agreements in 04.05.2000.

[45] See further Leht, H., The Development of Bilateral Trade Agreements between Estonia and States not Members of the EU, paper forthcoming in Gothenburg University Anthology of Symposium on Europe Agreements in 04.05.2000.

goal as declared in the Preamble to the EA, may find itself in a rather difficult situation after the accession. The Agreement also provides marginal rights in the chapter on the movement of workers, establishment and services, providing only for a right of non-discrimination instead of a right of free movement of workers.

One of the few substantial returns for Estonia is EU financial and technical assistance. However, the financial assistance is far from comparable with the assistance provided to the Mediterranean countries. Almost a third of the PHARE funds has actually returned to the West as remuneration for consulting services.[46] The Agreement also provides to Estonia some other rights of an Associated State such as participation in the Fifth Framework Programme for Research and Technological Development, youth and education exchange programme and cooperation in some specific fields. One important indirect benefit resulting from the Europe Agreement is also potential investors' enhanced confidence in the country thereby drawing in more foreign direct investment.

We could conclude along with Kennedy and Webb that:

> '[t]hese efforts, ... while significant, do not constitute a coherent and bilateral commitment to coordinate legal and regulatory policies and institutions. This perhaps represents the worst of both worlds: the Association Countries *cede a level of independence* at a crucial time in their democratic reform and economic restructuring programmes and *receive little that is tangible in return* [emphasis added]'.[47]

As we saw from the previous chapters, the harmonisation obligation undertaken by the Estonian authorities through the Europe Agreement means a unilateral submission to extensive adaptation to the EU *acquis* as the law of a foreign legal entity, from internal market spheres to social and foreign policy. Estonia has no say in the formation of this law and, having to take over the full *acquis* for accession, has very little say in the process of accession negotiations and receives 'little that is tangible in return'. Together with other European adaptations such as the accession application, institutional reorganisations, accession negotiations and financial resources appropriated for this end, the integration process is most likely irreversible, while the EU on its side does not even have a legal obligation to accept Estonia's entrance into the organisation. In the light of the above discussed austere constitutional safeguards on sovereignty, reinforced by the Expert Commission interpretation of Article 1 of the Constitution, according to which the unilateral domination of one treaty party violates sovereignty, it is difficult to interpret the Europe Agreement as compatible with these requirements.

[46] Report by Court of Auditors, OJ No. C/175, cited in Grabbe, Hughes, 1998, supra, p. 38.
[47] Kennedy, Webb, supra, p. 1115.

2.5 Legitimacy of harmonisation and European adaptations

The harmonisation process, reorganisation of institutions, accession application and accession negotiations furthermore touch on the fundamental constitutional principle of popular sovereignty, which is established in the second part of Article 1 of the Constitution: 'Estonia is an independent and sovereign democratic republic, *wherein the supreme power of the state is vested in the people'*. Among several concretising principles, the Estonian Constitutional Expert Commission interprets popular sovereignty as involving the requirement that (a) the people as *pouvoir constituant* have determined in the Constitution the competences of state bodies, (b) no foreign body can exercise higher power in Estonia, and (c) the principle of democracy.[48]

In the present process of EU integration, the Estonian authorities' policy-making is altogether extensively subjected to the norms and politically obligatory guidelines from the EU, which, until Estonia's eventual membership, is a foreign power. Considering that Estonia's people have subjected the authorities' activity by the Constitution to the inflexible principle of inalienability of sovereignty, one could well argue that the authorities, in concluding the Europe Agreement and particularly in the light of the European adaptations as a whole, have not acted within these constitutionally restricted competences.

Furthermore, the Estonian parliament *Riigikogu* has had no participation in the contents of the 'eurorequirements' so as to provide legitimacy by the Estonian people and take account of the interests of the Estonian state and of different national interest groups.[49] Although the *Riigikogu* has given its authorisation to the integration process by ratifying the EA and legitimacy could partially be based on the popular will expressed by the parliamentary elections – all the major political parties have declared the EU accession to be a foreign policy priority in their

---

[48] Põhiseaduse 3. Peatükk 'Rahvas' [3 Chapter of the Constitution 'People']. In: Eesti Vabariigi Põhiseaduse Ekspertiisikomisjoni Lõpparuanne. [Final Report of Constitutional Expert Commission of Estonian Republic]. Internet: http://www.just.ee/pohiseadus/4rahvas.htm, ptk 1; Põhiseaduse 1. Peatükk 'Üldsätted'..., supra, ptk 3.3; Võimalik liitumine Euroopa Liiduga..., supra, p. 5.

[49] The democratic participation is deficient also in regard to the discretion left for harmonisation and accession negotiations, as the integration process concentrates power to the executive branch. The parliamentarians have on EU-related sessions pointed out the following problems: (a) the procedures of parliamentary involvement into the decision-making mechanism should be determined by law; (b) the harmonisation and accession negotiations proceed rather quickly so that there is left no time for coalition-opposition deliberation, whereby several important questions are in fact solved by 1-2 officials. For instance, a Working group on sugar did not include representatives of the Estonian food industries, result of which is that the sugar price on joining the EU rises four times, and is likely to launch a chain reaction of bankruptcies and social problems. Similarly, Estonian officials have sought no exceptions in regard of land sales to foreigners, while there is already today high foreign interest in buying cheap Estonian land for speculative purposes; (c) very few issues of the 80,000 pages of the *acquis* have been drawn to public discussion; (d) the Government positions submitted to Brussels are confidential. See Stenograms of *Riigikogu* sessions 04. and 08.06.1998, 19.01.2000, available on Internet: http://www.riigikogu.ee

programme – the implications of EU integration, as discussed, have very fundamental consequences, while the popular sovereignty principle *may be amended only by referendum and not by the Riigikogu* (Art. 162).

The EU integration process also lacks empirical legitimacy, that is, it has a low level of popular support. As public opinion research reveals, the Estonian population's support for European integration has been the lowest among the candidate states, over the last five years fluctuatingly between 29-42%. Furthermore, the population is uninformed about EU-related issues in general. The public debate about the European integration takes place mainly but at the elite level and concentrates on the historic, security and geopolitical aspects, while the people are largely uninformed about the implications of joining the EU, such as its economic and social aspects or impact on their daily lives.[50] Although the EU is not a security organisation, the Baltic states deem the EU membership important primarily because it would mean a decisive move out of the Russian influence sphere. Two-thirds of Estonia's population, mainly Estonians, see in Russia a threat to independence and the positive answer in the referendum to EU accession may largely depend on developments in Russia.[51] Such data further show a lack of legitimacy for the political bodies to engage Estonia in developments having such fundamental consequences for state sovereignty.

3. THE EXPERT COMMISSION OPINION ON PRE-ACCESSION IMPACTS ON SOVEREIGNTY

The need for constitutional authorisation for the European adaptation process has been to a certain extent acknowledged also by the Constitutional Expert Commission in its recent Report on the constitutional consequences of EU accession.[52] The ECEC suggests as a parenthetical option a two-step constitutional amendment, introducing in the near future norms

> '... *creating legal preconditions for the Estonian Republic's accession to the Union. These should ensure that Estonia's accession application, negotiations, which concern the conclusion of an accession treaty constraining the sovereign state powers, and ul-*

[50] Grabbe, H., Hughes, K., Central and East European Views on EU Enlargement: Political Debates and Public Opinion. In: Back to Europe, ed. by K. Henderson, London: UCL Press, 1999, p. 185, p. 186, p. 189; Kirch, M., Avalik arvamus Euroopa Liidu laienemisest liikmes- ja kandidaatriikides [Public Opinion on the European Union Enlargement in the Member and Candidate States]. Riigikogu dokument no. 295, 06.04.99, Internet: http://www.riigikogu.ee/osakonnad/msi/tel295.

[51] Kivirähk, J., Eestlased kardavad Venemaad, muulased mitte [Estonians are afraid of Russia, non-Estonians not]. – Eesti Päevaleht, 29.03.2000, and Kirch, M., Eestlaste otsus tulevasel euroreferendumil sõltub Venemaast [Estonians' decision in the euroreferendum depends on Russia]. – Eesti Päevaleht, 28.03.2000. Internet: http://www.epl.ee

[52] Võimalik liitumine Euroopa Liiduga..., supra.

> *timately the whole process of harmonisation of legislation, reorganisation of institutions, etc, which takes place on the basis of the state budget resources so as to carry out the pertinent state politics, would be in accordance with the Constitution.* The norms introduced in the first step would form a general basis for the accession to the European Union and a possibility to delegate to this end certain state powers [emphasis added]'.[53]

However, the Expert Commission prefers a one-stage amendment shortly before the actual accession, since the amendments would require a referendum, the organisation of which twice in a short period of time is complicated. The Commission further explains that a referendum carried out 6-7 years before the actual accession, so as to obtain the people's approval to accede in the far future, would not express the popular will regarding what would probably have became a changed EU in the meantime.[54] Rather than authorising the integration process by constitutional amendment, the Expert Commission suggests, somewhat inappropriately, that the citizens, according to Article 54 of the Constitution, have a right to defend the independence of Estonia in the form of initiating resistance.[55] As the Expert Commission apparently disregards the expression 'change of the constitutional order *by force*', the initiation of resistance as a means of protecting the constitutional order cannot be applicable because of the unfeasibility of using force in carrying out the process of EU integration.

Thus, the Expert Commission implicitly acknowledges that the pre-EU-accession adaptation process may not be in accordance with the sovereignty requirement of the Constitution, but does not consider the matter serious enough to require constitutional amendment. On the other hand, the Expert Commission applies a rather strict interpretation to the member State status. Emphasising strongly the legal thinking in the paradigm of the sovereign nation state, the ECEC concludes that accession would affect sovereignty and require constitutional amendment, since the law-making power in broad fields would be accorded to the Union bodies, whereby the will of these and the other member States would be binding upon Estonia, even in the case Estonia that has voted against a decision.[56] The Expert Commission further sets strict limits to European integration: based on the independence requirement, Estonia's Constitution would never allow Estonia's participation in the EU were the latter to adopt its own, European Constitution, since this would mean the development of the EU into a federation[57,58].

---

[53] Võimalik liitumine Euroopa Liiduga ..., supra, p. 19 [Author's translation].

[54] Voimalik liitumine Euroopa Liiduga ..., supra, p. 19.

[55] Võimalik liitumine Euroopa Liiduga ..., supra, p. 20 [Author's translation].

[56] Võimalik liitumine Euroopa Liiduga ..., supra, p. 4, p. 11.

[57] Võimalik liitumine Euroopa Liiduga ..., supra, pp. 8-9, pp. 14-15.

[58] The Expert Commission's positions on EU membership status have been discussed further by the author elsewhere, suggesting that the ECEC has taken a German Constitutional Court *Maastricht*-decision type intergovernmental attitude to issues of sovereignty, democratic legiti-

The ECEC's lenient position to pre-accession implications seems to contradict its conservative interpretation on sovereignty in the case of the eventual status of EU membership. Differently from EU membership, where Estonia would have a participation in the decision-making process, the pre-accession harmonisation takes place as a unilateral subordination without any corresponding legal entitlement, entailing, along with other European adaptations, an irreversible transformation of economic, legal, political and institutional structures under the *de facto* EU governance.

4. STATUS OF RATIFIED UNCONSTITUTIONAL TREATIES

The previous sub-chapters show that in the light of the strict protection of sovereignty by the Estonian Constitution, there are substantial reasons to question the constitutionality of the Europe Agreement, particularly in the context of the European adaptations as a whole. This situation takes us to a rather complicated legal and political problem in regard to the potential unconstitutional treaties adopted by ratification into the Estonian legal order. Article 123.1 of the Constitution prohibits the conclusion of unconstitutional treaties, but, since *a posteriori* constitutional review is not possible in the Estonian legal system and *a priori* constitutional control takes place only in regard of a marginal number of treaties adhered to Estonia, the possibility of unconstitutional treaty provisions may therefore not always be precluded. So far, none of the treaties already in force have been the subject of litigation nor public discussion on unconstiutionality. The issue has been addressed at a theoretical level by the Expert Commission, with divergent conclusions.

The Expert Commission has offered the following interpretations to Article 123.1:[59] (a) firstly, it may be regarded as a confirmation that in the Estonian legal order there are no treaties incompatible with the Constitution; (b) alternatively, not taking a position on the potential existence of unconstitutional treaties, the provision forms a prohibition against the conclusion of unconstitutional treaties by analogy with the prohibition on internal bodies from issuing unconstitutional acts; (c) moving then implicitly towards acknowledging the possibility of the existence of unconstitutional treaties, the ECEC suggests that the treaties are subject

misation and judicial review in the EU, and that the statal concepts of 1930s legal writings should be updated so as to match the EU and general internationalisation context. Albi, A., Euroliit ja kaasaegne suveräänsus [Eurounion and Contemporary Sovereignty. One potential response to Constitutional Expert Commission's call for discussion]. Tartu University Law Faculty Journal *Juridica* 2000/3 (in Estonian, with English summary).

[59] Põhiseaduse 9. Peatükk 'Välissuhted ja välislepingud'. [9 Chapter of the Constitution 'External Relations and Treaties']. In: Eesti Vabariigi Põhiseaduse Ekspertiisikomisjoni Lõpparuanne. [Final Report of Constitutional Expert Commission of Estonian Republic]. Internet: http://www.just.ee/pohiseadus/10valissuhted.htm

to interpretation for conformity with the Constitution. Since the National Court cannot review the treaties already entered into force, the treaty is compatible for the formal reason that it cannot be declared unconstitutional; (d) however, when a treaty in its application appears to be manifestly incompatible with the Constitution, the Vienna Convention on the Law of Treaties, which is itself below the Constitution, allows Estonia to refer to Article 46, according to which Estonia's consent would have been expressed in violation of a very important national norm, such as Article 123.1 of the Constitution; (e) in case of manifest unconstitutionality, the Estonian state bodies should not act in violation of the Constitution and should decline from complying with the treaty obligation. If international law does not provide grounds for non-compliance, it results in state liability.

Firstly, solutions (a) and (b), denying the existence of unconstitutional treaties in the Estonian legal order, are, given the rare preventative control by the National Court, not necessarily true. We have seen in this paper one example of a potentially unconstitutional treaty. Solutions (d) and (e), insisting on non-compliance of the unconstitutional treaty, are at least in the case of the Europe Agreement obviously politically unfeasible, considering that EU membership is Estonia's foreign policy priority. There remains option (c), namely, to interpret the treaty so as to achieve conformity with the Constitution. However, considering the strict inflexibility of the protection of sovereignty by the Estonian Constitution, the lack of provisions on international cooperation and the interpretation provided to the sovereignty provision by the Expert Commission, this option would be conceivable only by a radical change in the traditional interpretation given to the sovereignty concept. This option will be discussed later.

The author suggests that there is also a sixth and feasible option, namely, to introduce promptly into the Constitution a provision authorising international and European cooperation. This solution was parenthetically also proposed by the Expert Commission, although the later referendum shortly before the EU accession was preferred.

5. CONSTITUTIONAL AMENDMENT BY REFERENDUM

With regard to the constitutional amendment by referendum, the Expert Commission's argumentation can be supported to the extent that two referendums in a short period of time is unfeasible on economic and participatory considerations. Since these referendums would virtually overlap in the question posed, the rate of participation, particularly of the latter, is likely to be problematic. Furthermore, the constitutional amendment is made technically rather difficult by the Constitution itself so as to avoid frequent constitutional amendments

(Arts.161-168).[60] The amendment procedure lasts, at a minimum, seven months and the amendment cannot be re-initiated for one year. The quorum of 3/5 of the *Riigikogu* for constitutional amendment further requires a broad consensus among the political parties represented in the *Riigikogu.*

However, the Expert Commission's argumentation for a preference for the later-in-time referendum, based on the consideration that in this case the popular will would be most in accordance with the stage of EU development then reach, deserves questioning. Does the potential closer accordance of the people's will to the future stage of EU development indeed outweigh the virtual violation of the fundamental constitutional principles of national and popular sovereignty, which has been happening by virtue of unilateral law harmonisation to a foreign legal order, accession application, institutional rearrangements, negotiations and expenditure of state budget resources for this purpose, leaving the strict protection of sovereignty in the Constitution a historic relic without real substance?

In other words, the possibly earlier referendum with pertinent constitutional amendments would ensure the legitimacy of the whole European adaptations process, while the *late referendum* is quite *predetermined of choice* and has relatively smaller effect, since the potential differences in the then EU stage of development would not amount to the fundamental process which Estonia has undertaken. Furthermore, when the referendum takes place after the harmonisation and other European adaptations have been completed, there is virtually no way back, whereby the people's choice in the referendum is but illusory, rather than being a *posterior legitimising nature.* As has also been suggested by Küpper, the transfer of sovereignty to a supranational organisation – particularly at a time when the transferring state is not yet a member and has no say in the law-creating process – is a decisive and hardly reversible process, which on legal policy considerations necessarily requires constitutional amendment.[61]

The amendment is further prompted by the fact that there is also the necessity for a general provision enabling the delegation of powers to an international sphere, so as to formalise the present situation where Estonia is a member of numerous international organisations, which inevitably encroach to some extent on the sovereign decision-making. In order to avoid the country's accession to organisations based on the former Soviet Union, which has obviously been the purpose of the strict protection of Estonia's sovereignty, a formulation used by the Lithuanian Constitution could be used, which explicitly prohibits Lithuania's participation in ex-USSR-based organisations.[62]

---

[60] Põhiseaduse 15. Peatükk 'Põhiseaduse muutmine' [15 Chapter of the Constitution 'Constitutional Amendment'] In: Final Report..., supra, Internet: http://www.just.ee/pohiseadus/16pohiseaduse muutmine.htm

[61] Küpper, H., Integration mit Hindernissen – Die 'Europa-Entscheidung' des ungarischen Verfassungsgerichts. Im: Recht in Ost und West, 1998/8, p. 335.

[62] Art. 150(3), Constitution of Lithuania (unofficial translation), adopted Oct 25, 1992, Internet: http://www.uni-wuerzburg.de/law/lh00000 .html.

6. CHANGE OF INTERPRETING SOVEREIGNTY – 'OPEN STATEHOOD'?

An alternative to a fast referendum introducing a constitutional amendment would be the option suggested above of *interpretation of conformity with the Constitution*. In this case, the interpretation given by the Expert Commission to the fundamental provisions of independence and sovereignty should be changed. As we saw before, the Expert Commission, basing its conclusions on definitions from legal writings of the inter-war period, interprets independence to mean prohibition from becoming part of another state/federation, while sovereignty implies that state decision-making must not be subjected to a higher power. It explains that while conclusion of and subordination to international treaties forms part of sovereignty in the contemporary world, unilateral submission to the domination of another power would not be compatible with sovereignty.

Proceeding from this interpretation, the Europe Agreement and European adaptations would not mean a *loss* of *independence*, since they do not render the state part of the European supranational order. However, these largely irreversible adaptations are oriented to membership of the EU, whereby they affect independence, at least when adhering to the Expert Commission interpretation that adoption of the EU constitution, which is a feasible future development, would render it a federation.

As to *sovereignty*, the above chapters show that, based on the Europe Agreement and other EU accession-aimed documents which should be read together with the EA, Estonia has subjected itself to a unilateral harmonisation of its law to the *acquis communautaire*. The content of Estonia's policy-making is largely determined by the EU institutions and Estonia is subjected to EU control to the effect that in the case of non-compliance, sanctions are applied by suspending financial assistance and EU membership postponed/denied. It is problematic to interpret this situation so as to be in conformity with the austere sovereignty protection provided by the Constitution, particularly if one proceeds from the sovereignty-interpretation provided by the Expert Commission.

Instead of the Expert Commission interpretation of sovereignty and independence notions, the Europe Agreement as well as imminent EU accession would provide an *appropriate time to rethink the traditional interpretation given to these constitutional concepts*. In comparison with the state theory of the nineteen-thirties during the First Estonian Republic, present-day writings on state and sovereignty suggest that these concepts have undergone a transformation, internationalisation processes requiring from states more openness so as to fulfil their tasks on the international/supranational level on the basis of efficiency. It has been suggested that openness to international co-operation in delegating certain tasks on the basis of efficiency to the supranational/international level could have become a fourth element of state, beside population, government and territory.[63] Regardless of disputes over how far the European integration is to go so as to be efficient, it is generally acknowledged that a supranational organisation such as the EU has proved effective in tackling its major policy areas. Meanwhile, the EU has not led and will not lead to erosion of member States' statehood, but rather shows that the traditional concepts may need rethinking so as not to foreclose on EU future substantive integration, while the question of further integration should rather be subject to limits of economic/political efficiency.

The author suggests that the Estonian Constitution may provide a basis for interpreting the independence and sovereignty notions in a way more open to European integration. The Preamble of the Constitution sets forth as one of the purposes of the Constitution to 'protect internal and external peace' and to be 'a pledge to present and future generations for their social progress and welfare'. Considering that security, particularly the 'external peace' of the Estonian state requires the military guarantees of NATO as well as the soft security provided by the EU, while 'social progress and welfare' presumes participation in the EU economic and social integration, the will of *pouvoir constituant* should be interpreted by taking account this social reality.[64]

The change of interpretation may be also supported by two following moments. Firstly, we must bear in mind the fact that the strict formulation of sovereignty was designed during the first years of Estonia's independence, where its primary concern was to assert itself as an independent republic in regard of an unstable Russia, whose troops were still in the country. Presently, the priorities have switched towards an openness to Western cooperation. Secondly, the change of interpretation should be considered as due by the fact that the definitions used by the Expert Commission were suggested as long ago as 1935, after which the world order has undergone fundamental changes towards globalisation, interdependence and various exceptions to state sovereignty. However, it is likely that in order to be feasible, this change of interpretation, based on mere academic thoughts, needs a supporting expeditious constitutional amendment, similar to that discussed in the previous section. It may also be that since the norms themselves can be amended only by referendum, a radical change of interpretation requires also authorisation by the people.

---

[63] See e.g., Hobe, S., Statehood at the End of the 20th Century – The Model of the 'Open State': A German Perspective – AJIEL, 1997, n. 2, pp. 127-154.

[64] A sign of revolution in interpreting sovereignty may be distinguished in the official answer of L. Hänni, Chairman of Riigikogu Constitutional Commission, to the above noted communication of K. Kulbok, where she states that 'Estonian foreign policy priorities conform to the Constitution and are aimed at ensuring Estonia's independence and sovereignty'. Letter of 14.06.2000, available in e-mail list ut.juura.vestlus@lists.ut.ee, 14.06.2000.

CONCLUSION

While it is usually EU membership that is regarded as an encroachment on the state's sovereignty, this paper suggests that also the pre-EU-accession adaptations such as the harmonising of law to the *acquis communautaire* under the Europe Agreement the law of foreign states in the formation of which CEECs have no participation, as well as institutional reorganisations, accession negotiations and expenditure of state budget for this end, require authorising constitutional amendment. This is particularly the case with Estonia, whose constitution, as a reflection of the country's oppressive history, protects sovereignty exceptionally strictly through several safeguards. Alternatively, it is suggested that the interpretation of the sovereignty concept deriving from constitutional writings of the inter-war period Republic be replaced by a modern concept open to international and European cooperation, such as 'open statehood'. The main positions of this paper could in principle be applicable also to several other CEE countries, depending on the level of constitutional protection of sovereignty provided in their constitutions.

INTRODUCTION TO THE PARTNERSHIP AND COOPERATION AGREEMENTS

Christophe Hillion*

1. INTRODUCTION

The Partnership and Cooperation Agreements (PCAs) are the contractual instruments linking the EC and its member States with most countries from the former Soviet Union, the so-called Newly Independent States (NIS).[1] The latter are not recognised by the EU to be *official* candidates for EU membership, although some of them would like to. Consequently, the NIS do not, *a priori*, have to modify their constitution the way the candidate countries are expected to do.

Nonetheless, the constitutional impact of a third country's relationship with the EU does not exclusively derive from the former's preparation for accession. Constitutional change can also be stimulated by links of a different nature, e.g., the Partnerships established by the PCAs, which in the case of Russia and Ukraine were consolidated by the recently adopted Common Strategies (CSs).[2] The CSs were introduced by the Amsterdam Treaty as a new instrument of the Common Foreign and Security Policy (CFSP).

Indeed, as a growing number of external agreements signed by the Community and its member States, the PCAs illustrate the potential influence the EU exercises on the constitutional life of its partners, although in a less direct and less formal way than in the case of the candidate countries.[3] This general trend goes hand in hand with the development of EC and CFSP 'competences' for promoting respect for human rights and democracy. Some see in this evolution the de-

---

* Deputy-Director, Centre for European Legal Studies, University of Cambridge.

[1] Armenia, Azerbaïjan, Belarus, Georgia, Kazakhstan, Kyrgyzstan, Moldova, the Russian Federation, Tadjikistan, Turkmenistan, Ukraine, Uzbekistan.

[2] Respectively OJ 1999 L157, OJ 1999 L331.

[3] I refer here to Joseph Weiler who once wrote that 'constitutional changes' can be 'direct and formal', touching on the constitution itself or 'thought of in less formal ways'; in this case, non-legal yet symbolic historical events and the constitutional change they reflect may be 'indirect and informal'. See Weiler, *The Constitution of Europe* (Cambridge University Press, 1999), p. 3.

A.E. Kellermann et al. (Eds.), EU Enlargement: The Constitutional Impact at EU and National Level

velopment of the EU towards an 'organisation of general human rights competence'.[4]

In this context, the PCAs deserve particular attention because they are agreements signed with the NIS. Firstly, these countries are in a process of transformation which has entailed the creation of new constitutions[5] and also, to a variable extent, the (re)definition of a constitutional culture.[6] Secondly, the NIS are increasingly affected by the EU enlargement process. That is particularly the case for those which are, like Russia, or which will be European neighbours of the enlarged Union, viz. Belarus, Moldova and Ukraine, let alone Armenia and Georgia, once Turkey accedes. With a view to moderating the negative impact of the enlargement and as part of a more general domestic political choice, some 'excluded' countries, such as Ukraine and Moldova, have spontaneously adopted a candidate-like behaviour, i.e., giving signs of political, economic and legal 'acculturation'.[7] In doing so, the NIS have shown how the Union may be regarded as a political reference, despite the fact that it cannot be, as such, a constitutional model to be followed.

Indeed, by 'drawing from the constitutional traditions common to the member States'[8] and through the EC external relations and the CFSP, the EU itself may want to influence the transformation process undertaken by the NIS, particularly to secure a stable neighbourhood and more generally to 'assert its identity on the international scene'.[9]

This contribution does not pretend to provide for a thorough qualitative assessment of the PCAs.[10] It will rather present the political aspects of the Partnership that have a clear constitutional nature, that is the object of the first part. The following section will explore the mechanisms for influence linked to the Part-

[4] See for instance McGoldrick, The European Union after Amsterdam: an organisation with general human rights competence, in O'Keeffe and Twomey, *Legal Issues of the Amsterdam Treaty* (Hart, 1999), pp. 249-270.

[5] See on that Mullerson, Fitzmaurice and Andenas (eds.) *Constitutional Reform and International Law in Central and Eastern Europe* (Kluwer, 1998); Ludwikowski *Constitution-making in the region of former Soviet dominance* (Duke University Press, 1996).

[6] Georgia, Moldova, Russia and Ukraine have become members of the Council of Europe, Armenia is special guests to its Parliamentary Assembly.

[7] See on that Mullerson, Fitzmaurice and Andenas, op. cit.

[8] To paraphrase what the Court of Justice pointed out in *Internationale Handelsgesellschaft* (Case 11/70 [1970] ECR 1125): 'respect for fundamental rights forms an integral part of the general principles of law' that it shall protect. The protection of such rights 'whilst inspired by the constitutional traditions common to the member States must be ensured within the framework of the structure and objectives of the Community'. See also, Opinion 2/94 [1996] ECR I-1759, para. 36.

[9] Article 2 TEU.

[10] In that respect, the reader may want to see the analysis of Maresceau, On Association, Partnership, Pre-Accession and Accession, in Maresceau, *Enlarging the European Union – Relations Between the EU and Eastern Europe* (Longman, 1997); see also his contribution Les relations entre l'Union européenne et la Russie à un tournant de leur histoire in Raux & Korovkine (eds.) *Le Partenariat entre l'Union Européenne et la Fédération de Russie* (Apogée, 1998).

nership. Finally, the limits of the EU's constitutional influence vis-à-vis the NIS will be underlined.

2. THE POLITICAL NATURE OF THE PARTNERSHIP: A REFLECTION OF COMMON 'CONSTITUTIONAL TRADITIONS'

Both the PCAs and the CSs include political objectives reflecting principles having a constitutional nature. The latter are inspired by the members States' 'constitutional traditions' and international commitments.[11]

2.1 **The political aspects of the PCAs**

PCAs were first concluded with Ukraine, the Russian Federation, Belarus, Kazakhstan, Kyrgysztan and Moldova. The network of Partnerships was then extended to other Central Asian and Caucasian countries.[12] For reasons the author explored elsewhere,[13] the Community did not consider signing Association Agreements such as the Europe Agreements with the NIS. That was especially

[11] Case 4/73 *Nold* v. *Commission* [1974] ECR 491. In the aftermath of *Internationale Handelsgesellschaft*, the ECJ introduces a further source of fundamental rights in Community law: 'international treaties for the protection of human rights on which the member States have collaborated or of which they are signatories'.

[12] Tajikistan excluded. To date, nine of these agreements have entered into force: Council and Commission Decision of 30 October 1997 on the conclusion of a PCA between the EC and their member States, of the one part, and the Russian Federation, of the other part (OJ 1997, L 327); Council and Commission Decision of 26 January 1998 on the conclusion of the PCA between the EC and their member States, of the one part, and Ukraine, of the other part (OJ 1998, L 49); Council and Commission Decision of 28 May 1998 on the conclusion of a PCA between the EC and their member States, of the one part, and the Republic of Moldova, of the other part (OJ 1998, L 181); Council and Commission Decision on the conclusion of a PCA between the EC and their member States, of the one part, and Armenia, of the other part (OJ 1999, L 239); Council and Commission Decision on the conclusion of a PCA between the EC and their member States, of the one part, and Azerbaijan, of the other part (OJ 1999, L 246); Council and Commission Decision on the conclusion of a PCA between the EC and their member States, of the one part, and Georgia, of the other part (OJ 1999, L 205); Council and Commission Decision on the conclusion of a PCA between the EC and their member States, of the one part, and the Republic of Kazakhstan, of the other part (OJ 1999, L 196); Council and Commission Decision on the conclusion of a PCA between the EC and their member States, of the one part, and the Kyrgyz Republic, of the other part (OJ 1999, L 196); Council and Commission Decision on the conclusion of a PCA between the EC and their member States, of the one part, and Uzbekistan, of the other part (OJ 1999, L 229); see also the proposal for a Council and Commission Decision on the conclusion of the PCA between the EC and its member States, on the one hand, and Belarus, on the other hand (COM(95)44); the proposal for a Council and Commission Decision on the conclusion of the PCA between the EC and its member States, on the one hand, and Turkmenistan, on the other hand (OJ 1998, C 50/2).

[13] Hillion, Partnership and Cooperation Agreements between the European Union and the New Independent States of the Ex-Soviet Union, 3 EFA Rev. (1998), pp. 399-420, at pp. 406-408; see also Maresceau, op. cit., note 10.

true after EU membership was recognised to be the ultimate goal of the latter agreements.[14] Indeed, one may see the PCAs as an alternative to the Europe Agreements and define their nature accordingly: the PCAs are neither association agreements nor, *a fortiori*, an instrument preparing for accession to the EU.[15]

Moreover, unlike association agreements (Art. 310 EC) and agreements signed with developing countries (Art. 177 EC), the PCAs have no specific legal basis in the EC Treaty. Rather, they borrow the traditional legal grounds of the trade and cooperation agreements, viz. Articles 133 and 308 EC.[16] Indeed, the PCAs are mixed agreements involving both EC exclusive competences relating to the common commercial policy, and competences shared between the Community and its member States, considering not only the PCAs provisions on economic cooperation[17] but also the considerable political dimension of the agreements.

---

[14] The Conclusions of the June 1993 Copenhagen European Council read as follows: 'the associated countries of Central and Eastern Europe that so desire shall become members of the European Union.'

[15] To use the *Demirel* definition *a contrario*, the NIS do not have any 'special, privileged links with the Community' and they do not 'take part, at least to a certain extent, in the Community system' (see Case 12/86, *Demirel* v. *City of Schwäbish Gumd* [1987] ECR 3719, para. 9). For more on that point see Maresceau, op. cit, note 10; see also Hillion, Partnership and Cooperation Agreements between the European Union and the New Independent States of the Ex-Soviet Union, 3 EFA Rev. (1998), pp. 399-420.

[16] As the PCA also covers matters relating to the European Coal and Steel Community and European Atomic Energy Community, a general reference to the ECSC Treaty, particularly Art. 95, and to Art. 101 EAEC was made in the Council and Commission Decisions on the Conclusion of the PCAs.

[17] Following ECJ's Opinion 1/94 (*WTO* [1994] ECR I-5267), the legal basis of the PCA was developed; for instance, the Council and Commission Decision on the Conclusion of the PCA with Russia includes: Art. 44(2) (ex Art. 54(2)), the last sentence of Art. 47(2) (ex Art. 57(2)) and Art. 55 (ex Art. 66) for the PCA provisions on services and establishment; Art. 57(3) (ex Art. 73c(3)) for the provisions on payments (connected with the movement of goods) and capitals; Art. 71 (ex Art. 75), Art. 80(2) (ex Art. 84(2)) for the provisions on transports; Art. 93 (ex Art. 99), and Art. 94 (ex Art. 100) for the provisions on direct and indirect taxation, in conjunction with the second sentence of Art. 300(2) (ex Art. 228(2)) and the second subparagraph of Art. 300(3) EC, together with Art. 95 of the Treaty establishing the European Coal and Steel Community and Art. 101 of the Treaty establishing the European Atomic Energy Community. See also the Commission Document on the amended proposal for a Council and Commission Decision on the conclusion of the PCAs with Belarus, Kazakhstan, Kyrgyzstan, Moldova and Ukraine (OJ 1995 C127/2). For an analysis on this inflation of legal basis, see Flaesch-Mougin, 'Quel partenaire européen pour la Fédération de Russie: Union européenne, Communauté, Etats membres?' in Raux & Korovkine (eds.) *Le Partenariat entre l'Union européenne et la Fédération de Russie* (Apogée 1998) at p. 66; Peers, 'EC frameworks of international relations: Cooperation, Partnership and Association' in Dashwood and Hillion, *The general law of EC external relations* (Sweet & Maxwell, 2000). For analysis on Opinion 1/94, see for instance, Tridimas and Eeckhout, 'The external Competence of the Community and the Case-law of the Court of Justice: Principles versus Pragmatism'; 14 YEL (1994) p. 143; Simon, 'La compétence de la Communauté pour conclure l'accord OMC: l'avis 1/94 de la Cour de Justice', *Europe* (1994) Chronique 9.

Firstly, the Agreements underline the Parties' 'firm' commitment to the full implementation of all principles and provisions contained in the Final document of the Conference on Security and Cooperation in Europe (CSCE), the Concluding documents of the Madrid and Vienna follow-up meetings, the document of the CSCE Bonn Conference on economic cooperation, the Charter of Paris for a New Europe and the CSCE Helsinki document 1992, 'The Challenges of Change'.[18]

Secondly, Art. 2 of the PCA with Russia states that:

> 'respect for the democratic principles and human rights as defined in the Helsinki Final Act and the Charter of Paris for the New Europe[19] underpins the internal and external policies of the Parties and constitute an *essential element* of partnership and of the Agreement' (italics added).

This type of human rights clause is not exclusive to the PCAs. It has appeared in an increasing number of bilateral trade and cooperation agreements, association agreements such as the Europe Agreements, since the early 1990s.[20] Yet, a specific policy applies to agreements concluded with European countries which are members of the OSCE, such as the CEECs and the NIS. A Joint Declaration to the PCA with Russia indicates the basis of such a clause by referring to 'the Council Declaration of 11 May 1992,[21] requiring the inclusion of this reference in cooperation or association agreements between the Community and OSCE partners'.

The substantive obligations encapsulated in the concept of 'essential element' are not explicitly spelled out in the PCAs. Echoing Article 2 of the Agreement with Russia, the Joint Declaration indicates that 'the reference to the respect for human rights ... flows from the attachments of both Parties to the relevant obligations, arising in particular from the Helsinki Act and the Charter of Paris on the New Europe'. The latter includes a chapter on 'Human Rights, Democracy and Rule of Law', the first sentence of which states that the participating states undertake 'to build, consolidate and strengthen democracy as the only system of government'. The text further elaborates on democracy, which, 'with its representative pluralist character, entails accountability to the electorate, the obligation of public authorities to comply with the law and justice administered impartially. In-

[18] See the Preamble of the PCAs.

[19] Both documents are stated in Art. 11 (ex J.1) TEU. They can be found on the OSCE website, for the Charter of Paris: http://www.osce.org/docs/english/1990-1999/summits/paris90e.htm; for the Helsinki Final Act, http://www.osce.org/docs/english/1990-1999/summits/helfa75e.htm

[20] On this point, see Brandtner and Rosas, Human Rights and the External Relations of the European Community: An Analysis of Doctrine and Practise, 9 EJIL (1998) pp. 469-490 at p. 473. See also Reidel and Will, Human rights clauses in external agreements of the EC, in Alston (ed.) *The EU and Human Rights* (Oxford University Press, 1999) pp. 723-753.

[21] Council Declaration of 11 May 1992, Press Release no. 6326/92.

deed, "[d]emocratic government is based on the will of the people, expressed regularly through free and fair elections ...".[22]

By being mentioned in the Agreement, such international political documents are given a legal value by and for the Parties, not only in their mutual relations but also internally as required for instance by Article 2 of the PCA with Russia.[23] The Community's external relations are in that sense used as a tool to give a legal dimension to political principles to which the member States are committed in international arenas,[24] but also in the context of the EU.

Such a commitment corresponds to one of the CFSP objectives enshrined in Article 11 TEU (ex J.1), one of which is:

> 'to develop and consolidate democracy and the rule of law, and respect for human rights and fundamental freedoms'.

Moreover, it also refers to the *obligation* of result stemming from the combination of paras. 2 and 4 of Article 6 included in the common provisions of the TEU, and which, despite its reference to the 'General Principles of Community law', applies to the whole EU:[25]

> '2. The Union shall respect fundamental rights, as guaranteed by the European Convention for the Protection of Human Rights and Fundamental Freedoms signed in Rome on 4 November 1950 and as they result from the constitutional traditions common to the member States, as general principles of Community law.
> 4. The Union shall provide itself with the means necessary to attain its objectives and carry out through its policies.'

The political dimension of the Partnerships established by the PCAs was strengthened by the Common Strategies adopted by the European Council on Russia and Ukraine.[26]

---

[22] The Helsinki Final Act of 1975 is more restrictive, on state institutions and political system and rather focuses on *Respect for human rights and fundamental freedoms, including the freedom of thought, conscience, religion or belief* (part 1.VII).

[23] Neither of these documents is legally binding. The Final Act of Helsinki Summit reads: '... the undersigned High Representatives of the participating States, *mindful of the high political significance which they attach to the results of the Conference, and declaring their determination to act* in accordance with the provisions contained in the above texts, have subscribed their signatures below' (italics added); the Charter of Paris follows the same line: '...we, the undersigned High Representatives of the participating States, mindful of the high political significance we attach to the results of the Summit Meeting, and declaring our determination to act in accordance with the provisions we have adopted, have subscribed our signatures below'.

[24] COM(95) 216.

[25] See in that respect Fouwels, The European Union's Common Foreign and Security Policy and Human Rights, 3 NQHR 1997, pp. 291-325 at p. 294.

[26] See from the same author, Institutional aspects of the Partnership between the European Union and the New Independent States of the former Soviet Union- case studies of Russia and Ukraine, 37 CMLRev. (2000), Sept-Oct.

2.2 The Common Strategies' inventory of constitutional principles promoted by the EU

The objectives of the two CSs adopted respectively with Russia and Ukraine are as follows:

Consolidation of democracy, the rule of law and public institutions in Russia:

> 'The establishment of efficient, transparent, public institutions is one of the prerequisites for confidence and wider adherence to democratic guidelines and the operation of the rule of law.
> ... The Union wishes to support Russia in the consolidation of its public institutions, particularly, its executive, legislative and judicial bodies and its police, in accordance with democratic ... The European Union will attach particular importance to regional and local administrations, within their powers. Relations between central, regional and local authorities are an essential factor in the future of the Federation. The emergence of civil society in all areas is indispensable for the consolidation of democracy in Russia.'[27]

Support for the democratic and economic transition in Ukraine:

> 'The EU supports Ukraine in all its efforts aiming at the consolidation of democracy and good governance, human rights and the rule of law ... The EU supports Ukraine's efforts to reform the legal system in the framework of the PCA. A properly functioning independent judiciary, a professional police force, the development of a meritocratic, well-trained public administration at national, regional and local levels are all key elements in the effective implementation of government decisions. The EU encourages Ukraine's efforts to develop the efficiency, transparency and democratic character of its public institutions, including the development of free media.'[28]

Also mentioned are the development of civil society, the encouragement to create links between peoples and NGOs of the Union and Ukraine, support for the protection and promotion of the rights of minorities. Indeed the EU '*urges* Ukraine to fulfil its commitments and to adapt its legislation to meet the norms of the Council of Europe' (italics added).[29]

These objectives, although stated in broad terms in the CSs, refer to certain constitutional principles the EU Partner is invited to work on, under EU's 'guidance'. The CSs state that the EU and its member States will work closely together with [Russia and Ukraine] to implement [the] CS, in particular through the PCA and its institutions'.[30]

---

[27] CS on Russia, part II, paras. 1 and 2.
[28] CS on Ukraine, part II (Principal Objectives), I(i), second para.
[29] Ibid., third para.
[30] See for instance pt. 48 of the CS on Ukraine.

To sum up, the constitutional principles promoted through the EU-NIS Partnerships are mediated through a complex combination of the EC developing 'competence' in the field of human rights and the CFSP objective to consolidate democracy, the rule of law, respect for human rights and fundamental freedoms. The PCAs, consolidated by the CSs in the case of Russia and Ukraine, require the NIS to effectively observe a set of fundamental principles to which they are already committed, either legally (Council of Europe) or politically (OSCE). Interestingly, the EU (i.e., Community and its member States acting in the framework of the European Union by the Treaty on European Union) acts as the guardian of other European organisations' principles without being, neither itself nor the Community, a member of these organisations. It is through the international commitments of the EU member States as well as by 'drawing on their constitutional traditions', that a certain constitutional *culture* is reflected by the Partnership. Indeed, the latter establishes several mechanisms for these constitutional principles to be observed.

3. THE MECHANISMS FOR INFLUENCE LINKED TO THE PARTNERSHIP

Two types of mechanisms are envisaged to ensure that the conditions laid out in the Partnership are observed: political dialogue and Community technical assistance (Tacis) on the one hand, and the suspension or termination of the relationship on the basis of the conditionality on the other.

3.1 **Dialogue and assistance**

As pointed out earlier, the nature and substance of the Partnerships' principles refer to various external political documents. Observance of these principles is likely to lead to discussion, to put it mildly, as it actually depends on the two Parties' interpretation of their obligations.[31] In order to bring some common understanding of the PCAs' contents, a framework for political dialogue has been established.[32] Such a political dialogue is regarded as an instrument of 'EU foreign policy'.[33] As such, it may, depending on how it is effectively used, constitute a means to further the process of political transformation and influence the constitutional life of the EU's Partner. It represents, together with the technical assistance a *positive* policy in promoting certain values.

[31] Given that the Joint Declaration annexed to the PCA with Russia mentions that the human rights provisions of the Partnership are based on the Community's human rights policy (see above) on the one hand and 'Russia's policy in the field of human rights' on the other, the question arises whether the two policies imply different approaches.

[32] Art. 1 PCA with Ukraine, Art. 1 PCA with Russia; also in other PCAs.

[33] Fouwels, supra, at p. 301.

The Agreement with Russia provides for consultations at the highest level between the President of the Council of the EU and the President of the Commission on one side and the President of the Russian Federation on the other. The practice has also developed in relation to Ukraine, although not explicitly provided by the PCA.[34] This formula has become the so-called 'EU-Russia/Ukraine Summits', in which the Secretary-General of the Council/High Representative for CFSP assists the President of the European Council.[35] Noteworthy, such a presence institutionalises further the inter-penetration of first and second pillars within the Partnership.[36] The 'EU-Ukraine Summit' in September 2000 clearly recalled that the EU-Ukraine 'Strategic Partnership ... is founded on the principles of democracy, respect forpmd1000@hermes.cam.ac.uk human rights, the rule of law'. The 'importance' attached to the 'democratic character of political reforms in Ukraine' was indeed underlined.[37] Also, the Joint Statement of the 'EU-Russia Summit' in May 2000 stated that '[the] Partnership and [the] reinforced political dialogue aim at promoting a stable and prosperous Europe, and are founded on the principles of democracy, respect for human rights, the rule of law and on the market economy.'[38]

At a lower level, the Cooperation Council is, in principle, in charge of monitoring the implementation of the Agreement.[39] It assembles once a year the members of the Council of the EU and members of the Commission on the one hand and members of the Partner's Government on the other. The Cooperation Council can adopt recommendations on further developments and interpretation of the Agreement. It is assisted by a Cooperation Committee in performing its duties.[40] In addition, sub-committees and working parties operating under its aegis assist the Committee. Finally, the dialogue also involves parliamentarians.[41] Such regular, high-level political meetings between the EU member States and the NIS can be used to further the Partnerships' political objectives although in a limited way

[34] See the Joint Press Release of the first EU-Ukraine Summit, 16 Oct. 1998; no. 12113/98.

[35] See Joint Statement EU-Russia Summit, 29 May 2000, Press Release no. 8976/00.

[36] For more on that point, see from the same author, Common strategies and the interface between EC external relations and the CFSP: lessons of the partnership between EU and Russia in Dashwood and Hillion (eds.), The General Law of EC External Relations (Sweet & Maxwell, 2000), p. 287.

[37] See Joint Statement of the EU-Ukraine Summit of 15 September 2000, Press Release no. 11241/00.

[38] This statement was reiterated at the sixth EU-Russia Summit in Paris on 30 October 2000.

[39] See Art. 90 PCA with Russia; Art. 85 PCA with Ukraine.

[40] It is composed of representatives of the members of the Council of the EU and members of the Commission on the one hand and representatives of the Partner's Government on the other, at senior civil servant level.

[41] The Parliamentary Cooperation Committee, consisting of members of the European Parliament on the one hand and of members of the partner's parliamentary body, may require information on the Agreement's implementation. It shall be informed of the recommendations adopted by the Cooperation Council, who is free to publish them, and can itself make recommendations to the latter.

as it will be developed later. At least the Partners may have an exchange of views.[42]

In parallel to the political dialogue, the Community technical assistance (Tacis) also plays a role in influencing the political developments taking place in the NIS. The Tacis political objectives are fairly clear. Restructuring of public administration, legal assistance, including approximation of legislation and in particular the strengthening of the civic society are among the indicative areas for assistance to the NIS and Mongolia.[43]

If dialogue and cooperation through assistance fail to influence the political development, the 'stick policy' might ultimately be used, viz. suspension of the PCAs.

3.2 The 'stick policy': suspending the Partnerships

The concept of 'essential element' contained in the PCAs implies that its violation by any of the Parties constitutes a 'case of material breach of the Agreement'.[44] As such it is a 'case of special urgency' which, in derogation to the rules attached to the dispute settlement mechanism established by the PCAs, allows the injured Party to suspend unilaterally the implementation of the Agreement. This is an exceptional procedure both in the context of the PCAs[45] and in view of international law.[46] To date, suspension has only been applied at the level of ratification. For instance, the ratification process of the PCA with Belarus has been and still is suspended due to the dictatorial regime established by Lukashenko.

---

[42] The press release of the third Cooperation council between the EU and Russia reads as follows : 'the partnership allows both partners to speak candidly to each other when views diverge, as now on regard to the situation in Chechnya'; see Press Release 7534/00.

[43] See Annex II of the 1996 Tacis Regulation, Council Regulation 1279/96 concerning the provision of assistance to economic reform and recovery in the New Independent States and Mongolia [Tacis], OJ 1996 L1/6.

[44] A Joint Declaration to Art. 107, annexed to the PCA with Russia (the same Declaration exists in the PCA with Ukraine, concerning Art. 102) defines 'the material breach' by reference to Art. 60(3) of the Vienna Convention on the Law of Treaties (1969) as either a repudiation of the Agreement not sanctioned by the general rules of international law or a violation of the essential elements of the Agreement.

[45] The PCA dispute settlement mechanism normally requires that before a Party retaliates in response to the other Party's non compliance with its obligations, the former supplies the Cooperation Council with all the relevant information required for a thorough examination of the situation with a view to seeking a solution acceptable to the Parties. Hence dialogue is sought until the last moment.

[46] Art. 61(1) of the Vienna Convention provides that the 'material breach' by one Party allows the other Party to terminate the Agreement or suspend, partly or wholly its implementation, in observance of the procedure set out in Art. 65 which requires three months between the notification and the suspension. The 'case of special urgency' allows a derogation from the obligations set out in Art. 65 of the Vienna Convention.

Suspension of the Agreements themselves has never been used in relation to the NIS. Whether it is a sign of success or weakness is open to discussion.[47]

Article 3 of the Tacis regulation 1279/96 of July 1996 echoes this mechanism:[48]

> 'when an essential element for the continuation of cooperation through assistance is missing in particular in cases of violation of democratic principles and human rights, the Council may, on a proposal from the Commission, acting by qualified majority, decide upon appropriate measures concerning assistance to a partner State.'

An example of 'appropriate measures' is the Tacis Civil Society Development Programme for Belarus. As a result of the 1996 constitutional crisis in the country, all bilateral assistance was suspended as no programme could be negotiated with Belarusian authorities. Although the situation was condemned by the Council, the possibility was maintained for potential Community assistance to promote human rights and freedom of the media. Eventually, a Decision on a Tacis Civil Society Development Programme for Belarus was adopted by the Council.[49] This was the first measure based on the human right clause of the Tacis Regulation and as underlined by some authors, the first measure ever to be formally decided by the Council under a human right clause with the objective of helping to restore human rights and democracy in a country in serious constitutional crisis.[50] However, the absence of political change in Belarus illustrates the limited impact of EU influence on the former's political situation. The continuing Russian campaign in Chechnya is another example. What are the main reasons for such a limited impact?

4. THE LIMITS OF THE CONSTITUTIONAL INFLUENCE THROUGH THE PARTNERSHIP: A REFLECTION OF THE EU INSTITUTIONAL ARCHITECTURE

Without trying to be exhaustive, one may point out two reasons to explain the limited political influence of the EU on its Partners. The first derives from the absence of accession perspective for the NIS, combined with a lack of clear alternative policy/perspective. The second reason which might explain the first is more related to the internal shortcomings of the EU institutional system, particularly in the field of external policy.

[47] Noteworthy, the decision to suspend involves, on the EU side, a complex procedure which can actually be dissuasive, see Brandtner and Rosas, Trade Preferences and Human Rights in Alston (ed.) *The European Union and Human Rights,* op. cit., pp. 699-722, at p. 708.

[48] OJ 1996 L165/1.

[49] OJ 1998 L1/6, on a proposal by the Commission, COM(97)441, amended by COM(97)602.

[50] See Brandtner and Rosas, op. cit., at p. 482.

Given that the PCAs do not entail the perspective of accession for the Partners, the incentive for the latter to conform to the constitutional principles advocated by the EU is limited. It depends on the Partners' conviction and good will. It also result from the EU's persuasion capacity as well as its way of adequately handling the membership aspirations of certain Partners. The lack of substantial alternatives underlined by some authors[51] reduces the NIS' acceptance of the EU's influence on their domestic affairs.

Indeed to date, the political dialogue has remained fairly modest in its capacity to influence the Partners' constitutional life. First, the Cooperation Council in charge of developing the Partnership may only adopt *recommendations* which, in contrast to decisions adopted by the Association Council established by the Europe Agreements[52], do not have binding effect.[53] At no point can the Cooperation Council oblige the Parties to act, be it for taking additional measures in order to strengthen the relationship, or for settling a dispute arising in the framework of the PCAs.[54] Second, the EU position advocated at the various levels of the political dialogue, including at the summit level, is subject to a prior convergence of member States' views, which often turns out to be a difficult exercise. Finally, the impact of the EU policy on its Partners also depends on the coherence between the various instruments constituting the Partnership.[55]

Aside from those legal obstacles, the Partnerships' political dimension has shown its limits on several occasions, particularly when it comes to using the stick policy, viz. suspension or the threat of suspension. The signature of the Interim Agreement with Russia, whilst engaged in the first Chechnian campaign, was illustrative of the essential conflict of interests that regularly appears with regard to the EU's external 'action'. The dilemma for the Union was either to suspend the establishment of the Partnership as a sanction to Russia's recorded violation of human rights, or rather to adopt a pragmatic, *realpolitik* attitude aiming at reducing the causes of such crisis, in order to prepare for long term change. Given certain trade interests and under the pressure of various member States, the latter position prevailed, seemingly at the expense of the Union's general political principles. Indeed, the External Relations Commissioner at that time, commenting on the decision, declared that the EU should not neglect long term consider-

---

[51] See Maresceau, op. cit., note 10.

[52] The Association Council established by the Europe Agreements has the power to take decisions which are binding on the Parties, see for instance the EA with Poland, OJ L 348/1, 31 December 1993.

[53] Art. 101(3) PCA with Russia, Art. 96(3) PCA with Ukraine.

[54] The final title on 'Institutional, General and Final Provisions' of the PCAs provides that the Cooperation Council 'shall supervise the implementation of the Agreement'. It shall also 'examine any major issues arising within the framework of the Agreement and any other bilateral or international issues of mutual interest for the purpose of attaining the objectives' of the PCA.

[55] See from the same author, Common strategies and the interface between EC external relations and the CFSP: lessons of the partnership between EU and Russia, op. cit..

ations for Russia at a crucial point of its development. The reassessment of the relationship with Russia was partly, officials privately admit, the recognition that the latter is simply too big and too important for the EU to permit its policy-making to be dominated by the Chechnian war, seen as a serious but essentially short-term problem.[56] Such an equivocal policy has made the credibility of the EC political conditionality and, indeed, the political dimension of the Partnership rather questionable.[57]

The Amsterdam Treaty, described as 'neither a bang nor a whimper'[58] has not dramatically changed the general EU approach. Indeed, despite a strong declaration on Chechnya adopted by the 1999 Helsinki European Council and the consequent suspension of some Tacis programmes – including money for academic research! – the same EU pragmatism has prevailed with regard to Russia's second campaign in Chechnya and it remains to be seen if any reaction will follow the current media policy of the current Russian authorities. This being said, it can be argued that such compromises are partly understandable considering that the political 'strength' of the EU is conditional. The latter's position always remains subject to member States' convergence of interests. In this context, one may wonder whether the adoption of the European Charter of Fundamental Rights by the European Council in Nice will further commit the member States to shape an EU's external policy in favour of these rights. Moreover, should the Charter be binding on the institutions, there would be less excuse for the EU not to act or react, all the less if it is granted at some stage a full-fledged legal personality.[59]

5. CONCLUSION

In the framework of their relations with the EU, the NIS do not have to modify their constitutions the way the candidate countries are having to do. Nevertheless, the bilateral Partnerships established on the basis of the PCAs require that certain fundamental principles, which have a constitutional nature, be observed.

---

[56] See *Euro-East*, no. 34 – June 1995, p. 15; see also the Declaration of the EU's Presidency on the situation in Chechnya, *Communication à la presse*, 17 January 1995, 4215/95.

[57] See opinion of MEP Catherine Lalumière, PE 189.493. One could point out the ambivalent position of the EP concerning Russia, see the analysis of Christine Delcourt 'Un partenariat subordonné à l'approbation du Parlement européen: la procédure de l'avis conforme' in Raux & Korovkine, *Le partenariat entre l'Union européenne et la Fédération de Russie* (Apogée, 1998) pp. 85-109.

[58] See the editorial comment, 34 CMLRev. (1997) p. 767. For particular opinions on the Amsterdam reforms in the particular field of external policy, see Dashwood, External Relations Provisions of the Amsterdam Treaty, 35 CMLRev. (1998) p. 1019; Monar, The European Union's Foreign Affairs System after the Treaty of Amsterdam: A Strengthened Capacity for External Relations?, 2 EFA Rev. (1997) p. 413.

[59] See the Contribution of Prof. Schemers in this Volume.

The potential for an EU constitutional influence derives in particular from the following:

- the NIS, some of which are future neighbours of the enlarged EU, are in a process of transformation that includes the (re)definition of a constitutional culture; for domestic political reasons they may choose to observe values advocated by the EU;
- the EU may be in a position to influence the NIS transformation process through its *involvement* for promoting respect for human rights and democracy through EC external relations and CFSP.

Such promotion is currently based on the 'the constitutional traditions common to member States' and their international commitments, particularly within the Council of Europe and the OSCE. Although behaving as the guardian of the latter's principles, neither the Union, deprived of legal personality, nor the Community, officially participate in those organisations. This is an obvious weakness not to say inadequacy in the EU's attempt to become a political reference. For the EU to be a credible advocate of a certain constitutional culture, it should itself be bound by the principles it promotes.

CONSTITUTIONAL QUESTIONS RAISED BY THE PROPOSED ACCESSION OF MALTA TO THE EUROPEAN UNION IN THE GENERAL CONTEXT

Peter G. Xuereb*

1. IS CONSTITUTIONAL AMENDMENT REQUIRED AND WHAT WOULD THE PROCEDURE BE? [Questions 1 and 2]

This question has not yet been the subject of in-depth study or discussion in academic circles, and therefore this Conference provides an excellent occasion for such discussion to take place in as informed a framework as the subject deserves. The governing and the opposition parties have, of course, their stances and recent statements from both sides indicate their thinking on the difficult issues involved in the context of something of a 'moving target'. The opposition Labour Party remains opposed to Malta's membership of the Union in the foreseeable future. Ultimately, it would be for the Constitutional Court to decide these questions when the time came.

Membership of the EU, in terms of the 'Union constitutional acquis' as expressed in the judgments of the European Court of Justice, involves a limited or partial transfer of sovereignty, although how 'limited' it can be said to be forty years or so after such judgments were delivered is arguable in terms of range. Any further development of the EU would herald yet further transfer of sovereignty albeit circumscribed by as yet not fully developed principles of subsidiarity. The central issue is that as a dualist state, international law is not automatically part of Maltese law. The Constitution is the supreme law of the land. Yet Community Law, according to the caselaw of the ECJ, is supreme over all national law.

There are two issues.

The first issue is raised by the Community law position that Community law prevails over national constitutions themselves, as a matter of Community and evolving Union law. The second issue is that Community law prevails, according to the ECJ, over national acts of parliament, past and future. The big question is

* Professor Peter G. Xuereb LL.D. (Malta), LL.M.(Lond.), Ph.D (Cambridge), Professor of European and Comparative Law, and Chairman of the European Documentation and Research Centre, University of Malta.

A.E. Kellermann et al. (Eds.), EU Enlargement: The Constitutional Impact at EU and National Level

whether the Constitution can be interpreted as providing or (if deemed necessary) be made to provide a secure constitutional basis for the adoption of the constitutional and other acquis coupled with the preservation of the principle of the supremacy of the Constitution, the Constitution reflecting Malta's international obligations as signatory to the Treaties while remaining the expression of the ultimate sovereignty of the people.

The Constitution[1], in Section 6, provides that 'Subject to the provisions of subsections (7) and (9) and of Section 66 of this Constitution, if any other law is inconsistent with this Constitution, this Constitution shall prevail and the other law, to the extent of the inconsistency, shall be void.'

The Section was drafted at a time when membership of the EU (then EEC) was not an immediate, though possibly a foreseeable, prospect. In classic terms the Constitution declared the Constitution supreme over 'any other law'. Implied, possibly, is the phrase 'of the Maltese legislature' as indicated especially by the phrase 'shall be void'. Arguably, this phrase indicates the context. Maltese law cannot declare 'non-Maltese law' 'void'. At most it could declare such law inapplicable and inoperative in Malta, in the same way that Community law and the European Court of Justice cannot and will not declare any law even of a member state void, but rather point out the duty of national courts not to apply it in a 'Community context'. For the same reason, no specific provision for the 'limitation' or 'transfer' or 'pooling' of sovereignty or the exercise of sovereignty as linked to membership of the Community, as found in the Constitutions of some of the current member States of the Union, was made.

It is not possible here to enter into fully into the arguments as they may develop in the Maltese context. The issues are beginning to emerge in public debate and this is to be welcomed, but what is also needed is for the legal experts to make their contribution. As a start, perhaps, I here highlight the main issues and relevant provisions as I see them.

First some background. It is of interest to recount the view of the EC Directorate[2] as expressed in a report to the Prime Minister and the Minister of Foreign Affairs back in 1990 (the year in which Malta applied for membership). The report[3] stated (p. 160) that '(Section 6) "should" be amended to read that the Constitution is, however, also subject to Community law.' The report then went on to point out that amendment of the section would, however, require a two-thirds majority of all the members of the House of representatives [Section 66(2)(b)]. Obtaining such a majority can be regarded as being out of the question for the foreseeable future as far as the Maltese scene is concerned. There is no realistic prospect of such a majority being secured in practice, in a country where the electoral swings are relatively small and government majorities are always slim, as

[1] The Independence Constitution 1964 as amended.
[2] Within the Ministry of Foreign Affairs, and now known as the EU Directorate.
[3] Department of Information, March 1990.

long as Labour Party policy remains as it is (there is no sign of any change in this regard). The Deputy Leader of the Labour Party, Dr. George Vella was recently reported (The Times, July 28) as 'inviting' legal experts to comment on how Malta, through a simple majority, could adopt a 'constitution of European laws' that would be above the Maltese Constitution. (Of course, this paper is a response to T.M.C. Asser Institute's invitation and not to Dr. Vella's). He was reported as being of the view that this should only happen with the approval of two-thirds of the members of the House of Representatives or a vote of at least 75% at a referendum. He also reiterated that, in his party's view, participation in NATO military programmes (read here Partnership for Peace) would be unconstitutional, while saying that the Labour Party was not against participation by Malta in military exercises with neighbouring countries aimed at strengthening co-operation as this had nothing to do with military alliances, he is quoted as saying.

The 1990 Report went on to argue that short of an amendment of Section 6, 'a declaration that Community law prevails over Maltese internal law contained in an ordinary Act of Parliament (that is one which does not purport to amend the Constitution) would always be advisable though not essential'. The reader will see that the compilers of the report were of the view that while section 6 '"should" be amended' yet in the absence of such amendment, an ordinary law could resolve the second issue raised above, i.e., the issue of supremacy of Community (Union) laws over Maltese Acts of Parliament, but argued further that even without such a declaration in an Act of Parliament this issue could be settled by a reference to the Court of Justice and a ruling therefrom that Union law was supreme. I comment on this below. As far as the question of Supremacy of Union law over the Constitution itself is concerned, the Report stated (at p. 161) that

> 'The declaration above mentioned would not change the legal situation in so far as the issue relating to the supremacy of Community law versus the supremacy of Constitutional law is concerned. Unless and until Article 6 of the Constitution is amended the question will still remain as to whether it is the Community law which is supreme or the Constitution on the basis of Article 6, in case of conflict between the two'.

It continued:

> '(i)f Article 6 is not amended any dispute relating to the supremacy of Community Law -vs- Supremacy of Maltese Constitutional Law would presumably arise before the Maltese Constitutional Court which, as has been stated above, will be obliged to refer the matter to the European Court for a preliminary ruling thereon under Article 177 of the EEC Treaty. The Constitutional Court must make such a reference since from its decisions there is "no judicial remedy under national law". The findings of the European Court would then be binding on the Constitutional Court, and the European Court ruling would then have to be applied by the Constitutional Court.'

With respect, as to this proposed solution, this approach totally misconceives the role and jurisdiction of the European Court of Justice, which will not pronounce itself on national constitutional questions, and would probably not be repeated today that the position is clearer in people's minds. The understanding of the situation seems to have been at the time that the European Court could somehow resolve the Maltese constitutional issue for the Maltese by reference to European Law. The confusion is only compounded by the statement that the Maltese Constitutional Court might, rather than refer the question to the Court of Justice, rule that 'the issue does not require any interpretation and that it is absolutely clear – an "acte clair"', and that the Court would, in such eventuality, 'go for the supremacy of Community law, at all costs, if not for any other reason at least for the sake of uniformity and of conformity with the European Court dictates.'

Clearly government advisors needed, in 1990 (as this Conference acknowledges that all Members and applicants need now), to engage in the comparative study of the various positions in the member States as a matter of constitutional law for whatever guidance they can offer as to the possible approaches on such matters. Such a comparative analysis will show that various approaches are possible, not all of which, however, may be available to all applicants. Some will argue at the Conference that the member States do not afford a model for Constitutional amendment in the light of accession. It is true that no single model emerges, but a common denominator can certainly be found. Some would seek to take their starting point for Constitutional reform in the Applicant States from the Community (or Union) constitutional acquis, arguing for a new start or new approach which would require the incorporation in the Treaties (or a European Constitution) and in national constitutions in textual terms of the relevant European Court rulings, but much could be said about the feasibility or desirability of this at a time when the 'ultimate goal' or 'shape' or 'nature' of the Union is still very much an open question. The comparative analysis which I argue is still an appropriate point of departure would throw up various examples as to how member States' constitutional traditions have 'accommodated' (as it has been put) the rulings of the European Court of Justice and how they view the question as to whether, and if so how, 'ultimate sovereignty' (in some sense such as the reservation of the core, or core identity, of the Constitution and who has the last say on the compatibility of EC law with such core) could be retained as a matter of Constitutional Law and also European Law in the known *acquis* context.

However, to anticipate argument on the question, one could raise the point that before assuming that Section 6 is an obstacle to membership, another question should be asked, namely: Does membership involve *per se* a conflict with the Constitution so that an amendment of the Constitution is required, bearing in mind that it would be a Maltese Act of Parliament which brought in the Treaties? Or, more precisely, would a law ratifying the Treaties (Treaty) be 'inconsistent with the Constitution' as per Section 6? One implicit subquestion is whether the 'transfer of law-making power' to the Union institutions *per se* involves a conflict with the Constitution. The second implicit subquestion is whether, apart from this first issue, there is any present or foreseeable future unresolvable conflict between the Acquis Communautaire, including the Constitutional acquis, and the Constitution? I take these points in turn.

On the first subquestion, one argument which might be raised, leading to an affirmative reply, would be that the Constitution vests law-making power in the Maltese Parliament. Section 65(1) reads: 'Subject to the provisions of this Constitution, Parliament may make laws for the peace, order and good government of Malta', and, according to the argument this is to be interpreted in the sense that only the Maltese Parliament (and acting alone) may make laws which have effect in Malta and, further, some may argue that although there is no reference in the entrenchment clause (Section 66) to Section 65 nevertheless this provision should be regarded as alterable only by a two-thirds majority. I would foresee a counter argument being made to the effect that Section 65 does not in terms provide that it is only Parliament which can legislate directly, and delegated legislation (at least, downwards) is as much a feature in Malta as elsewhere. But according to the first argument the sense is that Parliament should have legislative monopoly subject to the Constitution unless the latter is amended to provide otherwise. Equally clearly (this argument would run) this 'supremacy', used in the sense of 'monopoly', would 'go', in legal terms, on membership. The main counter-argument, I imagine, would be that Section 65 vests in Parliament the power to make laws for the peace, order and good government of Malta, and that membership of the Union (the passing of a law which gave effect in Malta to such membership) comes within that authority, i.e., that these aims are only achievable, in the 'post-sovereign' context and in the corresponding spheres of 'sovereignty' or competence of the Union (and limited to that), *by* joining the Union and pooling sovereignty with other member States. Hence, on this interpretation of Section 65 in the context of the Constitution and modern Constitutional theory, Parliament can pass an Act of Parliament to this effect. On this argument, there is no alteration of Section 65 involved. Nor would such a law be inconsistent with the Constitution, so that it would not be void in virtue of Section 6. All international treaties involve a transfer of sovereignty, the argument could run. Perhaps other arguments are possible. The case might also be advanced that, as said above, Section 65 is not an entrenched clause. Is this because the framers of the Constitution foresaw the possibility of 'sovereignty – pooling' as a matter of evolving international relations? Therefore, this argument would run, Section 65 might be amended by majority vote. The anterior question *whether it needs to be*, and the questions as to whether and how it could be, would be questions for the Maltese Constitutional Court alone. This makes the role of the Constitutional Court central.

1.1 Reservations and 'Ultimate Sovereignty' ('the last word')

The 1990 Report had indeed noted (p. 161) that 'it is sometimes argued that the transfer of sovereign powers is not recognised unreservedly by the member States, even in those where the Constitutions recognise the principle'. For example, the Luxembourg Constitution spoke of a 'temporary devolution' of law-making power. Given consensus on membership across the Maltese political spectrum, there is no doubt that Constitutional arguments of the type described above could be resolved but that would leave the question as to whether a 'holier than thou' model scrupulously synthesising the various 'constitutional' statements of the ECJ needs to be incorporated by appropriate amendment of the Constitution, after reference also to the position in the member States and the line taken by other applicant states. There certainly is no such model in being; the closest would appear to be the Polish model. Otherwise, actual constitutional provision falls short of that 'ideal'. Thinking proceeds in general on the lines of current member State practice. For example, the contributor from the Czech Republic has made suggestions which would allay many fears on 'loss of sovereignty' or 'the dilution of democracy' among people in applicant states. The Danish paper is also instructive. The German and Italian supreme courts' 'constitutional reservations' are well known. Absent such consensus, much debate appears to be in the offing as to the Constitution as it stands on the lines tentatively drawn above and we cannot anticipate a replication in Malta of the balanced analysis and development of their Constitutions anticipated by the contributors to this Conference from some other applicant states. The debate is and will probably remain on the 'can or cannot' level rather than on the 'how far and how best' premise. What is clear as to the current position is that the wording of national Constitutions is not on the negotiating agenda, but that the European Commission is taking an interest in how applicant states address the question as to the supremacy, direct effect etc. of Community law, even if this be only at the level of the role of the courts.

1.2 Incorporation of Treaties

This leads to the question of the procedure for incorporation of Treaties and resulting *acquis* into the Maltese legal system. The matter is covered by Act V of 1983, Section 3 of which states that:

> '1. Where a Treaty to which Malta becomes a party after the coming into force of this Act is one which affects or concerns:
> (a) the status of Malta under international law or the maintenance or support of such status, or
> (b) the security of Malta, its sovereignty, independence, unity or territorial integrity, or

(c) the relationship of Malta with any multinational organisation, agency, association or similar body,
such Treaty shall not enter into force with respect to Malta unless it has been ratified or its ratification has been authorised or approved in accordance with the provisions of this Act.

2. A Treaty to which subsection (1) of this Section applies shall be ratified or shall have its ratification authorised or approved as follows:
(a) where such treaty concerns a matter referred to in paragraph (a) or (b) of subsection (1) of this Section or contains any provision which is to become, or be enforceable as, part of the law of Malta, by Act of Parliament;
(b) in any other case, by Resolution of the House of Representatives.

3. No provision of a treaty shall become, or be enforceable as part of the law of Malta except by or under an Act of Parliament.

4. The instrument of ratification shall be issued under the signature of the minister responsible for foreign affairs.

5. Any act of a foreign state relating to any of the matters mentioned in paragraph (a) or (b) of subsection (1) of this section shall be laid on the Table of the House as soon as practicable by the minister responsible for foreign affairs together with a motion giving an opportunity to the House to express itself on such act.'

The first point to be made is that taking subsections (1) and (2) together, an Act of Parliament would be required for the ratification of a Treaty concerning or affecting Malta's status under international law, its security, sovereignty, independence, unity or territorial integrity [paras. (a) and (b)]. Of course, this provision falls to be interpreted by reference to international law concepts. Besides that, the 1983 Act is itself subject to the Constitution and must be interpreted in the light of the Constitution. The Constitution entrenches a status of neutrality, and a change in such status would arguably require an amendment of the Constitution, which would mean interpreting the phrase 'affects and concerns' restrictively so that it would not permit an ordinary Act of Parliament to alter or debunk such status. This raises two issues: (a) whether Union law now requires or will in future require such debunking without reference to the sovereign decision of the member States concerned, and (b) issues of interpretation and definition of Malta's neutral status, as a matter now not only of the 1983 Act but of the Constitution. This is considered further below.

The second point is that while, according to subsection (2)(b), a Resolution of the House would appear to suffice for the ratification of a Treaty which falls within Subsection (1) para (c), which refers to Treaties affecting or concerning 'the relationship of Malta with any multinational *organisation, agency, association or similar body*', yet, according to subsection (3), 'no provision of a Treaty shall become, or be enforceable as part of the law of Malta except by or under an

Act of Parliament, so that it seems clear that an Act of Parliament is required.'

Again, it may still be useful to refer to the views of the EC Directorate expressed in the 1990 Report already referred to above. The Report stated (p. 145) that

> 'Having mentioned this Act of 1983 it is advisable that before Membership an amendment should be made whereby an Act of the Maltese Parliament would not be needed in so far as Community measures which are directly applicable in member States, that is those which do not need any internal implementation, are concerned. If this is not done the Maltese legislature would have to undertake the mammoth task of passing Acts of Parliament for each and every one of such Community measures.'

In my view, as long as the Treaties were incorporated, it would follow that no further action was needed in order that directly applicable Community law be so. Of course, it could be added to this that according to Community law member States should not resort (and should therefore have eliminated the need to resort) to internal implementation of directly applicable measures. It was the opinion of the compilers of the 1990 Report that

> 'otherwise, the Constitution ... does not require any special formalities since nowhere is it mentioned that a special majority in Parliament, or a referendum or any other special procedure is needed to ratify any such agreement, or, at that, any international convention or treaty.'[4]

1.3 **Neutrality**

This brings me to the issue of neutrality. As was said above, the fact that an Act of Parliament can be used for ratification purposes and for the introduction of any treaty as part of the law of Malta, as well as for the amendment of the 1983 Act (as proposed in the 1990 Report) for the purpose of rendering applicable in Malta directly applicable Community law, does not necessarily resolve the issues related to any perceived needed amendments of the Constitution. One issue which will be raised in this context is that of neutrality, as adverted to above. I turn briefly to this issue.

According to Section 1 of the Constitution, Malta is a neutral state actively pursuing peace, security and progress among all nations by adhering to a policy of non-alignment and refusing to participate in any military alliance. Such status is expressed to imply in particular that:

> '(a) no foreign military base will be permitted on Maltese territory;
> (b) no military facilities in Malta will be allowed to be used by any foreign forces except at the request of the government of Malta, and only in the following cases:

[4] EC Directorate Report, 1990, p. 146.

(i) in the exercise of the inherent right of self-defence in the event of any armed violation of the area over which the Republic of Malta has sovereignty, or in pursuance of measures or actions decided by the Security Council of the United Nations: or
(ii) whenever there exists a threat to the sovereignty, independence, neutrality, unity or territorial integrity of the Republic of Malta;
(c) except as mentioned above, no other facilities in Malta will be allowed to be used in such manner or extent as will amount to the presence in Malta of concentration of foreign forces;
(d) except as mentioned above, no foreign military personnel will be allowed on Maltese territory, other than military personnel performing or assisting in the performance of, civil works or activities, and other than a reasonable number of military technical personnel assisting in the defence of the Republic of Malta;
(e) the shipyards of the Republic will be used for civil commercial purposes, but may also be used, within reasonable limits of time and quantity, for the repair of military vessels which have been put in a state of non-combat or for the construction of vessels; and in accordance with the principles of non-alignment the said shipyards will be denied to the military vessels of the two superpowers.'

Of course it is arguable that the second clause of paragraph (e) in particular may be regarded as redundant in the light of the ending of the cold war. It has also been argued (e.g., in the 1990 Report, mentioned above)[5] that the entire constitutional provision centres around non-alignment 'much more than neutrality', and that non-alignment is not a fixed concept in international law and must in any case bear reference again to the climate prevailing at the time of the provision's adoption. The conclusion reached in 1990 by the drafters of the Report cited above was that

> 'it appears abundantly clear that there would be no Constitutional constraint against Malta adopting the same foreign policy as that adopted by the rest of the Community were it to become a Member and were the stage to be reached, also involving changes to the EEC Treaty, whereby the Community adopts its own foreign policy rather than simply going for "European Co-operation in the sphere of foreign policy" and "as things stand, the position of Malta as a neutral and non-aligned state in the sense of Article 1(3) of the Constitution in no way conflicts with the EEC Treaty[6]".'

The Report cited above was written in 1990. The Berlin Wall had already fallen. Since then, we have seen the development of the Common Foreign and Security Policy through Maastricht and then Amsterdam. We are currently seeing what some refer to as the 'militarisation of the Union', as it was described most recently in Malta by Irishwoman Patricia Mckenna, a member of the European Parliament brought over to Malta as a guest of the local Campaign for National Independence, which is opposed to membership. No doubt, we can anticipate further

[5] Ibid., p. 153.
[6] Ibid., p. 154.

debate in Malta as to the direction of CFSP, and in legal terms whether it has developed or is likely to develop in a direction which is contrary to the proper interpretation of the neutrality clause in the Constitution (again a question ultimately for the Constitutional Court). The government points out that there are other neutral states in the EU. The Labour Party insists that Malta's neutrality is specific, arguing that this specific concept comes within the Constitutional clause and that it is incompatible with the CFSP obligations which Malta is being asked to assume. The government's position is that there is no conflict between the CFSP and the Constitution and that the constructive abstention provisions in the Treaty safeguard sovereignty in this regard. In the meantime, Malta and the member States have closed (provisionally, of course) negotiations on the relevant chapter (it is declared, to mutual satisfaction) and one presumes that there is no perceived problem on either side. The Progress Report on Malta's application due out in October 2000 may shed further light on the matter. If the current framework of the Treaty is maintained and constructive abstention remains a feature of CFSP (or other mechanisms for respect for such sovereignty as is retained on this issue are put in place) up to and beyond any time when Malta may join the EU then arguably Malta, with other neutral members, can maintain its status, or such of it as is still considered relevant, as described in the Constitution and no amendment will be necessary. The Labour Party would argue otherwise, viewing the CFSP as it stands even now as being incompatible with Section 1 of the Constitution. In any case, a careful assessment of the future of CFSP and its implications remains an ongoing imperative.

2. WHICH SPECIFIC NATIONAL CONSTITUTIONAL PROVISIONS MAY BE CONTRARY TO AND CONTRADICTING THE ACQUIS? [Question 3]

Rather than simply stating my opinion, I have sought above to indicate which main constitutional provisions are felt either by the government side or by the opposition to be an issue. Any amendment would require the two-thirds Parliamentary majority referred to above, and in the final analysis it would fall to the Constitutional Court to interpret and apply the Constitution. Aside from the above, it would need to be studied what other constitutional provisions are or could be incompatible with the Acquis. It is, however, for constitutional law experts in all applicant states and current member States also to seek to anticipate possible conflict scenarios in view particularly of the evolving debate on the possible further 'constitutionalisation' of human rights at European level, via the proposed Charter on Fundamental Rights. This is still very much an open issue. I here say a few words on the subject by way of background and the current position in Malta.

In 1987, by virtue of Act XIV of 1987, the European Convention for the Protection of Human Rights and Fundamental Freedoms was in substance made enforceable in Malta. Malta had long been a signatory to the Convention in any event. This does not exclude the possibility that a provision of Maltese law may ex post be found to conflict with the Convention, and this has been the subject of some recent cases before the European Court of Human Rights, but this does not in my view raise serious constitutional issues as long as the mechanism to respond appropriately is in place and the hierarchy of norms is clear. I say more about this under the heading 'The role of the National Courts'.

3. WOULD THE CONSTITUTION REQUIRE AMENDMENT FOR THE HOLDING OF A NATIONAL REFERENDUM? [Question 3a]

The real question is what force the result of a referendum would have. The Constitution does not provide for (require) as a general principle the amendment of the Constitution by referendum, and there would need to be an amendment of Section 66, therefore, for the Constitution to so provide. As it happens, the government is committed to holding a referendum 'on membership' as a political commitment. The party in opposition has said it will not consider itself bound by the result of a referendum inasmuch as it would have no legal effect.

4. THE ROLE OF THE NATIONAL COURTS

It is clear that the national courts will have an important role to play in clarifying the constitutional issues related to accession just as they have done in all of the member States. In particular the Constitutional Court may be called upon to interpret the Constitution, as indicated above.

The general position is that the courts will respect the Constitution as the supreme law of the land. They will do all in their power to interpret national law, including national law incorporating international treaties, in accordance with the relevant international obligations, and are likely to follow UK case law on this score.

As far as the validity of a law incorporating the Treaties upon accession is concerned, it may be that such a law, if and when passed, will be challenged. The general rule adopted by our courts is that of a presumption of constitutionality, so that a law is presumed valid as long as its invalidity is not clear beyond all reasonable doubt. An Act of Parliament will be deemed 'inconsistent' or 'in conflict' with the Constitution, and be 'invalid', when that law and the Constitution cannot `stand together' in the context of the whole. These principles were affirmed, for example, in the case of *Luis Vassallo et.* v. *Hon. Prime Minister.*[7]

---

[7] Constitutional Decisions, Vol. 2, 1967-1978, p. 618.

As far as the protection of human rights is concerned, our Constitution has long provided for such. The 1964 (Independence) Constitution contained provisions drawn heavily from the European Convention. Hence, the judgments of the European Court of Human Rights have long been cited and relied upon, as having strong persuasive force, by our courts,[8] arguably on occasion even in such a manner as to 'supplement' the language of the Maltese provision. Our courts also regularly referred to Commission decisions, the decisions of the national courts of states party to the Convention, and the writings of noted jurists. The Courts have on occasion noted, however, that each case will turn, nevertheless, on its facts and context and in the past tended to stress the 'relevant terms of the provisions of the Maltese Constitution'.[9]

In 1987, Malta recognised the competence of the European Court of Human Rights to receive individual petitions and the compulsory jurisdiction of that Court. The European Convention Act (Act XIV of 1987) came into force on 19 August 1987. It incorporated the substantive provisions of the Convention and its First Protocol into domestic law. Since then, the Convention has the force of law in Malta. The Act provides that the rights and freedoms set out in Articles 3 to 18 of the Convention and 1 to 3 of the First Protocol are to be part of the law of Malta and enforceable as such, subject to the declaration and reservations made on the signing of the Convention in 1966.

The Act provides, in Section 3, that where any ordinary law is inconsistent with such rights and freedoms then these are to prevail, and such ordinary law is, to the extent of the inconsistency, to be void. Section 2 defines 'ordinary law' as 'any instrument having the force of law and any unwritten rule of law, other than the Constitution of Malta'. So here again we have the anticipated operation, in the event of clear conflict with an ordinary law, of the supremacy of the Constitution. The view expressed by a leading constitutional expert, former Chief Justice and Judge of the European Court of Human Rights, Professor J.J. Cremona, is that these developments led to the following hierarchy of norms being established in 1987: at the apex, the Constitutional provisions, next the European Convention norms and then the ordinary law.[10] If we had an ordinary law introducing the *acquis*, then the Community human rights acquis would *prima facie*, from the above perspective, be at level three. However, as far as I am aware, all Union proposals to further constitutionalise human rights take as their starting point and end, in legal terms, as opposed to political declarations (which latter the proposed Charter will probably remain), the European Convention. If we take this into account, and seek to analyse the situation that would arise on membership, the human rights acquis would at the lowest be at the Convention level (level two), subject to what is said in the next paragraph.

---

[8] See, e.g. *Galea* v. *Secretary for Housing*, 20 July 1971, Constitutional Decisions, Vol. 2, 1964-1978, p. 541 at p. 547.

[9] *Cuschieri* v. *Hon. Prime Minister*, ibid., p. 570 at pp. 593, 606, 614.

[10] J.J. Cremona, 'Selected Papers 1946-1989' (PEG Ltd., 1990) p. 229.

Of course, we would not anticipate unresolvable conflict. Yet in theory, it is said, there is this hierarchy. What would the position be on membership in theory and in practice? What could be said is that the European Community *acquis* must, after Maastricht and Amsterdam, but even on the basis of prior European Court of Justice case law, evolve in harmony with the European Convention, in legal terms. The European Convention is part of our law already, so the question is whether real conflict can arise between the Convention and the Constitutional provisions. So far as I am aware this remains a hypothetical question, but if a conflict did appear to arise, the Constitutional Court would be called upon to reconcile the texts and their interpretation. Moreover, Section 6 of the European Convention Act of 1987 requires the Maltese Constitutional Court to give effect to the judgments of the European Court of Human Rights to which a declaration by the Government of Malta in accordance with Article 46 of the Convention applies, in the same manner as judgments delivered by the Constitutional Court itself. Furthermore, the European Convention is of course itself binding on Malta as a matter of international law, and the 1987 Act simply ensures the fulfilment by Malta of its international obligations. The assumption is that it is simply not contemplated that there could be any truly irreconcilable conflict between the Convention and the Constitution. Clearly, there has been a strong evolution of constitutional human rights protection in line with the European Convention, as Professor Cremona put it. This analysis does not resolve all difficulties *ex ante* and, as in all member States, there is always the possibility of conflicting interpretations but EU membership and the incorporation of the Treaty will not, it is thought, add to them, for it is the European Convention which remains at the centre.

On the general question whether the Maltese courts recognise a rule of interpretation whereby national law must be interpreted in conformity with international obligations, it is clear that they do.

5. CONCLUDING REMARKS

It seems to the author that the clarification of a number of difficult issues, if this were possible, might be desirable from the point of view of a fuller debate at least. The answer to some questions is in some cases express and in others implicit in the stances of some (if not all) current member States, or is otherwise a matter for them in a later IGC, if they wish to open such questions for themselves, or a matter for them outside that context. I flag them because they have been considered important by a number of the contributors to this Conference in their provisional papers. They include:

1. In the event of some exercise in Constitutional drafting would it be fair to say that a formula of 'delegation' with reservation of 'ultimate sovereignty' (e.g.,

re human rights, national identity) was the acceptable common denominator among the member States?
2. How far will national parliaments be involved in the decision-making process?
3. Is it likely that the current member States' attitude towards neutrality (and CFSP development) will undergo any radical change?

It appears to me from the excellent national papers, but also from the equally helpful general papers with their comparative analyses, that as a common denominator among what are in effect disparate approaches which have been adopted by the current member States the following emerges. There is a need for:
(a) A constitutional basis in the light of generally accepted 'post-modern' constitutional theory and practice for the decision to 'delegate' or 'transfer' as an internal constitutional matter (of course with international legal effect) of the exercise of legislative, executive and judicial competence from the purely domestic decision-making sphere to the common decision-making level, limitedly to the areas of competence of the institutions as defined in the Treaties and in so far as necessary (subsidiarity/proportionality) for the achievement of those common objectives.
(b) Adequate mechanisms, with the ultimate support of the national supreme courts, for the giving of full effect in the domestic sphere to the Treaties and to all binding Community (Union) law as legitimately adopted by the institutions to which such exercise of power had been passed.

To put it any higher in terms of the manner of fulfilment of the Constitutional *acquis* would be for Community (Union) law to take a step which the member States and the ECJ have not made and will probably not be ready to make in the foreseeable future. The ECJ has, of course, stated the Community position in terms of Community principle and of national effect; it has never required any particular form of national constitutional textualisation of its own statements. Nor would it ever do so, I would think. But a new Treaty could and, some would argue, should. Recently re-floated ideas for the drafting of a Constitution for the Union raise this issue directly. The questions which such a proposal raises can only be answered by the member States themselves, by unanimity, and, if it meant a radically new concept in national constitutional terms of what membership of the Union involved, and seen from the perspective of what they have all so far been prepared to accept without equivocation and caveats, would mean, I suggest, a wholesale review even by several current member States of their constitutional positions. I have not argued here either in favour of, or against, either Professor Weiler's call for constitutional tolerance or de Witte's view (as I understand it) that the time will come for a revision of (member States') constitutions. I have sought simply, in the interests of constructive debate, to state the Maltese position in the general context of the existing and foreseeable Union and member State reality.

THE CONSTITUTIONAL IMPACT OF ENLARGEMENT AT EU AND NATIONAL LEVEL: THE CASE OF THE REPUBLIC OF CYPRUS

Nicholas Emiliou*

THE CONSTITUTIONAL ORDER OF THE REPUBLIC OF CYPRUS – AMENDMENT PROCEDURES

The foundation for the constitutional structure of the Republic of Cyprus,[1] which comprises the Constitution together with two Annexes (containing the Treaty of Guarantee and the Treaty of Alliance), was laid by the Zurich and London Agreements[2] which were thought to provide the final settlement of the Cyprus problem. The Treaty of Guarantee[3] and the Treaty of Alliance[4] have been given constitutional force.[5]

The Constitution of the Republic of Cyprus of 1960 is rigid, detailed and complex. The 1960 Constitution '... stands out as the centrepiece of an intricate net-

* Ambassador of the Republic of Cyprus.

[1] The Republic of Cyprus was set up by means of the Treaty of Establishment between Cyprus, Britain, Greece and Turkey. The Treaty provides that the Republic 'shall comprise the island of Cyprus ... with the exception of two areas defined in Annex A of this Treaty, which areas shall remain under the sovereignty of the United Kingdom.' This secured British military bases on the island.

[2] The Zurich and London Agreements (of 11 and 19 February 1959, respectively) declared Cyprus an independent Republic, whose independence, constitutional order and territorial integrity were guaranteed by the United Kingdom, Greece and Turkey.

[3] The Treaty of Guarantee, between Cyprus, on the one hand, and Britain, Greece and Turkey on the other, aimed at the protection of the constitutional order created by the Zurich and London agreements and the exclusion of political or economic union of the island with any state. The three guarantor powers guaranteed the continuation of existence and maintenance of the constitutional order, as well as, the independence and territorial integrity of Cyprus. By means of Article IV, each of the three guarantor powers reserved 'the right to take any action with the sole aim of re-establishing the state of affairs established by the present Treaty' provided that 'common or concerted action may not prove possible.'

[4] The Treaty of Alliance was concluded between Cyprus, Greece and Turkey and provided that military contingents of each state should be stationed in the territory of the Republic. This had the purpose of securing the parties' responsibility to resist any attack or act of aggression directed against the independence or territorial integrity of Cyprus.

[5] Article 181 of the 1960 Constitution.

work of international agreements and undertakings, delicately but inextricably interwoven with one another and with the Constitution itself ...'.[6]

According to paragraph 21 of the Zurich Agreement, several of its provisions had to be included in the Constitution of the Republic of Cyprus as fundamental – basic Articles, not subject to any revision or amendment. These basic Articles, stipulated by the Constitution itself to be unalterable,[7] include the whole or parts of forty-eight separate Articles out of 199.

On the other hand, according to Article 182(2) and (3) of the 1960 Constitution, any other provision of the Constitution (that is, non-basic provisions) 'may be amended, whether by way of variation, addition or repeal' by law passed by a majority vote comprising at least two-thirds of the total number of the Representatives belonging to the Greek Community and at least two-thirds of the total number of the Representatives belonging to the Turkish Community.

As a result of the deliberate withdrawal of Turkish Cypriots and their refusal to participate in the state organs of the Republic since 1964, the Supreme Court of Cyprus in its landmark judgment *Attorney General of the Republic* v. *Ibrahim*[8] adopted the doctrine of necessity. This doctrine has been further elaborated by case law as an integral part of the legal and constitutional order of the Republic, so much so, that it is possible to deviate temporarily from strict compliance with constitutional provisions. In other words, the doctrine has been applied in Cyprus to validate public acts facing procedural difficulties which it is impossible to remedy because of political boycott by the Turkish Cypriot leadership and, later, foreign invasion.

Thus, pending the solution of the political problem, any necessary constitutional amendments of non-basic constitutional provisions may be adopted by a law passed by a majority of at least two-thirds of Greek Cypriot members of the House of Representatives.[9]

Given the fact that all parliamentary (and non-parliamentary) political parties in Cyprus are strongly in favour of EU accession no practical problems are foreseen in securing the minimum two-third majority vote required for any constitutional amendment necessitated by accession.

The Constitution of the Republic makes no reference to the possibility of holding referenda on any issue whatsoever, but, on the other hand, there is nothing in the 1960 Constitution precluding that possibility.

Given the constitutional impact of accession to the EU and the fact that the decision to pursue Union membership is one of the most serious decisions ever

---

[6] S.A. de Smith, The New Commonwealth and its Constitutions (1964), p. 285.

[7] Article 182(1) of the 1960 Constitution. A list of these basic Articles of the Constitution is to be found in Annex III thereto.

[8] (1964) CLR 195.

[9] On this basis, there have been, since 1985, a number of amendments on non-basic provisions of the 1960 Constitution such as Article 111.

made on behalf of the people, it may be argued that any proposals for amendment of the Constitution necessitated by EU accession should be submitted by referendum to the will of the people of Cyprus.

Such a course of action would conform with the inalienable, indefeasible and sovereign right of the people to choose its own form of government, to determine its relations with other nations and to develop its political, economic and cultural life in accordance to its own wishes. Furthermore, in democratic states all powers of government, legislative, executive and judicial derive from the people whose right it is, in final appeal, to decide all questions of national policy. A most authentic form of exercise of this right by the people is through a referendum.

Given that no provision is made for referenda in the 1960 Constitution or any other law of the Republic, holding a referendum on any issue would require the adoption of a relevant law by the House of Representatives which will provide the legal basis for it. Such a law will also lay down the relevant organisational details for a referendum and, most importantly, decide the issue of the majority required for the approval of the measure subject to referendum.

THE POSITION OF INTERNATIONAL AGREEMENTS IN THE LEGAL ORDER OF THE REPUBLIC

Article 169 of the 1960 Constitution deals with both, the means of ratification of treaties, conventions and international agreements and their effect on internal law. The Constitution of Cyprus vests the power to ratify in different authorities of the Republic, depending on the subject matter of the treaty, convention or international agreement.

Cyprus is a monist country. In the Republic of Cyprus a treaty negotiated or signed under a decision of the Council of Ministers and ratified by a law made by the House of Representatives and published in the official Gazette of the Republic acquires superior force to any municipal law.[10] A ratifying law comes into operation on the date of its publication in the Gazette unless otherwise provided.[11]

According to Article 169 of the Constitution, subject to the provisions of Article 50 and paragraph (3) of Article 57 of the Constitution,[12]

- all international treaties and agreements relating to commercial matters, economic co-operation (including payments and credit) and *modus vivendi* are concluded under a decision of the Council of Ministers;
- every other international treaty, convention or agreement, negotiated and signed under a decision of the Council of Ministers, is concluded and becomes

[10] See Article 169(2) and (3) of the 1960 Constitution.

[11] See Article 82 of the 1960 Constitution.

[12] Articles 50 and 57(3) of the 1960 Constitution concern the right of veto of the President and the Vice-President of the Republic respectively.

operative when approved by law made by the House of Representatives; and
- every treaty, convention and agreement (concluded in accordance with the provisions above) is published in the official Gazette of the Republic and on its application has superior force to any municipal law, on condition that such treaty, convention or agreement is applied by the other party thereto.[13]

However, the Constitution, under the terms of Article 179(1), is the supreme law of the Republic and is not, therefore, within the ambit of the definition of 'municipal law' within the meaning of Article 169(3) which covers any ordinary law prior or consequent to an international treaty.[14] Thus, the hierarchy of norms in the Cypriot legal order is (a) the Constitution; (b) international treaties; and (c) ordinary laws.[15] A treaty is, therefore, inferior to the Constitution and the latter prevails in case of any inconsistency between constitutional provisions and the provisions of the treaty.[16]

On the other hand, it is clear that European Community law – which is based on treaties between the EC member States – forms a distinct legal system which is capable of creating directly effective rights for those subject it. These Community rights are not only independent of national laws but are also to be regarded as superior to them. The acceptance by national courts of the supremacy of Community law is the pre-requisite to its full reception into national law.

THE CASE LAW OF THE SUPREME COURT

According to the Supreme Court case law,[17] an international treaty, being inferior to the Constitution by virtue of Article 179(1), is subject to judicial review in the sense that the constitutional provisions prevail in case of any inconsistency between them and the provisions of the treaty. A treaty does not, *stricto sensu*, repeal municipal law but has only superior force to it taking precedence in its application. Such a treaty retains its nature as part of international law. Having regard to its nature, however, and its connection with the international obligations of the Republic, it cannot be amended or repealed by any posterior law contrary to its provisions or the provisions of the Vienna Convention on the Law of Treaties.[18]

---

[13] See the *Malachtou* judgment, infra, for a clear statement by the Supreme Court as to when such reciprocity is excluded.

[14] For the definition of the term 'law' see Article 186(1) of the 1960 Constitution. See also the *Malachtou* judgment, infra.

[15] See, for example, *Eracleous* v. *The Municipality of Limassol* (Appeal no. 5793), judgment of the Supreme Court of 14 December 1993, which recalled the above hierarchy.

[16] See *Malachtou* v. *Armefti,* supra.

[17] See *Malachtou* v. *Armefti* (1987)1 CLR 207.

[18] The Vienna Convention on the Law of Treaties was ratified under Article 169 of the 1960 Constitution by Law 62/76.

According to the Supreme Court, a ratified treaty delineates not only the international obligations of the State, as defined therein, but also the internal law until the day that, under its provisions or the Vienna Convention on Treaties, it ceases to be operative.

Article 169 of the 1960 Constitution does not apply only to treaties affecting rights and obligations of the State but also covers all treaties, conventions and agreements ratified and concluded in conformity with paragraph 2 thereof, provided that all other requirements are satisfied.[19]

According to the Supreme Court case law, the requirement of reciprocity under Article 169(3) is waived in the case of:

> '... treaties whose nature, objective and function in the international relations and the international legal order exclude the condition of reciprocity. Such are multilateral conventions the object of which is not to create any subjective or reciprocal rights for the contracting parties themselves but their objective and their intent is to promote certain principles of law, moral and legal values and which a contracting party signs and ratifies only for the realisation of this objective. Examples are: Conventions for the protection of human rights and the improvements and formulation of common rules and the achievement of social justice.
>
> ...
>
> Where there is any international mechanism of control or supervision, the condition of reciprocity again cannot validly be raised'.[20]

Self-executing treaties are directly applicable:

> 'We agree ... That for a treaty to be applicable it must be self-executing. ... We need not in this case attempt to give a general definition of the term "self-executing treaty". Pious declarations and provisions relating to political and international relations in a convention are not self-executing provisions. Only such provisions of a Convention are self-executing which may be applied by the organs of the State and which can be enforced by the Courts and which create rights for the individuals; they govern or affect directly relations of the internal life between the individuals, and the individuals and the State or the public authorities. Provisions which do not create by themselves rights or obligations of persons or interests and which cannot be justiciable or do not refer to acts or omissions of State organs are not self-executing. International law is primarily a law between States and normally treaties have effect upon States only. As it has been pointed out by the Permanent Court of International Justice (Series B. No. 15), this rule can be altered by the express or implied terms of the treaty, in which case its provisions become self-executing. If treaties contain provisions with regard to rights and duties of the subjects or the contracting States, their courts, officials, and the like, these States must take such steps as are necessary, according to their Municipal Law, to make these provisions binding upon their subjects, courts, officials and the like – (*Oppenheim's* International Law, 8th edition, vol. 1, p. 924).

---

[19] Ibid.

[20] Ibid. See also *Shipowners Union* v. *The Registrar of Trademarks & Others* (1988) 3 CLR 457.

The question whether or not treaties are self-executing is influenced by the wording of the convention, its provisions and the relevant constitutional law in a given country ...'.[21]

In the same case, Pikis, J. observed:[22]

'Ratification by the legislature incorporates the treaty or convention, as the case may be, into domestic law by virtue of the legislative power vested in the House of Representatives (Art. 61 of the Constitution); and if its provisions are self-executing they acquire the force of law quite independently of paragraph 3 of Article 169 (of the Constitution) or its impact on domestic legislation. The point is exemplified by the decisions of the Supreme Court in *Mizrahi* v. *The Republic*[23] and *Kannas* v. *The Police*[24] in which the Court referred to the European Convention on Human Rights ratified by Law 39/62 as an integral part of our domestic legislation without at all inquiring into the question of reciprocity. A provision of a treaty or convention is self-executing if the rights vested or the obligations imposed thereby are comprehensively defined to the extent of making them, without further addition or modification, enforceable before a court of law ...'.

In respect of the question whether the courts in Cyprus recognise a rule of interpretation whereby national law must be interpreted in conformity with international obligations, there are indications, in the case law of the Supreme Court, that such a rule has been adopted, at least as far as treaties whose 'intent is the promotion of values and the protection of human rights' are concerned.

In its judgment in the *Shipowners Union* v. *The Registrar of Trademarks & Others*[25] case, the Supreme Court stated (per Stylianides J.):

'The aforesaid international instruments[26] are not only relevant, but should serve as a guide to the interpretation of our constitutional provisions. ...
Before concluding I would like to stress that it is the duty, not only of the Courts, but all authorities of the Republic, including executive – administrative and legislative, to secure within the limits of their respective competence the efficient application, both of the Part II of the Constitution – Fundamental Rights and Liberties – and the ratified International Conventions for the enjoyment of the rights and freedoms declared and safeguarded thereby ...'.

---

[21] Per Stylianides J. in *Malachtou* v. *Armefti,* supra.
[22] Ibid., pp. 234-236.
[23] (1968) 3 CLR 404.
[24] (1968) 2 CLR 35.
[25] (1988) 3 CLR 457.
[26] Author's note: i.e., the European Convention on Human Rights, the ILO Convention No. 87, Concerning Freedom of Association and Protection of the Right to Organise, and the UN Covenant on Civil and Political Rights.

THE IMPACT OF ACCESSION: SPECIFIC CONSTITUTIONAL PROVISIONS REQUIRING AMENDMENT[27]

In the Cypriot constitutional order, the executive power is ensured by the President (and the Vice-President) of the Republic (Art. 46(1) of the 1960 Constitution) and it is exercised by the Council of Ministers (Art. 54(1) of the 1960 Constitution). The legislative power of the Republic is exercised by the House of Representatives 'in all matters' except those expressly reserved to the Communal Chambers under the Constitution (Art. 61 of the 1960 Constitution).[28] The Supreme Court exercises all the judicial power of the Republic, including constitutional matters, such as the constitutionality of laws, conflict of competence between the organs of the Republic and electoral petitions.[29]

Under Article 179(1), the Constitution is the supreme law of the Republic. On the other hand, European Community law by its own terms is supreme and takes precedence over all national law, including national constitutions themselves. It should, however, be noted that Article 179 is not a basic provision of the Constitution and can, therefore, be amended under the procedure provided for by Article 182.

Moreover, membership of the European Union involves a partial loss or transfer of sovereignty in favour of the Union. This, *prima facie*, appears to sit uneasily with Article 61 of the 1960 Constitution providing that the House of Representatives exercises the legislative power of the Republic 'in all matters'. Article 61 is a basic Article and, therefore, unamendable.

A way of overcoming the above difficulties would be by means of an amendment of Article 169 of the 1960 Constitution (a non-basic provision), following the procedure prescribed in Article 182, by adding specific paragraphs reflecting, *mutatis mutandis*, the contents of Articles 29(4)(3), 29(4)(4), 29(4)(5) and 29(7) respectively of the Irish Constitution. Article 29 of the Irish Constitution provides, inter alia, that:

> 'The State may become a member of the European Coal and Steel Community (established by Treaty signed at Paris on the 18th day of April, 1951), the European Economic Community (established by Treaty signed at Rome on the 25th day of March, 1957) and the European Atomic Energy Community (established by Treaty signed at

[27] N.B. Rather than simply presenting his personal opinion, the author discusses briefly key constitutional provisions which were highlighted in a report prepared in September 1998 by the Group for the Study of the Constitution set up by the Attorney General of the Republic in order to deal with the constitutional implications of the Republic's accession to the EU.

[28] The Communal Chambers were designed to serve as legislative, executive and economic authorities in religious, educational, teaching and cultural affairs of the two Cypriot communities as well as issues of personal status. See Articles 86-111 of the 1960 Constitution.

[29] See Articles 133-164 of the 1960 Constitution. The jurisdiction of the Supreme Court is derived from Articles 136 and 152 of the Constitution. See also Law 33/64.

> Rome on the 25th day of March, 1957). The State may ratify the Single European Act (signed on behalf of the member States of the Communities at Luxembourg on the 17th day of February 1986 and at The Hague on the 28th day of February 1986). (Art. 29(4)(3))
> The State may ratify the Treaty on European Union signed at Maastricht on the 7th day of February, 1992, and may become a member of that Union. (Art. 29(4)(4))
> The State may ratify the Treaty of Amsterdam amending the Treaty on European Union, the Treaties establishing the European Communities and certain related Acts signed at Amsterdam on the 2nd day of October, 1997. (Art. 29(4)(5))
> No provision of this Constitution invalidates laws enacted, acts done or measures adopted by the State which are necessitated by the obligations of membership of the European Union or of the Communities, or prevents laws enacted, acts done, or measures adopted by the European Union or by the Communities or by institutions thereof, or by bodies competent under the Treaties establishing the Communities, from having the force of law in the State'. (Art. 29(7))

The adoption of such an amendment would cover the actual accession of the Republic to the Union as well as the transfer of national executive, legislative, judicial and treaty-making powers to the EU institutions thus pre-empting the potential problems posed by Articles 54(1), 61(1), 136, 152 and 169 of the 1960 Constitution.

Moreover, for reasons of clarity and legal certainty, Article 179(1) of the Constitution (also a non-basic provision) could be amended as follows: '*Subject to the provisions of Article 169* (...) [T]his Constitution shall be the supreme law of the Republic'.

Such an amendment would ensure that constitutional provisions do not affect in any way the Treaty of Accession and European Community law and would safeguard their supremacy over the Constitution.

Turning now to the legal/constitutional objections expressed by the Turkish side concerning the Republic's accession to the EU, the following should be noted.

Both the Turkish Government and the Turkish Cypriot leadership reacted strongly to Cyprus's application to join the EU. Turkey attempted, using both political and legal arguments, to block Cyprus's accession course. In the summer of 1997, when, following the publication of *Agenda 2000*, it became obvious that accession negotiations with Cyprus would begin in the next few months, Turkey circulated an opinion signed by Professor Mendelson of the University of London claiming that Cyprus's application to join the Union as such was unconstitutional.

This Opinion claimed that (a) the 1960 Treaty of Guarantee (b) Article 50 and (c) Article 170 of Cyprus's Constitution precluded Cyprus from joining the European Union.

Cyprus countered this legalistic effort by Turkey by obtaining a joint opinion (of 27 September 1997 – henceforth 'the Opinion') by three well-known international law experts, Professor Crawford of the University of Cambridge, Professor Häfner of the University of Vienna and Professor Pellet of the University of Paris.

(a) Article I(2) of the Treaty of Guarantee provides that the Republic of Cyprus: '... undertakes not to participate, in whole or in part, in any political or economic union with any state whatsoever ...'

However, according to the three experts, this provision does not prohibit Cyprus from becoming a member of a regional organisation such as the European Union. Membership of the Union would not constitute participation, 'in any political or economic union with any state whatsoever' within the meaning of Article 1(2) of the Treaty of Guarantee. In arriving at this conclusion the three professors, examined:

- the Vienna Convention on the Law of the Treaties (Arts. 31-33);
- the legal nature of the European Union (with particular reference to the judgment of the German Constitutional Court in the *Maastricht Treaty Constitutionality Case*);
- the *travaux preparatoires* of Article I(2) of the Treaty of Guarantee;
- the case of Austria (in whose case there was also an analogous guarantee against political union);
- the attitude of the international community to the Cyprus application for EU membership.

More specifically, Professors Crawford, Häfner and Pellet refer to the precursor of Article I(2) of the Treaty of Guarantee, that is, point 22 of the Zurich Agreement, and the *travaux preparatoires*. Point 22 of the Zurich Agreement provides that:

> 'It shall be recognised that the total or partial union of Cyprus with any other State, or a separatist independence for Cyprus (i.e., the partition of Cyprus into two independent States), shall be excluded'.

On the basis of the above provision, as well as the *travaux preparatoires*, the three Professors conclude that the purpose was then quite obviously to exclude both union and partition and, by invoking Articles 31-33 of the Vienna Convention on the Law of the Treaties,[30] they suggest that the interpretation of Article I(2) must be based in good faith and that the actual language must be seen in 'its context and in the light of its object and purpose'. By further reference to Articles 50 and 169 of the 1960 Constitution, which refer to 'international organisations

[30] Articles 31-33 of the Vienna Convention deal with the interpretation of international treaties.

and pacts of alliance'[31] or international agreements 'with a foreign State or any International Organisation, relating to commercial matters, economic co-operation ... and *modus vivendi'*,[32] the Opinion indicates that the Treaty of Guarantee makes a clear distinction between 'political and economic union with any State' and any other form of international co-operation. Thus, what is prohibited is union with another State, not co-operation with a group of States in establishing a supranational organisation of a political and/or economic union. Moreover, 'a distinction has always been drawn between membership of multilateral or plurilateral organisations of States (whatever their title), and the political or economic union with another State'. Clearly, the EU is not a State; it is a 'supranational organisation' or an 'independent legal order', a legal system of transnational character, although it aspires to a 'more perfect union'. Hence, membership of the EU does not involve 'political or economic union with any State'. The Opinion also clearly distinguishes the *Austro-German Customs Union Case* as Cyprus would be less dependent on any single member State of the EU by virtue of EU membership, in contrast, to the then eventual domination of Austria by Germany.

Another argument put forward by Professor Mendelson was that the two EU member States which are also Guarantors, that is Greece and the United Kingdom, 'are under an obligation of their own to refrain from promoting Cyprus' membership of the EU and, indeed to use their veto to prevent it' since they undertook by virtue of Article II(2) of the Treaty of Guarantee to prevent the union of Cyprus with any other State. However, this argument does not seem valid if one follows the line of argument of the three Professors in respect of Article I(2) of the Treaty of Guarantee, that is, accession to the EU does not imply 'political or economic union with any State'. Moreover, the Opinion of the three Professors refers to constant State practice and the attitude of the international community on the issue of Cyprus's accession to the Union. The EU itself considers Cyprus eligible for membership; the Resolutions of the UN Security Council have been affirming, since 1990, that a settlement of the Cyprus problem must, inter alia, 'must exclude union in whole with any other country or any form of partition or secession'[33] whilst, at the same time, approved of the EU decision to open accession negotiations with Cyprus.[34] In addition, the Opinion points out to the fact that neither Turkey nor the United Kingdom ever protested that the EC-Cyprus Association Agreement (1972) was contrary to the Treaty of Guarantee.

---

[31] Article 50(1)(a) of the 1960 Constitution.

[32] Article 169(1) of the 1960 Constitution.

[33] See, e.g., UN Security Council Resolutions 649(1990), 716(1991), 750(1992), 939(1994), 1092(1996), 1117(1997), 1146(1997), 1179(1998), 1217(1998), 1251(1999).

[34] UN Security Council Resolutions 1062(1996), 1092(1996), 1117(1887), 1146(1997) recognise that 'the decision of the European Union concerning the opening of accession negotiations with Cyprus is an important new development that should facilitate an overall settlement'.

The Opinion also refers to the case of Austria's membership of the EU and to Article 4(1) of the Austrian State Treaty (1955) by means of which Austria undertook not to 'enter into political or economic union with Germany in any form whatsoever' in order to prevent another *Anschluss*. It was unanimously held in that case that Austria's accession to the EU would not contravene that provision.

(b) Article 50 of the 1960 Constitution grants the President and Vice-President (a Turkish-Cypriot) a veto over any foreign policy decision, particularly any decision on joining an international organisation or alliance that does not count both Greece and Turkey among its members. However, with regard to the Vice-President's veto, the 1960 Constitution prescribes a specific mechanism based on the assumption of his participation in the administration. In other words, that veto is the prerogative of the Vice-President as an office holder and can only be exercised by him when in office. Thus, under the Constitution of 1960 that veto cannot be exercised by the Turkish Cypriot community as such but only by the holder of the Vice President's office. In the case of deliberate abstention of the Vice-President from his duties, the intentional refusal to play his constitutional role and in the face of an invasion by foreign forces, one could clearly argue that the vice-presidential veto provided for in Article 50 cannot be exercised.

(c) Article 170 of the Constitution provides for most-favoured nation treatment to be extended by Cyprus to the three guarantor powers 'for all agreements whatever their nature may be'. Such treatment has only to be extended 'by agreement on appropriate terms'. In common with other most-favoured-nation clauses, Article 170 does not prohibit Cyprus from entering into agreements which confer benefits on third states; it envisages that benefits extended to the most favoured nation will also be extended to each of the guarantors. Thus, Article 170 does not prohibit Cyprus from acceding to any agreement whatever.

In fact, EC membership is not regarded as triggering general most-favoured nation obligations under the GATT or otherwise. Turkey as a GATT contracting party and applicant for EU membership is well aware of this practice. Both Turkey and Greece, in bilateral treaties concluded with Cyprus after independence, have recognised that most-favoured nation obligation in respect of trade in products do not apply 'to privileges ... preferences or concessions ... granted ... in the future to other countries on account of ... participation, entry or association ... [to] a customs union, a free area or an economic community'. For these reasons Article 170 would not require Cyprus to extend any additional benefits of EU membership to Turkey.

Thus, by circulating the opinion of the three Professors, the Government of the Republic has dealt effectively with the Turkish efforts to invent legal arguments against Cyprus's accession to the European Union. This view is reflected by the European Commission's Opinion on Cyprus's application for accession where it is stated, after citing the Turkish arguments mentioned above, that:

'The Community, however, following the logic of its established position, which is consistent with that of the United Nations where the legitimacy of the Government of the Republic of Cyprus and non-recognition of the "Turkish Republic of Northern Cyprus" are concerned, felt that the application was admissible and initiated the procedures laid down by the Treaties in order to examine it'.

Furthermore, the Court of Justice of the EC in the *Anastasiou*[35] case stated that:

'The problems resulting from the *de facto* partition of the island must be resolved exclusively by the Republic of Cyprus, which alone is internationally recognized'.

ISSUES ARISING FROM THE POLITICAL PROBLEM OF THE ISLAND

The issues raised in Professor Soysal's paper concerning the problems related to the existence of the so-called 'Turkish Republic of Northern Cyprus' call for the following comments:

a) The issues raised in the above paper have their background in the Turkish invasion of Cyprus in 1974 and the continuing illegal occupation by Turkey of approximately thirty-seven per cent of the territory of the Republic. The invasion resulted into a *de facto* division of Cyprus into an area which the authorities of the Republic continue to exercise full jurisdiction and an area – the part north of the UN Buffer zone – where the authorities of the Republic cannot in fact exercise their constitutional powers.

The Turkish invasion and the subsequent *de facto* division of the island have been the subject of numerous resolutions adopted by the UN Security Council and the UN General Assembly.[36] The main thrust of those resolutions was that the external military intervention should be brought to an end, Cyprus's territorial integrity should be respected and the parties encouraged to seek a peaceful solution.

In November 1983, the Turkish side in the occupied part of the Republic proclaimed itself an independent State with the name 'Turkish Republic of Northern Cyprus' ('TRNC'). The UN Security Council reacted strongly against the attempt to set up such a State. By resolution 541/1983, the Security Council pronounced the declaration of secession to be 'legally invalid and [called] for its withdrawal'. In its Resolution 550/1984, the Security Council repeated the 'call upon all States not to recognize the purported state of the "Turkish Republic of Northern Cyprus" set up by secessionist acts and [called] upon them not to facilitate or in

[35] Case C-432/92 [1994] ECR I-3087, para. 47 of the Judgment.

[36] See, e.g., Security Council Resolutions 353/1974, 354/1974, 355/1974, 357/1974, 358/1974, 360/1974 and 365/1974 and General Assembly Resolution 3212/XXIX.

any way assist the aforesaid secessionist entity'. No States (or international organisations) other than Turkey have recognised the so-called 'TRNC'.

By declarations of 16 and 17 November 1983, the European Parliament, the Commission and the Foreign Ministers of the EC member States, in the framework of European Political Cooperation, rejected the unilateral declaration of secession and expressed their continued support for the legitimate Government of the Republic of Cyprus. By a declaration of 27 March 1984, in the framework of European Political Cooperation, the Foreign Ministers expressed their support for UN Security Council Resolution 541/1983 and regretted that Turkey had taken the step of recognising the so-called 'TRNC'.

Furthermore, the Court of Justice of the EC in the *Anastasiou*[37] case stated that:

> '... cooperation is excluded with the authorities of an entity such as that established in the northern part of Cyprus, which is recognized neither by the Community nor by the member States; the only Cypriot State they recognize is the Republic of Cyprus.
>
> ....
>
> The problems resulting from the *de facto* partition of the island must be resolved exclusively by the Republic of Cyprus, which alone is internationally recognized'.

The above position is also demonstrated by the reactions of the Council of Europe system. As the European Court of Human Rights declared in *Loizidou* v. *Turkey* (*Preliminary Objections*):

> 'The Court confines itself to noting, with reference, inter alia, to the consistent practice of the Council of Europe and the decisions of the Commission in the inter-state cases of *Cyprus* v. *Turkey*, that the applicant Government have been recognised by the international community as the Government of the Republic of Cyprus (see in this connection, Applications nos. 6780/74 and 6950/75, *Cyprus* v. *Turkey,* 26 May 1975, Decisions and Reports (DR) 2, p. 125, at pp. 135-136; no. 8007/77, *Cyprus* v. *Turkey,* 10 July 1978, DR 13 p. 85, at p. 146). Its *locus standi* as the Government of a High Contracting Party to the Convention cannot therefore be in doubt.' (Series A, no 310, §40).

This position was reaffirmed by the Court in *Loizidou* (*Merits*):

> 'Moreover it is only the Cypriot Government which is recognised internationally as the Government of the Republic of Cyprus in the context of diplomatic and treaty relations and the working of international organisations (see the Commission's decisions on the admissibility of applications nos. 6780/74 and 6950/75, *Cyprus* v. *Turkey*, 26 May 1975, DR 2, pp. 135-136; no. 8007/77, *Cyprus* v. *Turkey,* 10 July 1978, DR 13, p. 146).' (§42).

---

[37] Case C-432/92 [1994] ECR I-3087, paras. 40 and 47 of the Judgment.

The position was further underlined in paragraph 44, where the Court emphasised that 'the Republic of Cyprus has remained the sole legitimate Government of Cyprus'.

Moreover, in *Loizidou (Merits)*, the Court declared the so-called 'constitution' of the 'TRNC' as lacking 'legal validity'.[38]

On the basis of the above, therefore, one cannot talk about the necessity of any amendments to the 'constitution' of the 'TRNC for purposes of accession to the EU. Obviously, both the 'TRNC' and its 'constitution' are null and void and legally non-existent.

Finally, looking beyond the European Union and the Council of Europe, it is crucial to note that no State in the world (with the sole exception of Turkey for obvious political purposes) and no regional or international inter-Governmental institution recognises any authority as the legitimate Government of Cyprus other than the Government of the Republic.

b) The settlement of the Cyprus problem is subject to the following general principles:
(i) The object of the negotiations is not to create a new State of Cyprus but to find a new constitutional arrangement for the Republic of Cyprus.
(ii) The settlement must be based on a State of Cyprus with a single sovereignty and international personality and a single citizenship, with its independence and territorial integrity safeguarded and comprising two politically equal communities as defined in paragraph 11 of the Secretary-General's Report (S/27780) in a bi-communal and bi-zonal federation and that such a settlement must exclude union in whole or in part with any other country or any form of partition or secession.[39] Consequently, confederation is excluded and cannot be accepted.
(iii) Fundamental human rights as recognised and protected by the European Convention for the Protection of Human Rights, the UN instruments concerning human rights and other international instruments and conventions binding on the Republic of Cyprus should be safeguarded and respected.
(iv) In view of Cyprus's application to join the European Union, the new constitution must be compatible with the *acquis communautaire* and it should not include provisions which will prevent proper implementation of decisions of the European Union executive or legislative in Cyprus or hinder the country's effective participation in the institutions and processes of the Union.

c) It is clear in the Helsinki Conclusion of the European Council that there is no linkage between Cyprus´s accession to the Union and the solution of the Cyprus problem or to the outcome of Turkey's relations with the European Union.

---

[38] See paras. 44-46 of the Court's judgment.

[39] See, e.g., UN Security Council Resolutions 649(1990), 716(1991), 750(1992), 939(1994), 1092(1996), 1117(1997), 1146(1997), 1179(1998), 1217(1998), 1251(1999).

The Government of Cyprus considers Cyprus's irreversible accession course as being at the service of the solution of the Cyprus problem because it could act as a catalyst for the solution of the problem. But if Cyprus´s accession course is to play an effective catalyst role, it must remain free of any conditions or restrictions and proceed unhindered.

Turkish reactions to the prospect of Cyprus's accession to the Union indicate very clearly two things. First, Turkey realises that Cyprus's accession process will be the agent that will compel it to revise its current stance on the political problem and cooperate for a solution; secondly, Turkey attempts, at the same time, to use the fact that it holds the key for the solution of the Cyprus problem as a leverage to obtain from the European Union significant concessions regarding its own accession course.

This is why Turkey's position regarding Cyprus's accession varies from a total rejection of the prospect of accession on the ground that that the application of Cyprus is allegedly illegal, despite the clear position taken by the Commission in its Opinion as well as by the member States of the European Union, to an inextricable linkage of Cyprus's accession to Turkey's own accession, in the sense that Cyprus´s accession can only be contemplated after the solution of the Cyprus problem and depending on whether Turkey itself would start accession negotiations or not.

With regard to the role of the Turkish Cypriots in the accession process, one should recall President Clerides' invitation to the Turkish Cypriot community in March 1998 to nominate their representatives to join as full members the Republic's negotiating team. The proposal, which was characterised as fair and generous by the then President of the Council of Ministers Robin Cook, has not yet been taken up but still remains open

Cyprus's accession into the EU would serve the interests of all the parties involved into the political problem. It would offer security to both Cypriot communities and would foster mutual trust. It would serve as a guarantee for the respect of human rights and democratic principles for the people of Cyprus. It would also strengthen the economic development of Cyprus, the benefits of which would be enjoyed by both Cypriot communities. Finally, it would contribute to the long term stabilization and peace in Southeastern Mediterranean.

INTRODUCTION TO THE CONSTITUTIONAL PROBLEMS OF THE ACCESSION OF TURKEY

Mümtaz Soysal*

The present Constitution of the Republic of Turkey reflects the philosophy of and is a typical nation-state modelled on the 'Jacobine' principles of the French Revolution (supremacy of the national sovereignty 'without restrictions or conditions', unity of the state's territory with its nation, indivisibility of the national territory – Arts. 3, 5 and 6).

The Constitution also prohibits any amendment and even any proposed amendment of Article 1 (the republican character of the state), Article 2 (democratic, secular, social nature of the Republic, respecting human rights and the rule of law) and Article 3 (indivisibility of the national territory and the unity of the state).

On the other hand, the Constitution stipulates that 'the nation exercises its sovereignty through authorized organs in accordance with the constitutional principles' and then enumerates these organs together with their powers:

Article 7: 'The legislative power shall vest in the Grand National Assembly of Turkey on behalf of the nation. This power cannot be delegated.'

Article 8: 'The executive power and function is carried out and exercised by the President of the Republic and the Council of Ministers in accordance with Constitution and the laws.'

Article 9: 'The judicial power is exercised on behalf of the nation by independent courts.'

Considering that the European Union is not an international organization, but a 'supranational' entity, its membership implies the transfer or delegation of a part of the national sovereignty to the organs of the Union or, more correctly, sharing the sovereignty with the Union for the conduct of national affairs. Although the supranational character of the EU was not explicitly mentioned in any of its founding agreements, already at the earliest stages of its development several judgments of the European Court of Justice in Luxemburg had underlined this character of the new 'economico-political entity' (e.g., *Walt Wilhelm* case, 1969; *Handelsgesellschaft* case, 1970; *Nold* case, 1974; *Simmenthal* case, 1978). Even such a partial transfer, delegation or sharing of such constitutionally defined

* Professor of constitutional law, University of Ankara.

A.E. Kellermann et al. (Eds.), EU Enlargement: The Constitutional Impact at EU and National Level

sovereign powers is definitely against the conception of the present Turkish system on the exercise of national sovereignty, thus making the accession of the country to the EU completely impossible without a drastic amendment of the Constitution.

However, the last paragraph of Article 90 in the present Constitution, as did Article 65 of the previous Constitution of 1961, may at first glance seem to make the problem relatively easier to solve: 'International treaties which have been duly put into operation shall have the force of law. Recourse cannot be made to the Constitutional Court in respect of such treaties on the grounds of unconstitutionality.' The Turkish constitutional system, adopting the dualist approach and trying to incorporate it within its own rules, never recognized the supremacy of international treaties above the national legislation. So, under the present rules the effect of an international treaty can be easily modified by an ulterior law, at least as regards its domestic implications. It is also interesting to note, in this respect, that the Constitutional Court, in one ground-breaking case (the text of the judgment has not been officially published), agreed to the admissibility of a recourse on the grounds of unconstitutionality of a law granting parliamentary authorization for the ratification of international treaties, but claimed to be unconstitutional by one fifth of the legislators. The Court, although refuting the claim on the unconstitutionality of the wording of the treaty itself, has opened, by this verdict in favour of admissibility, a previously unforeseen possibility of judicial review of international treaties, at least prior to their ratification. This means that, in the absence of the required constitutional amendments, many provisions of an eventual accession treaty between Turkey and the European Union and most of the following acts stemming from such a membership are likely to be declared void by the Turkish Constitutional Court, even if a general provision for a symbolic reference to 'shared sovereignty' is made by amending one of the introductory articles of the Constitution.

It would not be wrong to conclude, after this short and general introduction, that the harmonization and adaptation of Turkey's Constitution to the legal obligations to be assumed under the EU Treaties will be an extremely difficult task requiring changes that from the point of view of the constitutional principles cherished throughout the history of the Republic, will be painfull changes.

Furthermore, in addition to this fundamental difficulty concerning the concept of sovereignty which arises when it comes to accession to EU, there are other aspects of the Turkish Constitution that certainly need to be changed in order to make it more democratic and more in line with the principles of the rule of law and universal conceptions of human rights. The enactment of such constitutional changes should not normally be very difficult because there is already a very large consensus on this point in Turkish public opinion and among the political cadres, with or without any consideration of EU membership.

Thus the list of constitutional amendments necessitated by the process of accession can be drawn up as follows:

1) There is an obvious need to change the basic principles of the Constitution concerning national sovereignty so as to allow its partial transfer to, or sharing with, the Union or its collective exercise with other members. At first one may be tempted to conclude that this could be accomplished by a single and general constitutional provision recognizing the supremacy of international law, as has been the case with the French, German, Spanish, Portugese and Greek constitutions, sometimes even before attempts at European integration. Such a simplistic solution would, according to some jurists, provide the necessary legal ground for sharing the exercise of sovereignty with other members of the EU as a consequence of the accession treaty if it were ever to be concluded. But in view of the fact that the constitutional principles of the Turkish system are extremely rigid and that 'European law' does not merely consists of a few international treaties, but of all sorts of directives, regulations, court decisions, etc., there is a need to amend the fundamental articles of the Constitution in this respect so as to allow the exercise of national sovereignty collectively with the supranational organs of EU in all legislative, executive and judicial fields.
2) As to the other amendments necessitated, not only by the Copenhagen Criteria, but by a national desire to create a more democratic system of government, these may fall into several categories according to the nature of the needed improvement:
   a) To abolish the exceptions constitutionally made to the general principle of judicial review of the constitutionality in the case of laws and ordnances enacted by the military regime between 1980-1983 which cannot at present be brought before the Constitutional Court and may only be superseded by new legislation;
   b) To introduce the possibility of judicial review as to the constitutionality of decrees having the force of law enacted, according to the present Constitution, by the Council of Ministers as presided over by the President of the Republic at times of emergency rule, martial law and war situations;
   c) To ensure that the personnel matters concluded by the High Military Council be also subjected to judicial review;
   d) To delete the phrase in Article 87 of the Constitution which indirectly gives constitutional legitimacy to the death penalty by listing the approval of the execution of death sentences among the powers of the Grand National Assembly.
   e) To enlarge the scope of the rights and liberties of the person so as to allow the free expression and effective protection of individual ethnic identities in accordance with the spirit of the Copenhagen Criteria without having recourse to the creation of collective minority status for the Moslem citizens of the Republic.

The Turkish Constitution is in the category of 'rigid' constitutions due to the fact that its amendment is subject to strict rules of qualified majority and detailed procedural regulations. A proposal to amend the constitution, partially or in whole, requires the signature of at least a third of the full membership of the Grand National Assembly and has to be adopted, in secret voting, by a majority of two thirds, i.e., by 367 members out of 550. The text of the amendment has to be approved by the President of the Republic who can return it to the parliament, only once, for reconsideration. If the legislators insist on their original text, the President of the Republic can submit it to a referendum. In the event of a majority falling below two thirds but above three fifths of the full membership, the President of the Republic has the option of either returning it or deciding to go to a referendum. A constitutional amendment put to referendum has to obtain more than half of the valid votes cast to be adopted.

The fundamental shift in the constitutional principles of a 77 year-old nation-state necessitated by its eventual accession to the EU and the strict rules for the enactment of the required constitutional changes will make this constitutional adaptation one of the most interesting episodes in Turkish political history.

On the other hand, in line with the jurisprudence of the Italian and German constitutional courts on the primacy of EU law, one should expect the Turkish Constitutional Court, with its long and solid record of upholding 'the fundamental values and principles of the Constitution', to act similarly in cases where the rules of EU law eventually are in conflict with the basic provisions of the Turkish constitutional order on such values and principles. (For the Italian concept of *'controlimiti'* (limits to the limitation of sovereignty allowed by the national constitution), see the *Frontini judgment* (1973) and *Fragdt rulings* (1989) and *the German Constitutional Court's rulings* in *Solange-I* (1974) and *Solange-II* (1986)).

Of course, in the case of a constitutional system, such as that of Turkey, which makes provision for the necessities of 'nation-building' and rapid social progress in a developing society, the definition of such fundamental values and constitutional principles is a very delicate and controversial task. One may venture to cite the following, just to show the complexity of the problem: the principle of national unity (can the Copenhagen criterion on the 'protection of minorities' go as far as granting statutory autonomy to ethnic or other minorities as opposed to the protection of personal ethnic identities by a constitutionally recognized right of collectively exercising individual liberties?); the principle of 'sozialstaat' as one of the unchangeable fundamental characteristics of the Republic; the necessity of strategic economic and social planning foreseen by the Constitution (is it compatible with the 'free market economy' criterion?).

These are complicated legal issues, but neither the political elite nor the general public are fully aware of their critical importance. Open debate on them is just starting.

ADDENDUM

(Without prejudice to the Report presented for the 'Republic of Cyprus', this Chapter is added to the Report on Turkey, for academic purposes and in order to make up for the absence of a presentation by the Turkish Cypriot side, considering the eventuality of a confederal solution on the island, as advocated by the Turkish Cypriot delegation at the United Nations talks for the resolution of the conflict. The author is a constitutional adviser to the Turkish Cypriot delegation at these talks.)

PROBLEMS RELATED TO THE EXISTENCE OF THE TURKISH REPUBLIC OF NORTHERN CYPRUS

Events since 1963 have caused a series of developments leading to the proclamation of the Turkish Republic of North Cyprus (abbreviation: TRNC), a state recognized by Turkey. This fact added a new dimension to the conflict. The status of this state constitutes one of the most crucial issues of the talks at the United Nations.

There the Turkish Cypriot side advocates a confederal solution based on an agreement recognizing the equal status of two co-founding states, each with its own territory and constitutional order. The confederation will have a single international personality, but the states will retain their right to enter into agreements and relations with foreign governments and international organizations in their areas of competence and may maintain separate offices abroad within this context. The special relationship between the confederated states and their respective motherlands will be preserved by the confederation agreement. In short, according to the Turkish Cypriot approach, it is this package agreement, and not a common constitution, which should define the parameters, principles and procedures concerning the EU membership of the confederal Cyprus.

Synchronization of the accessions of the future confederation and of Turkey in the EU is essential for the Turkish Cypriot side. Furthermore, in order to exclude any possibility of domination in any form the Turkish Cypriot side would like to introduce in the agreement some restrictions on settlement and property ownership as a precaution against the recurrence of past tragedies. Similarly, special arrangements should be worked out with regard to the free movement of goods, labour, services and capital and these should be included in the agreement package and the accession treaty as necessary exceptions to the EU rules for at least a determined period of transition.

It is obvious that the agreement package on a comprehensive settlement is seen by the Turkish Cypriot side as the basis of the membership status of the confederal Cyprus in the European Union and therefore should be made part of the accession treaty.

Considering that the future bi-national confederation will have a single international personality, its relations with the EU will be conducted by a single but bi-national delegation composed of equal numbers of members of both sides and operating in accordance with the principle of parity. The delegation will formulate its joint positions on all European matters on the basis of consensus. On issues which fail to generate a consensus position, the delegation will abstain. In cases where the government or the parliament of either confederated state declares that a proposal or draft decision of an EU institution risks causing serious harm to the relations between the two confederated states, the bi-national reaction of the confederation to such proposal or draft will be determined within a conciliation structure in which Turkey and Greece may participate on an ad hoc basis. If a decision harmful to the relationship of the two confederated states is taken, either of them will be able to appeal to the European Court of Justice.

Of course, these considerations or proposals put forth by the Turkish Cypriot side with regard to a possible solution and its implications for the relations with the EU need to be agreed to by the Greek Cypriot side in order to become the basis of a future partnership within the European context. This is why reaching a political settlement at the present negotiations is crucial from the point of view of determining the modalities of the accession of Cyprus to the EU. Will it be the accession of a Cyprus where a comprehensive settlement has been reached whereby both peoples of the island will enjoy the benefits of having their respective states and at the same time benefitting from the advantages of a bi-national membership of the EU? Or will the integration of only one of the sides with Europe leave the island as the restless arena of uresolved conflicts and force the other side to seek the same degree of integration with its motherland, thus eternalizing the present division?

The attitude of the Union before this dilemma has not been of a nature to make the conclusion of a comprehensive settlement an essential requirement for accession to the EU. The relevant paragraph of the 1999 Helsinki decision on enlargement reads as follows:

> 'The European Council underlines that a political settlement will facilitate the accession of Cyprus to the European Union. If no settlement has been reached by the completion of accession negotiations, the Council's decision on accession will be made without the above being a precondition. In this the Council will take account of all relevant factors.'

The ambiguity of the style, although at first giving the impression of equally compelling both sides to a settlement, in fact favours the side which, by virtue of its status as a recognized state, is already engaged in the accession negotiations with the EU while withholding its assent for a settlement at the UN talks. It will be a pity if the opportunity for a comprehensive settlement is missed because of this unfortunate linkage and rather short-sighted tactics.

As to the amendments to be made in the present Constitution of the TRNC in case it becomes one of the founding states of a confederation in Cyprus, itself being admitted as a member of the EU, these would be practically the same as those for the Republic of Turkey as far as the principle of national sovereignty is concerned and almost no change would be required when it came to harmonize the Constitution with the requirements of the Copenhagen Criteria.

What makes the first operation even easier is the fact that the Constitution of the TRNC, although democratically debated and enacted by a Constituent Assembly and adopted by referendum, has been modelled, systematically, on the 1982 Constitution of the motherland with significant ameliorations so as to make it much more democratic and respectful of the rule of law. Naturally, in a revision of this Constitution for accession purposes, all references to national sovereignty have to be amended for two obvious reasons: first, because of the single international personality of the confederation necessitating an acknowledgment of confederal powers in external relations while making provision for cases where confederated states will retain their right to enter into agreements and relations with governments and international organizations in their areas of competence; and secondly, because of the EU membership of the confederation itself requiring a substantial transfer of sovereignty to the institutions of the Union as in the case of all members.

On the other hand, there is almost no need for amendment for the harmonization and adaptation of the TRNC Constitution with the requirements of the Copenhagen Criteria. The constitution system of the TRNC contains no exception to the judicial review of the unconstitutionality of laws and administrative decrees; the death penalty was abolished at the very beginnings of the political organization of the Turkish Cypriots at the time of their expulsion from the institutions of the then bi-communal Republic of Cyprus.

LEGAL AND QUASI-LEGAL TRESHOLDS OF THE ACCESSION OF THE CZECH REPUBLIC TO THE EC

Vladimír Balaš*

SOME INTRODUCTORY REMARKS ABOUT THE IMPLEMENTATION OF INTERNATIONAL LAW IN THE CZECH REPUBLIC

The Czech legal system is a typical example of the dualistic system. As far as the relation between international law and municipal law is concerned, some Czech authors traditionally distinguish four main methods of implementation of international law[1]:

Transformation

By transformation they mean promulgation or approval of the treaty in the form of municipal law by a formal legislative act, most often in the form of an Act (Statute) of Parliament. Through the process of transformation, a normative content of the international treaty becomes part of the internal legal order, part of municipal law. The international treaty loses its quality by becoming just an ordinary Act of the Parliament or Decree of Government, having its validity based on the authority of the State. The text of a treaty is translated into the Czech language and applied as an internal legal norm. There is no notice of the origin of the norm, and the courts, of course, interpret it by using municipal methods of interpretation that might sometimes lead to a different outcome than that expected if the norm were to be interpreted while using the standard means of interpretation in international law.[2] It is also quite clear that the Czech translation of a treaty might be far distant from the authentic text and the meaning of the translated text, as it is used in the Statute, is sometimes shifted, sometimes might be quite different.

* University of West Bohemia School of Law, Pilzen, Czech Republic.

[1] Malenovský, J.; Mezinárodní právo verejné (International Public Law), Doplnek Brno 1993, pp. 55 et seq.

[2] Teleological interpretation is generally not used by the Czech judiciary.

A.E. Kellermann et al. (Eds.), EU Enlargement: The Constitutional Impact at EU and National Level

Adaptation

The norms of international law become part of municipal law also by adaptation. By adaptation the Czech legal literature does not mean the promulgation of the verbatim (word-for-word) text of the international treaty in the form of the municipal regulation (precept or ruling). A content, not the text of the international legal obligation of the State, is transferred into the particular municipal regulations. It is similar with EU directives.

Incorporation

Incorporation, on the other hand, according to the prevailing opinion in Czech doctrine, means drawing the international treaty into the internal legal order while preserving its quality of international law. Treaty provisions are becoming internally generally binding. A typical example of incorporation is a reference to the international treaty in the municipal legal regulation (Statute). Such a reference is usually made in the particular Act. According to this reference, the municipal legal regulation is binding, unless the international treaty stipulates something else. Priority of international law in the Czech legal order can in some cases look like moderate dualism or moderate monism. As concerns the anchorage of the relationship of international law and municipal law into the Czech legal order and its legal bases, almost all authors have spoken for decades about the constitutional deficiency, since the only provision in the Czech Constitution deals with issues of incorporation of international law in a broader sense. Article 10 states that ratified and officially promulgated international treaties on human rights and fundamental freedoms, that bind the Czech Republic, are directly binding and have priority over the Statute. This provision can also serve as a demonstration of the incorporation principle in Czech law. The trouble is, that this is the only constitutional provision dealing with the relationship of international and municipal laws, and is a provision of a very limited scope. It deals only with a) international treaties b) on human rights and fundamental freedoms. It is clear that this wording is important but far from sufficient.[3]

Adoption

As far as adoption (incorporation) is concerned legal doctrine understands by it the implementation of the international law directly by the courts in their decision-making. As for adoption, it is quite obvious that the Czech courts cannot do that without express reference to the international law, usually an international treaty. There is a kind of confusion in the terminology between particular schools of thought

---

[3] Mikule, V.; Vnitrostátní platnost mezinárodních smluv, na které se nevztahuje cl. 10 Ústavy (Domestic Law Validity of International Treaties Not Provided For in Art. 10 of the Constitution), Acta Universitatis Carolinae, Iuridica 1/1997, pp. 65-72.

and among individual writers themselves not only abroad, but among Czech writers as well, and terms such as adoption and incorporation can hold different meanings in different works of different authors. We can easily put this kind of implementation under the heading 'Incorporation'. I would even fully agree with the opinion of another authoritative work of a Czech author dealing with this particular issue[4] and claim together with him, that there are only two basic means of implementation, i.e., 'transformation' and 'incorporation', each of them having various forms.

FORMAL LEGAL SOURCES AS THE BASIS OF THE DECISION OF THE CZECH COURT

According to Article 95 of the Czech Constitution, a court is bound only by the Statute (Act of the Parliament) and it is also entitled to judge (consider) the conformity of the other legal norm (especially a Decree of the Government or Regulation of the Ministry) with the Act of the Parliament. For the international law to become the formal source of municipal law in the Czech Republic, that every court is obliged to follow, the Czech legal order requires either its transformation (in a broader sense) or incorporation into the internal legal order of the Czech Republic. International law is incorporated not only by reference in the Constitution (as already shown in Art. 10 of the Constitution) but also by reference in the particular Statute. Otherwise the courts cannot use the international treaty or other norm of international law. There are, of course, a number of such references not only to international treaties but also to international customary law (I am aware of one such a case at least). To be frank, I can hardly imagine how this particular international customary law dealing with the sovereign immunity of the foreign State is to be applied by the Czech courts or what should be considered as a binding customary law (whether absolute or restrictive immunity). Some doubts also remain concerning international treaties and other sources of international law.

The Czech Constitution in Article 49 divides international treaties into treaties that are negotiated by the President and treaties that can by negotiated by the Government or Minister. So-called presidential treaties require approval by Parliament in a similar way as it approves Statutes. This approval should be given to the human rights and fundamental freedoms treaties, political treaties, economic treaties of a general nature as well as to the treaties that should be implemented by statute. For the presidential treaty to come into force internally it should be promulgated in the same way as a statute. I should note here that the text of this particular provision (Art. 52) of our Constitution is even more confusing and it states that promulgation is required for the statute to be valid and that the same applies to international treaties. This is of course nonsense. The legislator did not notice that there is a difference between

---

[4] Týc, V.; O vnitrostátní přímé závaznosti mezinárodních smluv (On Direct Internal Applicability of International Treaties), Masarykova univerzita, Brno 1996, pp. 25 et seq.

the international validity (entry into force) of the international treaty and its internal applicability.[5]

PROMULGATION OF INTERNATIONAL TREATIES

International treaties were published officially in the Official Gazette (Collection of Laws) until the end of 1999. The Act on the Collection of Laws of the Czech Republic No. 545/1992 Coll. has been derogated and replaced by Act No. 309/1999 Coll. on the Collection of Laws and the Collection of International Treaties. The new Statute has been in force since 1 January 2000. Neither the previous Statute nor the new one properly set up the time limit in which the newly ratified international treaty should be officially published. There were many ratified treaties that have been published years after they became binding for the Czech Republic or for Czechoslovakia, respectively. This was not the only insufficiency of the former legal regulation. Not all international treaties have been officially published (promulgated). The new Statute does not stipulate a requirement to promulgate all international treaties in full text. The particular provision of the new Statute might sound slightly strange. Article 5 paragraph 2 of the law stipulates that international treaties are promulgated by the publishing of their full text. International treaties that are not approved by the Parliament and that concern only a small number of natural or juridical persons can be promulgated without the publication of the full text of their annexes. In that case the Ministry of Foreign Affairs shall inform in its Notification also the number of annexes of the international treaty and shall provide the information where these relevant documents are available. Who is going to judge at the Ministry who might be the potential addressee, especially whether the group is small or big, is not very well known.

On the other hand, the new Statute brings some improvements. It extends the duty to publish international law documents to the decisions adopted by the international bodies and the organs of international organisations that are binding for the Czech Republic. Another improvement, compared to the previous regulation, lies in the promulgation of the official language of the treaty or the decision of the international organisation. The Czech language is used only as a translation of an official text or where it is the authoritative text itself.

[5] Hasenkopf, P.; Vnitrostátní závaznost mezinárodních smluv z hlediska ceského práva (Internal Applicability of International Treaties from the Point of View of the Czech Legal Order), Acta Universitatis Carolinae, Iuridica 1/1997, pp. 47-51.

HOW IS INTERNATIONAL LAW IMPLEMENTED IN THE CZECH LEGAL ORDER?

The most common method of implementation of international law into the national legal order in the Czech Republic is traditionally the transformation in a broader sense. To be more specific, it is probably adaptation, as mentioned above. International law is also implemented by incorporation. International treaties on human rights and fundamental freedoms are usually implemented by reference made in Article 10 of the Constitution. Other treaties are incorporated by the reference to them made in normal statutes. As I have already mentioned above, implementation may also cover international customary law. For example, Article 47 paragraph 1 of the Act on the International Private Law and the Procedure thereto states that the foreign States and persons that under international treaties or other rules of international law or particular domestic legal regulations enjoy immunity in the Czech Republic, are not subjected to the jurisdiction of the Czech courts (with some exceptions). This provision is not a typical one and most of the statutes refer only to the international treaties. Some particularity might be also seen in the fact that some statutes refer to the treaties promulgated officially in the Gazette (e.g., Criminal Procedure Act No. 141/1961 Coll. in current wording), some refer to international treaties without any requirement of official promulgation (Act on the International Private Law and the Procedure thereto No. 97/1963 Coll.) and some, which is even more confusing, require official promulgation in some cases while not in others (Customs Act No. 13/ 1993 Coll.).[6]

DOES THE CZECH CONSTITUTION ALLOW THE TRANSFER OF LEGISLATIVE POWERS TO INTERNATIONAL ORGANISATIONS WITH OR WITHOUT LIMITS?

The Czech Constitution is considered as 'anaemic' as far as it concerns the relationship between international law and municipal law and this fact is strongly criticised by many legal commentators in the Czech Republic.[7] Unfortunately, the

---

[6] See also Pauknerová, M.; Otázka klauzulí o prednostní aplikaci mezinárodních smluv (The Issue of Clauses on the Preferential Application of International Treaties), Acta Universitatis Carolinae, Iuridica 1/1997, pp. 73-78.

[7] Blahož, J., Balaš, V., Klíma, K.; Srovnávací ústavní právo (Comparative Constitutional Law) Codex 1998, pp. 293 et seq.; Malenovský, J.; 'Chudokrevnost' mezinárodního rozmeru Ceské ústavy a možné terapie ('Anaemia' of the International Dimension of the Czech Constitution and Possible Therapies) Právník 7/1997. Wagner, A.; První ústava Ceské republiky z hlediska mezinárodního práva (The First Constitution of the Czech Republic from the Point of View of International Law), Právník 3/ 1994, pp. 201, 207 and 209; Wagner, A., K meinárodneprávním aspektum nové ceskoslovenské ústavy (On the International Law Aspects of the New Czechoslovak Constitution), Právník 6/1991, pp. 487 et seq.

same is true with the transfer of legislative powers to international organisations. There is a lack of any constitutional provision that would allow the Czech authorities to transfer any legislative powers to international organisations. It is usually done ad hoc. There are just a few provisions that envisage to some extent the legislative or decision-making powers of international organisations. For example, Article 87 paragraph 1 letter i) stipulates that the Constitutional Court of the Czech Republic shall decide on measures necessary to the implementation of the decision of an international court that binds the Czech Republic and cannot be implemented by some other means. Another provision deals with the legislative process for the implementation of the decisions of UN Security Council on actions safeguarding the international peace and security, namely, the Procedural Order Act of the Chamber of Deputies of the Czech Parliament (Act No. 90/1995 Coll. as amended by the Act No. 47/2000 Coll.). This provision states that if this particular situation requires urgent adoption of the Law implementing such a decision of the UN Security Council, the Government can ask for the passing of a bill in a short procedure, while submitting such a draft. The most recent regulation, the Act on the Implementation of International Sanctions to Maintain International Peace and Security (No. 98/2000 Coll.) states that everybody is obliged to obey international sanctions imposed in accordance with this Act. Sanctions imposed by the UN Security Council and by the EU Council can be implemented by the Decree of the Government after it is approved by the particular Committee of the Chamber of Deputies of the Czech Parliament. As for the UN Security Council, sanctions should be imposed under the Article 41 of the UN Charter. As for EU Council sanctions, the Czech Republic should first join the call for sanctions stemming out from the common policy (common attitude) of the EU Council.[8]

One should add that these provisions represent a huge move forward in at least one direction. The previous practice was so rigid that the Laws imposing sanctions have been adopted by the Parliament even with more than one year's delay and the same was true for their subsequent removal.

WHAT IS THE LEGAL SITUATION IN CASE OF A CONFLICT OF THE CZECH CONSTITUTION WITH THE TREATY (PRIMARY LAW) OR COMMUNITY SECONDARY LAW, AND A CONFLICT OF A PRIOR OR LATER NATIONAL LAW WITH THE TREATY ON THE EU AND THE EC TREATY?

The current legal situation in case of a conflict of the Czech Constitution with the treaty is not solved by any provision in the Czech Constitution. There are two possible

[8] Janda, I.; Implementace rozhodnutí Rady bezpecnosti v našem vnitrostátním právním rádu (Implementation of the UN Security Council in Our Internal Legal Order), Acta Universitatis Carolinae, Iuridica 1/1997, pp. 53-55.

solutions to such a situation. Since some kinds of treaties to be ratified require the prior approval of the Parliament, no such treaty that conflicts the Czech Constitution would be concluded, unless the Constitution was amended. There would be no difference in this case between the primary or secondary law of the EU. Since there are no relevant constitutional provisions for supremacy of international law, the supremacy or direct effect of European law is not guaranteed so far.

Our Constitution would certainly require amendment for the ratification of the EU Treaty, EC Treaty, and Euratom Treaty. The procedure is quite simple and the Czech Constitution is rather flexible in this sense. The qualified 3/5th majority of all deputies in the Chamber of Deputies (120 deputies) and a 3/5th majority of the present members of the Senate is required for the amendment of the Constitution. To have the quorum in the Senate, at least one third of the whole Senate members are required to vote; thus the minimum number of votes required to pass the Constitutional amendment is 17 (3/5th out of the 1/3rd of the 81 Senate members).

The only practical problems we can face if the Czech Constitution has to be amended for accession to the EU are of the political nature. I would not dare to estimate what should be the position of the main political parties. It is quite sure that one of the strongest political parties in the Czech Republic is currently headed by the Euro-sceptically minded Mr. Klaus. There is no law that would require a referendum to join the EU. This situation might change and the last draft of the Constitutional Act on referendum might require it. Though it is not clear now what the outcome would be of the negative vote, whether the vote should have a decisive role or be understood only as a recommendation. As concerns the efforts to improve the Constitution I am aware of at least three unsuccessful attempts to amend the Constitution during the last 14 months to match the requirements of implementation of international law in the internal legal order in a more proper way. All three drafts have not been ideal but they were still much better than the current situation. All attempts failed for some unknown political reasons.

ROLE OF THE COURTS (SOME PRACTICAL ISSUES)

The role of the courts is definitely quite crucial if the Czech Republic is to join EC successfully. There is no constitutional law provision that would enable the Czech courts to accept and use the international law except the situations mentioned above with respect to international treaties on human rights and fundamental freedoms, ratified and officially promulgated in the Official Gazette (Art. 10 of the Constitution). As we have also mentioned above, there are references in statutes to international treaties and to customary law as well. Irrespective of these references, the situation is far from satisfactory. As was pointed out, statutory references are not uniform, some require promulgated treaties, some just binding ones. We have already mentioned Article 95 of the Czech Constitution but we did not mention the whole sad truth. The Czech Republic is one of the countries that underwent a quite complicated transition from the totalitarian to democratic state, from the direct economy system to the market oriented one. This transition has required a substantial change to the legal order. During the last decade, there were virtually hundreds of new statutes promulgated each year and thousands for the decade.[9] The quality of these laws is doubtful and the reasons for this phenomenon are manifold. Some laws are changing so quickly that some laws have been amended even earlier than they entered into force, others have been amended so often that nobody is really able to follow them. Let me give you an example. One of the most important transitional statutes was the Commercial Code. This code was promulgated in 1991 (Act No. 513/1991 Coll.) and during the last ten years has been amended 28 times. In only the first five months of the year 2000 the Commercial Code has been amended 7 times. There were at least 24 amendments of the Civil Code within the last 10 years, the Criminal Code has been amended 40 times and, what is quite embarrassing here, it is not only the fact that there are 4 or even more amendments of some laws in a year but also the fact that these amendments are done also indirectly, by some other laws. I did not mention tax laws in which the frequency of amendments can be counted by tens in a year. Mentioning tax laws I cannot but mention another example of the quality of the legislative process. The Value Added Tax Act (Act No. 588/1992 Coll.) has been amended twice in one day. One amendment was a direct one, by Act No. 17/2000 Coll., the other amendment was indirect by the Excise Duties Act. The same provision that reads slightly differently was promulgated by two different laws in the same day. Guess which one you can rely on?

What I would like to comment on here is not only the legislative chaos as such, but also its impact on the decision-making of the courts and the legal certainty of the addressee. One can understand why I consider the leading principle of our law *iura novit curia* as a false fiction. Can we expect the over-burdened Czech courts to apply European law properly in a situation of ever-changing domestic legislation? The Czech judiciary can hardly know the Czech law properly, and nobody can blame them for that. The reasons are quite obvious and I consider another illustration as redundant.[10]

---

[9] According to the digital system of legal information of the Institute of State and Law of the Czech Academy of Sciences LEGSYS, 681 legal documents were promulgated in 1990, 672 in 1991, 798 in 1992, 419 in 1993 (the lower number was caused by the split of the Czech and Slovak Federal Republics) 363 in 1994, 399 in 1995, 400 in 1996, 436 in 1997, 407 in 1998 and 442 in 1999. These numbers cover Statutes, Decrees, Regulations and international treaties promulgated officially in the Gazette which is called the Collection of Laws. We do not speak here on other hundreds and thousands of internal instructions and others not published but only registered the normative acts of Ministries and other administrative bodies. As can be seen, our Parliament approved in average at least one legal document a day, in some years even two a day.

[10] It would be interesting to ask an average Euro-citizen about the acquis. One can even doubt that this legislative system is designed to appeal to them directly. If mess was the model, the Czech Republic would be really a very diligent pupil. There is, of course, a great difference in the quality of the content of the legal norms, but certainly not in the system itself.

Another difficulty concerns the interpretation of international law. No doubt our legislators attempt to do their best by harmonising Czech laws with the European ones. We do that through transformation or adoption and our laws require sometimes even higher standards than is required by the legislation of the EU member States. Because of the nature of the harmonised legislation, the Czech courts interpret it by using the standard means of domestic interpretation. This interpretation differs from the international law interpretation and can also differ from the interpretation of the ECJ. What can then happen? The legislative branch is harmonising, while the judicial branch is disharmonising. The problem is not only the interpretation. The translation of some international treaties is quite suspicious and the quality of translations differs substantially. In many cases the international law was not, until January 1, 2000, available in the authentic version and even if it were, the majority of our current judges are not able to speak any foreign language at all.

Even if there were some young judges, fairly well trained in EC law, fluent in at least one of the most common EC languages, it would not solve the issue. There is no envisaged method in our current position of associated member to ask the ECJ about the proper interpretation. I am quite sure that we already have such qualified judges and that the situation might change quite quickly but they also need to have recourse to the ECJ and to ask for preliminary rulings (Art. 234/ex-Art. 177 of the EC Treaty). This complaint reminds me of another hidden danger that can hamper harmonisation. EC law is transformed into our legal order and nobody knows that this or that particular provision is of EC origin and that it should be interpreted as such. What can we do about this particular issue? One of the possibilities might be the amendment of the Czech Constitution, as proposed by one of my distinguished colleagues. This amendment would read as follows: The Constitution of the Czech Republic, Constitutional Acts and the Statutes of the Czech Republic cannot be interpreted and applied in a manner inconsistent with the obligations of the Czech Republic stemming from membership of the Czech Republic in the EU.[11] Is such a formulation sufficient? It might be sufficient vis-à-vis EU membership. On the other hand, I do not think that the amendment to be sufficient would require only the broadening of our limited incorporation clause in Article 10 of the Constitution for the general principles of international law and decisions of international organisations or its organs.[12] What if such an interpretation would lead to the improper interpretation of the fundamental constitutional law principles or would be inconsistent with another international law obligation of the Czech Republic?

---

[11] Král, R.; Zakotvení práva ES do naší ústavy (Anchoring the EC Law in Our Constitution), Právní Rádce 3/2000, p. 40.

[12] Šturma, P.; Prednostní jurisdikce mezinárodního trestního tribunálu pro bývalou Jugoslávii v. ceský právní rád (K jednomu príkladu vnitrostátní realizace mezinárodních závazku CR) – *Primacy of Jurisdiction of the International Criminal Tribunal for the Former Yougoslavia* v. *Czech Legal Order* (On one example of the implemention of international obligations of the Czech Republic), Acta Universitatis Carolinae, Iuridica 1/1997, pp. 83 and 84.

In any case, in practice the Czech courts do not note international law as an international law. In practice, one can hardly imagine our courts applying even the international law referred to in the statutes. The same applies to the principle of indirect effect. Even the Constitutional Court would rather resort to municipal law.[13] Even this court uses international treaties as a last resort. This does not mean that the Constitutional Court does not apply them at all. Even more difficult and rather theoretical is the question, whether our Court would give priority to a Community measure or the prior international commitment of the Czech Republic. I do not even know whether such a question can be of any practical importance. *Pacta sunt servanda* and international law, although mostly of a dispositive nature, once agreed it should be observed in good faith. Can we accept commitments inconsistent with our current international obligations? We should get rid of such commitments first and then adopt the new ones. Termination and suspension of the operation of treaties is envisaged in the Vienna Convention on the Law of Treaties. Some treaties might be terminated without difficulties, others not. Even here we should follow a general pattern and respect our international law obligations. As for the courts in the Czech Republic, I doubt that they are aware of any of the international commitments of the Czech republic at all, except in the field of human rights. The reason might be found in our totalitarian past and the attitude shown toward international law.

THE ROLE OF GOVERNMENT AND ADMINISTRATION

The last question posed asks to what extent do the Government and Administration in the Czech Republic implement and/or apply in practice the *acquis communautaire* and the Europe agreements. No doubt there is a great effort to change the last negative evaluation of this situation in the Czech Republic by the Commission. Hundreds if not thousands of laws have been harmonised already.[14] As you might know, our new social democratic Government proclaimed that it is ready to start a 'legislative tornado'. Let me remind you what might be the most common result of a tornado-destruction. And this is perhaps also apparent from my comments above. I do think that some rational signal should come from the EC Commission to slow down hasty legislative effort. Otherwise, the impact on the legal systems of the associated members can be devastating. Everyone knows that tornadoes hardly bring any positive effect. This effort of our Government might then easily turn upside down and bring quite opposite results than those expected. I suspect that we do not harmonise for the sake of harmonisation. Our aim should be to increase the effectiveness of the law. One can hardly imagine any other reason that would lead EC States, Council and

[13] Malenovský, J.; Ústavní soud Ceské republiky a mezinárodní právo (Constitutional Court of the Czech Republic and the International Law), Právník 2/2000, pp. 105 et seq.

[14] Volný, J., Kohout, A., Palivec, J.; Problémy a perspektivy prípravy na clenství v Eropské unii (Problems and Perspectives of Preparations for the EU Membership), Právní rádce 8/99, p. 5.

Commission in urging applicants for membership to approximate their legislation. Or is it foreseen that the admission of new applicants will be postponed? It would be not be too fair to use this reason as a disguise. Or would it?

As for the implementation of the acquis by the Czech Government the situation is quite foreseeable. There is, of course, a great will to do it. It should be noted though, that the situation of the Czech Republic is far from similar to the situation of the EU member States. One cannot forget that current EU members did not change their whole legal order in just a couple of years and that they absorbed EC legislation gradually, some of them for more than 40 years. What our Government really missed for a quite a long time was a proper methodology and a systematic approach. Our new Government did notice this insufficiency and adopted some measures that would bring order to the approximation and harmonisation of our law. This was done by Decision No. 432/97. The situation has improved but it is still not ideal.[15]

Talking about the application of the acquis, there is generally no fear in applying acquis by the top level administrative bodies. What I am afraid of is the application of the acquis at the bottom. As an example at the end of my paper might be the attitude of one charming lady working as a civil servant at the tax revenue office in one North Bohemian district that replied to the criticism that her way of administering some financial issue was not in the constitutional manner that however a Constitution did not attract too much if any of her attention. I suspect, this is not just an isolated view. Irrespective of the manifold obstacles mentioned above, the attitude of some of the first instance courts and lower administrative bodies will be probably the most difficult hurdle for the proper and fluent application of EU law in the Czech Republic. The same is probably true for application by the average Czech, although they might learn quite quickly that the acquis might be a powerful tool to serve in their own interest, much better than current Czech laws.

Let me add one optimistic view at the very end. I suppose that the most important element in the future proper interpretation and application of the acquis will not be the State and its bodies but citizens duly represented by qualified attorneys. This matter will become the most important and decisive training for our judges and civil servants.

[15] Král, R.; K metodice sbližování našich predpisu s predpisy ES (About the Methodology of the Approximation of Our Law with the EC Regulations), Právní rádce 8/99, p. 8.

THE IMPACT OF THE EUROPEAN INTEGRATION PROCESS ON THE CREATION OF THE BROAD LINES OF THE CONSTITUTION OF THE REPUBLIC OF POLAND AND ON THE POLITICAL PRACTICES OF THE COUNTRY

Janus Justynski*

INTRODUCTION

The issue of the Constitution of the European Communities is a matter of dispute.[1] The European Court of Justice also joined in this dispute by its judgment of 23 April 1986.[2] The echoes of this dispute could also be heard during the International Colloquium on European Law organised by the Asser Institute (The Hague, 20-23 September 2000).

At the present time the resolution of this dispute does not seem possible. The question concerning the necessity of the European Constitution is still being repeated ('*Does Europe need a formalisation of its Constitutional order*'). Further, this statement does not question the constitutional character of the European order, but it does, however, pose a question relating to the necessity of its formalisation.

The factor, that connects the divergent positions is the acceptance of the 'rule of law' as the basis of the European order. This rule is endorsed by the authorisation of the European Court of Justice to perform a judicial review, in spite of the fact that not all member States of the European Union have this institution in their legal order.[3]

If the Communities and the European Union constitute the same legal order which is their foundation, it means that this order must be transmitted also to the

* Nicolas Copernicus University, Torun, Poland.

[1] See J. H.H. Weiler, *Europe 2000 – The Constitutional Agenda,* p. 1; P. van Nuffel, *The Constitutional Issues in the IGC 2000 Agenda,* p. 149, also A. Whelan, *Specific Constitutional Normalisation of the Community and its Impact on the member States' Constitutional Systems* (in:) *Constitutional Changes Connected with the Membership in the European Union,* pp. 19-20.

[2] Case 294/ 83, 'Les Verts', ECR, p. 1339: '*Treaty is the "Basic Constitutional Charter" of the European Community*' while P. van Nuffel adds that '*a fortiori the Treaty on the European Union is the basic Constitutional Charter of the Union*', p. 149.

[3] See A. Whelan, op. cit., p. 20.

A.E. Kellermann et al. (Eds.), EU Enlargement: The Constitutional Impact at EU and National Level

legal systems of the member States.[4] This principle concerns all the member States, therefore, it should be reflected in their constitutional regulations. However, it can be observed that in this very field there occur significant discrepancies between particular member States. Nevertheless, these discrepancies are not expressed in questioning the primacy of Community law over the laws of the member States.

As far as the evaluation of the constitutional regulations of the countries aspiring to the European Union is concerned, a fundamentally different attitude can be detected. In most cases these are countries which a decade ago discarded both the communist system and the constitutional solutions characteristic of this system. They differed from the standards of a democratic system to such an extent that it is expected that they will have to make up for the historic distance. It also finds reflection in the expectation that these countries will in their constitutions expressly state the rule of the superiority of the European Community Law over the national legal order.

The review of the constitutional acts of the twelve countries qualified for the present round of negotiations indicates that only the Constitution of Poland of 2 April 1997 is adequate on this issue. The subject of this article is the characteristics of the resolutions of the Constitution of the Republic of Poland which concern the question of the supremacy of community law over Poland's legal order, along with the mechanism of transmitting the execution of acts of sovereignty to the community institutions.

SOME HISTORY

The constitution of every country constitutes the outcome of a number of factors. A particular role is played by historic experiences, the social structure, the cultural values adopted by the society, along with certain universal ideas, subscribed to and propagated by the most educated intellects of a given society. These factors influenced the creation of the broad lines of the oldest constitution in the world – the Constitution of the United States – along with the oldest European constitution – the Constitution of the Republic of Poland of 3 May 1791. They can also be found in the consecutive constitutional acts – the French Constitution of 1791, 1793, 1795, the German and the Italian constitutions and those of many other countries. A remarkably complicated situation arose when it came to the

[4] The rule of the 'superiority of the community law' was formulated as early as the *van Gend en Loos* v. *Nederlandse Administratie der Belastingen* (1963) ECR 1(15) and *Costa* v. *ENEL* judgments, Case 6/642 of 1964, ECR 585. It means that a national court, which finds a conflict between the national law and the community law, is obliged to apply community law. The only exception is a situation where a member State has the right of derogation, because of public security, public order or health protection. See also D. Lasok, Zarys prawa Unii Europejskiej, Toruñ 1995, p. 161.

creation of the totalitarian communist ideology which treated the Constitution as an additional tool for propaganda of the given system's ideas. It transformed the act into a kind of declaration having no practical application. In this period quoting the constitution was considered a manifestation of the political opposition, since in this very act one could find rights that had no reflection in the political practices of the communist countries.

It must be added that the range of the rights declared by communist constitutions recurrently misled the observers from democratic countries. Read in secluded offices, they might have seemed modern acts aimed at the promotion of social needs. However, more attentive reading demonstrated the leading role of the party, the dependence of the range of liberties on the degree of acceptance of socialist ideas, etc.

The breakthrough of 1989 constituted a deep shock for communist countries. Its extent depended to a large degree on the experiences of the communist era. Unquestionably, its extent was different in Poland and Hungary than in Bulgaria or Romania. Hungary had the experience of the many years of the so-called liberal economic policy of Kadar. Poland was continuously in the process of experiments, as the only country of the communist group that kept the concept of private property of peasant land and provided a certain freedom to the Church, which was becoming, against its mission, a significant political power. Paradoxically, the same authorities that introduced martial law in 1981 undertook to initiate political and economic experiments. In 1985, the Sejm (the lower chamber of the Polish Parliament) adopted the law on the Constitutional Tribunal and the Civic Rights Spokesman[5], and in 1987/88 experiments with the so-called social market economy were introduced, and the equality of all private sectors was declared.

Nevertheless, all the time the rule of the Party's leading role continued to dominate, and the Party did not intend to share its power with any other political organisation. All the time any free and democratic election and a multiparty system, along with the citizens' political freedom, were out of the question. This came about only in 1989.

THE CONSTITUTIONAL PRINCIPLES OF THE TRANSITIONAL PERIOD

Almost directly before the breakthrough of 1989 the Central European countries, the most advanced in the promotion of liberal market and political solutions, declared their readiness and willingness to accede to the European Communities (Czechoslovakia, Hungary and Poland). It imposed a number of constitutional

[5] The Act on the Constitutional Tribunal was adopted by Polish Parliament on 29 April, 1985 and the Act on the Spokesman for Human Rights on 15 July 1987.

obligations, which were defined in the Preambles to the European Agreements, establishing Association, reached on 16 December 1991. They included a constitutional guarantee of law and order, human rights, the establishment of a warranty for the development of a market economy and the confirmation of political rights characteristic of democratic societies, and thus a multiparty system, democratic elections, the proper role of the parliament, the mechanisms for power division, etc.

The introduction of these regulations was made possible either by immediate adoption of new constitutional acts or by the gradual introduction of new political ideas and solutions to the old system, which meant the necessity of its constant amendment; at the same time the political elite was exposed to the accusation of collaboration with the old system. It was the second method that was adopted in Poland, introducing two hundred amendments to the former constitution, subsequently establishing the so-called Constitutional Act[6] and finally deciding on a long and arduous procedure of political negotiations on the broad lines of the new Fundamental Statute which would reflect the society's aspirations, create an effective mechanism for the exercise of authority, and ultimately fulfil the demands of European integration.[7]

In the course of virtually a seven-year long debate, several drafts of the Constitution were presented, and finally the accepted text is the result of compromises that had to be made so that the act would the gain support of a sufficient number of the political elites. Ultimately, it was supposed to gain support expressed in referendum.

POLITICAL PRINCIPLES OF THE CONSTITUTION OF 2 APRIL 1997

The question whether the compromises did not in fact destroy the political basis, the construction of the civic rights and the principles of the market economy is of fundamental significance. It appears possible to state that the authors of the final draft of the constitution came out of these dilemmas well. In fact there is the implication that redundant statements were introduced into the Preamble and they sometimes may complicate the interpretation of the Constitutional Tribunal; nevertheless, the body of the Constitution was defended and its regulations do not cause more serious disputes.[8]

Therefore, today, three years after the Fundamental Statute came into force, we can say that a tremendous majority of the society regard the constitutional regulations as the ones reflecting their aspirations and creating bases for the proper functioning of the political mechanism of the country.

---

[6] Mała Konstytucja of 29 December 1989.

[7] See M. Kallas, *Projekty konstytucyjne 1989-1991,* Warszawa 1992.

[8] Compare W. Skrzydło, *Konstytucja Rzeczypospolitej Polskiej, Komentarz,* Kraków 1998, p.10.

However, the situation directly after the adoption of the Fundamental Statute by the National Assembly was totally different, it was an atmosphere indicative of a huge national dispute preceding the constitutional referendum. The dispute was concentrated on some basic political issues, but its dynamism was determined by the attitude towards Articles 90 and 91 of the Constitution of the Republic of Poland. The camp opposed to Poland's integration with the European Union managed, in the course of the intensive political campaign, to mobilise a huge part of the society to reject the presented draft to such an extent that it was adopted in the ratio of 51 to 49, thus with a minimal majority.[9]

The circumstance mentioned above provokes a closer analysis of the resolutions of these articles. Article 90, paragraph 1 states:

> 'The Republic of Poland may, by virtue of international agreements, delegate to an international organisation or international institution the competence of organs of State authority in relation to certain matters.'

Let us stop and analyse the essence and implications of this resolution.

It must be admitted that the doctrine on the constitutional law contains a number of disputes relating to the delegation of competence of the organs of State authority to an international organisation. They result from the fact that we are dealing here with a certain sort of restriction of independence, and therefore, of restrictions of this value which is very deeply rooted in the consciousness of societies. Obviously, the restriction of independence may have the character of a fundamental breach when the society's will is restricted by a brutal external interference, or the form incomparably milder when the restriction results from the 'sovereign will of a given society'. I do not have to convince anybody that we deal here with the latter case, all the more in that, by losing legislative power, Poland gains a broad power in the field of co-establishing law for the whole European Union. Moreover, it must be added that this delegation of competence, constituting a certain limitation of sovereignty, is made in the context of very far-fetched reservations introduced by paragraph 2 of Article 90. It states that:

> 'A statute, granting consent for ratification of an international agreement referred to in paragraph 1, shall be passed by the Sejm by a two-thirds majority vote in the presence of at least half of the statutory number of Deputies, and by the Senate by a two-thirds majority vote in the presence of at least half of the statutory number of Senators.'

Thus, to guard sovereignty, an additional requirement was placed, namely, to execute the act of delegation the support of an extremely high, two-thirds qualified majority of both chambers of parliament is required. Moreover, in paragraph 3 of Article 90 a possibility was added of granting consent for ratification of such an

[9] Ibid., pp. 85-86.

agreement in a nation-wide referendum. It is highly probable that the ratification of an accession statute will be achieved with the contribution of the Sejm, Senate and the whole society, expressing its opinion in this matter in the act of referendum.

Not less significant are the resolutions of Article 91 of the Constitution. They control the issue of the place of such a statute in the Polish legal order. Article 91 in paragraph 1 states that:

> 'After promulgation thereof in the Journal of Laws of the Republic of Poland (Dziennik Ustaw), a ratified international agreement shall constitute part of the domestic legal order and shall be applied directly, unless its application depends on the enactment of a statute.'

In this expression one can detect a remote echo of the resolution in the Van Gend case. Let us recall that in that case, which was being resolved in the European Court of Justice in 1963, the concept of the precedence of community law over the member States' legal order, along with the so-called theory of the closed area, was formulated. At that time, most theoreticians of community law declared that this position constituted the cornerstone in the construction of the European integration. One cannot imagine the effective development of the Communities and progress in the process of integration without harmonisation of the legal order of particular member States. In fact, it is not determined whether harmonisation needs to reach the level of the member States' Constitutions; however, there is much to support the view that also the member States' basic statutes should take into consideration all basic regulations of community law, since without that the authentic realisation of integration is not possible.[10]

The content of the Constitution of the Republic of Poland does not settle this dilemma. Although paragraph 2 of Article 91 explicitly states that

> 'An international agreement ratified upon prior consent granted by statute shall have precedence over statutes if such an agreement cannot be reconciled with the provisions of such statutes'

but this statement does not imply that such an agreement has precedence over the Constitution. In this view doctrine sticks to the traditional position that the Constitution is the highest manifestation of the nation's sovereignty and no act can prevail over its regulations.

Even the resolution of paragraph 3 of Article 91, saying that the law established by an international agreement 'is applied directly and has precedence in the event of a conflict of laws', does not settle the above-mentioned dispute. Undoubtedly, it means that Polish courts will be obliged to apply community law

[10] This issue was the subject of the seminar organised by the European Institute in Łódż and the European Law Academy in Trewir in January 30-31, 1997 in Łódż.

directly, therefore, with no delay resulting from delegation of the law to the Polish statute. In the case of doubt, they will be able to turn to the European Court of Justice for a preliminary ruling. But what of the dilemma of the constitution being the expression of the nation's sovereignty and the construction of the European integration process to which all member States are subject?

Although the issue of the relationship between the national legal order and *acquis communautaire* occupies a central position, there are also a number of other problems, among which are the problem of constitutional guarantees of the state of law, the market economic system, guarantees of political and civic rights or the introduction of the principle of subsidiarity in the functioning of local authorities.

Article 2 states that 'The Republic of Poland shall be a democratic state ruled by law and implementing the principles of social justice'. This principle was added to the Polish legal order in 1989, specifying in this manner the direction taken by works on the Constitution and, more generally, on the reform of the state. It reflects the postulate of placing law over the state and its institutions. This thesis is further developed in Article 7 which states that 'The organs of public authority shall function on the basis of and within the limits of the law'. An analogy can be found between the Communities and Poland. As the Communities are a legal order (J. Delors), Poland is a structure being an established legal order. Also A. Whelan emphasises that the rule of law, forcefully reflected in Articles 3 and 3b of the Treaty, had a huge influence on the constitutional solutions of particular member States, and also of Poland.

> 'In a democratic state of law the existence of a state organ is based on the Law, which both defines the competence of this organ and determines the borders of its activity'.[11]

The above-cited expression secures at the same time the society's participation in making law and its influence on the functioning of the country and its organs. It means not only securing the right of the majority, but also warrants the fundamental rights of the minority. The last statement finds support in the thesis that Poland, being a democratic state of law, implements the principles of social justice. Therefore, we can state that this article secures not only the principle of political pluralism expressed in the freedom of establishing political parties and their functioning, but also in the democratic representation of the society. Apart from mechanisms of direct democracy, the Constitution also provides for the referendum being the expression of direct democracy (Art. 4, para. 2). And finally, this act emphasises the role of social and territorial self-government as the concrete form of the society's participation in exercising authority.

Another significant resolution of the Constitution of the Republic of Poland, which at the same time means the acceptance of the basic political standard of the

[11] See W. Skrzydło, op. cit., p. 12.

European Communities, is the statement included in Article 10 paragraph 1, saying that

> 'The system of government of the Republic of Poland shall be based on the separation of and balance between the legislative, executive and judicial powers.'

In our political system that is not a new principle. It goes back to Locke's and Montesqieu's political doctrine, taking into consideration the experiences of the United States' system. However, it must be added that although the legislator mentions the separation of and balance between powers, the further rules indicate the quite clear domination of the legislative power; therefore, this balance has rather more a declarative than an actual character.

In the definition of the economic system, the Constitution of the Republic of Poland also evidently refers to the community pattern. Article 20 states that

> 'A social market economy, based on the freedom of economic activity, private ownership, and solidarity, dialogue and co-operation between partners, shall be the basis for the economic system of the Republic of Poland.'

In the commentaries to this article a distinctive discrepancy is evident. On the one hand, the social aspects of the functioning of the economy are emphasised,[12] and on the other the support of the economy on a liberal model of its functioning is stressed (L. Balcerowicz). These interpretations reflect distinct political perspectives characterising various political powers in Poland. If we take into account the long-term practice of imperative and separating ruling, it is evident that the creation of the market economy connected with the freedom of economic activity and private ownership is in the Polish economic interest. Nevertheless, the other components of this article included particularly the emphasis on the social character of the market economy and also the solidarity, dialogue and the co-operation between partners constitute supplementary elements, establishing the main direction of the market economy development. Actually, the same values are emphasised in the Communities' Treaties, particularly in the Amsterdam Treaty.

Significant regulations referring to basic community standards are included in Chapter II, which deals with freedoms, rights and duties of a human being and a citizen. In this chapter we can find not only reference to the political traditions of the Enlightenment, but also a direct implementation of the international conventions ratified by Poland, particularly the European Convention of Human Rights of 1950, International Pact of Civic and Political Rights and the Pacts of Economic, Social and Cultural Rights of 1966.

This chapter proclaims the principle of absolute equality, prohibition of discrimination for any reason (Art. 32, paras. 1-2), the rule of the equality of men

[12] Ibid., p. 24.

and women (Art. 33), full rights of national and ethnic minorities (Art. 35), absolute prohibition of torture or cruel, inhuman or degrading treatment or punishment (Art. 40), security proceedings fulfilling the contemporary European standards (Arts. 41-46), protection of personal data (Art. 51), freedom of faith and religion, and the freedom to express opinions (Art. 54).

Another category that is of great importance is political freedoms and rights (Arts. 57-63). They include the traditional catalogue of rights, thus, the freedom of peaceful assembly (Art. 57), the freedom of association (Art. 58), the freedom of association in trade unions (Art. 59), the right of access to the public service (Art. 60) and the right to obtain information on the activities of organs of public authority (Art. 61), which corresponds with the active movement in favour of access to information in the European Union.

A distinct category of rights constitutes economic, social and cultural freedoms and rights. The debate on the proposal to introduce these rights to the Constitution caused remarkably passionate disputes. The opponents of the introduction of these rights took the view that the state should not have the protective role, and consequently, should not make promises that can be empty promises. Therefore, they opposed, for example, the introduction of the right to work to the Constitution, since in reality there are no chances of its full realisation.[13] At the same time the followers of the idea of the introduction of this category of rights to the Constitution emphasised the necessity of confirmation of the State's responsibility on economic and social issues. Finally, this position was accepted by a sufficient constituent majority and was included in the resolutions of the Articles 64-76.

Even if we assumed that the above resolutions have both their followers and opponents in western countries, we could find there a number of expressions clearly inspired by community regulations. And it is not the economic rights that are significant, such as the right to ownership (Art. 64), the freedom to choose and pursue an occupation (Art. 65), or the right to safe and hygienic conditions of work (Art. 66), the right to social security whenever incapacitated for work (Art. 67), or the right to health protection (Art. 68). These regulations result from the achievements of the last one hundred and fifty years. I would like to draw attention to the category that is clearly connected with the development of the community legislation, and constitutes a sort of community standard, which must be a pattern for all the countries aspiring to the membership in the European Union: first of all, environmental protection regulations and consumer regulations must be included.

Article 74 states in paragraph 1: 'Public authorities shall pursue policies ensuring the ecological security of current and future generations'. At the same time, it adds in paragraph 2 that 'Protection of the environment shall be duty of public

[13] Compare W. Skrzydło, op. cit., p. 61.

authorities'. One can state that rules of this kind are indeed to be found in many modern Constitutions, which does not undermine the fact that it is the community legislation that constitutes their evident source. Article 130r of the Treaty and environmental Directives to a large extent changed the consciousness of the societies, especially the political elites of the aspiring countries. The fact that beside these regulations, there is also the expression of paragraph 3, which formulates the right of every citizen to information about the condition and protection of the environment, proves that the authors of the Constitution of the Republic of Poland took into consideration the newest tendencies, which are still the subject of debate among the community leaders. Transparency became a significant postulate of the Amsterdam summit meeting and found reflection in its amendments to the Community Treaty. It must be emphasised that this is the tendency that is still under fundamental debate, since the borders between the desirable range of openness and the range of confidentiality, indispensable because of commercial reasons, have not been clearly specified.[14]

In addition, Article 76 explicitly indicates the influence of community consumer legislation. It states that

> 'public authorities shall protect consumers, customers, hirers or lessees against activities threatening their health, privacy and safety, as well as against dishonest market practices'.

The authors of the Constitution take the position that, in fact, every member of society acts in certain situations as a consumer, and hence, his rights should be protected by the Fundamental Statute. However, because of the direct contact of the consumer protection issues with the market (and it is the market economy that constitutes the basis of the Community), detailed specification of the complex relationship between market and consumer rights is left for a separate statute.

According to community standards, the Constitution grants citizens the possibility of claiming their rights before ordinary courts of law, the Constitutional Tribunal (in the field of conformity of the legal act with the Constitution) (Art. 79) along with applying to the Commissioner for Citizens' Rights for assistance in ensuring protection of his freedoms or rights infringed by the organs of public authority (Art. 80). Pointing at the possibility of appealing to the European Court of Justice was premature, since such right will arise only at the moment of Poland's accession to the European Union.

A certain role in the adaptation of community law on the territory of Poland may be played by the Constitutional Tribunal. According to Article 188

---

[14] See D. Willis, 'Freedom of Information and Environmental Rights: Building Protection from Below' (in:) The Harmonisation of Polish Environmental Protection Law with European Standards – 2000, Przysiek 2000, pp. 64-65.

'The Constitutional Tribunal shall adjudicate regarding the following matters:
1. the conformity of statutes and international agreements to the Constitution,
2. the conformity of a statute to ratified international agreements whose ratification required prior consent granted by statute.'

Moreover, the Constitutional Tribunal adjudicates on the conformity of legal provisions issued by central State organs to the Constitution, ratified international agreements and statutes and the conformity to the Constitution of the purposes or activities of political parties.

Therefore, we can see that this organ possesses very substantial powers, that should be considered in the context of the sovereignty issue. This matter has already been the subject of an analysis on the occasion of the reflection on the ratification of international agreements. Nevertheless, then the matter concerned the precedence of international agreements over statutes, where such an agreement cannot be reconciled with the provisions of such statutes (Art. 91, para. 2). The provision mentioned above does not apply directly to the relations between an international agreement and the Constitution. However, the responsibility of the Constitutional Tribunal is to adjudicate on the conformity of international agreements with the Constitution. And here a serious political problem arises. The basis for the whole construction of the integration process constitutes the common binding force of community regulations. It is confirmed by many authorities. Dominik Lasok states that in the light of the jurisdiction of the European Court of Justice in the Van Gend case

> 'The conception of the Community law (...) resembles the theory of a federal state, where the component states and their citizens are also subjects to the federal law.'[15]

In this meaning the Community is a defined legal order which has precedence over the national legal order of the member States. In this context it also occurs that the range of sovereignty becomes limited depending on the obligations undertaken. Again, there arises the question whether the theory of the nation's sovereignty, which finds its reflection in the principles of parliamentary democracy and in the Fundamental Statute, becomes limited in favour of the community legal order. In this issue, Lasok's answer is not so explicit. He indicates that although the Treaty of the Union 'designates a new stage in the process of formation of a closer connection between European nations, the Community is still an organisation of States, not an organisation of nations'. Therefore, although the Community in its outline is thought of as a federation and its legal order is the legal order of a federal state, its law is applied by national institutions, as if it were the national law. It undermines the thesis of the federal character of Com-

[15] Compare D. Lasok, op. cit., p. 162, also A. Whelan, Specyficzne unormowania konstytucyjne Wspólnoty i ich wpływ na systemy konstytucyjne Państw Członkowskich, Łódź 1998, p. 24.

munity law, and thus its absolute supremacy over the whole legal order of the member States. The fact is that the European Court of Justice has worked out the construction of the precedence of Community law, its autonomy and direct application, but these rules do not settle definitively the issue of the precedence of this law over the constitutions of the member States. R. Hofman indicates that the ratification of the Maastricht Treaty entailed the need to amend the German Constitution, since the Treaty caused the transformation of the economic community into a political community.[16] Undoubtedly, we may deal with a situation where the necessity of adapting the constitutional order of particular member States to the Community regulations arises. However, the question concerns rather the evaluation of the situation where in a given country the order is not adjusted to these regulations.

The issue of the conformity of Constitution and community law was undertaken during the international conference organised by the European Institute in Łódż and the Academy of the European Law in Trewir on 30-31 January 1997 in Łódż.[17] Many speakers, among them particularly German scientists, recalled the complaints laid by German citizens to the Constitutional Tribunal which included the charge that the Maastricht Treaty infringed their basic rights guaranteed in the German Constitution. In its statement of October 1993, the Federal Constitutional Tribunal pronounced in defence of the German constitutional order towards community law. This judgment evidently indicated the power of the Federal Constitutional Tribunal to study the conformity of community law with the German Constitution.[18]

The duty of the Constitutional Tribunal, as it was stated in its judgment, is to ensure so that the Union does not do more than is allowed. Undoubtedly, it is an extremely 'sovereignty' point of view, since it is not the European Court of Justice, but the national court that decides whether the Union has overstepped its powers.

Although the point of view of the Federal Constitutional Tribunal has not been equally explicitly stated by the tribunals of other member States, it does bring about a certain theoretical problem. In fact, it raises the issue of the adjustment of the precedence of community law and the sovereign laws of the member States articulated particularly in their Constitutions.

---

[16] Ibid., p. 163

[17] Zmiany konstytucyjne związane z członkostwem w Unii Europejskiej – przykład Niemiec, Łódż 1998, pp. 45-53.

[18] Compare R. Hofman, op. cit., p. 52.

ESTONIAN CONSTITUTIONAL PROBLEMS IN ACCESSION TO THE EU

Tanel Kerikmäe*

INTRODUCTORY REMARKS

The new enlargement process has raised the question of the legal and ethical bases of delegating sovereignty. It is a peculiar historical situation in which clearly formulated legal questions require concrete answers. The legal analysis, of course, has to do with the nature of the constitution as the means of delegating competence.

The author of this article supports the idea that a constitution should be deemed to be a type of a contract.[1] As was stated by Zupanćić:

> 'If it is true to say that every contract presupposes a judge who will eventually interpret its clauses and who will, in turn, have the (state backed) power and the authority to enforce his interpretations, then the constitution, too, would be a dead letter unless there was an authority in the state to interpret it'.[2]

It is obvious that a law, especially the constitution, is provided on a certain level of abstraction. Although considered as a contract, it is still intended to regulate the future. The question is to what extent can the circumstances underlying the contract be binding on future interpretations. In this case, however, when talking about the need to amend the constitution in connection with accession to the European Union, not all questions can be answered by the Constitutional Review Chamber of the Supreme Court.

Delegated *pouvoir constituant* presumes that sovereignty can be re-delegated. According to that concept, whatever is delegated, can be re-delegated as a result of logical argument, i.e., the competence cannot be increased or decreased. However, if the competence delegated by a member State is determined by the inter-

---

* Associate Dean of Estonian Law at Concordia International University Estonia.

[1] B.M. Zupanćić, 'From Combat to Contract: What Does the Constitution Constitute?', in: (1998/1999) 1 European Journal of Law Reform. Although this article deals with the constitution of a nation state, I would suggest extending the so-called contractual doctrine to the process which could be called as 'the development of EU constitutionalism'.

[2] Ibid., p. 75.

A.E. Kellermann et al. (Eds.), EU Enlargement: The Constitutional Impact at EU and National Level

pretation of the member State, we may speculate that after the act of delegation, it will be determined through the European perspective.[3] It is therefore that a constitution is the document to determine the scope of delegated sovereignty. Unless we talk about a Europe without boundaries, competence is still determined on the state level and not on the level of individuals or a group of individuals.

Yet, what is sovereignty, the object of delegation? Just as there are different interpretations of *bona fide* when talking about the constitution of the European Union, the notion of sovereignty also causes confusion.[4] Already in 1957 an Estonian jurist N. Maim[5] wrote,

> 'sovereignty is important for a state as long as the state can be the highest communal phenomenon which provides people with the necessary communal/social dimension which would be impossible without the state ... As long as the state is a communal phenomenon which provides people with something that would not be achieved without the state, the notion of sovereignty was well-based because it represented a certain higher creative force which promoted communal life and better welfare.'

Being a people's patriot rather than being a patriot of the state, one could speak of delegating the people's sovereignty. When using the doctrine of the right of self-determination, the questions of interpreting sovereignty that we posed before would become irrelevant. However, it remains to be answered how the state would delegate the people's sovereignty and into what form the European Union will put the delegated sovereignty. And even if we take the state to be the mediator between an individual and the European Union, the constitution still remains the limiting factor in mediation.

Several authors have tackled the issue of delegating sovereignty to a world organisation in earlier articles (it was especially topical during the first years of the League of Nations and the United Nations). Whatever we call such a world organisation, the nature of it always entails mutual co-operation. In the European Union though, we can see that intergovernmental co-operation gives way to supranational right. It is up to the state to explain whether the evolving European Union can be communally beneficial for an individual or for an Estonian, for that matter, and how. On the level of the European Union, the so-called *communis opinio doctorum* should evolve.

---

[3] Certainly, we may suggest that the EU does not diminish sovereignty but rather strengthens it or increases through co-decision mechanisms. This is mostly supported by politicians and as such is opposed to the views of the euro-sceptics who claim that, in reality, Estonia lacks the possibility to influence the decisions taken in the European Union

[4] A member of the Riigikogu suggested in a discussion held 23.01.01 on 'Preparations for Estonia's accession to the European Union' not to use this term when addressing people because it would make the situation too 'black-and-white'.

[5] See: N. Maim, 'Suveräänsuse iganemine kaasajal' (Obsolescence of Sovereignty Nowadays), Akadeemia, 11th year's issue 1999, No. 3, (120) p. 479

This article bears reference to the report of the Expert Commission on Estonian Constitution, the purpose of which was for the government of a candidate country to try to determine the notion of sovereignty and the re-delegation of the competence delegated to the state thereby.

Lately, several high officials and politicians have expressed their opinion that the constitution need not be amended, but rather an EU-friendly interpretation of the Constitution would be enough. I would not agree with either position. The author of this article believes that although the latter would be choosing the easy way out, the Expert Commission of the Constitution, despite the long-winded, yet precise analysis, does not see the constitution as a 'living organism' that it should be.

Although the Commission has made several recommendations to the *Riigikogu* (the Parliament of Estonia) to adopt political decisions, the Commission states that these recommendations are not derived from the desires of the political forces of Estonia, but grounded in arguments of legal science (constitutional law). The Commission declared that the proposals presented have to be regarded as 'the starting point of discussion' in society. However, the statements deriving from the Commission's final report remained the most authoritative arguments to the present time.

I. ESTONIAN CONSTITUTION

To understand our constitution one must understand our history. Estonia has a single constitutional Act, the Constitution (*Põhiseadus*) of the Republic of Estonia, adopted by a referendum on 28 June 1992, which entered into force the following day. Since its adoption no amendments have been made to the Constitution.[6] The Constitution establishes the principle of legal continuity of the Republic of Estonia which was proclaimed independent on 24 February 1918, and occupied by the Soviet power on 17 June 1939. This reflects the idea of legal restoration (*restitutio ad integrum*), which served as a basis for the re-independence and liberation from the Soviet Union on 21 August 1991.

II. THE PROPOSED AMENDMENTS

The Government of Estonia appointed[7] the Commission for legal expertise of the Estonian Constitution (1992) on 14 of May, 1996 in order to review the need to amend the Constitution by looking at the whole body of it. The Commission de-

[6] However, there have been several attempts mainly in regard to presidential elections.
[7] *Riigi Teataja* (State Gazette) I 1996, 35, 725.

clares that EU accession would not directly harm national independence since the EU forms more of a confederation-like structure than a federation.[8]

As a result of its work,[9] the Commission reached a conclusion that the current constitution *does not enable* Estonia to become a full member of the European Union nor does it fulfil the requirements of the Union's legislation. The Commission report contains several amendment proposals which would help to solve the legal problem.[10]

In order to discuss whether the Constitution needs to be amended or not, we first have to find the teleological basis of the Constitution. The philosophical basis of the Constitution can be found in the Preamble and the Commission refers to it as 'the basic agreement of the Estonian society':

> 'With unwavering faith and a steadfast will to strengthen and develop the state, which is established on the inextinguishable right of the people of Estonia to national self-determination and which was proclaimed on 24 February 1918, which is founded on liberty, justice and law, which shall protect internal and external peace, and is a pledge to present and future generations for their social progress and welfare, which shall guarantee the preservation of the Estonian nation and culture through the ages, the people of Estonia, on the basis of paragraph 1 of the Constitution which entered into force in 1938, and by a referendum held on 28 June 1992, adopted the following Constitution'.

The Commission believes that the Preamble does not need to be amended since it does not hinder the development of Estonia's statehood,

> 'Moreover, it would be unnecessary to bring in the European Union in the Preamble – the preamble is primarily concerned with stating the principal values of Estonian people. If the European Union were to be mentioned in the preamble as the goal of the Republic of Estonia, there would be a danger of confusing the means and the goal, for the European Union being a supranational organisation cannot be a goal in itself.'

This argument probably determines the general view of the Commission whereby certain sections of the Constitution need to be amended. The Commission does not question the legally binding nature of the preamble.

Independence means that the Republic of Estonia cannot be made part of another state, a federate state of a federation. It must remain an independent state with no higher power than the state itself.

---

[8] However, the use of the term 'a closer union' in the EU has gradually been replaced by the ideas of Joschka Fischer who advocates a unified model of a federation in Europe. Our Prime Minister has also expressed his support of that idea.

[9] I do not agree with all the statements included to the final report. For example, I would like to emphasise still existing III pillar structure of EU law, which makes different legislative acts of having different legal bindingness.

[10] IX Chapter, Head of the Working-group, Prof. Heiki Pisuke.

The Commission maintains that the three European Communities are a threat to national independence since they establish the supranational right. The Commission points out the following aspects:

- giving up competence in certain fields of legislation (sole competence of the Community);
- giving up competence to enter into international agreements (change of legal subject);
- general jurisdiction of the European Court of Justice (decisions are binding on all legal subjects of member States).

The Commission concluded that due to the peculiar legal nature of the European Community, Estonia would be subordinated to the legislative will of another member State. Moreover, as a result of the wide jurisdiction of the ECJ, Estonia will become dependent on other countries as well as international organisations (the three Communities). The same argument has been used by euro-sceptics in Estonia. However, it is obvious that an argument like that cannot be absolute considering the wide scope of international relations the Republic of Estonia already has; another example would be certain dependence on the cases of the European Court of Justice. The European Convention on Human Rights is also based on the legal tradition of European states. This, however, cannot contradict the Constitution in any way. Section 3 of the Constitution states:

> 'The state authority shall be exercised solely pursuant to the Constitution and laws which are in conformity therewith. Generally recognised principles and rules of international law are an inseparable part of the Estonian legal system'.

The Commission finds that the Constitution does not allow for accession considering the provisions on independence and sovereignty. This derives mainly from subsection 1(1) of the Constitution, which reads:

> 'Estonia is an independent and sovereign democratic republic wherein the supreme power of the state is held by the people. Estonian independence and sovereignty is interminable and inalienable.'

The same wording could be found in the Constitutions of 1920 and 1938.

The arguments of the Commission are based on the so-called *travaux preparatoire*. In trying to interpret the meaning and the grounds for paragraph 1 of the Constitution, we can use the arguments made in the sessions of the Constitutional Assembly whereby the provision has its roots in the history of Estonia and is intended to protect against collaborationism. The principle that independence and sovereignty are inalienable probably means that independence and sovereignty must not be sacrificed. Yet the provision does not exclude the delegation of sovereignty, which according to the Commission, though, cannot be final. The problem relates strongly to the disputed question whether a member

State is able to quit the EU or change legal relations to demand re-delegation of some powers back to the nation State.

The Commission concludes that the re-delegation of sovereignty must be guaranteed; presently the treaties of the European Union do not allow for that. The analysis ends with Article 54 of the Vienna Convention on Law of Treaties. Indeed, if we read the provisions of the Vienna Convention, then pursuant to Article 56 the right of denunciation or withdrawal is directly dependent on the condition that prescribes that such a right arises if it is established that the parties intended to admit the possibility of denunciation or withdrawal. Considering that it would be hopeless to wait for a precedent in order to determine whether there is such a possibility, I suggest using Article 60 which provides for denunciation where the other party (or parties) is in material breach of the treaty (especially with regard to the goals of the treaty). This should be a sufficient guarantee that delegated sovereignty is not misused to suit the ambitions of the bigger states in the field of foreign politics.

As the Commission points out, sovereignty has two dimensions – internal and external. In its internal dimension, the State is the ultimate power in regard to its territory and members, and the decisions of the State cannot be appealed under any higher power. As stated above, this statement cannot be absolute as we already have some indisputably binding case law under the European human rights protective system. The ECHR is part of the Estonian legal system as a ratified international treaty and the Human Rights Court is the ultimate interpretor of the Convention.

The external view of sovereignty by the Commission means that States acting in reciprocal relations are not subject to a higher authority than international law. In that sense, the meaning of sovereignty is non-symmetric – absolute in its internal dimension and relative in its external dimension, where the *alter ego* of the State meets the sovereignties of other States. The Commission explained, that section 1 of the Constitution declares State sovereignty in general terms, describing both its external and internal dimensions.

As the amendment provision as well as the accompanying analysis in the Report shows, the Commission draws a distinction between the delegation and transfer of sovereignty, stressing that 'delegation' implies the development of the EU on the basis of national constitutions allowing the delegation of competences to the EU institutions. 'Delegation', according to the Commission, differently from 'transfer', allows the sovereign State to withdraw the competences, using international legal mechanisms. Thus, the Commission refers to the 'inalienable right of national self-determination'.

By way of protection, the Commission proposes to add the following sentence to the above-mentioned provision:

> 'Estonia may, on the basis of referendum, participate in the European Union, which is an association of States created by its member States on the basis of the Treaties'.[11]

Here the emphasis lies on the phrase 'association of states' which attempts to limit the object of accession and to provide it with a 'convenient meaning' for a nation State. It is understandable why the Commission tries to place the accession to the European Union in the traditional context of international law. Thus we find a subsection 123(1) added to Chapter IX of the Constitution 'Foreign Relations and Treaties':

> 'Estonia may, under the principles of reciprocity and equality, delegate to the European Union bodies the power competences deriving from the Constitution, in order to exercise them jointly with the European Union member States, to the extent necessary for the implementation of the Treaties the Union is based upon and on the condition that this does not violate the basic principles and functions of Estonian statehood, manifested in the Preamble of the Constitution'.

These, I would say 'protective' amendment proposals, take into account the nature of the European Union, especially the results that the supremacy of the supranational law may have on the independence of the Republic of Estonia. The European Union must thus meet certain requirements in order for the accession not to be contradictory to the Constitution. This way competence can be delegated without prejudice to the sovereignty of Estonia.

The Estonian Expert Commission also states that only the Estonian nation is the legitimate source of power exercised in Estonia. The Commission proceeds from section 1 of the Constitution, which sets forth that Estonia is a democratic republic where the highest authority is vested in the people. It reaches the interpretation that this clause does not allow any intergovernmental or other governmental organ authorised by a foreign nation to possess any higher power than the Estonian Parliament, since the former would then exercise higher power not only at the intergovernmental level but also in Estonia, which is prohibited by the Constitution. Moreover, under the right of national self-determination, it is the Estonian nation to whom the *pouvoir constituant* belong so as to adopt the Constitution as the act of the highest legal force determining the legal arrangement of the functioning of the State; the Estonian nation is the only source of legitimacy and therefore the European Parliament as the representative body of the nation cannot possess any higher legitimacy than the Estonian legislator. The Commission further states that in the European Union there is no parliament elected by people exercising the legislative power as the highest State authority body.

---

[11] The English translation of the Commission proposals and main generalisations are made by A. Albi (researcher/PhD student of European University Institute, Florence) in her bachelor's thesis on Estonian Sovereignty, Tartu 1999 (Councel: T. Kerikmäe).

In order to secure the Estonian Parliament's participation in the EU decision-making process, it is proposed to amend the IX Chapter 'Foreign Relations and Treaties' by adding section 123, the second sentence of which would read as follows:

> 'The Government of the Republic informs the Riigikogu at the earliest and the widest possible on the issues concerning the European Union and considers in its contribution for the European Union legislation the positions of the Riigikogu. The precise procedure will be regulated by law in case of Estonian Republic's membership'.

Another way of securing the people's position being vested in the supreme power of the state is to hold a referendum. Since the current section 106 of the Constitution prohibits referendums on foreign treaties, the new referendum clause on the EU would be added to the proposed section 1(3). A separate provision would legitimise the delegation of competences since it is a question that does not fall under the scope of international agreements specified in section 106. This would allow limits to be set to the delegated competence and guarantee the participation of the people in the exercise of state power.

Foreign legal experts in the field have held different positions. The Conference in Tallinn (26-27 September 1997, dedicated to 'Five years of Estonian Constitution') first discussed problems whether (and how) the Estonian Constitution must be amended in relation to the EU accession with the purpose of clarifying the necessity and the technical features of these possible amendments. Furthermore, the Report of the Expert Commission has been analysed to see whether the proposed amendments are justified.

Professor Gardner answered the question whether the current Estonian Constitution is in conflict with EC rules. He emphasised that the main question is political – whether we want to access, pointing out some evident contradictions (in regard to the current competence of the Bank of Estonia and the obligations deriving from the Monetary Union). If we want to join the EU, we have to change the Constitution (i.e., the competence of the National Bank). The amendment of those provisions which would otherwise be in conflict with the delegated competence is indeed necessary.

Professor Alexy declared that there is no ultimate need to change the current Constitution. However, he proposed to add a third sentence to section 1 which reads as follows: 'Estonian sovereignty and independence does not exclude of being a member State of the EU'. The adding of such a general provision seems to be the best solution for the author of this article, and I believe also for the Estonian people who are to decide the accession to the European Union. The sentence provides that sovereignty and independence are standing values for the Republic of Estonia and accession to the European Union cannot change those.

The Estonian author A. Leps[12] concludes his opinion with the idea that the legal problems deriving from Constitutional amendments are to be solved by the Estonian State, since there is no elaborated international model for taking account of being a member State of the European Union. However, I maintain my opinion that such a complex problem cannot be solved on the international level. Sovereignty can be delegated only by the decision of the Sovereign.

III. ROLE OF NATIONAL COURTS

By the Constitution paragraph 3:

> 'The powers of state shall be exercised solely pursuant to the Constitution and laws which are in conformity therewith. Generally recognised principles and rules of international law are an inseparable part of the Estonian legal system'.

By paragraph 123:

> 'The Republic of Estonia shall not conclude international treaties which are in conflict with the Constitution. If laws or other legislation of Estonia are in conflict with international treaties ratified by the Riigikogu, the provisions of the international treaty shall apply'.

Direct effect of international norms is determined by the Constitution.

Theories of monism and dualism and their techniques in the context of Estonia and the EU law are complicated to analyse. Estonia has not, despite political promises, delegated its sovereignty. The 'Europe treaty' (association treaty) must be treated as an international treaty in the sense of the Vienna convention 1969. The problem is that the 'Europe treaty' is closely linked with EC law and dichotomic international texts (possibly interpreted differently by the ECJ).

A separate opinion of the Estonian Supreme Court (the highest court) decision 3-4-1-4-98 of 27th May 1998 contains a direct reference to the 'Europe treaty' (i.e., association treaty); the Estonian Republic has made a political decision to accede to the EU. On 1st August 1995 the *Riigikogu* adopted a decision to ratify the association treaty, signed on 12th June 1995 in Luxembourg and enforced with regard to Estonia on 1st February 1998. According to this treaty, Estonia is obliged to harmonise domestic legislation with EU law and its principles (see Art. 68).

In the decision 3-4-1-1 of 10th May 1996, the Supreme Court replied to the opinion of the President. The President argued that Estonian law of non-govern-

---

[12] A. Leps, 'Eesti Põhiseaduse muutmisest' (On Amendment of the Constitution of the Republic of Estonia), Akadeemia, 1999/3, AS Akadeemia Trükk.

mental organisations is not in accordance with the EU legal system and this conflict, in terms of the rule of law, could be 'destructive'. Already in the decision of 30th September 1994, II-4/A-5/94, the Supreme Court stated that

> 'building up general principles of Estonian law, we must take account of not only the Constitution, but also the basic principles of EU law, as derived from general principles of member States with high legal culture'.

In the decision 3-4-1-97 of 11th June 1997, the Supreme Court also referred to the decisions of the ECJ.

Although there are few references to the legal system of the European Union, the application of EC law is supported by the Supreme Court. The 'Europe treaty' is used as a 'mediator' between the supranational level and implementation of international norms.

CONCLUSION

The Constitution has always been a symbol of the State's sovereignty. The EU leaves 'free hands' to modernise our constitution, if necessary. Even the Regular Report from the Commission of the European Communities on Estonia's progress towards accession[13] does not mention the constitutional issues. The possible accession of Estonia is planned to take place in 2003.

The constitutional amendments must certainly be adopted before the accession. However, there are still different approaches in the field of constitutional amendments in relation to the EU accession.

It is important to note that one of the obstacles in drafting indisputable amendments to the State Constitution is certainly the ongoing reform in the EU. The answer to the question: 'what is the constitutional future of the Union?' is also the answer to many questions of how to reach a compromise in our society.

[13] http://europa.eu.int/comm/enlargement/docs/index.htm

CONSTITUTIONAL AMENDMENTS DUE TO BULGARIAN FULL EU MEMBERSHIP

Evgeni Tanchev*

A positive description of the adaptation of the member States' national constitutional law to EC and EU law would emphasize the gradual process of amending the Constitutions aimed at securing the supranational, direct, immediate and horizontal effect of community legislation. In most of the countries this process has been facilitated to a great extent by the existing constitutional provisions on the status, supremacy and implementation of international law in the national legal order, especially during the period preceding the TEU. This has been a valid trend particularly in countries like Belgium, the Netherlands and Luxembourg where international agreements and EC founding treaties have been considered superior, according to their legal standing, to domestic law, including national Constitutions.[1] However, most national Constitutions provide that under certain conditions international norms become part of the national legal order and acquire the legal force of parliamentary legislation, or by superceding the statute law stand second only to the Constitution. National debates on sovereignty, functionalism and federalism between proponents of the integration and eurosceptics, this being the political background of the adaptation process, played a crucial role in the extent of the constitutional amending process in each of the EU member States. For the candidate countries to full EU membership, the body of constitutional formulae used during the process of adapting the 15 member States' national Constitutions might be considered to be the 'constitutional *acquis communautaire*'.

The 1991 Bulgarian Constitution is a typical rigid Constitution providing a dual (hybrid) regime for the exercise of the constituent power. The constitutional

* Professor, Sofia University, Bulgaria.

[1] To a certain degree concerning the overcoming of conflicting constitutional provisions with parliamentary supermajorities, Austria, Finland and Italy might be good examples of a precedence of the international treaties over the National Constitutions, see C. Economides, The Elaboration of Model Clauses on the Relationship between International and Domestic Law in The Relationship between International and Domestic Law, European Commission for Democracy through Law, Council of Europe, 1994, pp. 101-103; on the hierarchy of legal acts, see Law in the Making, ed. Al. Pizzorusso, Springer, 1988; Sources and Categories of European Union Law, ed. G. Winter, Baden-Baden, Nomos, 1996; L.M. Diez-Picazo, Sources of Law in Spain: An Outline, EUI, Working Paper, N 94/10, Florence.

A.E. Kellermann et al. (Eds.), EU Enlargement: The Constitutional Impact at EU and National Level

amendments are within the powers of the Grand National Assembly and the Parliament, with a special list of amendments being reserved exclusively for the Grand National Assembly.[2] The founding fathers provided a rationalized model of constituent power vested in the National Assembly for all the other amendments with the exception of those reserved as exclusive prerogatives of the Grand National Assembly. Though contrived along the modern fourth constitutional generation constitutional amendment lines, the Bulgarian model for constitutional revision has proven so far to be an effective barrier against quick, authoritarian and not well thought out constitutional amendments and an obstacle bringing to the flexibility of the Constitution in the transition. The procedure for constitutional amendment through the National Assembly requires an extremely high level of consent for constitutional amendments, since the latter should be passed by super majorities. Amendments are to be initiated by the President or one fourth of the members of Parliament. The amendments become part of the Constitution if they receive a three-fourths majority vote in the Assembly to be cast three times, and there is a possibility for drafting with a two-thirds majority if the bill on the constitutional amendment has been supported in the first and second ballot by less than three-fourths, but has received more than two-thirds support of the members of Parliament. In the context of a liberal constitutionalism and responsible government with limited powers, the purpose of super majorities in the constitutional amendment process has been to generate consensus behind the proposed revision, to defend opposition and parliamentary minority against unilateral and authoritarian decisions of the parties in power and to exclude potential encroachments on human rights. In a pluralistic, highly fragmented Parliament sometimes with fragile coalitions, to mobilize these majorities, has been nearly impossible, as the case with Bulgaria has proved.

There is much debate in society, among politicians and in academia about the different merits and demerits of the 1991 Bulgarian Constitution.

With this in mind, I will outline the possible amendments that have been circulating in the public discourse but have not acquired the status of official proposal for constitutional amendment.

Most of the proposals for constitutional amendment refer to the enhancement of both institutional and functional constitutional safeguards of individual rights:

- the establishment of an ombudsman which was an integral part of several draft constitutions is obligatory, all the more since this institution exists in most of

---

[2] Following the traditions and legacy of the Tirnovo 1879 Constitution the most important amendments to the Constitution should be drafted by a Grand National Assembly of 400, elected *ad hoc* for the constitutional revision. The exclusive prerogatives of this classic, though outdated, repository of constituent power are to adopt a new Constitution, to decide on changes related to the territory of the Republic and ratify any international instruments envisaging such problems, to decide on changes on the form of State (unitary, federal, confederal, or to grant autonomy) or the form of government, direct applicability of the Constitution and supremacy of international law, certain human rights guarantees and amendments relating to constitutional amendment.

the EU member States, some of the associated new democracies, as well as in the European Parliament;
- improvement of the functioning of the judicial system by taking the investigation office out of the judiciary, transferring the prosecution service to the executive power and introducing a limited term of office for judges;
- stipulation of the right to bring individual complaints to the Constitutional Court, legitimating citizens as parties to constitutional proceedings in defending their rights whenever infringed by unconstitutional laws.[3]

The constitutional amendments implied by the full EU membership of Bulgaria have not yet been drafted, introduced or pending on the legislative agenda now in the Bulgarian Parliament. The scope and content of the amendments will be effected by the trends in the development of the EU Constitutional order. They require a considerably more profound public discourse to generate a higher degree of public consensus.

A full EU membership requires adapting the Constitution to the requirements of the EC Treaties before signing and ratifying primary law. The current Association Agreement and the Commission's White Paper stipulating the obligations for approximation of the legislation do not contain requirements for amending the Constitution and they do not provide for the supremacy, direct, universal and immediate effect of EU law in the territory of the associated Members. The approximation of legislation resembles partly the transplant of certain foreign standards in Bulgarian legislation and partly the introduction of international law in the domestic legal order under the system of dualism. Adapting the national Constitutions to the requirements of EU primary law reflects not so much the supremacy of common international law over domestic law, rather it resembles the interdependence between the constitutional framework at national and international level.

The ratification of primary law, during which process most of the European Union member States amended their constitutions, reveals the trend of a necessity for constitutional amendments, which will go along with the adoption of new amendments in primary law of the European Union following some amendments to the TEU and even develop on the sounder grounds of a new treaty adoption or a Constitution of Europe. That is why the European Union member States will enact partial constitutional amendments each time during the ratification of the

[3] The Constitutional Court in Ruling N 1 of 1 July 1997 constitutional decision N 5 of 1997 took a radical step towards the transfer of the right of an individual claim in an indirect way through the empowerment of Supreme Court of Cassation panels and Supreme Administrative Court panels to suspend the hearing of a case and to refer the matter of the constitutionality of an act to the Constitutional Court. Each of the parties to such a case may claim the control of the constitutionality of an act, S.G., N. 54, 8 July 1997. This is, of course, the utmost power of the Constitutional Court in respect of complying with the effective constitutional provisions which the Court is not allowed to change.

amendments to primary law whenever they contradict the national constitutional law. The frequency and the scope of the constitutional changes in the EU member States depend on the scope of the envisaged transfer of sovereignty or the delegation of powers to supranational institutions. The future accepted EU full Members will have to adopt primary law in full and bring their Constitutions into compliance with the requirements of the latter on their actual entry. There is a conspicuous trend that each later accession will presuppose constitutional amendments that are more numerous and greater in ambit so that the degree of Community integration achieved will widen the gap between primary law and the Constitutions of non-member States.

The necessity for constitutional amendments before the accession of the Republic of Bulgaria stems from several factors. Their preliminary elucidation overwhelms the arguments of opponents and reveals to a considerable degree the imperatives of part of the future changes in the Basic Law of 1991.

Firstly, the amendments in the Constitution in relation to the accession arise from the inappropriateness of the existing constitutional provisions in respect of European law enforcement.

Secondly, the legal nature of primary and secondary Community law excludes the use of the subsisting constitutional mechanism in providing enforcement of the European law.

The content of the necessary amendments precludes the Constitutional Court from using an interpretative approach to adapt the constitutional provision mechanism which allows the incorporation of international law into the national legal system and thus prevent any amendments to the 1991 Bulgarian Basic Law.

The comparative analysis of the constitutional evolution in the European Union member States before and after the signing of the Treaty of Maastricht indicates the necessity for amendments to the Constitution of Bulgaria.

The Constitution of 1991, under Article 5, section 4, reflects the democratic principle of the primacy of international law. The latter is considered to be an integral part of the supremacy of the law proclaimed by the classic wording of the German *Rechtsstaat* doctrine which is the continental equivalent of the Rule of Law. Moreover, the Constitution adopts the monistic principle of integrating international norms into the national legal system. International treaties which are signed, ratified, and promulgated are part of the domestic legal order and no special national legislation has to be enacted for their enforcement. Furthermore, the Constitution explicitly states that international law norms which have become part of the domestic legislation prevail over any conflicting provisions of parliamentary acts.

Is there any option to the Constitution not being amended and the wording of Article 5, section 4 of the Constitution being used instead? Assuming that the primary law of the European Union is suitable for transplantation through the mechanism of adopting international law norms into the domestic legal order, then the issue of the *acquis communautaire* and the European law effect cannot be solved because of its specific character in comparison with public international law. This is so because of supranationalism, because of the supremacy, the direct, immediate and universal effect on all national legal subjects within the territory of the European Union member States.[4] Simultaneously, the supremacy of primary and secondary EU law does not require any consent on behalf of national institutions with respect to any new act through which EC law develops as an autonomous transnational legal order and which, therefore, should be applied by the authorities of the EU member States. In this particular sense, supremacy of EU law acquires also an infra-national effect and autonomous enforcement in the territories of member States, unlike either monism or dualism on the adoption into the domestic legal order of international law norms arising from the primacy of international law.

The supranational character of EU law implies, in the event of a conflict, supremacy over the provisions of national Constitutions, as well as giving rise to the obligations for member States to procure the enforcement of the European Union law provisions.

According to the subsisting constitutional provisions on the adoption of international law into the domestic legal order, the provisions of international treaties precede the provisions of any act belonging to the hierarchy of legal acts of the national legal system.[5] The 1991 Bulgarian Constitution seemingly does not solve the problem of the correlation between the legal force of international law norms that have become part of domestic law and of provisions of the Constitution. However, it is sufficient to interpret the text of Article 85, section 3 and Article 149, section 1, count 4 as indicating that the legal force of international law norms does not prevail over the intensity of the legal effect of the supremacy of the Constitution. The same could be concluded by means of the comparative analysis of the Constitutions in the States which have adopted legal monism and which reveals that international law norms do have a lower or, as an exception, equal legal force in comparison with the provisions of their Constitutions. Hence, the implicit provisions of Article 85, section 3 and Article 149, section 4 and the analogy with some legal systems of other European countries places the provisions of international treaties on an equal par with or above parliamentary acts,

[4] These undoubted characteristics of European law were formulated by the Court as early as the beginning of the 1960s, *N.V. Algemeine Transport- en Expedite Onderneming van Gend & Loos* v. *Netherlands Fiscal Administration*; Case 26/62; *Costa* v. *ENEL*; Case 6/64. See in detail E. Stein, Lawyers, Judges and the Making of a Transnational Constitution, AJIL, Vol. 75, January 1975, N 1, pp. 1-27; P. Pescatore, The Doctrine of Direct Effect, ELRev., 8, 1983, pp. 155-157; J.H.H. Weiler, The Community System: the Dual Character of Supranationalism, YEL 1, 1981; A. Easson, Legal Approaches to European Integration in Constitutional Law of the European Union, F. Snyder, EUI , Florence, 1994-1995.

[5] See, Law in the Making, ed. Al. Pizzorusso, Springer, 1988; Sources and Categories of European Union Law, ed. G. Winter, Baden-Baden, Nomos, 1996; L.M. Diez-Picazo, Sources of Law in Spain: An Outline, EUI, Working Paper, N 94/10, Florence.

but below the Constitution of the Republic of Bulgaria. The opposite assumption contravenes the Constitution. If international treaties were to have legal force equal to or above that of the Constitution, then Article 85, section 3 and Article 149, section 4 would be redundant. If they had had the same force as the provisions of the Constitution at the time of their signing and ratification, they would have been automatically incorporated into the constitutional text and there would have been neither a need to change the Constitution before concluding international treaties in conflict with it, nor any need to review the text of the Constitution, nor even any need to test the latter for its compliance with an international treaty before ratification for the Constitutional Court. Furthermore, the constitutional provisions would have been overridden and changed by the mere fact of signing and ratifying an international treaty whose provisions were in conflict with the subsisting constitutional provisions. Thus, in practice, the primacy of international law would acquire the dimensions of a constituent power and would directly do away with the fundamental principle of international law, that is to say, the recognition of national sovereignty. Finally, another option should be excluded: the Constitutional Court of the Republic of Bulgaria would hardly be able by means of an extensive interpretation to change the meaning or the scope of the constitutional provisions and at the same time prevent the intervention of the constituent power, because otherwise the Court would perform its functions in contravention of the content of the Constitution itself. Moreover, the Court is called upon to protect the latter and abide by it.

Here one could add other arguments, but the above-mentioned are sufficient to conclude that Article 5, section 4 of the 1991 Bulgarian Constitution is not capable to guarantee the supremacy, or the universal, direct and immediate effect of the secondary law comprising the fundamental bulk of the provisions of European law.

The adequate constitutional model needed to provide the effect of EU law involves a partial transfer of national sovereignty or devolution of powers of nation states to the European Union. This model is substantially different from the primacy of international over domestic law which according to Article 2 of the United Nations Charter involves full respect for national sovereignty.

The constitutional amendments implied by EU membership of the Republic of Bulgaria may be classified in two groups.

The first group includes all the amendments introduced in the member States:

- restriction of and a partial transfer of State sovereignty in certain areas to the EU and to EU institutions;
- European citizenship, a number of rights inherent in European citizenship and especially their passive and active voting rights both in local elections and in elections for European Parliament, the term of office and the immunities of its deputies;
- direct effect of Community law;

- parliamentary control and establishment of special parliamentary committees on matters concerning the European Union, information about the activity of the European institutions and forthcoming acts of community law to be followed by statements of national parliaments which have binding effect on the respective governments, the requirement for a consent in respect of nominated national candidates for members of the Commission, the European Court of Justice and Court of First Instance, of the Court of Auditors and the Board of Managing Directors of the European Investment Bank;
- the Economic and Monetary Union and the option of the European Central Bank to assume the competence bestowed chiefly on national banks;
- participation in the common foreign and security policy, according to Title V of the Treaty of the European Union and obligations for the national executive to inform the Parliament.

The second group includes amendments related to the fundamental rights of citizens. Article 22 of the 1991 Bulgarian Constitution pertains directly to full membership whereas the rest of the amendments only indirectly affect the accession because in their purpose they concern the reinforcement of the principle of the rule of law which constitutes one of the political criteria of the Agenda 2000.[6]

It is necessary that the subsisting ban on foreigners to acquire land under Article 22 of the Constitution be eliminated.[7] The legislative permission is a palliative which hardly encourages foreign investors. In a State governed by the rule of law, the overruling of a constitutional ban by a legislative regulation in respect of its legal effect is as inadmissible as the circumvention of the Constitution and the laws by any natural and legal persons using subtle, jeweller-like juridical constructions. By virtue of the supremacy and the direct effect of the Constitution under Article 5 of the 1991 Bulgarian Constitution, the subsisting constitutional ban of Article 22 could be enforced and precluded from being potential. Besides, there is a total discrepancy between preserving Article 22 unchanged and full membership of the European Union, as far as this is flagrantly in conflict with the fundamental principle of Community law concerning the free movement of persons, goods, services and capital. Preserving Article 22 would also be treated as an act of discrimination in respect of EU citizens.

Another specific constitutional amendment concerns Article 65, section 1 and Article 93, section 2 of the Constitution. Under these provisions persons holding exclusively Bulgarian citizenship can stand in the parliamentary and presidential elections. By the time Bulgaria joins the EU no person will be able to stand in these elections for every Bulgarian will be a EU citizen as well.

[6] Agenda 2000, For a Stronger and Wider Union, Bulletin of the European Communities, Supplement 5/97.

[7] This ban is delicately noted in the statement of the European Commission, op. cit., p. 46.

Second in order but not in significance, some of the proposals for the constitutional amendments refer to constitutional amendments in the member States during the ratification of the founding EC Treaties.

Depending on the scope of the amendments necessary for membership of Bulgaria in the European Union a fuller and more pragmatic revision of the Constitution might also have taken place, which probably would affect the functioning of the institutions.

The aim of adapting the Constitution will be to avoid the exclusively hard mode of a constitutional revision by the Grand National Assembly .

Amendments to the Constitution can be made within the rationalized procedure in the National Assembly given a maximum consent between the State institutions, among the political forces and on a consensus in the society concerning the purposes of the constitutional revision.

The enforcement of the accession agreement of the Republic of Bulgaria to the European Union will be a final result of several consecutive stages each preceding one preparing and being the ground for the following. Consequently, the following procedure shall be followed: a preparation of the agreement on the accession to the European Union; a preparation and passing in the National Assembly of a bill on the amendment to the Constitution (Art. 85, sect. 3); a carrying out of the procedure under Chapter IX of the Constitution on the passing of the amendments; the signing of the agreement and the making of a provision for time within which the ratification shall take place; referring to and ruling by the Constitutional Court under Article 149, section 1, count 4 on the compliance of the Agreement concluded with the Constitution before the ratification; passing of an act of the National Assembly on the ratification of the agreement.

By virtue of Article 85, section 3 of the Constitution of the Republic of Bulgaria the accession agreement for full EU membership may be signed only after amending the 1991 Bulgarian Basic Law. The negotiations for the agreement are normally conducted by the executive power presented by the Council of Ministers. When the final draft has been completed a precise estimation needs to be made as to the determination of the texts that do not comply with the constitutional provisions at the moment of the accession of the country. On the basis of this estimation a legislative bill should be drafted. The persons entitled to introduce the bill are the President of the Republic and one fourth of the members of the Parliament. It is usually understood that the President symbolizes the unity of the nation. The working out of the latter may be left to a larger scope of experts, both of political forces in the State and independent ones. Such expert groups on different social areas have already been set up at the presidency. Broad publicity and transparency should obviously be needed on the working out of this project. It could be possible that before the legislative bill has been brought before Parliament it can be published for public discussion which may lead to corrections until the final version is reached. Within this highly responsible task, the President of the Republic may conduct periodic consultations with the leading bodies of the political parties aiming at reaching a political consensus within the Parliament on the constitutional amendment(s) needed. Generally, the role of the Head of the State in this process would be that of a political arbitrator and a go-between both for the Parliament and the government and for the political elite and the society as a whole. The President shall pass the final draft bill in the National Assembly and shall trigger the procedure under Chapter IX of the Constitution.

Another, more complicated way of adopting amendments to the Constitution is possible. All the activity can be performed by the National Assembly. By a decision of the Parliament a special ad hoc commission can be set up for preparing the bill. Only lawyers can be members to that commission and membership is on the principle of proportional representation of parliamentary political parties. The parliamentary commission would work out and deliberate the constitutional amendments in open meetings. The commission, on the basis of a consensus among its members, would present the bill to the members of the Parliament, the latter expressing their support by signing it. The signatures of one fourth of the deputies shall be sufficient for the bill to be passed in the National Assembly (Art. 154, sect. 1). From this moment on the procedure under Chapter IX of the Constitution is in motion.

The constitutional amendment bill passed in the National Assembly goes through three readings with three votes under the procedure of Article 155, section 1 or section 2 of the Basic Law. The Parliament may establish a special commission for a preliminary deliberation on the bill when the latter has been passed in by the President of the Republic. In that case the President of the National Assembly may alternatively allocate the bill to the standing commission on legal issues. Whenever the bill has been passed in by one fourth of the deputies it is usually worked on by the parliamentary commission which has elaborated it.

The Parliament shall deliberate and vote on the bill on the first reading the report of the commission in principle having been heard. On the first voting the bill shall be deliberated in plenary session. The members of the Parliament shall express their opinion on the purpose of and the fundamental matters underlying the constitutional amendment.

Following the first reading the deputies may submit proposals concerning amendments. They shall be submitted through the president of the relevant parliamentary commission. The commission shall pass a reasoned report in the National Assembly containing the submitted written suggestions of the deputies together with the statement of the commission thereon as well as the suggestions of the commission.

The National Assembly shall deliberate and vote on the legislative bill on the second reading text by text. On this reading only the deputies' suggestions submitted in writing and passed in after the first reading as well as the suggestions of the commission incorporated in its report shall be deliberated on. Suggestions contravening the principles of the bill passed on the first reading shall not be subject to deliberation.

On the third reading of the legislative bill on the amendment of the Constitution the former shall be voted on provisionally a reasonable time having been left for the deputies to determine their final will. At the end of the third reading the bill shall be considered to be passed. The final text shall be signed by the president of the parliament and shall be promulgated within seven days in the Official Gazette. It is usual that the law comes into force on the day of its promulgation.

It is necessary that before the passing of the ratification bill in the Parliament the President of the Republic shall refer to the Constitutional Court a claim for a judgment on the compliance of the agreement with the already amended constitution (Art. 149, sect. 1, count 4 of the Constitution). It is usual for the Constitutional Court to constitute as interested parties on that constitutional case the President, the Government and the Parliament. Where the Constitutional Court rules by decision that there is compliance with the basic law the Council of Ministers shall pass in the Parliament the draft bill on the ratification of the agreement. From this point on the ordinary legislative procedure under the Rules of Procedure of the Parliament shall be followed. After the ratification law is passed it shall be promulgated by the President and by its entering into force the membership agreement shall effect its legal consequences.

The complicated procedure related to the accession agreement to the European Union requires from the political elite of this country as well as from the State institutions a quick generating of consensuses based on modern political discourse.

The content and phrasing of the amendments to the Constitution of the Republic of Bulgaria can only be formulated at present because they are a changing variable, depending on the future content of the *acquis communautaire*[8] at the moment of the accession of Bulgaria to the EU. A paradigm could be constructed stating that if the content of the Constitution being a constant dimension during the coming decades, of which one cannot be certain, the range of the amendments to the Bulgarian Constitution will be predetermined by the current evolutionary degree of the European Union at the time of Bulgaria's accession. The paradigm is becoming more and more complicated on the basis of two variable parameters which basically influence the content of the *acquis communautaire:* taking into account the impossibility of applying the formula of the growth of the Constitution (implicit virtual interpretation) to the European constitutions including the Bulgarian one, which is an impermissible heresy in the continental legal family. The second variable parameter is the condition of the European Union Constitutional order at the time of the accession which will probably enlarge the range of necessary amendments to the Constitution of Bulgaria during the coming decade.

---

[8] See, Carlo Curty Gialdino, Some Reflections on *Acquis Communautaire*, CMLR, 32, 1995, pp. 1089-1121.

CONSTITUTIONAL PROBLEMS OF ACCESSION IN ROMANIA*

Aurel Ciobanu-Dordea**

Firstly, I wish to say that I am speaking to you as the specialist, a scholar who is teaching international law at the University of Bucharest. From the official capacity that I act in, I would like to introduce you to the form and the contents of the amendments that need to be made to the constitution of Romania in the light of the accession to the EU.

Secondly, I have to say that the conference is scheduled at a time when a fierce debate is occurring in Romania. In this debate the politicians discuss the possible modifications to the constitution to be made in the light of the accession. In addition to this political turmoil, the general presidential elections are due in two months from now.

I find this coincidence to be significant for a number of reasons:

a) Our constitution provides for equal powers and identical composition of the two chambers of parliament. This has been subject to considerable criticism, which might or should in the end lead to the change facilitating the transposition of the *acquis* into our domestic legal order. In order to achieve this change, the parliament of Romania must be able to work more effectively.

b) The Constitutional assembly, which brought the constitution into existence in 1991, expressed the intention to make the basic law of the land 'carved in stone'. The result is that finally the constitution can be changed only when a rather difficult procedure is followed.

From my position I cannot judge how intelligent this solution was.

However, if the on-going constitutional debate is to result in a referendum amending the constitution, then this has to be seen as the opportunity to make the changes required by the accession to the EU.

The opportunity will be hard to find, if the procedure for the amendment is not made more flexible. Article 147 para. 3 provides that *any revision shall be final after approval by national referendum.*

---

* Summary report of the presentation held at the Conference.

** Assistant-Professor, University of Bucharest, Chief-Negotiator (September 2000) for Romania's Accession, Ministry of Foreign Affairs of Romania.

A.E. Kellermann et al. (Eds.), EU Enlargement: The Constitutional Impact at EU and National Level

Without being aware of this fact, the parliament has adopted the **Law on the Organisation of Referendums,** which again makes the referendum obligatory for accession to the EU.

This law makes a referendum obligatory in case more powers are delegated to EU institutions than to domestic institutions. The revision of the Constitution will be more difficult to make after Romania joins the EU.

The Europe Agreement signed in 1993 furthers the requirement for amending the constitution. By the Europe Agreement Romania was granted a 10 year transitional period to make the acquisition of land available to nationals of EU member States. Problems might arise here, since the current constitution prohibits the acquisition of land by foreigners.

The Constitution of Romania was adopted in 1991 after a referendum took place. It was inspired by the French, Spanish and Italian examples of constitutional systems concerning the limitation of sovereignty. However, the new formula was a mixed one, too rigid in many ways and containing considerable lacunae.

As far as the reception of international conventions is concerned, the treaties ratified by parliament become internalised in the domestic legal order. It was not made explicit that they rank higher than the domestic legislation. However, doctrine has consistently stressed that the reception clause in international treaties shall be interpreted as an acknowledgement of the supremacy of international law over domestic law.

It would be unthinkable to amend treaties through subsequent domestic legislation. The Constitutional Court has not clarified this point yet, so one is not sure what would happen if international treaties are contrary to constitutional provisions. The constitutional provision on the ownership of land can also serve as an example of uncertainty. It is doubtful that the Constitutional Court would have ventured to solve the issue in 1993 as at that time it had shown proof of judicial complacency.

Regarding international treaties, the constitution also provides in Article 20 for the basic principle of precedence of international treaties on human rights over national law:

> Constitutional provisions concerning the citizens' rights and liberties shall be interpreted and enforced in conformity with the Universal Declaration of Human Rights with the cognisance to other treaties Romania is party to. Where inconsistencies exist between the treaties on human rights and the internal laws, the international regulations shall take precedence.

The provisions of the Universal Declaration and of the European Convention on Human Rights (ECHR) serve as a basis for the Constitutional Court to declare the unconstitutionality of certain domestic laws.

Since 1997, this has been the case with a number of provisions of certain economic laws and of the Code of Criminal Procedure that were declared unconstitutional. The last judgments were generally welcomed by legal circles in Romania as bringing conformity with the ECHR, with the exception of a few ordinary judges who thought that difficulties may arise from the absence of the constitutional provisions as the basis for such judgment.

Another issue related to the provision of Article 20 of the constitution is linked to the supremacy and direct affect of the EU *acquis*. The provision will need an amendment with regards to the extension of the treaties covered by this article to the whole of the *acquis*. The primacy of the EU *acquis* in case of conflicts with the domestic legislation will have to be made more explicit and clear.

Article 58 para. 1, which says that *the parliament of Romania is the single legislative authority of the country*, will also require further amendments.

The issue of equality of rights between nationals of Romania and nationals of EU member States could also receive attention. So far the constitution provides in Article 18 that *foreign nationals enjoy the protection of persons and assets as warranted by the constitution and other laws.* Three particular points will come into question under this general label.

LAND OWNERSHIP

Today the climate in Romania is more relaxed when compared to 1991when the provision on the prohibition of land ownership by foreigners was enacted.

Later, the parliament laid down the general rules for setting up of foreign companies in the country. In 1997, the Constitutional Court was called upon to check the constitutionality of this law. The court rejected the challenge issued.

This could have been viewed by many as a progressive step towards a more relaxed view on land ownership. Perhaps that constitutional amendment in this way would be possible.

RIGHT TO VOTE AND TO BE ELECTED IN LOCAL ELECTIONS

The right to vote and run for local office will require an amendment of Articles 34 and 35 of the Constitution as well as a lifting of the ban on the access of nationals of EU member States to public offices.

EXTRADITION OF ROMANIAN NATIONALS

The Constitution contains a general prohibition of extradition in Article 19 para. 1. The Schengen *acquis* requires that member States allow for the extradition of their own nationals, but for the moment the accession to this convention is not compulsory for all member States and candidate countries.

However, this has been added to the official listing of the *acquis* that, according to the Amsterdam Treaty, require ratifications by the member States in order to create 'an area of freedom, security and justice.' Consequently, there is a need for mutual confidence between the domestic judicial systems, which imposes high standards of credibility and consistency of law enforcement of member States and candidate states including Romania in particular.

ADDENDUM
by
Alfred E. Kellermann

According to the Government Programme for the period 2001-2004, accepted by the Parliament by passing a vote of confidence in the Government by the Chamber of Deputies and the Senate in the joint sitting on December 28, 2000, was elaborated 'The Legislative Programme of the Romanian Government for 2001-2004 – Main Regulations' (Bucharest 2001).

The programme provides, by draft laws per fields of activity, the object of the regulation, the initiators and the terms for the ministries to submit the respective drafts to the Government.

The first field of activity mentioned under I is **Revision of the Constitution.** The object of the regulation – see point 4 – is achieving the compatibility of certain constitutional provisions with the exigencies of the process of Romania's integration into the European Union.

CONSTITUTIONAL QUESTIONS OF THE PREPARATION OF HUNGARY TO ACCESSION TO THE EUROPEAN UNION*

Attila Harmathy**

I. PRELIMINARY REMARKS

Hungary was one of the first countries (together with the other 'Visegrád States') of Central and Eastern Europe with which the European Communities and their member States concluded an Association Agreement, the so-called Europe Agreement.[1] The aim of Hungary, as expressed in the Preamble to the Agreement, was accession to the Communities but as the Communities were not willing to make any commitment concerning the accession the conditions of accession were, therefore, not agreed upon.[2] In 1993 the European Council in Copenhagen decided that the associated countries could apply for membership and the conditions were set consequently. The Agreements with Hungary and Poland were signed in December 1991, and entered into force on 1 February 1994. The formal application of Hungary for accession to the Community was presented in March 1994.[3]

The political conditions of the Copenhagen Summit were: achieving stability of institutions guaranteeing democracy, the rule of law, human rights, and respect for and protection of minorities. The conditions can be found in Articles 6 and 49 of the Treaty (as amended in Amsterdam) establishing the European Union. These Articles are of decisive importance from the point of view of the preparation for accession and they are also relevant for constitutional aspects.

In the Preamble to Hungary's Association Agreement reference had been made to the achievements of the new democracy rendering possible the establishment of

---

* The present paper expresses the personal opinion of the author and cannot be understood as representing any kind of official view. The author is grateful to Barna Berke, Vice-President of the Hungarian Competition Office for his assistance.

** Professor, Eötvös University, Budapest; Judge of the Hungarian Constitutional Court; Member of the Hungarian Academy of Sciences, Vice-President of the International Academy of Comparative Law.

[1] See an analysis of the Europe Agreements, M. Marescau, E. Montaguti, The Relations between the European Union and Central and Eastern Europe: A Legal Appraisal, *CMLRev.* 32 (1995), pp. 1327-1367.

[2] See the papers presented by two Hungarian negotiators: Endre Juhász, Társulási szerződésünk az Európai Közösségekkel és azok tagállamaival, János Martonyi, Csatlakozásunk az Európai Közösséghez, both published in: *Európajogi tanulmányok*, ed. Ferenc Mádl, Budapest 1993, pp. 130-131, pp. 166-167.

[3] Mihály Ficsor, Jogharmonizáció a Fehér Könyv elõtt és után, *Jogtudományi Közlöny* 1995, p. 647.

A.E. Kellermann et al. (Eds.), EU Enlargement: The Constitutional Impact at EU and National Level

relations of a new quality and also to the mutual commitment to the multiparty democratic system based on the rule of law, guaranteeing human rights and fundamental freedoms, a market economy and social justice.

In 1998 in Luxembourg the European Council decided that the Commission would make regular reports to the Council reviewing the progress of each Central and East European candidate State towards accession in the light of the Copenhagen criteria and evaluating the candidate States' ability to meet the economic criteria and fulfil the obligations deriving from accession. It has been stated in both the first and second Regular Report that Hungary fulfils the Copenhagen political criteria, the only matters still needing attention being the situation of the Roma and the fight against corruption. It has been noted also that Hungary had ratified all the most important international human rights conventions including the European Convention for the Protection of Human Rights and Fundamental Freedoms, and its various protocols.

The accession to the European Union also raises a series of important questions in the field of Constitutional Law. These questions are to be studied in the pre-accession period taking into consideration both the experiences of other countries and the Hungarian situation.

II. COMPARATIVE ASPECTS

Although there were important differences in the accession of different countries to the European Union one can learn much from the experiences of these countries. Furthermore, there are some constitutional problems which are not connected with accession but are of a general character. These general problems of the relationship between national Constitutional Law and European Law are to be studied on the basis of the legal theory of the member States.

1. **Accession and amendment of the Constitution**

In this short paper reference is made only to Austria as that country joined the Union only recently and, in addition, there are several similar features in the legal systems of Austria and Hungary. Austria's accession to the EU took place in 1994. Prior to the ratification of the Treaty on accession some basic rules of the Constitution were modified. Those rules concerned the republican or democratic principles (in connection with the adoption of legal rules), the principle of the rule of law as enshrined in the Austrian Constitution (administration of justice) and the federal principle. New rules were enacted which ensured Parliament and the local authorities having a part in the decision-making on the position of the representatives of Austria in the European law-making process.[4]

---

[4] P. Fischer, A. Lengauer, The adaptation of the Austrian legal system following EU membership, *CMLRev.* 37 (2000), pp. 764-765.

The amendment of the Constitution has meant a revision of basic principles. Even since the amendment of the Constitution the problem has been discussed what should happen if EU rules are found to be in conflict with the basic principles of the Austrian fundamental constitutional rules and the prevailing position seems to be that these EU rules cannot be considered as valid rules.[5] As it is clear from the sketchy treatment of the problem it is not restricted to the period of accession. The question can be mentioned here, however, as the solution can be worked out in connection with the amendment of the Constitution because of the accession.

In some countries (e.g., Germany and France) a rule was incorporated into the Constitution on European integration, on the partial transfer of sovereignty. According to some authors this solution can be a model providing an answer to the special question separating it from the general problems of the relationship between national legal rules and rules of international law.[6] This proposition could be taken into consideration if an amendment of the Constitution were to be drafted in connection with the accession.

On the basis of the experience of other countries the necessity of amending the Hungarian Constitution in connection with accession to the European Union is to be studied seriously.

2. Relationship between national constitutional laws and the law of the European Union

One of the important tasks in the preparation for the accession is the working out of a proper solution which will ensure the unproblematic relationship between the national constitutional law and the law of the European Union. When one sets oneself the task of finding the solution under the conditions of the national legal system a comparative study is inevitable.

a) The President of the European Court of Justice has recently summarised the opinion of the Court as elaborated out in its decisions.[7] The Court expressed the view already in 1963 that Community law constitutes a new legal order addressed not only to the states but to the people and confers rights on individuals having thus a direct effect without the need for implementing legislation.[8] In 1964 the Court stated that Community law has precedence over national law.[9] The European legal order has its

---

5 S.L. Frank, Altes und Neues zum Vorrang des Gemeinschaftsrechts vor staatlichem Recht, *Zeitschrift für öffentliches Recht* 55 (2000), p. 18.

6 J. Gerkrath, *L'émergence d'un droit constitutionnel pour l'Europe*, Bruxelles 1997, p. 279, see also I. Pernice, Multilevel Constitutionalism and the Treaty of Amsterdam: European constitution-making revisited? *CMLRev.* 36 (1999), p. 713, p. 716.

7 G.C.R. Iglesias, Gedanken zum Entstehen einer Europäischen Rechtsordnung, *Neue Juristische Wochenschrift* 1999, pp. 1-9.

8 Case 26/92 *Van Gend en Loos* v. *Nederlandse Administratie der Belastingen* [1963] ECR 3.

9 Case 6/64 *Costa* v. *ENEL* [1964] ECR 585.

roots in the international treaties but it is, at the same time, parallel to the national legal systems. It embodies common elements of the national legal systems as well as supranational law, namely, Community law and the European Convention for the Protection of Human Rights and Fundamental Freedoms. In 1970 it was declared that fundamental human rights are inspired by the constitutional traditions common to the member States.[10] These rights form an integral part of the general principles of law and besides the common constitutional traditions, guidelines to be followed within the framework of the Community law are supplied by international treaties for the protection of human rights on which the member States have collaborated.[11] A great part of the general principles are to be considered as mandatory rules having a constitutional character. The President of the ECJ has underlined the effect of directives on candidate countries of accession and later on referred to the possible role of general principles to be taken into consideration as standards in the process of the voluntary reception of Community law.[12]

b) The questions raised above have been discussed in the abundant legal literature for several years. Here I restrict myself to a few remarks which seem to be of relevance for the topic of this paper. At the beginning the principle of the supremacy of EC law over national rules was not accepted easily; agricultural regulations were felt to be contrary to national constitutional rules on fundamental rights but decisions of the European Court of Justice could surmount the difficulties.[13] However, for several years the principle seems to have been recognised by the member States.[14]

The scope of the recognition of the supremacy of EC law is, however, not clear and has led to controversies. The problems are formulated in different contexts. For some years there has been a discussion on the constitution of the EU and it has been observed that there are signals in the economic and political reality indicating that the concept of the existence of a Community constitution is not universally accepted without reservations. It means that there are different opinions on the relationship between Community law and the constitutions of the member States.[15]

In French legal literature one can find the expressions *désordre normatif*, *labyrinthe décisionnel*, and *échec de la hiérarchie des actes communautaires* and the views concerning these phenomena are connected with the relationship between EU

---

[10] Case 11/70 *Internationale Handelsgesellschaft* v. *Einfuhr und Vorratsstelle Getreide* [1970] p. 1125.

[11] Case 4/73 *Nold* v. *Commission* [1974] ECR 491.

[12] Iglesias, supra, n. 7, p. 4, p. 9.

[13] S.E. Finer, V. Bogdanor, B. Rudden, *Comparing Constitutions*, Oxford-New York, 1995, p. 38.

[14] B. de Witte, International Agreement or European Constitution, in: *Reforming the Treaty on European Union*, ed. J.A. Winter, D.M. Curtin, A.E. Kellermann, B. de Witte, The Hague-Boston-London, 1996, p. 13.

[15] J. Schwarze, Concept and Perspectives of European Community Law, *European Public Law*, 5 (1999), p. 236, p. 238.

law and the national legal systems.[16] In view of the difficulties it has been suggested that it would be better not to give a full list of sources of law in constitutions based on the concept of nation-state but to establish an open and flexible system of the sources of law ensuring the precedence of constitutional rules over others and referring to general principles of law in the part on international rules.[17]

In different member States the main ideas of constitutional law seem to be in conflict with the acceptance of the supremacy of Community constitutional rules without reservation (if the existence of a European constitution is accepted).[18] Although it is not probable, theoretically it is possible that national Constitutional Courts or institutions having an equivalent competence will reject the supremacy of Community law and will not apply Community rules whenever they become dissatisfied with the protection of human rights in the Community legal order and there are such signs in Germany, Italy, Denmark, and Greece.[19]

According to a more optimistic understanding of the problems, the constitutional rules (considering German law) do not constitute obstacles to integration and in its framework to the acceptance of the supremacy of Community rules, only the too ambitious interpretation of the national Constitution can cause difficulties.[20]

c) The analysis of the practice of the member States has shown that the States considered it necessary to ratify the Treaty of Maastricht and that they were not of the opinion that the Treaty would have direct effect without ratification. The Treaty itself expressly provided for ratification in case of any amendment including admission of new States 'the amendments shall enter into force after being ratified by all member States in accordance with their respective constitutional requirements'[21] and the agreement on conditions of admission and the adjustments to the Treaties on which the Union is founded 'shall be submitted for ratification by all the contracting States in accordance with their respective constitutional requirements'.[22]

The position of the member States was reflected also in the fact that the constitution was amended in Germany, Ireland, and Portugal to bring about accordance with the Treaty, and France and Spain joined their ranks after their Constitutional Courts had declared the Treaty to be incompatible with the constitution as it stood.[23]

---

16 H. Gaudin, Amsterdam: l'échec de la hiérarchie des normes? *Revue Trimestrielle de Droit Européen* 35 (1999), pp. 1-3 with references.

17 P. Häberle, Pluralismus der Rechtsquellen in Europa – nach Maastricht, *Jahrbuch des Öffentlichen Rechts der Gegenwart* N.F. Bd. 47, Tübingen (1999), pp. 96-97.

18 W. Hertel, Die Normativität der Staatsverfassung und einer Europäischen Verfassung, *Jahrbuch des Öffentlichen Rechts der Gegenwart* N.F. Bd. 48, Tübingen (2000), pp. 240-242.

19 S. Weatherill, P. Beaumont, *EU Law*, London 1999, 3rd edn., p. 452.

20 J. Schwarze, Ist das Grundgesetz ein Hindernis auf dem Weg nach Europa? *Juristen Zeitung* 54 (1999), p. 640.

21 Art. 48(3).

22 Art. 49(2).

23 B. de Witte, supra, n. 14, p. 13.

In the relationship between Community law and national laws the basis is that the Community has a limited special authorisation.[24] The question is whether there is a general agreement as to the extent of such authorisation, and the sovereignty conferred on the Community is limited by the basic principles of national identity, and fundamental rights and freedoms.[25] Although the position of the German Constitutional Court concerning the limits of the transferred sovereignty, and of Community legislation, is debated, eminent German constitutional lawyers are of the opinion that it is the nature of the European Community to handle a part of the tasks of the member States in common, the States exercising, to this extent, their sovereignty jointly, and 'European constitutional case law in other member States thus similarly confirms that it is the respective member State's constitution that is the basis of empowerment to collaborate in European integration, but sets justiciable bounds to this collaboration for primary and secondary Community law'.[26] The text of Article 23(1) of the *Grundgesetz*, as amended in 1992, seems to have formulated the restrictions in accordance with the view of the Constitutional Court.[27]

3. **General principles of law**

The general principles of law and common constitutional traditions have an important role in Community law particularly from the point of view of the protection of human rights. This topic seems to be important also in connection with the preparation for accession. In the vast field of questions concerned it is not easy to find clear answers. Here reference is made only to some of the problems.

One of the problems of an outsider is to define the meaning of general principles of law. The use of the term general principles has been particularly criticised in the French legal literature on the grounds that the term had been unknown prior to 1970, it is vague, uncertain, having different notions in different Conventions and other legal texts, its understanding is different in time, its connection with fundamental rights is different (and uncertain) depending on which country is taken as a basis.[28]

It is not easy to detect the exact meaning of common constitutional traditions either. As van Caenegem put it, in many countries the text of the Constitution remained unchanged while political institutions assumed different roles and the

---

[24] U. Everling, Comments on the article by B. de Witte, in: *Reforming the Treaty on European Union,* supra, n. 14, pp. 19-20.

[25] Pernice, supra, n. 6, p. 713.

[26] Paul Kirchhof, The Balance of Powers between National and European Institutions, *European Law Journal* 5 (1999), p. 241, see also p. 226.

[27] H.-J. Papier, Die Entwicklung des Verfassungsrechts seit der Einigung und seit Maastricht, *Neue Juristische Wochenschrift* 50 (1997), pp. 2843-2844.

[28] É. Picard, L'émergence des droits fondamentaux en France, *L'Actualité Juridique, Droit Administratif,* 1998, juillet-août, spécial 6, 10, 16; B. Genevois, Principes fondamentaux, principes généraux, *Revue française de droit administratif* 14 (1998), p. 478; F. Moderne, Actualité des principes généraux du droit, *Revue française de droit administratif* 14 (1998), p. 518; W. Pauly, Strukturfragen des unionsrechtlichen Grundrechtsschutzes, *Europarecht* 1998, pp. 253-254.

liberal welfare state is a mixed product of free market and private enterprise checked by state intervention and trade union influence in uncertain balance following the ups and downs of party politics.[29]

A critical point of the whole problem seems to be the role of the state. Under existing conditions the State cannot ignore asserted social problems and leave them to self-regulating forces within society. At the European level the consequence is a politicisation of Community law also in constitutional aspects. It has been pointed out that two approaches to integration have influenced the development of a European economic constitution right from the very beginning and they continue to be present. They reflect the two opposing views of the market system: one is integration by intervention, the other is integration by framework activities (based on the system of competition). Legal structures cannot be protected from the contradictory political tendencies.[30] Thus it is understandable that the European Union seems to lack a coherent policy of protecting human rights.[31] The uncertain position is particularly observable in connection with economic, social, and cultural rights and the collective rights of the third generation of human rights, where some member States have not ratified some international conventions but these are already requirements of the Union towards candidate countries of accession.[32]

The above tendencies, observable on the basis of a superficial, sketchy survey of a small part of the huge literature, will help one to understand the unease felt by lawyers of a candidate country trying to assist the constitutional development of the country. Constitutional development is itself a complicated process, particularly understanding it in the way that Philip Allott described it, taking place at the level of ideas, theories, at the level of political, social, economic events, and at the level of law. If one tries, in Allott's words,[33] to avoid disunifying Europe, by the creation of sub-unions, and to help in creating a coherent Europe, he needs a clear understanding of the situation.

---

[29] R.C. van Caenegem, *An Historical Introduction to Western Constitutional Law*, Cambridge 1995, p. 245.

[30] M.E. Streit, W. Mussler, The Economic Constitution of the European Community: From 'Rome' to 'Maastricht', *European Law Journal* 1 (1995), pp. 11-12; Ch. Joerges, European Economic Law, the Nation-State and the Maastricht Treaty, in: *Europe after Maastricht, An ever closer union*, ed. Renaud Dehousse, München 1994, p. 48.

[31] Ph. Alston and J.H.H. Weiler, An 'ever closer union' in need of a human rights policy: The European Union and human rights.in: *The EU and Human Rights*, ed. Ph. Alston, with the assistance of M. Bustelo and J. Heenan, Oxford-New York, 1999, p. 6.

[32] M. Nowak, Human rights 'conditionality' in relation to entry to, and full participation in the EU, in: *The EU and Human Rights*, supra, n. 31, p. 693.

[33] Ph. Allott, The crisis of European constitutionalism: reflections on the revolution in Europe, *CMLRev.* 34 (1997), pp. 486-487 and p. 476.

III. ON THE HUNGARIAN SITUATION

1. General remarks

In Hungary economic conditions have been in the forefront in connection with accession. Although the framework of the transition from a planned economy to a market economy were established at a relatively early date after the political changes (Hungary had started the transformation of the economic system prior to the changes), so that the monopoly of foreign trade was abolished in 1990 and privatisation has proceeded fast, it was evident that the structure of the economy would not soon reach the level of the member States.[34]

Pursuant to the Association Agreement detailed programmes of approximation of Hungarian law to Community law have been worked out and their realisation is proceeding. The process of approximation is complicated and covers a vast domain of legislative activities. It has been noted that the accession of Central and East European countries has become much more complex a process than it used to be because of the establishment of the Union and of the enlarged scope of the Communities' activities, and complications are aggregated with problems of the readiness of the Union to absorb the new members.[35] Other kind of problems are faced because of the fact that the harmonisation of law has been carried on mostly with regulations and directives and less attention has been paid to other parts of Community law.[36] It has been observed that as in the Central and East European countries the constitutional problems of European integration have not been dealt with in the constitution, the sovereignty regained is very much appreciated.[37] This observation is also correct in the case of Hungary.

2. Relevant constitutional rules

The following rules of the Constitution have particular importance from the point of view of the present paper:

---

[34] See relevant chapters in *Introduction to Hungarian Law*, ed. A. Harmathy, The Hague-London-Boston, 1998, F. Mádl, *Állam és gazdaság*, Budapest 1997, pp. 39 et seq., F. Mádl, L. Vékás, *Nemzetközi magánjog és nemzetközi gazdasági kapcsolatok joga*, Budapest 1997, pp. 206-207, J. Martonyi, Az Európai Közösség külkapcsolatai, in: Az Európai Közösség külkereskedelmi joga, Budapest 1994, II, pp. 236-237.

[35] Marescau, Montaguti, supra, n. 1, p. 1337.

[36] L. Kecskés, EK jog és jogharmonizáció, Budapest 1995, p. 310.

[37] M. Wyrzykowski, The Constitutions of the Eastern European Countries in the Structure of European Constitutionalism, in: *L'espace constitutionnel européen*, ed. R. Bieber, P. Widmer, Zürich 1995, p. 161; Z. Kedzia, Europäische Integration und nationales Verfassungsrecht der mit der Europäischen Union assoziierten Länder Mitteleuropas, in: *Europäische Integration und nationales Verfassungsrecht*, U. Battis, D. Th. Tsatos, D. Stefanou (Hrsg.) Baden-Baden 1995, p. 551, p. 565.

The Constitution[38] declares that Hungary is an independent, democratic state under the rule of law and all powers are vested in the people who exercise sovereignty through elected representatives and directly.[39] The supreme body of state authority and representation of the people is the Parliament. Exercising rights deriving from sovereignty the Parliament ensures the constitutional order and defines the organisation, orientation, and conditions of government. Among other activities within its sphere of authority the Parliament enacts the constitution and passes statutes.[40] The Constitution can be amended by the Parliament but a majority of two-thirds of the votes is required.[41]

Any question, except for those enumerated in Paragraph (5) Article 28/C, falling within the competence of the Parliament may be the subject of a national referendum.[42] A national referendum may not be held, inter alia, on the obligations arising from international treaties in force and on the content of the laws containing those obligations, nor, furthermore, on the provisions of the Constitution relating to a national referendum.[43]

Voters exercise local government through the representative body elected by them and by way of a local referendum.[44] Those entitled to vote are adult Hungarian citizens and immigrants residing in the territory of the Republic of Hungary.[45]

The Republic of Hungary recognises the inviolable and inalienable fundamental rights of man. Rules pertaining to fundamental rights shall be determined by statute, which, however, may not limit the essential content of any fundamental right. The exercise of the fundamental rights enshrined in specified Articles of the Constitution may not be suspended or restricted even in a state of national crisis, state of emergency, or state of danger.[46] Chapter XII on fundamental rights and duties contains rules not only on first generation human rights but also on economic, social and cultural rights. Rights of national and ethnic minorities are also protected.[47]

The constitutionality of laws is reviewed by the Constitutional Court. The Constitutional Court annuls any statute and other legal norms that it finds to be unconstitutional.[48]

Justice is administered by the Supreme Court and by the specified different kinds of courts. The Supreme Court ensures uniformity in the application of the law by the

---

[38] Act XX of 1949 revised and restated by Act XXXI of 1989 amended several times since 1989.
[39] Art. 2.
[40] Art. 19.
[41] Para. (3) Art. 28.
[42] Art. 28/B.
[43] Points (b) and (c) para. (5) Article 28/C.
[44] Art. 44.
[45] Art. 70.
[46] Art. 8.
[47] Art. 68.
[48] Art. 32/A.

courts; its resolutions on uniformity in the application of law are binding on the courts.[49]

The legal system of the Republic of Hungary accepts the generally recognised rules of international law, and shall further ensure harmony between domestic law and the obligations assumed under international law.[50]

3. Interpretation of the rules

At the time of the political changes no new Constitution was enacted but the Constitution of 1949 was amended in a fundamental way and it has also since been amended several times. Because of this situation, and also partly for other reasons, the Constitutional Court has played a particularly important role. The aim of the Court has been to develop the Constitution and its amendments into a coherent system and to join the standards of constitutionality common in developed democracies. In this respect, comparative law has been of significance. Decisions of the European Court of Justice have been studied and quoted, and the German influence, traditional in the Hungarian development, can be observed.[51]

In connection with the relationship between international law and national law the dualist approach has been prevalent.[52] In the Constitution there is no rule directly concerning the question. The only provision on international law is paragraph (1) of Article 7 (quoted above at the end of point 2). The meaning of the rule has been interpreted in some decisions of the Constitutional Court. The questions decided were also connected with the rules of Act XXXII of 1989 on the Constitutional Court. The Court's competence comprises both the *ex post* and *ex ante* review of legal rules. However, in the case of international treaties the rules are different. Prior to ratification of a treaty review may be initiated only by the Parliament, the President or the Government,[53] while there is no special rule on the review of the constitutionality of an international treaty after it has been promulgated by a legal act. The Court has stated that there is no constitutional basis under which to deal with a law promulgating a treaty differently from any other legal rule. If the Court declares a legal rule of the domestic law to be unconstitutional, it has no effect on the obligation assumed by the State under international law. Following upon such a decision the legislature is required – if necessary, by amendment of the Constitution – to achieve the harmony of domestic law and the obligations assumed under international law. Pending this process, the Constitutional Court may suspend its proceedings concern-

---

[49] Arts. 45, 47.

[50] Para. (1) Art 7.

[51] L. Sólyom, Introduction to the Decisions of the Constitutional Court of the Reublic of Hungary, in: *Constitutional Judiciary in a New Democracy, The Hungarian Constitutional Court*, ed. L. Sólyom, G. Brunner, Ann Arbor 1999, pp. 4-5.

[52] See a survey of different views L. Bodnár, *A nemzetközi szerzõdések és az állam*, Budapest 1987, pp. 28-52.

[53] Para. (1) Art. 36.

ing the determination of the date of annulment of the unconstitutional legal rule for a reasonable time.[54] In its reasonings the Court has referred to different decisions of the German Constitutional Court, including the Maastricht judgment, mentioning that, according to the German Constitutional Court, the task of protecting the Constitution cannot be renounced and this principle is also to be applied to the Treaty on European Union.

Another decision of the Court concerned the Europe Agreement promulgated by Act I of 1994.[55] In this case a rather complicated system of regulation was reviewed. Under Art. 62(2) of the Europe Agreement specified conduct was to be dealt with by the Hungarian authorities in accordance with criteria deriving from the application of Articles 85, 86, and 92 of the Treaty establishing the European Community. The rules of implementation were worked out by the Association Council and these rules were promulgated as an annex to a Government Decree. Under the rules of implementation the specified Hungarian authority was to apply in full the principles contained in the Communities' block exemption regulations in force. The Decision set the constitutional requirement not to apply the criteria referred to by Article 62(2) of the Act promulgating the Europe Agreement and declared the specified rule of the Annex to the Government Decree, promulgating the implementing rules, to be unconstitutional as the Government was not entitled to issue rules on the mandatory application of criteria contained in the Communities' rules, judicial and administrative practice without a previous authorisation given by the Parliament concerning the limitation of Hungary's sovereignty in a procedure provided for in cases of the amendment of the Constitution. The direct effect of foreign (present and future) rules in Hungary, not a member State of the Community, is contrary to Article 2 of the Constitution formulating the principles of the rule of law and sovereignty. These principles are infringed by the regulation under which rules are set and the criteria for their application are determined by bodies not legitimised by the people's sovereignty. The Court suspended the procedure in order to enable the legislator to take the necessary steps.

Paragraph (1) of Article 7 of the Constitution on the acceptance of generally recognised rules of international law and ensuring harmony between domestic law and the obligations assumed under international law has been referred to in court practice several times. There were two decisions of the Constitutional Court which tried to formulate some kind of principle of interpretation. In one of these decisions the Court stated that the provisions of paragraph (1) of Article 7 also means the

---

[54] Decision No. 4/1997. (I. 22.) AB határozat, ABH 1997, p. 41, abridged English text can be found in *Constitutional judiciary ...*, supra, n. 45, pp. 356-363.

[55] Decision No. 30/1998. (VI. 25.) AB határozat, ABH 1998, p. 220, see its discussion: A. Tatham, Constitutional Judiciary in Central Europe and the Europe Agreement: Decicision 30/1998. (VI. 25.) AB of the Hungarian Constitutional Court, *International and Comparative Law Quarterly* 48 (1999), pp. 913-920; J. Volkai, The Application of the Europe Agreement and European Law in Hungary: the Judgment of an Activist Constitutional Court on Activist Notions, Harvard Law School, The Jean Monnet Chair, Working Papers 1999.

obligation of the competent legislative body to issue the legal rules needed for meeting the assumed international obligations.[56] The other decision has stated that the generally recognised rules of international law are parts of the Hungarian legal system without transformation by special legislation as these rules have been transformed by the Constitution.[57] The decision has been criticised.[58]

There are signs of the growing awareness by lawyers of the constitutional problems associated with the accession to the European Union. The increased interest in European integration is manifested by the recommendations of the Congress of the Hungarian Lawyers' Association held in May 2000 containing some points on the preparation for Hungary's accession to the European Union.[59] According to those recommendations the Constitution should be amended thus enabling the transfer of some elements of sovereignty (some legislative and judicial powers) to the European Union, incorporating rules on the election of Hungarian members of the European Parliament and recognising the right of EU citizens, residing in Hungary to participate in the election of local government representatives, regulating the relationship between the Hungarian legal system and the law of the EU on the basis of the direct effect of the latter. It is clear that the solution to be adopted in Hungary has not been worked out yet but the work on it is going on.

---

[56] Decision No. 16/1993. (III. 12.) AB határozat, ABH 1993, p. 143 at p. 154.

[57] Decision No. 50/1993. (X. 13.) AB határozat, ABH 1993, p. 323 at p. 327.

[58] See an overview of the discussion I. Vörös, Az Európai Megállapodás helye a magyar jogrendszerben, *Állam- és Jogtudomány* 39 (1998), pp. 95-100.

[59] Az Ötödik Magyar Jogászgyûlés ajánlásai, *Magyar Jog* 2000, p. 321.

CONSTITUTIONAL ASPECTS OF THE ACCESSION OF THE SLOVAK REPUBLIC TO THE EUROPEAN UNION

Vlasta Kunová *

I have divided my report on the constitutional aspects of the accession of the Slovak Republic to the European Union into two parts.

In the first part, I am going to analyse and comment on the current legislation, in particular the relevant provisions of the Constitution of the Slovak Republic adopted on September 1, 1992.

In the second part, I will make some comments on the latest version of the Members of Parliament's proposal to amend the Slovak Constitution which focuses on the problems concerned. This proposal changes considerably the constitutional basis philosophy for the integration of the Slovak Republic into the EU.

Since no so-called 'integration articles' exist in the Slovak Constitution and the new proposal is only at the stage of the second reading in Parliament, my paper will probably be brief in comparison to the other reports.

I. THE PRESENT SITUATION IN THE LEGAL ORDER

'The Declaration of Sovereignty of the Slovak Republic' promulgated on July 17, 1992 by the National Council of the Slovak Republic, before the adoption of the Slovak Constitution, contains some provisions on the democratic and humanitarian legacy of Europe and the world.

Thus, in the Preamble to the Constitution we can read about the interest of continuous and peaceful cooperation with other democratic countries. These general statements are not, however, reflected in any particular constitutional articles.

The Constitution neither mentions the relations between the Slovak Republic and the European Union, nor does it contain any provisions on the integration of Slovakia into international structures, or economy or defence institutions.

Nevertheless, the Constitution and the other sources of law that I am going to mention later contain some international elements, which could be designated

* Institute of International Relations and Approximation of Law, Comenius University, Faculty of Law, Slovak Republic. Department of European Law, Faculty of Law, UMB Banská Bystrica, Slovak Republic.

A.E. Kellermann et al. (Eds.), EU Enlargement: The Constitutional Impact at EU and National Level

with some invention as a 'constitutional nucleus of the basis for the integration' of the Slovak Republic into the network of international alignments.

The constitutional provisions, which will be the subject of my analysis, are as follows:

- *Article 7 of the Constitution* on the manner of accession of the Slovak Republic into a union with other states and the right of secession from such unions.
- *Article 11 of the Constitution* which formulates the conditions of precedence over national laws of international treaties concerning human rights and freedoms ratified by the Slovak Republic and promulgated under statutory requirements.

Furthermore, there are:

- *Article 86 d)* of the Constitution which provides the National Council of the Slovak Republic with the possibility to grant approval, prior to ratification, to international political treaties, international economic agreements in general and to any international agreements provided their execution requires legislation.
- *Article 86 j)* of the Constitution allows the National Council of the Slovak Republic to declare war in the event of an act of aggression by parties hostile to the Slovak Republic or in the event that the obligations under international joint defence treaties must be fulfilled.
- *Article 102 a)* grants the President of the Slovak Republic the power to negotiate and ratify international agreements.
- *Article 125 e)* of the Constitution states that the Constitutional Court shall have jurisdiction over constitutional conflicts between generally binding rules and international treaties promulgated as fixed by law.
- *Article 144, paragraph 2* states that the courts shall also be bound by international instruments if so provided by the Constitution or the law.

Article 7 of the Constitution consists of only three sentences:

> 'The Slovak Republic may, by its own discretion, enter into a union with other states. The right of secession from such unions shall not be restricted. The decision to enter into a union with other states or to secede therefrom shall be subject to a constitutional statute and subsequent ratification by means of a public referendum.'

This Article has given rise to much controversy in the scholarly community.

Despite the fact that the accession of Slovakia to the EU is not a typical union with other states, we might justify the possible legitimacy of such step via this provision.

Such an interpretation demands not only a retreat from classical definitions of the terms such as state and state union, but at the same time the defenders of the interpretation realise the contradictions and obscurities which may possibly arise from such an extensive interpretation. As we can further observe, the proposal to amend the Constitution considerably broadens Article 7 of the Constitution, thereby determining the so-called *integration situations*.

The accession of the Slovak Republic to the EU is indisputably a contractual relationship, therefore our information on the actual constitutional basis for the integration of Slovakia will comprise the problem of international treaties, their position within the Slovak system of law, characteristics and so on.

As far as the relationship between national and international law is concerned, until the year 1989 the constitutional order applied the principle of precedence of national law over international law. A partial breakthrough in this doctrine was brought about by Constitutional Act No. 23/1991, adopted by the Federal Assembly of the Czech and Slovak Federal Republic, which introduced the Bill of Basic Rights and Freedoms. The text of this Bill provided a basis for Article 11 of the Constitution.

Current constitutional regulation does not contain any provisions on 'general priority' of international instruments and their precedence over national laws.

Article 11 of the Constitution states, that:

> 'International instruments on human rights and freedoms ratified by the Slovak Republic and promulgated under statutory requirements shall take precedence over national laws provided that the international treaties and agreements guarantee greater constitutional rights and freedoms.'

Some authors term such a conception a conditional priority, for example J. Klucka in his work International law and the Constitution of Slovak Republic.[1]

The work cited above contains the very interesting idea that Slovak legislation on the relations between international and national law can be characterised as a 'moderate dualistic approach'. I personally would prefer the expression 'partial dualism' or 'semi-dualism'.

With regard to the absence of any general reception clause in the Slovak Constitution, which would *expressis verbis* determine valid international treaties as a part of our system of law, their position therein is determined by Act of Parliament No. 1/1993. Under paragraph 6 of this Act, international treaties belong to the group of legal regulations which are promulgated in the Collection of Laws. The international instruments that are binding for the Slovak Republic, which means the valid agreements, are those:

a) ratified by the President;
b) other instruments if concerning the legal status of natural and legal persons or their justified interests.

---

[1] J. Klučka: International law and the Constitution of the Slovak Republic, Košice 1996.

In connection with the ratification of the Europe Agreement of 1993 establishing an association between the European Communities and their member States and the Slovak Republic, which came into force in 1995, a degree of confusion could be observed when the agreement was published in the Collection of Laws only in the year 1997 under the number 158.

International agreements with the EU should be approved by the Parliament prior to their ratification, as follows from Article 86 d) of the Constitution, which applies to international political treaties, economic treaties in general and any international agreements provided the execution thereof shall require legislation.

The above-mentioned list of international instruments, as stated by Article 86 d) of the Constitution, demands the precise content specification of each agreement and consequent appropriate procedure for its conclusion.

> 'The president shall represent the Slovak Republic in international relations, negotiate and ratify international agreements; he can delegate the power to the Government or, with the consent of the Government, to individual members of the Government or negotiate those international agreements for which no consent by the National Council of the Slovak Republic is required'. (Article 102 a) of the Constitution)

In general, we can qualify Slovak legal regulation of international agreements as rather unclear, too abstract and giving rise to several different interpretations. This is not only caused by the legal basis itself but by the process of succession as well. Under Article 153 of the Constitution, the Slovak Republic shall be the successor to all rights and duties ensuing from international treaties and agreements binding the Czech and Slovak Federal Republic to the extent fixed by a constitutional statute issued in the Czech and Slovak Federal Republic or to the extent specified in an agreement made between the Slovak Republic and the Czech Republic.

The effective law in the Slovak Republic does not enable the courts or other state bodies to decide independently whether there is a conflict between generally binding rules and international instruments. This power is granted to the Constitutional Court only, which under the Article 125 e) 'shall have jurisdiction over constitutional conflicts between generally binding rules and international instruments promulgated as fixed by law'. The Constitutional Court commences proceedings upon a petition submitted by a limited number of persons: not less than one-fifth of all members of the National Council of the Slovak Republic; the President of the Slovak Republic; the Government of the Slovak Republic; any court and the Attorney-General (Art. 130 para. 1).

More precisely the procedural conditions on consistency of laws are fixed in Act of Parliament No. 38/1993, paragraph 37-41.

The task of the courts with a view to our topic is emphasised in the Slovak Constitution, Article 144, paragraph 2, which states: 'Courts shall also be bound by international instruments if so provided by the Constitution or the law'.

The jurisdiction of the Slovak courts comprises such judicial decisions, as supported by international treaties on human rights and freedoms. The courts are aware of the importance of international elements in their jurisdiction. Based on Article 71 of the Europe Agreement, the European Union has prepared training for judges in the area of European law and law approximation.

On the other hand, in its regular reports the European Union criticises the situation in the Slovak judiciary, thereby emphasising the requirement for ensuring the independence of the judiciary and the ability of courts to apply the *acquis communautaire*.

Despite the drawbacks in our Constitution, which does not determine precisely the status of the Slovak Republic within a European and international context, Slovakia has achieved much success in the integration process. Currently, the negotiations on terms for the accession are still continuing, we have concluded eight chapters and the recent European Commission evaluation report of November 1999 was relatively positive. On the basis of the association agreement, jointly created bodies are functioning and we are quite successful in the fulfilment of duties in the area of approximation of law.

It seems that with the exception of the principle *pacta sunt servanda*, which is one of the European legal principles and can be found also in the Vienna Convention on the Law of Treaties, the integration process has its own rules and pragmatic standpoints where competitiveness between the CEECs, joint co-ordination of the activities in the process of integration as well as other phenomena are influencing the dynamic trend of the Slovak integration process.

II. INTEGRATION PROVISIONS IN THE PROPOSAL AMENDMENT OF THE CONSTITUTION OF THE SLOVAK REPUBLIC

Despite the optimistic results that the Slovak Republic has scored in the area of international relations and the gradual improvement of the image of Slovakia on the international scene, the outcome of the present inquiry has shown that it is necessary to amend the Constitution so as to adopt measures to prepare the legal basis for the accession of Slovakia to the European Union. This was performed by a group of Members of Parliament who submitted a proposed amendment to the Constitution on June 14, 2000. The Explanatory Memorandum to the proposal says that

> 'the experience with the Constitution in force up to now has shown, that there are some weak points in adherence to international commitments and in the regulation of the conduct of public administration bodies in carrying out the commitments which they are to ensure.'

The change of philosophy of the Constitution is indicated by *Article 1* of the amendment as proposed underlining that the 'Slovak Republic acknowledges and maintains general rules of international law – international treaties by which it is bound – and its further international commitments.'

The amendment proposed to the Slovak Constitution significantly changes Article 7 so that apart from the possibility of accession of the Slovak Republic to a union with other states and the right of secession from such a union (*Art. 7, para. 1*), it includes an integration standard, according to which the Slovak Republic can, via an international treaty or based on it, transfer a part of its sovereign rights to international organisations of which the Slovak Republic is a member, as fixed by an international treaty. In the event that this organisation issues legally binding acts, these are also directly binding in the Slovak Republic and have precedence over national law (*Art. 7 para. 2* of the proposal).

In the event of the adoption of the Article as proposed, the Constitution of the Slovak Republic would acquire a European standard dimension through declaring its willingness to transfer a part of its sovereign rights to an international organisation.

It is indisputable that the drafters of the amendment proposal had a problem in designing the character and legal identity of the European Communities and the European Union and finally they chose the not very appropriate expression 'international organisation' as the object to which sovereign powers are to be transferred.

The transfer of a part of its sovereign powers is a very significant step for each state. Therefore, the drafters of the proposal have, in *Article 7 paragraph 4,* embodied the requirement for the consent of Parliament prior to the ratification of international treaties, which also include a treaty establishing the membership of the Slovak Republic of an international organisation, as a condition for validity of such agreements. To pass this kind of international agreement, a quorum in the National Council of the Slovak Republic shall consist of a majority of all its members. For an effective resolution, the consent of a 3/5 majority of members present shall be required.

Under A*rticle 7 paragraph 5* of the proposal, the relationship between national and international law is solved through the inclusion of a new principle – international treaties ratified by the Slovak Republic and promulgated under statutory requirements binding for the Slovak Republic, provided their execution does not require new legislation, shall take precedence over national laws.

This provision permits the absence of any particular legislation for the execution of certain international treaties. This is the principle of the self-execution of treaties, which are according to their content directly applicable and have precedence over national law.

Under *Article 125 a)* of the proposal, the Constitutional Court shall have jurisdiction over constitutional conflicts between the Constitution of the Slovak Republic and constitutional laws, on the one hand, and international treaties from which membership of the Slovak Republic in international organisations arises, on the other.

A petition to commence proceedings before the Constitutional Court can be submitted by the President of the Slovak Republic or the Government, before submitting the concluded treaty to parliamentary debate. If the Constitutional Court rules that there is a conflict with the Constitution or other constitutional law, this international instrument can be ratified only after the Constitution or this constitutional law has been amended.

In connection with this, it is necessary to mention *Article 144* of the Parliamentary proposal which would determine the sources of law, binding for courts other than contemporary legislation. These are the Constitution, constitutional law and also self-executing treaties, as specified in Article 7 paragraph 5 of the proposal.

The problems which will come into existence by application of the respective articles, especially after the accession of the Slovak Republic to the European Union, will be connected with the question of character and competence of the European Communities and the European Union as well. These entities are understood in relation to the member States as supranational institutions.

Moreover, it will be necessary to determine the scope of the supranational rights, that will be transferred to the international organisation, by which will be verified the mechanism of their transmission from the conclusion of the international treaty, its ratification, up to the control of their conformity with the Constitution and other constitutional acts as well.

The uncertainties, which are induced by the interpretation of the proposed Constitutional amendment, also reflect the deficiency and chaos of the European legal order. This is probably caused by the fact that we are currently at a stage of radical change in the understanding of the basic principles of international law, such as state sovereignty, law-making sovereignty, etc. and we try to subordinate the new understanding to traditional definitions.

The proposed amendment of the Constitution of the Slovak Republic does not contain any rules by which a referendum upon the admission of the Slovak Republic to the European Union should be announced. Article 93, paragraph 1 of the Constitution of the Slovak Republic states, 'A constitutional statute on the formation of a union with other states or a secession thereof shall be confirmed by a public referendum.' This article also contains rules according to which, 'A referendum may also be used to decide on other crucial issues in the public interest.'

The parliamentary opposition, especially the Slovak National Party and the movement for Democratic Slovakia, require the announcement of a referendum upon the admission of Slovakia into the NATO and the EU.

Given the present situation it would seem to be politically prudent to hold such a public vote upon the admission of the Slovak Republic to the EU.

In conclusion, I would like to outline some trends that will probably appear in the Slovak constitutional development before adopting the legal regulation as proposed. These are as follows:

- The importance of the integration of the Slovak Republic into the European and international structures will be emphasised, and the legislative background for the accession of the Slovak Republic into the European Union will be formulated more clearly.
- The scope of international treaties having precedence over national law will be broadened.
- As a consequence of the rule of precedence of international treaties ratified by the Parliament over national legislation and their direct applicability, similarly as a direct effect of the Acts of the European Union, it will be a change-over from a partial dualistic conception towards monistic tendencies in the relationship between national and international law.
- It will be specified more precisely that courts are bound by self-executing treaties. It is supposed that, as stated in the Explanatory Memorandum to the amendment proposal, in the case of a conflict between an Act of Parliament and a directly applicable treaty ratified by Parliament, the courts will give precedence to this international treaty, which means that they will not apply the Act. A similar situation will occur in the case of conflict between national law and European law.
- The requirement of a 3/5 majority vote to pass the international treaty by which the Slovak Republic is to transfer a part of its sovereign rights to an international organisation, strengthens the position of the legislative body and thereby the democratic elements in the Constitution.
- The amendment of the Slovak Constitution would strengthen the control mechanism over conformity adherence and consistency with international treaties concerning integration by investigating the compliance of such treaty with the Constitution and constitutional law before submitting it to Parliament.

The submitted analysis of the amendment of the Constitution of the Slovak Republic, especially of those paragraphs relevant to the admission of the Slovak Republic to the EU, the mode of overtaking *acquis communautaire* and a possible adoption of this rule by courts of law in the Slovak Republic confirms that after the amended Constitution has been accepted, the legislative basis for the endorsement of these rules will be established.

However, the differences among the deputies of the National Council of the Slovak Republic are culminating now, which threatens to slow down the process of admission. Due to these differences, the moment of acceptance of the amended articles of the Constitution of the Slovak Republic is to be postponed to some future time. It also means that the optimal solution to the issue of constitutional preconditions inevitable for the admission of the Slovak Republic to the EU will be postponed as well.

Finally, let me express my personal conviction that the constitutional basis for the accession of Slovakia to the European Union will demonstrate standard European criteria. Hopefully, the improved legal regulation of the accession of the Slovak Republic to the European Union will be adopted by the end of the year 2000.

CONCLUSION

On February 23, 2001 the National Council of the Slovak Republic passed Constitutional Act No. 460/1992 amending the Slovak Constitution.

The amended Article 7 now provides for the scope of delegation and the rules by which the sovereign powers of the Slovak Republic can be delegated to the European Communities, the precedence of the laws of the European Communities and the European Union, and the method of incorporating the legal measures of the European Union into the laws of the Slovak Republic.

Thus, by an international treaty ratified and promulgated as prescribed by law, or based upon such treaty, the Slovak Republic can partially delegate the exercise of its powers to the European Communities and the European Union. And, under Article 120(2) of the Constitution, any legally binding acts of the European Communities requiring implementation can also be decreed by a governmental action. The Government of the Slovak Republic is empowered to make rules for the implementation of the European Agreement of the Association of the Slovak Republic to the European Union or other international treaties made with the European Communities and the European Union as specified in Article 7(2).

Through the above provisions, the approximation of laws will become more efficient as a result of the simplified legislative process required for the adoption of the legislative enactment in relation to the integration of the Slovak Republic in the European Communities and the European Union.

The final construction of the amended Constitution and its new integration articles have a clear and explicit format, and constructions superior to those contained in the draft of the amendments. Their pluses and minuses, however, will come to light only through their practical applications. At the moment, it is possible to conclude that the Amended Constitution of February 23, 2001 meets the basic requirements for integration of the Slovak Republic into the European Communities or the European Union.

The constitutional amendments were not sustained by the Opposition HZDS (Movement for the Democratic Slovakia) and SNS (Slovak National Party) as they considered them repugnant to the interests of the State.

Of 148 members of parliament present, 90 voted in favour of the amendments, 57 voted against , and one member abstained from voting.

THE IMPACT OF THE EUROPEAN INTEGRATION PROCESS ON THE CONSTITUTION OF LATVIA

Anita Ušacka*

1. THE NATIONAL CONSTITUTION AND ITS DEVELOPMENT

The Satversme (Constitution) of the Republic of Latvia, adopted in 1922, partly renewed in 1990 and fully renewed in 1993 is the Constitution of an independent and democratic state.

In its almost 82 years of existence the State has experienced great and also tragic events: the foundation of the state in 1918, the loss of its independence in 1940 and its restoration in 1990-1991. Joining the European Union will be the fourth biggest event in the history of Latvia and this new status has to be reflected in the Constitution.

When analysing the tendencies exhibited in relation to constitutional development in Latvia, including amendments, one notices several methods of modification of the Constitution.

First of all, small amendments of the Constitution have been accomplished four times. Thus, in 1933 two Articles of the Constitution on voting were been amended.[1]

In 1994 an Article of the Constitution was amended, determining age 18 (instead of the previous 21) as the age whereby the right to the vote is acquired.[2]

In 1996 the Constitution was supplemented with a new Article 85 and, in conformity with it, the Constitutional Court of the Republic of Latvia was established.

Several Articles, referring to the Parliament and the State President, were amended, determining a four-year term of authority (instead of the former three-year term) to the Parliament and the State President, and altering other norms as well.[3] The Article of the Constitution, envisaging that the Cabinet of Ministers

* Assoc. Prof. Ph.D. (Law). Justice of the Constitutional Court of the Republic of Latvia.

[1] The Constitution of the Republic of Latvia, adopted on 15.02.1922. Latvijas Vestnesis, 01.07.1993, No. 43. Arts. 74 and 79.

[2] Ibid., Art.8.

[3] Ibid., Arts. 10, 11, 13, 30, 35, 37, 39 and 45.

A.E. Kellermann et al. (Eds.), EU Enlargement: The Constitutional Impact at EU and National Level

may pass regulations, which have the force of the law, and one of the Articles on courts were amended.[4]

Secondly, the Constitution can be amended with the addition of new chapters. Although already in 1922 the second part of the Constitution on human rights and obligations was elaborated, it did not receive the support of the required Parliament majority. It was only in 1998 that the Constitution was supplemented with a new VIIIth Chapter 'Fundamental Human Rights'. Simultaneously several other Articles of the Constitution were amended.[5]

Thirdly, there is the adoption of constitutional laws. In 1991 the Law 'The Rights and Obligations of a Citizen and a Person'[6] was adopted. Up to 1998 the Constitution had lacked a section on citizens' rights. This Law in point of fact supplemented the Constitution, guaranteeing human rights and fundamental freedoms. Even though this Law did not have the legal status of the Constitutional Law,[7] as it was adopted under the common procedure of passing laws, up to the time of adoption of Chapter VIII of the Constitution 'Fundamental Human Rights', it served as the basic law for the protection of human rights in Latvia. As to Latvia joining the European Union, one of the motions is to adopt a special constitutional law, not amending the basic text of the Constitution. However, the Constitution does not envisage adoption of constitutional laws and thus must the Constitution first of all be amended. There are no traditions of adopting constitutional laws in Latvia.

Fourthly, there is the idea of elaborating a new Constitution.

The adoption of a new Constitution was envisaged in Article 4 of the May 4, 1990 Declaration 'On the Renewal of the Independence of the Republic of Latvia'. Even though the above Article of the Declaration has not been formally repealed, it was never implemented. After the renewal of independence, a new Constitution was not fully elaborated, but the Satversme of 1922 was renewed fully.

Professor of the Latvian University Edgars Melkisis has proposed to adopt a new Constitution in connection with Latvia joining the European Union.[8] There is a view that the Constitution, adopted almost 80 years ago, has not taken into account the dramatic changes in Latvia and therefore it has to be modernised. For example, it lacks a chapter or perhaps even an Article dedicated to local authorities. Joining the European Union would be an appropriate occasion for adopting a

---

[4] Ibid., Arts. 81 and 84.

[5] The Constitution. Arts. 4, 77 and 82.

[6] The Constitutional Law 'The Rights and Obligations of a Citizen and a Person', adopted on 10.12.1991, the Bulletin 'Augstakas Padomes un Ministru Padomes Zinotajs', 30.01.1992, No. 4.

[7] Edgars Melkisis, 'Development of Constitutionality in Latvia'. 'Reform of the Satversme in Latvia: for and against'. Riga, 1995.

[8] For this discussion see, 'The Constitution of the Republic of Latvia and EU'. The Law and the Rights. Vol. 2, No. 6, June, 2000. (This and the following articles are available in Latvian.)

new constitution. However, the idea of adopting a new constitution has not received much support from lawyers.

Even though even recently the issue of the possibility of amending the renewed Constitution (whether it would be permissible) has been discussed, today the above issue is not mentioned any more. The experience of the development of the Constitution proves that the endeavour of retaining the original text of the Constitution to testify to the national succession and emphasise the independence of Latvia should not become a factor hindering the development of the state.

2. LATVIAN CONSTITUTION AND THE EUROPEAN UNION

In the light of the upcoming accession to the European Union there is undoubtedly a necessity to approximate Latvian legislation and the Constitution to the legal principles and norms of the European Union. The necessity of amending the Constitution is determined by a new legal order in the European Union, in compliance with which

> 'The essential characteristics of the Community legal order which has thus been established are in particular its primacy over the law of the member States and the direct effect of a whole series of provisions which are applicable to their nations and to the member States themselves'.[9]

Advancement of Latvia towards the European Union undoubtedly demands the approximation of Latvian legal principles and norms to those existing in the European Union. Latvia has already undertaken certain liabilities, which determine that approximation of the Constitution of Latvia to the legislation of the European Union shall be ensured.

Already Article 69 of the Europe Agreement, establishing an association between the European Community and its member States, of the one part and the Republic of Latvia, of the other part,[10] signed in 1995, has established that:

> 'The Parties recognize that an important condition for Latvia's economic integration into the community is the approximation of Latvia's existing and future legislation to that of the Community. Latvia shall endeavour to ensure that its legislation will be gradually made compatible with that of the Community'.

Although the above Agreement was signed already in 1995, a real discussion on the required amendments to the Constitution started only last year. Only in Au-

---

[9] (1991) ECR I-6079, Point 21.

[10] 'Europe Agreement establishing an association between the European Communities and their member States, of the one part, and the Republic of Latvia, of the other part', signed 12.06.1995, Latvijas Vestnesis, 12.06.95, No. 138.

gust 2000 was a special working group for drafting amendments to the Constitution created by Decree of the Prime Minister. According to the Decree the amendments to the Constitution in connection with Latvia joining the European Union were to be worked out until 1 March 2001. The head of the group is the Minister of Justice, with representatives from the Parliament, the Ministries of Justice and Foreign Affairs, the European Integration Bureau, the State Chancellery as well as from the Constitutional Court participating in the working group.

The first Chapter of the Constitution contains four Articles, which are of great importance. These Articles are the basis for State independence and democracy. The fathers of the Constitution have consequently observed the principle that Latvia shall be an independent country. Therefore, the above four Articles are strict and may be amended only by a referendum.

The fundamental constitutional norm of Latvia – Article 1 of the Constitution – states that 'Latvia is an independent democratic republic'. The Article contains two elements. The first is 'independence'. It is an element directed outwards – towards the international legal sphere: Latvia shall be an 'independent' state. The second one is the element directed inwards – towards the national constitutional legal sphere: Latvia shall be a 'democratic' state.[11] When becoming a member State of the European Union, Latvia will not experience any major problems with respect to the second element – 'democracy'.

However, Latvia would lose part of its independence within the meaning of Article 1 of the Constitution, for in becoming one of the member States, it would transfer part of its competence to the EU. It means that when joining the European Union, Latvia should modify the interpretation of the concept 'independence' of Article 1 of the Constitution.

Article 2 of the Constitution states that 'The sovereign power of the State of Latvia is vested in the people of Latvia'. Several viewpoints have been expressed on the necessity of amending Article 2 of the Constitution. One of them is that, as the supreme power will not belong only to the Latvian people but to the institutions of the European Union as well, Article 2 of the Constitution should be amended.[12] However, the majority of lawyers hold that Article 2 of the Constitution should be left unaltered. The issue of 'sovereignty', determined by Article 2 of the Constitution, is interesting. In point of fact sovereignty means the right 'of saying the last word'. When joining the European Union, the member States by an agreement transfer a certain part of their competence to the institutions of the European Union. Thus, the European Union is based upon international agreements, and the members of it are separate states. The member States voluntarily admit being subordinated to the directives of the Union, even in cases where they

---

[11] 'The Satversme and the European Union' by Egils Levits, Justice of the European Court of Human Rights. Latvijas Vestnesis, 08.06.2000, No. 213/218.

[12] 'On Essential Amendments to our Satversme by Arnis Buka, student of the Faculty of Law of Latvian University. Latvijas Vestnesis, 02.03.2000, No. 71/72.

do not agree with them. However, the states retain the right of interrupting 'the limited independence' by discontinuing their membership in the European Union. Thus – 'the last word' – and that means sovereignty – remains to the member States. Therefore, if Latvia joins the Union, the meaning of Article 2 of the Constitution will not be noticeably changed.[13]

Some lawyers express the viewpoint that the most suitable solution would be to supplement Article 68 of the Constitution which reads, 'All international agreements which settle matters that may be decided by the legislative process shall require ratification by the Saeima (Parliament)', without amending Article 2 of the Constitution.[14] The norm, envisaging the possibility of transferring part of the realisation of the authority of the State of Latvia to supra-national institutions with an international agreement, should be included in Article 68.

3. JOINING THE EUROPEAN UNION AND THE NECESSITY OF THE POPULAR VOTE

From the principles included in the fundamentals of the Constitution and the essence of the Constitution, it clearly follows that a referendum is mandatory for joining the European Union. The meaning of the Articles analysed above and Article 77 of the Constitution demonstrates it. Article 77 of the Constitution states that

> 'If the Saeima (Parliament) has amended the first, second, third, fourth, sixth or seventy-seventh Article of the Constitution, such amendments, in order to come into force as law, shall be submitted to a national referendum.'

One should additionally stress that, at the present time, according to the Constitution and the Law on Referendum and on Legislative Proposals adopted in 1994 there are only four cases when popular votes in Latvia may be held:[15]

1) obligatory referendum (Article 77 of the Constitution);
2) optional referendum: if the President has withheld a law, it shall be put to a national referendum, if so requested by not less than one-tenth of the electorate;
3) automatic referendum: if the people have submitted a draft law to the Parliament, but the Parliament does not adopt it, shall it then be submitted to national referendum;

---

[13] Egils Levits, 'The Satversme and the European Union'.

[14] 'On Potential Amendments to our Satversme' by Arnis Buka, student of the Faculty of Law of Latvian University. Latvijas Vestnesis, 08.06.2000, No. 213/218.

[15] The Law on Referendum and on Legislative Proposals, adopted 31.03.1994. Latvijas Vestnesis, 20.04.1994, No. 47. Art. 1.

4) a popular vote must be held also where the President proposes the dissolution of the Parliament.

The above cases are exhaustive and one may conclude from the above that at the present moment the Constitution does not envisage the right of either the Parliament or the government to freely formulate the issue of referendum in a case of joining the European Union. Therefore, motions on supplementing Articles 73 and 79 of the Constitution have been expressed to envisage granting the people the right of reaching the decision on the sovereignty of the state and holding a popular vote.

Article 73 of the Constitution specifies those issues that cannot be solved by a referendum. In conformity with the Article, agreements with other nations may not be submitted for national referendum. Thus, it is necessary to amend the Article.

Article 79 refers to a quorum. The Constitution provides a different percentage of votes for obtaining a quorum to amend the Constitution and to amend the law. In compliance with Article 79 of the Constitution 'An amendment to the Constitution submitted for national referendum shall be deemed adopted if *at least half of the electorate has voted in favour.'*

The condition expressed in Article 79 of the Constitution that an amendment shall be deemed adopted if at least half of the electorate has voted in favour, is a really strict demand, directed to the defence of the fundamental principles of democracy and state sovereignty. A viewpoint has been expressed that it would be problematic to reach the above-qualified majority. Therefore, the necessity to amend the first part of Article 79, envisaging a smaller quorum only in the specific case of Latvia joining the European Union, arises. It is clear, that the issue will invite intense discussion both of the part of lawyers and the public. It is already necessary to inform society about the European Union more actively to achieve the support of the people on the issue of Latvia joining the European Union.

It is worth listening to the viewpoint of the Justice of the European Court of Human Rights, Judge Egils Levits,[16] which was recently expressed in the Government newspaper. He states that any amendment of the Constitution, mentioning membership of Latvia in the European Union, formally modifies the sense of the concept of 'independence' expressed in Article 1 and, possibly, also the sense of sovereignty of Article 2 of the Constitution. Therefore, any such amendment should be submitted to a national referendum, as envisaged in Article 77 of the Constitution. If the following amendments to the Constitution are formulated precisely (see below), then two national referendums are not necessary, as the people when voting 'for' or 'against' the precisely formulated amendments to the Con-

[16] Egils Levits, 'The Satversme and the European Union'.

stitution will simultaneously vote for the abstract issue of Latvia becoming a member State of the European Union.

4. WHAT AMENDMENTS TO THE CONSTITUTION ARE NECESSARY IN THE CASE OF LATVIA JOINING THE EUROPEAN UNION (LEGAL TECHNIQUE)

At the present moment several variants for amending the Constitution have been offered. One could divide them into two variants.

The minimum variant seems to be very attractive, because the constitutional stability as well as precision and laconicism of language of our basic law would be retained. Egils Levits has proposed stating the supplement to the Constitution in a special integration (European) clause, the wording of which could be like this: 'Latvia is a member State of the European Union. Latvia transfers to it a certain extent of authority of the State, determined in the European Union Treaties.'[17] The Article could be even shorter: 'Latvia is a member State of the European Union'. The supplement would be then directed to Latvia joining the European Union and not any supranational organisation. The above 'European Clause' could be numbered as Article 2a and placed just after Article 2 'The sovereign power of the State of Latvia is vested in the people of Latvia' or after Article 68 of the Constitution, which refers to international agreements. The 'European Clause' will come into legal force on the day of Latvia joining the European Union. If some day Latvia – on the basis of Article 2 of the Constitution – decides to discontinue membership in the European Union, the 'European Clause' would lose force.

One has to agree that supplementation of the Constitution with the 'integration clause', at the same time amending the first part of Article 79 on the quorum necessary for a national referendum, will demand a new interpretation of such notions as 'independence' and 'sovereignty' as well as a new interpretation of many other Articles of the Constitution. Proper interpretation of constitutional legal norms, in conformity with standards of methodology of the Western legal system, will be needed. Other issues, specifically connected with Latvia joining the European Union, could be solved by a special 'European Law', adopted by the Parliament.

As concerns the second variant, the proposal to amend several Articles of the existing Chapters of the Constitution, as well as supplementing the Constitution with a new Chapter on membership of Latvia in the European Union has been expressed. The positive element of the proposal is the possibility of taking into consideration the traditionally strong traditions of normative regulations in

[17] Ibid.

Latvia. Besides, it would correspond to the present structure of the Constitution and its historic development. The new Chapter could be placed after Chapter VIII of the Constitution, adopted only in 1998.

The new Chapter could regulate the following relevant issues:

1) restriction of sovereignty of Latvia, its objective and motivation;
2) transfer of the authority of the State of Latvia to the institutions of the European Union, the procedure of the process;
3) connection of the rights and principles of the European Union and the Latvian legal system;
4) co-ordination of the Parliament and government action in matters of the European Union;
5) the procedure of electing deputies to the Euro-Parliament in Latvia;
6) other vital issues.

5. ROLE OF NATIONAL COURTS

Article 68 of the Constitution states: 'All international agreements which settle matters that may be decided by the legislative process shall require ratification by the Saeima (Parliament)'.

According to Article 13 of the Law 'On International Agreements of the Republic of Latvia', adopted in 1994, 'If an international agreement affirmed by the Parliament provides for other provisions than those in the Republic of Latvia legislative acts, the provisions of the international agreement shall be applied.'[18] It means that the national courts when reviewing cases shall apply a hierarchy of legal norms in which the international norms are of a higher legal force than the national ones, with an exception for the norms of the Constitution.

If Latvia has ratified an international agreement, but the respective national normative act is not adopted, then the court shall directly apply international legal norms. Although in the practice of the courts of general jurisdiction one can find judgments in which the courts have applied international norms, such very small number is very small. The direct application of international norms is being implemented in Latvia very slowly.

Thus, for instance, in 1999 the Riga Ziemelu District Court in the case *Mentzena* v. *the Registry Office of the Riga Ziemelu District* applied the European Convention for the Protection of Human Rights and Fundamental Freedoms. Article 8 of the Convention guarantees the right to respect for private life and on the basis of it Mentzena's claim was satisfied. Mrs. Mentzena claimed to be entitled to enter her son's name and last name in the Register of Births in the same spell-

[18] The Law On International Agreements of the Republic of Latvia, adopted on 13.01.1994, Latvijas Vestnesis, 26.01.1994, No. 11.

ing as in his father's, who was a citizen of Germany. Documents (in compliance with rules effective in Latvia) the original spelling of names is not retained, they are spelled as they are pronounced.[19]

In 1996 the Riga Regional Court in the case *V.G.* v. *Latvia* (V.G. submitted a complaint against the State of Latvia in the person of the Ministry of Finance, claiming compensation for 7 years of imprisonment; she was imprisoned on the basis of an unlawful sentence, which was later quashed) applied Article 6 of the International Covenant on Civil and Political Rights, which establishes payment of compensation to a person if a trial error has occurred by which a person has been convicted and the court sentence is quashed or the person pardoned.[20]

In 1995 the Bauska District Court in the case *Kazarovecs* v. *Iecava High School* applied Article 19 of the UN Convention on the Rights of the Child, rejecting Kazarovec's claim have his right to the post restored (Kazarovecs, a teacher at the Iecava High School, was dismissed in compliance with the Code of Labour Law for immoral behavior, incompatible with the status of a teacher). The Convention on the Rights of the Child envisages that member States shall undertake all possible measures to protect children against any kind of violence (physical, psychological, insults, maltreatment, etc.) by grown-ups.[21]

Latvia has ratified many different international agreements, including documents on Human Rights. The above agreements are some of the most important legal instruments to be used by the courts. The fact that lately the judges of the courts of general jurisdiction have started applying contemporary methods of interpretation of legal norms is a positive one.

The situation at the Constitutional Court, which was established in 1996, is better. In its decisions, the Constitutional Court makes extensive use of the principles of the legal system of Continental Europe (trust in law, separation of power, proportionality, justice, state of rule of law), international legal norms as well as judgments of the European Court of Human Rights.

Thus, in its 1998 Decision 'On Expropriation of Real Estate in the State or Public Interest', the Constitutional Court, when evaluating the conformity of the disputable norm to Article 1 of the First Protocol of the European Convention for the Protection of Human Rights and Fundamental Freedoms, referred to two Decisions of the European Court of Human Rights.[22]

In one of its 1999 decisions the Constitutional Court declared the norm of the Cabinet of Ministers Regulations on confidentiality of government agreements to

---

[19] Judgement in the case '*J. Mentzena* v. *The Registry Office of the Riga Ziemelu District*'. Latvijas Vestnesis, 04.07.2000, No. 247/249.

[20] *V.G.* v. *Latvia,* Latvian Human Rights Quarterly, 1997, No. 2.

[21] *Kazarovecs* v. *Iecava High School,* Latvian Human Rights Quarterly, 1998, No. 3/4.

[22] The Decision of the Constitutional Court in the case No. 09-02(98) 'On Expropriation of Real Estate in the State or Public Interest', adopted 30.04.1998, Latvijas Vestnesis, 05.05.1998, No. 122; in English in the Bulletin on Constitutional Case Law, 1998, No. 2, LAT-1998-2-003.

be incompatible with Article 100 of the Constitution, determining the right to freedom of expression. In the conclusive part of the Decision norms of international instruments on the right to accessibility to information (the Declaration of Human Rights, the International Covenant on Civil and Political Rights, the European Convention for Protection of Human Rights and Fundamental Freedoms) were interpreted.[23]

Article 85 of the Constitution states that the Constitutional Court reviews cases concerning the compliance of laws with the Constitution and other matters, which are in its jurisdiction according to the law being the Constitutional Court Law.[24]

Article 16 of the Constitutional Court Law establishes what cases are within the competence of the Constitutional Court. Among other cases the Constitutional Court reviews:

> '2. Compliance with the Constitution of international agreements signed or entered into by Latvia;
> 9. Compliance of the national legal norms of Latvia with the international agreements entered into by Latvia, which are not contrary to the Constitution.'

According to Article 32 of the Law, if the Constitutional Court has recognised any international agreement signed or entered into by Latvia as being incompatible with the Constitution, the Cabinet of Ministers is immediately obliged to see that the agreement is amended, denounced, suspended or that the accession to that agreement is reversed.

We expect that in joining the European Union Latvia shall neither have to amend the norms of the Constitution Chapter VI 'Courts' nor the norms of the specific laws 'On Judicial Power'[25] and the Constitutional Court Law. When joining the European Union, the competence and authority of the courts shall be interpreted in compliance with the amended norms of the Constitution, transferring a certain measure of competence to the structures of the European Union.

After joining the European Union, the Constitutional Court of the Republic of Latvia will cease to be the court of last instance, reaching decisions on conformity of national legal norms with the rights of the European Union. All the courts of general jurisdiction as well as the European Court of Justice by applying the legal norms of the European Union will make decisions on compliance of the national legal norms with EU legislation. The competence of the Constitutional Court will continue to encompass reviewing compliance of international agreements with non-EU member States and international organisations with the Constitution and the community law.

---

[23] The Decision of the Constitutional Court in the case No. 04-02(99) 'On Conformity of the Cabinet of Ministers Regulations No. 46'. On Government Agreements 'with the Information Accessibility Law', adopted 06.07.1999. Latvijas Vestnesis, 07.07.1999; in English in the Bulletin on Constitutional Case Law, 1999-2-002.

[24] The Constitutional Court Law, adopted 14.06.1996. Latvijas Vestnesis 25.07.1996, No. 14

[25] The Law On Judicial Power, adopted 15.12.1992; 'Augstakas Padomes un Ministru Padomes Zinotajs', 14.01.1993, No. 1.

LITHUANIA: THE CONSTITUTIONAL IMPACT OF THE ENLARGEMENT AT NATIONAL LEVEL

Vilenas Vadapalas*

THE CONSTITUTION OF THE REPUBLIC OF LITHUANIA

1. The Lithuanian Constitution, which was adopted by referendum on 25 October 1992, created a solid legal basis for democracy, the rule of law and respect for human and minority rights, as well as for the implementation of the international obligations of Lithuania in its internal law.

The main principles declared by the Constitution of Lithuania, i.e., the rule of law (Preamble), freedom and democracy (Preamble and Art. 1), and respect for human and minority rights (Arts. 18-37 and 45), correspond to those of the European Union and its member States embodied in the Treaty on European Union: 'attachment to the principles of liberty, democracy and respect for human rights and fundamental freedoms and the rule of law' (Preamble); 'the Union is founded on the principles of liberty, democracy, respect for human rights and fundamental freedoms, and the rule of law, principles which are common to the member States' (Art. 6). In addition, Article 135 of the Constitution, which deals with the principles of foreign policy of Lithuania, contains the principles corresponding to the objectives of a common foreign and security policy of the Union.[1]

---

* Director General of the European Law Department, Government of Lithuania; Chairman of the Chair of International and EU Law, Faculty of Law, Vilnius University. The opinions expressed in this report represent the personal position of the author only.

[1] Article 135 of the Constitution stipulates:
'In conducting foreign policy, the Republic of Lithuania shall pursue the universally recognised principles and norms of international law, shall strive to safeguard national security and independence as well as the basic rights, freedoms and welfare of its citizens, and shall take part in the creation of sound international order based on law and justice.'
Article 11(1) of the EU Treaty stipulates:
'1. The Union shall define and implement a common foreign and security policy covering all areas of foreign and security policy, the objectives of which shall be:
– to safeguard the common values, fundamental interests, independence and integrity of the Union in conformity with the principles of the United Nations Charter;
– to strengthen the security of the Union in all ways;
– to preserve peace and strengthen international security, in accordance with the principles of the United Nations Charter, as well as the principles of the Helsinki Final Act and the objectives of the Paris Charter, including those on external borders;

A.E. Kellermann et al. (Eds.), EU Enlargement: The Constitutional Impact at EU and National Level

At the same time, the Constitution an emphasis on the independence and sovereignty principles (Arts. 1-5, 135 and 136, see below). In particular, the Constitutional Act on Non-alignment of the Republic of Lithuania to Post-Soviet Eastern Alliances of 8 June 1992 prohibits the accession of Lithuania to 'any new political, military, economic or any other state alliances or commonwealths formed on the basis of the former USSR' (Art. 1 of the Act). This Constitutional Act concerns, first of all, the Community of Independent States and has no relationship with the European Communities and the European Union. However, it shows once again the importance of the independence and sovereignty principles in the constitutional system of Lithuania.

The Constitution is based on a monistic approach and incorporates ratified international treaties into the Lithuanian legal system (Art. 138 of the Constitution). A monistic approach would facilitate the national implementation of future obligations deriving from the EC, the EU and other Community treaties. However, a question arises whether the monistic legal system creates *per se* a legal basis that would be sufficiently effective for ensuring direct effect and supremacy of the EC law in Lithuanian law.

The EC Treaty, EU Treaty, as all other primary and secondary legal acts of the European Union, have supremacy over the legal norms of the internal law of the member States.[2] As regards the future accession of the Republic of Lithuania, it should be pointed out that, according to the Constitution, these treaties should be ratified. Thereafter, these treaties would become the constituent part of the Lithuanian legal system on the basis of the provision of Article 138 of the Constitution of the Lithuania, which stipulates:

> 'International agreements that are ratified by the Seimas of the Republic of Lithuania shall be the constituent part of the legal system of the Republic of Lithuania'.[3]

This constitutional provision makes international treaties ratified by the Republic of Lithuania a constituent part of the Lithuanian legal system. It means that these treaties are directly applicable in the Lithuanian legal system, provided, of course, that these treaties contain self-executing provisions, i.e., provisions that

---

– to promote international cooperation;
– to develop and consolidate democracy and the rule of law, and respect for human rights and fundamental freedoms.'

[2] In *Simmenthal* (1978) the Court of Justice of the European Communities referred to this requirement as 'supremacy of Community law' which invalidates the norm of domestic law contrary to Community law and precludes adoption of national legislation contrary to it. CMLR 11978, 3, p. 263.

[3] A provision analogous to the provision of Article 138 of the Constitution of the Republic of Lithuania is established by the 1978 Constitution of Spain which lays down that validly concluded international treaties shall constitute part of the internal legal order but does not say anything about the relationship of such treaties with legislative and constitutional norms.

could be executed at the level of the internal legal order. All State institutions – the legislature, the judiciary, administrative and other institutions – must apply them and comply with them.

On 22 June 1999 the Seimas enacted a new Law on International Treaties which establishes the supremacy of ratified treaties over domestic law. Article 11 of the Law stipulates:

> 'Article 11. Binding force of international treaties of the Republic of Lithuania
> 1. International treaties of the Republic of Lithuania shall be executed in the Republic of Lithuania.
> 2. If a ratified international treaty of the Republic of Lithuania stipulates other provisions than the laws or other legal acts of the Republic of Lithuania, irrespective of whether they are in force at the moment of the conclusion of the treaty or enter into force following the conclusion of the treaty, the provisions of the international treaty of the Republic of Lithuania shall apply.
> 3. If the execution of an international treaty of the Republic of Lithuania requires that a law or other legal act should be enacted, the Government of the Republic of Lithuania shall submit a draft law to the Seimas according to established procedures, or shall issue a directive, either under its competence ensuring that the other legal act would be adopted.'

The monistic rules of Lithuanian law, i.e., incorporation of international treaties into the national legal system (Art. 138 of the Constitution and Art. 11(1) of the Law on International Treaties), as well as the supremacy of ratified international treaties over the ordinary laws and other (i.e., lower) legal instruments (Art. 11(1) of the Law on International Treaties) facilitates the national implementation of international treaties in Lithuania. As a matter of principle, this model does not require that the international treaties be transformed, through the enactment of internal legal instruments, into internal law. It is important, in particular, with regard to the Europe (association) Agreement with Lithuania of 12 June 1995. This monistic model creates possibilities for the direct enforcement of the self-executing provisions of the Europe Agreement into Lithuanian law, i.e., the provisions creating the rights and obligations on natural and legal persons. These are, for example, the provisions concerning the abolition of quantitative restrictions on exports in Lithuania and any other measures having equivalent effect (Art. 14(2), establishment (Art. 44), etc.

In respect to Lithuania, the Europe Agreement is a treaty of public international law, whereas with regard to the member States of the European Union the Europe Agreement is, first of all, a part of EU law. Thus, with regard to the member States, the Europe Agreement has direct effect and supremacy under the EU law itself notwithstanding the monistic or dualistic system of a particular member State. A distinction should be drawn between the direct effect and supremacy of international treaties under national law, on the one hand, and the direct effect and supremacy of the particular Community law under Community law, on the other. In this respect, the monistic system and supremacy of ratified international treaties over national laws and 'secondary' legislation *per se* are not sufficient to give full effect to EC law in the national legal system. First of all, the supremacy of the ratified international treaties of Lithuania does not mean their supremacy over the national Constitution, whereas it would be the case under Community law. Consequently, the conflict of rules problem could arise especially with regard to Lithuanian constitutional provisions which are problematic from the point of view of EU law: Article 47 (right to acquire land property) and Article 119 (right to take part in municipal elections). Secondly, the monistic model and the supremacy of international treaties under Lithuanian law, even with respect to the EC and the EU Treaties, do not necessarily mean the direct effect of and supremacy of secondary Community law.

Politically, it would be difficult to expect that the Lithuanian Constitution would be amended with the provisions that *expressis verbis* would establish the supremacy of Community law over the Constitution. Instead, amendments to the Constitution in order to adjust its particular provisions (Art. 47 and 119(2)) to the needs of a future accession to the EU seem to be necessary, as well as amendments introducing into the Constitution the so-called 'Community clauses' (the principles of the transfer of sovereignty, the direct effect of EU law, and a general clause on the supremacy of EU law over Lithuanian laws and other legal acts).

Procedures for the amendments of the Constitution are established in its Chapter 14 'Amendments to the Constitution' which reads as follows:

> 'Article 147
> In order to amend or append the Constitution of the Republic of Lithuania, a proposal must be submitted to the Seimas by either no less than one-fourth of the members of the Seimas, or by at least 300,000 voters.
> During a state of emergency or martial law, amendments to the Constitution may not be made.
>
> Article 148
> The provision of Article 1 of the Constitution that the State of Lithuania is an independent democratic republic may only be amended by a referendum in which at least three-fourths of the electorate of Lithuania vote in favour thereof.
> The provisions of Chapter 1 ('The State of Lithuania') and Chapter 14 ('Amending the Constitution') may be amended only by referendum.
> Amendments of other chapters of the Constitution must be considered and voted upon in the Seimas twice. There must be a lapse of at least three months between each vote. Bills for constitutional amendments shall be deemed adopted by the Seimas if, in each of the votes, at least two-thirds of all the members of the Seimas vote in favour of the enactment.
> An amendment to the Constitution which is rejected by the Seimas may not be submitted to the Seimas for reconsideration for a period of one year.

Article 149
The adopted law on an amendment to the Constitution shall be signed by the President of the Republic of Lithuania and officially promulgated within 5 days.
If the President of the Republic of Lithuania does not sign and promulgate such law in due time, the law shall become effective when the Chairperson of the Seimas signs and promulgates it.
The law on an amendment to the Constitution shall become effective no earlier than one month after the adoption thereof.'

2. There are no specific practical problems regarding the procedure for amendment of the Constitution in the case of accession. However, one problem could arise in the case where the question of accession were to be brought to referendum. In this regard, Article 9 of the Constitution stipulates:

> 'The most significant issues concerning the life of the State and the People shall be decided by referendum.
> In the cases established by law, referendums shall be announced by the Seimas.
> Referendums shall also be announced if no less than 300,000 of the electorate so request.
> The procedure for the announcement and execution of a referendum shall be established by law.'

The first paragraph of the Article ('the most significant issues (...) shall be decided by referendum') does not necessarily mean that a referendum on this matter should be held. However, if it were to be the case, the 1989 Law on Referendum is applicable. The provisions of this law could raise the most difficult problem, namely, the provision establishing the excessive requirement of an absolute majority of the citizens of Lithuania voting 'for'. Article 32, para. 6, of the Law on Referendum stipulates:

> 'The provisions of a law of the Republic of Lithuania or other issue raised by the referendum is considered as adopted, provided that during the referendum more than half of the citizens included in the lists approved it.'

Today, at least, it would be difficult to expect that such a majority of Lithuanian citizens would vote in a referendum for the accession of Lithuania to the European Union. According to the public opinionpolls of October 2000, 47 per cent of Lithuanians are for the accession, and 21 per cent against it.[4]

3. The Constitution of Lithuania does not contain any so-called 'Community clauses' providing for the transfer of sovereignty to the European Union, direct effect and supremacy of the EU law over national law, etc.

---

[4] Tests made by 'Vilmorus'. See http://rope.euro.lt/indexeng.html.

Membership of the European Union calls for a transfer by a member State to the Union of a certain portion of the competence of its State institutions in the areas defined by the constitutive treaties of the EC and the EU. Article 249 (ex Art. 189) of the EC Treaty stipulates:

> 'In order to carry out their task and in accordance with the provisions of this Treaty, the European Parliament acting jointly with the Council, the Council and the Commission shall make regulations and issue directives, take decisions, make recommendations or deliver opinions.
> A regulation shall have general application. It shall be binding in its entirety and directly applicable in all member States.
> A directive shall be binding, as to the result to be achieved, upon each member State to which it is addressed, but shall leave to the national authorities the choice of form and methods.
> A decision shall be binding in its entirety upon those to whom it is addressed.
> Recommendations and opinions shall have no binding force.'

The case law of the European Court of Justice is unequivocal about the meaning of the above provisions: member States transfer to the EU a part of their sovereignty, agreeing to limit their sovereign rights to pass binding legal acts in some areas defined by the EC and the EU Treaties. In *Costa* v. *ENEL (1964)* the Court held: 'By (...) a transfer of powers from the States to the Community, the member States have limited their sovereign rights (...).'[5]

Transfer of sovereignty to the European Union implies also the exercise of the sovereign powers of the member States in common in the European Union. This is clearly reflected, for example, in Article 88-1 of the Constitution of France:

> 'Article 88-1
> La République participe aux Communautés européennes et à l'Union européenne, constituées d'Etats qui ont choisi librement, en vertu des traités qui les ont instituées, *d'exercer en commun certaines de leurs compétences.*' (our emphasis added)[6]

In this connection it is necessary to determine whether the Constitution of the Republic of Lithuania does not prohibit the transfer of a part of the competence of the State institutions to the international organisations.

Article 1 of the Constitution declares: 'The State of Lithuania shall be an independent and democratic republic.'

---

[5] CMLR 1964, p. 425.

[6] English translation:
'Article 88-1
The Republic shall participate in the European Communities and in the European Union constituted by States that have freely chosen, by virtue of the treaties that established them, *to exercise some of their powers in common.*' (our emphasis added)

Accession to the European Union and transfer to its institutions of a portion of State sovereignty does not at all mean that this State loses its independence or features of its democratic system. It has been universally recognised and is beyond doubt that the member States of the European Union are fully-fledged members of international organisations. On the other hand, under the Treaty on European Union, through the implementation of its common foreign and security policy the Union might ensure the common defence of its members (Arts. 2 (ex Art. B) and 24 (ex Art. J.4)) and in this way protect the independence of its members; 'the Union shall respect the national identities of its member States, whose systems of government are founded on the principles of democracy' (Art. 6 (ex Art. F), para. 2).

Accession to the European Union does not mean loss of independence or its limitation; it means delegation of a part of one's State competence to the EU bodies along with the consent to transfer one's sovereign rights in certain areas defined in the treaties establishing the Communities and the Union. Reference to Articles 2 and 3 of the Constitution is relevant at this point:

> 'Article 2
> The State of Lithuania shall be created by the People. Sovereignty shall be vested in the People.
>
> Article 3
> No one may limit or restrict the sovereignty of the People or make claims to the sovereign powers of the People.
> The People and each citizen shall have the right to oppose anyone who encroaches on the independence, territorial integrity, or constitutional order of the State of Lithuania by force.'

Similar provisions were established in the constitutions of France, Italy, Spain, Portugal and some other States but they have not prevented those countries from becoming members of the European Communities, subsequently the European Union.[7]

The above provisions and similar constitutional provisions do not mean a prohibition on transfer of certain issues of state competence to international organisations; they point to the source of sovereignty – the people – and prohibit any usurpation of sovereignty in the hands of individuals or groups. The above provisions were not an obstacle for Lithuania when in 1991 it became a member of the United Nations. One of the bodies of the UN, the Security Council, is empowered to adopt resolutions for the maintenance of international peace and security which are binding on the UN member States (Art. 24 of the United Nations

[7] See: D. Kriaučiūnas. Konstitucinės Lietuvos narystės Europos Sąjungoje problemos. – Lietuvos integracija į Europos Sąjungą: būklės, perspektyvų ir pasekmių studija. Vilnius: Europos integracijos studijų centras, 1997, pp. 167-168.

Charter). Nor were those provisions an obstacle when in 1995 Lithuania ratified the European Convention for the Protection of Human Rights and Fundamental Freedoms which provides that judgments of the European Court of Human Rights are binding on the High Contracting Parties; and the Committee of Ministers of the Council of Europe shall supervise their execution (Art. 46 of the Convention). Of course, the essential distinction should be made between the 'traditional' international organisations, such as the United Nations, its specialised agencies (ILO, ICAO, etc.), the Council of Europe, etc., in which Lithuania is a State Member, on the one hand, and the European Union, on the other. Membership of the UN does not require the transfer of sovereign powers to the organs of the United Nations, even to the Security Council, whereas membership of the European Union means membership of a supranational organisation, since legislative powers in large areas are transferred by the States to the institutions of the Union. The same concerns the competence and jurisdiction of the International Court of Justice, on the one hand, and the competence and jurisdiction of the Court of Justice of the European Communities, on the other. The competence of the ICJ is to adjudicate, on the basis of public international law, on the disputes between States; its jurisdiction is optional. The ECJ is competent to adjudicate on cases, which from the traditional point of view of public international law, would be within the exclusive jurisdiction of a State, its *domaine réservé*.

Nevertheless, membership of the European Union is membership of an international organisation, even a supranational one. In this respect it should be noted that the Constitution of the Republic of Lithuania contains a special provision dealing with the accession of Lithuania to international organisations. Article 136 stipulates:

> 'The Republic of Lithuania shall participate in international organisations provided that they do not contradict the interests and independence of the State.'

As for the interests of Lithuania, it was showed above that the constitutional principles and objectives of the Community and the Union do not contradict the principles and objectives of Lithuanian Constitutional system. Moreover, in most cases they could be regarded as corresponding and coincident. With regard to independence, an additional argument could be found in favour of drawing the conclusion that after the accession to the EU Lithuania would not lose its independence under public international law. It seems that the States Members of the EU still possess the traditional customary international law qualifications of States, which have been codified in Article 1 of the 1933 Montevideo Convention on the Rights and Duties of States:

> 'The State as a person of international law should possess the following qualifications: (a) a permanent population; (b) a defined territory; (c) government; and (d) capacity to enter into relations with other States'.

The transfer of sovereignty to the Union in the areas defined by the EC and the EU treaties does not deprive the States Members of such traditional elements of statehood in international relations. Free movement of persons in the Community has nothing to do with the existence of 'a permanent population' of a State Member. The same concerns the citizenship of the Union: with the introduction of the notion of citizenship of the Union there was no intention to replace the national citizenship of a nation-State. Citizenship of the Union is limited only to those who have the nationality of one or other of the member States and implies that the member States retain the full powers to define the conditions of their nationality. The Union does not possess its own territory or power to change 'a defined territory' of the member States. As for 'government', the institutions of the Union, such as the Council and the Commission, acting within the powers conferred them by the EC and the EU treaty do not substitute for the governments of the member States. This is a matter of transfer of some defined sovereign powers, rather than the loss of control of any Government over population and territory. Finally, the 'capacity to enter into relations with other States' could be linked with the question of the external relations of the European Community, where, according to and within the limits of the EC treaty, the Communities have exclusive competence (common commercial policy, common fisheries policy and, to some extent, competition) or shares competence with its member States (transport, education, culture, public health, research and technological development, environment, development and assistance policy, protection of intellectual property). There is authority for the view that shared competence is the general rule, and exclusive Community competence the exception; certain provisions of the treaties *expressis verbis* provide that the existence of Community competence does not prejudice the competence of the member States to negotiate within international bodies and to conclude international agreements (Arts. 111(5), 174(4), 181, etc.).[8] Membership of the Union does not deprive a State of its general capacity to enter into relations with other States, i.e., of its international legal personality, including the capacity to conclude international treaties, to be admitted into international organizations and to bring international claims.[9]

The above analysis shows that the Constitution of the Republic of Lithuania does not prohibit the accession of Lithuania to the European Union and does not create obstacles in respect of the obligations which Lithuania would assume in connection with its membership of the European Union. It may also be presumed that under the provisions of Article 138 of the Constitution and Article 11 of the

---

[8] I. MacLeod, I.D. Hendry, S. Hyett. The External Relations of the European Communities. Oxford: Clarendon Press, 1996, p. 64, p. 235, etc.

[9] As the International Court of Justice stated in its advisory opinion in the *Reparation for Injuries (1949)* case: 'What it does mean is that it is a subject of international law and capable of possessing international rights and duties, and that it has capacity to maintain its rights by bringing international claims'. ICJ Reports 1949, p. 179.

1999 Law on the International Treaties, such legal acts of direct application as regulations and decisions passed by the institutions of the EU would become a part of the legal system of the Republic of Lithuania because this would stem from the treaties ratified by the Seimas (Art. 138 of the Constitution) and would even have supremacy over Lithuanian laws and other legal instruments (Art. 11 of the 1999 Law). However, this legal presumption is hardly a sufficient ground for solving this fundamental issue. The problem of transfer of sovereignty could arise with regard to interpretation of Articles 4 and 5 of the Constitution:

> 'Article 4
> The People shall exercise the supreme sovereign power vested in them either directly or through their democratically elected representatives.
>
> Article 5
> In Lithuania, the powers of the State shall be exercised by the Seimas, the President of the Republic and Government, and the Judiciary.
> The scope of the powers shall be defined by the Constitution. (...)'

First of all, since Articles 4 and 5 address the exercise of supreme sovereign power and the powers of the State directly, through democratically elected representatives, by the Seimas, the President, the Government and the Judiciary, then the transfer of even of a part of those powers to the EU institutions could raise questions about the constitutionality of such transfer. I would state the necessity of amendment of the Constitution with a provision devoted to the transfer of sovereignty or State competence to the European Union.

In preparing for membership of the EU, the Republic of Lithuania also has to make a provision in its Constitution that the binding legal acts adopted by the institutions of the European Union are directly applicable in the legal system of the Republic of Lithuania and have precedence when the laws and other legal acts of the Republic of Lithuania are contrary to them.

On the contrary, in Lithuania amendments to the Constitution dealing with the relations between the Seimas (Parliament) and the Government in respect of the proposals of Community measures (regulations, directives, etc.) seem to be unnecessary because this issue could be resolved through the procedure for amendment of ordinary legislation (e.g., Statute of the Seimas, Law on the Government, Rules of Procedure of the Government, etc.). Of course, membership of the European Union accords to every member State a right to take part in adopting acts of the EU institutions and at the same time the possibility to protect its national interests. This applies, in particular, to the participation of the member State in the adoption by the European Council of such binding legal acts as regulations. In connection with this, the legislative bodies of the member State must be informed about the drafts (proposals of the new regulations and directives, etc.) in order to give a possibility to the national Parliament to express its position on the adoption of such acts and on their contents, especially when these acts concern national interests. Because the interests of a member State in the European Council are represented by the representatives of the government of that State, the Government has a possibility to inform Parliament about the drafts (proposals) of the binding acts. One of the most modern legal solutions of this problem is Article 88-4 of the Constitution of the French Republic adopted on the basis of the Constitutional Law of June 25, 1992 (as amended after the Amsterdam Treaty), which amended the Constitution of the French Republic with Title XV 'On the European Communities and the European Union' in connection with the ratification of the 1992 Maastricht Treaty on the European Union. Article 88-4 of the Constitution of France sets forth:

> 'Article 88-4
> Le Gouvernement soumet à l'Assemblée Nationale et au Sénat, dès leur transmission au Conseil de l'Union européenne, les projets ou propositions d'actes des Communautés européennes et de l'Union européenne comportant des dispositions de nature législative. Il peut également leur soumettre les autres projets ou propositions d'actes ainsi que tout document émanant d'une institution de l'Union européenne.
> Selon les modalités fixées par le règlement de chaque assemblée, des résolutions peuvent être votées, le cas échéant en dehors des sessions, sur les projets, propositions ou documents mentionnés à l'alinéa précédent.'[10]

Similar provisions are established in Article 23 (European Union), para. 3 of the German Constitution (Grundgesetz):

> 'Artikel 23 [Europäische Union] (extract)
> (3) Die Bundesregierung gibt dem Bundestag Gelegenheit zur Stellungnahme vor ihrer Mitwirkung an Rechtsetzungsakten der Europäischer Union. Die Bundesregierung berücksichtigt die Stellungnahmen des Bundestages bei den Verhandlungen. Das Nähere regelt ein Gesetz.'[11]

---

[10] English translation:
'Article 88-4
The Government shall lay before the National Assembly and the Senate any drafts of or proposals for instruments of the European Communities or the European Union containing provisions which are matters for statute as soon as they have been transmitted to the Council of the European Union. It may also lay before them other drafts of or proposals for instruments or any document issuing from a European Union institution.
In the manner laid down by the rules of procedure of each assembly, resolutions may be passed, even if Parliament is not in session, on the drafts, proposals or documents referred to in the preceding paragraph.'

[11] English translation:
'Article 23 [European Union] (extract)
(3) The Federal Government shall give the Bundestag the opportunity to state its opinion before it takes part in drafting the European Union laws. The Federal Government shall take account of the opinion of the Bundestag in the negotiations. Details shall be the subject of a law.'

In addition to the issues of 'the Community clauses', it should be noted that there are two provisions of the Lithuanian Constitution that could raise difficult questions of their inconsistency with the *acquis communautaire*, i.e., Article 47, paras. 1 and 2 (right to acquire land property) and Article 119, para. 2 (right to take part in municipal elections). In addition, Article 125, para. 2 (exclusive right of the Bank of Lithuania to issue bank notes) could give rise to a restrictive interpretation of its provisions with regard to the possibility of introducing a single currency into Lithuania.

1) Article 47, paras. 1 and 2, in the context of the right of acquisition of land, raises questions of their conformity with the principle of non-discrimination in relation to three of the four fundamental freedoms of the European Community: free movement of persons (including the right of establishment), the services and capital (Arts. 39, 43, 54, 58(3)). Those provisions establish very strict limits on the right of foreign nationals and corporate persons, including citizens and legal persons of the European Union, to acquire land in Lithuania. Article 47, para. 1, stipulates that 'land, internal waters, forests, and parks may only belong to the citizens and the State of the Republic of Lithuania by the right of ownership.' This provision does not apply even to the Lithuanian corporate persons. Para. 2 allows some categories of foreign nationals and corporate persons to acquire non-agricultural land but in fact only for the purposes of certain economic activities.[12]

These restrictions should be examined, first of all, from the perspective of Articles 43-48 of the EC Treaty, which provide a general framework for the right of establishment. In particular, Article 43 prohibits any restrictions on the right of establishment based on nationality in a member State. Article 44, which is devoted to the means of implementation of the right of establishment, stipulates that the Council and the Commission shall carry out their duties in this field by enabling a national of one member State to acquire and use land and buildings situated in the territory of another member State.

As for the free movement of capital, it should be noted that Article 56 of the EC Treaty prohibits all restrictions on the movement of capital and payments between member States and between member States and third countries. Although Article 57(1) of the EC Treaty contains a stand-still clause allowing member States to maintain restrictions, that existed before December 31, 1993 in respect

[12] More detailed rules are set forth in the 1996 Constitutional law on the implementation of provisions of Article 47, para. 2, of the Constitution. Article 4 of the Constitutional law allows only citizens or corporate persons of the EU, of the associated countries, NATO and the OECD to acquire non-agricultural land in Lithuania for the purposes of economic activities. Under Article 3, para. 5, the term 'economic activities' means 'unlimited and permanent activities of industrial, commercial and professional character and the activities of craftsmen or other activities in Lithuania, which have been established and registered in accordance with the procedure established by law whereby profit is sought in compliance with the procedure and conditions established by the laws of the Republic of Lithuania.'

of the free movement of capital (including direct investments in real estate), this provision is valid only in respect to third states – restrictions between member States shall be unconditionally abolished. Additionally, the Directive 88/361 further liberalizes the free movement of capital between member States. Its scope is more narrow than the scope of Article 56 of the EC Treaty for it does not cover third states. Under its Article 1, all restrictions on capital movements between persons resident in member States shall be abolished. Annex I of the Directive provides for the list of capital movements and refers to direct investments (including investments in land and buildings) by non-residents. Nevertheless, according to Article 6(4) of Directive, member States may maintain existing national legislation regulating the purchase of secondary residences until a separate decision of the Council is taken.

As far as the free movement of persons is concerned, it should be noted that Article 39 of the EC Treaty provides for the free movement of workers within the Community. Regulation 1612/68 on freedom of movement for workers (Art. 9, para. 1) provides that a worker who is a national of a member State and who is employed in the territory of another member State shall enjoy all the rights and benefits accorded to national workers in matters of housing, including ownership of the housing he needs.

At the same time, it should be emphasized that according to the ECJ case law member States may establish certain restrictions on the above freedoms and rights, but these restrictions should fulfil the following conditions:

a) they should not discriminate on grounds of nationality;
b) restrictions should be necessary in the public interest;
c) the principle of proportionality should be observed.

In the case *Commission* v. *Hellenic Republic* (C-305/87) the ECJ found that the provisions of the Decree of the President of Greece prohibiting foreigners (including nationals of member States) from acquiring land in the frontier regions of Greece was incompatible with Articles 39 (free movement of workers), 43 (right of establishment) and 49 (free movement of services) of the EC Treaty.[13] In the case *Klaus Konle* v. *Republic of Austria* (C-302/97) the ECJ pointed out that the system of prior authorizations for the acquisition of land might be justified only in exceptional circumstances for the public interest – for example, town and country planning.[14] In both cases the Court applied the principles of proportionality and public interest.

Furthermore, it should be mentioned that Protocol 16 to the EC Treaty provides for an exemption for Denmark which allows it to restrict the right of foreigners to purchase secondary residences in Denmark. This also covers the right to acquire land. As for the experience of the accession negotiations of other mem-

[13] ECR 1989, p. 1461.
[14] ECR 1999, p. 1.

ber States, it should be noted that it is common to negotiate certain transitional periods in this field – for example, Austria, Finland and Sweden negotiated 5 year transitional periods concerning the acquisition of secondary residences, and Portugal a 5 year period concerning acquisition of agricultural land.

Finally, it should be pointed out that it is only in Slovenia and Lithuania that the acquisition of land by foreigners is or was a matter of constitutional legislation, whereas in all the other countries these kinds of questions are governed by ordinary laws. Nevertheless, Lithuania remains the only country still retaining constitutional restrictions in this area, because Slovenia has already amended its Constitution in 1997 prior to the ratification of the Europe Agreement.

As far as the situation in Lithuania is concerned, it should be emphasized that the constitutional and the negotiation options of Lithuania in this field have still not been finally defined. In principle, there are two options: first, to allow all foreign natural and corporate persons to acquire land in Lithuania, and second, to negotiate the possibility of some restrictions (transitional periods rather than exemptions) and refer to these restrictions in a possible new Constitutional Law on Implementation of Article 47 of the Constitution (for both options of the constitutional amendments see the Annex to this paper).

In both cases Lithuanian legislation will follow the above rules of the *acquis communautaire* concerning the right to acquire land.

2) Article 119, para. 2, allows only citizens of the Republic of Lithuania to participate in municipal elections:

> 'Article 119
> (...)
> Members of local government Councils shall be elected for a two-year term on the basis of universal, equal and direct suffrage by secret ballot by the residents of their administrative unit *who are citizens of the Republic of Lithuania* (our emphasis added).
> (...)'

This provision could be regarded as inconsistent with the provisions of Article 19 of the EC Treaty Every, which, inter alia, stipulates that 'every citizen of the Union residing in a member State of which he is not a national shall have the right to vote and to stand as a candidate at municipal elections in the member State in which he resides, under the same conditions as nationals of that State'.[15] Nevertheless, Article 19 of the EC Treaty does not aim at the harmonisation of national electoral systems, all it requires is the abolition of any requirement of na-

---

[15] Article 19 (ex Art. 8b)
1. Every citizen of the Union residing in a member State of which he is not a national shall have the right to vote and to stand as a candidate at municipal elections in the member State in which he resides, under the same conditions as nationals of that State. This right shall be exercised subject to detailed arrangements adopted by the Council, acting unanimously on a proposal from the Commis-

tionality. It should be added that this right was also included in Article 40 (Right to vote and to stand as a candidate at municipal elections) of the Draft Charter of Fundamental Rights of the European Union.[16] In general, this right is a constituent part of citizenship of the Union.[17]

Directive 94/80 sets out more detailed provisions on the exercise of this right. First, it establishes three general requirements concerning the exercise of the right: citizenship of the Union; residence in that member State and, other conditions of eligibility also required from nationals of the host State, e.g., certain age limits (Art. 3). Second, it gives definitions: municipal elections are elections by direct universal suffrage of members of the representative council and, where appropriate, the head and members of the executive of 'a basic local government unit'. The 'basic local government unit' are those specified in the Annex and empowered to administer, at the basic level of political and administrative organisation, certain local affairs on their own responsibility (Art. 2). Third, it establishes residence requirements: if national law provides for minimum periods of residence in the electoral territory, this condition must be fulfilled (Art. 4). Fourth, it contains provisions related to candidates and grounds for disqualification (Art. 5 para. 1 – non-discrimination – civil and criminal law grounds; Art. 5 para. 3 – member States may provide that only their nationals may hold the office of elected head of the executive of a basic local government unit). Fifth, the directive provides for the possibility of derogations (Art. 12) (currently only Luxembourg qualifies): if the proportion of citizens of the Union who are not nationals of that member State exceeds 20 per cent of the total number of voters, that member State may: 1. restrict the right to vote; 2. restrict the right to stand as a candidate; 3. take appropriate measures with regard to the composition of the list of candidates.

---

sion and after consulting the European Parliament these arrangements may provide for derogations where warranted by problems specific to a member State.

2. Without prejudice to Article 190(4) and to the provisions adopted for its implementation, every citizen of the Union residing in a member State of which he is not a national shall have the right to vote and to stand as a candidate in elections to the European Parliament in the member State in which he resides, under the same conditions as nationals of that State. This right shall be exercised subject to detailed arrangements adopted by the Council, acting unanimously on a proposal from the Commission and after consulting the European Parliament these arrangements may provide for derogations where warranted by problems specific to a member State.

[16] Article 40

Right to vote and to stand as a candidate at municipal elections

Every citizen of the Union has a right to vote and to stand as a candidate at municipal elections in the member State in which he or she resides, under the same conditions as nationals of that State.

[17] Part II of the EC Treaty spells out the following rights for every citizen of the Union: a) rights of free movement and residence; b) rights to vote and to stand in municipal elections in the member State of residence; c) rights to vote and to stand in elections to the European Parliament in the member State of residence; d) rights of diplomatic and consular protection; e) rights to petition the European Parliament and to apply to the Ombudsman.

Lithuanian legislation will follow the above mentioned rules of *acquis communautaire* concerning the right to vote and to stand in municipal elections.

3) An analysis of the constitutional questions of the future accession of Lithuania to the EU would be incomplete without a short examination of Article 125, para. 2, of the Constitution, which deals with monetary issues and, therefore, is relevant to the Economic and Monetary Union. Of course, the introduction of Euro is a separate matter from the EMU, which should be separated from the general question of the accession to the EU. Nevertheless, it should be mentioned that the provision of Article 125, para. 2, of the Constitution could be interpreted in such a way that it does not allow for the introduction of single European currency in Lithuania.

> 'Article 125 *(extract)*
> The Bank of Lithuania shall have the exclusive right to issue bank notes.'

This constitutional provision will be examined with regard to the third stage of the EMU, which started on 1 January 1999, after the European Central Bank was established on 1 June 1998 and the independent European System of Central Banks (ESCB) comprising the European Central Bank and the national central banks was created. The Euro was introduced on 1 January 1999. The Euro-denominated banknotes and coins will be brought into circulation by 1 January 2002.

According to Article 105 of the EC Treaty the ESCB has the following tasks: to define and implement the monetary policy of the Community (according to the Statute of the ESCB its main element is to maintain price stability within the Community); to conduct foreign exchange operations; to hold and manage the official foreign reserves of the member States; to promote the smooth operation of the payments systems. A member State may participate in the third stage of the EMU only if it satisfies certain macro-economic requirements. Once a member State begins to participate, it acquires the right to participate in a decision-making process on monetary issues (both in the ECB and the Council). However, according to Protocol 10 of the EC Treaty the understanding was reached that participation in the third stage of the EMU is compulsory once a member State fulfils necessary requirements.[18] At the same time, if a member State does not comply with the established macro-economic requirements (e.g., has too excessive budget deficits) it may have sanctions imposed by the Council or the ECB. At the same time, even if a member State is not participating in the third stage of the EMU, it has to avoid too excessive budget deficits.

---

[18] The decision concerning Greece had already been taken in Lisbon this year. Denmark and the United Kingdom are covered by special Protocols – these member States have the right to chose – whether to participate or not. For the time being, Sweden does not qualify for the third stage of the EMU.

Going back to Article 125 of the Constitution of Lithuania, it should be pointed out that the term 'to issue bank notes' is a matter of interpretation. It could mean only national currency (Litas) and, therefore, would not be in contradiction with the powers of the European Central Bank to issue a single European currency. In any case, the accession of Lithuania to the European Union does not mean that Lithuania would automatically participate in the third stage of the EMU. Therefore, the above provision of Article 125 of the Constitution could not *per se* be regarded as incompatible with the *acquis communautaire*, and, thus, could be an obstacle to the accession of Lithuania to the EU.

ROLE OF NATIONAL COURTS

4. The courts of Lithuania do accept the principle of direct effect and supremacy of international obligations, and this is based on the dispositions of Article 138 of the Constitution (ratified international treaties are incorporated into the Lithuanian legal system), as well as Article 11, para. 2, of the Law on International Treaties (ratified international treaties have supremacy over laws and secondary legal acts). It would be premature to speculate whether it is also applicable to secondary community law notwithstanding the fact that there are no legal obstacles to the extension of these dispositions to secondary law.

5. There is no case law proving that the Lithuanian courts recognize a rule of interpretation whereby national law must be interpreted in conformity with international obligations. However, there is a constitutional ground for assuming that this recognition would be given in future in relevant case law. Article 135, para. 1, of the Constitution provides for the binding force of 'universally recognized principles and norms of international law'. It provides:

> Article 135
> 'In conducting foreign policy, the Republic of Lithuania shall pursue the universally recognized principles and norms of international law, shall strive to safeguard national security and independence as well as the basic rights, freedoms and welfare of its citizens, and shall take part in the creation of sound international order based on law and justice.'

Notwithstanding the fact that this constitutional provision is devoted to foreign policy, it seems that the conclusion could be drawn that Lithuanian law should be interpreted in conformity with 'universally recognized principles and norms of international law' including the principle *pacta sunt servanda*. Of course, it is not directly related to EU law. However, this rule of interpretation will be applicable to the future obligations of Lithuania, which will derive from the EC and the EU treaties (EU Treaty, EC Treaty, Euratom Treaty, etc.).

6. With respect to the applicability of international legal instruments in the Lithuanian legal system, the most interesting is the case law of the Constitutional Court of Lithuania.

In its Opinion of January 24, 1995 on the conformity of Articles 4, 5, 9, and 14 of the European Convention for the Protection of Human Rights and Fundamental Freedoms and of Article 2 of Protocol No. 4 of the Convention to the Constitution of the Republic of Lithuania, the Constitutional Court gave the following conclusion with regard to the legal force of the Convention in the Lithuanian legal system:

> 'This constitutional provision with regard to the Convention means that a ratified and effective Convention will become the constituent part of the legal system of the Republic of Lithuania and will have to be applied in the same way as legislation of the Republic of Lithuania.'[19]

Such legal force of ratified international treaties (they have the force of law) has been endorsed by the Constitutional Court in its Decision of October 17, 1995 on the conformity of para. 4 of Article 7 and Article 12 of the Law of the Republic of Lithuania on International Treaties to the Constitution of the Republic of Lithuania.[20]

The Supreme Court of Lithuania has, on many occasions, confirmed these principles and has given priority to the international treaties of Lithuania in cases where the law allows it (e.g., Art. 606 of the Civil Code of Lithuania). For example, in the civil case No. 3K-3-337, 1999 concerning trade marks the Supreme Court based its decision on the direct effect of international treaties. In that case, the Court applied the 1967 Convention establishing the World Intellectual Property Organisation (WIPO) and the 1957 Nice Agreement concerning the International Classification of Goods and Services for the Purposes of Registration of Marks. [21]

7. If a Community measure is inconsistent with the prior international commitments of Lithuania, do Lithuanian courts give priority to the prior international commitments? First of all, Lithuanian legislation does not contain dispositions concerning this matter. As a matter of fact, Community measures are not yet directly applicable in Lithuania. Secondly, there is no comparable Lithuanian case law on this matter. Finally, the answer, even theoretical, could be very complex. For example, one specific answer could be drawn from the provisions of the 1995 Europe Agreement concluded by Lithuania. Article 64 para. 5 of the Europe Agreement (anti-competitive agreements between undertakings) refers to a con-

---

[19] Valstybės Žinios, 1995.01.27, No. 9 -199.
[20] Valstybės Žinios 1995.10.20, No. 8 -1949.
[21] Teismų praktika, Nr. 12 (1999), p. 74.

crete Community measure: Council Regulation No. 26/1962, and, in fact, makes this measure directly applicable. One may suppose that this measure, as a part of the dispositions of the Europe Agreement, will prevail over the prior international commitments (treaty commitments). In practical terms, the question of point 7 may also be relevant with regard to the accession negotiations: Lithuanian free trade agreements with Latvia and Estonia, as well as with Ukraine, may be regarded as incompatible with Community measures. The only way to resolve this contradiction would be to denounce these treaties before the accession or, eventually, to ask for transitional periods. The last solution seems unrealistic.

On January 7, 1998, the Chancellery of the Seimas (Lithuanian Parliament) established a working group, which was asked to draft the legal acts necessary for the accession of Lithuania to the European Union.[22] On September 15, 1998, this working group submitted to the Chancellery the first draft consisting of draft amendments to Articles 135 and 138 of the Constitution of the Republic of Lithuania. In its scope this draft was limited to so-called 'Community clauses', which, in the opinion of the Working group, should be introduced into the Constitution of Lithuania, i.e., the transfer of a part of the State competence to a supranational international organisation, the internal procedures concerning proposals of Community measures, the principles of direct effect and supremacy of Community measures, etc.[23] At the same time, it should be noted that this draft, in comparison to the drafts referred to below, did not concern some special provisions of the Constitution, which could raise questions as to their compatibility with the *acquis communautaire*, i.e., acquisition of land (Art. 47 of the Constitution) and local elections (Art. 119). The draft of September 15, 1998 was discussed in the Committee of European Affairs of the Seimas without, however, any follow up.

The issue of the conformity of the Constitution with Community law was further discussed during the seminar-workshop on the 'Constitution of the Republic of Lithuania and accession to the European Union' organized by the European Law Department of the Government of Lithuania together with SEIL/PHARE Project in Vilnius on 28 July 2000. The participants of the seminar-workshop discussed draft proposals prepared by the author of this present paper.[24]

---

[22] The working group was composed of three members: Mr. Stasys Stačiokas, Member of the Seimas, Chairman of the Legal Committee of the Seimas (head of the Working group), Mr. Vytautas Sinkevičius, Director of Legal Department of the Chancellery of the Seimas, and the author of this report (a rapporteur of the Working group).

[23] See: Stojimas į Europos Sajungą ir Konstitucija. Seminaro medžiaga 1999 06 29-30. Vilnius: Eugrimas, 200, pp. 125-161; Vilenas Vadapalas. Independence and Intergration – Constitutional Reform in Lithuania Preparing its Accession to the European Union. In: Verfassungrechtliche Reformen zur Erweiterung der Europäischen Union. Forum Constitutionis Europae – Band 2. Baden-Baden: Nomos Verl., 2000. S.9-22.

[24] See: Vilenas Vadapalas. Questions concerning National Level in Lithuania. In: The Constitutional Impact of Enlargement at the EU and National Level. Reader: Provisional Reports and Docu-

The drafting of proposals for the constitutional amendments relating to the future accession of Lithuania was also included in the Action Plan for the Implementation of the Programme of the Government of the Republic of Lithuania (1999/2000). Under the Action Plan, on 23 October 2000, the European Law Department of the Lithuanian Government submitted the draft to the Government (see annex), which was prepared taking into consideration the opinions and comments of Lithuanian and foreign experts and the experience of previous *travaux préparatoires*.

Annex

Draft of October 23, 2000
Prepared by the European Law Department of the Government of Lithuania
(Unofficial translation, draft amendments are in bold letters)

REPUBLIC OF LITHUANIA
LAW ON THE AMENDMENT OF ARTICLES 47, 119 AND 136 OF THE CONSTITUTION OF THE REPUBLIC OF LITHUANIA

Article 47 (*Option I*)

Land, internal waters, forests, and parks may only belong to the citizens **or legal persons** of the Republic of Lithuania, the State of the Republic of Lithuania by the right of ownership, **as well as to the citizens or legal persons of other States.** (N.B. – *Paragraph 2 of the Article, as well as the Constitutional Law on the Subjects, Procedure, Terms and Conditions and Restrictions of the Acquisition Into Ownership of Land Plots Provided for in Article 47, Paragraph 2 of the Constitution of the Republic of Lithuania of June 20, 1996 shall be repealed and the following paragraphs of the Article shall become paragraph two, three and four respectively*).

Plots of land may belong to a foreign state by the right of ownership for the establishment of its diplomatic and consular missions in accordance with the procedure and conditions established by law.

The right of ownership of entrails of the earth, as well as nationally significant internal waters, forests, parks, roads, and historical, archaeological and cultural facilities shall exclusively belong to the Republic of Lithuania.

The Republic of Lithuania shall have the exclusive rights to the airspace over its territory, its continental shelf, and the economic zone in the Baltic Sea.

---

ments. Colloquium on European Law. Millenium Session XXX. The Hague, 20-23 September 2000, pp. 139-140.

Article 47 (*Option II*)

Land, internal waters, forests, and parks may only belong to the citizens **or legal persons** of the Republic of Lithuania, the State of the Republic of Lithuania by the right of ownership.
Land, internal waters, forests, and parks may as well belong to the citizens or legal persons of other States according to the constitutional law of the Republic of Lithuania. (N.B. – *a new constitutional law should make, inter alia, a reference to the Treaty on Accession of the Republic of Lithuania to the EU*).
Plots of land may belong to a foreign state by the right of ownership for the establishment of its diplomatic and consular missions in accordance with the procedure and conditions established by law.
The right of ownership of entrails of the earth, as well as nationally significant internal waters, forests, parks, roads, and historical, archaeological and cultural facilities shall exclusively belong to the Republic of Lithuania.
The Republic of Lithuania shall have the exclusive rights to the airspace over its territory, its continental shelf, and the economic zone in the Baltic Sea.

Article 119

Administrative units provided by law on State territory shall be entitled to the right of self-government. This right shall be implemented through local government Councils.
Citizens of the Republic of Lithuania and the European Union shall be elected the members of local government Councils for a two-year term on the basis of universal, equal and direct suffrage by secret ballot by the residents of their administrative unit who are citizens of the Republic of Lithuania **and citizens of the European Union.**
The procedure for the organisation and activities of self-government institutions shall be established by law.
Local government Councils shall form executive bodies which are accountable to them for the direct implementation of the laws of the Republic of Lithuania and the decisions of the Government and the local government Council.

Article 136

The Republic of Lithuania shall participate in international organisations provided that they do not contradict the interests and independence of the State.
With the view of taking part in European integration and common European affairs, thus assuring the security of the Republic of Lithuania and the welfare of its citizens, the Republic of Lithuania shall participate in the European Union and transfer to the European Union competence of the State institutions in the spheres defined by the constituent treaties of the European Union in order to exercise this competence in common with other States Members to the European Union.

Provisions of the law of the European Union shall be a constituent part of the legal system of the Republic of Lithuania and shall have supremacy over the provisions established by the laws and other legal acts of the Republic of Lithuania.

CONSTITUTIONAL PROBLEMS IN THE PERIOD OF PRE-ACCESSION IN THE REPUBLIC OF SLOVENIA

Primož Vehar*

This report focuses on some practical problems arising from the constitutional questions concerning the approximation process in the Republic of Slovenia.

1. THE CONSTITUTION OF THE REPUBLIC OF SLOVENIA

1.1 Background

After the Slovenian people and the citizens of the Republic of Slovenia expressed their will on the issue of the independence and sovereignty in a plebiscite held in December 1990 the National Assembly enacted the basic Constitutional Charter on the Independence and Sovereignty of the Republic of Slovenia in June 1991. With this 'sui generis' constitutional act the Republic of Slovenia was constituted as an independent and sovereign state and the Constitution of the Socialist Republic of Yugoslavia ceased to have effect in the Republic of Slovenia, and Slovenian authorities assumed all the rights and obligations that had been transferred to the authorities of the Yugoslav federation.

The basic Constitutional Charter on the Independence and Sovereignty of the Republic of Slovenia and the Statute for its implementation enabled the first 'packet' of statutes needed for the functioning of a new State to be issued.

The Constitution of the Republic of Slovenia was enacted by the National Assembly on 23 December 1991 and entered into force the same day. Since its adoption an amendment has been made regarding property rights of foreigners[1] in July 1997. As a result of this amendment Slovenia is the only candidate country

* Dipl. iur., Adviser to the Government, Government of the Republic of Slovenia, Office for Legislation.

The opinions expressed are purely personal.

[1] The Constitution, Art. 68 '... Foreigners may not acquire title to land ...', was amended to: 'Foreigners may acquire ownership rights to real estate under conditions provided by law or if so provided by a treaty ratified by the National Assembly, under the condition of reciprocity. Such law and treaty from the preceding paragraph shall be adopted by the National Assembly by a two-thirds majority vote of all deputies.'

A.E. Kellermann et al. (Eds.), EU Enlargement: The Constitutional Impact at EU and National Level

that allows EU member States citizens to acquire real estate before the accession to the EU. This amendment was needed to make ratification of the Europe Agreement,[2] specially its Annex XIII,[3] possible.

1.2 The Constitution and Accession to the EU

Accession to a supranational organisation is not admitted by the Slovenian constitutional order due to the fact that the transfer of sovereign rights implied by an accession was not foreseen and is not allowed by the current Constitution.[4]

This situation has to be changed by future amendments of the Constitution that is now based on the idea that all powers are derived from the nation and are executed by the national institutions.[5]

This is quite opposed to the supranational character of the EC Treaty where some legislative, executive and also judicial powers are given to EC institutions, and where a single member State has no control over these powers. Even more, due to direct application (where it is possible) in the case of a conflict of legal norms, the national courts and other institutions have to give precedence to EC law over the national constitution and of course, also over any other national legal norms. Alternatively, the principles of direct effect and primacy of Community law, which cannot be found in the Treaties because they have been developed by ECJ judgments in the 1960s, constitute a part of Community law for all EU member States.

These facts are scarcely understood or credible to many traditionally oriented lawyers and politicians who insist on the position that the Constitution is hierarchically the highest legal act and all state authorities, no matter if they are from the legislative, executive or judicial branch, have to ensure this hierarchy and respect it.

The future accession of Slovenia opens also some other constitutional aspects, not only the hierarchy of legal acts and transfer of sovereign rights, but also the relationship Government-National Assembly in EU matters, elections to the EU Parliament and others.

It should be realized that accession to the EU is not possible without amending the Constitution and that requires a high level of political consent.

---

[2] Europe Agreement Establishing an Association between the European Communities and their member States, acting within the framework of the European Union, of the one part and the Republic of Slovenia, of the other part, signed on 10 June 1996, entered into force on 1 February 1999.

[3] See n. 12.

[4] The Constitution, Art. 3 para.(2): 'In Slovenia supreme power is vested in the people. Citizens exercise that power directly at elections, and consistently with the principle of the separation of legislative, executive and judicial powers'.

[5] See also an analysis concerning Slovenian future membership in the EU and Constitution: Šinkovec, B.: Približevanju clanstvu v Evropski uniji in ustava, published in: Pravna praksa 1999, No. 6, pp. I-VI.

1.3 The Constitution and 'Europe Agreement'

For the legal effect of the Europe Agreement in the internal legal order, the status of international treaties in the Slovene legal order has to be investigated and generally the relationship between international treaties[6] and the internal legal order.

In the Slovenian constitutional order the Constitution is the highest legal act followed by international agreements ratified by the National Assembly.[7]

In the relationship between international law and internal law in Slovenia, the position is that only the Constitution is hierarchically superior to ratified and proclaimed international treaties that on the basis of the Constitution[8] have precedence over all legal acts adopted by the National Assembly.

But the fact that an international treaty has been ratified and published in the Official Gazette and acquires the character of internal law[9] does not mean that it has also a direct effect in the sense of establishing rights and obligations for subjects.[10] This effect (which belongs to the so-called 'self-executing treaties') can be decided only before the national court, it is namely, a question of internal law.[11]

Slovenia was the last of the Central and East European Countries to have signed a Europe Agreement and did not do so until June 1996 due to the EU member State requirements concerning real estate. The result was Annex XIII to the Europe Agreement or so-called 'Spanish compromise' that allowed the acquisition of real estate by EU member States citizens, under some conditions, before the Slovenian accession to the EU.[12] The Europe Agreement was ratified by the

[6] In this case a Europe Agreement, which is no more and no less than an international treaty under the Vienna Convention from 1969.

[7] The Constitution, Art. 8: 'Laws and regulations must comply with generally accepted principles of international law and with treaties that are binding on Slovenia. Ratified and published treaties shall be applied directly' and Art. 153 para. (2): 'Laws must comply with generally accepted principles of international law and with international treaties currently in force and adopted by the National Assembly; regulations and other legislative measures must comply also with other ratified international treaties.'

[8] We have to take care concerning international treaties ratified by the National Assembly and other ratified international treaties.

[9] The Constitution, Art. 8.

[10] A Treaty provision: '... Slovenia shall endeavour to ensure that...' is, in the author's opinion, an example of a non-self-executive provision.

[11] Concerning the Europe Agreement and its effects in the Slovenian legal order see also: Ilešič, Mi.: Pridružitveni sporazum in njegovi učinki v notranjem pravnem redu, published in: Podjetje in delo 1996, No. 8, pp. 731-750 and Pogačnik, M.: Pravna narava Evropskega sporazuma o pridružitvi, published in: Dolčič, T., Pogačnik, M., Šinkovec, B., Vehar, P.: Evropski sporazum o pridružitvi z uvodnimi pojasnili, Ljubljana 1999, pp. 35-45.

[12] In Annex XIII the Government committed itself to take the necessary measures to allow the citizens of the EU member States, on a reciprocal basis, the right to purchase property in Slovenia on a non-discriminatory basis by the end of the fourth year from the entry into force of the Europe Agreement and to grant to the citizens of the EU member States, having permanently resided on the present territory of the Republic of Slovenia for a period of three years, on a reciprocal basis, the right to purchase property from the entry into force of the Europe Agreement.

Slovenian Parliament in July 1997 after the required constitutional amendment[13] and came into force only in February 1999 due to its mixed character and ratification needed in all EU member States.

The Constitutional amendment was needed in the Republic of Slovenia before ratification as a result of the opinion of the Constitutional Court that was requested by the Government who sought a prior evaluation of the constitutionality of the some provisions of the Europe Agreement, as the provision of the Annex XIII is contrary to the provision of the Constitution according to which foreigners may not acquire title to land except by inheritance and then also subject to reciprocity.[14]

In its opinion the Constitutional Court clearly expressed the view that the competent State body may not approve any such commitment under international law as to be in conflict with the Constitution. A commitment under international law would be in conflict with the Constitution if, by an international agreement coming into force, it created directly applicable unconstitutional norms in internal law or if it bound the State to adopt any such instrument of internal law which is in conflict with the Constitution.

According to the Constitution,[15] the Constitutional Court has been empowered to decide upon the conformity of a law on ratification of an international agreement with the Constitution.[16] If in the process of such assessment the Constitutional Court should find a provision of the international law to be in conflict with the Constitution, it may abrogate the law on ratification, but such a decision has effect only in the internal legal order. Such decision does not have any effect on the obligation of the state under international law, which remains unchanged.

Such *a priori* constitutional review of an international agreement in the process of adoption has a preventive objective, namely, to prevent any international agreement, which might introduce unconstitutional norms or would be in conflict with the Constitution, from being concluded.

In the opinion of the Constitutional Court[17] provisions of an international agreement are integrated in the internal legal system upon such an agreement

[13] Article 68 was amended allowing foreigners to acquire title to land under certain conditions. See n. 1.

[14] Other provisions requested for the evaluation of constitutionality related to subsidiaries of Community companies and their right to acquire and sell real property (Arts. 45, para. (7.b) and (7.c) of the EU Agreement).

The provision of Article 65, para. (2), concerning competition: 'Any practice contrary to this Article shall be assessed on the basis of criteria arising from the application of the rules of Articles 85, 86 and 92 of the Treaty establishing the European Community', should be, in the author's opinion, also a subject of constitutional review.

[15] The Constitution, Art. 160.

[16] The Constitutional Court shall provide such an opinion, but only upon the proposal of the President of the Republic, of the Government or of not less than one third of the Deputies of the National Assembly. The National Assembly shall be bound by any such opinion of the Constitutional Court (The Constitution, Art. 160, para. 2).

[17] Case No. RM-1/97, Decision of 5 June 1997, Uradni list RS (Official Gazette), No. 40/97.

coming into force. Of course, only under the condition that it has been ratified in accordance with Slovenian internal law. But we have to be aware that rights and obligations are created by an international agreement only for the state, which is the party to the agreement, and a subject of international public law. They are created also for natural and legal persons if the provisions make it possible[18] – but that remains to be determined by a court decision in each specific case.

1.4 The Procedure for Amending the Constitution

The Procedure for amending the Constitution[19] consists of two stages and starts with a proposal of not less than twenty Deputies of the National Assembly[20], by the Government or by not less than thirty thousand voters. Such a proposal shall only be proceeded upon if it secures the vote of a two-thirds majority of the Deputies of the National Assembly who are present. The National Assembly may then enact an act to amend the Constitution upon the vote of a two-thirds majority of all elected deputies. There is also a possibility for the people to take part in the amending procedure if that is demanded by not less than thirty of the National Assembly Deputies. An amendment could be adopted at such a referendum by a majority of voters eligible to vote and voting in the referendum.

2. THE ROLE OF NATIONAL COURTS

There is a question of the application of international law by the national courts that have to be bound by the Constitution and other internal acts.

The Constitution in Article 8 states that ratified and published international agreements are directly applicable, but this, in author's opinion, does not mean that they have also a direct effect in the sense of establishing rights and obligations for individual subjects. The decision on this question is left to the national court itself.

The most interesting case in Slovenia is on this point the above opinion of the Constitutional Court which held:

> 'Thus, provisions of an international agreement are integrated in the internal legal system of the Republic of Slovenia with the coming into force of such agreement on condition that they have been ratified in accordance with the internal law of the Republic of Slovenia. By an international agreement, rights and obligations are created for the State. When the international agreement has been approved by the law on ratification, it can create rights and obligations also for natural and legal persons in the country if

---

[18] In the case of a self-executing treaty.

[19] The Constitution, Arts. 168-171.

[20] The National Assembly consists of ninety Deputies.

its provisions are by their nature such that they make this possible (in the case of the so-called “self-executing treaty”)’.[21]

3. CONCLUSION

The precondition for the accession of the Republic of Slovenia to the EU will be constitutional amendments, as the National Assembly cannot ratify the Accession Treaty, that allow the supremacy of EC law and its direct effect against the Constitution, which, as has already been explained, does not allow for the transfer of sovereign powers.

Amendments to the Constitution are needed before the ratification of the Accession Treaty but the procedure for changing the Constitution is a quite complicated political question and could be long lasting. Nevertheless, it seems that there will be enough time for the ratification of the Accession Treaty, not only due to the fact that negotiations need time to come to the end but also because the EU needs time to prepare itself for the enlargement through the adoption of internal institutional changes.

Slovenia will be prepared for accession in the very near future[22] through having harmonized its legal system and also amending its Constitution[23], but will the EU and its member States be equally prepared for the enlargement?

How to amend the Constitution – no matter how – but a practical harmonisation must be achieved with direct or ‘hidden’ recognizing the supremacy of EC legal order in the Republic of Slovenia, being in the future one of the EU member States. But this has to be done before ratification of the Treaty of Accession because an amended Constitution is a precondition for ratification.

To sum up, it is not only the amendment of the Constitution by the National Assembly, but also the confirmation of such parliamentary decision by referendum could be the solution. It could be followed by a plebiscite for joining the EU, so demonstrating the highest level of democracy and confirming that Article 3 of the Constitution reading, ‘Slovenia is a state of all its citizens and is based on the permanent and inalienable right of the Slovenian people to self-determination’, is not a dead sentence on the page.

---

[21] Case No. RM-1/97, Decision of 5 June 1997, Uradni list RS (Official Gazette), No. 40/97.

[22] The readiness of Slovenia for the accession to the EU is planned to be in 2003.

[23] Other Copenhagen criteria (democratic system and market economy) are less problematic.

CONSTITUTIONAL IMPACT OF THE EASTWARD ENLARGEMENT IN CENTRAL-EASTERN EUROPE. REPORT ON SESSION III

András Nikodém*

INTRODUCTION

After the second dramatic *memento* of the evil forces of human destruction of the last century, Western Europe witnessed a qualitatively new development of international relations, an ongoing integration process of greatest historic importance. As the epochal East-West conflict has been eased at the turn of the 1980s to the 1990s, the chance to involve the other part of the European continent into this integration process has increased significantly.

The prospective eastern enlargement of the European Union, among other crucial factors, challenges the legal architecture of both the European Union and the candidate countries. What is the nature of this challenge? Does it follow from the prospective enlargement exclusively or did the EU of 15 reach a level of integration in the course of time at which the reconsideration of the whole legal regime is a must? What kind of legal problems arise in making the next enlargement, in making the enlarged EU work? What possible responses can lawyers, coming from the current member States and candidate countries, articulate to the necessary constitutional amendments preceding the accession? What lessons could the history of previous accessions to the Communities and the pre-accession phase in the Central-Eastern European countries teach us? What grade would we, lawyers and citizens of the unified Europe, receive in a class on constitutionalism, legitimacy, democratic and accountable decision-making? Can we improve this grade? Can we, by joint actions, ensure that the quantitative change will not result in a reduced quality?

These questions are not be answered overnight but to bring them out into the open, to identify them, to be confronted with them was one of the valuable purposes of Session III, and, of course, of the whole conference. By sharp contrast with the Intergovernmental Conference, where the candidate countries are not present, though their future is largely dependent upon the results of the IGC, the conference on 'The Constitutional Impact of Enlargement at EU and National

* Istvan Bibo College of Law, Hungary

Level' brought together the representatives of both candidate and EU countries, internationally recognized learned experts in the area of law concerned, to discuss the common elements and specialties of the constitutional preparation for accession. Session III exemplifies this attempt of the organizers with a remarkable message: the candidate 'student' countries in pre-accession may even teach lessons to the EU of 15, so the learning process is a two-way road.

It is also worth noting that in many candidate countries the prospective accession to the European Union will most likely contribute to the constitutional modernization of the country. The lack of political consensus in many of these countries blocked constitutional reform but the accession will likely give impetus to fundamental changes in this respect.

To summarize the reports in an orderly fashion, one has to take step by step common elements in the constitutional procedures such as the constitutional amendments themselves, the role of the courts, and the question of human rights protection.

GENERAL 'EUROPEAN INTEGRATION' CLAUSE

With regard to the necessary constitutional amendments, the process is under way in the countries concerned. A general model is difficult to draw. Two types of amending provisions are possible: a general constitutional clause authorizing the transfer of the exercise of sovereign powers and specific provisions dealing with specific rights and obligations.[1] What the general clause should contain is of key importance. The history of the Communities shows that many difficulties arose out of the lack of constitutional responses to the specific characters of the emerging EC law regime. Naturally, at the beginning of the process, the present well-known specific features of the legal order of the Communities were not clear at all. It was the jurisprudence of the European Court of Justice that added its significant contribution to the development of EC law. However, the candidate countries can be better prepared for the challenge by having express reference in their constitutional acts authorizing the transfer of sovereign powers to the European Union and reference to the most fundamental principles of the EC legal system, to supremacy and the direct effect of Community law.[2]

[1] Francis G. Jacobs writes about three broad categories of constitutional amendment: (1) general provisions allowing for the transfer of certain powers to international organisations, (2) general provisions allowing for the transfer of powers but directed specifically to the EC or EU, (3) specific amendments, for example removing special rights for nationals: e.g., the ownership or publishing of journals in Portugal. See his report at p. 183.

[2] See Francis G. Jacobs's report on the typology of potential conflicts between national constitutions and European law according to the three broad categories of constitutional amendment he identifies at pp. 183 of his report.

The specific historic circumstances of the establishment of the newly-born Central Eastern European democracies make it necessary to note that the transfer of sovereignty in countries that have just recently regained their independence is a very sensitive issue. Since the recent national achievement of the free and independent status of these countries gives a different viewpoint on the possible loss of sovereignty, and on the symbolic value of sovereignty in the minds of the people, communication policies play a crucial role in helping the political process progress

One should also remember that this political process was initiated by a small sector of the society and the issue of legitimization of the process will be a challenge of a different nature than drafting laws and harmonizing legal systems. The requirement to meet basic democratic principles should not be the last one to be concentrated on in the process.

A country-by-country approach reveals that most of the candidate countries have yet to complete the constitutional processes necessary before accession. The case studies of the countries showed that various approaches exist and the interpretation of the existing national constitutional provisions, and the desirability and feasibility of constitutional changes influence what actual steps are made in the process in each country.

Bulgaria

The Bulgarian constitutional provisions on the relationship between international and municipal law are examples of a monist solution. Those international legal instruments that have been properly signed, ratified and promulgated become part of the domestic legal order without any further need for national legislation on their enforcement. In case of conflict with acts of parliament these international law norms prevail. The specific character of EC norms, however, question the necessity of the constitutional amendments.

The Bulgarian reporter mentioned the following elements in this regard:[3]

- transfer of sovereign powers to the EU and its institutions
- European citizenship and the rights it encompasses particularly passive and active voting rights both in local and parliamentary elections
- parliamentary control on integration matters
- direct effect of EC law
- the participation in the European Monetary Union and its consequences for the national monetary policy and the activities of the national central bank
- the participation in the common foreign and security policy of the European Union

[3] See p. 301 of the report of Professor Evgeni Tanchev.

– specific constitutional provisions to be changed such as the ban on foreigners acquiring land.

Czech Republic

The Czech constitutional provisions on the relationship between international and domestic law are very similar to the Bulgarian ones. As in Bulgaria, under the current Czech system properly ratified international norms have supremacy over parliamentary acts but the supremacy of EC law over the constitution as well as the application of the direct effect doctrine of EC law require constitutional amendment in the Czech Republic.

A possible difference is the implication of Article 2 Section 2 of the Czech Constitution calling for a nation-wide referendum on the would-be Accession Treaty. Open questions remain concerning the implementation and effect of such a referendum.

In the Czech Republic too, there is a minimum variant of constitutional amendment and a broader one resulting in a more extensive constitutional incorporation of the EC norms.[4] Czech constitutional lawyers put emphasis on the possibility,[5] through the powers of the national parliament and the implications of the maintenance of unanimous decision-making rules in the Council, of controlling the law-making mechanism of the EU.

Estonia

Legal experts appointed by the Estonian Government made a study of the constitutional situation in Estonia and concluded that without constitutional changes Estonia cannot become a full member of the European Union.[6] The provision 'Estonia is an independent and sovereign democratic republic wherein the supreme power of the state is held by the people. Estonian independence is interminable and inalienable' is to be amended, according to the Commission, with the following paragraph: 'Estonia may, on the basis of referendum, participate in the European Union, which is an association of States created by its member States on the basis of the Treaties.' Under the Chapter of the Constitution entitled Foreign Relations and Treaties, the delegation of power clause should be set out pursuant to the Commission's proposal. The Commission explains that this solution would demonstrate that European integration matters belong to international law actions not endangering the independent statehood of Estonia. The transfer of powers would be conditional upon the assumption 'that it does not violate the ba-

---

[4] See p. 423 of the report of Professor Zemanek.

[5] Ibid., p. 423.

[6] See Riigi Teataja (National State Gazette) I. 1996,35,725 found at p. 1 of the report of Professor Kerikmae.

sic principles and functions of Estonian statehood manifested in the Preamble of the Constitution.'[7]

Hungary

The Hungarian Constitution declares that Hungary is an independent, democratic state ... where all powers are vested in the people. The implications of the prospective amendment before accession are therefore similar to other candidate countries.

The constitutional amendment in Hungary might be coupled with an overall reform of the constitution since the democratic political processes for political change could not reach consensus on the adoption of a new constitution, though the constitution of 1949 had been several times modified.

An interesting specialty is that the Hungarian approach is dualistic to the relationship of international and municipal law. The Hungarian constitution contains one provision on the relationship between international law and domestic law stating that the Republic of Hungary accepts the generally recognized rules of international law and ensures the harmony between domestic law and obligations under international law. On the interpretation of this constitutional provision the Constitutional Court in 1993 declared that the rule obliges the legislative organ to enact norms in order to meet assumed international obligations.[8] Another decision of the Constitutional Court stated that the generally recognized rules of international law are part of the Hungarian legal system without the requirement for any further national law-making.[9] According to the Court, the Constitution has transformed these rules. That has been a move away from the dualist theory ...

Latvia

Article 1 of the Latvian Constitution states that Latvia is an independent democratic republic while Article 2 declares that the sovereign power of the State of Latvia is vested in the people of Latvia. The legal experts in Latvia are divided on the issue whether Accession would be possible without amending these provisions.[10] Those stressing the necessity of the amendment argue that part of the sovereign powers will be transferred to and practised by the EU and not by the Latvian people. Others follow a different line of argument and explain sovereignty as 'the right to say the last word' and that is kept for the Latvian people since they can terminate their participation in the EU.

---

[7] Ibid., p. 2.

[8] See Decision no. 16/1993. (III.12.) ABH 1993, p. 143 at p. 154 found at p. 315 of the report of Professor Harmathy.

[9] See Decision no. 50/1993. (X.13.) ABH 1993, p. 323 at p. 327 found, ibid.

[10] See p. 337 of the report of Professor Ušacka.

In Latvia, similarly to other candidate countries, a minimum, 'laconic' integration clause and a more detailed amendment scenario exist.[11] The minimum variant might only include the sentence 'Latvia is a member State of the European Union', attached to Article 2. The other variant includes those issues that have been already discussed in other country reports.

As for the referendum on joining the European Union, the Latvian Constitution does not establish the possibility to hold a referendum on a freely formulated abstract issue such as Latvia's accession to the EU. An integration clause would, however, modify the understanding of the concept of independence expressed in Article 1 of the Latvian Constitution as well as that of sovereignty laid down in Article 2. The amendment of these articles is only possible by way of a referendum.[12] Hence, the Latvian people voting 'for' or 'against' the amendment will simultaneously vote for the abstract issue of Latvian membership in the European Union.

Lithuania

The Constitution of Lithuania mentions neither the transfer of sovereign powers to supranational organizations, nor the direct effect or the supremacy of EC law.

Article 138 of the Lithuanian Constitution reads 'international agreements which are ratified by the Seimas of the Republic of Lithuania shall be the constituent part of the legal system of the Republic of Lithuania'. At a statutory level, legislative provisions recognize the supremacy of ratified international treaties.[13]

The possibility of a specific conflict between the constitution and EC law still exists. Either explicit reference in the constitution to the supremacy of EC law could be made to incorporate the statutory reception of the supremacy of international law at the constitutional level or specific amendments should ease the obvious tensions between the existing EC norms and, for instance, the Lithuanian rules on the right to acquire land, the right to take part in municipal elections or the exclusive right of the Bank of Lithuania to issue bank notes.

With regard to the possibility of a referendum, Article 9 of the Constitution stipulates 'The most significant issues concerning the life of the State and the People shall be decided by referendum'.[14]

---

[11] Ibid.
[12] Ibid.
[13] See p. 347 of the report of Professor Vadapalas.
[14] Ibid.

Poland

Poland is a peculiar case because she had already adopted a constitution before accession negotiations took place. In the new constitution express reference is made to the transfer of sovereign powers to international organizations.[15] It is also important that the constitution was popularly legitimated by the people in 1997.

Article 90 of the Constitution states that Poland may delegate the competence of the organs of State authority to an international organization. Furthermore, Article 91 states that properly promulgated and ratified international agreements shall constitute part of the domestic legal order and shall be applied directly, unless application is dependent on the enactment of a statute. Similarly to the Lithuanian situation, at the statutory level precedence is given to ratified international agreements.

The issue of the 'last word', however, returns to greet us if, in a hard case, a conflict between a constitutional norm and EC law provision should arise. This question is, however, not resolved in the EU of 15 either.

Slovakia

The Constitution of Slovakia, similarly to many of the examined countries in question, does not have reference to the transfer of sovereign powers to supranational organizations. Article 7 of the Constitution declares that 'The Slovak Republic may, by its own discretion, enter into a union with other states ... The decision to enter into a union with other states or to secede therefrom shall be subject to a constitutional statute and subsequent ratification by means of a public referendum'. To read this provision as authorizing the accession of Slovakia into the EU would require an expanded understanding of the terms set out in the provision.[16]

In line with this view, Slovak MPs submitted a proposal, currently pending, to amend the Constitution.[17] The amendment would change Article 7 as follows: 'the Slovak Republic can via an international treaty or based on it, transfer a part of its sovereign rights to international organisations of which the Slovak Republic is a member, as fixed by an international treaty'.[18]

With regard to the prospective relationship between national law and EC law the proposed amendment to the Slovak constitution reads that 'in the event that this organisation issues legally binding acts, these are also directly binding in the Slovak Republic and have precedence over national law'.[19]

---

[15] See p. 279 of the report of Professor Justynski.

[16] As Professor Vlasta Kunová expresses her view on this point at p. 327 of her report.

[17] Ibid.

[18] Ibid.

[19] Ibid.

A parliamentary three-fifth majority requirement exists in the proposal to pass an international treaty transferring a part of sovereign rights of the Slovak republic to an international organisation. On the issue of a referendum the proposal is silent, here one can quote Article 93 of the current Constitution stating 'A constitutional statute on the formation of a union with other states or a secession thereof shall be confirmed by a public referendum' ... furthermore 'a referendum may be also used to decide on other crucial issues in the public interest'.[20]

Slovenia

Article 3(2) of the Slovenian Constitution declares that 'in Slovenia supreme power is vested in the people'. The transfer of sovereign powers is not mentioned in the basic law adopted in 1991 after the country gained independence. On the relationship of international treaties and internal law, Articles 8 and 153(2) of the Slovenian Constitution places ratified international agreements below the constitution in the legal hierarchy of sources of law. The Constitutional Court of Slovenia has expressly stated that the Slovenian Parliament cannot approve any commitment under international law that is in conflict with the Constitution.[21] Article 160 empowers the Court to decide a priori the constitutionality of the law on ratification before the law would operate to incorporate the international agreement into the domestic order. The above mechanisms in the Slovenian legal order aim at protecting the independence of the newly-born state as well as its legal order.

Under a literally reading of the constitutional norms, which seems to be widely accepted in Slovenia, the Parliament of Slovenia would not be able to ratify the would-be accession treaty unless the present constitutional provisions not allowing the transfer of sovereign powers are changed.[22] The amendment of the constitution is therefore a precondition for ratification of the treaty. Concerning the specific nature of EC law, particularly the supremacy of EC law and direct effect, Articles 8 and 153(2) should also be explicitly changed in order to avoid a negative decision by the Constitutional Court on the ratification.[23]

It would be highly desirable to gain popular legitimacy for such changes of fundamental importance in Slovenia. Upon the request of at least thirty parliamentarians the Slovenian people may take part in the amending process itself. The Amendment is adopted if the majority of voters approve it.

To sum up, existing constitutional provisions must be amended, though how and to what extent are questions to be resolved on a case-by-case basis. A further problem is when should the constitutional amendments be made. Since the date

---

[20] Ibid.

[21] See p. 369. of the report of Mr Vehar.

[22] Ibid.

[23] Ibid.

of accession is the least clear even for well-informed future tellers, the evolution of the EU acquis, i.e., the problem of the 'moving target' phenomenon, might result in new changes in the amending provisions that have already been made. Maybe one of the most striking examples is the case of the Charter of Fundamental Rights. At this stage, one may think of the alternatives that can happen with the Charter but obviously the important, and quite frequent, 'constitutional' developments at the EU level severely challenge the preparation of the acceding countries.

Having briefly overviewed the issues concerning 'the European integration clause', focus should be shifted to those specific constitutional provisions that are not in conformity with the legal norms of the European Community.

SPECIFIC PROVISIONS

The specific constitutional provisions, if they are to be adopted, will be in response to the unique legal issues to be resolved. General examples might be formulated as follows. In the case that a national constitutional rule is in collision with EC norms, for instance with the requirements of the four freedoms, a possible solution is a constitutional amendment, i.e., removal of the national rule. Judicial interpretation of the rules is also an element to be taken into account and this leads us to consider the role of the courts in the process.

A country-by-country analysis below will highlight examples of specific provisions to be removed as a precondition before accession takes place.

The property rights in real estate is a general source of problem throughout the candidate countries. As an illustration, in Slovenia, the signing of the Europe Agreement had to be postponed because of a prohibition on EU member State citizens acquiring real estate in the country. The Slovenian Constitutional Court expressed in its opinion on the issue that a constitutional amendment would be necessary. The Europe Agreement could only be signed after the constitutional amendment of Article 68 of the Constitution allowing foreign citizens to acquire title to land under special conditions. The problem is present in almost all the countries involved.

Another general example might be the right to take part in municipal elections. Where the constitution defines eligibility in terms of citizenship of the country concerned, the norm has to be changed in order to give effect of the EC norm allowing every citizen of the Union residing in a member State of which he is not a national to vote and to stand as a candidate at municipal elections.

In the light of the European Monetary Union, the exclusive right of the national banks of the candidate countries to issue bank notes must be reconsidered too.

The above examples show that besides the question of a general clause specific constitutional provisions draw the attention of constitutional lawyers in the candidate countries working on the removal of obstacles before accession.

THE ROLE OF NATIONAL COURTS

Evidently, the work of the courts and the quality of the work of the courts is a core element. The preparation of the judges for the challenges they are to handle is under way in the candidate countries. Would ordinary courts be able to deal with conflicts between national and EC law? When would the matter fall under the competence of the constitutional court and when under that of ordinary courts? The resolution of these questions determine to what extent the candidate countries will contribute to the reduction of discrepancy and to the increase of predictability and coherency when the *order* of EC law is at stake.

The lack of case law in the candidate countries gives a possibility to consider theoretical questions only but the evolution of the ECJ-national/constitutional courts discourse still causes headache for constitutional lawyers.

In light of the above consideration, it is quintessential to advance the awareness of national justices of the problems of the application of EC law and of their future role as Community judges. To this aim, providing adequate training in the field of EC law for national judges of the candidate countries is a must.

A strongly inter-linked, highly relevant issue is the protection of human rights. In this respect, the evolution of EC law with the prospective but yet unknown way of adopting the Charter of Fundamental Rights may be a good example of the problem of moving targets that do not contribute to a higher level of coherency.

In the light of what has been said above, it seems to be only a technical matter that the number of cases referred to the European judicial organs will overburden them unless reform is undertaken.

The national courts will also have to face the challenge of the application of the preliminary ruling procedure and their cooperation with the European judicial organs will be the cornerstone of the European legal order. Criticism that it is actually an order might be anticipated.

However, it was not the attitude 'to stay where we are' that powered the integration train of Europe. The final destination, the *finalité politique*, is still debated even though attempts to handle the differences between the various levels of development are being undertaken. Flexibility is clearly attempting experimentation with the hope of achieving a possibly higher quality, so as to prevent quantity making a qualitative change being for the worse. Earlier accessions proved that the *aim* to accept new members to the European family is not a particularly significant danger for Europe, but *the forms and methods*, to use 'the directive terminology', have to be drawn carefully.

The architects of the legal system, the lawyers of the candidate and member countries, have to work together on the creation of the new European order by maintaining the ideals of the founding fathers upon which the European *édifice* has been built.

SESSION IV
IGC and Future Perspectives for the European Architecture

THE CONSTITUTIONAL ISSUES ON THE IGC 2000 AGENDA

Pieter Van Nuffel*

1. The Feira European Council underlined that the aim of the present Intergovernmental Conference (IGC) is to ensure '*that the Union continues to have properly functioning, efficient and legitimate institutions after enlargement*'.[1] It is indeed generally accepted that the institutional framework of the Union, if it were, as in the past, only to be adjusted for the entrance of the new member States, would face major difficulties in a Union with 28 or more member States. Institutional reforms are therefore a prerequisite for enlargement. Does that mean that the IGC is preparing 'constitutional changes' for the European Union?

2. The answer to that question depends on what one considers as being the 'Constitution' of the European Union. Clearly the Union does not have a written constitution in the sense that (most) sovereign states have; so, arguably, no constitutional changes are being prepared. On the other hand, the Court of Justice has stated that the EC Treaty is the 'Basic Constitutional Charter' of the European Community[2]; a fortiori the Treaty on European Union is the basic Constitutional Charter of the Union. So, since the IGC is being convened to determine the amendments to be made to those treaties, arguably all the work undertaken by the IGC can be considered as preparing constitutional changes for the European Union.

Both paths are not very helpful for this Colloquium. Therefore, and for the sole purpose of this paper, without any claim that this definition is suitable in another context, I will consider as the 'constitutional provisions of the Union' those basic institutional provisions of the treaties which govern the functioning of the Union and the Communities: the Institutions, their composition, functions, powers and competences, the interinstitutional relations, etc.; in short: the institutional framework of the Union.[3]

* European Commission – Head of Unit IGC on Institutional reforms (SG-1), Views expressed are strictly personal.

[1] Feira European Council (19-20 June 2000), Presidency conclusions, point 3; the Cologne European Council (3-4 June 1999), that decided that an IGC would be convened in 2000, used similar language (Presidency Conclusions, points 52-54).

[2] Judgment of 23 April 1986 (case 294/83, 'Les Verts', ECR 1986 p. 1339), point 23.

[3] As a single institutional framework serves the European Union and the European Communities (Art. 3 TEU), a reference in this paper to 'the Union' has to be understood – unless specifically indicated – as a reference to 'the Union and the Communities'.

A.E. Kellermann et al. (Eds.), EU Enlargement: The Constitutional Impact at EU and National Level

However, not all modifications of the institutional provisions of the Union are to be considered as *real* 'constitutional changes': only if the 'pillar structure' of the Union were to be changed or abolished, if new competences were to be bestowed on the Union or if the basic features of the composition, functioning or powers of an Institution were to be changed would this signify, in my view, a change of the 'Constitution' of the Union.

3. It can be recalled that every accession requires unavoidably the adjustment of the provisions concerning the composition of some of the Institutions and those concerning the territorial application of the Treaties;[4] but these changes should not be considered as 'constitutional changes', because they are (or should be) strictly limited to those 'technical' modifications necessitated by the accession of one or more new member States. Article 49 TEU (which lays down the procedure to be followed for accession of new member States) allows indeed only for 'adjustments to the Treaties which the admission of a new member State to the Union entails'.

It is certainly not easy to draw a precise and clear dividing line between the adjustments to the Treaties to be made under Article 49 TEU and the amendments to the Treaties which are required following the procedure of Article 48 TEU. However, as both procedures require ratification by all member States and as the Court of Justice cannot judge the validity of primary Community law, the distinction is more one of procedural than of fundamental importance:[5] an Accession Treaty not only requires (obviously) ratification by the acceding State, but also the assent of the European Parliament.

There seems to exist a general agreement that an Accession Treaty may not alter the functioning and powers of the Union and its institutions[6] nor the rationale behind the composition of the institutions or the respective weight of the member States.[7] In other words, an Accession Treaty cannot introduce 'constitutional changes' in the Union: these can only be adopted through an amendment of the Treaties according to the procedure of Article 48.

---

[4] See e.g., Articles 11 to 28 of the 1994 Act of Accession (OJ No. C 241 of 29.8.1994), as modified by Council Decision 95/1 of 1 January 1995 (OJ No. L 1 of 1.1.1995).

[5] Nevertheless, the distinction between an Accession Treaty and a Treaty making amendments to the existing Treaties may have consequences for the ratification procedure at the national level: e.g., the debate in Germany whether Accession Treaties come under Article 23(1) or Article 59(2) Grundgesetz (see *Vedder* in Grabitz/Hilf EUV Art. 49, Rdnr. 38-39).

[6] It is, however, interesting to note that Article 102 of the 1972 Accession Treaty, as the Court of Justice found in its Judgment of 5 May 181 (case 804/79, *Commission* v. *UK*, ECR 1981 p. 1045, points 17-18), has bestowed on the European Community the exclusive competence to adopt measures relating to the conservation of the resources of the sea, which was probably an extension of its competences as laid down in the Treaty of Rome.

[7] It is therefore questionable whether the change which the 1972 Act of Accession made in the relative weight of the vote in the Council for Luxembourg could be done in the framework of the

4. The IGC has been convened – in the framework of Article 48 TEU – to consider the institutional changes required in the prospect of a Union of 28 or more members. The member States agree that the present IGC should *only* tackle those issues that *need* to be decided upon in order to proceed with the envisaged enlargement. The IGC will therefore in principle not discuss issues such as new competences for the Union or a further transfer of competences from the 'third pillar' (police and judicial cooperation in criminal matters) to the 'first pillar' (the European Community). The only issues on the IGC agenda are the composition and functioning of the institutions and the decision-making process, while maintaining the overall interinstitutional balance.

A fortiori, the IGC is not looking into the even more fundamental questions on the future of Europe which have been raised in different political statements in the debate since the speech of the German Foreign Minister Fischer on 12 May 2000 at the Humboldt University in Berlin. As a matter of fact, these statements make clear the true distinction between what has to be decided at the conclusion of the present IGC, at the Nice European Council, and what are the issues to be tackled in the long term.

Consequently, the *first question* posed by the Organization Committee of this Colloquium must receive the reply that the IGC 2000 will not develop the 'Constitutional Order of the Union': it will leave untouched the present European architecture with its 'Pillar structure'; at this stage there is no prospect of any further 'communautarization'.

5. The debate among member States on what are the 'necessary changes' to the Union's institutional framework in the prospect of enlargement has been more or less settled by the mandate for the IGC, as laid down by the Cologne, Helsinki and Feira European Councils.

The Helsinki European Council decided that the IGC 2000

> 'will examine the size and composition of the Commission, the weighting of votes in the Council and the possible extension of qualified majority voting in the Council, as well as other necessary amendments to the Treaties arising as regards the European institutions in connection with the above issues and in implementing the Treaty of Amsterdam'.[8]

The Feira European Council considered moreover that

---

accession procedure (the weight of the vote of the original member States provided for in the Treaty of Rome was multiplied by 2,5 in order to create the possibility to insert Denmark and Ireland in the scale between Belgium and Luxembourg, but the weight of the vote of Luxembourg was only doubled).

[8] Helsinki European Council (10-11 December 1999), Presidency conclusions, point 16.

'the provisions on closer cooperation introduced into the Treaty of Amsterdam should form part of the Conference's future work, while respecting the need for coherence and solidarity in an enlarged Union'.[9]

6. The Presidency Report to the Feira European Council[10] gives a detailed description of the issues that are being discussed, on the basis of this mandate, in the IGC. They concern, almost exclusively, the institutional framework of the Union: the composition and functioning of the institutions and the decision-making process. Most of the IGC work is therefore indeed to consider 'constitutional issues' for the Union.

And yet it is in a way paradoxical that, due to the number of candidate States and their size, the mere adoption of technical adjustments to the institutional framework in the coming Accession Treaties, in the same way as has been done for the previous enlargements of the Union, would have led, as will be explained in this paper, *de facto* to major 'constitutional changes' in the Union, whereas the modifications of the institutional framework of the Union which are considered in the IGC are aimed to maintain in essence somehow, through new formulas, the basic features and the equilibria of the present Union notwithstanding the doubling of its member States.

My introductory question 'is the IGC preparing constitutional changes for the European Union?' can therefore not receive an unequivocal reply. From a formal point of view, the reply must doubtless be affirmative, as the IGC is preparing modifications to the institutional framework of the Union that would certainly exceed the scope of Article 49 TEU. Substantially, the reply will depend on the outcome of the IGC, since some of the solutions proposed aim at maintaining the present *status quo* in an enlarged Union, whereas others, although conceived to maintain the present overall equilibrium, would indeed alter the institutional framework of the Union. The reply may, in fact, differ from one issue to another, as I will try to explain below.

7. Before entering into these various issues, it should be noted that the IGC may address some questions which are definitively of a constitutional nature. It may not, however, decide on the substance, but only agree on a *procedure* on how to proceed 'after Nice'.

The Biarritz European Council is due to propose to the European Parliament, the Commission and the Council that they solemnly proclaim the European Charter of Fundamental Rights, which is presently being elaborated by the 'Convention'. The Cologne European Council decided, however, that 'consideration of whether, and if so, how the charter might be integrated into the treaties would be

---

[9] Feira European Council (19-20 June 2000), Presidency conclusions, point 3.

[10] Presidency report on the Intergovernmental Conference on institutional reform, CONFER 4750/00 of 14 June 2000 (http://db.consilium.eu.int/cigdocs/EN/04750en.pdf).

left until after this whole process was complete'.[11] Although advocated by some, in particular the European Parliament,[12] it seems unlikely that the present IGC will be in a position to take the decision whether or not to integrate the Charter into the Treaties. A possible compromise might be to take a procedural decision on how to continue the examination of this question after the Nice European Council.

Another theme is the reorganisation of the Treaties. At the request of the European Commission, the European University Institute (Robert Schuman Center for Advanced Studies) has drawn up a Report on this matter and has elaborated a draft '*Basic Treaty of the European Union*' which demonstrates the feasibility of such an operation.[13] The European Commission adopted on 12 July 2000 a Communication on this matter, which proposes that the IGC should decide, not on the substance, but on a procedure and a timetable for carrying out, without interfering with the enlargement process, the reorganization and simplification of the Treaties.[14] The Nice European Council could thus also agree on a procedural decision how to continue this issue afterwards.

8. With respect to *the second question* posed by the Organization Committee of this Colloquium, the following pages will try to give a short overview of the most significant institutional reforms the IGC is presently considering. The question whether these institutional reforms are to be considered real 'constitutional changes' is to be addressed issue by issue.

THE EUROPEAN COMMISSION

9. The Commission is composed of one or two nationals from each member State (cf. Art. 213(1) EC), in fact, from the outset, it has been composed of two from each of the larger member States and one from each of the others. Although, through the different accessions, the number of Commissioners has increased from 9 to 20, its composition was always characterised by the co-existence of two elements, equally important for its particular position in the Union's institutional system and for the legitimacy of its decisions: the presence of (at least) one national of each member State and the fact that the Commissioners formed together a relatively small group of persons, capable of acting genuinely according to the principle of collegiality, as the Treaty provides.

---

[11] Cologne European Council (3-4 June 1999), Presidency conclusions, Annex IV.

[12] Resolution A5-0086/2000 of 13 April 2000, point 33.1.

[13] http://europa.eu.int/comm/igc2000/offdoc/repoflo_en.pdf and http://europa.eu.int/comm/igc2000/offdoc/draftreaty_en.pdf .

[14] Commission Communication '*A Basic Treaty for the European Union*' (COM(2000)434 of 12 July 2000, http://www.europa.eu.int/comm/igc2000/offdoc/com434_en.pdf).

If the rules with respect to the composition of the Commission were not changed, the number of Commissioners would increase over successive accessions to 35 in a Union of 28 member States, i.e., almost four times as many as when it was first set up. It is generally accepted that this would seriously affect the Commission's capability to act efficiently and as a college, thereby weakening its position in the institutional architecture of the Union. By not changing the rules, the successive Accession Treaties would thus, gradually and silently, bring about an important *de facto* constitutional change for the Union.

10. However, a solution does not exist which allows for the preservation in the future of the co-existence of the above two characteristic elements (a small group of Commissioners comprising at least one national of every member State); a real 'constitutional change' is therefore unavoidable. In its Opinion of 26 January 2000 on the IGC,[15] the Commission presented the two possible approaches to the problem: either maintaining the principle of a Commission made up of one national from each member State with its structure overhauled to maintain its efficiency, or a Commission composed of a limited number of Commissioners irrespective of the number of member States.

The latter approach would constitute an important change with respect to the present situation, but would allow the Commission to maintain its present internal decision-making process and to continue to act as a real college. It obviously raises the question of how the Commissioners would be appointed. The Commission considered in its Opinion of 26 January that the only realistic possibility would be a system of rotation that would treat all member States strictly equal on the basis of a pre-set order; this solution would have the advantage of remaining relatively close to the present system. Others have proposed to leave it entirely up to the President to form a Commission, composed in such a way that it can receive approval both from the European Parliament and all the member States. Obviously, this solution would constitute a major constitutional change for the Union since such a Commission would, far more than presently, be a prefiguration of a European government, with an enhanced role for the President.

The more classical approach, a Commission which would continue to comprise one national of each member State, would require the introduction of drastic changes: the functioning of the college would need to be fundamentally reorganised, with in particular significantly increased powers for the President, the appointment of a larger number of Vice-Presidents with the task to coordinate and oversee the work of certain other Commissioners: a certain degree of hierarchisation of the college would seem unavoidable.

---

[15] Commission Opinion '*Adapting the Institutions to make a success of enlargement*' (COM-(2000)34 of 26 January 2000, http://www.europa.eu.int/comm/igc2000/offdoc/opin_igc_en.pdf, Bulletin of the EU – Supplement 2/2000).

THE WEIGHTING OF VOTES IN THE COUNCIL

11. The question of the weighting of votes in the Council has been linked to the composition of the Commission by the Protocol annexed to the Treaty of Amsterdam 'on the institutions with the prospect of enlargement of the European Union'. The question is fundamental: what will be the weight of each member State in the institutional framework of the enlarged Union?

The major difficulty in resolving this question is that the current system (cf. Art. 205(2) EC) was not built upon clearly defined premises, but on a simple political compromise between the original six member States, based on the particular composition of the Community at that time: the three larger States each had 4 votes, the three Benelux together 5 votes (2 for the Netherlands and 2 for Belgium, 1 for Luxembourg); qualified majority was fixed at 12 votes out of 17. With the successive accessions, no new political deals were made, but the new member States were grafted into that scheme, more or less on the basis of their population in comparison with the others, leaving the original relationship untouched,[16] the qualified majority remained unchanged through the years, around 71% of the total votes.

The number and the size of the candidate States[17] would mean that the present 'balance' between larger and less populated member States would be altered if the Accession Treaties were merely to adjust the Treaty provision on the weighting of votes, i.e., if they were merely to introduce the acceding States into the present scale: indeed the number of less populated member States will seriously increase and hence the relative position of the larger member States will be affected.[18] By not changing the rules, the successive Accession Treaties would thus, gradually and silently, bring about *de facto* an important constitutional change for the Union.

12. The debate in the IGC has focused on the various elements one should take into account with a view to agreeing on the premises for a reweighting of the votes in the Council. However, as is clearly shown by the Presidency report to the Feira European Council[19], this leads to a large number of possible parameters, variants and options; it is on that basis very difficult to predict the outcome of the IGC. But if one looks at the question from the angle of this Colloquium, the IGC

[16] But for the weight of votes of Luxembourg (see n. 7).

[17] Nine of the candidate States have a population equal to or less than the present 'median' member State (Belgium); six of them are less populated than Ireland.

[18] Already at the time of the last accession, the prospect of the accession of (at first four) 'smaller' States induced some member States to contest the mere adjustment of the Treaty, which eventually led to the 'Ioannina compromise' (Council Decision of 29 March 1994, OJ No. C105 of 13.4.1994, as modified by Council Decision of 1 January 1995, OJ No. C1 of 1.1.1995); see also Declaration No. 50 annexed to the Treaty of Amsterdam.

[19] See n. 10.

has, in my view, basically to make a choice between two approaches. Either the IGC decides simply to make, as in 1957, a new political compromise, based on the particular composition of the Union in the years to come, or the IGC opts for an entirely new system, that is a system of double majority.

The first approach (a simple reweighting) would not have to be considered as a 'constitutional change' for the Union,[20] because it would be nothing more than, as in 1957, a politically agreed balance between the member States, adjusted to take into account the changed composition of the Union.

The second approach (double majority) would constitute a 'constitutional change', certainly in the formula proposed by the Commission in its Opinion of 26 January 2000,[21] whereby a qualified majority would be reached if the decision has the support of at least a majority of the member States and of (member States representing) a majority of the total population of the Union ('double simple majority'). It would be a major change, because until now a qualified majority can only be reached by a number of member States that represented at least 58% of the Union's total population.[22] The Commission proposed to express directly within the system of qualified majority the fact that the Union is a Union of states and a Union of peoples. However, as shown by the Presidency Report to the Feira European Council, the IGC has also discussed other formulas of double majority, which in their analysis would come closer to a simple reweighting of the votes.

THE EUROPEAN PARLIAMENT

13. The composition of the European Parliament is a question similar to that of the weighting of votes in the Council. The current composition of the European Parliament (cf. Art. 190(2) EC) was agreed upon by the Edinburgh European Council (1992), on the basis of a Parliament proposal.[23] Although in the decision-making process in the Parliament some formulas were used, the final resolution only provides for an allocation of seats. The Treaty of Amsterdam has limited the number of members of the European Parliament to a maximum of 700 (cf. Art. 189 EC).

If the present provisions are not changed, the ceiling of 700 seats would be exceeded, probably already on the first accession.[24] There is a broad agreement in

---

[20] Unless the reweighting would make it possible to reach a qualified majority of votes with a minority of member States, a possibility which never existed in the past: a qualified majority comprised always a majority, or at least half, of the member States.

[21] See n. 15.

[22] This figure was until 1986 in the region even of 67-70 % (see the table in footnote 11 of the Commission's Opinion).

[23] Resolution A3-0186/92 of 10 June 1992, OJ No. C176 of 13.7.1992.

[24] The Parliament currently has 626 members; Poland has a number of inhabitants almost equal to Spain, which is represented in the EP by 64 members.

the IGC that this maximum must be maintained and it is anyhow questionable whether Article 189 EC could be modified by an Accession Treaty (see para. 3 above). Consequently, this IGC must decide on a reduction of the number of seats for each member State in order to allow the allocation to the acceding States of a corresponding number of seats in the European Parliament, whilst respecting the ceiling of 700 seats.

14. The question is how the present figures will be reduced. Broadly two approaches are possible. On the one hand, it would be possible to make a linear reduction of the number of seats with the same percentage; this would, in my view, not constitute a 'constitutional change' since the present relative differences between member States would remain unchanged. On the other hand, if the IGC were to adopt the formula proposed by the European Parliament itself, i.e., an allocation on a proportional basis according to population,[25] it would definitively introduce a 'constitutional change'. In any event, in both approaches the question remains of whether to maintain or reduce the assured minimal number of seats for each member State (presently 6).

Finally, the European Commission has proposed to elect a number of members of the European Parliament on 'European lists', presented to all voters throughout the Union. Adoption of this proposal would constitute a major 'constitutional change'; it has, however, to be noted that this proposal has received little support at this stage.

EXTENSION OF QUALIFIED MAJORITY VOTING

15. The Single European Act and the Treaties of Maastricht and Amsterdam have made 'constitutional changes' to the legal system of the European Community by introducing the co-decision procedure and extending qualified majority voting; today, the vast majority of Council decisions are founded on a legal basis that provides for qualified majority voting. These changes have been made in order to enhance not only the democratic legitimacy of Community rules but also the effectiveness of the decision-making process. Nevertheless, important issues remain subject to unanimity, in particular themes like taxation, social security, structural funds and cohesion fund, asylum and immigration, and also some international trade agreements.

It does not need to be explained that reaching unanimity was originally, with six member States, easier than today. The abandonment of the practice introduced after the 1965 Luxembourg compromise never to vote and the reduction by

[25] Resolution A5-0086/2000 of 13 April 2000, point 5.2. The Parliament does not propose a system of strict proportionality, because it provides for an allocation of a minimum of four seats for each member State.

the three above-mentioned Treaties of cases that require unanimity have to a large extent compensated for the effect of the increase in the number of member States on the decision-making process. It is generally accepted that the prospect of a Union with 28 or more members necessitates a further extension of qualified majority voting, to forestall possible blockages.

16. The Commission has, in its Opinion on the IGC,[26] proposed to change the previous approach and to decide that henceforth the Council would always act by qualified majority, except in a limited number of cases where serious and lasting reasons warrant unanimity. The European Parliament has taken an even stronger view, suggesting that a unanimity vote in the Council should be confined to decisions 'of a constitutional nature which, in accordance with the Treaty, require the assent of the national parliaments'.[27] Discussions in the IGC, however, have followed a more traditional approach through an examination of all relevant provisions; for some a straightforward transition to qualified majority voting is being considered, while other provisions might provide partly for qualified majority after a rewording of the text. It should, however, be stressed that there is not yet an agreement on any of the provisions considered.

Therefore, the outcome of the IGC on this question is highly uncertain. For the purposes of this Colloquium, however, it is clear that the move of an important number of provisions from unanimity to a qualified majority vote would constitute an important 'constitutional change' for the Union, certainly if the move were to be associated with a further extension of the application of the co-decision procedure for decisions of a legislative nature. But a disappointing result would also be, in my view, a *de facto* 'constitutional change' because maintaining the unanimity requirement in a Union with a doubling of the number of member States is not maintaining the *status quo*, certainly not in policy areas (as distinct from institutional provisions, where the risk of blockage is less): if the Community becomes unable to exercise certain competences with which it has been bestowed, it is as if these competences had been removed.

CLOSER COOPERATION

17. The Treaty of Amsterdam has provided for the possibility for a group of member States (at least a majority), which intend to establish closer cooperation between themselves, to make use of the institutions, procedures and mechanisms of the European Community (cf. Arts. 43-45 TEU and Art. 11 EC) or of the 'third pillar' (Police and Judicial Cooperation in criminal matters) (cf. Arts. 43-45 and 40 TEU).

---

[26] See n. 15.

[27] Resolution A5-0086/2000 of 13 April 2000, point 30.3.

The Feira European Council has endorsed the request from the Commission and some member States that the IGC look also into those provisions. They consider that in a Union of 28 or more members a more frequent recourse to the provisions on closer cooperation will prove to be unavoidable in order to maintain momentum in the European integration process. One has therefore to be certain that the provisions on closer cooperation are indeed practicable. The Commission has proposed three modifications: to delete the possibility for a member State to require that the authorisation for establishing a closer cooperation is subject to an unanimous decision, to lower the threshold of a minimum number of member States participating in a closer cooperation to one third and to make under certain conditions closer cooperation possible in the 'second pillar' (Common Foreign and Security Policy).

It is too soon to tell whether the IGC will agree on any of these – or indeed other – modifications of the provisions on closer cooperation. Negotiations on those provisions will be extremely delicate because they will tend implicitly or even explicitly to glide into the debate on the future of Europe (above, para. 4). It is in any event clear that any modification in this area would constitute a clear 'constitutional change' in the Union, as the possibility for establishing closer cooperation plays a key role in the present architecture of the Union.

OTHER ISSUES

18. As shown by the Presidency Report to the Feira European Council.[28] the IGC is considering other institutional reforms, e.g., the composition of the Court of Auditors, the Economic and Social Committee and the Committee of the Regions, a modification of Article 7 TEU, which may, depending on the kind of reforms that would be decided, be considered as 'constitutional changes'.

I would like, however, to draw attention in particular to the *Court of Justice*. There is broad agreement that the number of judges should remain equal to the number of member States, on the understanding that the number of judges participating in the Court's plenary session could be limited (Art. 15 of the Court's Statute allows already a plenary session with nine judges).

More important is that, in particular following a Communication of the Commission,[29] the IGC is considering a range of important reforms for the Court, in particular a redistribution of powers between the Court of Justice and the Court of First Instance with regard to direct actions so as to limit the role of the Court of Justice, in its capacity as the Union's supreme judicial body, to questions

---

[28] See n. 10.

[29] Additional Commission Contribution '*Reform of the Community Courts*' (COM(2000)109 of 1.3.2000, http://www.europa.eu.int/comm/igc2000/offdoc/cont04022000 en.pdf).

which are regarded as fundamental to the Community legal order. The IGC would also open the way for creating specialised judicial boards of appeal for specific and specialised matters.

REFLECTIONS ON A NEW EUROPEAN ARCHITECTURE

Frans Andriessen*

There is just one element of consensus between all those involved – in one way or another – with the enlargement of the European Union. That is that we cannot proceed in the future as we have in the past.

In itself, this is not a new consideration. When the extension of the Union to include Sweden, Finland and Austria was under review there was considerable debate concerning what was referred to in those days as the deepening or widening of the EU.

Deepening meant that before such an enlargement of the Union could take place we had to restructure the internal institutional framework to be able to remain an effective and efficiently functioning Union into the future. This was simply a continuation of what we had done in the past when we were extending the European Union to include such countries as the UK, Ireland, Denmark and Greece.

In hindsight an interesting change in attitude subsequently happened as far as such discussions were concerned. At the end of the 1980s a substantial body of opinion was in favour of giving priority to the deepening element, reflecting on the widening aspect of enlargement as very much a secondary consideration. The European Commission issued reports expressing this tendency perceived by the Commission and in fact the negotiations to create a European economic area with a number of former EFTA countries were merely an expression of the same way of thinking.

What it meant in fact was the extension of economic integration with these countries without establishing full membership – thereby avoiding all the institutional implications that such closer ties would have catalyzed. When, in the same period, so-called Europe Agreements were negotiated with a number of Central and Eastern European countries there was a broad reluctance to give these agreements the full status of Association Agreements.

The simple reason for this was that Association Agreements, following similar agreements with Turkey and Greece, came to be considered as the first step to full Union membership.

---

* Chairman and Member of the Independent Commission for the Reform of the Institutions and Procedures of the Union (ICRI), former member of the European Commission, Brussels.

A.E. Kellermann et al. (Eds.), EU Enlargement: The Constitutional Impact at EU and National Level

For this reason the Council refused during the negotiations to create a clause committing the Union to membership from the side of the EU in the Preamble of the so-called Europe Agreements, which finally took the form of an Association Agreement of a special kind.

It was later, particularly at the meeting in Helsinki in 1993, that the European Council accepted the notion that when a European Agreement has been established, the way forward for membership for the country involved would be open, provided that certain conditions were fulfilled. One of the conditions laid down was that not only the absorptive capacity of the adherent countries but also the absorptive capacity of the union should be taken into consideration as a vital condition for concluding new memberships.

That situation has now changed radically, due to the fact that at some point after the dismantling of the Berlin Wall and the implosion of the Soviet Union, member States in the Union began to recognize that extension of the EU into Central and Eastern Europe, and perhaps even beyond, had become an historical and political imperative. Europe's involvement in the cold war, which in itself was a major incentive for integration, no longer existed.

France and Germany were allies in the most constructive and positive sense in this connection. EFTA, being a kind of defensive alliance between European countries not able or prepared to join the EU, still existed – although most of its members were negotiating or preparing negotiations for entry to the European Union. In fact, securing or stabilizing Europe, normalizing relations with Russia and the acceptance of the historical and cultural necessity to promote Central and Eastern European involvement in the European integration process became strategic priorities for the Union. This drive has been further stimulated by a shift away from the over-cautious attitudes of many Union member States engaged in the extension of the European Union towards what amounts to a continental union. Even so, there are no clear definitions of what these geographical boundaries should be.

Until now, all decisions on the boundaries of the European Union have not been of a geographical, but of a political character. It is outside the scope of this paper to dwell in detail on this particular point, but it is clear that a Union negotiating with Cyprus (not a European country) and having declared Turkey as a candidate member, is having to face up to a highly important question: how in the near future should the frontiers of the European Union be framed? The geo-political, and indeed the legal implications – for instance regarding the protection of external borders – are of the greatest importance.

From all this it must be apparent that the motives and mechanisms of enlargement which will take place in the beginning of the 21st century will be completely different from the 1950s, the decade in which the concept of European integration was first developed. This leads to the conclusion that I started with, namely, that future enlargements cannot be pursued according to the norms, principles and procedures established in the past.

In fact, these original procedures were simple, since every enlargement was basically a specific ad hoc action focusing on a specific country or a limited number of countries. Moreover, the Union was able to focus virtually exclusively on the process of integration with new members. There was no reason for the Union to look into such questions as

- is it possible to continue with the same situational framework, or
- is the *acquis communautaire,* as we have established in the past, the best solution for an extended Union.

From the institutional point of view the first difficulties occurred when – at the end of negotiations with Finland, Austria and Sweden – the British and Spanish were not prepared to accept a weakening of their position as a blocking minority in an extended Union.

The famous Ioannina Compromise was established which was to a certain extent a variant on the so-called Luxembourg compromise. The need to look into the *acquis communautaire* from the point of view of substance was raised when preparing negotiations with the first wave of countries in Central and Eastern Europe.

Changes to structural and technical policies were, and are considered to be, major adjustments of the established *acquis communautaire* as it exists at present. For the first time in history the EU was prepared, with a view to enlargement, to discuss seriously such modifications.

At the same time, at the Amsterdam Euro-summit the notion of strengthened cooperation was introduced. This initiative was directed at creating possibilities for those member States not prepared to see progress and integration hindered by enlargement or internal hesitations to make special agreement for relevant forms of integration – not necessarily covering all EU member States.

Certainly one of the considerations for introducing into the Treaty the possibility of strengthened cooperation, although not meant for this particular purpose by the Germans who invented it some years ago, was the fact that by enlarging the Union to many countries, Eastern Europe could have a negative or at least a slowing down effect on the integration process in the EU.

All this emphasizes that the approach to opening up the Union for a new member – essentially on the basis of prior precedents of substance and institutions – became more and more difficult to realize. The discussion on what should be the priority, deepening or widening, was set aside – but was, of course, unavoidable. The interesting point here is that until now, although in practice recognizing that some elements of substance have to be discussed within the internal circle of the 15, the current discussion is focusing on the form, i.e., the institutional framework of the Union. There should be some adjustments to guarantee that in the future the Union continues to be an efficiently and effectively operating entity. All the outstanding considerations from Amsterdam are institutional in nature. Amsterdam did not deal with substance, if the decision to introduce strengthened cooperation is viewed as more of an institutional than a substantive issue. Obviously a more substantial integration between a certain number of member States is the objective of strengthened cooperation, but the conditions as laid down in the Treaty to make it possible to go in that direction are much more institutional than substantial.

So it would appear that the 15 can limit themselves specifically to look into the institutional aspects of enlargement and that the negotiators for the 15 should look into issues of substance with new member States. But that is not at all true. It is obvious that the way in which the Union modifies its institutional set-up is of the greatest importance for new members.

They, of course, will have to deal with the results of what the 15 are doing in relation to institutional adjustment. On the other hand, the 15 will be deeply immersed in the outcome of negotiations on vital elements of the *acquis communautaire*, including such dimensions as the free movement of persons or capital elements of the common market, such as agricultural and environmental issues and, last but not least, the budgetary implications of the extension of the structural funds to many new members, all eligible for the highest qualification under the terms of reference of these funds. This means that discussions and negotiations on form and substance – or to put it in other terms, on institutional reform and the development of the *acquis communautaire* – are of common interest for both the 15 and any new member State.

Looking at the past we have seen that trying to make progress in the integration of the Union has become increasingly complicated and delicate. That has, of course, to do with the fact that to a large extent economic integration has already been achieved.

The common market, with some exceptions, embodies a comprehensive competition policy backed by a highly developed legal framework and a common trade policy which underpins the Union's influence and position in world trade affairs. Moreover, the realization of economic and monetary union implies the transfer of monetary powers to a supranational entity, namely, the European Central Bank. This latter achievement, the creation of EMU, clearly manifests the fact that collective decisions with a major impact on national sovereignty are a mark of strengthened cooperation. The European Monetary System was established as a specific means for monetary cooperation between a number of EU members outside the Treaty. Even within that limited number of participating states there were specific provisions, for instance for Italy. The EMS initiative was introduced in Maastricht as a form of strengthened cooperation within the Treaty, although some member States were not prepared to join this association.

Notwithstanding the establishment of EMU, it is evident that member States are keen to defend their prerogatives as far as socio-economic policy is concerned.

Schengen is another example of strengthened cooperation or, in other words, differentiation. Again this initiative started *outside* the treaty, and is now an element *inside* the treaty. Even some countries' coordinating policies in the so-called Nordic cooperation, not being members of the Union, are implementing the Schengen agreement. These are two examples of differentiation in the so-called First Pillar.

In the Second Pillar we have seen cases of differentiation. As far as foreign policy is concerned these examples are more of a diminished rather than a strengthened nature in terms of cooperation. In the context of foreign policy, member States can abstain from a decision to act, but cannot prevent other member States from so doing on the basis of some common position or ad hoc decision.

What seems relevant in this development is the fact that major decisions concerning the core policies of member States are increasingly being taken on the basis of differentiation. Either the decision is taken unanimously, which, of course, has an impact on all the member States of the EU, or it is taken on the basis that some member States have the right to abstain.

Looking at this from the point of view of strengthened cooperation one could say that this is a means of strengthening cooperation *avant la lettre*.

Formerly, and as a matter of fundamental principle, the Union rejected the concept of differentiation. But the EU has now effectively adopted this approach so as to able to press on with integration, without being constrained or obliged to include all member States in such a process.

In a report issued in January of this year, the Dutch Advisory Council for International Affairs recommended as one of the issues to be discussed and negotiated at the intergovernmental conference the possibility of changing institutional conditions to accelerate stronger cooperation. In the Treaty of Amsterdam this possibility was envisaged, but with heavy institutional and substantive conditions. Basically the Treaty requires that the majority of member States participate in strengthened cooperation and that decisions should be taken by a qualified majority. However, any member of the Union could veto the decision. There are other conditions but these are the most significant ones. It means in practice that it is extremely difficult under current conditions to start strengthening cooperation. The Advisory Council recommended that barriers to progressive cooperation should be systematically dismantled. This position has now been endorsed by the Dutch government. Jacques Delors, Valéry Giscard d'Estaing, Helmut Schmidt and most recently Joschka Fischer (the German Foreign Affairs Minister) have echoed this viewpoint and are now advocating that strengthened cooperation should be rendered easier to achieve. Such a measure would permit member States to proceed unfettered further down the road of integration, without having to wait for the final member to agree to move in a certain direction. If my impression is correct, I would venture to suggest that France is also in favour of easing conditions for strengthened cooperation. This may well prove to be one of the more important results of the IGC, which in itself is not a very ambitious exercise – being mainly limited to the so-called leftovers of Amsterdam.

In my view the importance of such an outcome should not be underestimated. The reason is that whilst Amsterdam reluctantly accepted the possibility of reinforced cooperation, at the same time it made it extremely difficult to implement; an outcome of the IGC giving way for minorities in the Union to start this kind of strengthened cooperation could give a new dynamic to the integration process in a very positive way. That means that wider integration might be more readily achieved between groupings of member States than was previously possible. We have already seen some forms of differentiation take shape. All such initiatives, however, were based on a majority of member States acting in a concerted manner. One might say that such an outcome would not be revolutionary but more evolutionary in essence. The importance of such an outcome would be that the idea of European integration along the lines of evolution at a greater number of speeds might become more common for European politicians and citizens. Implementing this possibility would give us some experience about the way in which to handle these forms of strengthened cooperation or differentiation institutionally.

When one examines existing forms of differentiation – such as EMU and Schengen, and within the realms of foreign policy – one can see that, in spite of the formal requirement to use common institutions, effectively specific institutions or coordinating bodies for these differentiated activities do exist.

There is nothing against it. It works well for cooperating member States. It could be an incentive for non-member States to try to make this qualitative jump to join.

In my view it is realistic to recognize that this will happen. All these recommendations to facilitate the establishment of strengthened cooperation differentiation indicate that the enlargement with so many countries might have negative impacts on the further development of the general *acquis communautaire*. Whether we like it or not the new member States – including the most sophisticated ones – will have the greatest difficulties to implement this code fully with all the bureaucratic, legal and juridical implications that this entails. In fact, the idea of differentiation was born from the notion that already within the union of the 15 more possibilities for further integration for a certain number of member States should be established. From the moment that we are confronted with an enlargement of 15 or perhaps 20 member States, we should not underestimate the risk that the development of an *acquis communautaire* that *is binding on every member State* might be slowed down.

To get a better view on that, we have to try to analyze what is happening now to enlargement as the top political priority of the European Union.

In the past, enlargement was a specific action regarding one or a limited number of new member States. And we took all the time in the world to negotiate. We negotiated over many years with Greece, Spain and Portugal. Today, it seems that we no longer have time to negotiate thoroughly the implications of enlargement. Timetables have been set by individual heads of government and that has resulted in heightening expectation within the countries concerned. We are similarly faced with rapidly increasing cultural diversity within potential new member States – in the way in which we approach such issues as democracy, the rights of minorities, national cultures, etc. Within the existing 15 member States there is already a wide degree of cultural and political diversity. Extending the frontiers of the Union to Russia, the Ukraine and finally to somewhere in the Middle East would represent an exponential increase in diversity. For this reason Articles 6 and 7 of the Treaty are important, as are efforts to bring about a convention on human rights.

The picture I have painted thus far means that skill, scope, pace and ever-increasing diversity in the Union will have their impact on the integration and enlargement process. We see this already within the Union of 15 when it is confronted with the necessity of differentiation inside or outside the Treaty. When we look at the longer term for European integration we have to accept that when we have finalized discussions with the 12 countries with which we are now negotiating – and with a 13th which is in the waiting room – we will have to negotiate with the Balkan countries. I will not complicate the issue further by including the Caucasian republics or countries around the Mediterranean in this context. The dimension of Central/Eastern Europe, including the Balkans and Turkey, is already enough. It means that from what was an ad hoc and comparatively small scale action, enlargement has now become a kind of process. For the next 25 years we will be busy in the European Union with enlargement. That is an enormous challenge. But it also provides a bit of time. Time to analyze the implications of numbers and diversity. On the other hand, it must be clear that addressing the institutional and common policy implications within a Union which in the meantime might have 20 or 25 members will be more difficult than it is now, by several orders of magnitude. The challenge is overwhelming. If what I said at the beginning of this presentation is true, that thinking and negotiating on form and substance are of equal concern – for both the 15 and new EU entrants, it is abundantly clear in this context that discussions on form and substance have to be significantly revised. Furthermore, substance should be placed at the forefront of discussion within the Union, and perhaps between prospective new member States.

The IGC which will result in the Treaty of Nice, whatever the content may be, is to a certain extent part and parcel of this process. If Nice becomes what it is generally supposed to be, it will confirm that the scope of intergovernmental conferences – in preparing this huge and ambitious enlargement strategy – is simultaneously metamorphosing from an ad hoc existence to some form of process. In fact what we have seen since Maastricht has already moved in this direction, even though we are not there yet.

Of course, it is impossible at this very moment to change the format of this IGC. We have to live with it and we have to live with the fact that whatever might happen, the French will secure the Treaty of Nice. So starting from the point of view of process development, which I referred to earlier, perhaps the best outcome of Nice would be an agreement between member States that IGCs are fundamental to the process of enlargement. That means that the timetable and agenda for the next IGC should already be set in Nice.

Given the attitude of many member States it will not be possible to make quantum leaps forward. However, step by step progress will ultimately secure the relevant institutional changes. It could possibly figure as one of the main objectives of the next or subsequent intergovernmental conference, in order to define clear proposals that take into account the need for the integration of up to 35 member States. Decisions on institutions and differentiation in the future could be realized with less cumbersome procedures than at present – which currently always implies changes to the Treaty, major internal institutional implications and a convoluted external ratification process.

This means that the next IGC – which most likely will take place within two or three years from the end of the current one – should not necessarily decide on the content of institutional and substantive differentiation, but would open the possibility to do so. If certain conditions have been fulfilled that should not sound as revolutionary as it seems. The mechanism for strengthened cooperation adopted in Amsterdam and most likely being developed in a more feasible sense in the Nice Treaty is, in fact, based on the same rationale. It provides member States with an institutional possibility to move away from the *acquis communautaire* in a positive sense.

I cannot see why we should not in the future have the same possibility to move away from the *acquis* in the negative sense. That means that we would have in the Union a possibility to have integration plus and integration minus. In fact, we are already implementing this, at least in theory, and perhaps sometimes in practice, in the field of foreign policy, where we have what we call the positive abstention.

Opening that possibility would significantly facilitate negotiations with new member States in the future, confronting them, of course, with the fact that if they do not engage in particular policies their say in the development or implementation of the policies will be in proportion to their engagement or non-engagement.

As regards Turkey, when discussing the pro's and cons of differentiation plus or differentiation minus, many people are concerned about the efficiency or transparency of the whole process. Let me say that whilst accepting differentiation plus, there is no reason to be afraid of the implications of differentiation minus, because the implications in terms of institutions will be exactly the same. Either one accepts that in both plus and minus situations the same institutional framework works, or one says that specific institutional arrangements will need to be. I am in favour of the latter view. In fact, this reflects what is happening currently. Moreover, it is more transparent than the other way round. In differentiation plus or minus only those member States involved in the policies participate in the decision-making. And the same would apply for the European Parliament. I do not see a problem for the Court of Justice and there is for sure no problem for the Court of Auditors. The Commission should, of course, take care of everything and everybody, and every institutional entity which lies within the framework of the European Union.

Of course, the dynamics of the integration process would imply that every member State at any time has the possibility to participate in any form of integration which has been established between whatever number and kind of member States. No discrimination at all.

On the other hand, we have to be realistic. I do not think it is realistic to expect that in such a differentiated European Union all member States should have the same ambitions or the same intentions to belong to the most integrated minority grouping. That will not be the case. It is not the case currently in the Union and it will not be the case in the Union 25 or 35 years hence. If we can live as a Union of 15 where integration embodies different vital elements, I do not see any reason why we should not be able to live at different levels of integration in a community or union of 30 or 35.

The important thing is that the citizens in a particular member State or perhaps even in a region of the European Union feel that they are essential components of this European integration process. If that experience is made on the basis of somewhat differentiated obligations and commitments towards that union, that should be acceptable in my view. It should be the more acceptable as long as we have not been able to create a real democracy in the European Union.

As long as that is not the case we will be dependent upon the way in which, according to their internal democratic systems, European citizens will have the feeling that they are engaged in one way or another in the European integration process. Of course, it is vital that the European Union, being a union of democratic nations, should be a democratic entity in itself. To achieve this it will be necessary to effect fundamental changes in the treaties of the Union. The introduction of European citizenship alone is not sufficient to achieve this, nor is the fact that the Nice intergovernmental conference will frame some form of EU convention on human rights.

Much more is needed to secure this. Perhaps one of the more remarkable conclusions of the ICRI report is that it is perfectly clear on this basic issue, the issue being that within the existing treaties a real democratic European Union cannot be established.

ICRI is a report that does not seek to add another blueprint on how the European Union should be shaped in the future. It mainly aims to contribute to the debate and to evaluate what the implications might be of the different options people might have when addressing European integration in its institutional form. Here ICRI is very clear. A real democratic dimension is vital for the Union in the long term and to get that we have to change fundamentally the Treaty of Rome.

Some suggestions in this regard have been made very recently, by the German Minister of Foreign Affairs, for instance. The ICRI report discusses different choices, one of which Mr. Fischer has endorsed. This focuses on the creation of a two chamber system for Europe. I personally believe that this would be of great importance. In my view it should be one of the cornerstones in the architecture of the new Europe. Through proportional representation the people of Europe would have a direct voice in one chamber; the other chamber being dedicated to the member States. Such a mechanism, I am sure, would stimulate people to identify more closely with Europe and to become more involved in current European Union affairs.

ICRI examined the merits of such a system, and the Advisory Council of International Affairs in Holland made a long-term recommendation to consider it. Of course, such an approach would change fundamentally the position of the different institutions. That is, of course, the very significance of the idea. Rejecting the idea, *because* it changes fundamentally the institutional framework, as the Dutch government has clearly stated, means in fact that one is not prepared to open up discussions in this regard. That is not very promising.

I think we should reflect on an institutional set-up where legislation would be the prerogative of a bicameral system. The execution and the right of initiative – but not the sole right of initiative – would reside with the European Commission. The Council of Ministers would become an intergovernmental entity coordinating and preparing all the issues which remain intergovernmental in a European Union which will in the near future undoubtedly be – for most member States – decidedly more intergovernmental in nature than in the past. Thus, nobody should fear that they would loose influence and importance. It would just be differently divided.

I think that this essential requirement for the creation of wider democracy is perhaps the most important building block for the house of the European Union. A house in which there are different apartments with different accommodation and different levels, but all of them sharing the common objective of strengthening European integration.

FINAL SESSION
Practical Implementation of the Challenges of Accession

PRACTICAL IMPLEMENTATION BY THE ACCEEDING CANDIDATE COUNTRIES OF THE CONSTITUTIONAL *ACQUIS* OF THE EU PROBLEMS AND CHALLENGES

Jenö Czuczai*

INTRODUCTION

In the history of the economic and political transformation process in Central and Eastern Europe – looking back over the last ten years – special attention has been devoted to the distinction made between the process of what may be called 'democratization' and the process entitled 'constitutionalization'.[1] It was obvious in late 1989 and in early 1990 in the former 'Soviet block' that the transition process from the former socialist authoritarian political system into a democracy based on the principle of the rule of law had to start with revolutionary political changes. Although most of these rapid institutional and legal changes were reflected somehow in the individual constitutions of the newly emerging democracies in East Central Europe, nevertheless many scholars believe that it cannot be stated that the process itself would inevitably have resulted in the necessary adoption of a new constitution in all the former socialist countries. The most important priority was the rapid democratization process of the old political and constitutional institutions in these countries in order that by completing this the even more urgent economic transformation process could start as soon as possible.

Another dimension of the above historical process in Central and Eastern Europe is reflected in the distinction that can be made between the notion of 'democratization' and the new qualitative aspect of this notion described either in the term of 'Europeanization' or by the expression 'modernization' especially within the framework of the Eastward enlargement process of the European Union.[2] This latter dimension, namely, the `Europeanization' process, should,

* The author is the Vice-President of the European Law Academy, and Adjunct Professor of Law of the Pázmány Péter Chatolic University, Budapest. The author's views, statements, conclusions developed and explored in this paper are strictly personal and stem exclusively from the author's academic activities.

[1] See: Wiktor Osiatynski, 'A brief history of the 1997 Polish Constitution' in East European Constitutional Review, Vol. 6, No. 2-3, 1997, pp. 66-76.

[2] See: 'Democratization and Europeanization in Hungary: The First Parliament (1990-1994)', (eds. Attila Ågh and Sándor Kurtán), 1995, Hungarian Centre for Democracy Studies, Budapest, in particular pp. 216-264.

A.E. Kellermann et al. (Eds.), EU Enlargement: The Constitutional Impact at EU and National Level

however, be closely linked to the recent `consitutionalization' process in Central and Eastern Europe. Both processes will generate new challenges for the CEECs (hereinafter CEE candidate countries) in the near future, a situation that will raise very important constitutional law-related questions for the concerned CEECs, in particular when they are on the cusp of actual EU accession.

In this article, therefore, my purpose is to address the most important issues of this nature that directly concern the accession process of the Central and Eastern European candidate countries to the EU, first of all from a practical implementation point of view and primarily with regard to the necessary constitutional changes the candidate countries will have to face soon. I wanted to elaborate the subject in the following order:

I. The pre-accession period for the candidate countries from the point of view of 'constitutionalization'. Is there a Europe-Agreement-based constitutional (legal) framework for the pre-accession environment?

II. Towards the conclusion of the 'Accession Treaties' – the call for accession-related constitutional 'reforms' in the acceding candidate countries. Is there a model wording that could be adopted?

III. The '*constantly evolving constitutional acquis of the EU*' and the related challenges in a 'United Europe' the CEE candidate countries will have to face. Can we develop general conclusions?

I. The pre-accession period for the candidate countries from the point of view of 'constitutionalization'. Is there a Europe-Agreement-based constitutional (legal) framework for the pre-accession environment?

Under this heading, we can address the following questions.

(1) Can we find anything which relates to the EU constitutional *acquis* in the so-called Europe Agreements concluded between the European Communities and their member States and the Central and Eastern European Countries, the CEECs?

(2) How can we assess the so-called '*Democracy Clause*' put in the 2nd and 3rd generation Europe Agreements?

(3) What is the significance of the 1st (political) membership criterion of the so-called Copenhagen criteria laid down in June 1993?

(4) Is there an EU constitutional *acquis*, defined clearly by the Accession IGC for the candidate countries within the pre-accession framework?

(5) In the association-driven period how can the principles of 'direct effect' and 'direct applicability' be treated by the CEE associated countries in the light of the 'ratio decidendi' of the Hungarian Constitutional Court Ruling 30/1998 (VI. 25)

to the issue whether EC law can be directly applicable in the territory of the Republic of Hungary before accession?

Concerning the above questions, the following points can be underlined:

Ad. (1) In order to be able to answer this question, we should divide the ten Europe Agreements (hereinafter EAs) into three blocks. The first block (which we could also call 'the first generation Association Agreements') concerns those which were negotiated with the so-called 'Visegrád Countries' (Hungary, Poland and the former Czechoslovakia) in 1991.[3] They did not contain specific provisions that would reflect on the EU constitutional *acquis* most probably because those countries were at that time considered as the frontrunners in the economic transformation process as well as in the legal transitology proceedings in Central and Eastern Europe. After 1993, however, in both generation EAs (namely, in terms of the 2nd block concluded with Romania and Bulgaria as well as with regard to the 3rd block concluded with the Baltic States and Slovenia in 1995-1996) the so-called 'Democracy Clause' was introduced (Title II/General Principles).[4] To give an example this model clause in the EA concluded with Romania stipulates the following:

> 'Respect for *the democratic principles and human rights* established by the Helsinki Final Act and the Charter of Paris for a New Europe, as well as the *principles of market economy*, inspire the domestic and external policies of the Parties and *constitute essential elements of the present association.*' (Article 6)[5] (emphasis added)

---

[3] For further literature see, for example: M. Maresceau and E. Montaguti. '*The relations between the EU and Central and Eastern Europe: A Legal Appraisal*', (1995) 32 CMLRev. 1327, A. Mayhew.: '*Recreating Europe. The EU's policy towards Central and Eastern Europe*', Cambridge University Press, 1998, in particular p. 18 et seq., or J. Czuczai: '*Lessons and Challenges learned from the Approximation of Laws' Process in the CEECs*' in Implications of the Eastward Enlargement of the EU, Bibó István College of Law, Budapest, 1999 Year Book, pp. 53-59. I should also mention here that under this article I use the terms 'Europe Agreement' and 'Association Agreement' as synonyms, although I should stress that the term 'Europe Agreement' is more accurate and better reflects the specificities of this type of 'Association Agreement' (TEC Art. 310 (ex. Art. 238)) in particular from a historical point of view, but also in terms of content.

[4] It might be worth mentioning that a similar 'Democracy Clause' was also introduced in the legal text of the so-called 'Partnership and Cooperation Agreements' concluded with certain NISs (former member States of the former Soviet Union). See as further literature on this implication: Christophe Hillion: 'Partnership and Cooperation Agreements between the EU and the New Independent States of the Ex-Soviet Union', in European Foreign Affairs Review, Vol. 3, 1998, issue 3, Kluwer Law International, pp. 399-420, or the Report from the Commission to the Council and the European Parliament on 'The Implementation of Measures Intended to Promote Observance of Human Rights and Democratic Principles in External Relations for 1996-1999', COM(2000) 726 final, in particular point 2.3 on pp. 66-70.

[5] See: COM(92) 511 final, p. 5. It needs to be mentioned that the introduction of the so-called 'Democracy Clause' in the EAs after 1993 for political reasons was very much supported (and influenced) by the European Parliament. In this respect special reference should be made to the Briefing No. 20 of the European Parliament, Secretariat Working Party Task-Force 'Enlargement', entitled: 'Democracy and Respect for Human Rights in the Enlargement Process of the EU', Luxembourg,

But it is important to recognize that even after 1993 in the EAs – I think quite understandably – no specific reference was made to any of the statutory (or primary law) elements of the EU constitutional *acquis*. Nevertheless, following the above international legal patterns and the subsequent implementation practice of the related EAs, we may conclude by submitting that there was a kind of 'EA-based constitutional (legal) framework' put in place between the contracting parties already for the pre-accession period under the established 'Association' structure (this is true even in relation to those EAs in which no specific 'Democracy Clause' can be found, see below point (3)).[6]

Ad (2) I think that the incorporation of the so-called '*Democracy Clause*' in the relevant EAs gave an additional political and legal guarantee to the EU which might had been felt necessary at the time when such clauses were negotiated first of all for geopolitical security reasons, and in practice such an action from the EU side was also in line at that time with the newest developments of the European integration process especially after the Treaties of Maastricht were concluded.[7]

Ad (3) Under point (1) above I concluded that we can talk about a kind of 'EA-based constitutional (legal) framework' between the contracting parties to the EAs referred. Such a statement can be supported further by the fact that the so-called 'Membership criteria' were laid down by the Copenhagen European Council Summit in June 1993, in particular, if we take into consideration the first so-called political criterion which reads: '*an applicant country shall assure ... stability of institutions guaranteeing democracy, rule of law, respect for human rights, respect for and protection of minority rights*'. It is clear from the scientific literature that the establishment of the 'Membership criteria', and for the purpose of this paper in particular, of the first 'political criterion' – read jointly with the 3rd

---

April 1998, PE 167.582. In addition to this I should also point out that special attention was devoted to the EA-incorporated 'Democracy Clauses' later in the course of the adoption of the Accession Partnerships (in March 1998) in particular in terms of the so-called '*conditionality clause*' for the provision of further Community pre-accession financial instruments to the candidate countries. For instance see point 5 of the Accession Partnership for Hungary, COM(1999) 525 final, 13.10.1999, p. 11.

[6] Certainly a similarly important legal and institutional guarantee is that all the CEE candidate countries have in the meantime become member States of the Council of Europe as well as they have joined the universal *acquis* of the UN human rights regulatory framework. In this context see the standard Annex, developed by the European Commission, on 'Human Rights Conventions Ratified by the Candidate Countries' which was decided should be attached to each Progress Report. For example see: Regular Report 2000 from the Commission on Hungary's Progress towards Accession, COM(2000) 705 final, p. 92.

[7] It should be noted that after the former Czechoslovakia was dissolved in late 1992, the already signed Europe Agreement with the former Czechoslovakia was renegotiated in early 1993 which resulted in the conclusion of two seperate EAs, one with Slovakia and another one with the Czech Republic. These renegotiated EAs were already affected by the new approach of the EU in terms of the protection of human rights and democratic principles.

criterion about the related *acquis* – all this resulted in a significant political reorientation of the EAs in 1993, mainly by reshaping these Agreements so that they *could serve thereafter in practice for a contractual legal and institutional framework in the pre-accession period with the already mutually confirmed ultimate purpose of a future EU membership.*[8] Nonetheless, it needs to be stressed that the CEECs *accepted* the above-referred criteria *and the related EU acquis* in fact 'only' *by 'concludens factum'* (e.g., by submission of the application request for membership or by a declaration of the acceptance of the new *acquis* within the screening framework) since formally, from a public international law point of view, the EAs (e.g., the Preamble, etc.) in this respect have not been amended since June 1993.

Ad (4) I am convinced that there is an existing (and in practice constantly evolving and developing) constitutional *acquis* of the Union, especially in the light of the last three amendments to the founding Treaties (Maastricht, Amsterdam, Nice). But as far as the accession negotiations in terms of the so-called 'Eastward enlargement' are concerned, and certainly the related IGC framework, we can see that *no specific screening chapter was identified and set out for the 'constitutional issues'* (among the thirty-one screening chapters). The reason for this could have been that *this part of the EU acquis was considered by the member States to be not negotiable*. It is also generally known that the candidate countries will have to take on fully the constitutional *acquis* of the Union 'as it stands at the time of accession'. There is, therefore, no option (opportunity) for derogation or for any other transitional period. Nevertheless, the identification task of the so-called 'EU constitutional *acquis*' is still with the EU (member States) which task ('obligation') will be carried out, I think, in close cooperation with the acceding countries and especially on time.[9]

Ad (5) In 1998 the Hungarian Constitutional Court (hereinafter the Court) examined the relationship of the legal system of an 'associated country' such as Hun-

[8] See: M. Maresceau: 'On Association, Partnership, Pre-accession and Accession' in Enlarging the EU (ed. M. Maresceau), 1997 Longman, London and New York, pp. 3-22.

[9] See in this respect for example as a good summary: Warner.: '*The Relationship between European Community Law and the National Laws of the member States*' (1977) 93 LQR. p. 351 et. seq. As regards the last enlargement for comparative analysis see for example: Allan Rosas: '*Finland's Accession to the EU: Constitutional Aspects*', 1 European Public Law (1995), pp. 165-170, Niilo Jaaskinen: '*The Application of Community Law in Finland*' (1999) 36 CMLRev. pp. 407-441, or Wolfram Kaiser: '*Austria in the EU*', JCMS (1995) 33, pp. 411-425. In order to see how difficult is the identification exercise of the constitutional *acquis* of the Union we shall take as an example the current implications of the recently adopted European Charter of Fundamental Rights from the point of view of the CEECs. Are the candidate countries for instance supposed to take on this Charter as if it is deemed to be part of the constitutional *acquis* of the EU or not? The issue, beyond any doubt, is very sensitive. See as further literature for example: Communication from the Commission to the Council on: 'The Legal Nature of the Charter of Fundamental Rights of the EU', COM(2000) 644 final.

gary with the Community legal order under the established Association 'status iuris', in terms of the application of Article 62(1)-(2) of the EU-HU EA on competition rules. The main question raised by the Court was whether any existing or future Community law (or to be more precise in relation to the EC competition law – any piece of the Community *acquis* in this area) could have direct effect in the territory of Hungary as being a non-member State, or in other words whether any EC Competition *acquis* could be directly applied (invoked) before a Hungarian anti-trust authority (or before the competent court in a concrete case) without the prior enactment of the necessary transposing national law? The answer of the Court was a definitive `no'. The main reasoning of this ruling was based on the constitutional doctrine of `sovereignty' of the Republic of Hungary (Art. 2(1)-(2)), developed by the Court since 1990.[10]

II. Towards the conclusion of the 'Accession Treaties' – the call for accession-related constitutional 'reforms' in the acceding candidate countries. Is there a model wording that could be adopted?

It is clear that before accession all the acceding CEE countries shall take into consideration whether they are really ready – also from the constitutional law point of view – for accession? From this comparative law point of view we can discern the following three models that can be found now in Central and Eastern Europe.

A. The special case of Albania. Why is first of all this case special? It is special because, as is well-known, Albania at present in legal terms is neither a 'candidate country', like, for example, Hungary, nor even an 'associated country', like, for instance, Israel, from an EC external relation point of view. Nevertheless, from our point of view it should be reported that Albania adopted a very modern Constitution in 1998.[11] From the point of view of the CEE acceding countries it can be very instructive to analyse especially the relevant provisions of this Constitution concerned with international agreements. These articles read as follows (emphasis added).

> 'The Republic of Albania applies international law that is binding upon it. (Art. 5)

---

[10] See: B. Berke.: '*National Legal Orders facing Community Law. Encounters, Adjustments, Reservations in Hungary*' in 'From the Europe Agreement to a member State Status in the EU' (eds. F. Mádl- P. Müller-Graff), Budapest 1996, pp. 91-109.

[11] The Constitution of the Republic of Albania was approved by the National Assembly of the Republic of Albania on 21 October 1998. It was confirmed by a nationwide referendum on 22 November 1998.

> (1) The ratification and denunciation of international agreements by the Republic of Albania is done by law if *they have to do with:*
>
> ...
>
> c. *membership of the Republic of Albania in international organizations*
> d. the undertaking of financial obligations by the Republic of Albania. (Art. 121)
> (1) Any international agreement that has been ratified constitutes part of the internal juridical system after it is published in the Official Journal of the Republic of Albania. *It is implemented directly*, except for cases when it is not self-executing and its implementation requires issuance of law ...
> (2) *An international agreement that has been ratified by law has superiority over laws of the country that are not compatible with it.*
> (3) The norms issued by an international organization have superiority, in case of conflict, over the laws of the country if the agreement ratified by the Republic of Albania for its participation in the organization expressly contemplates their direct applicability.' (Art. 122)

The real proof for that the above provisions can also be of some usefulness for other CEE countries is that – as will be explored in more detail below – Poland, which is a candidate country, drew up in its new Constitution of 1997 very similar provisions in relation to international agreements, but was already specifically concentrating on the preparation for EU accession.

B. The 'pre-prepared constitutional legal model for EU accession'. The Polish case.

One could ask why I consider the Polish constitutional model as '*pre-prepared for EU accession*'. Because it was adopted in 1997 (also confirmed by a referendum in 1997), thus before the Accession IGC was opened with the CEECs, which took place on 31st March 1998 in Brussels. Secondly for the time being Poland is the only CEE candidate country which could *de lege lata* even immediately join the EU because there would not appear, at least in principle, to be any constitutional obstacle to such an action.

Now let me quote the relevant articles from the Polish Constitution of 1997 (emphasis added).

> 'The Republic of Poland shall respect international law binding upon it. (Art. 9)
> (Very similar to Art. 5 of the Albanian Constitution quoted above).
> (1) Ratification of an international agreement by the Republic of Poland, as well as renunciation thereof, shall require prior consent granted by statute, if *such agreement concerns: ...*
> (3) *the Republic of Poland's membership in an international organization,*
> (4) considerable financial responsibilities imposed on the state. (Art. 89) (In content also very similar to Art. 121(1) of the Albanian Constitution, quoted above).
> (1) The Republic of Poland may, by virtue of international agreements, delegate to an international organization or international institution the competence of organs of State in relation to certain matters.

(2) A statute, granting consent for ratification of an international agreement referred to in para. 1 shall be passed by the SEJM by a two-thirds majority vote in the presence of at least half of the statutory number of Deputies, and by the Senate by a two-thirds majority vote in the presence of at least half of the statutory number of Senators.
(3) Granting of consent for ratification of such agreement may also be passed by a nation-wide referendum …
(4) Any resolution in respect of *the choice of procedure* for granting consent to ratification shall be taken by the SEJM by an absolute majority vote taken in the presence of at least half of the statutory number of Deputies. (Art. 90) (The formula of the "delegation of state powers to an international organization" in content is also similar to Art. 123(1) of the Albanian Constitution quoted above).[12]

(1) After promulgation thereof in the Journal of Laws of the Republic of Poland (Dziennik Ustaw), *a ratified international agreement shall constitute part of the domestic legal order and shall be applied directly*, unless its application depends on the enactment of a statute.
(2) *An international agreement ratified* upon prior consent granted by statute *shall have precedence over statutes* if such an agreement cannot be reconciled with the provisions of such statutes.
(3) *If an agreement, ratified by the Republic of Poland, establishing an international organization so provides, the laws established by it shall be applied directly and have precedence in the event of a conflict of laws.'* (Art. 91) (Also to a certain extent similar to Art. 122 of the Albanian Constitution quoted above, but with the obvious difference that the Polish Constitution speaks about 'an international agreement establishing an international organization' in terms of the 'precedence clause'.)

In conclusion, it needs to be seen that both Constitutions speak about 'international organizations' without specifying the European Union at all. This is a much more flexible approach when compared to the model followed in the past by many member States as, for example, is the case today with the French Constitution which – under Chapter XV – specifically addresses the '*European Communities and the European Union'*.[13] Therefore, if one would like to have a kind of 'model wording' in terms of our subject, then we can conclude by saying that some examples can be found.

[12] The reason why the Polish Constitution is much more detailed here is that in Poland there is a 'bicameral parliamentary system' whereas in Albania only a 'one-chamber National Assembly' was established by virtue of the adoption of the 1998 Constitution. This means that from the point of view of how to amend the national constitutions in the acceding countries in light of the forthcoming EU accession, it could also be of some significance to pay attention to the structural device of the national parliamentary system.

[13] Similar experiences can be found in the Irish, Swedish and Austrian constitutional models where the European Communities or (since November 1993) the European Union as special (supranational) international organization were/was specifically addressed either before accession or in parallel with accession.

C. All the remaining CEE candidate countries (except for Poland) are currently thinking of their constitutional reforms in the light of the forthcoming EU accession. These countries could be called *'candidate countries not yet prepared for EU accession* from the constitutional law point of view'. Hungary belongs to this group of CEECs.[14]

In relation to this group of countries and in the light of the future EU accession-driven constitutionalization process – from a methodological point of view – I think that the following points will under all circumstances need to be examined by them.

(i) Whether the EU accession process should call for the adoption of a totally new national constitution in any of the concerned candidate countries? If yes, why?

(ii) It is clear that in these countries the existing national constitutions will have to be amended before accession. The question is: when exactly? There are many options here like, for example: (1) before the accession negotiations are completed or, in other words, in the course of the pre-accession preparatory phase; or (2) this constitutional amendment can be made in parallel with the ratification process of the would-be Accession Treaty, which means between the period when the Treaty of Accession has already been initialled by a candidate country but before the national promulgation law in the given candidate country is enacted; finally, (3) it is also an option to amend the national constitution in parallel with the adoption of the necessary national ratification law in fact in the same text.[15]

(iii) what are the *minimum standards* for the necessary constitutional changes at national level in terms of the forthcoming EU accession? What should the relevant provision(s) in the national constitutions contain as a minimum (supremacy of EU law, doctrine of direct effect and of direct applicability, EMU-related items, electoral rules in terms of directly electing MPs to the European Parliament or what concerns the implementation of TEC Article 19 (ex. Art. 8b), human rights-related modifications, or very specific items like, for instance, rules on acquisition of real property by foreigners, etc.)?[16] Is it reasonable and useful to standardize a model wording in this respect (like a *'constitutional à la carte'*) for the candidate countries?

---

[14] Please note that the detailed Hungarian experiences (including even *de lege ferenda* legislative plans) were explored by Prof. Attila Harmathy as country-Panel Rapporteur.

[15] For practical reasons I would opt for chosing the 2nd option. Such a decision could be justified on the following grounds: (i) the candidate country can know already the agreed content of the whole Accession Treaty, (ii) the candidate country can separate the necessary (to a large extent technical) constitutional amendment from the adoption process of the promulgation law of the Treaty of Accession which can easily become a topic for very sensitive internal political debates.

[16] A special problem for the Baltic States will be how they can align the so-called 'independency clause' in their constitutions with the EU constitutional legal order!?

(iv) should the EU specifically be addressed in the modified national constitutions of the candidate countries or is it sufficient just to address the international agreement-related rules in general in terms of joining any international organization?[17]
(v) what will be the constitutional impact of the enlargement process on the constitutional courts in the candidate countries? and on the working of the National Parliaments?[18] Such an issue can be relevant especially in terms of the national human rights concept developed so far in the acceding countries (for example, by the established case law of the constitutional courts) vis-à-vis the currently emerging human rights policy of the EU? Does all this need to be reflected somehow in the national constitutions in the acceding candidate countries?
(vi) what should we talk about: 'delegation of the exercise of certain state powers stemming/deriving from the sovereignty of the EU as a supranational organization' or 'transfer of the exercise of certain part of the (state) sovereignty (rights) to a supranational organization'? and why? Is there any relevance that the EU is a 'supranational organization' and not just a 'simple international organization'?[19]
(vii) how should we approach the constitutional need for a referendum in terms of the EU accession?[20]

III. The '*Constantly Evolving Constitutional Acquis of the EU*' and the Related Challenges in a 'United Europe' the CEE Candidate Countries Will Have to Face. Can We Develop General Conclusions?

The following preliminary statements can be made.

a. It is beyond doubt that by now there is already an EU constitutional *acquis*, which is 'constantly evolving'. The evolving and developing nature of this *acquis*

[17] Regarding this question, for me the solution of addressing at constitutional level the EU specifically as an international organization is more sympathetic especially because one can thus give special emphasis to the fact and to the moral and political significance that his/her country is a member State of the EU.

[18] See for further literature for example: Briefing No. 38 of the European Parliament Secretariat Working Party Task-Force for 'Enlargement', entitled: 'The Role of the European Parliament in the enlargement process', Luxembourg, January 1999, PE 168.065, or Attila Ágh: 'Europeanization of Policy-making in East Central Europe: the Hungarian Approach to EU Accession' in Journal of European Public Policy 6:5 December 1999, pp. 839-854, in particular point 3.

[19] As far as I am concerned I believe that the term 'delegation of the exercise of certain state powers deriving from sovereignty' is more accurate at least in dogmatic terms. This is because in my view sovereignty (or rights belonging to it) as such cannot be transferred to a 'supranational organization' since: (1) sovereignty is indivisible , (2) sovereignty is not transferrable because it is directly attributed to the status of an independent statehood.

[20] As for the question of whether it is necessary to hold a referendum before accession in the candidate countries in terms of their future accession to the EU, my personal opinion is 'yes'.

is becoming more and more significant within the EU. This process creates remarkable challenges for the acceding CEE countries as well in particular because – at least for the time being – they cannot take part in the formulation proceedings of the new constitutional architecture of the EU. It is highly likely that any future reshaping of the EU constitutional legal order would be even more difficult without the involvement of the future new member States, especially taking into consideration the recent declarations on the obvious need for developing the constitution of the EU.

b. As stated by the EU Presidency – in office on 31st March 1998 in Brussels – when the Accession IGC was opened in terms of the Eastward Enlargement of the EU: 'you (meaning the candidate countries) have to adopt and *apply the whole acquis of the EU* ... as it stands at the time of accession'.[21] This means that the term 'whole *acquis* of the EU' will involve the so-called 'constitutional *acquis* of the Union' as well, and, moreover, that 'constitutional *acquis*' which will be in force in the EU at the time of accession. But this date is not yet known for the candidate countries whereas the 'EU constitutional *acquis*' is very intensively developing in the EU (see: point c below).

c. The biggest challenges in terms of the '*constantly developing EU constitutional acquis*'[22] for the candidate countries are, inter alia, the following: (i) the new European Charter for Fundamental Rights (including the different dimensions of the EU human rights policy),[23] (ii) the latest developments in the EU constitutional *acquis* brought by the Amsterdam Treaty (e.g., Arts. 6.(1)-(2)-7. of the TEU, and Art. 13. of the TEC, etc.) and the related new legislative developments at secondary law-making level within the EU (including in this respect also the relevant changes in the judicial *acquis communautaire*), (iii) the new dimension of the EU 3rd Pillar *acquis* after the Tampere European Council Summit in terms of completing the 'Area for Freedom, Security and Justice', which involves fundamental challenges for the candidate countries as well, since this segment of the *acquis* is really a 'moving target' from their point of view, especially considering that in the formulation of this new *acquis* the candidate countries cannot participate.

For the last question, whether we can develop any general conclusion in terms of the forthcoming Eastward enlargement of the Union as far as its constitutional impact is concerned, I think one can answer 'yes', for at least three general con-

---

[21] See: General EU position/Ministerial Meeting Opening the Intergovernmental Conference on the Accession of Hungary to the EU (Brussels, 31 March 1998), CONF-H 2/98, p. 7.

[22] In a broader sense see: J. Czuczai: '*The Notion of the Constantly Evolving EU Acquis*', Bibó István College of Law Budapest, Year Book 2000, under publication.

[23] In this respect see as the most relevant documents of the European Parliament: (1) Draft EU Constitution A3-0064/94 in OJ of the European Communities (28.2.94) No. C 61/155, (2) European Parliament Resolution on the Drafting of a EU Charter of Fundamental Rights. A5/0064/2000.

clusions can be drawn up, one at EU law and two at the level of the Candidate Countries.

1. (*at EU level*). I think that the candidate countries must be involved in the next IGC on the 'Future of Europe. Developing the Constitution of the EU'.[24] Without the active involvement of the would-be Member Countries the next IGC (or if you wish the Post-Nice IGC) cannot be successful either in historical terms or in political terms. *The constitutional traditions of the acceding CEE countries shall be made an inherent part of the* new constitutional architecture of the recently-formulated *new United Europe*.

2. (*at the level of the candidate countries*). I think that there is no 'ready-made constitutional model (pattern)' which the acceding CEE countries should and/or could copy in terms of making their own constitutional order ready for EU accession. A flexible approach should be put in practice and each candidate country should find its own way to adjust its respective constitutional regime (let it be either dual or monist) to the constitutional order of the EU. As shown above examples are available even in Central and Eastern Europe (not speaking about the current member States' relevant experiences), nevertheless, I do not think that any of them could be considered as perfect for other countries in Europe. The most important aspect in this respect, however, is that *the EU constitutional acquis could remain fully and effectively implementable* in all future member States after accession.

3. *(at the level of the accession negotiations)* Finally, it seems to me that the identification task of the constitutional *acquis* of the EU is such a complicated and comprehensive challenge even for the present member States of the Union that the CEE candidate countries should be given the opportunity in the near future for this part of the EU *acquis* to somehow be screened with them within the framework of the Accession IGC.

[24] It should be noted that in the Presidency Conclusions of the Nice European Council Summit (held on 7-10 December 2000) – on a German proposal – it was decided that a new IGC will be convened sometime in the course of 2004.

THE AMENDMENTS OF THE CZECH CONSTITUTION FOR THE ACCESSION TO THE EUROPEAN UNION

Jiří Zemánek*

1. INTRODUCTION

The Central and Eastern European countries candidating for membership of the European Union are expected to accept the *constitutional acquis* of the EU since the entry into force of the Treaty on Accession, even if there is no explicit request in this respect articulated within the negotiations. They are trying to enhance the chance to become members as soon as possible through confidence building measures. Therefore, they undertake a review of their constitutions and (intend to) draft respective amendments. However, the object of our present discussion seems to be too much focused on the wordings of constitutional texts (constitutions 'in books') instead of reflecting on their interpretation and application by national courts in practice ('living' constitutions). This could cause some misunderstandings due to the lack of lasting democratic development during the communist era in the CEECs.

To give just two examples: even if Article 10 of the Czech Constitution (Act no. 1/1993 Coll.) stipulates the direct effect and supremacy of international conventions on human rights and fundamental freedoms agreed by the Czech Republic, their application by courts is too often far from fair and correct. The extension of the direct effect and supremacy doctrines for the whole *acquis communautaire* could not be guaranteed by mere amendments to the Constitution. A profund judicial reform including re-training of judges would be necessary. Article 2(4) stipulates: 'All citizens may do what is not prohibited by law. Nobody may be compelled to do something that is not imposed upon him or her by law'. But, such an explicit constitutional statement of the rule of law principle cannot prevent citizens from misbehaviour by public administration to the extent that the gap between some not yet abolished 'old' (communist) statutory provisions and 'new' democratic statutes still exists.

Therefore, the constitutional impact of the EU enlargement at the national level of the candidating countries should not be understood only in terms of making amendments to constitutions prior to their accession, but also in supporting a

* Charles University, Prague.

A.E. Kellermann et al. (Eds.), EU Enlargement: The Constitutional Impact at EU and National Level

far-reaching process of bringing them to a position coherent with the values shared by the established democracies-member States of the EU.

Implications arising from accession of the Czech Republic to the European Union for its Constitution result from the fact that the EC/EU with supra-national features is an international entity *sui generis* and community law is not a mere set of international law rules, but an autonomous legal system. Therefore, these implications significantly exceed the scope of issues arising from the approximation of laws that is currently taking place on the basis of the European Agreement on Association. Under the complete take-over of the Union's *acquis*, stated in the Copenhagen criteria (1993), a number of future membership rights and duties with constitutional concern need to be identified and anticipated during the period of preparation for accession.

National courts and administrative bodies, which carry the main responsibility for the exercise of community rights and obligations in the member State, still remain authorities independent of the EU institutions and are subject to national procedures. Nevertheless, they must guarantee an effective enforcement of community law within the national legal system in conformity with the principle *effet utile* and with the case law of the European Court of Justice unifying its interpretation. Even the application of national laws must comply with the duty of loyalty (indirect effect). Furthermore, national Parliaments in member States have to play a different role in a decision-making process on European laws than the one they used to play in the legislative process at the national level. Authorities of the member State, although they enjoy a certain autonomy for the selection of the means of transposition of community directives, must follow rules of common discipline, etc.

The exercise of membership rights and duties calls for changes in the functioning of constitutional rules at the national level. The restriction on the scope of national exclusivity, frustrating States-candidates for accession, should be compensated by offering more opportunities for indirect influence of national authorities on the decision-making processes within the EU. This necessitates measures on two levels:

- to support the implementation of the principle of subsidiarity and raise the transparency and accountability of the EC/EU by reforming, i.e., strengthening the democratic legitimacy of their institutions
- to re-shape the institutional balance and mutual communication between national authorities, to introduce adequate methods of participation of self-governing territorial units and non-governmental structures of civic society, to develop new controlling and supervisory mechanisms independent from decision-makers, to accompany such unprecedented changes by new selection and training methods of civil servants and favouring a Community-friendly style in their thinking and working.

2. THE QUESTIONS

Among a number of steps which are to be undertaken during the pre-accession period by the Czech Republic, it is clear that the hardest task will be to manage the internal discussion about checks and balances ('ins' and 'outs') of joining the European integration process, not the negotiations in Brussels themselves. During the course of debates in the Chamber of Deputies of the Czech Parliament some conservative representatives expressed their worries about the implied restriction of State sovereignty. Reflecting the stressful and emotional parliamentary debates in the Sejm on the occasion of the adoption of Articles 90 and 91 of the new Polish Constitution (May 1997), the correct understanding of the following questions prior to the considered constitutional manoeuvre should be achieved:

- what is the nature of the EC/EU institutional and legal system at present and which developments could be expected in the future: an extension of 'the Community method' in the second and the third pillars?, drafting of a Charter of Fundamental Rights of the EU?, a constitutionalization of the basic Treaties? (remains open: IGC 2000)
- which of the existing principles and procedures of community law must be incorporated into the Czech constitutional order from the perspective of accession?[1]
- does the Czech Constitution provide the space necessary for execution of membership rights and duties or – if not – could such a space be based on the case law of the Constitutional Court?
- to what extent must the Czech Constitution undergo – if any – changes and which adaptations would be subject to statutes? How should the consistency of the prior international commitments of the Czech Republic with its membership status be guaranteed? (the experience of some present member States and – when already available – the approach of other candidate countries from the Central and Eastern Europe should be consulted).

3. DOES THE CZECH CONSTITUTION PROVIDE THE SPACE NECESSARY FOR THE CONCLUSION OF THE TREATY ON ACCESSION AND FOR THE EXECUTION OF MEMBERSHIP RIGHTS AND DUTIES?

3.1 **Transfer of sovereign powers to the EU**

The Czech Constitution is locked in this respect: '*The Czech Republic is a sovereign ... State ...*' (Art. 1). The Preamble offers a somewhat more favourable im-

---

[1] (On this subject see: Jiří Zemánek-Richard Král: Ústavneprávní aspekty vstupu Ceské republiky do Evropské unie/The Constitutional Law Aspects of the Accession of the Czech Republic to the European Union/, in: Rocenka evropského práva 1998/Yearbook of European Law 1998/ *Masarykova univerzita* v. *Brne* 1999, pp. 41-90)

pression '*We, the citizens ... as a part of the family of democracies in Europe ...*' The exhaustive list of competencies of the Constitutional Court (Art. 87 sec. 1 Const.) does not give any ground for the assumption that the delegation of powers could be instrumentalized through its decision (as was the case, for instance, in Denmark, Greece and Spain in relation to their accession). An authorization to the conclusion of the Treaty on Accession, which would imply such a delegation, cannot be based on a statute only (*a maiori ad minus).* The conclusion of the Treaty on Accession should necessitate the special constitutional authorization, 'an integration clause'. Yet Article 1 may remain untouched.

3.2 **Democratic legitimisation of ratification of the Treaty on Accession**

The Constitution of the Czech Republic is a rigid one as it does not allow any change either by an interpretative decision of the Constitutional Court, or by statute, or by an international agreement (Art. 9 sec. 1 Const.). The procedure for its amendment would be one requiring a qualified majority of 3/5 of all Deputies and 3/5 of all Senators present (Art. 39 sec. 4 Const.). The Treaty on Accession will be a treaty (a) '*concerning human rights and fundamental freedoms*', (b) a '*political treaty*', (c) an '*economic treaty of a general character*' as well as (d) a '*treaty which requires an implementing law*' (Art. 49 sec. 2 Const.). For the reason ad (a) the consent of the same qualified majority in both Chambers of the Parliament would be *de lege ferenda* required (Art. 39 sec. 4 Const.).

As mentioned already above, pursuant to Article 10 Const., international treaties concerning human rights and fundamental freedoms – duly ratified and promulgated and by which the Czech Republic is bound – are directly applicable and take precedence over statutes, but not over the Constitution itself. Thus, the total superiority of community law within the national constitutional and legal system would need an additional legitimisation. The authority of the State, which 'emanates from the people', is entrusted to national legislative, executive and judiciary bodies (Art. 2 sec. 1 Const.). Therefore, the approval required for its transfer to the extent necessary for the implementation of the basic Treaties should not be left to the Parliament only. With regards to the far-reaching implications for the division of powers in the State which the Treaty on Accession will enhance, the consent of the Parliament as pouvoir constitué would be insufficient. The direct expression of the people's vote as pouvoir constituant seems to be indispensable. A nation-wide referendum based on the constitutional act is anticipated by Article 2 sec. 2 Const., without, however, specifying the criteria as to how this is to happen. It is not clear whether the constitutional act should stipulate the general rules for calling the referendum or only the rules for an individual case. It is also not clear whether the referendum should have only a facultative (consultative, nonbinding) force for the Parliament where the quorum is not reached, or an obligatory force, replacing the Parliament´s consent where the quorum is not reached.

In any case, the timely determination of the manner of approving the Treaty on Accession would influence the behaviour of all political entertainers, both coalition and opposition ones. If, with regards to the lasting critical balance of power on the Czech political scene, a clear majority cannot be expected in the coming years, including the period just prior to the accession to the Union, then the requirement of the qualified 3/5 majority combined with the referendum can bring them near to consensual behaviour: it would be certain that none of them could obtain the necessary majority without the votes of a substantive part of the opposition.

Currently, the constitutional act on referendum has been drafted three times (recently passed by the Chamber of Deputies on 9 December 1999, but failed later in the Senate). It was always coupled with other questions than the EU accession only. Next time, it would be desirable to have it consensually drafted by all the major relevant political subjects. It could cumulate the referendum and voting of the Parliament as mentioned above.

3.3 The effects of the Community law in the Czech Republic since the accession

The approach of the Czech Constitution to international commitments is strictly a dualistic one. It admits – as we have just seen – direct application and precedence over statutes only to international agreements on human rights and fundamental freedoms (Art. 10 Const.). Although the internal effects of the provisions of some other international agreements having a *self-executing* nature are based on some statutory references (for instance § 756 Commercial Code, § 2 Act on Private International Law, etc.), there is no general rule. The insufficiencies of such a case-by-case approach are quite obvious.

Moreover, the effects of community law in the member States are based on community law itself, not on the national constitutions. Therefore, the lack of opening of the Czech constitutional system as a barrier to enforcement of community law would be removed by the constitutional authorization for the conclusion of the Accession Treaty ('integration clause'), and all effects would then run immediately. The only question is, whether this extension of 'the international dimension' of the Czech Constitution is to be made for the purposes of the EU Accession only) or rather more generally, i.e., in favour of provisions of all international agreements with a *self-executing* nature. As the effects of community law will occur automatically (with the enforcement of the Treaty on Accession), their expressive declaration in the Constitution need not be required.

4. SHOULD THE CHANGE IN THE CONSTITUTION REACH BEYOND THE SCOPE OF 'THE INTEGRATION CLAUSE'?

The question arises, whether it will be necessary or appropriate to undertake some other amendments to the Czech Constitution, which should reflect some standards – or just lack of standards – of the *acquis communautaire*. Two options could be employed:

- A minimum variant, justified by the identical reasons as mentioned in connection with the declaration of the effects of community law within the constitutional order: parts of the *acquis communautaire,* directly applicable in the member State (the respective provisions of the basic Treaties, regulations, etc.), do not require (allow!) any transposition into the national constitutional and legal system at all. Amendments to the Constitution – if any – could occur concerning not directly applicable parts of the *acquis communautaire* (other provisions of basic Treaties, directives, etc.). This option would be more 'clean' as regards avoiding any parallel regulation – a community one and a national one – endangering the unity of community law. On the other hand, it would be harder for national authorities enforcing community law as they would have to learn and know community law more profoundly.
- The other variant would be just the extensive incorporation of community law provisions into the Constitution, disregarding the dangers just stated. Some constitutional guarantees not evoked directly by the provisions of community law might be justified

4.1 Aims of joining the EU

The will of the Czech Republic to share the responsibility of member States for creating an ever closer union among the peoples of Europe through its full participation in this process could be expressed in 'the integration clause' as an interpretative provision.

4.2 Respect of human rights and rule of law

The delegation of powers could be linked to the maintenance by the EU of equal respect to '*the essential requirements for a democratic State governed by the rule of law*' as protected by the Czech Constitution (Art. 9 sec. 2), as in the German Constitution (Art. 23 sec. 1 GG with reference to Article 79 sec. 3 – 'Struktursicherungsklausel'). This condition emerged when the national constitutional courts of some member States were faced with the priority of community law over constitutional standards of human rights. Their reaction reflected the fear of a gradual erosion of national statehood as a result of the progressive invasion of the supra-national regulation into the domain of international and constitutional regulation. It clearly indicated that the more the national legislator leaves a space for the European one, the greater the importance of guarantees for the standard of protection of values they both have to share. The candidate countries have to accept the *status quo* of the Community's own standard, as developed first by the EJC case law and based now on the European Convention for the Protection of Human Rights and Fundamental Freedoms and '*resulting from the constitutional traditions common to the member States, as general principles of community law'* (Art. 6 sec. 2 EU Treaty). Breach of the same standard by a member State could be sanctioned by suspension of certain membership rights (Art. 7 EU Treaty). The candidate countries may have to rely on further developments in the drafting of a Charter of Fundamental Rights of the European Union passing within the IGC 2000. Therefore, 'the integration clause' of the Czech Constitution need not be accompanied by an additional guarantee, although the Czech Constitutional Court has not yet had the opportunity to interpret Article 9 sec. 2 Const.

Respect of the principles set out in Article 6 sec. 1 EU Treaty is the pre-condition of the application for membership (Art. 49 EU Treaty). The respect for '*the democratic principles and human rights established by the Helsinki Final Act and the Charter of Paris for a new Europe ... inspire the domestic and external policies ... and constitute essential elements'* of the association of the Czech Republic under Article 6 of the Europe Agreement (such a clause had not been introduced into the earlier Europe Agreements concluded by the EU with Hungary, Poland and the former CSFR in 1991). It is worth mentioning that although the constitutional developments in the CEE candidate countries after 1990 have set guarantees of the respect for human rights and the rule of law, the 'integration clauses' in the Polish Constitution (Art. 90 sec. 1) or in the Draft Constitution of Hungary (1997, Art. 3) and in the constitutional amendments drafted in Lithuania (1998, Art. 136) and Estonia (1996, Art. 1 sec. 3) do not refer to the equal respect of these principles by the EU.

4.3 The Czech Parliament and EU law-making

The balance of powers among the national authorities will be changed after the accession to the EU:

- the passing of an act by the Parliament or by the Government within the scope of the exclusive power of the EU will be an *ultra vires* activity and such an act will be invalid from the beginning (*ex tun*)
- the law-making potential of the Government will become much stronger at the expense of the Parliament during the process of the drafting of a community act as well as during its transposition into the national law (directives)
- the strong position of the national judiciary as a power enforcing community law vis-à-vis the Parliament and the Government (non-application of the national legal provision contrary to community law, interpretation of national laws in conformity with the ECJ criteria, taking decisions on compensation for damage caused to an individual by the undue transposition of a directive by the State, etc.).

In order to balance this 'lack of influence',

- the Czech Parliament should be linked with the law-making process in the EU by stipulating the obligation of the Government to inform the Parliament on

community acts already drafted by the Commission, to consult the Parliament or ask it for an opinion, which could be binding for the Government, or allow a certain space for negotiation in the Council (on issues of majority voting), including rules for the Government's accountability in cases of disregard of the mandate and reporting on the subject (Protocol on the role of national parliaments in the European Union 1997)
– the general control of the Czech Republic as the member State over the further development of the EU should be exercised by maintaining the principle of unanimity required for the ratification of amendments to the basic Treaties on any fundamental issues like a new redistribution of powers between the EU and its member States, and the same qualified 3/5 majority or referendum as for the Accession Treaty should apply.

The most suitable approach to the balancing of influence between the Government and the Parliament in relation to secondary community law seems to be not the constitutional, but the statutory regulation. This could allow a flexible reaction to the dynamic process of changes in the law-making system of the EC/EU and to the strengthening of the role of the European Parliament in it. Mutual communication between the Government and the Parliament must be entirely fluent, and subject to change. The entire legislative process is going to be analysed in detail from this perspective soon. The Committees for European Integration in both parliamentary Chambers (or a Joint Committee based on their merger) would have to be entrusted with the authority to take decisions (opinions) in more simple matters on behalf of the plenary meeting. As for the rigidity of the Czech Constitution, some new constitutional customs might also be established.

4.4 The role of the Constitutional Court

The role of the Czech Constitutional Court as an authority for the control of the constitutionality of laws and other legal regulations as well as in relation to the execution of international agreements on human rights and fundamental freedoms pursuant to Article 87 par. 1 letters a/ and b/ will not apply in the settlement of conflicts between the national law and community law. After accession the Constitutional Court will lose its position of an ultimate arbiter of legality. All national courts will play this role in co-operation with the European Court of Justice.

However, the Constitutional Court could obtain new powers to decide on the compatibility of drafted international agreements of the Czech Republic with non-EU member States and with international organisations, with the Constitution and with community law, i.e., before their ratification by the Czech Parliament (such a preliminary control is used in Germany, France and in Poland). Any revealed contradiction would then be avoided either by re-negotiation of the drafted agreement, by its non-ratification or by the respective change of the Constitution, which would then enable ratification of the agreement. A constitutional amendment would be necessary for such extension of the competences of the Constitutional Court. Just for the ratification of the Treaty on Accession, negotiated over many years, the preliminary control could be a suitable guarantee and outlet for social stress accompanying the unprecedented transfer of sovereign powers to the EU. This clearance could also be helpful in case of a future fundamental change in the basic Treaties. Ratification could not take place before the removal of constitutional barriers.

With regard to the principle of supremacy of community law, national law provisions no longer applicable due to the lack of their compatibility could cause a degree of confusion among national courts, mainly within the period immediately following the accession. Unless the application of such provisions could be justified in pure national (non-community law-based) matters, it would seem to be more appropriate to eliminate them for reasons of legal certainty and transparency from the Czech legal system. Community law leaves this entirely up to the individual member States. The derogating power of the respective national law-making authorities might be used, but the initiative must first come from the law-applying bodies.

4.5 The preliminary ruling procedure and Czech courts

The jurisdiction to bring the matter (submit a question) concerning the interpretation of the basic Treaties or the community act before the ECJ (Art. 234 EC Treaty) will be given to Czech courts by the enforcement of the Treaty on Accession. Any change of the Constitution will not be necessary, but an adaptation of the Code on Civil Procedure (because of a withdrawal of the exclusive position of the Czech Constitutional Court in deciding cases of non-application of statutes) would be helpful.

4.6 Nomination of representatives to the EU-institutions

An instrumental regulation at the statutory level supported by a new constitutional custom seems to be a quite adequate solution.

4.7 Right to vote

The extension of the right to vote for elections to local and regional assemblies and to the European Parliament for all EU-citizens residing on the territory of Czech Republic as well as for Czech citizens (in the case of the European Parliament) will take place with the enforcement of the Treaty on Accession. Therefore, no amendment to the Constitution is necessary.

4.8 Responsibility for non-implementation of a directive

Well-known recent ECJ cases *(Francovich, Brasserie du Pêcheur, Dillenkofer,* etc.) could be difficult to settle on the basis of the Czech law in force at present. The Act No. 82/1998 Coll. on Responsibility for Damage Caused by a Public Power through a Decision or Incorrect Official Procedure does not address this issue and should be amended. No constitutional change will be necessary.

4.9 The enforcement of EJC and Commission decisions

The issue of enforcement of foreign judicial (not administrative) decisions on the territory of the Czech Republic (Act no. 97/1963 Coll. on Private International Law, Art. 63) will not be applicable: decisions of the ECJ and of the Commission will no longer be 'foreign' decisions, but 'own' decision, just like community law will become a part of the national legal system. Constitutional amendment will not be necessary because the effects of such acts will be immediate ('internalised') on the basis of the enforcement of the Treaty on Accession.

5. CONCLUSION

The relocation of the establishment of necessary constitutional pre-conditions for the membership of the Czech Republic in the European Union for a time subsequent to the drafting of the Treaty on Accession does not seem to be adequate to the issue or even dangerous. The timely undertaking of the respective measures would support the process of approximation of laws in the pre-accession period and offer the opportunities for a more comfortable take-over of rules and principles on the functioning of community law and institutions, which will have to be applied from the very beginning of the Czech membership.

Therefore, the following 'integration clause' might be incorporated into the Constitution:

Alternative I
The legislative, executive and judicial powers to the extent necessary for the membership of the Czech Republic may be transferred, by means of an international treaty, to the European Union.

Alternative II
For participation in the creation of a unified Europe, the Czech Republic, by means of an international treaty, may transfer its sovereign rights to the extent necessary to the European Union.

The question asked in the referendum on the Treaty on Accession could read as follows:

> 'Do you agree that the Czech Republic, in the aim of participating in the creation of a unified Europe, should join the European Union, which is established on the principles of democracy, rule of law, respect for human rights and fundamental freedoms, subsidiarity and solidarity, and respect for the national identity of its member States?'

Concerning the effects of community law within the Czech legal system, the following amendments to the Constitution – if any – could still be acceptable:

Alternative I
Constitutional laws, international agreements, statutes and other legal regulations cannot be interpreted and applied in a way incompatible with the duties ensuing from the Czech Republic's membership in the European Union.

Alternative II
Should it ensue from the Treaty on Accession, the law of the European Union forms part of the law of the Czech Republic with the effects stipulated by it.

P.S. When the Czech Parliament debated the first Draft Amendment to the Constitution submitted by the Government in the Spring of 1999, many misunderstandings occurred. In order to avoid such failure in the next round of drafting, more knowledge based on expertise should be available to the MPs. The international research project comparing experiences in core issues collected by the present member States as well as approaches of some candidating countries, initiated by the T.M.C. Asser Instituut, could contribute to the success of this venture.

THE GERMAN EXPERIENCE TO MEET THE CHALLENGES OF REUNIFICATION

Michael Bothe*

1. INTRODUCTION

What has German unification to do with the subject-matter of a conference on EU enlargement? As will be shown, German unification constituted the first case of EC enlargement towards a territory which had formally been part of the socialist block and economic system. Thus, the question may be asked whether this first and very fast enlargement can teach us any lessons as to the problems of the enlargement which is now before us.

The paper will first explain the legal construction of German unification, secondly describe the extension of EC law to the territory of the former German Democratic Republic and will finally address the question of financial transfers made to that territory in order to achieve an equalisation of living conditions.

2. THE LEGAL CONSTRUCTION OF THE GERMAN UNIFICATION

2.1 The pre-unification phase

Discussions about a possible unification of Germany started soon after the wall in Berlin fell on November 9, 1989. On February 6, 1990, the Federal Chancellor offered the creation of a monetary union to the GDR. On March 18, 1990, democratic elections were held in the GDR which resulted in a change in government. Thereafter, during the month of May, decisive steps were taken. These were the start of privatisation in the GDR, the creation (May 16) of a 'German Unity Fund' (*Fonds Deutsche Einheit*) in the Federal Republic in order to provide the resources for the financial transfers necessary for the development of the economy in the GDR and, finally, the treaty between the Federal Republic and the German Democratic Republic on a Monetary, Economic and Social Union, concluded on May 18, which entered into force on July 1st.[1] During this pre-unification phase, we can thus observe a stepwise transition process in the political,

* Professor of Public Law, Johann Wolfgang Goethe University, Frankfurt am Main.
[1] ILM 1108 (1990).

A.E. Kellermann et al. (Eds.), EU Enlargement: The Constitutional Impact at EU and National Level

social and economic order of the GDR, a stepwise extension of the legal order of the FRG to the territory of the GDR and a stepwise development of financial transfers.

The treaty on the creation of a Monetary, Economic and Social Union established far-reaching obligations for the GDR relating to the harmonisation of its laws with the laws of the Federal Republic. This concerned many areas of the law relating to the functioning of the economy and the social security system. In the implementation of this treaty, the GDR adopted a number of laws introducing laws of the Federal Republic of Germany as the law of the GDR. A very important example is the Framework Law on Environmental Protection of June 29, which introduced major parts of the environmental legislation of the Federal Republic into the law of the GDR. Although this process took place in great haste, the differences in the factual situation were not forgotten and, therefore, some adaptations were made and transition periods were granted.

Thus, as a result of this pre-unification phase, there existed in the GDR, at the time of unification on October 3, 1990, a legislation the content of which already corresponded to a certain extent to that of the Federal Republic. Measures implementing EC law, in particular EC directives, were, thus, also in place in the GDR to the extent that laws which had been enacted in the Federal Republic of Germany in order to implement EC law had been taken over by the GDR.

2.2 The unification process

Before unification, a considerable constitutional debate took place concerning the appropriate way to achieve it in terms of constitutional law.[2] There was, on the one hand, the option, favoured by many, to adopt a new constitution which could then be put into force by some kind of referendum process. The other option was to use the possibility that was expressly provided for in Article 23 of the Basic Law, namely that the Basic Law was open to accession by other German *Länder*. The political decision-making process very soon concentrated on the latter option. On August 23, 1990, the Parliament of the GDR (*Volkskammer*) adopted a declaration of accession to the 'scope of application of the Basic Law of the Federal Republic of Germany in accordance with the terms of Article 23 thereof', effective October 3. This was then implemented by the Unification Treaty signed August 31.[3] The relevant parts of the treaty read as follows:

---

[2] See (also for further references) Konrad Hesse, Grundzüge des Verfassungsrechts der Bundesrepublik Deutschland, 15th edn. 1995, p. 38 et seq.; Christoph Degenhart, 'Verfassungsfragen der deutschen Einheit', Deutsches Verwaltungsblatt 1990, p. 973 et seq.

[3] ILM 457 (1991).

'Art. 1
Länder
(1) Upon the accession of the German Democratic Republic to the Federal Republic of Germany in accordance with Art. 23 of the Basic Law taking effect on October 3, 1990, the Länder of Brandenburg, Mecklenburg-Western Pommerania, Saxony, Saxony-Anhalt and Thuringia become Länder of the Federal Republic of Germany ...

Art. 3
Entering into force of the Basic Law
Upon the accession taking effect, the Basic Law of the Federal Republic of Germany ... shall enter into force in the Länder of Brandenburg, Mecklenburg-Western Pommerania, Saxony, Saxony-Anhalt and Thuringia and to that part of Berlin where it has not been valid to date ...'

This constituted for all practical purposes[4] an enlargement of the territory of the Federal Republic of Germany, while the German Democratic Republic ceased to exist as a subject of international law. As a consequence, the law of the Federal Republic of Germany entered into force in the former GDR, the 'accession territory', subject to restrictions provided for in the treaty itself, while the law of the former German Democratic Republic remained valid only to the extent that it was compatible with the Basic Law and the federal law now in force in the accession territory, subject to certain modifications provided for in the treaty itself and the relevant Annex thereto (Art. 9 of the Unification Treaty).

As far as the international legal obligations of the Federal Republic of Germany are concerned, this construction is a case for the application of the principle of moving treaty frontiers, which means that the treaties which had been concluded by the Federal Republic of Germany apply to the entire enlarged territory.[5] This is expressly recognised by Article 11 of the Unification Treaty. It also applies to the treaties establishing the European Communities. This is expressly reflected in Article 10 of the Unification Treaty. Thus, the territory of the European Communities is enlarged as a consequence of the German unification.

---

[4] This is not the place to dwell upon the legal niceties of the controversy concerning the 'true' status of the GDR and the FRG in relation to the *Deutsches Reich*, and, as a consequence of the latter, to each other. On the historic development of this question see Michael Bothe, 'Deutschland als Rechtsproblem', in: Hans-Jürgen Schröder (ed.), Die deutsche Frage als internationales Problem, Stuttgart 1990, p. 39 et seq.

[5] Wilfried Fiedler, 'State Succession', in R. Bernhardt (ed.), EPIL, instalment 10, 449; K.-D. Schnapauff, 'Der Einigungsvertrag', Deutsches Verwaltungsblatt 1990, p. 1249 et seq. at p. 1254.

3. THE APPLICATION OF EC LAW TO THE ACCESSION TERRITORY

Solving the problem of how German unification might affect European integration (or vice versa), was by no means a matter of course.[6] The German unification process was accompanied by a political consultation process within the European Communities.[7] The European Council held in Dublin on April 28, 1990, determined the basic positive attitude of the European Communities towards German unification. A united Germany should remain a member of the Communities, no amendment to the treaties would be made on that occasion, the principle of respect for the *acquis communautaire* would be applied, but a specific transition regime would be granted.

With the wisdom of hindsight, this was a logical consequence of the legal construction of German unification which was eventually adopted. But from the relatively early perspective of April 1990, i.e., before the conclusion of even the treaty on the monetary, economic and social union, this was a decision of fundamental legal and political importance. It should be noted that, on the occasion of the ratification of the Rome Treaties 1957, the German Government of the day had declared that a revision of those treaties was expected in the case of any future German unification.

A major aspect of the decision not to amend the EC treaties was the maintenance of the existing voting balance in the Community organs, despite the fact that Germany was to become the country with by far the largest population in the Communities. It was only two years later that the Maastricht Treaty augmented the number of German seats in the European Parliament, but not the German voting weight in the Council. This problem has remained with us for a while and was rediscussed at the European Council held in Nice in December 2000.

The major practical difficulty was, of course, the application of the principle of the *acquis communautaire*. It was clear to everybody that it was physically impossible to introduce the entire highly developed legal order of the Communities from one day to the other, as it was also not possible to extend the legal order of the Federal Republic to the accession territory without modifications and adaptations. Problems existed, for instance, regarding the single market, in particular rules relating to products traded in the Community, consumer protection, freedom of movement, in particular recognition of diplomas, common agricultural policy, fisheries policy, industrial safety, environmental protection, energy, and subsidies.[8]

---

[6] For some of the problems involved see Eberhard Grabitz/Armin von Bogdandy, 'Deutsche Einheit und europäische Integration', Neue Juristische Wochenschrift 1990, p. 1073 et seq., written from the perspective of the early months of the year 1990.

[7] See H.-W. Rengeling, 'Das vereinte Deutschland in der Europäischen Gemeinschaft: Grundlage zur Geltung des Gemeinschaftsrechts', Deutsches Verwaltungsblatt 1990, p. 1307 et seq.; Reinhard Priebe, 'Die Beschlüsse des Rates zur Eingliederung der neuen deutschen Bundesländer in die Europäischen Gemeinschaften', EuZW 1991, p. 113 et seq.

[8] Dieter Carl, 'Die Gemeinschaft und die deutsche Einigung', EuZW 1990, p. 561 et seq.

It was a logical consequence of the decision not to amend the EECT on this occasion that the necessary adaptations had to be made at the level of secondary Community law. As the process of unification took place under extreme time pressures, the transition regime was divided into two phases. Only in the second phase was the transition regime based on the rule that only those provisions of Community law that were determined by a specific legal act of the Council and the Parliament did not apply. It was not possible to perform the necessary screening of EC legislation within a few weeks. For the first phase, which would end on December 31, 1990 at the latest, the Council authorised the Commission to authorise the German Federal Government to maintain the legal rules of the law of the former German Democratic Republic which were not in conformity with Community law. It is quite telling for the extreme time pressure of the entire process that the relevant Council regulation was adopted on September 17, the Commission decision on September 27 and the relevant regulation of the German Federal Government on September 28, that means five days before unification went into effect.

Criteria for admitting a modified application of Community law during the transitional period were formulated by the Commission.[9] Respect for the *acquis communautaire* was to be the point of departure and the final goal. Special rules of transition were only admissible to the extent that they were necessary for economic, social or legal reasons. Any exception to the applicable Community law had to be of limited duration and should in the least possible way impair the functioning of the common market. The second step, then, was a bundle of Council decisions adopted on December 4, 1990,[10] which provided for specific exceptions from rules of secondary Community law during a transition period which was to end, as a matter of principle, on December 31, 1992.

The transition periods are now over. The integration of the accession territory, i.e., the former GDR, into the legal order of the European Community was achieved in a rather smooth way. This problem was, on the level of legal technicality, relatively easy to solve once the fundamentals of the legal construction of German unification had become clear. The problems of the adaptation of the legal order or the accession territory must, however, not be belittled. There was the danger, which has fortunately been overcome to a great extent, that the adaptation of the law on paper would not correspond to an adaptation in reality. The new legal system required new institutions which did not exist before, and trained personnel to work with them. They have been created and are now in place. There is also the problem of liquidating the mortgages of the past: physical and political contamination. In the field of environmental protection there is the task of cleaning up contaminated sites, the inheritance of a system which for economic and military reasons gave a low priority to the health of the population and the preser-

[9] Carl, loc. cit., p. 561.
[10] Priebe, loc. cit., p. 113 et seq.

vation of a clean environment. On the social and political level the systematic injustice which had happened must be dealt with in one way or the other. This raises the question of how to assist and rehabilitate the victims and how to deal with the perpetrators.[11] Thus, the uniformisation of the law could not eliminate the social and economic border continuing to cut across Germany where the iron curtain had been before. That dividing line cannot be regulated away. It proved to be more persistent than anticipated. It is a political, a social and, last not least, an economic problem. In order to address the economic aspects of this problem, we must now turn to some of the financial and economic aspects of German unification, in particular the transfers needed to achieve an equalisation of living conditions in the two parts of the country.

4. THE PROBLEM OF UNIFORMITY OF LIVING CONDITIONS AND FINANCIAL TRANSFERS

The problem of uniformity of living conditions raised two different problems, namely, that of the difference of living standards between East and West, on the one hand, and that of the difference in the economic systems, on the other.

As to the first problem, there was (and is) indeed a notable difference in living standards. At the time of unification, the average income of an employee in the GDR was about 40% of that in the FRG.[12] Another figure may also indicate the discrepancy between the two parts of Germany: In 1991 the average tax revenue per inhabitant of the municipalities in East Germany was 13.5% of that of the corresponding local units in the West. For the taxation revenue of the *Länder*, the figure is 33.7%.[13] This was, of course, not politically acceptable after unification. It was not only a political issue, it also posed a legal problem because the uniformity of living conditions ('*Einheitlichkeit der Lebensverhältnisse*') is a fundamental constitutional principle of the Basic Law. It is implied in the principle of the social state, but also expressly mentioned in certain provisions of the Basic Law, in particular in Article 72 para. 2, the basic provision on federal legislative powers. Article 104a provides for a federal power to make grants to equalise differences in the economic capabilities of the *Länder*. Article 107, finally, imposes the duty on the federal legislature to enact a law providing for the equalisation of differences in financial capabilities.[14]

---

[11] Cf. Steffen Heitmann, 'Rechtangleichung zwischen Ost und West – Eine Bilanz', Neue Juristische Wochenschrift 2000, p. 3039 et seq.

[12] See the tables in: Das Parlament 2000, no. 35/36, p. 9; no. 37/38, p. 4.

[13] Norbert Andel, 'Finanzpolitische Aspekte der deutschen Wiedervereinigung', Frankfurter Volkswirtschaftliche Diskussionsbeiträge no. 32, 1992, p. 26 et seq.

[14] On the notion of '*Einheitlichkeit der Lebensverhältnisse*' see Hans Peter Bull, in: E. Denninger et al. (eds.), Kommentar zum Grundgesetz für die Bundesrepublik Deutschland, Reihe Alternativkommentare, 2nd edn. 1989, vor Art. 83, MN 89; Dieter Birk, ibid., Art. 106 MN 31 and 35.

As to the latter problem, that of the difference in the economic systems, it was taken for granted that a fundamental change was indeed necessary. It was, after all, the poor performance of the socialist economic system which had led to its final breakdown and the ensuing willingness of the Soviet leaders to make compromises with the West. Thus, the transition to a market economy was not really controversial as a matter of principle. The great question was how to achieve it. The leaders of the GDR accepted the principle of fast transition, a kind of shock therapy.[15] This raised tremendous problems as the economy in the GDR was not really prepared for it. But, in addition, this approach was combined with a measure taken for purposes of dealing with the first issue, namely, the difference in living standards, and that was the determination of the exchange rate between the East German Mark and the Deutsche Mark in the formation of the Monetary, Economic and Social Union. As a kind of political gift to the consumer population, it was decided that this exchange rate should be 1:1. This made unification politically more attractive in the East, but was, on the other hand, very problematic from an economic point of view. It amounted to a revaluation by 300 per cent of the old currency of the GDR. This was a kind of death blow to the already inefficient industry of the GDR. Even a stronger industry would have had difficulties to survive a 300 per cent revaluation combined with the abolition of any protection at the border. But this was exactly what was taking place. The result of that was only logic, as everybody knows now, but only a few realised at that time. Massive unemployment developed and the gross national product in the accession territory decreased in a dramatic way.[16] All this further increased the need for transfers.

Thus, transfers were necessary: for supporting the labour market, for keeping the social security system operational, for creating or re-establishing the necessary infrastructure, in particular for traffic and telecommunications, for running the health system and an efficient state administration. According to earlier publications,[17] the net transfer of public finance was in the order of DM 107 billion for 1991, and DM 126 billion for 1992. The exact calculation of the net transfer is somewhat controversial. According to a recent publication, the net transfer for the last 10 years (1991-2000) has been DM 1,4 trillion, i.e., DM 140 billion per year,[18] or about DM 82,000 per inhabitant of the accession territory.

---

[15] Heiner Flassbeck/Wolfgang Scheremet, 'Wirtschaftliche Aspekte der deutschen Vereinigung', in: Eckhard Jess/Armin Mitter (eds.), Die Gestaltung der deutschen Einheit, 1992, p. 279 et seq., at p. 281 et seq.

[16] In 1991, the GNP decreased by 30.3%, see Werner Weidenfald/Karl-Rudolf Korte (eds.), Handbuch zur deutschen Einheit, 1993, at p. 753: Detlef Pollack, 'Wirtschaftlicher, sozialer und mentaler Wandel in Ostdeutschland', Aus politik und zeitgeschichte, no. B40/2000, p. 13 et seq., at p. 14.

[17] Norbert Andel, op.cit., p. 20.

[18] Frankfurter Allgemeine Zeitung, 11 August 2000, p. 2.

The need for such transfers had been grossly underestimated in the beginning. One of the major errors was the overestimation of the value of the enterprises which were in the hands of the state. It was thought that the revenue to be derived from the privatisation of the enterprises would be able to pay back the major part of the early transfers. That was the concept which was at the basis of the treaty for the formation of a Monetary, Economic and Social Union. Thus, certain transfers were conceived as just bridging short-term gaps. But it was the contrary which eventually happened. The *Treuhandanstalt*, the agency in charge of the privatisation process, had to take over old debts and to engage in activities to save jobs, instead of collecting big revenues from sales. Thus, there was a big loss in the final balance sheet of the Agency. Important disparities between East and West continue to exist in Germany, in terms of per capita income, productivity (in the secondary and tertiary sectors, the figures for the accession territory are about 70% of those for West Germany) and employment (which in certain areas of East Germany is more than double that of the national average).[19] It is all too well known that this has resulted in frustrations which are a major cause of right wing violence. But as the current transfer scheme ('*Solidarpakt*'[20]) is to phase out in 2004, it is controversial how much longer the privileged transfer system for the former GDR is going to continue.[21] Whatever the result of this debate, it is fair to state that the problem of the difference is not yet solved, although the increase in personal income in the accession territory has been considerable over the last decade.[22]

The transfers were essentially organised in four different ways.[23] The first type was through the creation of a special fund, the *Fonds Deutsche Einheit*, the German Unity Fund. Secondly, there were additional special purpose funds, one of them addressing the specific problems of the Currency Union (*Ausgleichsfond 'Währungsumstellung'*),[24] the other that of the old debt of the GDR and its subdivisions (*Kreditabwicklungsfonds*). Third, a major actor in the transfer system is social security. Finally, specific federal spending programmes relate to particular activities such as building roads and railways.

In the federal system of the FRG, it had to be decided which level of government would be financially responsible for these public transfers. Difficult negotiations between the federal Government and the *Länder* were necessary to solve

---

[19] Unempoyment rate 2000: 7% West, 17% East; productivity: 100% West, 65% East; see Detlef Pollack, 'Wirtschaftlicher, sozialer und mentaler Wandel in Ostdeutschland', Aus politik und zeitgeschichte no. B40/2000, p. 13 et seq., at p. 14 et seq.

[20] Thomas Lillig, 'Die Finanzierung der deutschen Einheit', in: Werner Weidenfeld/Karl-Rudolf Korte (eds.), Handbuch zur deutschen Einheit, 1993, p. 289 et seq., at p. 296 et seq.

[21] Frankfurter Allgemeine Zeitung, loc. cit.

[22] Pollack, loc. cit.; Thomas Bulmahn, 'Zur Entwicklung der Lebensqualität im vereinten Deutschland', Aus politik und zeitgeschichte, no. B40/2000, p. 30 et seq.

[23] Lillig, loc. cit., p. 289 et seq.

[24] Andel, op. cit. p. 9.

this problem. The *Länder* have paid a share, but somewhat reluctantly. In part, they were compensated by concessions which the federal Government made in relation to the distribution of the revenue of certain taxes, in particular VAT.

The second question is how that money could be raised. Essentially, there are four possibilities: tax increase, increase of social security contributions, spending cuts and recourse to the financial markets. As a matter of fact, all four possibilities were used, but in different combinations. In 1990, the federal Government of the day was rather inclined to have recourse to the financial markets, as this postponed the distribution problem and was less visible. It allowed the Federal Government to avoid discussing the problem of who would have to foot the final bill. Not addressing this issue was quite helpful for the Government in its campaign for the first election after unification. The social security system also played a major role, in particular through the *Bundesanstalt für Arbeit*, the agency which manages the unemployment insurance system. Whether it is appropriate to charge the persons paying contributions to the social security system with the financial burdens involved in unification is, however, questionable. Spending cuts were used with moderate success, as this created immediate victims. Finally, major tax increases were unavoidable. They took the form of a supplement to the income tax ('*Solidarzuschlag*'), of increasing some special taxes[25] and finally of increasing the VAT. The tax reform which is under way will reduce some of this burden, but not all.

These transfers also raise important questions of Community policy and law. On the one hand, the intra-German transfers just described have been supplemented by Community subsidies.[26] The area of East Germany is entitled to EC funds available from the Structural Funds, i.e., the European Regional Development Fund (ERDF), the European Social Fund (ESF), the European Agricultural Guidance and Guaranty Fund (EAGGF) and the Financial Instrument for Fisheries Guidance (FIFG), under a special promotional concept, altogether 6,8 billion ECU for 1994-1999.[27] This was more than doubled for the following six-year period.[28] In the next period, governed by the 'Agenda 2000', East Germany still qualifies for subsidies from the ERDF, in particular under Objective 1 (regions whose development is lagging behind, or with less than 75% of the average per capita GDP).[29]

On the other hand, the European Commission has considered some of the German government spending for purpose of promoting private investment to be

[25] For details see Lillig, loc. cit., p. 293 et seq.

[26] Karl-Peter Repplinger, 'Hilfen der EG für die Einheit Deutschlands', EuZW 1991, p. 79 et seq.

[27] Carl, loc. cit., p. 564.

[28] EuZW 1993, p. 523.

[29] Lothar Jung/Helge Hassold, 'Die Neuordnung der deutschen und europäischen Regional-/Strukturförderung vor dem Hintergrund der Beihilfenkontrolle und der Agenda 2000', Die Öffentliche Verwaltung 2000, p. 190 et seq., at p. 195.

problematic as regards its compatibility with EC subsidies law,[30] and the Court of First Instance has upheld the Commission's decision.[31] This question has to be solved on the basis of the general rules concerning government subsidies (Art. 87, former Art. 92 ECT). Without going into the details of what is permissible under this provision, it is acknowledged (and corresponds to the Commission policy on EC subsidies) that East Germany qualifies as an area where 'the standard of living is abnormally low or where there is serious underemployment' (Art. 87 para. 3(a)).[32] Thus, aids to promote the economic development of these areas may be considered compatible with the Common Market, subject to the control by the Commission.[33] Certain attempts designed to promote industrial activities in East Germany have also raised the problem of discrimination of nationals of other Community members and in particular with the government procurement directives. The latter makes it difficult, for instance, to give any preference to local enterprise in such matters as building contracts.

5. CONCLUSIONS

To what extent can the German experience tell us any lessons for the current enlargement process? On the one hand, it constitutes an example of a smooth extension of the *acquis communautaire.*[34] But, on the other hand, it is a warning not to underestimate the problems involved in the economic differences. There is no doubt that massive transfers of resources to the acceding countries will be necessary in order to fulfil the requirements of cohesion and the reduction of disparities (Art. 158, former 130a ECT).[35] The estimates concerning these costs vary in a most confusing way, depending, inter alia, on the enlargement scenario and the reform of the common agricultural policy that goes with it.[36] On the other hand, the difficulties involved in the current enlargement process will, hopefully, be of

[30] Carl, loc. cit., p. 562; Robert Uerpmann, 'Der europarechtliche Rahmen für staatliche Subventionen in Ostdeutschland', Die Öffentliche Verwaltung 1998, p. 226 et seq; Ben Perry, 'State Aids to the Former East Germany: A Note on the VW/Saxony Case', ELRev. 22 (1997), p. 85 et seq.

[31] Cases T-132 and 143/96, Judgment of 15 December 1999, Europarecht 35 (2000), p. 420 et seq.

[32] Uerpmann, loc. cit. p. 231.

[33] The specific provision of Art. 87 (former 92) concerning the partition of Germany has only played a limited role after unification, Uerpmann, loc. cit., p. 227 et seq.

[34] Priebe, loc. cit., p. 113.

[35] See Jürgen Stehn, Agenda 2000: Ouvertüre oder Finale der Reformen im Zuge der Osterweiterung?, Kiel 1999; Thomas Oppermann, 'Der Europäische Traum zur Jahrhundertwende', Juristen-Zeitung 54 (1999), p. 317 et seq, at p. 322.

[36] Thomas Lenk/Andreas Mathes, 'EU-Osterweiterung – finanzierbar?', in: Spiridon Paraskewopoulos (ed.), Die Osterweiterung der Europäischen Union. Chancen und Perspektiven, Berlin 2000, p. 61 et seq., at p. 94.

a lesser magnitude than those encountered in the German unification process. There are several good reasons for that hope.

The most important difference is the time element. The accession of the GDR took place under extreme time pressure. The current accession candidates have had the benefit of an adaptation process of several years, which the GDR did not. The principle of early adaptation, with the help of EU programmes already in existence, is important. Pre-accession adaptation is the essence of the conditions formulated by the European Council in Copenhagen 1993 (so-called Copenhagen criteria). They relate to fundamental questions of the political, legal and economic system. Furthermore, some of the problems of homogeneity of economic conditions, which in Germany arose already before unification with the creation of the Monetary, Economic and Social Union, will arise later in the enlargement process when the acceding countries finally become full members of the European Economic and Currency Union.

On the level of political and legal principles, the EU does not require the same type of homogeneity that is demanded by the constitutional and political system of the Federal Republic of Germany. It can, however, not neglect the problem. Solidarity is not only required in the constitutional systems of states, it is also a principle of the Constitution of Europe. This has been made explicit in the goal of economic and social cohesion (Art. 3(1)(k) ECT). The welfare goals established in Article 2 ECT shall be achieved 'throughout the Community'. This remains a major challenge.

THE IMPACT OF THE EU CHARTER OF FUNDAMENTAL RIGHTS IN THE PERSPECTIVE OF ENLARGEMENT

Koen Lenaerts*

This paper inquires into the legal nature of the several mechanisms of enforcement of respect for fundamental rights by the EU institutions, member States and European States applying for EU membership. The analysis should shed some light on the potential significance of the EU Charter of Fundamental Rights for the legal order of the Union in general and with a view to enlargement of the Union in particular. Attention is being drawn to the operation of the present Union system of protection of fundamental rights in which the Charter is to be inserted.

INTRODUCTION

With Philip Alston and Joseph Weiler, it may be said that '[t]he Union cannot be a credible defender of human rights in multilateral fora and in other countries while insisting that it has no general competence of its own in relation to those same human rights'.[1] The latter was nevertheless the verdict of the Court of Justice in its Opinion 2/94 of 1996 on the question whether the European Community had the competence to accede to the European Convention for the Protection of Human Rights and Fundamental Freedoms (hereinafter 'Convention' or 'the European Convention on Human Rights'), where it stated that no provision of the Treaty establishing the European Community confers on the Community institutions any general power to enact rules on human rights or to conclude international conventions in this field.[2] This thinly veiled appeal to the Community legal order's constituent power to assume its responsibilities by amending the 'consti-

* Judge of the Court of First Instance of the European Communities. Professor of European Law, Leuven. All opinions expressed are personal to the author.

[1] Ph. Alston and J.H.H. Weiler, 'An "Ever Closer Union" in Need of a Human Rights Policy: The European Union and Human Rights', in Ph. Alston (ed.), *The EU and Human Rights*, Oxford, Oxford University Press, 1999, p. 15.

[2] In its view 'accession to the Convention would ... entail a substantial change in the present Community system for the protection of human rights in that it would entail the entry of the Community into a distinct international institutional system as well as integration of all the provisions of the Convention into the Community legal order'. Such a modification 'would be of constitutional

tutional charter'[3] of that legal order did not, however, find favour with the framers of the Treaty of Amsterdam, signed on 2 October 1997, since that Treaty does not grant the general powers that the Court considered necessary to open the way for the Community to accede to the Convention.[4]

One month after the entry into force of the Treaty of Amsterdam, the Cologne European Council of 3 and 4 June 1999 decided that a Charter of Fundamental Rights of the European Union should be drawn up.[5] This decision to draft a genuine Union Charter of Fundamental Rights was taken against the background of a legitimacy and credibility crisis of the European Union culminating in the forced collective resignation of the Commission because of allegations of corruption and incompetence and resulting in an impressive abstention from the European Parliament elections by the voters later that month. To alter this growing indifference shown by the public towards the present EU – let alone the future enlarged

significance and would therefore be such as to go beyond the scope of Article 235'. The Court consequently concluded that it could be brought about only by way of Treaty amendment. Opinion 2/94 *Accession by the Communities to the European Convention for the Protection of Human Rights and Fundamental Freedoms* [1996] ECR I-1759, paras. 27-28, 31 and 34-35. For an assessment of the relative merits of the arguments developed by the Court and the various criticisms that have been levelled against them, see M. Waelbroeck, 'La Cour de Justice et la Convention européenne des droits de l'homme', 32 *Cahiers de droit européen*, 1996, pp. 549-553, S. Mathieu, 'L'adhésion de la Communauté à la CEDH: un problème de compétence ou un problème de soumission?', 414 *Revue du Marché commun et de l'Union européenne,* 1998, pp. 31-36, N. Burrows, 'Question of Community Accession to the European Convention Determined', 22 *ELRev.,* 1997, pp. 58-63, and P. Wachsmann, 'L'avis 2/94 de la Cour de justice relatif à l'adhésion de la Communauté européenne à la Convention de sauvegarde des droits de l'homme et des libertés fondamentales', 32 *Revue trimestrielle de droit européen,* 1996, pp. 467-491, F. Chaltiel, 'L'Union européenne doit-elle adhérer à la Convention européenne des droits de l'homme?', 404 *Revue du Marché commun et de l'Union européenne,* 1997, pp. 34-50.

[3] Judgment in Case 294/83 *Les Verts* v. *Parliament* [1986] ECR 1339, para. 23, and Opinion 1/91 Draft Agreement between the Community, on the one hand, and the countries of the European Free Trade Association, on the other, relating to the creation of the European Economic Area [1991] ECR I-6079, para. 21. See also G.F. Mancini, 'The Making of a Constitution for Europe', 26 *CMLRev.* 1989, pp. 595-614.

[4] For further details, see K. Lenaerts and E. De Smijter, 'Le traité d'Amsterdam, 6 *Journal des Tribunaux – Droit européen,* 1998, pp. 25-36.

[5] The idea originally stems from a proposal of Germany, inspired by the activist attitude of the German *Bundesverfassungsgericht* in its judgments *Solange* and the *Maastricht Urteil,* where it considered that it was necessary to conduct a second review of the Community legislation in the light of the fundamental rights guaranteed by the *Basic Law so long as* the Community lacked, next to a democratically elected parliament with legislative powers and powers of scrutiny, a codified catalogue of fundamental rights, (first*) Solange* judgment of 29 May 1974, BverfG versus EuGH *re* 'Grundrechte' (1975 EuR. 1-19). This stance was later turned into a conditional acceptance of the primacy of Community law *so long as* the case law of the Court of Justice continued to guarantee the observance of fundamental rights as part of the requirements that Community acts have to satisfy in order to be valid (Judgment of 22 October 1986 *(Solange II)* (1986) BverfG p. 73 at p. 339 and *the 'Maastricht-Urteil'* (1993) Eu.GR.Z. 429). Cf. K. Lenaerts and P. Van Nuffel, *Constitutional Law of the European Union*, London, Sweet & Maxwell, 1999, pp. 518-519, paras. 14-017 to 14-019.

Union – the European Council concluded that '[t]here appears to be a need, at the present stage of the Union's development, to establish a Charter of Fundamental Rights in order to make their overriding importance and relevance more visible to the Union's citizens'.[6] The European Council entrusted the task of drafting the Charter to a 'Convention' made up of 15 representatives of heads of state or government, 16 Members of the European Parliament, 30 members of national parliaments and a Commissioner representing the President of the Commission. The working methods of the Convention were agreed upon at the European Council meeting in Tampere on 15 and 16 October 1999. By now more than 700 amendments to the working text of the Presidency of the Convention have been proposed by members of the Convention, by observers and by civil society, most of these of a merely textual, but some of them of a very substantial nature. No agreement could be reached on a preliminary draft, which was to be presented at the European Council meeting in Feira of 17 and 18 June 2000. Since then, a complete text of the Charter has been proposed by the Praesidium of the Convention on 28 July 2000,[7] accompanied by explanatory notes drafted by the Secretariat of the Convention at the request of the Praesidium.[8] The Draft Charter adopted by the Convention was submitted to the European Council meeting on 13 October 2000 in Biarritz, in preparation for the Nice European Council in December 2000.

In the present contribution we will examine – taking into account the developments introduced by the Treaty of Amsterdam – first, the mechanisms for judicial enforcement of respect for fundamental rights by the EU institutions (under 1.) and, second, the political and judicial control by the EU over the way in which respect is shown for fundamental rights by the member States (under 2.) and the European States applying for EU membership (under 3.). All of this should shed some light on the potential significance of the EU Charter of Fundamental Rights, in particular with a view to enlargement of the European Union.

1. EU INSTITUTIONS

1.1 Articles 6(2) and 46 of the Treaty on European Union and Article 220 of the Treaty establishing the European Community

As though to make up for its failure to grant the necessary powers required by the Court of Justice to accede to the European Convention on Human Rights, the

[6] European Council Decision on the drawing up of a Charter of Fundamental Rights of the European Union, Annex IV to the Conclusions of the Presidency of the Cologne European Council of 3 and 4 June 1999, http://www.europarl.eu.int/dg7/summits/en/kol2.htm#UP.

[7] Document CHARTE 4422/00 CONVENT 45.

[8] Document CHARTE 4423/00 CONVENT 46 of 31 July 2000. In the meantime, on 28 September 2000 the Convention adopted the Draft Charter of Fundamental Rights of the European Union

Treaty of Amsterdam has strengthened the constitutional basis for the protection of fundamental rights by the *Union* itself. The new Article 46 (ex Art. L) of the Treaty on European Union has extended the exercise of the Court's powers to Article 6 (ex Art. F)(2) of that Treaty 'with regard to action of the institutions, in so far as the Court has jurisdiction under the Treaties establishing the European Communities and under this Treaty'. Article 6(2) provides that 'the Union shall respect fundamental rights, as guaranteed by the European Convention for the Protection of Human Rights and Fundamental Freedoms signed in Rome on 4 November 1950 and as they result from the constitutional traditions common to the member States, as general principles of Community law'.[9] Since that was one of the 'common provisions' (Arts. A to F, now Arts. 1 to 6) of the Treaty on European Union, the former Article L had not included it within the Court's jurisdiction *ratione materiae*, a singular omission when considered in the light of the case law of the Court, which for thirty years has been engaged in determining whether Community acts (and national measures which fall within the scope of Community law) are compatible with fundamental rights as now defined in Article 6(2) of the Treaty on European Union. The aim was probably not to weaken the protection of fundamental rights in the Community legal order, an essentially praetorian form of protection which in any case depends ultimately for its legitimacy on Article 220 (ex Art. 164) of the Treaty establishing the European Community, under which the Court is required to ensure that 'the law is observed' in the interpretation and application of that Treaty.[10]

The anomaly thus revealed has, for actions undertaken by the EU institutions, been remedied by the new wording of Article 46 of the Treaty on European Union. This empowers the Court to examine the compatibility of 'action of the institutions' with fundamental rights, in the normal exercise of its powers under the Treaty establishing the European Community and the Treaty on European Union. Article 46 referring to Article 6(2) of the Treaty on European Union thus

---

(Document CHARTE 4487/00 CONVENT 50), which met with general approval during the Biarritz European Council. The explanatory notes were updated in document CHARTE 4471/00 CONVENT 48 of 20 September 2000.

[9] Apart from references to the European Convention, the Treaties equally contain references to the 1961 European Social Charter of the Council of Europe and the 1989 Community Charter of the Fundamental Social Rights of Workers. In the fourth recital of the Preamble of the Treaty on European Union, the member States confirm their attachment to fundamental social rights as defined by these Charters. In Article 136 (ex Art. 117) of the Treaty establishing the European Community, both Charters serve as guidelines for the development of a social policy by both the Community and the member States.

[10] In Opinion 2/94, cited in n. 2 above, the Court stated that 'it is well settled that fundamental rights form an integral part of the general principles of law whose observance the Court ensures' (para. 33). Cf. G.C. Rodríguez Iglesias, 'The Protection of Fundamental Rights in the Case Law of the Court of Justice of the European Communities', *1 Columbia Journal of European Law*, 1994-1995, pp. 169-181, and A.G. Toth, 'The European Union and Human Rights: the Way Forward', 34 *CMLRev.*, 1997, pp. 491-529, in particular pp. 493-494.

requires the Court of Justice to examine the compatibility of action of the institutions with the provisions of the European Convention on Human Rights, regarded by the 'basic constitutional charter'[11] of the Union as the key reference for the protection of fundamental rights within the Community legal order. In addition to this hard core, the constitutional traditions common to the member States, likewise mentioned in Article 6(2) of the Treaty on European Union, are another source of rules to add to the level of protection afforded by the European Convention on Human Rights, should the need arise.[12] By committing itself to that Convention in the context of its internal legal order, the Union has undertaken to require its institutions to respect fundamental rights at the very least in so far as they can be invoked in proceedings against any public authority in the wider Europe represented in the Council of Europe, to which all the member States must – of necessity – belong. Beyond that minimum protection, it is only in so far as the member States of the Union, representing a narrower range of legal traditions, have enough in common to add to it, that the Union is also bound, by virtue of the above-mentioned provisions of the Treaty on European Union, to require its institutions to respect such additional protection. In this connection, it is significant that Article 6(2) of the Treaty on European Union mentions the European Convention on Human Rights first and the constitutional traditions common to the member States second, as defining sources of fundamental rights which the Union must respect.

1.2 **Articles 13 and 141 of the Treaty establishing the European Community**

Although the Amsterdam Treaty may have failed in respect of enlisting fundamental rights in the Treaties, it did provide for two interesting new legal bases allowing the Community to adopt rules with a view to securing their protection. In addition to the general rules for the protection of fundamental rights within the European Union, Articles 13 and 141 define some aspects of the principle of non-discrimination. Apparently without wishing to call into question the established case law on the subject, the constituent power of the European Union has chosen to anchor the principle of equal treatment even more firmly in the text of the Treaty establishing the European Community.[13]

---

[11] See for this expression the references to the case law of the Court mentioned in n. 3 above.

[12] See, to the same effect, the article by O. Due and C. Gulmann, 'Community Fundamental Rights as Part of National Law', in *Scritti in onore di Giuseppe Federico Mancini*, Milan, A. Giuffrè Editore, 1998, II, pp. 405-422, in particular p. 407. For a critical exposition on this particular source of fundamental rights: L.F.M. Besselinck, 'Entrapped by the Maximum Standard: on Fundamental Rights, Pluralism and Subsidiarity in the European Union', 35 *CMLRev.*, 1998, pp. 633-638.

[13] The Treaty establishing the European Community had previously imposed only two prohibitions to ensure equal treatment: Article 6 (now Art. 12) prohibits within the scope of application of that Treaty any discrimination on grounds of nationality, and Article 119 (now Art. 141) prohibits any discrimination between men and women with regard to pay. These two provisions, together with

First of all, there is Article 13 of the Treaty establishing the European Community, empowering the Council, within the limits of the powers conferred by that Treaty upon the Community and after consultation of the European Parliament, to take appropriate actions to combat discrimination based on sex, racial or ethnic origin, religion or belief, disability, age or sexual orientation.[14] That article is not presented as a provision having direct effect, which would prohibit outright any discrimination on the grounds listed. It provides, rather, an additional legal basis, which is intended to enable the Council to act, within the limits of the material scope of Community law, to eliminate discrimination on those grounds.[15] As the right to non-discrimination (and the duties it entails) is a core element of a great deal of other fundamental rights, Article 13 of the Treaty establishing the European Community might provide an ideal foundation upon which to build a comprehensive fundamental rights policy.[16] The Union's constituent power has thus assigned to the legislative process the responsibility of making the social choices underlying the application of the above aspects of the principle of non-discrimination. The caution shown by the Court in its judgment in *Grant* confirms that it has picked up the signal sent out by the Union's constituent power.[17] However, that does not mean that in future the Court will no longer be required to refer to the general principle of Community law constituted by equal treat-

---

a substantial body of Community legislation on social policy and some other provisions of the Treaty establishing the European Community, notably on agriculture, have contributed to the Court's development of the prohibition on any form of discrimination as a general principle of Community law which must be respected both by the Community institutions and by the member States in any action falling within the scope of Community law.

[14] The list contained in Article 13 of the Treaty establishing the European Community is not the same as other similar lists, such as the list contained in Article 14 of the European Convention on Human Rights.

[15] For the first application of this provision, see Council Directive 2000/43/EC of 29 June 2000 implementing the principle of equal treatment between persons irrespective of racial or ethnic origin (OJ L 180/22-26).

[16] L. Flynn, 'The Implications of Article 13 EC – After Amsterdam, will some Forms of Discrimination be more Equal than Others?', 36 *CMLRev.*, 1999, pp. 1151-1152.

[17] Judgment of 17 February 1998 in Case C-249/96 *Grant* [1998] ECR I-621 in which, after an analysis of Community law, the national law of the member States and the case law of the European Commission and Court of Human Rights, the Court held that 'in the present state of law within the Community, stable relationships between two persons of the same sex are not regarded as equivalent to marriages or stable relationships outside marriage between persons of opposite sex' (para. 35). The Court considered that in those circumstances 'it is for the legislature alone to adopt, if appropriate, measures which may affect that position' (para. 36). The Court referred in that connection to the possibilities offered by Article 13 inserted in the Treaty establishing the European Community under the Treaty of Amsterdam (para. 48). For a critical analysis of that decision, see A. Weyembergh, 'Les droits des homosexuels devant le juge communautaire', 6 *Journal des Tribunaux – Droit européen*, 1998, pp. 110-113; compare E. Brems, case note in 5 *Columbia Journal of European Law*, 1998-1999, pp. 141-151 and J. McInnes, 'Case C-249/96, *Lisa Jacqueline Grant* v. *South West Trains Ltd.*, Judgment of the Full Court of 17 February 1998, [1998] ECR I-636', 37 *CMLRev.*, 1999, pp. 1043-1058.

ment, as gradually established by the case law. It is difficult to believe that, in the absence of Community legislation adopted under Article 13, the Court will have no power to censure an act of the Community institutions, or even of the member States when they are directly implementing such an act, if the act is discriminatory on one of the grounds mentioned or on some other ground such as the language or 'nationality' of natural or legal persons other than nationals of a member State (the personal scope of Article 12 [ex Art. 6] of the Treaty establishing the European Community being in fact limited to nationals of member States).

Secondly, the Treaty of Amsterdam has amplified the wording of Article 141 (ex Art. 119) of the Treaty establishing the European Community to allow the Council, acting jointly with the European Parliament in accordance with the co-decision procedure referred to in Article 251 (ex Art. 189b), and after consulting the Economic and Social Committee, to adopt measures to ensure the application of the principle of equal opportunities and equal treatment of men and women in matters of employment and occupation, including the principle of equal pay for equal work or work of equal value [Art. 141 (3)].[18] That provision now provides a specific legal basis, including an effective and democratic decision-making procedure (the new co-decision procedure) in place of Article 94 (ex Art. 100) or Article 308 (ex Art. 235) of the Treaty establishing the European Community, which had previously served as a legal basis for legislation on the subject (adopted by the Council, acting unanimously after consulting the European Parliament). Lastly, the new Article 141(4) allows the member States to maintain or adopt measures of positive action in order to make it easier for the under-represented sex to prevent or compensate for disadvantages in professional life.[19]

1.3 The problem of a possible divergence between the case law developed by the Community Courts and that of the European Court of Human Rights

As Community law now stands, the challenge for the Community legal order is to ensure that the European Convention on Human Rights, respect for which is a

[18] Promotion of equality between men and women – in general and not just in working relationships – is one of the tasks of the Community listed in Article 2 of the Treaty establishing the European Community, and Article 3(2) of that Treaty provides that in all the activities referred to in Article 3(1) the Community shall aim to eliminate inequalities, and to promote equality, between men and women. For the way in which such a horizontal objective must be reconciled with the specific objectives arising from the Article in the Treaty establishing the European Community which serves as a legal basis for the Community activities in question, see the judgment in Case C-233/94 *Germany* v. *Parliament and Council* [1997] ECR I-2405, paras. 46-49.

[19] This provision echoes the Court's case law: judgment in Case C-450/93 *Kalanke* [1995] ECR I-3051, qualified by the Court in its judgment in Case C-409/95 *Marschall* [1997] ECR I-6383. For the limits set to the application of Article 141(4) see the judgment of 6 July 2000 in Case C-407/98 *Abrahamsson, Anderson/Fogelqvist* [2000] ECR nyr.

condition of the lawfulness of acts of the Community institutions,[20] is correctly applied within that order without any system of outside control over its application. In this connection, the problem is often raised of a possible divergence between the case law developed by the Community Courts and that of the European Court of Human Rights.[21] There are two points to be made here. First, as the living law will ultimately be determined by the decisions of the Community Courts[22] and if they are to remain credible in their application of the European Convention on Human Rights as a direct source of the fundamental rights protected within the Community legal order (Art. 6(2) in conjunction with Art. 46 of the Treaty on European Union), the Court of Justice and the Court of First Instance must explicitly include in their own judgments precedents from the case law of the European Court of Human Rights, in order to explain whether those precedents are relevant to the interpretation of fundamental rights in the specific context of a review of the legality of a particular act of the Community institutions.[23] Such an approach not only increases the transparency of the Courts' grounds of judgment but also improves the consistency with which the Convention is applied by the competent courts of both the wider and the narrower Europe. If the Union is serious in declaring that it is bound by the substantive content of the Convention, the approach described also appears to be the least it can do to ensure that the Community legal order incorporates in the interpretation of the Convention developments in the case law of the European Court of Human Rights. For this purpose, the Community Courts must be prepared, if need be, to modify earlier case law to keep in line with interpretations of the Convention given by the European Court of Human Rights at a time later than the Community case law on the same point. Neither the Court of Justice nor the Court of

---

[20] This point is made by the Court in Opinion 2/94, cited in n. 2 above, para. 34.

[21] See the examples quoted in the article by M. Waelbroeck, cited in n. 2 above, p. 550, n. 3. See the Order of the Court of Justice of 4 February 2000 in Case C-17/98 *Emesa Sugar* [2000] ECR nyr, in which the application of Emesa Sugar for leave to submit written observations in response to the Opinion delivered by the Advocate-General was dismissed on grounds that distinguish the position of the Advocate-General from that of the 'ministère public' in issue in the judgment of the European Court of Human Rights of 20 February 1996 in *Vermeulen* v. *Belgium* (Reports of Judgments and Decisions, 1996, I, p. 224). The European Court of Human Rights will possibly have the opportunity to pronounce on the compatibility of the order of the Court of Justice with Article 6 of the European Convention on Human Rights as Emesa Sugar has brought a case in the European Court of Human Rights against the Netherlands (No. PN 15 690), or even before that – albeit indirectly – on the occasion of a ruling involving the position of the *Commissaire du Gouvernement in the French Conseil d'État* and the possibility, under Article 6 of the Convention, for parties to reply to his Opinion in proceedings before the *Conseil* which come under the purview of Article 6 (Case *Kress/France*, decision on admissibility of 29 February 2000, merits of the case sent to a Grand Chamber).

[22] European Commission, *Affirming Fundamental Rights in the European Union. Time to Act*, Brussels, Report of the Expert Group on Fundamental Rights, February 1999, p. 20.

[23] See, for example, judgments in Joined Cases T-213/95 and T-18/96 *SCK and FNK* v. *Commission* [1997] ECR II-1739, paras. 53-57, and Case C-185/95 P *Baustahlgewebe* v. *Commission* [1998] ECR I-8417, para. 29.

First Instance has the power to refer questions to the European Court of Human Rights for a preliminary ruling on the interpretation of provisions of the Convention in a given context, even in cases where those provisions have not yet been the subject of any relevant case law.[24] The Community Courts are consequently obliged, when the occasion arises, to steer their own course – as any national court called upon in similar circumstances to apply the Convention in its own legal order would do[25] – while at the same time remaining open to possible developments in interpretation that may occur at some future time.

The second point to be made is that a 'divergence' in case law is not always easy to detect because of the very nature of the fundamental rights most often at issue. Very few are absolute rights. The enforcement of most of the fundamental rights invoked in the Community context is based to some extent on an assessment of the circumstances of the particular case. In the context of litigation, the assessment must be made by the court and the result may vary according to the subject-matter involved or the society in which the case arises. One has only to think, for example, of the 'reasonable time' mentioned in Article 6 of the European Convention on Human Rights, within which courts – including the Community Courts – must hear cases pending before them or, by analogy, administrative authorities may be required to take certain decisions.[26] Moreover, the exercise of a considerable number of fundamental rights protected by the Convention may be subject to such limitations as are prescribed by law and are necessary in a democratic society in respect of certain general interests specified in the Convention. The relevant provisions of the Convention in this connection are those stating that everyone has the right to respect for his private and family life, his home and his correspondence (Art. 8 of the Convention), freedom of thought, conscience and religion, including freedom to manifest one's religion or beliefs (Art. 9 of the Convention), freedom of expression (Art. 10 of the Convention), freedom of peaceful assembly and freedom of association (Art. 11 of the Convention), that every natural or legal person is entitled to the peaceful enjoyment of his possessions (Art. 1 of the Protocol No. 1 to the Convention), and that everyone has the right to liberty of movement and freedom to choose his residence (Art. 2 of Protocol No. 4 to the Convention). A comparison of these lists of general interests

---

[24] After Opinion 2/94, cited in n. 2 above, it must be concluded that, as the Treaties on which the Union is founded now stand, the Union likewise has no power to set up, in agreement with the members of the Council of Europe, machinery for referring questions for preliminary ruling. Here, too, an enabling clause to that effect would probably have to be inserted in the Treaties before this could be done. See K. Lenaerts, 'Fundamental Rights to be Included in a Community Catalogue', 16 *ELRev.*, 1991, pp. 367-390.

[25] Cf. the observation to this effect made in a different context by Advocate-General Jacobs in his Opinion in Case C-168/91 *Konstantinidis* [1993] ECR I-1191, point 50.

[26] See the judgments cited in n. 23 above. See also, for further examples, W. Wils, 'La compatibilité des procédures communautaires en matière de concurrence avec la Convention européenne des droits de l'homme', 32 *Cahiers de droit européen*, 1996, pp. 329-354.

that may in a democratic society justify restrictions prescribed by law on the exercise of the fundamental rights in question reveals, on the one hand, a diversity as to the precise grounds that may be invoked to justify such restrictions and, on the other, a similarity as to the issue at stake, namely the need to strike the right balance between respect for the fundamental right in each case and the general interests that may require certain restrictions to be imposed by law on the exercise of that right. Striking that balance inevitably entails the exercise of a power of assessment, the result of which may vary, depending on the – democratic – society in which the assessment is made.[27] That is why the European Convention on Human Rights assigns this responsibility in the first instance to the legislature, referring in the various provisions cited above to restrictions prescribed by law. In accordance with this basic position, reflected in the actual wording of the Convention, the European Court of Human Rights is inclined in most cases to respect the national legislatures' decisions on the subject, provided that they appear to be reasonable, particularly if they are essential to reconcile the exercise of fundamental rights by different parties or to render the exercise of such rights compatible with one of the general interests referred to in the Convention.[28]

It follows that, when the Court of Justice or the Court of First Instance review the legality of a Community act by which the legislature, in the specific context of the Community's economic or other policies, has imposed on a fundamental right certain restrictions necessary to protect one of the general interests mentioned in the Convention, it will not be easy to determine whether or not their assessment coincides with the assessment that would be made by the European Court of Human Rights, were it to exercise outside control. The assessment of the Court of Justice and the Court of First Instance must be reasonable, when these courts rule on the legality, with regard to fundamental rights, of the choices made by the Community legislature. This should, in principle, be enough to ensure that their case law is consistent with that of the European Court of Human Rights, in view of the latitude which the Human Rights Court accords to national authorities to make a reasonable assessment of the application of the fundamental rights at issue here. In some cases, it will merely be a matter of interpreting the Commu-

---

[27] Cf. the article by O. Due and C. Gulmann, cited in n. 12 above, pp. 409-410, and J.H.H. Weiler, 'Fundamental Rights and Fundamental Boundaries: on Standards and Values in the Protection of Human Rights', in N. Neuwahl and A. Rosas (ed.), *The European Union and Human Rights*, The Hague, Martinus Nijhoff, 1995, pp. 51-76, in particular pp. 56-66.

[28] See, in this connection, Advocate-General Van Gerven's Opinion in Case C-159/90 *Grogan* [1991] ECR I-4685, points 34-38, and particularly the case law of the European Court of Human Rights cited in the judgment in Case C-299/95 *Kremzow* [1997] ECR I-2629, para. 15. See also the judgment in Case C-144/95 *Maurin* [1996] ECR I-2909. For an interesting analysis, see L.F.M. Besselinck, cited in n. 12 above, pp. 633-650.

nity act in question in such a manner as to ensure that it is in any event consistent with respect for a particular fundamental right.[29]

1.4 Conditions under which EU member States can be held responsible under the European Convention on Human Rights for infringements of the Convention committed by Community institutions

The European Union's real 'problem' will be to make it clear, by its internal control over respect for fundamental rights by Community institutions, that it deserves the restraint shown by the organs of the European Convention on Human Rights in dealing with member States of the Union whenever they are perceived to be merely instruments for implementing rules enacted by Community institutions.[30] The Convention organs have justified their restraint on the ground that the Community itself is a Community based on the rule of law which enforces respect for fundamental rights so that the member States consequently incur no liability of their own in assisting in the implementation in their territory of rules enacted by the Community institutions.[31] Since the prospect of outside control by the European Court of Human Rights appears to be receding, at least for the time being, the European Union will have to continue to earn respect for its internal control machinery so that its member States may in a sense have 'blind' faith in that machinery without compromising their own responsibilities under the Convention. The (old) European Court of Human Rights still seemed to be strongly committed to an approach of self-restraint in this respect, as is demonstrated by the judgment of 26 February 1998 in *Pafitis and Others* v. *Greece*.[32] Asked to determine whether judicial proceedings before the Athens Regional Court had

---

[29] The judgment in Wachauf is a case in point: Judgment in Case 5/88 *Wachauf* [1989] ECR 2609, para. 18. The Court noted that the fundamental rights it recognises are not absolute but must be considered in relation to their social function. Consequently, restrictions may be imposed on the exercise of those rights, in particular in the context of a common organisation of a market, provided that those restrictions correspond in fact to objectives of general interest pursued by the Community and do not constitute, with regard to the aim pursued, a disproportionate and intolerable interference, affecting the very substance of those rights. For another example of the Court interpreting an act of a Community institution in a manner consistent with fundamental rights, see the judgment in Case 63/83 *Kirk* [1984] ECR 2689.

[30] The crucial passage in the Strasbourg jurisprudence on this point is still the paragraph of the *M. & Co.* decision of the European Commission of Human Rights, delivered on 9 February 1990 (Decisions and Reports, vol. 64, March 1990, pp. 138-157), which reads as follows: '[T]he transfer of powers to an international organisation in not incompatible with the Convention provided that within that organisation fundamental rights will receive an equivalent protection. The Commission notes that the legal system of the European Communities not only secures fundamental rights but also provides for control of their observance'.

[31] Compare, however, M. Waelbroeck, 'La Convention européenne des droits de l'homme lie-t-elle les Communautés européennes?' in *Droit communautaire et droit national*, Semaine de Bruges 1965, Bruges, Collège d'Europe, 1966, pp. 305-318, at p. 317.

[32] Judgment in Case 163/1996/782/983.

lasted longer than the reasonable time referred to in Article 6(1) of the European Convention on Human Rights, the European Court of Human Rights decided that it could not take the period during which the matter had been referred to the Court of Justice into consideration in assessing the length of the proceedings in each particular case: 'even if it may at first sight appear to be relatively long, to take it into account would be detrimental to the system established by Article 177 of the EEC Treaty and to the essential aim pursued by that article'.[33] Although it shows due respect for the preliminary ruling procedure as the key-stone in the judicial system designed to secure the uniform application of Community law – a system without which it would be difficult for that law to maintain its position as an instrument of European integration – the decision arrived at by the European Court of Human Rights has been criticised on the ground that it might allow the member States that are parties to the Convention to escape all responsibility for the poor performance of a judicial procedure which they themselves introduced through the Treaties establishing the European Communities.[34] It has been observed, in this connection, that the States parties to the Convention are held responsible if the reasonable time referred to in Article 6(1) of the Convention is exceeded because of delay in the production of a report by an expert appointed by the court.[35] It is therefore quite possible that the case law of the European Court of Human Rights could evolve further if preliminary ruling proceedings were to take not merely a period of time which 'may at first sight appear to be relatively long' but a period of time which is clearly intolerably long, or if it were apparent that such proceedings served no useful purpose and merely allowed the national court to gain time in a manner acceptable only ostensibly. The European Commission of Human Rights took the view that this was an important factor but concluded that it had not been the case in *Pafitis*.

The (new) European Court of Human Rights has further specified the conditions under which EU member States can be held responsible under the European Convention on Human Rights for infringements of the Convention committed by Community institutions. This was done in the judgment of 18 February 1999 in case *Matthews* v. *United Kingdom*.[36] The Court found that the United Kingdom, together with all other EU member States as Contracting Parties to the European Convention on Human Rights, should be held responsible for the exclusion of Gibraltar from the scope of application of the Act of 20 September 1976 concern-

---

[33] Para. 95 of the judgment.

[34] See R.A. Lawson, case note in 46 *Sociaal-Economische Wetgeving*, 1998, pp. 220-223, and – more elaborately in the same sense – R.A. Lawson, *Het EVRM en de Europese Gemeenschappen* (Europese Monografieën 61), Deventer, Kluwer, 1999, pp. 410-416.

[35] See the case law of the European Court of Human Rights to this effect mentioned by R.A. Lawson in his article cited in n. 34 above, p. 223, n. 12.

[36] Application No. 24833/94. See H.G. Schermers, case note in 36 *CMLRev.*, 1999, pp. 673-681 and G. Cohen-Jonathan and J.-F. Flauss, A propos de l'arrêt *Matthews c/ Royaume-Uni* (18 février 1999), 35 *Revue trimestrielle de droit européen,* 1999, pp. 637-657.

ing the election of the representatives of the European Parliament by direct universal suffrage, which was attached to Council Decision 76/787 taken in accordance with Article 138(3) of the EEC Treaty. The crucial passage of the Court's reasoning in this respect reads as follows: 'The Council Decision and the 1976 Act ... constituted international instruments which were freely entered into by the United Kingdom. Indeed, the 1976 Act cannot be challenged before the European Court of Justice for the very reason that it is not a "normal" act of the Community, but is a treaty within the Community legal order'.[37] Subsequently the Court held that by excluding Gibraltar from the scope of application of the system of direct election of the Members of the European Parliament the United Kingdom, together with the other EU member States, had infringed Article 3 of Protocol No. 1 to the Convention according to which 'the High Contracting Parties undertake to hold free elections at reasonable intervals by secret ballot, under conditions which will ensure the free expression of the opinion of the people in the choice of the legislature'.

For the purposes of our analysis, the most relevant aspect of the case is that the European Court of Human Rights distinguishes between primary and secondary Community law as to the possibility of holding EU member States responsible under the Convention for infringements of fundamental rights committed by Community institutions. The criterion for distinction between the two categories of Community law lies, according to the European Court of Human Rights, in the possibility to challenge before the Court of Justice the acts of Community institutions said to infringe fundamental rights protected by the Convention. If the act concerned can be so challenged and therefore, in the words of the Human Rights Court, constitutes 'a "normal" act of the Community', the *M. & Co.* jurisprudence (1990) continues to apply, which means that EU member States will incur no responsibility under the Convention because the international organisation which they have set up contains a system of judicial review offering an 'equivalent protection'.[38] The 'only' thing which the Community legal order has to do, to remain worthy of the credit it enjoys at present in this matter, is to continue to make it clear that indeed it possesses a system of judicial review offering an 'equivalent protection' against the acts or failures to act of Community institutions said to be incompatible with the fundamental rights guaranteed by the Convention. If, on the contrary, the 'act' concerned cannot be the object of judicial review inside the Community legal order, the 'equivalent protection' test clearly cannot be met. Furthermore, the European Court of Human Rights does not shy away from itself analysing the proper characteristics of the Community legal order to draw the distinction between reviewable and non-reviewable acts of Community law.

[37] Para. 33 of the judgment.
[38] See n. 30 above.

It goes without saying that this judgment of the European Court of Human Rights marks an important development in the relationship between the Community legal order and the European Convention on Human Rights. The judgment looks 'classical' at first sight in that it confirms implicitly the 'equivalent protection' test excluding direct EU member State responsibility under the Convention in relation to 'normal' Community acts subject to judicial review inside the Community legal order. But, at the same time, the judgment indicates that in the absence of any such possibility of judicial review the EU member States may be held responsible under the Convention for any infringement of the provisions of the latter resulting from 'international instruments which [they] freely entered into'.[39] It remains to be seen whether this holding of the European Court of Human Rights might lead one day to some qualification of the *Pafitis* jurisprudence.

Similarly, the judgment of the Court of Justice of 17 December 1998, *Baustahlgewebe* v. *Commission*[40] concerning Article 6(1) of the European Convention on Human Rights and the general principle of Community law that everyone is entitled to fair legal process, raises questions on the absence of any mechanism of 'judicial review' of the decisions of the Court of Justice itself, which is a court of last instance. In case of criticisms leveled against its decisions, on the ground that the proceedings before the Court of Justice did not respect Article 6(1) of the European Convention on Human Rights, no 'equivalent protection' of the rights contained in that Article – which, according to the Court of Justice, are 'inspir[ing] the general principle of Community law that everyone is entitled to fair legal process' – appears to be available inside the Community legal order. The question then follows whether the EU member States – all of them as Contracting Parties to the European Convention on Human Rights, or else the EU member State called upon to enforce a decision of the Court of Justice said to be handed down in breach of Article 6(1) of the Convention – can be held responsible because they 'freely entered into' the Community Treaties, the Statutes of the Court of Justice and its Rules of Procedure which they approved unanimously, all of which instruments – of 'primary' Community law – confirm the Court of Justice in its status of supreme court of the Community legal order against whose decisions no further remedies will lie.[41] Quite obviously the best way for both Community Courts to answer this question is to stated beyond any doubt as to the conformity of the proceedings conducted before them with Article 6(1) of the Convention. But at least as a matter of principle the question should be raised and the answer to it seems to be more open after the *Matthews* v. *United Kingdom* judgment than before that decision.

---

[39] For this wording see again para. 33 of the judgment.

[40] See the judgment in *Baustahlgewebe* v. *Commission*, cited in n. 23 above.

[41] Compare para. 33 of the judgment *Matthews* v. *United Kingdom*, cited in the text accompanying n. 37. See at present the challenge to the *Emesa Sugar* order of the Court of Justice, mentioned in n. 21 above.

2. EU MEMBER STATES

2.1 Control by the EU over the way in which the member States generally respect fundamental rights

In the matter of control over the way in which the member States generally respect fundamental rights, the European Union relies in principle on the good offices of the European Court of Human Rights and, where need be, on its own political control.

2.1.1 *The 'good offices' of the European Court of Human Rights*

The Treaty of Amsterdam has elevated respect for human rights and fundamental freedoms to the status of a principle on which the Union is founded, a principle common to the member States, on a par with liberty, democracy and the rule of law. All these principles, to which the member States had so far merely confirmed their attachment in the preamble to the Treaty on European Union, are thus to be seen as the cornerstone of integration in the European Union (Art. 6(1) of the Treaty on European Union). Respect for human rights and fundamental freedoms (hereinafter 'fundamental rights') by the member States, which had previously been presented as an implicit condition of their membership of the Union, has now become an explicit condition of that membership.[42]

2.1.2 *Political control (Arts. 6 and 7 of the Treaty on European Union; Art. 309 of the Treaty establishing the European Community)*

The Treaty of Amsterdam has introduced provisions in the Treaty on European Union and the Treaty establishing the European Community, which allow measures to be taken against a member State guilty of a serious and persistent breach of the principles on which the Union is founded, including the principle of respect for fundamental rights. To that end, the Council, meeting at the level of the Heads of State or Government and acting by unanimity on a proposal of one third of the member States or of the Commission and after obtaining the assent of the European Parliament (given by a two-thirds majority of the votes cast, representing a majority of its members), must determine the existence of the serious and persistent breach in question (Art. 7(1) of the Treaty on European Union). Clearly, such a determination, which necessarily involves a careful assessment, can be made only if it is based both on a unanimous decision of the member States, excluding the member State concerned (though abstentions do not prevent

---

[42] The first mention of the European Convention on Human Rights as such occurred in the preamble to the Single European Act, which entered into force on 1 July 1987, a fact noted by the Court in its judgment in Case 249/86 *Commission* v. *Germany* [1989] ECR 1263, para. 10.

unanimity), and on a particularly broad consensus in the European Parliament. In other words, the procedure is ponderous and political, and depends ultimately for its legitimacy on the democratic character of the two Community institutions called on to make the determination, namely the Council which, indirectly, represents the people as nationals of the various member States and the European Parliament which represents them as citizens of the Union.[43] If and when the first stage of the procedure has been completed, the Council, acting by a qualified majority, may decide to suspend certain of the rights deriving from the application of the Treaty on European Union or the Treaty establishing the European Community to the member State in question, including the voting rights of the representative of the government of that member State in the Council.[44]

The obligations of the member State in question under those two treaties remain in any case binding on that State.[45] A suspension of the totality of rights or a suspension of the entire membership of the concerned State (the latter including also the suspension of the State's obligations) seems excluded: Article 309 of the Treaty establishing the European Community requires the Council to 'take into account the possible consequences of such a suspension on the rights and obligations of natural and legal persons'.[46] *A fortiori*, the same applies for the draconian measure of total expulsion, which anyhow would run counter to the purpose of European integration itself, since isolating the nationals of the member State in question would deprive them of their European citizenship and all the more, of

---

[43] For an analysis of the democratic character of these two Community institutions, see K. Lenaerts and E. De Smijter, 'The Question of Democratic Representation: On the Democratic Representation through the European Parliament, the Council, the Committee of the Regions, the Economic and Social Committee and the National Parliaments', in J.A. Winter, D.M. Curtin, A.E. Kellermann and B. De Witte (eds.), *Reforming the Treaty on European Union – The Legal Debate,* The Hague, Boston, London, Kluwer Law International, 1996, pp. 173-197.

[44] See Article 7(2) of the Treaty on European Union and Article 309 of the Treaty establishing the European Community. The procedure laid down in Article 7 of the Treaty on European Union could prove to be important in the context of the protocol on asylum for nationals of member States of the European Union, annexed to the Treaty establishing the European Community under the Treaty of Amsterdam (OJ 1997 C-340/103). According to that protocol, any application for asylum made by a national of a member State may be taken into consideration or declared admissible for processing by another member State only if (1) the member State of which the applicant is a national has taken measures derogating from its obligations under the European Convention on Human Rights, or (2) the procedure referred to in Article 7 of the Treaty on European Union has been initiated or has resulted in a determination of the existence of a serious and persistent breach of the principles on which the Union is founded. See K. Lenaerts and E. De Smijter, article cited in n. 4 above, p. 34, point 71.

[45] Article 309(2) of the Treaty establishing the European Community.

[46] The Council of Europe, on the contrary, does know the possibility of suspension of membership. See A. Verhoeven, 'How Democratic Need European Union Members Be? Some Thoughts After Amsterdam', 23 *ELRev.*, 1998, p. 222-223 and in particular n. 26; and E. Bribosia, O. De Schutter, T. Ronse and A. Weyembergh, 'Le contrôle par l'Union européenne du respect de la démocratie et des droits de l'homme par ses États membres: à propos de l'Autriche', 8 *Journal des Tribunaux – Droit européen*, 2000, pp. 61-62.

their right to seek judicial protection against violations of EU law by their national authorities.[47]

Recently, some member States have – out of fear that the mechanism contained in Article 7 of the Treaty on European Union would appear to be mere lip service to the principles of liberty, democracy, respect for human rights and fundamental freedoms and the rule of law – insisted on the need to develop a strategy on how to make use of the enforcement procedure with a view to preventing breaches of fundamental rights from occurring (for instance, by applying a system of prior warnings).[48] It might indeed seem not very probable that the sanction mechanism as it now stands will easily be applied, given the reluctance member States show in general to make use of the procedure contained in Article 227 (ex Art. 170) of the Treaty establishing the European Community to bring an action against another member State for an alleged infringement of an obligation arising under that Treaty.[49] In any event, one should not underestimate the potential deterrent effect, also towards European States applying for EU membership, that the sanction mechanism may have on authorities tempted to breach fundamental rights.

The Court of Justice plays no part in the procedure for determining the existence of a serious and persistent breach by a member State of the principle of respect for fundamental rights, since it is not involved in the procedure,[50] and it is

[47] A. Verhoeven, cited in n. 46 above, p. 223. However, in a recent Resolution, the 'Comité d'avis pour les questions européennes' of the Belgian Parliament called for a revision of the relevant Articles of the Treaties allowing sanctions that go as far as exclusion of a member State which does not respect the European Union's fundamental values (*Agence Europe*, 9 June 2000, p. 4).

[48] At the Conference of the Representatives of the Governments of the member States of 2 May 2000 in Brussels, the Belgian delegation submitted a draft amendment to Article 7 of the Treaty on European Union, containing a warning mechanism aiming at the prevention of a serious and persistent breach by a member State of the principles laid down in Article 6 of the Treaty on European Union. The Belgian delegation further proposed to replace the present unanimity requirement within the Council, meeting in the composition of the Heads of State or Government, to determine the existence of the serious and persistent breach in question by a qualified majority requirement. CONFER 4739/00 and http://db.consilium.eu.int/cigdocs/EN/04739en0.pdf. On 7 June 2000, the Austrian delegation submitted to the Conference of the Representatives of the Governments of the member States a draft amendment to both Articles 7 and 46 of the Treaty on European Union, with the aim of introducing a warning mechanism (different from the Belgian proposal, the Council would be required to decide with unanimity in this phase), of ensuring due consultation of the member State concerned throughout every single phase of the procedure, of obliging the member States to solely take – proportionate – measures within the framework of Article 7, and of extending the jurisdiction of the Court of Justice to measures taken under Article 7. CONFER 4748/00, http://db.consilium.eu.int/cig/default.asp?lang=en. For the suggestions of the IGC Presidency on the matter, see *Agence Europe*, 17 June 2000, pp. 5-6, and of the Commission, *Agence Europe*, 5 October 2000, p. 3.

[49] Compare E. Bribosia, O. De Schutter, T. Ronse and A. Weyembergh, cited in n. 46 above, pp. 63-64.

[50] This in contradiction to an earlier draft of the Treaty on European Union (14 February 1984) designed by the European Parliament, which foresaw a possible declaration of a 'serious and persistent breach' by the European Court of Justice. See A. Verhoeven, cited in n. 46 above, p. 223.

not attributed the power to review the legality of such a determination by the Council and the European Parliament as Article 7 of the Treaty on European Union, which provides the basis on which those institutions act in this area, is one of the common provisions of the Treaty on European Union with regard to which Article 46 has not conferred any jurisdiction on the Court.[51]

2.2 Judicial control by the Court of Justice of respect for fundamental rights by the member States acting within the scope of Community law

2.2.1 *Article 46 of the Treaty on European Union*

The new wording of Article 46 of the Treaty on European Union, which confers on the Court of Justice the necessary powers to rule on matters of compatibility with the fundamental rights standard exposed in Article 6, falls short in respect of enforcement of this standard vis-à-vis the member States.[52] It only authorises the Court to examine the compatibility of 'action of the institutions' with fundamental rights, in the normal exercise of its powers under the Treaty establishing the European Community and the Treaty on European Union.[53] It follows that the case law, which for thirty years has carried out this review, must continue to be based solely on Article 220 (ex Art. 164) of the Treaty establishing the European Community in so far as it recognises the Court's jurisdiction to examine the compatibility of member States' legislation with the fundamental rights protected within the Community legal order, when such legislation implements Community rules[54] or when a member State relies on an exception contained in a provision of the Treaty establishing the European Community[55] or in the case law of the Court[56] to justify national legislation that is likely to obstruct the exercise of free

[51] According to A. Verhoeven, cited above in n. 46, p. 224, an *a posteriori* control by the Court of Justice on the way the specific enforcement procedure is applied and thus on the legality of the decision to suspend the rights of a member State derived from the Treaties (not on the legality of the Council's determination of a serious and persisitent breach) might nevertheless be possible to the extent the decision has effect within the Community legal order. See as well E. Bribosia, O. De Schutter, T. Ronse and A. Weyembergh, cited above in the same footnote, p. 61: the member State concerned might even bring an action for annulment before the Court of Justice and that Court would then be competent to rule on the existence of a breach of one of the fundamental rights guaranteed within the Union.

[52] For the development of the Court's case law on the compatibility of national legislation with fundamental rights as guaranteed by the Community legal order, see O. Due and C. Gulmann, cited in n. 12 above.

[53] The powers in question are new powers conferred on the Court in the third pillar relating to police and judicial co-operation in criminal matters. See Article 35 (ex Art. K.7) of the Treaty on European Union.

[54] Judgment in Case 5/88 *Wachauf* [1989] ECR 2609, para. 19.

[55] Judgment in Case C-260/89 *ERT* [1991] ECR I-2925, para. 43.

[56] Judgment in Case C-368/95 *Familiapress* [1997] ECR I-3689, paras. 24-25. See also n. 75 below and accompanying text.

movement within the common market. It is difficult to believe that at the very time when it was consolidating the status of the principles on which the Union is founded, including the principle of respect for fundamental rights, the Intergovernmental Conference should have sought to restrict the scope of the Court's case law in this area.

Indirect support for this interpretation of the intentions of the Union's constituent power is to be found in the express provision that the Court shall have no jurisdiction to review the validity or proportionality – and therefore, in a broader sense, the compatibility with respect for fundamental rights – of 'operations carried out by the police or other law enforcement services of a member State or the exercise of the responsibilities incumbent upon member States with regard to the maintenance of law and order and the safeguarding of internal security' (Art. 35 [ex Art. K.7](5) of the Treaty on European Union). Similarly, the Treaty establishing the European Community expressly provides, in the new title on visas, asylum, immigration and other policies related to the free movement of persons, that the Court shall not have jurisdiction 'to rule on any measure or decision taken pursuant to Article 62 [ex Art. 73j](1) relating to the maintenance of law and order and the safeguarding of internal security (Art. 68 [ex Art. 73p](2) of the Treaty establishing the European Community). Article 62(1) confers on the Council the power to adopt 'measures with a view to ensuring, in compliance with Article 14 (ex Art. 7a of the Treaty establishing the European Community), the absence of any controls on persons, be they citizens of the Union or nationals of third countries, when crossing internal borders'. Here too, therefore, in so far as such measures contain elements relating to the maintenance of law and order and the safeguarding of internal security, neither the measures themselves (even though issued by a Community institution!) nor decisions taken by the member States for the purpose of implementing them may be reviewed by the Court in respect of their compatibility with fundamental rights. The effect of this is that the European Court of Human Rights is free to exercise its jurisdiction in this area with respect to the member States, even in cases where they are fulfilling obligations under Community law. In this context, there is now no reason for that court to exercise its customary restraint in dealing with the member States of the European Union when those States are merely fulfilling obligations under Community law because that law has its own system for controlling observance of fundamental rights.[57] It may appear paradoxical that the Union's constituent power should have removed this aspect of judicial enforcement of respect for fundamental rights from the jurisdiction of the Court of Justice and should thus prefer to be bound by a machinery for controlling actions of member States that are parties to a Convention to which it did not want the Union as such to accede, probably because it feared that all its actions would be constantly subject to out-

[57] See nn. 30 to 41 above and accompanying text.

side scrutiny that might differ from review by the Court of Justice as regards the balance to be struck between protection of individual rights and protection of the general interest as conceived at the level of the European Union.

However that may be, the express provision that the Court of Justice is not to have jurisdiction to examine the compatibility with respect for fundamental rights of certain national measures falling within the scope of Community law or the third pillar does at least confirm that, except with regard to those measures, the Court has such jurisdiction and this is reflected in the case law on the subject as it now stands.

2.2.2 *The 'scope of Community law' within which national legislation must fall in order to be subject to review by the Court of Justice*

In any event, the judicial review exercised by the Court of Justice is limited. The Court itself has explained that, where national legislation falls within the field of application of Community law, the Court, in a reference for a preliminary ruling, must give the national court all the guidance as to interpretation necessary to enable it to assess the compatibility of that legislation with the fundamental rights – as laid down in particular in the Convention – whose observance the Court ensures. However, it has also stated that the Court has no such jurisdiction with regard to national legislation lying outside the scope of Community law.[58]

The whole problem, therefore, is to determine whether national legislation falls 'within the scope of Community law'. This is clearly the case when the national legislation implements Community law[59] and when a provision of the Treaty derogating from the principle of free movement is invoked to justify a restriction on free movement contained in national legislation.[60] Despite doubts on the subject raised in the legal literature,[61] the Court has very fortunately extended the second case to include a situation where a member State, citing the *Cassis de Dijon* judgment,[62] relies on overriding requirements to justify rules which are likely to obstruct the exercise of free movement of goods, holding that such justification must also be interpreted in the light of the general principles of law and

[58] Judgment in Case C-299/95 *Kremzow* [1997] ECR I-2629, para. 15. See also the judgment in Case C-144/95 *Maurin* [1996] ECR I-2909.

[59] See the judgments in Case 222/84 *Johnston* [1986] ECR 1651, para. 15; *Wachauf*, cited in n. 29 above. Cf. the judgment in Joined Cases C-286/94, C-340/95, C-401/95 and C-47/96 *Molenheide and Others* [1997] ECR I-7281 (the principle of proportionality as understood in Community law is applicable to measures adopted by a member State in the exercise of its powers relating to VAT, in that, if they went further than was necessary to attain their objective, they would undermine the principles of the common system of VAT, in particular the conditions governing deductions which are an essential component of that system).

[60] See the judgment in *ERT*, cited in n. 55 above.

[61] See A.P.W. Duijkersloot, 'Nationale maatregelen, communautaire grondrechten en de vrij verkeersjurisprudentie', 45 *Sociaal-Economische Wetgeving*, 1997, pp. 218- 224.

[62] Case 120/78 *Rewe* v. *Bundesmonopolverwaltung für Branntwein* [1979] ECR 649.

in particular of fundamental rights.[63] Indeed, there can be little doubt that such legislation is 'within the scope of Community law', since only after a closely argued case has been made, entirely in terms of that law, including general principles of Community law and in particular fundamental rights, can it be concluded that the legislation in question is not caught by one of the prohibitions laid down in the Treaty establishing the European Community. Thus, in its judgment in *Familiapress*, the Court twice cites Article 10 of the European Convention on Human Rights, which protects freedom of expression, in the course of its investigation to resolve in the light of *Cassis de Dijon* the apparent paradox that, in order to encourage freedom of expression by promoting press diversity, it is first necessary to prohibit the sale of certain publications. The Court of Justice did not hesitate to rely on the wisdom of the European Court of Human Rights, referring to the judgment of 24 November 1993 in *Informationsverein Lentia and Others* v. *Austria* Series A No. 276, in which that Court held that Article 10 of the Convention does permit derogations from freedom of expression for the purposes of maintaining press diversity, in so far as they are prescribed by law and are necessary in a democratic society.[64]

It may be wondered whether the decision in *Familiapress*, in which the Court ruled on national legislation which was certainly 'within the scope of Community law' despite the fact that it did not fall within the ambit of one of the prohibitions contained in the Treaty establishing the European Community, foreshadows a greater willingness on the part of the Court of Justice to review the conformity of member States' legislation with the fundamental rights whose observance is guaranteed in the Community legal order. Nothing appears to be less certain. Indeed, as the judgment in *Annibaldi*[65] shows, in approaching the question of its own jurisdiction to give the national court the necessary guidance as to interpretation to enable it to assess the compatibility of national legislation with the fundamental rights whose observance the Court ensures, the Court has always considered whether material competence in the area covered by the national legislation in question rests with the member States or the Community.[66]

That ruling must be approved inasmuch as it accurately reflects the particular nature of the Community system for the protection of fundamental rights in regard to the member States which, unlike the system in the United States of America, does not apply generally irrespective of the subject-matter at issue, that

---

[63] See, in this connection, Advocate-General Van Gerven's observations on the subject of freedom to supply services, in his Opinion in *Grogan*, cited in n. 28 above, points 23 and 31.

[64] Ibid., para. 26.

[65] Judgment in Case C-309/96 *Annibaldi* [1997] ECR I-7493.

[66] Thus, the Court held that, even if it were capable of affecting indirectly the operation of a common organisation of the agricultural markets, the Italian law establishing a nature and archaeological park was aimed at the protection and enhancement of the value of the environment and the cultural heritage of the area concerned, a situation which does not fall within the scope of Community law as it stands at present. Ibid., paras. 21-24.

is to say irrespective of whether it falls within federal or State competence. The fourteenth amendment to the American Constitution, a provision that is addressed to all the States of the Union, served as the legal basis for 'incorporating' the entire *Bill of Rights* – an enumeration of fundamental rights which according to its wording may only be relied upon in proceedings against the federal authorities – so as to protect those rights vis-à-vis the States even when they act within their own sphere of competence.[67] Federal protection of fundamental rights against any violation of such rights by the States has thus become an important catalyst for the judicial construction of a constitutional order shared as *ius commune* by every public authority of the American nation. Europe chose not to follow that course and this is implicitly confirmed by the new wording of Article 46 of the Treaty on European Union, introduced by the Treaty of Amsterdam: the Court's jurisdiction with respect to the application of Article 6(2) of that Treaty is expressly recognised only with regard to 'action of the institutions'. Even if that provision was not intended to call into question the established case law on the protection of fundamental rights by the Court with respect to the member States within the material scope of Community law itself,[68] there is no denying that the signal from the constituent power of the Union is that the Court of Justice should proceed with caution in this respect. It is probably still possible, despite that caution, to take into account the content of the fundamental rights protected by the European Convention on Human Rights in interpreting the material scope of Community law in order to determine whether national legislation that is criticised for failure to conform with fundamental rights comes 'within that scope'.[69]

Developments in the case law are therefore possible. The judgment in *Demirel* is a case in point.[70] In that case, the Court was asked to interpret certain provisions of the Association Agreement between the Community and Turkey in order to enable the national court in Germany to decide whether further restrictions imposed by the Land Baden-Württemberg on the spouse and children under the age of majority joining a Turkish worker established in the Community were contrary to that Association Agreement. It ruled that, as 'at present there is no provision of Community law defining the conditions in which member States must permit the family reunification of Turkish workers lawfully settled in the Community',[71] the question whether the conditions subject to which the spouse and minor children of a Turkish worker established in the Community may join him are covered by the concept of freedom of movement within the meaning of the Agreement was

[67] For further details, see K. Lenaerts, *Le juge et la constitution aux États-Unis d'Amérique et dans l'ordre juridique européen*, Brussels, Bruylant, 1988, pp. 227-242, sections 222-234.

[68] See nn. 52 to 57 above and accompanying text.

[69] This is now the acid test for determining whether national legislation may be reviewed by the Court of Justice as to its compatibility with the fundamental rights guaranteed by the Community legal order. See, for example, the judgment in *Annibaldi*, cited in n. 65 above, para. 13.

[70] Case 12/86 *Demirel* [1987] ECR 3719.

[71] Ibid., para. 28.

therefore irrelevant. So too, according to the Court, was the point 'whether Article 8 of the European Convention on Human Rights has any bearing on the answer to that question', since the national legislation at issue '[lies] outside the scope of Community law'. The Court went on: 'there is at present no provision of Community law defining the conditions in which member States must permit the family reunification of Turkish workers lawfully settled in the Community'.[72] On this precise point, some development in the case law does appear possible, albeit without calling into question the fundamental rule that the Court has jurisdiction to examine the compatibility of national legislation with the European Convention on Human Rights only in so far as that legislation is within the scope of Community law. While it is clearly right to note – as the Court does – that Article 12 of the Association Agreement merely provides that the contracting parties agree to be guided by Articles 39, 40 and 41 (ex Arts. 48, 49 and 50) of the Treaty establishing the European Community for the purpose of progressively securing freedom of movement for workers between them, and that the Council of Association had adopted no decision in the sphere of family reunification, the fact remains that any further restriction on family reunification is likely to obstruct freedom of movement for workers rather than progressively secure it. Consequently, despite the fact that Article 12 'essentially serves to set out a programme',[73] the purpose of that provision is patently clear, particularly if it is interpreted in the light of a fundamental right recognised by the European Convention on Human Rights, which unquestionably now forms part of the Community legal order. The fact that a Turkish worker who is already duly integrated in the labour force of a member State may not, according to the relevant provisions, be subject to any further restrictions on the conditions governing access to employment should therefore, of itself, suffice to secure his right to be joined by his family as a fundamental right guaranteed by Community law, even if no material provision of Community law refers expressly to that right. Clearly, in that case, the content of the fundamental rights guaranteed by Community law provides an interpretative yardstick for determining the 'scope of Community law' within which national legislation must fall in order to be subject to review by the Court of Justice in relation to its compatibility with the European Convention on Human Rights.[74]

The same considerations may apply when a citizen of the Union, who exercises his or her right of free movement in a member State other than his or her own, seeks protection with regard to his or her fundamental rights as guaranteed by the Community legal order.[75] A common basis of protection of fundamental

[72] Ibid., para. 28.

[73] Ibid., para. 23.

[74] See, to the same effect, J.H.H.Weiler, 'Article 25', in R. Bieber, K. De Gucht, K. Lenaerts and J.H.H. Weiler (eds.), *Au nom des peuples européens. Un catalogue des droits fondamentaux de l'Union européenne*, Baden-Baden, Nomos Verlag, 1996, pp. 328-335, in particular pp. 332-334.

[75] Cf. Advocate-General Jacobs's Opinion in *Konstantinidis*, cited in n. 25 above, points 46-51.

rights is indeed an essential requirement for a federal type of legal order within which the citizens of all the States of the federation must be assured that there is a sufficient community of values shared by all the States before making so bold a move as to organise their professional and personal lives in a 'global' context inside the federation.[76] On this view, citizenship of the Union acquires its full meaning only when it includes – albeit implicitly – an assurance that all the member States respect the fundamental rights guaranteed by the Community legal order. The case law of the Court, as it now stands, is based on the premise that fundamental rights as guaranteed by the Community legal order must have a material connection with the rights conferred by citizenship of the Union which may be claimed in a member State by a national of another member State.[77] If that material connection were to be loosened so as to enable citizens of the Union to ask for protection of fundamental rights as guaranteed by the Community legal order in all the member States irrespective of the subject-matter at issue, the independent content of the concept of citizenship of the Union would definitely increase. It must, however, be recognised that, in that case, the member States would have to respect the fundamental rights guaranteed by the Community legal order in every area – possibly including rights over and above those protected under the European Convention on Human Rights – with regard to all citizens of the Union (including their own nationals), which would mean that the Court of Justice would have a review function in areas manifestly outside the scope of Community law.[78] In that case, the only link with Community law would be the Union citizenship of the person claiming protection of his fundamental rights as against a member State. Even if the Treaty of Amsterdam has included respect for fundamental rights among the principles on which the Union is founded and with which the member States must comply in all circumstances (Art. 6(1) and Art. 7 of the Treaty on European Union), the fact remains that the constituent power of the Union has not conferred upon the Court of Justice the task of reviewing the

---

[76] The European Union is clearly aware of this, since it has elevated respect for fundamental rights by all its member States to the status of a principle on which the Union is founded (see Articles 6(1) and 7 of the Treaty on European Union).

[77] See in this connection the judgment of 12 May 1998 in Case C-85/96 *María Martínez Sala* [1998] ECR I-2691, in which the Court does not confine itself, for the purposes of Article 12 (ex Art. 6) of the Treaty establishing the European Community (prohibiting any discrimination on grounds of nationality 'within the scope of application of this Treaty'), to the fact that as a national of a member State lawfully residing in the territory of another member State Mrs Martínez Sala comes within the scope *ratione personae* of the provisions of the Treaty on citizenship of the Union (para. 61), but notes that Article 17 (ex Art. 8(2)) of the Treaty attaches to the status of citizen of the Union the rights and duties laid down by the Treaty, including the right, laid down in Article 12 of the Treaty, not to suffer discrimination on grounds of nationality within the scope of application *ratione materiae* of the Treaty (para. 62). See further the comments by S. O'Leary, 'Putting Flesh on the Bones of European Union Citizenship', 24 *ELRev.*, 1999, pp. 68-79.

[78] See also the caution contained in the articles by J.H.H. Weiler, cited in n. 74 above, pp. 334-335, and O. Due and C. Gulmann, cited in n. 12 above, p. 422.

way in which the member States respect fundamental rights with regard to citizens of the Union (including their own nationals) in areas that have no material connection with the legal position of those citizens under Community law itself.[79] After all, Article 7 of the Treaty on European Union only provides for political control by the institutions of the Union. All this clearly does not mean that the Court is not free to approach any investigation to determine whether such a material link exists in a manner that brings the content of the fundamental rights concerned to bear on the outcome of that issue.[80]

3. EUROPEAN STATES APPLYING FOR EU MEMBERSHIP

3.1 Human rights and 'democracy clauses'[81] in co-operation and association agreements between the European Union and European States applying for EU membership

In almost all its agreements concluded with the Central and Eastern European countries since the fall of the Berlin Wall in 1989, the Community has made co-operation, aid, liberalisation of trade or the establishing of trade preferences con-

[79] In fact, the constituent power was so cautious that it even expressly precluded the Court from exercising its normal jurisdiction in this connection under the new title on visas, asylum immigration and other policies related to the free movement of persons, in the Treaty establishing the European Community (Art. 68(2) of the Treaty establishing the European Community). See n. 57 above and accompanying text.

[80] See nn. 70 to 74 above and accompanying text.

[81] Advocate-General La Pergola considers that it follows that, to comply with the specific wording of Article 177 (ex Art. 130u)(2)) of the Treaty establishing the European Community, which requires Community policy in the sphere of development co-operation to 'contribute to the general objective of developing and consolidating democracy and the rule of law, and to that of respecting human rights and fundamental freedoms', the Community must include in co-operation agreements concluded with developing countries the 'democracy clause', which is designed to allow the Community to exercise the right to terminate the agreement, in accordance with Article 60 of the Vienna Convention on the Law of Treaties between States and International Organizations or between International Organizations 1986, (UN Doc. A/Conf. 129/15, International Legal Materials, 1986, Vol. 25, p. 543), where the non-member State has failed to respect human rights (see Opinion in Case C-268/94 *Portugal* v. *Council* [1996] ECR I-6177, points 28-29). See further Council Regulation (EC) No. 975/1999 of 29 April 1999 laying down the requirements for the implementation of development co-operation operations which contribute to the general objective of developing and consolidating democracy and the rule of law and to that of respecting human rights and fundamental freedoms, OJ 1999 L 120/1 (legal basis: Article 179 [ex Art. 130w] of the Treaty establishing the European Community), and Council Regulation (EC) No. 976/1999 of 29 April 1999 laying down the requirements of the implementation of Community operations, other than those of development co-operation, which, within the framework of Community co-operation policy, contribute to the general objective of developing and consolidating democracy and the rule of law and to that of respecting human rights and fundamental freedoms in third countries, OJ 1999 L 120/8 (legal basis: Article 308 [ex Art. 235] of the Treaty establishing the European Community).

ditional upon the fulfillment of requirements of respect for fundamental rights and democracy. Already the Preambles to the 'first generation' of agreements, the Trade and Co-operation Agreements, otherwise concerned exclusively with trade, contained clauses pointing at a broader value-laden significance than merely trade liberalisation.[82] The 1988 Rhodes European Council had made clear that the Community would take the opportunity 'to promote the Western values and principles which the member States have in common', requiring at the time respect for the provisions of the Helsinki Final Act of the Conference on Security and Co-operation in Europe (including the Concluding Document of the Vienna Meeting), promotion of human rights and fundamental freedoms (on which, given the ideological contrasts between East and West, there was initially little agreement), and the establishment of more open societies in Eastern Europe.[83] The European Community actually did make use of its right to suspend negotiations or agreements in case of non-compliance with the established principles.[84]

In a second phase, at the beginning of the nineteen-nineties, the European Community gradually moved from Co-operation to Association Agreements with the so-called 'Europe Agreements', concluded with the ten Eastern and Central European States applying for EU membership, establishing free trade, a high-level political dialogue, the progressive introduction of the principles of free movement of persons, services and capital, legal approximation and co-operation in other fields, including culture, industry, environment, transport and customs.[85] The Europe Agreements are accompanied by a programme of financial support to assist the reform of the Eastern and Central European economies and institutions (PHARE).[86] The Preambles to the Europe Agreements are far more ambitious in

---

[82] See T. King, 'The European Community and Human Rights in Eastern Europe', *26 Legal Issues of European Integration,* 1999, p. 99. See also K. Pollet, 'Human Rights Clauses in Agreements between the European Union and Central and Eastern European Countries', 7 *Revue des Affaires européennes*, 1997, pp. 290-301.

[83] EC Bulletin 12/1988, para. 1.1.10.

[84] In 1989, concerned about infringements of the linguistic and religious rights of the Turkish minority, the Community suspended negotiations conducted with Bulgaria; it imposed economic sanctions on Romenia under the Ceaucescu regime. See European Commission, *Implications of Recent Changes in Central and Eastern Europe for the Community's Relations with the Countries Concerned,* 23 January 1990, SEC (90) 111, p. 7; see further in this respect, T. King, cited above in n. 82, p. 101.

[85] The first Europe Agreements were concluded with the Republic of Hungary and the Republic of Poland in 1991. The European Community had already established similar Association Agreements with Turkey (1963) – also aiming to achieve a Customs Union, which entered into force in December 1995, Malta (1970) and Cyprus (1972). http://europa.eu.int/comm/enlargement/intro/index.htm.

[86] I.e., the PHARE Programme, Regulation 3906/89 of 18 December 1989 on economic aid to the Republic of Hungary and the Polish People's Republic, OJ L 375/89 and, later on, TACIS, the equivalent of PHARE for the Commonwealth of Independent States, Regulation 2053/93 of 19 July 1993 concerning the provision of technical assistance to economic reform and recovery in the independent states of the former Union of Soviet Socialist Republics and Mongolia, OJ L 187/93.

referring to fundamental rights principles than the Trade and Co-operation Agreements, committing the Parties not only to respect human rights and the rule of law, but likewise to establish a pluralist democracy, a multiparty system and a market economy.[87] A further step was taken in the 1992 Agreements with Albania and the Baltic States. For the first time 'the importance of guaranteeing the rights of ethnic and national groups and minorities, in accordance with the undertakings made within the context of the Conference on Security and Co-operation in Europe', was recognised.[88] And for the first time as well, references to fundamental rights were no longer confined to the Preamble, but formed an essential part of the Agreement itself. In addition, they were equipped with the so-called 'Baltic clause', a non-execution clause allowing the Community to unilaterally – without even consulting the third State concerned – suspend the Agreement with immediate effect where the Community were to establish a serious violation of the essential provisions of the Agreement.[89] This unduly severe approach by the Community has been rightfully criticised by its trade partners. The Commission decided to replace it by a new, softer form of non-execution clause, known as the 'Bulgaria clause' in view of its first application in the Community's Association Agreement with Bulgaria, containing a consultation requirement and the principle that reprisals be proportionate to the breach committed. Still, no minimum time limit for consultation was prescribed, and an escape clause was maintained in order to enable the Community to rapidly take reprisals without consultation in cases of 'special urgency'.[90] The 'Bulgaria clause', together with references in the Preamble and the provision that respect for democracy and fundamental rights constitutes an essential element of the Agreement, has been incorporated in many subsequent agreements with the countries of the Conference for Security and Co-operation in Europe.[91]

3.2 The requirement of respect for fundamental rights in the Agenda 2000 pre-accession strategy

At the Copenhagen European Council of 21-22 June 1993, the member States officially took a stand in favour of a considerable enlargement of the European

---

[87] European Commission, Association Agreements with the countries of central and eastern Europe: a general outline, 27 August 1990, COM (90) 398, p. 2.

[88] See the Agreements between the European Economic Community and the Republic of Albania, the Republic of Estonia, the Republic of Latvia and the Republic of Lithuania on trade and commercial and economic co-operation, 11 May 1992, OJ L 343/92 (Albania) and L 403/92 (Baltic States).

[89] T. King, cited above in n. 82, p. 108.

[90] Ibid., pp. 109-110.

[91] Notably in the bilateral 'Europe' Association Agreements with Romania (1993) and with the Republic of Estonia, the Republic of Latvia and the Republic of Lithuania (1995), and in the Partnership and Co-operation Agreements with the Republic of Belarus, the Republic of Kazakhstan, the Kyrgyz Republic, the Republic of Moldava, the Russian Federation, the Ukraine (1994).

Union eastwards. As accession to the European Union is now the main focus of the European States applying for EU membership, the Europe Agreements have become part of the pre-accession framework within which these countries are preparing for membership. The member States seized the opportunity to clarify the principles with which European States applying for EU membership have to comply in order to be eligible for European Union membership. The 'Copenhagen criteria' require the European States applying for EU membership to give an undertaking to achieve stability of institutions guaranteeing democracy, the rule of law, human rights and respect for and protection of minorities, the latter as envisaged by the Organisation for Security and Co-operation in Europe (Conference on Security and Co-operation in Europe, at the time).[92] Since then, Accession Partnerships and National Programmes for the Adoption of the Acquis (NPAA), containing these Copenhagen criteria, are concluded with every one of the thirteen States negotiating for accession to the Union.

Recently, the emphasis has changed from a negative approach of human rights in external relations, merely confined to the insertion of clauses in trade or association agreements prohibiting the violation of fundamental rights, to a positive, pro-active approach promoting the democratisation of the institutions, strengthening the rule of law, creating civil society platforms, etc.[93]

What is striking in this regard is the general absence of any systematic and coherent approach to monitoring and reporting on the actual human rights situation in the countries candidate for accession, as compared to the requirements contained in the bilateral association agreements, or on the concrete implementation of the projects financed by the European Union. This overall lack of transparency in the external human rights policy of the European Union is highly unsatisfactory for the countries applying to join the Union, who are not aware of the basis on which their performances will be evaluated by the EU, for the EU institutions – evidently, if only for budgetary reasons, given the huge amounts spent on projects supporting the development of democratic institutions and on specific human rights initiatives – especially for the European Parliament, which is entirely dependent on transparent and systematic information to be able to exercise its scrutinising role, and for the European civil society, which is equally handicapped in its function of watch-dog of the performances of the EU institutions.[94]

---

[92] Cf. European Commission, 'Agenda 2000. For a stronger and wider Union', EU Bulletin, Suppl. 5/97, p. 44.

[93] See Ph. Alston and J.H.H. Weiler, cited in n. 1 above, pp. 10-11. For an example of this evolution, see Council Regulation (EC) No. 976/1999 of 29 April 1999 laying down the requirements of the implementation of Community operations, other than those of development co-operation, which, within the framework of Community co-operation policy, contribute to the general objective of developing and consolidating democracy and the rule of law and to that of respecting human rights and fundamental freedoms in third countries, cited in n. 81 above.

[94] See in this sense Ph. Alston and J.H.H. Weiler, cited in n. 1 above, p. 13.

3.3 A closer look at the membership requirement of respect for and protection of minorities

Relatively new is the explicit demand by the 1993 Copenhagen European Council of respect for (negative obligation) and protection of (positive duty) minority rights by the European States applying for EU membership as a pre-condition for accession. In its recommendations on the matter, the Commission draws inspiration for the concrete filling in of this Copenhagen requirement from the texts agreed upon within the framework of international fora such as the United Nations, the Organisation for Security and Co-operation in Europe and the Council of Europe, especially from the latter's 1995 Framework Convention for the Protection of National Minorities and the 1992 European Charter for Regional or Minority Languages.[95] This is somewhat surprising if one considers the fact that minority protection is almost a non-issue within the Union itself and its member States. The ratification record of the above-mentioned instruments by the EU member States is far from complete[96] and, apart from a few non-binding statements made by the European Parliament,[97] the European Union has shown little commitment to undertake action on the matter within its own borders.[98] Furthermore, national legislation aimed at the protection of minorities is being scrutinized by the Court of Justice on its compatibility with Community law: measures introduced with a view to the protection of minority languages, for instance, have been considered in view of the free movement principles.[99] In this respect, it may be regretted that 'language' is not included in the list of grounds of discrimination which Article 13 of the Treaty establishing the European Community seeks

---

[95] Some of the core instruments of the United Nations of concern for minority protection are the 1992 Declaration on Minorities and the Convention on the Elimination of All Forms of Racial Discrimination. Within the context of the Organisation for Security and Co-operation in Europe, the Concluding Documents of the Human Rights Dimension Conferences of Vienna and Copenhagen and the 1995 Pact on Stability in Europe are of importance. See generally, K. Henrard, *Individual Human Rights, Minority Rights and the Right to Self-Determination*, The Hague, Kluwer Law International, 2000.

[96] The Framework Convention has not yet been ratified by Belgium, France, Greece, Luxembourg, the Netherlands and Portugal and the European Charter for Regional or Minority Languages has so far been ratified by only four member States (Finland, Germany, the Netherlands and Sweden).

[97] E.g., the European Parliament's Resolution on a Community Charter of Regional Languages and Cultures and on a Charter of Rights of Ethnic Minorities, 1981, OJ C-278/106-107 and its Resolution on Linguistic and Cultural Minorities in the European Community, 1994, OJ C-61/110-113 and its Annual Reports on respect of human rights within the Union.

[98] See A. Verhoeven, cited in n. 46 above, p. 232.

[99] K. Lenaerts and P. Van Nuffel, *Constitutional Law of the European Union*, cited in n. 5 above, pp. 235-236, para. 4-211: the Court now recognizes the protection of an official language of a member State (or a region thereof) as an overriding or mandatory requirement in view of which member States may place reasonable restrictions on the free movement of goods, persons and services. See in the same sense the judgment of 4 July 2000 in Case C-424/97 *Haim* [2000] ECR nyr, paras. 59-60.

to eliminate within the scope of Community law.[100] Racial or ethnic origin and religion or belief are part of the list and of special concern for minorities, but none of these grounds can be relied upon as such by individuals belonging to minority groups, as it is clear from the outset that Article 13 has no direct effect. It does, however, constitute a potential base on which to build a genuine minority policy.[101]

The records of ratification of the above-mentioned Conventions by the European States applying for EU membership, on the contrary, are, in the context of the assessment of the fulfillment of the EU membership conditions, subject to severe scrutiny by the European Union.[102] The best strategy for the European Union to enhance the attachment to fundamental rights principles in general and respect for minority rights in particular within the broader Europe undoubtedly is to lead by example.[103] That, in turn requires the European Union to adopt an attitude of reciprocity and consistency.[104]

3.4 The requirement flowing from Article 49 of attachment to the principles of liberty, democracy, respect for human rights and the rule of law, as set forth in Article 6(1) of the Treaty on European Union as a legal condition for EU membership

An important innovation by the Treaty of Amsterdam is the requirement, inserted in the first paragraph of Article 49 of the Treaty on European Union, that any European State wishing to become a Member of the European Union must respect the principles on which that Union is founded, set out in Article 6(1) of that Treaty. This is a firm political signal to the European States that have applied to join the Union.[105] Thus, respect for fundamental rights by European States applying for EU membership has now become a legal condition of that membership. In principle, fulfillment of that condition may be the subject of judicial review by the Court of Justice, since the Court's jurisdiction extends to Article 49 of the Treaty on European Union [see Art. 46(e) of that Treaty].[106] In practice, however,

---

[100] A. Verhoeven, cited in n. 46 above, p. 233.

[101] See, for a more general discussion, L. Flynn, cited in n. 16 above, pp. 1132-1133.

[102] See as well Ph. Alston and J.H.H. Weiler, who accuse the Union of carrying out an inconsistent, untransparent, uncommitted and ambiguous fundamental rights policy, illustrated by the ruling of the Court of Justice of 12 May 1998 that calls into question the legal bases for the funding of several internal and external human rights and democracy projects, cited above in n. 1, pp. 7-9.

[103] Leading by Example: A Human Rights Agenda for the European Union for the Year 2000, Report of the Comité des Sages of the European University Institute, October 1998.

[104] Compare Ph. Alston and J.H.H. Weiler, cited in n. 1 above, pp. 8-9.

[105] Cf. European Commission, 'Agenda 2000. For a stronger and wider Union', EU Bulletin, Suppl. 5/97, pp. 42-44.

[106] That jurisdiction is not affected by the fact that the legal conditions for the accession of new member States remain to be defined in the context of the procedure laid down in Article 49 of the Treaty on European Union, without it being possible to determine their content judicially in advance

it will once again be a matter for political assessment by the Council acting by unanimity and the European Parliament acting by an absolute majority of its members. It appears to be somewhat unlikely that the Court will be called upon to review the legality of such a decision, for example at the request of the Commission or of a member State that has failed to exercise its veto.

It must therefore be concluded that the European Union requires both member States and European States applying for EU membership to respect fundamental rights in all circumstances, in order to preserve one of the principles set out in Article 6(1) of the Treaty on European Union and on which it is founded. However, to ensure compliance with that requirement, the Union relies essentially on the *political* decisions of its democratic institutions and on the machinery for controlling respect for fundamental rights established by the European Convention on Human Rights. Indeed, participation in that Convention by member States of the Union appears to be the principal – if not the only – objective criterion for determining their commitment to respect fundamental rights. There is, therefore, some justification for the view that a European State cannot be accepted as a member of the European Union, respecting the principles on which the Union is founded, without first acceding to the European Convention on Human Rights.[107] However, in the near future this requirement will probably still be a necessary but no longer a sufficient condition for accession in the field of compliance with human rights, as European States applying to join the Union are required to respect fundamental rights as enumerated in the – possibly higher standard – EU Charter of Fundamental Rights.

In the meeting of the Convention and Representatives of the European States applying for EU membership held on 21 June 2000, these States unanimously welcomed the Charter, but some of them expressed their concern about the higher standard – compared to compliance with the European Convention on Human Rights – currently being drafted (a standard which could contain, for instance, the right of minorities to special protection). There was near unanimity among the European States applying for EU membership against the granting of legally binding force to the Charter in the Treaties – at least for the time being – and against its possible insertion into the founding Treaties and the process of 'constitutionalisation' of the protection of fundamental rights – and thus of the entire European Union – this could entail. Most of the European States applying for EU membership appear to fear that this whole undertaking could make con-

(see judgment in Case 93/78 *Mattheus* v. *Doego* [1978] ECR 2203, para. 8), since the condition of respect for the principles set out in Article 6(1) of the Treaty on European Union follows from Article 49 itself and cannot therefore be the subject of the procedure laid down in that article for the purpose of determining its content.

[107] Thus, the Commission notes that 'respect for fundamental rights is, in principle, guaranteed in most of the applicant countries. All have acceded to the Council of Europe's Convention for the Protection of Human Rights and Fundamental Freedoms and the Protocol allowing citizens to take cases to the European Court of Human Rights'. See 'Agenda 2000', cited in n. 105 above, p. 43.

siderably more onerous the conditions to be met in the field of respect for fundamental rights as required by the 1993 Copenhagen European Council, and that this in turn could cause serious delays in the enlargement process. Therefore, most European States applying for EU membership advocate a Charter that is to be considered a mere political declaration.[108]

CONCLUSION

Whatever status the EU Charter of Fundamental Rights is to be granted by the Nice European Council in December 2000, it will in any event be a strong statement on the values and principles the European Union stands for and this both vis-à-vis the present member States and the other European States applying for EU membership.

Should the Charter be inserted into the Treaties on which the Union is founded, it will not replace the present *acquis* of Union law in the field of protection of fundamental rights. It will instead make that *acquis* more visible, as the Cologne European Council requested. The core of the said *acquis* indeed already belongs to 'primary' Union law as the preceding analysis has shown. It is of course possible – and frankly even to be hoped – that the Charter will lead to an increased level of protection through the formulation of rights that had not been stated so far, or else through the non-inclusion in the formulation of rights stemming from other instruments, of some limitations attaching to these rights. In either case the Charter contains a potential for growth of the material scope of protection of fundamental rights beyond the sources of those rights mentioned in Article 6(2) of the Treaty on European Union. It is in that sense that Article 52(3) of the text of the Charter proposed by the Praesidium of the Convention should be understood:

> 'Insofar as this Charter contains rights which correspond to rights guaranteed by the Convention for the Protection of Human Rights and Fundamental Freedoms, the meaning and scope of those rights shall be the same as those laid down by the said Convention. This provision shall not prevent Union law providing more extensive protection'.[109]

---

[108] *Agence Europe*, 22 June 2000, p. 6.

[109] Article 53 makes it clear that the existing law should in any case be seen as the minimum level of protection: 'Nothing in this Charter shall be interpreted as restricting or adversely affecting human rights and fundamental freedoms as recognised, in their respective fields of application, by Union law and international law and by international agreements to which the Union, the Community or all the member States are party, including the European Convention for the Protection of Human Rights and Fundamental Freedoms, and by the member States' constitutions'.

Yet, on the other hand, the same text indicates that operation of the Charter is to draw heavily on the concepts and categories of legal reasoning that govern the present *acquis* of Union law in the field of protection of fundamental rights, in spite of the difficulties of application which they may contain (and which the foregoing study has hopefully helped to elucidate to some extent). Thus, the Charter is addressed to the member States 'only when they are implementing Union law' (Art. 51(1)) and 'rights recognised by this Charter which are based on the Community Treaties or the Treaty on European Union shall be exercised under the conditions and within the limits defined by those Treaties' (Art. 52(2)).

Finally, even if the Charter becomes part of 'primary' Union law, the fact that it is addressed 'to the institutions and bodies of the Union' (Art. 51(1)) should not diminish the importance of accession of the European Community or Union (when the latter receives legal personality) to the European Convention on Human Rights. Only such accession can indeed give the EU member States, as Contracting Parties to that Convention, the watertight guarantee that they will in no circumstances be held responsible – under some future development of the *Matthews* case law of the European Court of Human Rights – for the infringement of fundamental rights by the EU institutions.

THE CONSTITUTIONAL IMPACT OF ENLARGEMENT AT EU AND NATIONAL LEVEL

SUMMING-UP AND CONCLUSIONS

Jaap W. de Zwaan*

1. THE SUBJECT OF THE CONFERENCE

The subject of the Conference has been well chosen and well timed. In fact we find ourselves in an advanced stage of the negotiations in the framework of the Intergovernmental Conference (IGC) 2000 which should lead to a Treaty of Nice, to be agreed upon during the European Council session of December 2000 in Nice (France). What is hoped for is that this treaty will bring about a certain number of institutional reforms enabling the institutions of the Union to function properly and efficiently in an enlarged Union. In this same period of time intensive negotiations are going on related to the accession of 12 candidate countries to the Union.[1]

It is a great pleasure to see all applicant countries represented at our Conference. Furthermore, we are pleased to notice that representatives of so many other countries – member States and third countries – have shown an interest in participating in this Conference.

The subject of our Conference is the more attractive because the 'constitutional' impact of enlargement is an essential element in the overall context of the 'rule of law' as one of the general principles of the Union.[2] Indeed, the impact accession has on the constitutional provisions of the legal order of a country, is closely related to the achievement, at the national level, of objectives such as a transparent system of government, a democratic legislative process, an independent judiciary and an adequate system of legal protection.

This being said, the discussions have been of utmost importance also for the participants originating from the existing member States since it has appeared that

* Chairman of the Conference. Professor of the Law of the European Union. Jean Monnet Chairholder. Erasmus University Rotterdam, The Netherlands. President of the Scientific Council of the Asser Institute.

[1] In his contribution to the Conference Professor Bothe has dedicated attention to the broader, economic, context of the enlargement process.

[2] Art. 6(1) EU.

A.E. Kellermann et al. (Eds.), EU Enlargement: The Constitutional Impact at EU and National Level

in fact each individual country has developed over time its own approach and modalities aimed at bringing its constitutional provisions into conformity with the requirements of European law.

Our Conference may be looked at as a unique occasion enabling a variety of interested circles to discuss fundamental issues: the academic world, politicians, civil servants of the national and European administrations, members of the national and European judiciary, and practitioners of the liberal professions. A first conclusion to be drawn from this feature is that through the Conference a valuable network of expertise and contacts has been developed which we should try to maintain and further develop in the course of time.

2. A EUROPEAN CONSTITUTION?

One of the questions raised by Professor Joseph Weiler during the Conference concerned the need and appropriateness to establish a European 'constitution'. Professor Weiler showed himself not in favour of such an idea since it could easily give rise to new debates on fundamental issues the outcome of which is at least uncertain. He also, in view of the already existing treaty texts, questioned the necessity of establishing such a constitutional text at the European level. Indeed, it seems that European provisions having a constitutional character do already exist in either the Treaty on European Union (EU)[3] or the European Communities treaties (EC). Our guest speaker, the British MEP Richard Corbett, was also of the same opinion in his dinner speech.

Now, in this context the question of course arises whether the existing treaty texts need not to be restructured in such a way that, inter alia, as a first and most important European Union text, a treaty of a 'constitutional' character arises. Such a treaty could be called the 'European Constitution'. Here a relationship does exist with the proposals put forward by the so-called Group Dehaene in October 1999 as well as with the work done by the European University Institute in Florence (Italy) the results of which have been presented to the Commission on 15 May 2000. Indeed, the Florence Institute has proposed establishing a European 'basic' text containing a selected number of fundamental provisions. Apart from that a consolidated text of the EC Treaty, an updated version of the Treaty on European Union as well as a number of Protocols could be developed. Professor De Witte, who was himself a participant in this valuable exercise, has provided the Conference with ample information on this work.[4]

[3] Also to be called: 'Maastricht Treaty', 'Treaty of Maastricht' or 'Union Treaty'.

[4] Professor De Witte explained that Part Two of the research done by the Florence Institute concerns new modalities of a treaty revision procedure. However, because this part of the study is still under examination with the Commission, he was not able to give further details here.

This being said, these questions have to be taken up at any rate since, as a follow up of the so-called 'Humboldt' speech of the German Minister of Foreign Affairs, Joschka Fischer, of 12 May 2000 in Berlin, it has already been agreed upon that – after Nice – a further European debate with a 'constitutional' character will be held in the framework of a new Intergovernmental Conference to be held in the year 2004. In the context of this debate the ultimate status of the European Union – in this context Minister Fischer referred to the model of a European 'Federation' – will be subject, inter alia, of discussion. However, it seems to me that we have to be prudent here. European integration so far has developed as a dynamic and continuous but gradual process. It was only when the time was considered ripe that amendments or additions to existing texts and structures have been agreed upon. Progress in the process of European integration has therefore always been the result of ad hoc developments without, however, it being clear beforehand what the ultimate objective, the final goal, of the exercise would be.[5] As a consequence of progressing in this way, the modalities of European cooperation are the result of 'tailor made' constructions. To that extent one may wonder if a discussion on the final modalities of European integration is not to be considered premature. Would it not be preferable to continue working on the improvement of the democratic character and the efficiency of the existing Union structures? For the moment at least it seems if such a 'fundamental' discussion would better not be forced. The least that may be hoped for is that such a discussion will not result in any steps backward. At any rate all interested circles and groupings should be allowed to participate in this fundamental discussion.

A final element raised during the discussions on this subject concerns the invitation put forward by Professor Jeno Czuczai to establish the boundaries of – what may be considered – the 'constitutional acquis' of the Union at this moment and this in order to illustrate notably to the candidate countries which are the requirements that must be complied with in this respect. Now, of course, it is not possible to give a precise and final answer to this question. Indeed, as is the case with the whole of the law of the European Union, we face a dynamic process which is gradually but constantly developing. Each day, in fact, the acquis may be amended, a phenomenon which, by the way, also results from the jurisprudence of the Court of Justice of the EC. Therefore, the only possibility is in fact to give a global 'print' of today's situation. However, once, for example, the Charter of Fundamental Rights of the European Union[6] will have been awarded a status within the legal order of the Union, this text will also form part and parcel of the 'constitutional' acquis of the European Union. Thus, this subject matter is better looked at in close connection with the other – just mentioned – elements

---

[5] In this context it is to be remembered that, at the occasion of the 'Maastricht' negotiations in 1991, the option of a European federation (the so-called 'f' word) was already in discussion, but strongly rejected by at least one of the partners, the United Kingdom.

[6] See infra, para. 3 of the Summing-Up.

related to the future 'constitutional' debate to be held in the context of the 2004 'post-Nice' IGC.

3. CHARTER OF FUNDAMENTAL RIGHTS

The Conference has intensively discussed the state of affairs relating to fundamental and human rights in the European Union. In this particular context it is notably the contributions of Professors Schermers and Hirsch Ballin that are to be mentioned.

The origin of this discussion relates to the absence in this period of time of concrete competences of the European Community to develop a proper human rights policy. Indeed, as was concluded by the Court of Justice in its Opinion 2/94 concerning the possible accession of the Community to the European Convention for the Protection of Human Rights and Fundamental Freedoms of the Council of Europe, the Community lacks competences in this particular area and Article 308 of the EC Treaty does not represent a sufficient legal basis to create such a competence.[7] The Amsterdam Treaty has not changed this situation. In fact, although without filling the 'lacuna' mentioned, the first paragraph of Article 6[8] as well as the new Article 7 (sanction procedure) have been introduced into the Treaty on European Union by way of an alternative solution.

Nonetheless, both Professor Joseph Weiler and Director-General of the Legal Service of the European Parliament Garzón Clariana expressed their preference for a fully fledged accession by the Community to the European Convention, as the most important and fundamental European catalogue in the area of human rights. Both interveners pleaded in favour of the creation of a Community competence to that extent, to be realised through an amendment of Article 3 of the EC Treaty. Moreover, they recommended the creation of a genuine infrastructure – a Directorate General – for human rights within the Commission, and proposed that fundamental rights be the substance matter of a separate portfolio of one of the Commission members.

Apart from the (absence of) Community powers in the area of human rights, the Conference also discussed the nature and content of the so-called Charter of Fundamental Rights of the European Union. This text, asked for by the European Council meeting in June 1999 in Cologne (Germany), has been prepared and negotiated in the framework of a separate 'Convention' composed of representatives of national governments, national parliaments and other experts.[9] As to con-

---

[7] [1996] ECR I-1759.

[8] This provision is worded as follows: 'The Union is founded on the principles of liberty, democracy, respect for human rights and fundamental freedoms, and the rule of law, principles which are common to the member States'.

[9] The final version is to be found in document CHARTE 4487/00 of 28 September 2000, CONVENT 50.

tents, the Conference was of the opinion that, in order to be significant, the Charter should aim at more than simply reflecting the existing acquis of the Council of Europe and that of the United Nations. Indeed, if at all important, the Charter should be made 'tailor made' for the purposes of the European Union, and have an 'added value' in that respect. It should include rights and principles reflecting the specific nature of (the forms of cooperation practised in) the Union. As to the 'status' of the document the Conference warned against giving a too low profile to the Charter. Indeed, more particularly, if it were to appear that the Charter as to contents only reflected the existing situation and, moreover, was to be given only a political character, the whole exercise could easily be interpreted, politically and legally, as a dangerous exercise, a step backwards. In such a case the Charter could even represent a threat to the prestige and the working of the European Convention of the Council of Europe.

On both aspects – status and content – Professor Ernst Hirsh Ballin, member of the negotiating Convention and member of the First Chamber of the Dutch Parliament, recalled that, although not representing an alternative for accession of the Union to the European Convention of the Council of Europe, the Charter offers ambitious and interesting opportunities. He explained that, as presently drafted, the Charter contains more rights and principles than are at present covered by the instruments of the Council of Europe and the United Nations. In this respect by way of example mention was made of the 'right to good administration' (Art. 40), the 'right of access to documents' (Art. 41) as well as of specific social and economic rights such as the 'right of freedom of the arts and sciences' (Art. 13), the 'right to education' (Art. 14) and the 'freedom to conduct a business' (Art. 16).[10] Also Professor Hein Schermers qualified the Charter as 'politically and constitutionally' important. It will contribute to the legitimacy of the Union, he said. However, as to the final status of the document – will it be a legal text or only a political declaration? – it seems that for the moment no decision will be taken. Therefore, it is probable that the European Council meeting in December 2000 in Nice will adopt the Charter as a – for the moment – purely political text, the decision on its final status being postponed until later. Also here it is expected that the Charter will appear as a separate subject for the agenda of the 'post-Nice' IGC in 2004.

As to this final aspect, the Conference was clearly of the opinion that at this next occasion of intergovernmental negotiations it should be decided to award the Charter a legal status, assuming it still represents added value compared to the existing texts and after a proper refinement of its drafting. On that occasion it also should be decided to integrate its contents into the relevant parts of the – by that time simplified – Treaty on European Union, not to say in the text of a 'European

---

[10] On the other hand, it has been established that the Charter contains no provision regarding the protection of minorities.

Constitution'.[11] Meanwhile, and this point was made more particularly by Professor Schermers, it has to be awaited to what extent the national and European judiciary will view the Charter, (provisionally) qualified as a Solemn Declaration, as a valuable 'source of inspiration' and apply it accordingly in concrete cases.[12]

4. THE REFORM OF THE EUROPEAN JUDICIARY

On this topic it was explained that reforms to be introduced in the organisation of the European judiciary (the Court of Justice and the Court of First Instance) are put surprisingly high on the agenda of the Intergovernmental Conference 2000. More particularly Advocate-General Francis Jacobs gave an inside view as to the present state of the negotiations regarding the reorganisation of the EC Court's infrastructure. So it appeared that the principle according to which all member States have the right to designate a candidate as a member of the Court of Justice,[13] will be maintained in the perspective of enlargement of the European Union. In this respect, however, it was observed that most probably there will be sufficient work to be done by a college composed of one judge per member State. On the other hand, deliberations within the Court should be dealt with as a rule in small chambers, composed of 3 or 5 judges. Also it was mentioned that in all probability the IGC will provide for the possibility for the Court to sit in 'grand' chambers, composed of a limited number of judges, say eleven. At any rate the Court should only in exceptional circumstances sit in full plenary session.

Advocate-General Francis Jacobs as well as former Advocate-General Walter van Gerven recalled the importance of the role played by the Advocate-General in representing the 'public interest' and providing the Court with an independent opinion. More particularly, Van Gerven argued that the work accomplished by Advocates-General represents a precious contribution to the coherence of the Court's jurisprudence. On the other hand, according to both speakers there is no need to designate an Advocate-General in each case appearing before the Court. Therefore there is no reason to increase further the existent number of eight Advocates-General.[14]

The number of members of the Court of First Instance (CFI) will be increased. Here is not only the implications of the enlargement process that are to be recalled for also possible changes in the division of the jurisdiction between the Court of Justice and the Court of First Instance are of relevance. Indeed, it seems that the number of future CFI judges will not so much depend on the number of

[11] Supra, para. 2 of the Summing-Up.

[12] Reference is made to the jurisprudence of the Court of Justice with regard to the interpretation of political declarations.

[13] Arts. 221(1) and 223(1) EC.

[14] See Art. 222(1) EC.

member States but will be more related to the workload of that Court. In this context it was observed that in all probability the IGC will decide to grant the Court of Justice jurisdiction to deal with several categories of 'direct' appeals, referred to in Article 230 EC Treaty, irrespective whether these are initiated by individuals, member States or institutions. On the other hand, member States apparently still manifest reluctance to delegate – to the CFI – jurisdiction on so-called infringement procedures, the direct appeal procedures referred to in Article 226 of the EC Treaty. In the framework of an infringement procedure the Commission may bring a case before the Court of Justice against a member State which, according to the Commission, has violated its Treaty obligations. Now, in this respect it was argued that also infringement procedures are much better suited to be dealt with by the CFI at first instance. Indeed, whereas these cases as a rule require an examination of facts, proceedings in two instances in fact contribute to a more fully developed system of legal protection, in this particular context to the benefit of member States and institutions.

Furthermore, it was recalled that discussions are going on to 'delegate' certain specialised categories of preliminary questions – such as cases on social security, customs tariff, VAT and intellectual property questions – to the CFI, and this without awarding to parties an automatic right of appeal to the Court of Justice itself. On this point, however, final decisions have not been taken as yet. Indeed, it seems that prudence is required here. The exclusive jurisdiction of the Court of Justice to make rulings providing for a uniform interpretation throughout the whole Community reflects a 'constitutional' responsibility of the Court of Justice. Because Community law is not to be divided into different categories of questions of law, and therefore constitutes a 'unity', one indeed should be extremely reluctant to delegate jurisdiction on preliminary questions to other instances than the Court of Justice itself.

Other ideas being discussed in the IGC framework regarding the (re-)organisation of the European judiciary relate to the creation of 'specialized chambers' within the CFI as well as the establishment of separate and autonomous 'bodies' or 'panels', with jurisdiction to deal with certain specialised categories of cases.[15] A possibility to appeal against decisions of these separate bodies of panels would be introduced with the CFI.

On the contrary, the Conference was of the opinion that the idea of specialised chambers within the Court of Justice itself should not be considered. In this context it was stressed that the Court of Justice should consist of 'generalists', thus legal experts possessing a broad and general knowledge and expertise on a wide variety of legal subjects.

Professor Joseph Weiler advocated the idea of a 'European High Court', composed of a limited number of judges (depending on the workload of such a court)

---

[15] By way of example reference was made to staff cases.

and competent to deal with a limited number of fundamental cases having a constitutional character. In his opinion this court should also have exclusive jurisdiction with regard to preliminary rulings. Now, it seems that a European supreme court must first and foremost have competence to decide on fundamental constitutional topics as well as on preliminary rulings. However, so far it has not been discussed if such a court should consist of fewer judges than there are member States. In fact, it is still possible that in the end it will be decided that the Court of Justice itself should perform all these responsibilities. Indeed, as earlier mentioned, such a solution appears to be the most logical one.

As to the current IGC 2000 both Weiler and Professor Jan Wouters furthermore proposed to strive at more uniformity in the system of the Court's jurisdiction in the three 'pillars' of the European Union. In concrete terms it was argued that the deviating modalities as embodied in Article 68 of the EC Treaty – related to the Court's jurisdiction concerning visa, asylum, immigration and civil law cooperation – and in Article 35 of the EU Treaty – related to the jurisdiction of the Court of Justice in the Third Pillar cooperation – should be adapted to the modalities of jurisdiction of the Court under the First Pillar cooperation. Along the same line of thinking it was proposed to confer upon the Court of Justice full jurisdiction as to the Second Pillar cooperation.[16] The Conference welcomed these suggestions.

5. THE CHARACTERISTICS OF COMMUNITY LAW: THE IMPLICATIONS OF MEMBERSHIP FOR THE NATIONAL CONSTITUTIONAL ORDERS

This subject, dealing with the question to what extent national constitutional provisions have to be amended because of the membership of a state of the European Union, was in fact the most important item of the Conference. On this subject many written contributions have been presented in connection with the Questionnaire prepared by the Asser Institute. The answers given on the different questions of the Questionnaire allow a clear impression. To arise as to experiences at the national level in this regard.

As a point of departure in this discussion it was signalled that the appropriateness of, even, necessity to amend national constitutional texts in view of the accession of a country to the Union, is not an explicit and specific item to be discussed during the accession negotiations. Such items are considered not so much a concern related to the 'take over' of the existing Union acquis, but – in principle at least – a purely national matter.

On the other hand, it was recognized that the way member States constitute their national legal orders has a relationship with the implementation of the gen-

[16] In this context it would suffice to include a reference to Title V EU in Art. 46 EU.

eral principles referred to in Article 6(1) of the EU Treaty. Indeed, national legal orders have to be made suitable to contribute to the 'effectiveness' of Union law.[17] To that extent national legal orders – here we are confronted with responsibilities not only of the national authorities but also of the judiciary – have to be adapted and organised in such a way that they are able to 'receive' Union law properly and to make Union law effective vis-à-vis individuals, the ordinary citizen and undertakings.

In this discussion the characteristics of Community law have to be taken into account, such as the principle of transfer of powers, primacy of Community law,[18] direct application and direct effect. Except of the principle of direct applicability, which, of course, is a characteristic inherent in the instrument of the regulation,[19] all these principles have been developed in the course of time by the Court of Justice, in its jurisprudence. The doctrine according to which the creation of the Community legal order reflects a process in the context of which a transfer of powers has taken place, from the national level to the European one and resulting in a parallel – and voluntary accepted – limitation of national sovereignty, has already been developed by the Court in its early jurisprudence, namely, in the decisions Van Gend & Loos as well as Costa/ENEL.[20] Equally, the principle according to which Community law takes priority over national law which is not in conformity, has been embodied in the jurisprudence of the Court of Justice.[21] Direct effect, the doctrine according to which an individual may directly invoke provisions of Community law to the extent they are clearly drafted, are unconditional in character and leave no margin of discretion to the member States, has also been developed by the Court as a remedy for the ordinary citizen who is confronted with public authorities not (fully) complying with their Treaty obligations, e.g., in the context of the implementation of a directive. These principles were also referred to in the oral contribution of Doctor Jit Peters, the representative of the Minister of the Interior in the Hague.

Now, on the basis of the written contributions and the discussions on this subject it has been concluded that even in the national legal orders of the present member States no uniform approach has been developed in order to cope with these specific Community law characteristics and requirements. Indeed, it appears – and here reference may be made to the resumé of Advocate-General

[17] Here does exist a relation with the principle of 'loyalty' as embodied in Art. 10 EC. This provision reads: 'member States shall take all appropriate measures, whether general or particular, to ensure fulfillment of the obligation arising out of this Treaty or resulting from action taken by the institutions of the Community. They shall facilitate the achievement of the Community's tasks. They shall abstain from any measure which could jeopardise the attainment of the objectives of this Treaty.' See also infra, n. 24.

[18] Also to be referred to as 'priority' or 'precedence'.

[19] Art. 249(2) EC.

[20] Case 26/62 [1963] ECR 1 respectively Case 6/64 [1964] ECR 585.

[21] Case 106/77, Simmenthal, [1978] ECR 629.

Jacobs,[22] which will not be repeated here – that some of the national constitutions – such as that of the Netherlands – do not refer to the Dutch membership of the Union at all, whereas others – such as the Austrian one – have developed specific modalities thereto.

On the contrary, it was striking to note – and here I refer to the other resumé, that of former Advocate-General Walter van Gerven covering the situation in the candidate countries as well as certain third countries maintaining special relations with the Community – that in fact all candidate countries are at least reflecting on the expediency to include explicit and specific clauses in their national constitutions. Most of them have already elaborated texts for that purpose. In so far, one could argue, the present member States may learn something from their new partners!

Now, of course, in this context the question arises if special 'European Union' clauses are really necessary. Indeed, to the extent member States have removed existing obstacles in the national legal order which may hinder a full application of Community law, one may argue that special constitutional clauses are not indispensable. Because, if – and this is the situation in the Netherlands – 'priority' of Community law over national law as well as 'direct application' and 'direct effect' are guaranteed in practice, through the efforts of the national judiciary and other authorities, one can do without 'tailor made' clauses in the national constitutional texts.

However, in view of the importance of the interests at stake, it is still to be recommended that member States, the present ones as well as the candidates, include in their national constitutions, albeit exclusively for political reasons, special clauses related to their membership of the Union. In this respect one could think, more particularly, of clauses concerning the principle of transfer of powers, the principle of primacy and the principle of direct effect.

As to the wording of the 'transfer of power' clause, a special reference to the European Union would seem to be indicated. In this respect it was noticed that certain draft texts prepared in candidate countries refer to a 'delegation of the exercise of national sovereignty' to the European Community. Now, such an approach does not correspond to the philosophy according to which powers are transferred, from the national level, to a higher – in this case the European, supranational – level. Therefore, a 'bottom up' approach is to be preferred over a 'top down' approach. For another reason also the wording 'delegation' seems not to be appropriate since it implies the power (of a member State) to 'withdraw' the delegated powers in certain circumstances, an option, however, which does not correspond with the reality of Community cooperation.

The responsibility of national courts and tribunals to make Community law really 'effective' was also stressed. This aspect was underlined more particularly by

[22] Supra, p. 183

Professor Jiri Zemanek. The obligation of Article 10 EC Treaty is in this context also of importance.[24] In fact in the jurisprudence of the Court of Justice references to this fundamental treaty provision are found each time the Court stresses the obligation of national courts and tribunals to provide for an adequate system of legal protection for the ordinary citizen. In the discussion in this particular context reference was made to the need to take appropriate measures e.g., in the area of training of members of the national judiciary.[25] It was also suggested to put this aspect on the agenda of a possible follow-up meeting of the Asser Conference.

In connection with the discussion related to the appropriateness of including amendments in the national constitutional texts, in one of the parallel sessions the question was raised – reference was made here to the tragic experiences of the (former federal states and now) independent successor states of the Republic of Yugoslavia – if the inclusion, in the Treaty on European Union, of – what was called – a 'withdrawal' clause should not be recommended. Now, obviously the option to withdraw from the European Union is a principle contrary to the clear intention of the Contracting Parties to provide for a continuous framework for co-operation to the benefit of all participating states. Therefore, it is not without reason that whereas the treaties do not contain a provision referring to the possibility to withdraw from the Union, an explicit clause has been introduced in the Union Treaty regarding the unlimited duration of the cooperation.[26] Moreover, when the possible 'withdrawal' of Greenland from the European Community was discussed, at that time the model of an amendment of the Danish Act of Ratification of the EEC Treaty was preferred over a construction according to which Greenland could withdraw from the Community.[27]

This being said, in cases of real urgency, the absence of a special withdrawal clause should not necessarily mean that a withdrawal is to be excluded in all circumstances. Indeed, here a reference to the principle of international law concerning the 'clausula rebus sic stantibus'[28] may be made.

A final element in this discussion concerned the phenomenon of 'regionalisation' of the European integration process. In this context it was observed that more and more the position of autonomous regions in certain member States and, in a more general context, the national arrangements with regard to the inter-

---

[24] See also supra, n. 17.

[25] Here a reference may be made to the FIDE Congress held in Helsinki in June 2000, which dealt with the respect paid by the national judiciary and other authorities of the member States to Art. 10 of the EC Treaty.

[26] Art. 51 EU reads: 'This Treaty is concluded for an unlimited period'.

[27] As a consequence of the amended version of the Danish ratification act, Greenland has become a so-called 'OCT', an overseas country and territory in the sense of Part IV of the EC Treaty (see Art. 188 EC).

[28] Art. 62 – fundamental change of circumstances – of the Vienna Convention on the Law of Treaties (23 May 1969).

nal division of powers in certain member States have to be taken into account. Therefore it was suggested that analyze the position of such autonomous regions in (quasi-)federal states vis-à-vis Community law should be analyzed. Now, in this discussion it was recalled that the obligation to respect the Treaties rests upon the central level of the national administration, thus the level of the member States themselves.[29] Indeed, according to Community law internal modalities with regard to the division of powers are qualified as an 'internal' affair for the member States concerned. Moreover, it seems that the consequences of regional autonomy within a member State do not represent an important problem for all candidate states. Therefore, it was decided not to further deepen the discussion on this point.

6. PARTNERSHIP AND COOPERATION AGREEMENTS

Parallel to the discussion with regard to possible amendments to be included in the constitutions of the present and future member States in order to ensure a good 'reception' and implementation of Community law, the Conference also paid attention to the consequences of agreements concluded by the Community (and its member States) with third countries for the national legal orders of the third countries concerned. In this context particular reference was made to the contributions to the Conference of Marc Maresceau and Christoffe Hillion. Indeed, these agreements concluded with countries many of which do find themselves in a process of transition to an open market economy do as a rule contain chapters regarding human rights, the protection of minorities, political dialogue, technical assistance and the like. It was observed that such agreements do represent an important instrument for the Union and its member States to contribute to the respect for human and fundamental rights in the whole world.

7. THE INTERGOVERNMENTAL CONFERENCE 2000 AND THE TREATY OF NICE

The Conference held ample discussions about the current negotiations in the framework of the Intergovernmental Conference (IGC) 2000.[30] As is well known, the IGC 2000 discusses proposals on how to prepare the institutions of the Union for enlargement. The Dutch State Secretary of Foreign Affairs Dick Benschop discussed this subject in his opening speech to the Asser Conference, whereas Commissioner Gunter Verheugen was the guest of the Conference for dinner.

---

[29] See, as an example, the Court's decision in the case C-302/97, Konle, [1999] ECR I-3099.

[30] The IGC 2000 is a 'conference of representatives of the governments of the member States' in the sense of Art. 48 EU.

Moreover, the former Dutch State Secretary of Foreign Affairs Michiel Patijn, presently member of the Dutch parliament, intervened on the subject during one of the working sessions of the Conference.

In the context of the IGC 2000 questions are at stake such as the efficiency of the decision-making process, the democratic character thereof and the capability of the European judiciary to ensure a sufficient degree of legal protection. The main concrete topics in the IGC 2000 relate to the composition of the Commission, the (re-)weighting of the votes within the Council, the scope of (qualified) majority voting, and the working of the Court of Justice. A discussion also takes place regarding possibilities to make the conditions for closer cooperation[31] more flexible.

As to the composition of the Commission the maximum number of commissioners in an enlarged European Union is the central issue in the discussion. Whereas the Commission at the moment is composed of 20 members, the concern has been expressed that if the existing practices – in the context of which 'bigger' member States[32] may designate two candidates and the other member States only one[33] – are still to be applied in an enlarged Union, the size of the Commission will become too large and disproportionate. Indeed, a Commission composed of 33 members[34] will give rise to more bureaucracy and inefficiency, whereas also no feasible portfolios may be created for such a huge number. The Conference recognized, of course, the political sensitiveness of the issue at stake. Indeed, in view of the extreme importance of the tasks and prerogatives of the Commission, in which context notably the exclusive right of initiative is to be mentioned, it is understandable that in principle each member State wants to be 'represented' in this college. And, it was said, that the same attitude is to be expected from the candidate states. Now, whether or not this last observation is correct or not, it was stressed during the discussions that the Commission in reality is not an organ representing the interests of the individual member States but an institution taking care of the 'general interests' of the Union as a whole. To that extent there is no necessity for member States to be always 'represented' in this institution. A fair system of rotation, to the extent it is based on a strict equality between the member States, could suffice in this respect. Thus, during the Conference wide support was expressed for the idea to limit the number of commissioners to 15 or 20. On the other hand, the Conference was not in favour of ideas circulating in the IGC according to which member States, which happen to be not represented in the Commission, will be compensated with a right to designate 'deputy' or 'junior' commissioners. Moreover, attention was given to the position

[31] See Title VII EU.

[32] France, Germany, Italy, the United Kingdom and Spain.

[33] Art. 213(1) EC.

[34] The idea being that Poland, like the present 'bigger' member States, also should have the right to designate 2 members, whereas the other – 11 – new member States would have the right to designate only one member.

of the President of the Commission. On this point the Conference was of the opinion that the role and responsibilities of the President should be strengthened.[35] It was suggested, inter alia, that the President should have the right to 'force' an individual member of the Commission to resign once it appears that his/her functioning has become controversial.

As to the issue concerning the re-weighting of the votes to be cast in the Council, the 'representativeness' of the present system laid down in Article 205(2) of the EC Treaty is at stake. Indeed, the 'bigger' member States claim that, in view of the fact that – with the exception of Poland and, to a certain extent, Rumania, – all candidate states are small if not very small states, the present system has to be adapted in order it make it more acceptable. Therefore, the number of populations of the (candidate) member States has been put forward as a new criterion to be taken into account once this weighting system is adopted. Ideas under discussion in the IGC 2000 relate, on the one hand, to an adaptation of the system of Article 205(2) and, on the other, to the introduction of a 'double' majority. This last option refers to the introduction of a second 'key' connected to the size of the overall population of the whole European Union. In this context the level to be acquired in order to enable a qualified majority decision could be fixed, for example, at 55 or 60% of the overall Union population. A third idea consists of a combination of both solutions mentioned. Now, whereas the Conference has accepted the principle of an adaptation of the present weighting system, it has also been argued that the size of the population is certainly not the only factor to be taken into account once re-adapting the numbers of votes to be cast by member States. Also other factors – such as the economic growth of the economy of a state, the military-strategic importance of a country, the geographical size of a country – are to be taken into account then. Furthermore, it was observed that the size of the populations of the member States is more suited to be reflected in the composition of the European Parliament, as the representative body of the peoples of the member States. Therefore, there was a tendency in the Conference in favour of (only) a slight adaptation of the present system of Article 205(2) of the EC Treaty. In this context also reference was made to the appropriateness of avoiding too complicated decision-making procedures.

As to the third item – the scope of qualified decision-making – the view was clearly expressed in the discussion that, in order to have the cooperation system survive in an enlarged Union, more majority voting is indispensable. In fact the idea was put forward that if unanimity is to be acceptable as a requirement for decision-making in certain policy areas, a justification has to be provided for. Indeed, with the exception of 'constitutional' dossiers such as the revision of the treaties,[36] unanimous decision-making has to be excluded in a Union composed

[35] In order to achieve this goal, the drafting of Art. 219 EC could be amended.

[36] Art. 48 EU.

of 27 or, taking into account a possible Turkish membership, 28 countries.[37] As 'sensitive' policy areas which in future also should allow for qualified majority decision-making, social security policy (Art. 42 EC), asylum and immigration policy (Art. 67 EC), taxation policy (Art. 93 EC), social policy (Art. 137 EC) and environmental policy (Art. 175 EC) were mentioned.

Furthermore, it was stressed that majority voting as a principle should not be 'mixed up' with full transfer of powers, from the national to the European level, in the areas concerned. Therefore, once majority voting is accepted for certain policy fields, this does not mean that the Community acquires exclusive competences in the areas concerned. What majority voting in such areas does mean, however, is that member States accept certain limitations as to the way they exercise their sovereign rights in the policy fields concerned.

The discussion on the working of the Court of Justice related more particularly to the composition of this institution and the division of jurisdiction between the Court and the Court of First Instance. For this discussion reference is made to what has said above, under paragraph 4, on this topic.

The principle of 'closer cooperation' is also under discussion in the IGC 2000. This principle refers to the possibility for a smaller group of member States to act as 'forerunners' in the process of implementation of the treaty objectives in certain policy fields. Although only introduced in the Amsterdam Treaty,[38] the conditions for application of this principle are currently under review. More particularly it is said that the present conditions to be fulfilled in order to allow an initiative on closer cooperation are too onerous. The IGC 2000 notably discusses a suggestion to delete the reference to a right of a member State to block a vote on an initiative for closer cooperation.[39] It is proposed also to alter the requirement that closer cooperation should concern a majority of member States.[40] Instead the number of eight (member States) has been put forward as the minimum number to participate in an exercise of closer cooperation. Generally speaking the Asser Conference supported the idea that more flexible arrangements are needed to make the principle of 'closer cooperation' workable. More particularly, the relationship with enlargement of the European Union was mentioned here. On the other hand, it was recognised that closer cooperation, because it allows deviation from the ordinary way of cooperation according to which all member States participate at the same 'time' and 'speed', should not be accepted too easily.

---

[37] And, indeed, it is most probable that the number of member States will not stop there. Indeed, in future applications for membership are to be expected from countries like Croatia, Albania, Macedonia, Bosnia-Herzegowina, Serbia-Montenegro as well as Moldavia. Also applications are not to be excluded from countries like Switserland, Norway and Iceland.

[38] See Title VII EU for the general arrangements concerning closer cooperation, and Art. 40 EU as well as Art. 11 EC for the specific modalities of closer cooperation in the Third respectively First Pillar.

[39] Art. 40(2)(2) EU respectively Art. 11(2)(2) EC. On such initiatives the Council may in principle decide by qualified majority.

[40] Art. 43 under d. EU.

A final aspect in this institutional debate was raised by former Advocate-General Walter van Gerven. He asked for attention for – what was called – the 'internal' dimension of democracy. In this context Van Gerven referred – not only – to the need for transparency of the activities of the institutions,[41] but also to the necessity to ensure the integrity and accountability of the members of the institutions. In this discussion reference was made to the resignation – in the beginning of 1999 – of the former Commission chaired by the former Luxembourg Prime Minister Jacques Santer, and the recommendations put forward by the Committee of Independent Experts.[42] Van Gerven was a member of that committee. Van Gerven stressed that, in order to function properly, the fulfilment of conditions to enable a proper 'external' functioning – such as independence and competence – does not suffice. Rules governing the 'internal' handling of affairs need also to be observed. Therefore Van Gerven pleaded in favour of the establishment of a 'Code of Conduct' to be subscribed to by European political leaders. The Conference supported this idea.

The Asser Conference did not discuss the complications flowing from the increase in the number of official languages, once enlargement will become effective. Nonetheless, it was observed several times that, although no amendment in the system of official languages[43] is required, in the area of 'working' languages flexibility and reforms are indicated. Referring to the restricted language regime already applicable, e.g., in the meetings of the Committee of Permanent Representatives,[44] at least in the framework of the negotiations within the Council further reforms – in the sense of practical language arrangements – were deemed feasible.

8. QUALITY OF LEGISLATION

During the Conference a topic dealt with during an earlier Asser Conference was recalled. This topic concerns the 'Quality of legislation' which represented the main theme of discussion in the framework of the 1997 Conference organised by the Asser Institute.[45] Referring to these earlier discussions, the present Conference underlined once more that a good quality of legislation to be adopted in the

[41] See the principle of Art. 255 EC which is also applicable in the Second and Third Pillar context: Arts. 28(1) and 41(1) EU.

[42] See the First Report on Allegations regarding Fraud, Mismanagement and Nepotism in the European Commission (15 March 1999); and the Second Report on Reform of the Commission: Analysis of current practice and proposals for tackling mismanagement, irregularities ad fraud (10 September 1999).

[43] Art. 290 EC.

[44] Art. 207(1) EC.

[45] See: A.E. Kellermann a.o. (ed.), Improving the Quality of Legislation in Europe, 1998 T.M.C. Asser Instituut, Kluwer Law International.

framework of the European Union is the more important in an enlarged European Union. Indeed, in order to ensure a uniform interpretation and application of European Law all over the territory of the Union, certain minimum requirements as to the quality of legislation are to be met. In the course of the 1997 discussions a variety of criteria and conditions have already been developed in order to ensure such a quality.

Furthermore, reference was made to the Declaration included in the Final Act of the Treaty of Amsterdam 'on the quality of the drafting of Community legislation'.[46] In this declaration it is underlined that the quality of (the drafting of) Community legislation is crucial if it is to be properly implemented by the competent national authorities, and better understood by the public and in business circles. Moreover, an appeal was made to the three institutions involved in the Community legislative process (the European Parliament, the Council and the Commission) to agree on common guidelines on the quality of the said legislation. Before the Treaty of Amsterdam formally entered into force such guidelines had already been established.[47]

The Conference welcomed these developments and emphasized the need to extend them to legislation developed in the framework of the other forms of Union cooperation, foreign and security policy (Title V of the EU Treaty) and justice cooperation (Title VI).

9. FOLLOW-UP OF THE CONFERENCE

At the end of the Conference it is useful to recall the importance of a gathering of experts in constitutional law originating from all the states involved, i.e., present member States, candidate States, and third states with whom the Union has developed cooperation relations in different policy areas.

As has been recalled earlier, the impact accession has on the national 'constitutional' provisions of (candidate) States is not as such a matter for negotiation in the context of accession. In fact, this subject is to be appreciated in the context of what may be called the 'pre-conditions' for membership. Indeed, principles such as priority of European law, direct applicability, and direct effect have to be applied by the public authorities and the judiciary of the member States in order to ensure the 'effectiveness' of European law. To that extent the wide variety of subjects dealt with during this Asser Conference under the heading 'the Constitutional impact of enlargement at the EU and national level' form part of a wider concept, the 'rule of law'.[48]

[46] Declaration No. 39.

[47] Interinstitutional Agreement of 22 December 1998 on common guidelines for the quality of Community legislation, OJ C 73/1-4 of 17 March 1999.

[48] Referred to in Art. 6(1) EU.

Because of the unique composition of the audience of this Conference an interest has been shown, by several participants, to keep this network of expertise intact, in order to have it further developed. Indeed, a group of outstanding experts as present here may play a useful role – not only – in the process of how to prepare (the authorities and judiciaries of) the candidate states for membership, but also in the format of a network periodically to discuss themes of common interest. The broader field of interest includes topics such as the drafting of standard clauses to be incorporated in national constitutions; the responsibility of the national judiciaries to ensure full effectiveness of European law; as well as improvements to be made in the system of legal protection of the European Union itself. As a means for these future discussions and activities one could think of trainings, seminars, round tables or bigger conferences such as the present one.

For more information on this subject related to the follow-up of the Asser Conference I refer to – paragraph V of – the 'Report on the Conference' prepared by Alfred Kellermann.[49]

Last but not least I recall that the main conclusions of this Conference[50] will be presented in a concise and written form to the Dutch State Secretary Dick Benschop, who is disposed to pass them on to the other delegations participating in the Intergovernmental Conference 2000.

---

[49] Supra, p. XXIX.

[50] See paragraph IV of the 'Report on the Conference' prepared by Alfred Kellermann.

POSTSCRIPTUM
The Irish referendum on the Treaty of Nice and Article 10 EC – A recent example of constitutional problems of enlargement –

A.E. Kellermann

The Irish referendum on the Treaty of Nice is a recent example of the importance of national constitutions and its impact on enlargement. The Nice Treaty was concluded by the Representatives of the member States of the EU, meeting within the European Council held in Nice in December 2000. By common accord they agreed to amend the Treaty on European Union, the Treaties establishing the European Communities and certain related acts. According to Article 48 Treaty on European Union (TEU), the amendments will enter into force after being ratified by all the member States in accordance with their respective constitutional requirements. In Ireland one of the constitutional requirements for the ratification of a treaty is to hold a referendum. The result of the referendum held on Thursday 7 June 2001 not to ratify the Nice Treaty (the actual percentages were: **YES** 46,13%, **NO** 53,87%), does raise several political and constitutional questions for legal solutions that would finally allow for the ratification of the treaty. It is, however, not for the first time that referenda form obstacles for the ratification of a European Treaty. There was a near failure to have the Maastricht Treaty ratified in Denmark and in France. In Norway accession was rejected twice in referenda, the first time in 1973 and the second time in 1994. The Agreement on the European Economic Area was rejected in a subsequent national referendum in Switzerland in 1992.

In the following we like to give some suggestions as a contribution to an exchange of ideas to the finding of legal and political solutions for these constitutional problems focusing on the recent Irish referendum.

The Irish complaints against the Nice Treaty were quite varied, reflecting everything from fears over loss of influence in an enlarged EU to concerns that the EU's military plans might threaten Ireland's traditional neutrality. The reasons for the **NO** vote had not only to do with enlargement, but to a large extent reflected disenchantment with further integration, which has been foisted on an unwilling electorate by political elites. The referendum culture in Ireland is very strong and, due to a series of political funding scandals, there is a deep cynicism towards politicians. Moreover, the electorate were assured in 1972 that with each significant step towards integration that there would be a referendum. The next move for Ireland is unclear. Its EU partners have already ruled out a complete

A.E. Kellermann et al. (Eds.), EU Enlargement: The Constitutional Impact at EU and National Level

renegotiation of the complex treaty. The alternative is a political declaration attached to the treaty which seeks to meet Irish concerns.[1]

One of the central questions to be answered from a European law point of view, is whether Article 10 EC Treaty is applicable in this situation and, if so, whether the Irish Government complied with the duty of loyalty to the Community as mentioned in Article 10 EC Treaty. Article 10 EC reads as follows:

> 'Member States shall take all appropriate measures, whether general or particular, to ensure fulfilment of the obligations arising out of this Treaty or resulting from action taken by the institutions of the Community. They shall facilitate the achievement of the Community's tasks. They shall abstain from any measure which could jeopardise the attainment of the objectives of this Treaty'.

The principal and essential question which arises is whether Article 10 EC applies at all in the case of the Irish referendum. In other words, can the ratification provisions of Article 48 TEU jo. Article 313 (EC Treaty) be considered as obligations arising out the EU and EC Treaty as required in the wording of Article 10 EC Treaty? Or can these obligations only be considered as obligations arising out of international law after signing a treaty according to the 1969 Vienna Convention on the Law of the Treaties?

National constitutional lawyers argue that Article 10 EC will only apply to existing Treaty obligations which will enter into force only after ratification.

Would it not be possible, as the European Court of Justice has done in some earlier cases, to give a teleological interpretation also to the provisions of Article 313 EC Treaty ('This Treaty shall be ratified by the High Contracting Parties ...') so that these provisions can be considered as a community obligation of loyalty in the meaning of Article 10 EC?

Perhaps a teleological interpretation of these articles may enlarge the applicability of Article 10 EC to agreements concluded in unanimity by all the governments meeting within the European Council. Would it not be possible to interpret these agreements as decisions of the representatives of the governments of the member States meeting within the Council? These acts or decisions have generally a character of international law, but may in certain cases form part of Community law and as such they are not subject to any rules of national constitutional law on the conclusion of international agreements.[2]

If the answer is in the affirmative and if therefore Article 10 EC or its principles do apply, the question may arise whether it would have been possible for the Irish Government to avoid all the problems of the **NO** vote. Was it wise to hold a referendum for treaty amendments? Was the Irish Government guilty of not informing the Irish people satisfactorily about the objectives of the Treaty of Nice and of not stimulating enough **YES** votes? If that were the case, then the

---

[1] Financial Times, June 12, 2001, by John Murray Brown.

[2] P.J.G. Kapteyn and Verloren van Themaat, Introduction to the Law of the European Communities, Third Edition, 1998 p. 341, edited by Laurence W. Gormley, Kluwer Law International.

Irish Government is responsible for the delay in ratification. As mentioned in *the Financial Times* of 14 June 2001, Brian Cowen, the Irish foreign minister, indicated there would be no early move to put a new referendum to the people to reverse the decision rejecting the Nice Treaty on enlargement of the European Union.

Although it is in accordance with the principle of subsidiarity, the differences in the constitutional requirements between the member States for the ratification of treaties may lead to bad results for European integration if the objectives of the proposed referenda are not sufficiently achieved by some governments of the member States. Given the importance of the outcome of the referendum, should the Irish Government, which after all signed the Treaty of Nice, not have indicated that it would resign in the case of a **NO** vote?

On the one hand, it is constitutionally advisable to hold a referendum in order to comply with the requirement of Article 6 TEU which refers to the principles of democracy on which the Union is based; on the other hand, this case shows that using referenda for amendment procedures of rather complicated treaties is not always an efficient procedure and may result in unexpected and unpleasant outcomes for further European integration.

Assuming that Article 10 EC or its principles will apply in this Irish case, a short comment on the interpretation of its provisions and reference to some ECJ Decisions may be useful.

In its present wording Article 10 EC refers only to the relationship between the Community and its member States and is formulated, moreover, as if it were a one-way-street, that is as a duty imposed on the member States to take all measures to promote the Community interests ... .[3] The Community interests are in this case the speedy ratification of the Nice Treaty by all the member States.

The notion of 'member State' is a global and wide one. It covers not only the central authorities, the 'executive' (the central Government), but also the local and/or regional authorities of a member State.[4]

Where clear breaches of Community law are at hand, as in violating the prohibition against discrimination, the Court is not impressed, generally speaking, by a member States invoking constitutional provisions to justify such a breach. A number of examples illustrate this attitude.[5]

A member State cannot rely upon provisions of its Constitution for the purpose of justifying a failure to comply with obligations and time-limits resulting from directives.[6]

---

[3] Report of the XIX FIDE Congress, Helsinki 1-3 June 2000, p. 9, W. van Gerven.

[4] Report of the XIX FIDE Congress, Helsinki 1-3 June 2000, p. 229, Jaap W. de Zwaan, Idem, Tijdschrift voor Europees en Economisch Recht (SEW), 48e jaargang no. 4 april 2000, pp. 132-154, Jaap W. de Zwaan.

[5] ECJ Court Decisions Case 77/69 *Commission* v. *Belgium* (1970 ECR 237, para. 15 and several judgments of 2 February 1982 of the ECJ in cases of the *Commission* v. *Belgium.* See Jan Wouters – National Constitutions and the European Union (Legal Issues of Economic Integration, Vol. 27, 2000-I, pp. 56-57, nn. 127 and 128.

[6] ECJ Case 100/77 *Commission* v. *Italy* (1978) ECR 887, para. 21. See Lenaerts/van Nuffel, Constitutional Law of the European Union, pp. 574-575, Sweet & Maxwell, London, 1999.

According to the opinion of de Zwaan, Article 10 EC encompasses an obligation of a general and broad, but not very precise, character. Thus although its merits and importance have only been increasing over the years, also in the jurisprudence of the Court of Justice, the significance of Article 10 EC in the context of the present discussion is to be seen as the reflection of a general attitude to be expected from an average and loyal member State rather than serving as a basis to impose specific and concrete conduct on the State concerned. It may be considered as a source of inspiration for the national judiciary, nothing less but also nothing more.[7] In our opinion, it may be also considered as a source of inspiration for the national governments.

From all the above-mentioned considerations, we may conclude and suggest the following two legal and political solutions for the constitutional problems in the Irish case.

In the first place, in our opinion Article 10 EC may be also considered as a source of inspiration for the Irish Government to

> 'take all appropriate measures, whether general or particular, to ensure fulfilment of the obligations arising out of this Treaty or resulting from action taken by the institutions of the Community ...'

to improve the support of the Irish people for its government policies and stimulate greater participation of the Irish people at these referenda. In this situation a more succesful and government friendly outcome of referenda may be expected.

In the second place, Article 10 EC may inspire the Irish Government to propose to its electorate an amendment of its constitution for example by proposing for some cases a replacement in the Constitution of referenda by a parliamentary procedure, especially for complicated treaties. As such texts are not easy to understand by ordinary Irish people, it seems better to submit these texts to members of Parliament who may consult their legal staff. The text of the Treaty on European Union of 1991 was already very complicated, and the text of the Treaty on European Union after the Amsterdam amendment is still more inaccessible and difficult to consult because of the insertion of many new Articles, Protocols and Declarations and the renumbering of the Consolidated Treaty text.[8] The text of the Treaty after Nice is even more inaccessible, complicated and difficult to understand. It was therefore to be expected that the ordinary people of Ireland might say **NO** in a Referendum to a text which they did not understand, except perhaps if they were experts in european law!

The Hague, 18 June 2001

---

[7] Supra n. 2, p. 247 and SEW, p. 146.

[8] See 'Improving the Quality of Legislation in Europe', T.M.C. Asser Instituut, Kluwer Law International, Alfred E. Kellermann et.al., eds., The Hague. 1998, Report of the Conference, pp. XXXV and XXXVI.

ANNEXES

ANNEX I

OPENING AND DINNER SPEECHES

Dick Benschop*

The Asser Institute and COLPI have ambitious plans for the next few days. This conference will be the arena for a probing study of the European architecture.

'The constitutional impact of enlargement at EU and national level' is a highly topical theme, given the new architectural plans that are now being drawn up all over Europe: rough sketches, panoramic vistas, and in some cases complex and detailed blueprints for new European constructions. In preparation for enlargement, the Union's foundations need reinforcing, its institutions need renovating and more room must be created for the further deepening of integration. I hope that this conference provides not only inspiration and vision, but also some useful practical suggestions.

ENLARGEMENT AND DEEPENING

Though the EU's forthcoming enlargement is an unparalleled event with far-reaching implications, it is not the only reason for reflecting on the structure of the Union at this time. Europe has an ambitious agenda. The advent of the euro; the need to respond to the challenges of globalisation, the new economy and the knowledge society; European defence; and a European policy on asylum and migration, are all ambitious projects that will deepen integration.

All these projects touch upon the division of labour between member States and the Union. Powers that were exercised solely at national level in the past, are increasingly being employed within a European framework. This is not undermining the role of national governments, but adding a European dimension, as national sovereignty is pooled and policy is coordinated at EU level. This is another development that has stimulated debate on the future of Europe.

This Asser conference focuses on three main issues relating to the wider question of Europe's future:

---

* State Secretary for Foreign Affairs of the Netherlands.

- what will accession to the European Union mean for the constitutions of the applicant countries and the relationship between European law and national laws, in particular constitutional law;
- the proposed Charter of Fundamental Rights for the European Union;
- the IGC on the reforms of the European Union's institutions.

Allow me to make a few remarks on these three themes in reverse order.

THE IGC

In the coming months, the Dutch government will put all its weight behind the necessary institutional reforms and the strengthening of the European institutions. Strong institutions are the cornerstone of the European integration process – about this, there can be no doubt. Strengthening these institutions is our key objective. The agenda is set. I should like to highlight several elements that I believe need extra attention in the run-up to Nice.

Some of the issues to be debated are rather technical in nature. But they are far from trivial. For the Netherlands, the main topic in this category is the reform of the European Court of Justice. More and more legal questions are being put before the Court, a trend set to continue. The Court cannot be left as it is. We need to introduce reforms that ensure that preliminary rulings are given within six months instead of the two years that our citizens and companies have to wait, on average, at present. Cases concerning the free movement of persons should also be settled within a six-month period.

- The size and composition of the European Commission and the weighing of votes in the Council are major issues at the IGC. We must take decisions on both. This requires political sensitivity, some mathematical skills and even some psychological insight. We need to do justice to demographic realities whilst maintaining the overall balance that exists within the Union.
- The most important issues at Nice are extending decision-making by qualified majority voting (QMV) and widening the scope for enhanced cooperation, or 'flexibility'. These are the issues that will determine how successful – or how far-reaching — the reforms prove to be. Both issues are crucial to safeguarding the decision-making capacity of an enlarged Union. They are essential if the dynamic thrust of the integration process is to be sustained. Unfortunately, I am rather pessimistic at the moment as to the direction of the IGC's debate on QMV. We must make a real effort to go forward, in four fields in particular:
  - where asylum and migration policy is concerned, we must make maximum progress;
  - the same applies to the environment, including the fiscal aspects of environmental policy;
  - we should take several steps forward on social policy, bearing certain nuances in mind;

– we should also make cautious headway with QMV on taxation. QMV should be introduced for so-called secondary aspects of tax regulations and anti-fraud measures. Major decisions on tariffs and tax bases must, however, be based on unanimity.

On enhanced cooperation, I am optimistic. The explicit debate on this subject in Feira produced a clear result on flexibility. The modalities still need to be discussed. But it is now a political fact that something substantial will be worked out on this issue in preparation for Nice. This is very important. The alternative to flexibility built into the Treaty and based on the Union's institutions, would be enhanced cooperation outside the Treaty and outside the Union's institutions. That would not be desirable. At the same time, it is essential that enhanced cooperation will have an open character. Any 'avant-garde' of member States must remain open to others wishing to join at a later stage. Let us have no closed shops. That would create new dividing lines in Europe. It would cripple the engine of European integration instead of enhancing its performance.

EU CHARTER OF FUNDAMENTAL RIGHTS

Simultaneously with the IGC, work is under way on a Charter of Fundamental Rights. At Nice a draft version should be ready. The unique character of this project is clear from the composition of the 'Convention' working on the draft. The Netherlands wants the Charter to be broad in scope, that is to say, to constitute a complete and modern definition of fundamental rights. This formulation must reflect the texts of existing international instruments, such as the European Convention for the Protection of Human Rights and Fundamental Freedoms – the ECHR – in order to rule out, if at all possible, differences in interpretation. The Netherlands also favours the accession of the European Community and – if possible – the European Union, to the ECHR.

Once the text has been agreed, we must decide on the Charter's place within the corpus of European law. There is no point in having an eloquent text without any binding force. Of course, this is easier said than done. Many problems will be raised and discussed at this conference. I hope that solutions will also be forthcoming, so that this great political aspiration may come to fruition.

NATIONAL CONSTITUTIONAL ORDERS

After Nice, the accession negotiations have to be upgraded to political level. For the Union as well as for the applicant countries, it will be time to take the plunge. For the aspiring member States it will mean making some very far-reaching decisions – in some cases, perhaps, amending their national constitutions. These constitutions may not contain any impediment to the direct application of European legislation. Amending legislation and reorganising the administrative apparatus are far from simple projects, and both therefore need to be tackled vigorously – with the Union and its member States lending a helping hand.

The present member States' constitutions will not in principle be affected by enlargement. They do have to ratify the accession treaties, of course, but the accession of new countries to the Union does not necessitate any review of the national constitutions of the existing member States.

A EUROPEAN CONSTITUTIONAL ORDER

So what will be the 'constitutional impact of enlargement at EU level'? What constitutions – including unwritten ones – have in common is that they contain fundamental rules for the actions of the state; the government has to observe certain formal requirements and procedures. Constitutions determine the powers of the legislature, the executive and the judiciary. They determine the relationships between the central, local and regional authorities. Last but not least, constitutions enshrine fundamental rights: classical human rights, the rights of citizenship, and often social and economic rights as well.

Given this definition, it seems to me irrefutable that the European Union possesses a constitutional order. I scarcely need to summarise the features of the EC and EU Treaties to remind you of how much they resemble a European constitution. Nonetheless, certain elements are absent or poorly developed. Fundamental rights, in particular, occupy as yet a humble place in the Treaties. Nor is their cohesiveness all it could be. Some have even spoken of 'a Europe of bits and pieces'.

It is therefore imperative, as I have said, for us to reach agreement in the IGC about vigorous reforms of the institutions. This is essential in the short term. In the longer term we shall have to consider further measures. For the Netherlands, the most important criteria are conserving, and where possible improving, the effectiveness, legitimacy and unity of the Union.

In the next few years, we must tackle the incorporation of the Charter of Fundamental Rights into European law. The revision of the Treaties – a topic on which the European University Institute in Florence has already done some hard thinking – is another important theme that will have to be addressed in the near future. In this context, a debate about the relationship between the powers of the Union and those of the member States will be unavoidable.

So enlargement has unleashed a fundamental debate about the future of the Union. We find ourselves confronting crucial questions about the set-up and responsibilities of the EU's institutions. Should they be better structured?

Is there a need for a review of the principles on which the Union is based? How should we incorporate the Charter of Fundamental Rights into the Treaties?

Basically, all these questions have to do with the development of a European constitutional order.

The Netherlands would welcome an exchange of views on this topic, and will be happy to contribute to further debate. The Dutch government sent Parliament a memorandum this week, called the 'State of the European Union', outlining our priorities for the forthcoming institutional reforms and putting forward for consideration certain ideas on the future of the Union.

Our compass for the course to be taken by the Union will be determined by unity, effectiveness, democracy and legitimacy. We must preserve the unity and cohesiveness of the Union. At the same time, we must improve the Union's internal and external effectiveness and strengthen its democracy and legitimacy.

LEGITIMACY

In conclusion, I should like to add a few words on the subject of democracy, legitimacy and transparency. Great European projects, such as enlargement, need courage and leadership. But courage needs people, and leadership needs listening. Modern leadership in Europe means absorbing, addressing, setting a course based on interaction, communication and explaining – just like modern management. Europe needs openness, not secrecy. People expect openness from Europe. They expect to be taken seriously by Europe's institutions. The European project is far too important to be carried forward without a solid base of popular support. Europe can only be built on the people's trust, on communication, and on respect for the identity of each and everyone. This sets high standards for those who determine Europe's course. Heads of government, ministers, state secretaries, or individual Commissioners have to live up to them. But it also sets high standards for our European institutions. If they do not live up to these same standards of interaction with people, building confidence and respecting differences, they will never feel like they are really 'ours'.

One important element of these standards is transparency. The Netherlands has a tradition of openness and transparency in government. We need to have the same at European level. We need to make Europe more open and accountable. It all has to do with the trust of our citizens. We voted against the recent change – deterioration I should say – in the transparency regime of the Council. For the same reason, we oppose the Commission's recent proposal for a transparency regime covering all the EU's institutions.

The grounds for excluding documents from the public are still too numerous and the terms in which they are formulated are far too general. We should change that. I believe in openness. Trust and legitimacy. It is becoming a key issue for Europe.

CONCLUSION

Let me conclude by saying, Ladies and Gentlemen, that with your knowledge and expertise you can make a vital contribution to the debate on the future of the European Union and its present and future member States. I hope that you encourage each other to engage in open dialogue and vigorous debate. I wish you an inspiring conference, rich in vision.

Thank you.

ANNEX I

OPENING AND DINNER SPEECHES

G . Verheugen*

A Vice-President of the European Parliament said ten years ago that if the European Community were a country, it would never be admitted as a member. I am not sure what conclusions a Commissioner responsible for Enlargement should draw from this. This was at a time when the European Union did not yet exist. But after having observed closely the attitude of the present candidates for accession, I can say two things: first, that they are determined to join the EU as soon as possible; and second, I believe that the goal of EU membership is well within their reach.

Ladies and Gentlemen,

You are here to debate the institutional implications of enlargement. It is clear why this is necessary: because enlargement without institutional reform is not a credible proposition. Sooner or later the European Union will consist of 28 or more countries, nearly double the number of its present members. And it goes without saying that the new members will be as keen as the present members to participate fully in European affairs. In these circumstances it becomes a pressing matter to review the set-up of our common institutions, in order to make sure that they will operate efficiently in the future.

All this is neither new nor disputed. The IGC on institutional reform has already been launched and the agenda is clear. There is even a natural deadline for wrapping up the negotiations, the European Council at Nice. I cannot overemphasise that success at Nice will be an indispensable step forward in the enlargement process. It will be a signal to the candidate countries that the European Union has managed to put its own house in order and that the accession process is well on track.

The stakes are high. The present enlargement has unprecedented historical significance. Most of the candidate countries were former communist states, and the prospect of EU accession facilitated their difficult transition to stable democracies and market economies. It would be unthinkable to reverse this process now. It is

* EU Commissioner for Enlargement, European Commission, Brussels.

an urgent priority of the European Union to work together with the applicants so that membership becomes a reality in the near future.

STATE OF PLAY IN THE NEGOTIATIONS

The single question that I am most persistently, and forcefully, asked as a Commissioner for Enlargement is: when the European Union will finally set dates for the accession of the candidate countries? The impatience of candidate countries to join the EU is fully understandable. But the question itself can be misleading, because it may give the impression that accession is only a question of political will, or whim if you like, and that all that needs to be done is to set a date.

Of course, the political will must be there – and I can assure you that it is: the Commission, the European Parliament, the member States, all are ready to welcome the applicant countries to the European Union as soon as possible. All recent political signals point in the same direction. I will name three: last year's Helsinki European Council, which decided to open negotiations with six more candidate countries and to grant Turkey the status of an official candidate; the progress in the accession negotiations made during the Portuguese Presidency; and the intention of the Commission and the French Presidency to accelerate the pace even further by starting to tackle the easier issues so that the table is clear before the final bargaining begins.

There is, therefore, no doubt that the political momentum has not abated. On the other hand, accession is not a one-way street. The candidate countries must also make the necessary efforts to restructure their societies and their economies in order to be able to comply with the policies and rules of the European Union once they join. Remarkable progress has already been made, but there are, of course, still challenges ahead. Let me give you three examples: structural and economic reform should be completed; the judiciary should be strengthened; and the capacity of the administration to enforce the Community *acquis* should improve.

Speed in the negotiations is important, but quality is also essential. We need quality to ensure that the new Members will be successfully integrated into the EU, to everyone's benefit. We also need quality in order to be able to address any public fears about enlargement so that the European citizens are fully behind it. The better the final product of the negotiations, the easier it will be to convince the public that enlargement is an opportunity, not a threat. Hence my call for a public debate on enlargement. As you may know, this call has been received enthusiastically.

For these reasons it would be irresponsible, or even meaningless, for the European Union to say to the candidates 'you will all become members by a particular year, come what may, ready or not ready'. What we can and should do is to help the applicants in their preparations for membership – and we are already doing this, by providing pre-accession aid of three billion Euro each year, and by giving guidance and expertise.

What we should also do is to try and keep the momentum in the accession negotiations. You may have heard a cynic's definition of a Committee: a Committee is a group that keeps minutes and loses hours. This is not my idea of negotiations. I would like to tackle the real, substantive issues as soon as possible. In order to do this, it is best to follow a pragmatic approach: first deal with the issues which appear to be the least problematic, and once these are out of the way, then attack the 'hard core' of the negotiations. On this, I am glad to say, the Commission and the French Presidency are of one mind. Together, we hope to make, by the end of the year, real headway in dealing with some of the numerous requests for transitional periods put forward by the candidate countries.

As negotiations advance, I expect that target dates will then naturally emerge at the appropriate time. I must stress *at the appropriate time*, that is, when we have a clear overall picture of the state of the negotiations and of the way ahead. Only then could we, for instance, set a date by which negotiations can be concluded with all candidates that will be ready to join.

CONSTITUTIONAL IMPLICATIONS

In parallel to the accession negotiations, one should also keep in mind the constitutional requirements to be met before new Members can join the EU.

As you know the constitutional implications of enlargement are manifold. At the national level, the accession treaties will need to be ratified by the existing and future member States according to their own constitutional requirements. As the contributions to this Conference demonstrate there is also another side of the coin that is often forgotten: any constitutional changes or other constitutional implications in the candidate countries themselves which will be necessary to meet the obligations of EU membership. These issues are indeed very important; the earlier we know exactly what will be needed, the more time will be gained later when the applicants are about to cross the threshold of membership.

IGC

You will hear in detail from the distinguished national experts participating in this Conference what the specific national situation in each country is. I would like to focus instead on the constitutional implications of enlargement at EU level and on the present IGC.

As we are marching full steam ahead towards Nice, and the clock is ticking, questions inevitably arise about the chances of success. The worries expressed concern both the agenda and the timing. Are the issues on the agenda, it is asked, sufficient to prepare the EU for enlargement or are we artificially limiting ourselves to a minimum on which agreement can be found? And second, can we really accomplish the task at hand by Nice?

My view is that the IGC agenda is necessary and sufficient for enlargement. Three of the core IGC items may be known, somewhat misleadingly, as the 'Amsterdam leftovers', but they are by no means minor matters. They are politically sensitive issues, which were left over precisely because they were so difficult to handle.

What we are talking about here is whether in a EU of 28 or more members, each member State should continue to have one Commissioner, with two Commissioners reserved for each of the larger member States. Personally, in the interest of efficiency I would opt for a smaller Commission, which can retain its dynamism when this situation arises, but on this as well as on all IGC matters the decision, of course, rests with the member States.

Another question is whether the present system of voting in the Council, which is deliberately tilted against bigger countries, can remain as it is in a future Union dominated by small or medium-sized members? My view is that the current imbalance should not be left to deteriorate any further. Adjustments should, therefore, be made so that a country's voting power in the Council will more closely correspond to the size of its population.

Finally, there is the question whether, with an additional thirteen or more potential vetoes in the Council, we can afford to continue having unanimity in important areas of EU decision-making? I am an advocate of a generous extension of qualified majority voting because otherwise the risk of a stalemate in EU affairs will be too great. Not because I believe that the new member States will be less integration-friendly than the existing ones, but because statistically the increase in numbers will inevitably make consensus much harder to achieve.

The increase in numbers also poses the question whether the existing Treaty arrangements for closer co-operation between a limited number of member States should be strengthened. I would be in favour of making closer co-operation more flexible, as long as three conditions are met: closer co-operation must stay within the institutional framework of the Treaties, it must not go against existing Community policies, and participation must be open to all member States able and willing to join. If these conditions are met, closer co-operation will not weaken the EU. It will promote further integration, by allowing some pioneer member States to make the first steps ahead in new areas, whilst others can join later, at their own pace.

These are only some of the issues on the agenda, but they give a flavour of the scale of the exercise. Settling these issues will imply making some hard, but indispensable decisions by Nice. We will most probably not know the final outcome of the talks until the very last minute, but I am optimistic that there will be a Nice Treaty. Failure would indeed be unacceptable to all involved. The real question in my view is not whether we will have *an* agreement but rather how ambitious this agreement will be. For the sake of a well-functioning EU after enlargement, I very much hope that the changes agreed will be at least the minimum required for the European institutions to operate efficiently in the future. We should not only have a Nice Treaty, but also a 'nice' Treaty.

It looks more and more certain, however, that the debate on the future of Europe will not be limited to the Nice agenda. In fact, it has already been broadened to cover the Charter of Fundamental Human Rights. It is expected that a draft Charter will be adopted by the Convention in September with a view to its submission to the European Council at Biarritz in October. I cannot but stress how important it will be to have the Draft Charter endorsed by all the member States. It should enhance the legitimacy of the Union and should bring it closer to its citizens for whom fundamental rights matter a great deal.

In addition to the Charter, the institutional debate looks increasingly likely to focus in the future on topics such as the re-organisation of the Treaties, the division of responsibilities between the Commission and the member States or even a European Constitution or the final destination of the European project.

These are fundamental questions on the future of Europe, which seem to fall outside the scope of the current IGC. In a joint Article in today's FAZ, Chancellor Schröder and PM Giulano Amato called for a new IGC to deal with these issues, whose launching should be decided already at Nice.

If a new IGC were to be launched, it should not be a condition for enlargement. There is a big difference between the present and a possible new IGC: the Amsterdam leftovers and the rest of the Nice agenda concern issues intrinsically linked to the efficient functioning of the EU after enlargement. The post-Nice agenda is different: the wider institutional debate is legitimate in its own right, and the applicant countries should have the opportunity to participate and express their views.

Thank you for your attention, Ladies and Gentlemen.

ANNEX I

OPENING AND DINNER SPEECHES

Richard Corbett*

One of the problems in discussing a European constitution is that the word 'constitution' evokes different responses and emotions from one country to another. In some, the constitution is an almost sacred document, adopted at a key moment in a country's history following independence or a revolution, probably drawn up by a constituent assembly, the annals of which feature prominently in history books. In others, the constitution is a more pragmatic notion. Take the UK, where the constitution is not even codified in a single text, and has evolved without there being a one single agreed starting point.

In this pragmatic sense, the EU already has a constitution: the treaties. They may be a bit messy, they are not codified in a single text, and they leave much to be desired in terms of their content. Nonetheless, in that they laid down the field of competence of the EU, the composition and the powers of its institutions and the details of the legislative and budgetary procedures, they do fulfil the role of a constitution.

Many would object that they cannot be dignified with the title constitution for a number of reasons: they are too detailed, they take the form of a treaty, they are not codified and have not been legitimised by a constituent assembly or a referendum.

Let us look at some of these objections more closely.

First, the point about too much detail. It is true that the treaties amount to over one thousand articles, most of them laying down detailed policy objectives rather than being of a typically constitutional nature. However, the EU is not alone in having such a constitution. I have in my hand the constitution of the state of California, in a book at 283 pages long. Let me read you just one paragraph: Article XIII, section 10 says:

> 'Real property in a parcel of ten or more acres which, for two or more years immediately preceding, has been used exclusively for non-profit golf course purposes, shall be assessed for taxation on the basis of such use, plus any value attributable to mines,

* Member of the European Parliament, Strasbourg.

quarries, hydrocarbon substances, or other minerals in the property or the right to extract hydrocarbons or other minerals from that property.'

California, as in many things, is perhaps an atypical example. But it is not alone. Here in Europe, the Swiss constitution has similar features, mixing institutional specifications with policy specifications that have often been added by popular referendum.

Second, the point about it being a treaty not a constitution. These are held to be incompatible. Why? Constitutions have emerged in many ways and need not be confined to the classic model of a constituent assembly. The Canadian constitution was, until recently, a simple Act of the British Parliament. Part of the UK constitution is the Act of Union between England and Scotland, which was an international treaty ratified by the two national Parliaments concerned, but which laid down in detail the composition of the common Parliament to be formed thereafter as well as an number of other constitutional questions. To claim that the EU treaties are not a constitution because they are treaties is too simplistic.

Third, the point about codification. I have already cited the UK as an example of a constitution that is not codified in a single text.

Fourth, the point about the legitimacy. The treaties, it is alleged, have never been approved by a constituent assembly or by a referendum. May be. They have at least been approved by the national Parliaments of all the member States, some of which have held a national level referendum. In one sense, the IGC is a constituent assembly, albeit with an unusual composition – or perhaps not so unusual when one remembers that the Philadelphia convention was also composed of representatives of the states.

If, then, we can accept that the treaties form the constitution of the Union, then we can turn to the real debate, namely how to improve this constitution. That, of course, is what the current IGC is about. It is addressing the efficiency, and accountability of , an enlarged EU.

I shall mention the IGC issues only briefly, as they have been covered by Commissioner Verheugen. First, the size of the Commission. At this stage, two alternatives are on the table: one Commissioner per member States or a fixed figure. The first alternative has the advantage that every member State can feel that it is present in the Commission (although Commissioners do not have the task of representing their own country, they do bring a knowledge of that country with them) but the disadvantage of the Commission appearing intergovernmental and remaining somewhat oversized. The second alternative is opposed by those who fear that they would not have a representative in the Commission – although it would inevitably be tied to an equitable rotation system. Indeed, Commissioner Barnier said that it is not a question about whether every country should have a Commissioner: the only issue is whether they should all have one at the same time!

Which ever solution is chosen, the president of the Commission must have a stronger role. In this regard, it is essential to put in the treaty the right, secured by President Prodi in practise, for the President to be able to dismiss individual Commissioners – a power sadly lacking in the last Commission.

Regarding the weighting of the votes in the Council and the importance of extending qualified majority voting, I have little to add to what Commissioner Verheugen said. Suffice to say that I think it essential that QMV be extended to appointments as well: imagine what would happen if unanimity is still required to appoint the president of the central bank, but there is gridlock while the euro falls still further on international exchanges!

Besides the three Amsterdam leftovers, the IGC is dealing with a number of other important constitutional questions: the number of seats per member State in the Parliament, the size of the various consultative bodies, the procedure for suspending a member State for ceasing to respect the fundamental rights, the rule of law and democracy, the issue of European political parties, and whether to give treaty status to the Charter of Rights.

I know you have dealt with these questions in your conference, so I shall not dwell on them here. I shall instead focus on two questions, namely the powers of the Parliament and the issue of codification and reorganisation of the treaties.

The Parliament hopes very much that the IGC will extend its powers of co-decision over EU legislation. Many of you will know that, at until recently, Parliament's powers were largely consultative. Since the entry into force of the Amsterdam treaty last year, Parliament has enjoyed the power of co-decision over most EU legislation. Proposals are subject to up to three readings each in Council and Parliament, requiring the agreement of both to become law. We now have a bi-cameral legislature in the EU.

We think that this is important. Draft legislation must pass two tests to become law: acceptability to the national governments meeting in the Council and acceptability to the directly elected MEPs. Parliament sits in political groups and examines proposals from a different perspective from ministers in the Council. It therefore brings added value and greater pluralism to European decision taking.

Of course, the European Parliament is not the sexiest of Parliaments! Its debates cannot match the cut and thrust of the House of Commons. When it comes to the theatre and drama of politics, it is rather pedestrian. Because of the need for interpretation, debates can be dull, and there are many amusing anecdotes about linguistic misunderstandings (...). But when it comes to shaping legislation, many of our national Parliaments merely rubber stamp what the government has put forward. This is not the case in the European Parliament where we re-shape Commission proposals line by line. Parliament is an extra guarantee as to the quality and acceptability of the European legislation

But co-decision still does not apply to all legislation. This IGC is an opportunity to rectify that.

Now to codification and reorganisation of the treaties. This is a subject that Parliament has pushed strongly for a number of years. Indeed, the fact that the Amsterdam Treaty began at this process is largely thanks to the European Parliament having advocated taking such a course of action. We have continued to do so and have gained strong support from the Commission and the committee of independent experts chaired by Jean Luc Dehaene that the commission set up a to advise it on the subject of the IGC.

The European University Institute in Florence has now produced a draft which shows that such a course of action is entirely feasible. Taking the current disparate set of treaties and protocols and turning them into a single codified text would not only make them more comprehensible for those having to deal with them and more accessible to a wider public – it would also make the treaties more recognisably a constitution, which brings us neatly back to the subject of your conference.

There are many who fear the idea of a constitution because it smacks of a federal state – and they oppose such a development in the EU either as such or, as is the case of many of my country, because they mistakenly equate federalism with centralism. Federalism is, indeed, another term that evokes different responses and emotions in different countries. Yet taken objectively, the EU has always been a federal type system – which does not mean a centralised system.

From near its beginning, the EU has enjoyed a legal system in which the European law prevails over national law; an institutional system in which States may be bound against their will by a majority decisions and which features an executive that, once appointed, is independent of national governments and cannot be recalled by them; an elected Parliament; and its own (albeit limited) budgetary resources. Each and every IGC has strengthened those federal characteristics. This is true even of the last couple of IGCs, which many people claim have developed the intergovernmental dimension at the expense of a more federal, communautaire system: rather, the new intergovernmental field has been developed on issues that were previously not within the remit of the EU at all. As we have seen with the parts of the third pillar that were transferred by the Amsterdam treaty to the community legal system, such intergovernmental, a co-operation can even be a stepping stone towards a more integrated system.

All in all, it is far from absurd to argue that what we have in the EU already is a sort of decentralised federal system with its own constitution, a system that is evolving, albeit untidily and in unequal steps, further in that direction. The fact that it is composed of strong member States with different cultures, and which will both retain large areas of their own competence as well as play a major role in the EU's own decision-taking, will make it an unusually decentralised federation, and one of which many people will prefer not to think of as such. But others will, perhaps, begin to perceive it as a federation with its own constitution.

ANNEX I

OPENING AND DINNER SPEECHES

A.H. Korthals*

Ladies and Gentlemen,

I am grateful to the T.M.C. Asser Instituut for their invitation to address you at this conference on European law. I am honoured to make a contribution to this conference on the importance of law for the future of Europe.

INTRODUCTION

Over the last fifteen years, Europe has undergone rapid change. The most critical political steps have already gained legal form – in which context I refer only to the treaties of Amsterdam and Maastricht and to the earlier Single European Act. The European Economic Community evolved into a European Union, from an internal market to an economic and monetary union. From Schengen cooperation to an area of freedom, security and justice. In this dynamic period, the European Union expanded considerably from nine to fifteen member States. Each enlargement also involved new legal issues. The coming enlargement – which could result in twenty-seven member States – assumes a new dimension. In which regard, the timing of your colloquium is politically topical.

I would like to begin by seeing the enlargement as a kind of mirror. The expansion reflects the EU and the member States in terms of the area of law. The issue of the form and architecture of a closer European Union would not have been raised in this way were it not for the imminent enlargement.

Classic constitutional law concerns national states and their democratic embedding, with which the political context for a national legal system is a relatively obvious given. However, the nature of the EU is unique, typified by community, inter-governmental and federal elements. Soon to include almost thirty member States, the character of the European architecture and with this of democracy and the Rule of Law is no longer so clear-cut.

In a nutshell, my angle is: how will the enlargement affect the functioning of the Rule of Law in the member States, the applicant member States and, in this regard, the EU institutions?

* Netherlands Minister of Justice, The Hague.

DEVELOPMENTS

After the changes in Central and Eastern Europe, there was considerable public attention for some time for the economic and financial aspects of the transformation and too little for the political, legal and institutional factors. The focus on constitutional consequences intensified primarily after the actual accession negotiations commenced in March 1998.

First and foremost, I believe that the good functioning of the Rule of Law is essential for sound government action and with this for orderly social and economic transactions.

Since 1993, the focus on the development of law on the basis of the EU Treaty mainly concerned cooperation in the field of criminal law, private law and aliens law. The European Council of Tampere last year was a last step in this direction.

The IGC on institutional reforms that commenced last February prompted a constitutional debate that is set to continue in the years to come.

CONSTITUTIONAL ORDER

Recent political discussions on the future of Europe not only dealt with democracy but also with the nature of the state under the Rule of Law of the member States and the EU.

The most politically advanced expression of concern for the Rule of Law is the draft Charter on fundamental rights of the European Union, which is unfortunately faced with resolving a number of drawbacks.

Firstly, I think that the concurrence of this Charter and the European Convention for the Protection of Human Rights and Fundamental Freedoms of the Council of Europe can pose a obstacle: for citizens, for the member States and, last but not least, for the administration of justice. The long-term practical and political complications cannot be underestimated.

Secondly, I anticipate that granting social rights at the European level will have an unintentional impact on national legislation. This may give rise to social, financial and legal consequences that will place the equilibrium of rights and duties under pressure.

Thirdly, I refer to the complex relationship between the national courts and legislation. The interaction between European and national areas of law will also increase as the duties of the European Court of Justice grow.

Enlargement entails greater diversity and differentiation in the national systems of law. These legal systems are linked to social, cultural and political features of the member States. This applies to some parts of the law more than others. What springs to mind here is criminal law. For this reason, I dismiss at this moment any further transfer of power to the Community of police and judicial cooperation in criminal matters. It is precisely in this area that for the time being a close relationship between citizen and national government is imperative.

TOPICALITY

The scale and composition of the Commission, the weight of votes in the Council, the expansion of decision-making with a qualified majority and the distribution of seats in the European Parliament are at the heart of the agenda for the IGC. The European Council of Nice must make treaty amendments to these 'left-overs' although they are not essential for the Rule of Law.

However, I have concerns about the capacity of the Court of Justice and the Court of First Instance, specifically with regard to the long duration of the procedures. The workload of the Court and Court of First Instance will become heavier as they are assigned new duties and as new member States accede. This point is being addressed by the IGC.

The idea of Commissioner Verheugen to hold a referendum is, in my opinion, an attempt to overcome, via direct democracy at national level, what apparently cannot be adequately dealt with in parliaments. However, I am no supporter of the referendum, which has limited significance as a revision of the political process. It inhibits rather than stimulates accession, both in the member States and in the applicant member States – which does no service to the Rule of Law.

Safeguarding the legal nature of the acts of national and European legislators and administrators is more important. Which is why attention for the judiciary and the quality of legislation is essential.

THE JUDICIARY AND ENLARGEMENT

The legal systems of the member States and applicant member States and of the EU are still developing – a development that will continue. For citizens, internal security is a key government duty. The media rightly focus on crime, drugs, corruption, fraud and illegal immigration which, in political terms, is translated into concern for border control, law enforcement and the operation of the judiciary.

I would like to emphasize the importance of cooperation with the new member States in these areas of law. This is reflected by the technical assistance provided by my ministry in the field of law and justice to countries in Central and Eastern Europe which gave rise to the realisation of a PHARE project on 'The Reinforcement of the Rule of Law' in the framework of the European Union.

Fundamental rights are a constitutional basis that can best be safeguarded in the EU by the accession of the EC and the EU to the European Convention for the Protection of Human Rights and Fundamental Freedoms. This also requires closer collaboration between the EU and the Council of Europe, which will also benefit the Rule of Law.

CONCLUSION

Ladies and Gentlemen,

Your participation in this conference shows that interest in the constitutional dimension of European developments thrives in many circles. The enlargement of the EU is a constitutional challenge of the first order.

Accordingly, I would like to express my regard for the T.M.C. Asser Instituut, which has once more succeeded in linking the development of national and European law with current political concerns.

I conclude with the wish and expectation that the Rule of Law will attract increasing interest in public debate.

Thank you.

ANNEX II

OVERVIEW BY EVGENI TANCHEV OF CEEC NATIONAL CONSTITUTIONAL PROVISIONS*

Contents

The Relevant Constitutional Provisions in the Candidate Countries

A. STATUS OF INTERNATIONAL LAW

Bulgaria
Article 5
(4) Any international instruments which have been ratified by the constitutionally established procedure, promulgated, and have come into force with respect to the Republic of Bulgaria, shall be considered part of the domestic legislation of the country. They shall supersede any domestic legislation stipulating otherwise.

Czech Republic

Article 10 [Human Rights Treaties]
Ratified and promulgated international accords on human rights and fundamental freedoms, to which the Czech Republic has committed itself, are immediately binding and are superior to law.

Estonia

Article 3 [Rule of Law, International Law]
(1) Governmental power shall be exercised solely on the basis of this Constitution and such laws which are in accordance with the Constitution. Universally recognized principles and norms of international law shall be an inseparable part of the Estonian legal system.

---

* The text for the Slovak Republic has been updated by the editors with the text accepted by the Parliament. Entry into force expected 1 July, 2001.

Hungary

Article 7 [International Law]
(1) The legal system of the Republic of Hungary accepts the generally recognized principles of international law, and shall harmonize the country's domestic law with the obligations assumed under international law.
(2) Legislative procedures shall be regulated by law, for the passage of which a majority of two-thirds of the votes of the Members of Parliament present is required.

Latvia

Article 89
The State shall recognise and protect fundamental human rights in accordance with this Constitution, the laws and international agreements binding upon Latvia.

Poland

Article 9
The Republic of Poland shall respect international law binding upon it.

Article 87
(1) The sources of universally binding law of the Republic of Poland shall be: the Constitution, statutes, ratified international agreements, and regulations.

Article 91
(1) After promulgation thereof in the Journal of Laws of the Republic of Poland (Dziennik Ustaw), a ratified international agreement shall constitute part of the domestic legal order and shall be applied directly, unless its application depends on the enactment of a statute.
(2) An international agreement ratified upon prior consent granted by statute shall have precedence over statutes if such an agreement cannot be reconciled with the provisions of such statutes.
(3) If an agreement, ratified by the Republic of Poland, establishing an international organization, so provides, the laws established by it shall be applied directly and have precedence in the event of a conflict of laws.

Slovak Republic

Article 7
(4) In order for international treaties on human rights and fundamental freedoms, international political treaties, international treaties of a military character, international treaties which provide for a membership of the Slovak Republic in international organizations, international economic treaties of a general character, international treaties which need to be implemented by a statute, and international treaties which directly provide for rights and duties of natural persons or legal persons, to enter into force, the consent of the National Council of the Slovak Republic is required prior to the ratification.
(5) The international treaties on human rights and fundamental freedoms, international treaties which do not require implementation by a statute, and international treaties which

directly provide rights and duties of natural persons or legal persons and which were ratified and promulgated in a manner set by a statute, have priority over the Slovak laws.

Slovenia

Article 8
Laws and regulations must comply with generally accepted principles of international law and with treaties that are binding on Slovenia. Ratified and published treaties shall be applied directly.

Article 13
In accordance with treaties, aliens in Slovenia enjoy all the rights guaranteed by this Constitution and laws, except for those rights which only citizens of Slovenia enjoy pursuant to this Constitution or law.

Article 153 (Conformity of Legal Acts)
Laws, regulations and other general legal acts must be in conformity with the Constitution.

Laws must be in conformity with generally accepted principles of international law and with valid treaties ratified by the National Assembly, whereas regulations and other general legal acts must also be in conformity with other ratified treaties.

Regulations and other general legal acts must be in conformity with the Constitution and laws.

Special legal acts and actions of state authorities, local community authorities and bearers of public authority must be based on a law or regulation adopted pursuant to law.

B. INTERNATIONAL TREATIES CONCLUSION, RATIFICATION, INTERPRETATION

Bulgaria

Article 85 [International Instruments]
(1) The National Assembly shall ratify or denounce by law all international instruments which:
1) are of a political or military nature;
2) concern the Republic of Bulgaria's participation in international organizations;
3) envisage corrections to the borders of the Republic of Bulgaria;
4) contain obligations for the treasury;
5) envisage the state's participation in international arbitration or legal proceedings;
6) concern fundamental human rights;
7) affect the action of the law or require new legislation in order to be enforced;
8) expressly require ratification.
(2) Treaties ratified by the National Assembly may be amended or denounced only by their built-in procedure or in accordance with the universally acknowledged norms of international law.

(3) The conclusion of an international treaty requiring an amendment to the Constitution shall be preceded by the passage of such an amendment.

Article 98 [Functions]
The President of the Republic shall:
3) conclude international treaties in the circumstances established by the law.

Article 149 [Functions]
4) rule on the compatibility between the Constitution and the international instruments concluded by the Republic of Bulgaria prior to their ratification, and on the compatibility of domestic laws with the universally recognized norms of international law and the international instruments to which Bulgaria is a party.

Cyprus

Article 37
The President of the Republic as Head of the State -
(a) represents the Republic in all its official functions;
(b) signs the credentials of diplomatic envoys appointed under Article 54 and receives the credentials of foreign diplomatic envoys who shall be accredited to him;
(c) signs -
(i) the credentials of delegates appointed under Article 54 for the negotiation of international treaties, conventions or other agreements, or for signing any such treaties, conventions or agreements already negotiated, in accordance with, and subject to, the provisions of this Constitution;
(ii) the letter relating to the transmission of the instruments of ratification of any international treaties, conventions or agreements approved as provided in this Constitution;
(d) confers the honours of the Republic.

Article 50
1. The President and the Vice-President of the Republic, separately or conjointly, shall have the right of final veto on any law or decision of the House of Representatives or any part thereof concerning -
(a) foreign affairs, except the participation of the Republic in international organisations and pacts of alliance in which the Kingdom of Greece and the Republic of Turkey both participate. For the purposes of this sub-paragraph "foreign affairs" includes -
(i) the recognition of States, the establishment of diplomatic and consular relations with other countries and the interruption of such relations. The grant of acceptance to diplomatic representatives and of exequatur to consular representatives. The assignment of diplomatic representatives and of consular representatives, already in the diplomatic service, to posts abroad and the entrusting of functions abroad to special envoys already in the diplomatic service. The appointment and the assignment of persons, who are not already in the diplomatic service, to any posts abroad as diplomatic or consular representatives and the entrusting of functions abroad to persons, who are not already in the diplomatic service, as special envoys;
(ii) the conclusion of international treaties, conventions and agreements;
(iii) the declaration of war and the conclusion of peace;
(iv) the protection abroad of the citizens of the Republic and of their interests;
(v) the establishment, the status and the interests of aliens in the Republic;

(vi) the acquisition of foreign nationality by citizens of the Republic and their acceptance of employment by, or their entering the service of, a foreign Government;
(b) the following questions of defence:-
(i) composition and size of the armed forces and credits for them;
(ii) (nominations des cadres - äéïñéóìïß óôåëå÷þí - kadrolara tayinler) and their promotions (êáé ç ðñïáãùãÞ áõôþí - ve bunlardaki terfiler);
(iii) importation of war materials and also explosives of all kinds;
(iv) cession of bases and other facilities to allied countries;
(c) the following questions of security:
(i) (nominations des cadres - äéïñéóìïß óôåëå÷þí - kadrolara tayinler) and their promotions (êáé ç ðñïáãùãÞ áõôþí - ve bunlardaki terfiler);
(ii) distribution and stationing of forces;
(iii) emergency measures and martial law;
(iv) police laws.
It is specified that the right of veto under sub-paragraph (c) above shall cover all emergency measures or decisions, but not those which concern the normal functioning of the police and the gendarmerie.
2. The above right of veto may be exercised either against the whole of a law or decision or against any part thereof, and in the latter case such law or decision shall be returned to the House of Representatives for a decision whether the remaining part thereof will be submitted, under the relevant provisions of this Constitution, for promulgation.
3. The right of veto under this Article shall be exercised within the period for the promulgation of laws or decisions of the House of Representatives as in Article 52 provided.

Article 57
1. On a decision being taken by the Council of Ministers such decision shall be transmitted forthwith to the office of the President and of the Vice-President of the Republic respectively.
2. The President or the Vice-President of the Republic or both shall have the right of return, within four days of the date when the decision has been transmitted to their respective offices, of such decision to the Council of Ministers for reconsideration, whereupon the Council of Ministers shall reconsider the matter and if they persist in such decision the President and the Vice-President of the Republic shall, subject to paragraph 4 of this Article, promulgate by publication such decision:
Provided that the exercise of the right of return shall not, in cases where the right of veto exists, prevent either the President or the Vice-President of the Republic or both from exercising the right of veto, within four days of the transmission to their respective offices, of the decision persisted upon.
3. If a decision relates to foreign affairs, defence or security as in Article 50 set out, the President or the Vice-President of the Republic or both shall have a right of veto which they shall exercise within four days of the date when the decision has been transmitted to their respective offices.
4. If the decision is enforceable and no right of veto or return has been exercised as in paragraph 2 or 3 of this Article provided, such decision shall be forthwith promulgated by the President and the Vice-President of the Republic 'by publication in the official Gazette of the Republic' unless the Council of Ministers otherwise states in that decision.

Article 169
Subject to the provisions of Article 50 and paragraph 3 of Article 57-

(1) every international agreement with a foreign State or any International Organisation relating to commercial matters, economic co-operation (including payments and credit) and modus vivendi, shall be concluded under a decision of the Council of Ministers;
(2) any other treaty, convention or international agreement shall be negotiated and signed under a decision of the Council of Ministers and shall only be operative and binding on the Republic when approved by a law made by the House of Representatives whereupon it shall be concluded;
(3) treaties, conventions and agreements concluded in accordance with the foregoing provisions of this Article shall have, as from their publication in the official Gazette of the Republic, superior force to any municipal law on condition that such treaties, conventions and agreements are applied by the other party thereto.

Article 170
1. The Republic shall, by agreement on appropriate terms accord most-favoured-nation treatment to the Kingdom of Greece, the Republic of Turkey and the United Kingdom of Great Britain and Northern Ireland for all agreements whatever their nature might be.
2. The provisions of paragraph 1 of this Article shall not apply to the Treaty concerning the Establishment of the Republic of Cyprus between the Republic, the Kingdom of Greece, the Republic of Turkey and the United Kingdom of Great Britain and Northern Ireland concerning the bases and military facilities accorded to the United Kingdom.

Czech Republic

Article 39 [Quorum, Majorities]
(1) The Chambers constitute a quorum if at least one third of their members are present.
(2) The passage of a resolution of the respective Chamber requires the consent of an absolute majority of deputies or Senators present, if not prescribed otherwise by the Constitution.
(3) The passage of a resolution on the declaration of the state of war and a resolution approving the presence of foreign troops on the territory of the Czech Republic requires the consent of an absolute majority of all deputies and of all Senators.
(4) The passage of a constitutional law and the approval of an international agreement under Article 10 shall require the consent of a three-fifths majority of all deputies and a three-fifths majority of all Senators present.

Article 49 [International Accords]
(1) International accords requiring consent from Parliament are passed by Parliament in the same way as draft laws.
(2) Accords on human rights and fundamental freedoms, political agreements, and economic agreements of a general nature, as well as agreements on the implementation of which a law must be passed, require consent from Parliament.

Article 63 [Powers]
(1) The President of the Republic further:
a) represents the state in external affairs,
b) negotiates and ratifies international treaties; he may transfer the negotiation of international agreements to the Government or, with its approval, to its individual members,
c) is commander-in-chief of the armed forces,
d) receives heads of diplomatic missions,

e) accredits and recalls heads of diplomatic missions,
f) calls elections to the Chamber of Deputies and to the Senate,
g) appoints and promotes generals,
h) confers and awards state distinctions, unless he authorizes another body to do so,
i) appoints judges,
j) has the right to grant amnesty.
(2) The President of the Republic is also entitled to exercise powers which are not expressly specified in the constitutional law, if it is stipulated so by law.
(3) Decisions of the President of the Republic issued in accordance with Paragraphs (1) and (2) require a signature of the Premier, or a member of the Government entrusted by the Premier, to come into effect.
(4) The Government is responsible for decisions of the President of the Republic which require the signature of the Premier or a member of the Government authorized by the Premier.

Article 87 [Competencies]
(1) The Constitutional Court resolves:
a) the nullification of laws or their individual provisions if they are in contradiction with a constitutional law or an international agreement under Article 10,
b) the nullification of other legal regulations or their individual provisions if they are in contradiction with a constitutional law, legislation, or international agreement under Article 10,
c) constitutional complaints by bodies of territorial self-administration against unlawful interference by the state,
d) constitutional complaints against authorized decisions and other interference by bodies of public power with fundamental rights and freedoms guaranteed by the Constitution,
e) legal remedies against decisions on matters of the verification of election of a Deputy or a Senator,
f) doubts concerning a loss of eligibility of a Deputy or a Senator and incompatibility of the discharge of his or her function according to Article 25,
g) a constitutional indictment by the Senate against the President of the Republic according to Article 65(2),
h) a proposal by the President of the Republic to repeal a resolution by the Chamber of Deputies and the Senate according to Article 66,
i) measures necessary to effect a decision by an international court which is binding for the Czech Republic, if it cannot be effected otherwise,
j) the congruency of a decision to dissolve a political party or other decisions concerning the activities of a political party with constitutional laws and other acts,
k) controversies on the scope of powers of state bodies and bodies of territorial self-administration, if, according to law, these do not fall under the jurisdiction of another body.
(2) The law may stipulate that instead of the Constitutional Court the Supreme Administrative Court shall pass decisions on:
a) the annulment of legal regulations or their individual provisions, if they are at variance with law,
b) controversies concerning the scope of powers of state bodies and bodies of territorial self-administration, if, according to law, these do not fall under the jurisdiction of another body.

Estonia

Article 121 [Ratification of Treaties]
The Parliament shall ratify and denounce treaties of the Republic of Estonia:
1) which amend state borders;
2) the implementation of which requires the adoption, amendment or annulment of Estonian laws;
3) by which the Republic of Estonia joins international organizations or leagues;
4) by which the Republic of Estonia assumes military or assets obligations;
5) where ratification is prescribed.

Hungary

Article 19
(1) The Parliament is the supreme body of State power and popular representation in the Republic of Hungary.
(2) Exercising its rights based on the sovereignty of the people, the Parliament shall ensure the constitutional order of society and define the organization, orientation and conditions of government.
(3) Within this sphere of authority, the Parliament shall –
a) adopt the Constitution of the Republic of Hungary;
b) pass legislation;
c) define the country's social and economic policy;
d) assess the balance of public finances, approve the State Budget and its implementation;
e) decide on the Government's programme;
f) conclude international treaties of outstanding importance to the foreign relations of the Republic of Hungary;
g) decide on the declaration of a state of war and on the conclusion of peace;
h) declare a state of national crisis and establish the National Defense Council, in the case of war, or imminent danger of armed attack by a foreign power (danger of war);
i) declare a state of emergency, in the case of armed actions aimed at overturning constitutional order, or at the acquisition of exclusive control of public power, in the case of acts of violence committed by force of arms or by armed groups which gravely endanger the lives and property of citizens on a mass scale, and in the event of natural or industrial disaster;
j) decide on the use of the armed forces, both abroad and within the country;
k) elect the President of the Republic, the Prime Minister, the members of the Constitutional Court, the Parliamentary Ombudsmen, the President and Vice-Presidents of the State Audit Office, the President of the Supreme Court and the General Prosecutor;
l) upon recommendation made by the Government, which shall first be submitted to the Constitutional Court for its review, dissolve representative bodies of local government whose actions have been found unconstitutional, decide on the territory of counties, their designation and seat, as well as the declaration of cities with county-level rights and the establishment of the Districts of the Capital;
m) exercise general amnesty.
(4) A majority of two-thirds of the votes of the Members of Parliament is required for the decisions specified in points g), h), i) and j) of Paragraph (3).
(5) The Parliament shall have the right to call a national referendum. A majority of two-thirds

of the votes of the Members of Parliament present is required to pass the law on national referenda.

Article 19A
(1) Should the Parliament be obstructed in reaching such decisions, the President of the Republic shall have the right to declare a state of war, a state of national crisis and establish the National Defense Council, or to declare a state of emergency.
(2) The Parliament shall be considered to be obstructed in reaching such decisions, if it is not in session and convening it is impossible due to lack of time or due to the events responsible for the declaration of the state of war, state of national crisis or state of emergency.
(3) The Speaker of Parliament, the President of the Constitutional Court and the Prime Minister shall jointly determine whether the Parliament is obstructed, and whether a declaration of a state of war, a state of national crisis or a state of emergency is justified.
(4) At its first meeting following the end of the obstruction, the Parliament shall review the justification of the declaration of a state of war, state of national crisis or state of emergency, and shall rule on the legality of the measures taken. A majority of two-thirds of the votes of the Members of Parliament is required for this decision.

Article 19B
(1) During a state of national crisis the National Defense Council shall decide on the use of the armed forces abroad and within the country, and on the introduction of emergency measures as defined in a separate law.
(2) The National Defense Council is chaired by the President of the Republic, and is composed of the following members: the Speaker of Parliament, the floor leaders of the political parties represented in Parliament, the Prime Minister, the Ministers, and the Commanding Officer and the Chief of Staff of the Hungarian Army.
(3) The National Defense Council shall exercise –
a) the powers transferred to it by the Parliament;
b) the powers of the President of the Republic;
c) the powers of the Government.
(4) The National Defense Council may pass decrees, which may suspend the application of certain laws or which may deviate from the provisions of certain laws. Furthermore, it may take other extraordinary measures, but may not, however, suspend the application of the Constitution.
(5) Decrees passed by the National Defense Council shall lose validity upon cessation of the state of national crisis, unless the Parliament extends the validity of such decrees.
(6) The operation of the Constitutional Court may not be restricted during a state of national crisis.

Article 19C
(1) Should the Parliament be obstructed upon a declaration of a state of emergency, the President of the Republic shall decide on the use of the armed forces.
(2) The President of the Republic shall introduce emergency measures, which are defined in a separate law, by decree during a state of emergency.
(3) The President of the Republic shall immediately inform the Speaker of Parliament of any emergency measures that have been introduced. The Parliament or, should the Parliament be obstructed, the Parliamentary Defense Committee shall remain in session during a state of

emergency. The Parliament, or the Parliamentary Defense Committee, shall have the right to suspend emergency measures introduced by the President of the Republic.
(4) Emergency measures introduced by decree shall remain in force for a period of thirty days, unless the Parliament or, should the Parliament be obstructed, the Parliamentary Defense Committee extends their validity.
(5) In other respects the regulations pertaining to a state of national crisis shall apply to a state of emergency.

Article 19D
A majority of two-thirds of the votes of the Members of Parliament present is required to pass the law specifying the detailed regulations to be applied during a state of national crisis and a state of emergency.

Article 19E
(1) In the event that the territory of Hungary is subject to unexpected attack by foreign armed units, immediate measures shall be taken to repel such attack and defend the territorial integrity of the country with the standing air and air defense forces of the Hungarian Army, in accordance with the defense plan approved by the Government and the President of the Republic and with forces commensurate to the gravity of the attack and equipped for such a role, up to the declaration of a state of emergency or state of national crisis, in the interests of ensuring constitutional order and the security of the lives and property of citizens, as well as the protection of public order and safety.
(2) In the interest of determining further measures to be taken, the Government shall immediately inform the Parliament and the President of the Republic on the measures taken on the basis of Paragraph (1).
(3) A majority of two-thirds of the votes of the Members of Parliament present is required to pass the law specifying the regulations applicable to immediate measures to be taken by the Government.

Article 28
(1) The term of Parliament commences from its inaugural sitting.
(2) The Parliament has the right to declare its dissolution prior to the completion of its term.
(3) The President of the Republic has the right to dissolve the Parliament, simultaneously with the announcement of new elections, if –
a) the Parliament passes a motion of no-confidence in the Government on no less than four occasions in a period of twelve months during the course of one term, or;
b) in the event that the mandate of the Government ends, a candidate for Prime Minister proposed by the President of the Republic is not elected by the Parliament within a period of forty days from the day upon which the first candidate is nominated.
(...)
(5) Prior to dissolving the Parliament, the President of the Republic is required to request the opinions of the Prime Minister, the Speaker of Parliament and the floor leaders of the parties represented in the Parliament.
(6) A new Parliament shall be elected within a period of three months following the expiration of the previous Parliament's mandate, declaration of the Parliament's dissolution or the Parliament having been dissolved. The Parliament shall continue to operate until the inaugural sitting of the new Parliament.

Article 28A
(1) During a state of national crisis or a state of emergency the Parliament may neither declare its dissolution nor be dissolved.
(2) Should a term of Parliament expire during a state of national crisis or a state of emergency, its mandate shall be extended until the cessation of the state of national crisis or state of emergency.
(3) During a state of war, the danger of war or an emergency, the President of the Republic may reconvene a Parliament which has declared its dissolution or which has been dissolved. The Parliament itself shall pass a resolution on the extension of its mandate.

Article 28B
(1) The subject of national referenda or popular initiatives may fall under the jurisdiction of the Parliament.
(2) A majority of two-thirds of the votes of the Members of Parliament present shall be required for the Parliament to pass the law on national referenda and popular initiatives.

Article 28C
(1) A national referendum may be held for reaching a decision or for an expression of opinion. Carrying out a national referendum may be mandatory or may be the result of the consideration of a matter.
(2) A national referendum shall be held if so initiated by at least 200,000 voting citizens.
(3) If a national referendum is mandatory, the result of the successfully held national referendum shall be binding for the Parliament.
(4) Based on its consideration, the Parliament may order a national referendum upon the initiative by the President of the Republic, the Government, by one-third of Members of the Parliament or by 100,000 voting citizens.
(5) National referendum may not be held on the following subjects:
a) on laws on the central budget, the execution of the central budget, taxes to the central government and duties, customs tariffs, and on the central government conditions for local taxes,
b) obligations set forth in valid international treaties and on the contents of laws prescribing such obligations,
c) the provisions of the Constitution on national referenda and popular initiatives,
d) personnel and restructuring (reorganization, termination) matters falling under Parliamentary jurisdiction,
e) dissolution of the Parliament,
f) the Government's programme,
g) declaration of a state of war, a state of emergency or a state of national crisis,
h) use of the Armed Forces abroad or within the country,
i) dissolution of the representative body of local governments,
j) amnesty.
(6) A national referendum shall be considered successful if more than half of the voting citizens cast valid votes, but at least more than one-quarter of all voting citizens gave the same answer for the subject.

Article 28D
At least 50,000 voting citizens are required for a national popular initiative. A national popular initiative may be for the purpose of forcing the Parliament to place a subject under its

jurisdiction on the agenda. The Parliament shall debate the subject defined by the national popular initiative.

Chapter III The President of the Republic

Article 30
(1) The office of President of the Republic is incompatible with all other public, social and political offices or mandates. The President of the Republic shall not be otherwise gainfully employed and shall not accept remuneration for other activities, with the exception of such activities which fall under the protection of copyright.
(2) A majority of two-thirds of the votes of the Members of Parliament present is required to pass the law on the amount of compensation, allowances and reimbursement due to the President of the Republic.

Article 30A
(1) The President of the Republic shall –
a) represent the State of Hungary;
b) conclude international treaties in the name of the Republic of Hungary; if the subject of the treaty falls within its legislative competence, prior ratification by the Parliament is necessary for conclusion of the treaty;
c) accredit and receive ambassadors and envoys;
d) announce general parliamentary or local government elections, and the date of the national referendum;
e) have the right to participate and speak at sittings of the Parliament and of its committees;
f) have the right to petition the Parliament to take action;
g) have the right to initiate national referenda;
h) appoint and dismiss State Secretaries, in accordance with regulations specified in a separate law;
i) appoint and dismiss the President and Vice-Presidents of the National Bank of Hungary, and university professors upon the recommendation of persons or organizations specified in a separate law; appoint and dismiss the university rectors; appoint and promote Generals of the armed forces; confirm the President of the Hungarian Academy of Sciences;
j) confer titles, orders, awards and decorations specified by law and authorize the use thereof;
k) exercise the right to grant individual pardons;
l) issue rulings in cases of citizenship;
m) issue rulings in all issues assigned to his sphere of authority on the basis of separate laws.
(2) The counter-signature of the Prime Minister or responsible Minister is required for all of the measures and actions of the President of the Republic listed in Paragraph (1), with the exception of the items specified in Points a), d), e), f) and g).

Latvia

Article 41
The President shall represent the State in international relations, appoint the diplomatic representatives of Latvia, and also receive diplomatic representatives of other states. The President shall implement the decisions of the Saeima concerning the ratification of international agreements.

Article 68
All international agreements which settle matters that may be decided by the legislative process shall require ratification by the Saeima.

Lithuania

Article 67
The Parliament shall:
1) consider and enact amendments to the Constitution;
2) enact laws;
3) adopt resolutions for the organization of referendums;
4) announce presidential elections of the Republic of Lithuania;
5) form State institutions provided by law, and shall appoint and dismiss their chief officers;
6) approve or reject the candidature of the Prime Minister proposed by the President of the Republic;
7) consider the programme of the Government submitted by the Prime Minister, and decide whether to approve it or not;
8) upon the recommendation of the Government, establish or abolish ministries of the Republic of Lithuania;
9) supervise the activities of the Government, and may express non-confidence in the Prime Minister or individual Ministers;
10) appoint judges to, and Chairpersons of, the Constitutional Court and the Supreme Court;
11) appoint to, and dismiss from, office the State Controller as well as the Chairperson of the Board of the Bank of Lithuania;
12) announce local government Council elections;
13) form the Central Electoral Committee and change its composition;
14) approve the State Budget and supervise the implementation thereof;
15) establish State taxes and other obligatory payments;
16) ratify or denounce international treaties whereto the Republic of Lithuania is a party, and consider other issues of foreign policy;
17) establish administrative divisions of the Republic;
18) establish State awards of the Republic of Lithuania;
19) issue acts of amnesty; and
20) impose direct administration and martial law, declare states of emergency, announce mobilization, and adopt decisions to use the Armed Forces.

Article 84
The President of the Republic shall:
1) settle basic foreign policy issues and, together with the Government, implement foreign policy;
2) sign international treaties of the Republic of Lithuania and submit them to the Parliament for ratification;
3) appoint or recall, upon the recommendation of the Government, diplomatic representatives of the Republic of Lithuania in foreign states and international organizations; receive letters of credence and recall of diplomatic representatives of foreign states; confer highest diplomatic ranks and special titles;
4) appoint, upon approval of the Parliament, the Prime Minister, charge him or her to form the Government, and approve its composition;

5) remove, upon approval of the Parliament, the Prime Minister from office;
6) accept the powers returned by the Government upon the election of a new Parliament, and charge it to continue exercising its functions until a new Government is formed;
7) accept resignations of the Government and, as necessary, charge it to continue exercising its functions or charge one of the Ministers to exercise the functions of the Prime Minister until a new Government is formed; accept resignations of individual Ministers and commission them to continue in office until a new Minister is appointed;
8) submit to the Parliament, upon the resignation of the Government or after it returns its powers and no later than within 15 days, the candidature of a new Prime Minister for consideration;
9) appoint or dismiss individual Ministers upon the recommendation of the Prime Minister;
10) appoint or dismiss, according to the established procedure, state officers provided by law;
11) propose Supreme Court judge candidates to the Parliament, and, upon the appointment of all the Supreme Court judges, recommend from among them a Supreme Court Chairperson to the Parliament; appoint, with the approval of the Parliament, Court of Appeal judges, and from among them, the Court of Appeal Chairperson; appoint judges and chairpersons of district and local district courts, and change their places of office; in cases provided by Law, propose the dismissal of judges to the Parliament;
12) propose to the Parliament the candidatures of three Constitutional Court judges, and, upon appointing all the judges of the Constitutional Court, propose, from among them, a candidate for Constitutional Court Chairperson to the Parliament;
13) propose to the Parliament candidates for State Controller and Chairperson of the Board of the Bank of Lithuania; if necessary, propose to the Parliament to express non-confidence in said officials;
14) appoint or dismiss, upon the approval of the Parliament, the chief commander of the Army and the head of the Security Service;
15) confer highest military ranks;
16) adopt, in the event of an armed attack which threatens State sovereignty or territorial integrity, decisions concerning defence against such armed aggression, the imposition of martial law, and mobilization, and submit these decisions to the next sitting of the Parliament for approval;
17) declare states of emergency according to the procedures and situations established by law, and submit these decisions to the next sitting of the Parliament for approval;
18) make annual reports in the Parliament about the situation in Lithuania and the domestic and foreign policies of the Republic of Lithuania;
19) call, in cases provided in the Constitution, extraordinary sessions of the Parliament;
20) announce regular elections to the Parliament, and, in cases set forth in Article 58(2), announce pre-term elections to the Parliament;
21) grant citizenship of the Republic of Lithuania according to the procedure established by law;
22) confer State awards;
23) grant pardons to sentenced persons; and
24) sign and promulgate laws enacted by the Parliament or refer them back to the Parliament according to the procedure provided for in Article 71.

Article 105
(1) The Constitutional Court shall consider and adopt decisions concerning the conformity

of laws of the Republic of Lithuania and legal acts adopted by the Parliament with the Constitution of the Republic of Lithuania.
(2) The Constitutional Court shall also consider the conformity with the Constitution of:
1) legal acts of the President; and
2) legal acts of the Government.
(3) The Constitutional Court shall present conclusions concerning:
1) the violation of election laws during presidential elections or elections to the Parliament;
2) whether the President of the Republic of Lithuania's health is not limiting his or her capacity to continue in office;
3) the conformity of international agreements of the Republic of Lithuania with the Constitution; and
4) the compliance with the Constitution of concrete actions of Parliament members or other State officers against whom impeachment proceedings have been instituted.

Poland

Article 89
(1) Ratification of an international agreement by the Republic of Poland, as well as denunciation thereof, shall require prior consent granted by statute if such agreement concerns:
1) peace, alliances, political or military treaties;
2) freedoms, rights or obligations of citizens, as specified in the Constitution;
3) the Republic of Poland's membership in an international organization;
4) considerable financial responsibilities imposed on the State;
5) matters regulated by statute or those in respect of which the Constitution requires the form of a statute.
(2) The President of the Council of Ministers (the Prime Minister) shall inform the House of Representatives (Sejm) of any intention to submit, for ratification by the President of the Republic, any international agreements whose ratification does not require consent granted by statute.
(3) The principles of and procedures for the conclusion and renunciation of international agreements shall be specified by statute.

Article 133
(1) The President of the Republic, as representative of the State in foreign affairs, shall:
1) ratify and renounce international agreements, and shall notify the House of Representatives (Sejm) and the Senate thereof;
2) appoint and recall the plenipotentiary representatives of the Republic of Poland to other states and to international organizations;
3) receive the Letters of Credence and recall of diplomatic representatives of other states and international organizations accredited to him.
(2) The President of the Republic, before ratifying an international agreement may refer it to the Constitutional Tribunal with a request to adjudicate upon its conformity to the Constitution.
(3) The President of the Republic shall cooperate with the Prime Minister and the appropriate minister in respect of foreign policy.

Article 144
(1) The President of the Republic, exercising his constitutional and statutory authority, shall issue Official Acts.
(2) Official Acts of the President shall require, for their validity, the signature of the Prime Minister who, by such signature, accepts responsibility therefor to the House of Representatives (Sejm).
(3) The provisions of (2) above shall not relate to:
1) proclaiming elections to the House of Representatives (Sejm) and to the Senate;
2) summoning the first sitting of a newly elected House of Representatives (Sejm) and Senate;
3) shortening of the term of office of the House of Representatives (Sejm) in the instances specified in the Constitution;
4) introducing legislation;
5) proclaiming the holding of a nationwide referendum;
6) signing or refusing to sign a bill;
7) ordering the promulgation of a statute or an international agreement in the Journal of Laws of the Republic of Poland (Dziennik Ustaw);
8) delivering a Message to the House of Representatives (Sejm), to the Senate or to the National Assembly;
9) making a referral to the Constitutional Tribunal;
10) requesting to the Supreme Chamber of Control to carry out an audit;
11) nominating and appointing the Prime Minister;
12) accepting the resignation of the Council of Ministers and obliging it to temporarily continue with its duties;
13) applying to the House of Representatives (Sejm) to bring a member of the Council of Ministers to responsibility before the Tribunal of State;
14) dismissing a minister in whom the House of Representatives (Sejm) has passed a vote of no confidence;
15) convening the Cabinet Council;
16) conferring orders and decorations;
17) appointing judges;
18) exercising the power of pardon;
19) granting Polish citizenship and giving consent for renunciation of Polish citizenship;
20) appointing the First President of the Supreme Court;
21) appointing the President and Vice-President of the Constitutional Tribunal;
22) appointing the President of the Chief Administrative Court;
23) appointing the presidents of the Supreme Court and vice-presidents of the Chief Administrative Court;
24) requesting the House of Representatives (Sejm) to appoint the President of the National Bank of Poland;
25) appointing the members of the Council for Monetary Policy;
26) appointing and dismissing members of the National Security Council;
27) appointing members of the National Council of Radio Broadcasting and Television;
28) establishing the statute of the Presidential Chancellery and appointing or dismissing the Chief of the Presidential Chancellery;
29) issuing orders in accordance with the principles specified in Article 93;
30) resigning from the office of President of the Republic.

Article 146
(1) The Council of Ministers shall conduct the internal affairs and foreign policy of the Republic of Poland.
(2) The Council of Ministers shall conduct the affairs of State not reserved to other State organs or local self-government.
(3) The Council of Ministers shall manage the government administration.
(4) To the extent and in accordance with the principles specified by the Constitution and statutes, the Council of Ministers, in particular, shall:
1) ensure the implementation of statutes;
2) issue regulations;
3) coordinate and supervise the work of organs of State administration;
4) protect the interests of the State Treasury;
5) adopt a draft State Budget;
6) supervise the implementation of the State Budget and pass a resolution on the closing of the State's accounts and report on the implementation of the Budget;
7) ensure the internal security of the State and public order;
8) ensure the external security of the State;
9) exercise general control in the field of relations with other States and international organizations;
10) conclude international agreements requiring ratification as well as accept and renounce other international agreements;
11) exercise general control in the field of national defence and annually specify the number of citizens who are required to perform active military service;
12) determine the organization and the manner of its own work.

Romania

Article 91 [Treaties, Diplomacy]
(1) The President shall, in the name of Romania, conclude international treaties negotiated by the Government, and then submit them to Parliament for ratification within 60 days.
(2) The President shall, on proposal by the Government, accredit and recall diplomatic envoys of Romania, and approve the setting up, closing down, or change in rank of diplomatic missions.
(3) Diplomatic envoys of other states shall be accredited to the President of Romania.

Slovak Republic
Article 86
The jurisdiction of the National Council of the Slovak Republic comprises, above all:
a) deciding upon the Constitution and constitutional and other laws and controlling compliance with them,
b) approving by means of a constitutional law a treaty on the Slovak Republic's enering into an alliance with other states and on its abrogation of such a treaty,
c) deciding on proposals to call a referendum,
d) voicing consent prior to the ratification with international treaties on human rights and fundamental freedoms, international treaties of a political nature, international treaties of a military nature, international treaties which provide for membership of the Slovak Republic in international organizations, international economic treaties of a general character, international treaties which need to be implemented by a statute, and international treaties

which directly provide for rights and duties of natural persons or legal persons to enter into force, and to decide whether they are international treaties pursuant to Art. 7 para. 5.
e) establishing ministries and other state administration bodies by means of law,
f) discussing the policy statement of the Government of the Slovak Republic, controlling the Government's activity, and passing a vote of confidence in the Government or its members,
g) approving the state budget, checking on its fulfillment, and approving the state closing account,
h) discussing the basic domestic, international, economic, social, and other policies,
i) electing and recalling the chairman and the depute chairman of the Supreme Control Office of the Slovak Republic and three members of the Court Council of the Slovak Republic,
j) deciding on the declaration of war if the Slovak Republic is attacked or as a result of commitments arising from international treaties on common defense against aggression and on settling peace after the end of a war,
k) giving consent to sending armed forces outside the territory of the Slovak Republic unless it is the case pursuant to Art. 119 letter p,
l) giving consent to the presence of foreign armed forces on the territory of the Slovak Republic.

Article 87
(2) If the President of the Slovak Republic returns a law with comments, the National Council of the Slovak Republic will discuss the law again, and in the event of its approval, such law must be promulgated.
(3) Laws are signed by the President of the Slovak Republic, the Chairman of the National Council of the Slovak Republic, and the Prime Minister of the Slovak Republic. If the National Council of the Slovak Republic reapproves a law after it has been returned by the President of the Slovak Republic despite the comments and the the President of the Slovak Republic does not sign the law, the law shall be promulgated without the signature of the President of the Slovak Republic.
(4) Laws become valid by promulgation. The details about the promulgation of laws, international treaties, and legally binding acts of an international organization pursuant to Art. 7 para. 2 will be set by a law.
(5) *Para. 5 is cancelled.*

Article 119
f) about the international treaties of the Slovak Republic whose conclusion has been delegated to the Government by the President of the Slovak Republic,
g) about the consent with the delegation of the conclusion of international treaties pursuant to Art. 102 para. 1 letter a) to its individual members,
h) on submitting a proposal to the Constitutional Court of the Slovak Republic to decide whether a concluded international treaty which requires a consent of the National Council of the Slovak Republic is in compliance with the Constitution and constitutional law, principal questions of domestic and foreign policy,
j) submitting a draft law or any other important measure to the public discussion, k) requesting the passing of a vote of confidence,
l) awarding amnesty for misdemeanons.

Article 125

(1) The Constitutional Court decides on the compatibility of

a) laws with the Constitution, constitutional laws, and international treaties which were consented to by the National Council of the Slovak Republic and which were ratified and promulgated in the manner prescribed by a law.

b) decrees issued by the Government and generally binding legal regulations issued by ministries and other central bodies of state administration with the Constitution, constitutional laws, and international treaties which were consented to by the National Council of the Slovak Republic and which were ratified and promulgated in the manner prescribed by law and laws,

c) generally binding decrees pursuant to Art. 68 with the Constitution, constitutional laws, and international treaties which were consented to by the National Council of the Slovak Republic and which were ratified and promulgated in the manner prescribed by law and laws, if they are not decided upon by other courts,

d) generally binding decrees adopted by local state administration bodies and generally binding decrees of the territorial self-administration bodies pursuant to Art. 71 para. 2 with the Constitution, constitutional laws, and international treaties promulgated in the manner prescribed by law, laws, Government decrees, generally binding decrees of the ministries and other central state administration bodies, if they are not decided upon by other courts.

(2) If the Constitutional Court accepts a proposal to start an action pursuant to para. 1, it may temporarily stop the effects of the legal acts in question, their parts, or some of their provisions, if their further implementation may threaten basic rights and freedoms, if there is a threat of a substantial economic damage or any other unrepairable consequence.

(3) If the Constitutional Court establishes by its verdict that legal regulations listed under para. 1 are mutually incompatible, the relevant legal acts, their parts, or, as the case may be, some of their provisions cease to be effective. Within six months after the announcement of the Constitutional Court's ruling, the bodies which adopted those legal acts must bring them into compliance with the Constitution, constitutional laws, and international treaties promulgated in the manner prescribed by law, and if the legal acts listed in para. 1 letter b) and c) are concerned, also with the Government decrees, generally binding decrees of the ministries and other central state administration bodies. Should they not comply with this, such legal acts, their parts, or their provisions shall cease to be valid after six months of the announcement of the ruling.

(4) The Constitutional Court does not decide upon the compliance of a law draft or a draft of any other generally binding legal act with the constitution, or international treaty which was promulgated in the manner prescribed by law or constitutional law.

(5) The validity of the rulings on the temporary stop on the effects of legal acts in question, their parts or provisions cease to exist with the announcement of the Constitutional Court's ruling in the prima facie case. This is so if the ruling on the temporary stop was not cancelled by the Constitutional Court because the reasons for its adoption ceased to exist.

(6) The ruling of the Constitutional Court concluded pursuant to paras. 1, 2, and 5 is promulgated in the manner described for the promulgation of laws. The valid ruling of the Constitutional Court is generally binding.

Aricle. 125a
(1) The Constitutional Courts rules upon the compliance of concluded international treaties which require the consent of the National Council of the Slovak Republic with the Constitution or constitutional laws.
(2) The proposal pursuant to para. 1 may be initiated by the President of the Slovak Republic or the Government prior to the discussion of the international treaty in the National Council of the Slovak Republic.
(3) The Constitutional Court shall decide about the proposal pursuant to Art. 2 in a period set by a law. If the Constitutional Courts rules upon the incompatibility of the international treaty with the Constitution or a constitutional law, such international treaty cannot be ratified.

Article 125b
(1) The Constitutional Court decides whether the subject of a referendum which shall be announced on the basis of a petition of the citizens or on the basis of an act of the National Council of the Slovak Republic pursuant to Art. 95 para. 1 is in compliance with the Constitution and constitutional laws.
(2) The proposal to the decision pursuant to para. 1 may be given to the Constitutional Court by the President of the Slovak Republic prior to the announcement of the referendum, if he has doubts whether the subject of such referendum to be announced on the basis of a petition of the citizens or on the basis of an act of the National Council of the Slovak Republic pursuant to Art. 95 para. 1 is in compliance with the Constitution and constitutional laws.
(3) The Constitutional Court decides on the proposal pursuant to para. 2 in a 60 days period since the day of its receiving. Shall the Constitutional Court in its rulings claim that the subject of the referendum on the basis of a petition of the citizens or on the basis of an act of the National Council of the Slovak Republic pursuant to Art. 95 para. 1 is not in compliance with the Constitution and constitutional laws, the referendum cannot be announced.

Slovenia

Article 86 (Decision-making)
The National Assembly may pass decisions if a majority of deputies are present at the session. The National Assembly adopts laws and other decisions and ratifies treaties by a majority of votes cast by those deputies present, save where a different type of majority is provided by the Constitution or by law.

Article 107 (Powers of the President of the Republic)
The President of the Republic:

- calls elections to the National Assembly;
- promulgates laws;
- appoints state officials where provided by law;
- appoints and recalls ambassadors and envoys of the Republic, and accepts the letters of credence of foreign diplomatic representatives;
- issues instruments of ratification;
- decides on the granting of clemency;
- confers decorations and honorary titles;
- performs other duties determined by this Constitution.

Where required by the National Assembly the President of the Republic must express his opinion on an individual issue.

Article 160 (Powers of the Constitutional Court)
The Constitutional Court decides:

- on the conformity of laws with the Constitution;
- on the conformity of laws and other regulations with ratified treaties and with the universal principles of international law;
- on the conformity of regulations with the Constitution and with laws;
- on the conformity of local community regulations with the Constitution and with laws;
- on the conformity of general acts issued for the exercise of public authority with the Constitution, laws and regulations;
- on constitutional complaints stemming from the violation of human rights and fundamental freedoms through specific acts;
- on jurisdictional disputes between the state and local communities and among local communities themselves;
- on jurisdictional disputes between courts and other state authorities;
- on jurisdictional disputes between the National Assembly, the President of the Republic and the Government;
- on the unconstitutionality of acts and activities of political parties; and
- on other matters vested in the Constitutional Court by this Constitution or laws.

In the process of ratifying a treaty, the Constitutional Court, on the proposal of the President of the Republic, the Government or a third of the deputies of the National Assembly, issues an opinion on the conformity of such treaty with the Constitution. The National Assembly is bound by the opinion of the Constitutional Court.

Unless otherwise provided by law, the Constitutional Court decides on a constitutional complaint only if legal remedies have been exhausted. The Constitutional Court decides whether to accept a constitutional complaint for adjudication on the basis of criteria and procedures provided by law.

Turkey

Article 87
The functions and powers of the Turkish Grand National Assembly comprise the enactment, amendment, and repeal of laws; the supervision of the Council of Ministers and the ministers; authorisation of the Council of Ministers to issue governmental decrees having the force of law on certain matters; debating and approval of the budget draft and the draft law of the final accounts; making decisions regarding printing of currency and declaration of war; ratifying international agreements, deciding on the proclamation of amnesties and pardons, excluding those who have been convicted for activities set out in Article 14 of the Constitution; confirming death sentences passed by the courts; and exercising the powers and executing the functions envisaged in the other articles of the Constitution.

B. Introduction and Debate of the Laws

Article 90
The ratification of treaties concluded with foreign states and international organisations on behalf of the Republic of Turkey shall be subject to adoption by the Turkish Grand National Assembly by a law approving the ratification.
Agreements regulating economic, commercial, and technical relations, and covering a period of no more than one year, may be put into effect through promulgation, provided they do not entail any financial commitment by the state, and provided they do not infringe upon the status of individuals or upon the property rights of Turkish citizens abroad. In such cases, these agreements must be brought to the knowledge of the Turkish Grand National Assembly within two months of their promulgation.
Agreements in connection with the implementation of an international treaty, and economic, commercial, technical, or administrative agreements which are concluded depending on an authorisation given by law shall not require approval by the Turkish Grand National Assembly. However, agreements concluded under the provision of this paragraph and affecting the economic, or commercial relations and private rights of individuals shall not be put into effect unless promulgated.
Agreements resulting in amendments to Turkish laws shall be subject to the provisions of the first paragraph.
International agreements duly put into effect carry the force of law. No appeal to the Constitutional Court can be made with regard to these agreements, on the ground that they are unconstitutional.

C. CONSTITUTIONAL AMENDMENT PROCEDURES

Bulgaria

CHAPTER NINE AMENDMENTS TO THE CONSTITUTION, ADOPTION OF A NEW CONSTITUTION

Article 153 [Amendment by National Assembly]
The National Assembly is free to amend all provisions of the Constitution except those within the prerogatives of the Grand National Assembly.

Article 154 [Amendment Bill]
(1) The initiative to introduce a constitutional amendment bill shall belong to one-fourth of the Members of the National Assembly and to the President.
(2) An amendment bill shall be debated by the National Assembly not earlier than one month and not later than three months from the date on which it is introduced.

Article 155 [Majorities]
(1) A constitutional amendment shall require a majority of three-fourths of the votes of all Members of the National Assembly in three ballots on three different days.
(2) A bill which has received less than three-fourths but more than two-thirds of the votes of all Members shall be eligible for reintroduction after not fewer than two months and not more than five months. To be passed at this new reading, the bill shall require a majority of two-thirds of the votes of all Members.

Article 156 [Promulgation]
An amendment to the Constitution shall be signed and promulgated in The National Gazette by the Chairman of the Grand National Assembly within seven days following its passage.

Article 157 [Grand National Assembly]
A Grand National Assembly shall consist of 400 Members elected by the generally established procedure.

Article 158 [Functions]
A Grand National Assembly shall:
1) adopt a new Constitution;
2) resolve on any changes in the territory of the Republic of Bulgaria and ratify any international instrument envisaging such a change;
3) resolve on any changes in the form of state structure or form of government;
4) resolve on any amendment to Article 5 (2) and (4) and Article 57 (1) and (3);
5) resolve on any amendment to Chapter Nine.

Article 159 [Initiative]
(1) The initiative to introduce an amendment bill pursuant to the preceding Article shall belong to one-third of the Members of the National Assembly and to the President.
(2) The draft of a new constitution or a proposed amendment to the existing Constitution, and any bill to introduce a change in the territory of the country pursuant to Article 158 shall be debated by the National Assembly not earlier than two months and not later than five months from the date on which it is introduced.

Article 160 [Grand National Assembly Elections]
(1) A resolution by the National Assembly announcing elections for a Grand National Assembly shall require a majority of two-thirds of the votes of all Members.
(2) The President shall schedule the elections for a Grand National Assembly within three months from the passage of the National Assembly's resolution.
(3) The mandate of the National Assembly shall expire with the holding of the elections for a Grand National Assembly.

Article 161 [Majority]
To pass a bill, the Grand National Assembly shall require a majority of two-thirds of the votes of all Members, in three ballots on three different days.

Article 162 [Functions]
(1) A Grand National Assembly shall resolve only on the constitutional amendment bills for which it has been elected.
(2) In an emergency, a Grand National Assembly shall further perform the functions of a National Assembly.
(3) The prerogatives of a Grand National Assembly shall expire after it resolves on all matters for which it has been elected. The President shall then schedule elections by a procedure established by law.

Article 163 [Promulgation]
An act of the Grand National Assembly shall be signed and promulgated in The National Gazette by the Assembly's Chairman within seven days following its passage.

Cyprus

Article 179
1. This Constitution shall be the supreme law of the Republic.
2. No law or decision of the House of Representatives or of any of the Communal Chambers and no act or decision of any organ, authority or person in the Republic exercising executive power or any administrative function shall in any way be repugnant to, or inconsistent with, any of the provisions of this Constitution.

Article 180
1. The Greek and the Turkish texts of this Constitution shall both be originals and shall have the same authenticity and the same legal force.
2. Any conflict between the two texts of this Constitution shall be determined by the Supreme Constitutional Court by reference to the text of the draft of this Constitution signed at Nicosia on the 6th April, 1960, in the Joint Constitutional Commission together with the Schedule of amendments thereto signed on * by representatives of the Kingdom of Greece, the Republic of Turkey and the Greek and Turkish Cypriot communities, due regard being had to the letter and spirit of the Zurich Agreement dated the 11th February, 1959, and of the London Agreement dated the 19th February, 1959.
3. In case of ambiguity any interpretation of the Constitution shall be made by the Supreme Constitutional Court due regard being had to the letter and spirit of the Zurich Agreement dated the 11th February, 1959, and of the London Agreement dated the 19th February, 1959.

* Note: date to be inserted later.

Article 181
The Treaty guaranteeing the independence, territorial integrity and Constitution of the Republic concluded between the Republic, the Kingdom of Greece, the Republic of Turkey and the United Kingdom of Great Britain and Northern Ireland, and the Treaty of Military Alliance concluded between the Republic, the Kingdom of Greece and the Republic of Turkey, copies of which are annexed to this Constitution as Annexes I and IE, shall have constitutional force.

Article 182
1. The Articles or parts of Articles of this Constitution set out in Annex III hereto which have been incorporated from the Zurich Agreement dated 11th February, 1959, are the basic Articles of this Constitution and cannot, in any way, be amended, whether by way of variation, addition or repeal.
2. Subject to paragraph 1 of this Article any provision of this Constitution may be amended, whether by way of variation, addition or repeal, as provided in paragraph 3 of this Article.
3. Such amendment shall be made by a law passed by a majority vote comprising at least two-thirds of the total number of the Representatives belonging to the Greek Community and at least two-thirds of the total number of the Representatives belonging to the Turkish Community.

Czech Republic

Article 9 [Constitutional Laws]
(1) The Constitution may be amended or altered solely by constitutional laws.
(2) Any change of fundamental attributes of the democratic law-observing state is inadmissible.
(3) Legal norms cannot be interpreted as warranting the removal or threatening of the foundations of the democratic state.

Article 39 [Quorum, Majorities]
(1) The Chambers constitute a quorum if at least one third of their members are present.
(2) The passage of a resolution of the respective Chamber requires the consent of an absolute majority of deputies or Senators present, if not prescribed otherwise by the Constitution.
(3) The passage of a resolution on the declaration of the state of war and a resolution approving the presence of foreign troops on the territory of the Czech Republic requires the consent of an absolute majority of all deputies and of all Senators.
(4) The passage of a constitutional law and the approval of an international agreement under Article 10 shall require the consent of a three-fifths majority of all deputies and a three-fifths majority of all Senators present.

Article 41 [Initiative]
(1) Draft laws shall be submitted to the Chamber of Deputies.
(2) A draft law may be submitted by deputies, groups of deputies, the Senate, the Government, and representatives of a higher territorial self-governing entity.

Estonia

CHAPTER XV AMENDMENTS TO THE CONSTITUTION

Article 161 [Initiative]
(1) The right to initiate amendments to the Constitution shall rest with at least one-fifth of the complement of the Parliament and with the President of the Republic.
(2) Amendments to the Constitution may not be initiated, nor the Constitution amended, during a state of emergency or a state of war.

Article 162 [Referendum]
Chapter I 'General Provisions' and Chapter XV 'Amendments to the Constitution' may be amended only by referendum.

Article 163 [Proceedings]
(1) The Constitution may be amended by a law which is adopted by:
1) referendum;
2) two successive complements of the Parliament;
3) the Parliament, in matters of urgency.
(2) A draft law to amend the Constitution shall be considered during three readings in the Parliament, whereby the interval between the first and second readings shall be at least three months, and the interval between the second and third readings shall be at least one month. The manner in which the Constitution is amended shall be decided at the third reading.

Article 164 [Majority for Referendum]
In order to put a proposed amendment to the Constitution to a referendum, the approval of a three-fifths majority of the complement of the Parliament shall be mandatory. The referendum shall not be held earlier than three months from the time that such a resolution is adopted in the Parliament.

Article 165 [Majority for Adoption by Parliament]
(1) In order to amend the Constitution by two successive complements of the Parliament, the draft law to amend the Constitution must receive the support of the majority of the complement of the Parliament.
(2) If the next complement of the Parliament adopts the draft which received the support of the majority of the previous complement, without amendment, on its first reading and with a three-fifths majority of its complement, the law to amend the Constitution shall be adopted.

Article 166 [Very Qualified Majority]
A proposal to consider a proposed amendment to the Constitution as a matter of urgency shall be adopted by the Parliament by a four-fifths majority. In such a case the law to amend the Constitution shall be adopted by a two-thirds majority of the complement of the Parliament.

Article 167 [Proclamation]
The law to amend the Constitution shall be proclaimed by the President of the Republic and it shall enter into force on the date determined by the same law, but not earlier than three months after its proclamation.

Article 168 [Limit to Re-Introduction]
An amendment to the Constitution dealing with the same issue may not be re-introduced within one year of the rejection of the respective draft by referendum or by the Parliament.

Hungary

Article 19
3) Within this sphere of authority, the Parliament shall –
a) adopt the Constitution of the Republic of Hungary;

Latvia

Article 76
The Saeima may amend the Constitution in sittings at which at least two-thirds of the members of the Saeima participate. The amendments shall be passed in three readings by a majority of not less than two-thirds of the members present.

Article 77
If the Saeima has amended the first, second, third, fourth, sixth or seventy-seventh Article of the Constitution, such amendments, in order to come into force as law, shall be submitted to a national referendum.

Article 78
Electors, in number comprising not less than one tenth of the electorate, have the right to submit a fully-elaborated draft of an amendment to the Constitution or of a law to the President, who shall present it to the Saeima. If the Saeima does not adopt it without change as to its content, it shall then be submitted to national referendum.

Article 79
An amendment to the Constitution submitted for national referendum shall be deemed adopted if at least half of the electorate has voted in favour. A draft law submitted for national referendum shall be deemed adopted if the number of voters is at least half of the number of electors that participated in the previous Saeima election and if the majority has voted in favour of the draft law.

Lithuania

Article 147
(1) In order to amend or append the Constitution of the Republic of Lithuania, a proposal must be submitted to the Parliament by either not less than one-fourth of the members of the Parliament, or by at least 300,000 voters.
(2) During a state of emergency or martial law, amendments to the Constitution may not be made.

Article 148
(1) The provision of Article 1 that the State of Lithuania is an independent democratic republic may only be amended by a referendum in which at least three-fourths of the electorate of Lithuania vote in favor thereof.
(2) The provisions of Articles 1 and 14 may be amended only by referendum.
(3) Amendments of other chapters of the Constitution must be considered and voted upon in the Parliament twice. There must be a lapse of at least three months between each vote. Bills for constitutional amendments shall be deemed adopted by the Parliament if, in each of the votes, at least two-thirds of all the members of the Parliament vote in favor of the enactment.
(4) An amendment to the Constitution which is rejected by the Parliament may not be submitted to the Parliament for reconsideration for the period of one year.

Article 149
(1) The adopted law on an amendment to the Constitution shall be signed by the President of the Republic of Lithuania and officially promulgated within 5 days.
(2) If the President of the Republic of Lithuania does not sign and promulgate such a law in due time, this law shall become effective when the Chairperson of the Parliament signs and promulgates it.
(3) The law on an amendment to the Constitution shall become effective no earlier than one month after the adoption thereof.

Malta

Section 66 [Qualified Majority]
(1) Subject to the provisions of this section, Parliament may alter any of the provisions of this

Constitution and (in so far as it forms part of the law of Malta) any of the provisions of the Malta Independence Act, 1964.
(2) In so far as it alters –
(a) this section; or
(b) Section 1, subsection (2) of section 2, subsection (1) of section 3, subsection (1) of section 5, section 6, sections 32 to 48 (inclusive), sections 51, 52, 56, 57, 60 and 61, subsection (3) of section 65, subsection (2) of section 75, section 76 (other than subsection (2) thereof), sections 77 and 78, section 80, section 91 sections 95 to 100 (inclusive), sections 102 to 110 (inclusive), sections 113, 114, 118, 119 or 120 of this Constitution: or
(c) section 124 of this Constitution in its application to any of the provisions specified in paragraph (a) or (b) of this subsection,a bill for an Act of Parliament under this section shall not be passed in the House of Representatives unless at the final voting thereon in that House it is supported by the votes of not less than two-thirds of all the members of the House.
(3) In so far as it alters –
(a) this subsection or subsection (4) of this section; or
(b) subsection (2) of section 76 of this Constitution, a bill for an Act of Parliament under this section shall not be presented to the President for his assent unless not less than three nor more than six months after its passage through the House in the manner specified in subsection (2) of this section it has been submitted to the electors qualified to vote for the election of members of the House of Representatives and the majority of the electors voting have approved the bill.
(4) The provisions of subsection (10) of section 56 of this Constitution shall apply to the voting on a bill submitted to the electors under subsection (3) of this section as they apply to voting at the election of members of the House of Representatives, and subject as aforesaid the vote on such bill shall be taken in such manner as Parliament may prescribe.
(5) In so far as it alters any of the provisions of this Constitution other than those specified in subsections (2) and (3) of this section, a, bill for an Act of Parliament under this section shall not be passed in the House of Representatives unless at the final voting thereon in that House it is supported by the votes of a majority of all the members of the House.
(6) An Act of Parliament altering the number of members of the House of Representatives shall not affect the membership of the House before the dissolution of Parliament next following its enactment.
(7) In this section –
(a) references to any of the provisions of this Constitution or of the Malta Independence Act, 1964 include references to any law that amends or replaces that provision; and
(b) references to the alteration of any of the provisions of this Constitution or of the Malta Independence Act, 1964 include references to the amendment, modification or re-enactment, with or without amendment or modification, of that provision, the suspension or repeal of that provision and the making of a different provision in lieu of that provision.

Poland

Article 235
(1) A bill to amend the Constitution may be submitted by the following: at least one-fifth of the statutory number of Deputies; the Senate; or the President of the Republic.
(2) Amendments to the Constitution shall be made by means of a statute adopted by the House of Representatives (Sejm) and, thereafter, adopted in the same wording by the Senate within a period of 60 days.

(3) The first reading of a bill to amend the Constitution may take place no sooner than 30 days after the submission of the bill to the House of Representatives (Sejm).
(4) A bill to amend the Constitution shall be adopted by the House of Representatives (Sejm) by a majority of at least two-thirds of votes in the presence of at least half of the statutory number of Deputies, and by the Senate by an absolute majority of votes in the presence of at least half of the statutory number of Senators.
(5) The adoption by the House of Representatives (Sejm) of a bill amending the provisions of Chapters I, II or XII of the Constitution shall take place no sooner than 60 days after the first reading of the bill.
(6) If a bill to amend the Constitution relates to the provisions of Chapters I, II, XII, the subjects specified in Paragraph (1) above may require, within 45 days of the adoption of the bill by the Senate, the holding of a confirmatory referendum. Such subjects shall make application in the matter to the Marshal of the House of Representatives (Sejm), who shall order the holding of a referendum within 60 days of the day of receipt of the application. The amendment to the Constitution shall be deemed accepted if the majority of those voting express support for such amendment.
(7) After conclusion of the procedures specified in Paragraphs (4) and (6) above, the Marshal of the House of Representatives (Sejm) shall submit the adopted statute to the President of the Republic for signature. The President of the Republic shall sign the statute within 21 days of its submission and order its promulgation in the Journal of Laws of the Republic of Poland (Dziennik Ustaw).

Romania

Article 146 [Initiative]
(1) Revision of the Constitution may be initiated by the President of Romania on the proposal of the Government, by at least one quarter of the number of Deputies or Senators, as well as by at least 500,000 citizens with the right to vote.
(2) The citizens who initiate the revision of the Constitution must belong to at least half the number of the counties in the country, and in each of the respective counties or in the City of Bucharest, at least 20,000 signatures must be recorded in support of this initiative.

Article 147 [Majority, Referendum]
(1) The draft or proposed revision must be adopted by the Chamber of Deputies and the Senate by a majority of at least two-thirds of the members of each Chamber.
(2) If no agreement can be reached by a mediation procedure, the Chamber of Deputies and the Senate shall decide thereupon, in joint session, by the vote of at least three-quarters of the number of Deputies and Senators.
(3) The revision shall be final after approval by a referendum held within 30 days from the date of passing the draft or proposed revision.

Article 148 [Limits to Amendment]
(1) The provisions of this Constitution with regard to the national, independent, unitary, and indivisible character of the Romanian State, the Republican form of government, territorial integrity, independence of the judiciary, political pluralism, and official language shall not be subject to revision.
(2) Likewise, no revision shall be made if it results in the suppression of the citizens' fundamental rights and freedoms, or the safeguards thereof.

(3) The Constitution shall not be revised during a state of siege or emergency or in wartime.

Slovak Republic

Article 72
The National Council of the Slovak Republic is the sole constituent and legislative body of the Slovak Republic.

Article 87
(1) Bills can be tabled by committees of the National Council of the Slovak Republic, Deputies, and the Government of the Slovak Republic.
(2) Laws of the National Council of the Slovak Republic shall be signed by the Chairman of the National Council of the Slovak Republic, the President of the Slovak Republic, and the Prime Minister of the Slovak Republic.
(3) If the President of the Slovak Republic returns a constitutional or other law with comments, the National Council of the Slovak Republic will discuss the constitutional or other law again and, in the event of its approval, such a law must be promulgated.
(4) The President of the Slovak Republic will return a law with comments, in line with Section (3), whenever requested to do so by the Government of the Slovak Republic.
(5) A law becomes valid with its promulgation. Details will be set out in a law.

Slovenia

Article 168 (Proposal to Initiate the Procedure)
A proposal to initiate the procedure to amend the Constitution may be made by twenty deputies of the National Assembly, the Government or at least thirty thousand voters.
Such proposal is decided upon by the National Assembly by a two-thirds majority vote of deputies present.

Article 169 (Acts Amending the Constitution)
The National Assembly adopts acts amending the Constitution by a two-thirds majority vote of all deputies.

Article 170 (Confirmation of Constitutional Amendments by Referendum)
The National Assembly must submit a proposed constitutional amendment to voters for adoption in a referendum, if so required by at least thirty deputies.
A constitutional amendment is adopted in a referendum, if a majority of those voting voted in favour of the same, provided that a majority of all voters participated in the referendum.

Article 171 (Promulgation of Constitutional Amendments)
Constitutional amendments enter into force upon their promulgation in the National Assembly.

Turkey

Article 175
The constitutional amendment shall be proposed in writing by at lest one-third of the total number of members of the Turkish Grand National Assembly. Proposals to amend the Constitution shall be debated twice in the plenary session. The adoption of a proposal for an

amendment shall require a three-fifths majority of the total number of members of the Assembly by a secret ballot.
The consideration and adopting of proposals for the amendment of the Constitution shall be subject to the provisions governing the consideration and adoption of legislation, with the exception of the conditions set forth in this Article.
The President of the Republic may refer the laws related to the Constitutional amendments for further consideration. If the Assembly adopts the draft law referred by the President by a two-thirds majority, the President may submit the law to referendum.
If a law is adopted by a three-fifths or less than a two-thirds majority of the total number of votes of the Assembly and is not referred by the President for further consideration, it will be published in the Official Gazette and shall be submitted to referendum.
A law on the Constitutional amendment adopted by a two-thirds majority of the total number of members of the Turkish Grand National Assembly directly or if referred by the President for further consideration, or its articles as considered necessary may be submitted to a referendum by the President. Laws or related articles of the Constitutional amendment not submitted to referendum shall be promulgated in the Official Gazette.
Laws related to Constitutional amendment which are submitted for referendum shall require the approval of more than half of the valid votes casted.
The Turkish Grand National Assembly, in adopting the laws related to the Constitutional amendment, shall also decide on which provisions shall be submitted to referendum together and which shall be submitted individually.
Every measure including fines shall be taken to secure participation in referenda, general, by- and local elections.

D. DELEGATION OR TRANSFER OF STATE POWERS

Poland

Article 90
(1) The Republic of Poland may, by virtue of international agreements, delegate to an international organization or international institution the competence of organs of State authority in relation to certain matters.
(2) A statute, granting consent for ratification of an international agreement referred to in Paragraph (1), shall be passed by the House of Representatives (Sejm) by a two-thirds majority vote in the presence of at least half of the statutory number of Deputies, and by the Senate by a two-thirds majority vote in the presence of at least half of the statutory number of Senators.
(3) Granting of consent for ratification of such agreement may also be passed by a nationwide referendum in accordance with the provisions of Article 125.
(4) Any resolution in respect of the choice of procedure for granting consent to ratification shall be taken by the House of Representatives (Sejm) by an absolute majority vote taken in the presence of at least half of the statutory number of Deputies.

Slovak Republic

Article 1
(1) The Slovak Rebublic is a sovereign, democratic, and law-governed state. It is not linked to any ideology or religious belief.

(2) The Slovak Republic acknowledges and adheres to the general rules of international law, international treaties by which it is bound, and its other international obligations.

Article 7
(1) On the basis of its free decision, the Slovak Republic can enter into a state alliance with other states. The decision on entering into a state alliance with other states or on secession from such alliance will be made by a constitutional law and a subsequent confirmative referendum.
(2) The Slovak Republic can by an international treaty which was ratified and promulgated in a way prescribed by the law or on the basis of such a treaty transfer the exercise of part of its powers to the European communities and the European Union. The legally binding acts of the European communities and the European Union have priority over Slovak statutes. The legally binding acts which require implementation will be adopted by a statute of the Parliament or by the Government decree pursuant to Article 120 para. 2.
(3) The Slovak Republic may, with the aim of promoting peace, security, and a democratic order and pursuant to conditions set by an international treaty, obtain access to an organization of common collective security.

ANNEX III

OVERVIEW OF RELEVANT LITERATURE AND DOCUMENTS ON THE ASSER CONFERENCE WEBSITE AT THE TIME OF THE CONFERENCE

SESSION I

- European Commission - Employment, Industrial Relations and Social Affairs, Affirming fundamental rights in the European Union: time to act - Report of the expert group on fundamental rights (President: S. Simitis). - Brussels, February 1999
- Draft Charter of Fundamental Rights of the European Union - Draft list of fundamental rights, 27-01-2000
- Draft Charter of Fundamental Rights of the European Union - Draft articles, 15-02-2000
- Draft Charter of Fundamental Rights of the European Union - Proposed Articles (Articles 10 to 19), 24-02-2000
- Draft Charter of Fundamental Rights of the European Union, 04-03-2000
- Draft Charter of Fundamental Rights of the European Union - Complete text proposed by the Preasidium, 28-07-2000
- Charter of Fundamental Rights
- European Commission - Justice and Home Affairs, Draft Charter of Fundamental Rights
- European Parliament, EU Charter of Fundamental Rights, A5-0064/2000
- European Parliament, Charter of Fundamental Rights
- President's Report to the European Council on the IGC
- European Landowners' Organisation (ELO), Charter of Fundamental Rights - Comments
- Giampierro Aldaheff, A European Union Charter of Fundamental Rights - the Heart of Europe
- Mathew Heim, 'A European Union Charter of Fundamental Rights - A Legal View'
- Giuliano Amato and Hervé Bribosia, Quelle Chartre constitutionelle pour l'Union Européen? Stratégies et options pour renforcer le caractère constitutionnel des traités, San Domenico di Fiesole
- Assemblée Nationale, Colloque: La charte des droits fondamentaux de l'Unuion européenne, 26 avril 2000 - Paris, Compte rendu des débats. - Les Documents d'Information de l'Assemblée Nationale No. 37/2000. - ISSN 1240-831-X
- Bultermann, Mielle and Rick Lawson, Het EU-Grondrechtenhandvest: méér dan een festijn voor juristen. - In: Internationale Spectator No. 9/2000, pp. 423-429
- Adviesraad Internationale Vraagstukken (Advisory Council on International Affairs), A European charter of fundamental rights? - The Hague: Ministry of Foreign Affairs (Occasional Paper No. 15, May 2000)

SESSION II

- Nationales Verfassungsrecht mit Blick auf die europäische Integration = Le droit constitutionnel national et l'intégration européenne = National constitutional law vis-à-vis European integration: 17. FIDE Kongress. - Baden-Baden: Nomos, 1996

- David Beatty, Law and politics: courts and the separation of powers. - In: L'espace constitutionnel européen = Der europäische Verfassungsraum = The European constitutional area, ed. by Roland Bieber and Pierre Widmer. - Zurich: Schulthess Polygraphiser Verlag AG, 1995 (pp. 165-185)
- George A. Bermann, The constitutional amendmet process. - In: L'espace constitutionnel européen = Der europäische Verfassungsraum = The European constitutional area, ed. by Roland Bieber and Pierre Widmer. - Zurich: Schulthess Polygraphiser Verlag AG, 1995 (pp. 291-311)
- Francis Delpérée, La constitution [de la Belgique] et l'Union européenne. - In: Constitutional Implications of European Union Membership, Phare Number BG 9316 04-06, pp. 41-51. - [s.l.], 1998
- F.F. Ridley, The British constitution and constitutional reform in Britain. - In: L'espace constitutionnel européen = Der europäische Verfassungsraum = The European constitutional area, ed. by Roland Bieber and Pierre Widmer. - Zurich: Schulthess Polygraphiser Verlag AG, 1995 (pp. 37-55)
- Théodore Tzonos, Les incidences du Traité de Maastricht sur l'ordre constitutionnel helénique. - In: Constitutional Implications of European Union Membership, Phare Number BG 9316 04-06, pp. 64-76. - [s.l.], 1998

SESSION III

Constitutions of the candidate countries
(The Relevant Constitutional Provisions in the Candidate Countries)

Bulgaria
Cyprus
Czech Republic
Estonia
Hungary
Latvia
Lithuania
Malta
Poland
Romania
– Draft
Slovakia
Slovenia
Turkey

Articles and reports

East European Constitutional Review

- Anneli Albi, 'Europe Agreements in light of sovereignty and legitimacy: Estonia'
  While it is usually the EU membership that is regarded as encroachment on state's sovereignty, this paper suggests that also the pre-EU-accession adaptations such as harmonising law under the Europe Agreement to the acquis communautaire, law of

foreign states in the formation of which CEECs have no participation, signify a subordination of state independent decision-making powers to the EU and should therefore require either authorising constitutional amendment or a rather open modern approach to sovereignty. This is particularly the case of Estonia, whose constitution, as a reflection of country's oppressive history, protects sovereignty exceptionally strictly through several safeguards. The main positions of this paper could, in principle, apply also to several other CEE countries, depending on the level of constitutional protection of sovereignty in their constitutions.

- Giuliano Amato and Judy Batt, 'Final Report of the Reflection Group. The Long-Term Implications of EU Enlargement: The Nature of the New Border', San Domenico di Fiesole, EUI: 1999
- Stanislaw Biernat, The impact of European integration of the organization and functioning of Poland's legislative and executive authorities. - In: Revue européenne de droit public = European Review of Public Law = Eur. Zeitschrift des öffentl. Rechts = Rivista europea di diritto pubblico No. 4/1997, pp. 1187-1207
- Stanislaw Biernat, Legitimationsfragen der polnischen Verwaltung unter dem Einfluss des Europarechts. - In: Entwicklungstendenzen des Allgemeinen Verwaltungsrechts und des Städtebaurechts: Referate und Diskussionsbeiträge des X. Deutsch-Polnischen Verwaltungskolloquiums vom 8.-12. September 1997 in Posen. - Stuttgart [usw.]: Richard Boorberg Verlag [s.a.]
- Stanislaw Biernat, Constitutional aspects of Poland's future membership in the European Union. - In: Archiv des Völkerrechts No. 4/1998, pp. 398-424
- Wladyslaw Czaplinski, Selected Jurisprudence of the Polish Supreme Court and Constitutional Court involving questions of public and private international law. - In: Polish Yearbook of International Law 1995-1996, pp. 201-219
- Leszek Garlicki, Necessity and functions of constitutions. - In: L'espace constitutionnel européen = Der europäische Verfassungsraum = The European constitutional area, ed. by Roland Bieber and Pierre Widmer. - Zurich: Schulthess Polygraphiser Verlag AG, 1995 (pp. 25-35)
- H.G. Heinrich et al, The Hierarchy of Legal Norms in CEE Constitutional Systems: Report to TAIEX, Brussels (with contributions from the Czech Republic, Estonia, Poland, Slovenia and Hungary)
- Bart Hessel and Piotr Hofmanski (eds.), Government policy and rule of law: theoretical and practical aspects in Poland and the Netherlands. - Bialystok / Utrecht: Uniwersytet w Bialymstoku / Universiteit Utrecht. - 1997
- Wiktor Osiatynski, The referendum, popular initiative and the issue of legitimacy in constitution-making in Poland. - In: L'espace constitutionnel européen = Der europäische Verfassungsraum = The European constitutional area, ed. by Roland Bieber and Pierre Widmer. - Zurich: Schulthess Polygraphiser Verlag AG, 1995 (pp. 345-358)
- Zoltán Péteri, The declaration of the rights of man and citizen and the Hungarian constitution. - In: Acta Juridica Hungaria No. 1-2/1991, pp. 57-73
- H.G. Heinrich et al, The Hierarchy of Legal Norms in CEE Constitutional Systems: Report to TAIEX, Brussels (with contributions from the Czech Republic, Estonia, Poland, Slovenia and Hungary)
- Zoltán Péteri, Constitution-making in Hungary. - In: Acta Juridica Hungarica No. 3-4/ 1994, pp. 149-161
- Miroslav Wyrzykowski, The constitutions of the Eastern European countries in the structure of European constitutionalism. - In: L'espace constitutionnel européen = Der

europäische Verfassungsraum = The European constitutional area, ed. by Roland Bieber and Pierre Widmer. - Zurich: Schulthess Polygraphiser Verlag AG, 1995 (pp. 151-163)
- Denis J. Galligan and Daniel M. Smilov, Administrative law in Central and Eastern Europe 1996-1998. - Budapest: Central European University Press, 1999. - ISBN 963-9116-40-8 / 963-9116-39-4
- Evgeni Tanchev, The Constitution of 1991 and the accession of Bulgaria to the European Union. - In: Constitutional Implications of European Union Membership, Phare Number BG 9316 04-06, pp. 25-40. - [s.l.], 1998

SESSION IV

- European Commission, IGC 2000 Website
- Council of the European Union, Work programma IGC 2000
- Dehaene, von Weizsäcker, Simon, The institutional implications of enlargement - Report to the European Commission (The "Dehaene-von Weizsäcker-Simon" report)
- European Commission, Adapting the Institutions to Make a Success of Enlargement - COM(1999)592
- European Commission, Adapting the Institutions to make a success of enlargement. - COM(2000)0034 fin.
- European Parliament, Resolution on the preparation of the reform of the Treaties and the next Intergovernmental Conference, A5-0058/1999. - In: Official Journal of the EC No. C 189/222 of 07-07-2000
- Contribution of the Court of Justice and the Court of First Instance to the IGC 2000 = Bijdrage Hof van Justitie en Gerecht van eerste aanleg aan de IGC 2000 = Contribution de la Cour et du Tribunal a la Conference Intergouvernementale
- European Commission, Reforming the Commission: consultative document
- European Commission, White paper: Reforming the Commission. - COM(2000)200 fin.
- Conference of the Representatives of the Governments of the Member States, Intergovernmental Conference on institutional reform: Presidency report to the Feira European Council. - Brussels, 14 June 2000. - CONFER 4750/00
- The Independent Commission for the Reform of the Institutions and Procedures of the Union (ICRI), Advancing the Union
- The Independent Commission for the Reform of the Institutions and Procedures of the Union (ICRI), Advancing the Union - Annex
- European Court of Justice and Court of First Instance, The Future of the Judicial System of the European Union - (Proposals and Reflections)
- Rethinking Europe for the new millennium: a new institutional framework for an enlarged Union: background material for the colloquium. 5-6 November 1999. - Maastricht: EIPA, 1999
- Greening the Treaty III: Proposals for the 2000 Intergovernmental Conference
- Roland Bieber, Verfassungsgebung und Verfassungsänderung in der Europäischen Union. - In: L'espace constitutionnel européen = Der europäische Verfassungsraum = The European constitutional area, ed. by Roland Bieber and Pierre Widmer. - Zurich: Schulthess Polygraphiser Verlag AG, 1995 (pp. 313-327)
- Pier Virgilio Dastoli, 'A Constitution for Europe'
- Stephen Hall, 'Tales from the Vienna Woods: EU Constitutional Law and Democracy in the Member States'. - European Policy Center, 2000

- Alfred E. Kellermann, Johan C. van Haersolte, Michael Hofstötter, 'National Constitutional Law and EU Law: A Comparative Study on Some Specific Aspects. A research done on behalf on the Parliament (Riigikogu) of Estonia'. - The Hague: T.M.C. Asser Instituut, 1999
- Jean-Claude Piris, Does the European Union have a constitution? Does it need one? . - In: European Law Review (1999) pp. 557-585
- Frank Vibert, 'How not to write a constitution - the Maastricht/Amsterdam treaties'. - in: Constitutional Political Economy No. 10 (1999) pp. 149-166
- Frank Vibert, Europe: a Constitution for the Millennium. - Aldershot: Dartmouth Publishing Company, 1995. - ISBN 1-85521-521-7
- J.H.H. Weiler, "... We Will Do, And Hearken" (Ex. XXIV:7): Reflections on a common constitutional law for the European Union. - In: L'espace constitutionnel européen = Der europäische Verfassungsraum = The European constitutional area, ed. by Roland Bieber and Pierre Widmer. - Zurich: Schulthess Polygraphiser Verlag AG, 1995 (pp. 413-468)
- Paul Craig and Carol Harlow, Lawmaking in the European Union. - The Hague [etc.]: Kluwer Law International, 1998 . - ISBN 90-411-9642-0
- Guido Biessen et al. (eds.), The second decade: prospects for European integration after ten years of transition. - The Hague: Ministry of Economic Affairs of the Netherlands / SDU Publishers, 1999. - ISBN 90-12-08807-0
- Willy Sigl, A New Institutional Architecture for an Enlarged European Union, Brussels: Université Libre de Bruxelles (CERIS), 2000 (Diss. Université Libre de Bruxelles, Master Programme of International Politics, June 2000)
- A.A.M. Schrauwen (ed.), Flexibility in constitutions: forms of closer cooperation in federal and non-federal settings. - Amsterdam: Hogendorp Centre for European Constitutional Studies, 1999
- K. Lenaerts et al. (eds.), Constitutional law of the European Union. - London: Sweet & Maxwell, 1999. - ISBN 0-421-65180-6
- Flexibiliteit en het Verdrag van Amsterdam: 28e zitting (1998) Asser Instituut Colloquium Europees Recht. - Den Haag: T.M.C. Asser Press, 1998. - ISBN 90-6704-108-4
- Report from the Florence European University Institute on the reorganisation of the European Treaties:
  Press release
  Draft for the basic treaty
  Final report

Contributions of the Member States

Austria
- Basic Principles of Austria's Position

Belgium
- Benelux Memorandum with regard to the IGC and the Institutional Reforms
- Proposed treaty changes for the Committee of Regions [Articles 21(3) and 151(4) EC treaty] and the Court of Justice, 12 May 2000
- Draft amendment to Article 7 of the TEU, 2 May 2000

Denmark
- Intergovernmental Conference 2000: Basis for Negotiations

Finland
- Background and objectives in the IGC 2000

France
- Bulletin de la Délégation pour l'Union européenne. - Paris: Assemblée Nationale
- Gérard Fuchs, 'La réforme des institutions de l'Union européenne'. - in: Bulletin de la Délégation pour l'Union européenne, No. 2242. - Paris: Assemblée Nationale, 2000
- Alain Barrau, 'Propositions pour la Présidence française de l'Union européenne'. - in: Bulletin de la Délégation pour l'Union européenne, No. 2138. - Paris: Assemblée Nationale, 2000
- Haenel, Hubert et al., Quelle réforme des institutions européennes pour l'an 2000? - Les rapport du Sénat No. 148
- Déclaration du Premier ministre sur les orientations de la Présidence française de l'Union européenne, Paris, le 9 mai 2000

Germany
- Policy Document on the Intergovernmental Conference on Institutional Reform

Greece
- Memorandum from the Greek Government to the Intergovernmental Conference on institutional reform of the European Union
- Memorandum on the reform of the judicial system of the EU, 12 April 2000

Ireland

Italy
- Position de l'Italie sur l'extension du vote à la majorité qualifiée
- Intergovernmental Conference on the Revision of the Treaties: Italy's position

Luxembourg
- Benelux Memorandum with regard to the IGC and the Institutional Reforms

The Netherlands
- Benelux Memorandum with regard to the IGC and the Institutional Reforms

An agenda for internal reforms in the European Union

Eric Philippart and Monika Sie Dhian Ho, The pros and cons of 'closer cooperation' within the EU: argumentation and recommendations. - WRR Working Document No. W 104. - The Hague: Netherlands Scientific Council for Government Policy, 2000
- A.J.G. Verheijen, Administrative capacity development: a race against time? - WRR Working Document No. W 107. - The Hague: Netherlands Scientific Council for Government Policy, 2000
- Jacques Pelkmans, Daniel Gros, Jorge Nunez Ferrer, Long-run economic aspects of the European Union's eastern enlargement. - WRR Working Document No. W 109. - The Hague: Netherlands Scientific Council for Government Policy, 2000

These texts can be obtained free of charge at the WRR (E-mail: langeweg@wrr.nl)

Portugal

Spain

Sweden

United Kingdom

- House of Commons, 'IGC: Reform for Enlargement - The British Approach to the European Union Intergovernmental Conference 2000'
- House of Commons, European Scrutiny, Seventeenth Report

ANNEX IV*

REPORTS ON THE ASSER INSTITUTE COLLOQUIUM IN AGENCE EUROPE

AGENCE EUROPE No. 7786

(EU) EU/ENLARGEMENT: Seminar, with Mr Verheugen, on constitutional impact of enlargement and Charter of fundamental rights on EU and candidate countries

The Hague, 28/08/2000 (Agence Europe) – The **T.M.C. Asser Institute in the Hague** is organising from the **20 to 23 September** in the Hague, in cooperation with the **Constitutional and Legal Policy Institute** (COLPI) from Budapest, a seminar on the theme "The constitutional impact of enlargement at EU and national level", so as to raise in particular the impact of the intergovernmental conference that should finish in Nice and the EU Charter of Fundamental Rights which should be proclaimed at the end of the year, and to help the European Union candidate countries to benefit from the experience of the present members in the adapting of their constitutions to the obligation resulting from belonging to the EU. The organiser drafted for the participants a series of questions, such as: How must the institutions be adapted for enlargement to succeed? What will be the legal impact of the Charter on national constitutions? To ratify the community treaties, will; it be necessary to amend your constitution? Do the courts of your country accept the principal of supremacy of community law?

The works, which will be opened by the Dutch Secretary of State to Foreign Affairs **Dick Benschop** and to which will participate several universities from EU member countries and candidate countries, Turkey included, will speak in several sessions especially covering:

– The European level (constitutional order and Charter of fundamental rights). This theme will be introduced by **Jaap W. de Zwaan**, Chairman of the Scientific Council of the T.M.C. Asser Institute, and discussed by, among others, **Joseph H.H. Weiler**, from the European University Institute Florence.

– The national level (impact of the constitutions and courts of the EU Member States and candidate countries). The theme will be introduced by Christiaan **W.A. Timmermans**, deputy Director-General in the European Commission's Legal Service, and by **Francis G. Jacobs**, Advocate-General at the EU Court of Justice, and among the participant will be the Commissioner responsible for enlargement **Gunter Verheugen** and the MEP **Richard Corbett**.

– The lessons to be learnt, future perspectives for the European architecture. Introduced by **Jan Jans** from the T.M.C. Asser Institute, this issue will be notably discussed by the Dutch Minister for the Interior **A.H. Korthals**, the former European Commissioner **Frans Andriessen**, Chairman of the Commission for the reform of the Institutions and Procedures of the Union, **Jean-Paul Jacqué**, Director of the Legal Service Council of the EU, and by the Dutch MEP **Michiel Patijn**, former Secretary of State for foreign affairs.

---

* Reproduced with the kind permission of the editor of Agence Europe.

– The practical implementation of the challenges of accession. Under the chairmanship of **Arie Bloed** and **Karoly Bard**, this last theme will in particular be discussed by **Koen Lenaerts** and by **Alfred E. Kellermann**, Secretary-General of the T.M.C. Asser Institute.

(Registration: Susanne van der Meulen, T.M.C. Asser Institute, R.J. Schimmelpennincklaan 20-22, P.O. Box 30461, NL 2500 GL The Hague).

AGENCE EUROPE No. 7809

(EU) EU/ENLARGEMENT: Another Intergovernmental Conference following up the Treaty of Nice "must not be a precondition for enlargement", says Commissioner Verheugen

Brussels, 28/09/2000 (Agence Europe) – Speaking last week before the "**Asser Institute Colloquium" of the Hague on "the Constitutional Impact of Enlargement at EU and National Level"**, Commissioner Gunter Verheugen considered that any further Intergovernmental Conference (IGC) that may follow the one that should be closed in Nice in December, had not to constitute a precondition for EU enlargement.

The current IGC is sufficient for EU enlargement to the current applicants: "should another Intergovernmental Conference be launched, it should not be a precondition for enlargement", Verheugen declared. According to the Commissioner, there is a "great difference" between the ongoing IGC and the one that could follow: the Amsterdam leftovers and the rest of the Nice agenda concern aspects "intrinsically linked" to the EU's functioning following enlargement, whereas the "post-Nice agenda" is different: the broader institutional debate is legitimate in itself, and applicant countries should have the opportunity to participate and express their opinions.

Mr. Verheugen also took stances on different issues currently being debated in the framework of the IGC on institutional reform, notably:

he spoke in favour of a smaller European Commission after enlargement, in which not all Member States would have "their" Commissioner;

he pleaded in favour of a correction (in favour of the larger States) of the current imbalance within the Council and for the establishment of a link between the number of votes and the population of a Member State;

he said he was in favour of a "generous" extension of qualified majority voting, not because he thought that the new member countries would be less "integration-friendly", but because statistically speaking, the increase in the numbers would invariably make consensus much harder to achieve;

he spoke in favour of flexibility of conditions for enhanced cooperation, on condition, however, that this:

- remains within the institutional framework of the Treaties;
- does not go against existing Community policies;
- remains open to all Member States wanting to participate.

AGENCE EUROPE No. 7824

(EU) EU/ENLARGEMENT: Asser Institute proposes project on development of "European models" of Constitution

The Hague, 18/10/2000 (Agence Europe) – The colloquium at the Asser Institute on "The Constitutional Impact of Enlargement at EU and National Level", held from 20 to 23 September in The Hague with the participation, above all, of representatives of applicant countries, European Commissioner Günter Verheugen, Dutch Justice Minister J.A. Korthals and Netherlands Secretary of State for Foreign Affairs Dick Benschop, resulted in a series of recommendations for the future (see programme of the colloquium in EUROPE of 28/29 August, p. 3).

Thus, the participants took a stance in favour of the suggestion made by the European University Institute in Florence to adapt the Treaty, and some of them (like Advocate-General Francis J. Jacobs) made proposals aimed at reorganising the work of the Court of Justice in order to improve the legal protection of citizens. Furthermore, the Institute, of which Jaap de Zwaan and Alfred Kellermann are President and Secretary-General respectively, hoped to continue work begun by this colloquium, by launching a multi-country project for the development of European models of Constitutions. The officials from the Institute (who recall that the European Commission does not cite the adjustment of national Constitutions in its reports on applicant countries, considering that the Constitutions "belong to the people" of each country) feel that such European models could help the applicant countries to adjust their Constitutions with a view to joining the EU. At the conference in The Hague, states a report by the Asser Institute, most representatives of applicant countries expressed the hope that they would be involved in this project, in which three persons per country could take part – a representative of the judiciary (for example a Constitutional Court, a representative of the government or parliament and a representative of the legal science

ANNEX V

PROTOCOL AND DECLARATION ON ENLARGEMENT ANNEXED TO THE TREATY OF NICE, AS FINALISED BY THE LEGAL/LINGUISTIC EXPERTS WORKING PARTY, BRUSSELS, 14 February 2001

PROTOCOLS

A. PROTOCOL ANNEXED TO THE TREATY ON EUROPEAN UNION AND TO THE TREATIES ESTABLISHING THE EUROPEAN COMMUNITIES

Protocol on the enlargement of the European Union

THE HIGH CONTRACTING PARTIES
HAVE AGREED UPON the following provisions, which shall be annexed to the Treaty on European Union and to the Treaties establishing the European Communities:

Article 1 Repeal of the Protocol on the institutions
The Protocol on the institutions with the prospect of enlargement of the European Union, annexed to the Treaty on European Union and to the Treaties establishing the European Communities, is hereby repealed.

Article 2 Provisions concerning the European Parliament
1. On 1 January 2004 and with effect from the start of the 2004-2009 term, in Article 190(2) of the Treaty establishing the European Community and in Article 108(2) of the Treaty establishing the European Atomic Energy Community, the first subparagraph shall be replaced by the following:
'The number of representatives elected in each Member State shall be as follows:

Belgium	22	Luxembourg	6
Denmark	13	Netherlands	25
Germany	99	Austria	17
Greece	22	Portugal	22
Spain	50	Finland	13
France	72	Sweden	18
Ireland	12	United Kingdom	72
Italy	72		

2. Subject to paragraph 3, the total number of representatives in the European Parliament for the 2004-2009 term shall be equal to the number of representatives specified in Article 190(2) of the Treaty establishing the European Community and in Article 108(2) of the Treaty establishing the European Atomic Energy Community plus the number of representatives of the new Member States resulting from the accession treaties signed by 1 January 2004 at the latest.

3. If the total number of members referred to in paragraph 2 is less than 732, a pro rata correction shall be applied to the number of representatives to be elected in each Member State, so that the total number is as close as possible to 732, without such a correction leading to the number of representatives to be elected in each Member State being higher than that provided for in Article 190(2) of the Treaty establishing the European Community and in Article 108(2) of the Treaty establishing the European Atomic Energy Community for the 1999-2004 term. The Council shall adopt a decision to that effect.

4. By way of derogation from the second paragraph of Article 189 of the Treaty establishing the European Community and from the second paragraph of Article 107 of the Treaty establishing the European Atomic Energy Community, in the event of the entry into force of accession treaties after the adoption of the Council decision provided for in the second subparagraph of paragraph 3 of this Article, the number of members of the European Parliament may temporarily exceed 732 for the period for which that decision applies. The same correction as that referred to in the first subparagraph of paragraph 3 of this Article shall be applied to the number of representatives to be elected in the Member States in question.

Article 3 Provisions concerning the weighting of votes in the Council
1. On 1 January 2005:
(a) in Article 205 of the Treaty establishing the European Community and in Article 118 of the Treaty establishing the European Atomic Energy Community:
(i) paragraph 2 shall be replaced by the following:
'2. Where the Council is required to act by a qualified majority, the votes of its members shall be weighted as follows:

Belgium	12	Luxembourg	4
Denmark	7	Netherlands	13
Germany	29	Austria	10
Greece	12	Portugal	12
Spain	27	Finland	7
France	29	Sweden	10
Ireland	7	United Kingdom	29
Italy	29		

Acts of the Council shall require for their adoption at least 169 votes in favour cast by a majority of the members where this Treaty requires them to be adopted on a proposal from the Commission.

In other cases, for their adoption acts of the Council shall require at least 169 votes in favour, cast by at least two-thirds of the members.'
(ii) the following paragraph 4 shall be added:
'4. When a decision is to be adopted by the Council by a qualified majority, a member of the Council may request verification that the Member States constituting the qualified majority represent at least 62 % of the total population of the Union. If that condition is shown not to have been met, the decision in question shall not be adopted.'
(b) In Article 23(2) of the Treaty on European Union, the third subparagraph shall be replaced by the following text:

'The votes of the members of the Council shall be weighted in accordance with Article 205(2) of the Treaty establishing the European Community. For their adoption, decisions shall require at least 169 votes in favour cast by at least two-thirds of the members. When a decision is to be adopted by the Council by a qualified majority, a member of the Council may request verification that the Member States constituting the qualified majority represent at least 62 % of the total population of the Union. If that condition is shown not to have been met, the decision in question shall not be adopted.'
(c) In Article 34 of the Treaty on European Union, paragraph 3 shall be replaced by the following:
'3. Where the Council is required to act by a qualified majority, the votes of its members shall be weighted as laid down in Article 205(2) of the Treaty establishing the European Community, and for their adoption acts of the Council shall require at least 169 votes in favour, cast by at least two-thirds
of the members. When a decision is to be adopted by the Council by a qualified majority, a member of the Council may request verification that the Member States constituting the qualified majority represent at least 62 % of the total population of the Union. If that condition is shown not to have been met, the decision in question shall not be adopted.'

2. At the time of each accession, the threshold referred to in the second subparagraph of Article 205(2) of the Treaty establishing the European Community and in the second subparagraph of Article 118(2) of the Treaty establishing the European Atomic Energy Community shall be calculated in such a way that the qualified majority threshold expressed in votes does not exceed the threshold resulting from the table in the Declaration on the enlargement of the European Union, included in the Final Act of the Conference which adopted the Treaty of Nice.

Article 4 Provisions concerning the Commission
1. On 1 January 2005 and with effect from when the first Commission following that date takes up its duties, Article 213(1) of the Treaty establishing the European Community and Article 126(1) of the Treaty establishing the European Atomic Energy Community shall be replaced by the following:
'1. The Members of the Commission shall be chosen on the grounds of their general competence and their independence shall be beyond doubt.
The Commission shall include one national of each of the Member States.
The number of Members of the Commission may be altered by the Council, acting unanimously.'

2. When the Union consists of 27 Member States, Article 213(1) of the Treaty establishing the European Community and Article 126(1) of the Treaty establishing the European Atomic Energy Community shall be replaced by the following:
'1. The Members of the Commission shall be chosen on the grounds of their general competence and their independence shall be beyond doubt.
The number of Members of the Commission shall be less than the number of Member States. The Members of the Commission shall be chosen according to a rotation system based on the principle of equality, the implementing arrangements for which shall be adopted by the Council, acting unanimously. The number of Members of the Commission shall be set by the Council, acting unanimously.' This amendment shall apply as from the date on which the first Commission following the date of accession of the twenty-seventh Member State of the Union takes up its duties.

3. The Council, acting unanimously after signing the treaty of accession of the twenty-seventh Member State of the Union, shall adopt:
– the number of Members of the Commission;
– the implementing arrangements for a rotation system based on the principle of equality containing all the criteria and rules necessary for determining the composition of successive colleges automatically on the basis of the following principles:
(a) Member States shall be treated on a strictly equal footing as regards determination of the sequence of, and the time spent by, their nationals as Members of the Commission; consequently, the difference between the total number of terms of office held by nationals of any given pair of
Member States may never be more than one;
(b) subject to point (a), each successive college shall be so composed as to reflect satisfactorily the demographic and geographical range of all the Member States of the Union.

4. Any State which accedes to the Union shall be entitled, at the time of its accession, to have one of its nationals as a Member of the Commission until paragraph 2 applies.

DECLARATIONS ADOPTED BY THE CONFERENCE

20. Declaration on the enlargement of the European Union [1]
The common position to be adopted by the Member States at the accession conferences, as regards the distribution of seats at the European Parliament, the weighting of votes in the Council, the composition of the Economic and Social Committee and the composition of the Committee of the Regions will correspond to the following tables for a Union of 27 Member States.

1. THE EUROPEAN PARLIAMENT

Member States	*EP seats*	*Member States*	*EP seats*
Germany	99	Bulgaria	17
United Kingdom	72	Austria	17
France	72	Slovakia	13
Italy	72	Denmark	13
Spain	50	Finland	13
Poland	50	Ireland	12
Romania	33	Lithuania	12
Netherlands	25	Latvia	8
Greece	22	Slovenia	7
Czech Republic	20	Estonia	6
Belgium	22	Cyprus	6
Hungary	20	Luxembourg	6
Portugal	22	Malta	5
Sweden	18	*Total*	*732*

[1] The tables in this declaration take account only of those candidate countries with which accession negotiations have actually started.

2. THE WEIGHTING OF VOTES IN THE COUNCIL

Members of the Council	*Weighted votes*	*Members of the Council*	*Weighted votes*
Germany	29	Bulgaria	10
United Kingdom	29	Austria	10
France	29	Slovakia	7
Italy	29	Denmark	7
Spain	27	Finland	7
Poland	27	Ireland	7
Romania	14	Lithuania	7
Netherlands	13	Latvia	4
Greece	12	Slovenia	4
Czech Republic	12	**Estonia**	**4**
Belgium	12	Cyprus	4
Hungary	12	Luxembourg	4
Portugal	12	Malta	3
Sweden	10	*Total*	*345*

Acts of the Council shall require for their adoption at least 258 votes in favour, cast by a majority of members, where this Treaty requires them to be adopted on a proposal from the Commission. In other cases, for their adoption acts of the Council shall require at least 258 votes in favour cast by at least two-thirds of the members.

When a decision is to be adopted by the Council by a qualified majority, a member of the Council may request verification that the Member States constituting the qualified majority represent at least 62 % of the total population of the Union. If that condition is shown not to have been met, the decision in question shall not be adopted.

3. THE ECONOMIC AND SOCIAL COMMITTEE

Member States	*Members*	*Member States*	*Members*
Germany	24	Bulgaria	12
United Kingdom	24	Austria	12
France	24	Slovakia	9
Italy	24	Denmark	9
Spain	21	Finland	9
Poland	21	Ireland	9
Romania	15	Lithuania	9
Netherlands	*12*	Latvia	7
Greece	12	Slovenia	7
Czech Republic	12	Estonia	7
Belgium	12	Cyprus	6
Hungary	12	Luxembourg	6
Portugal	12	Malta	5
Sweden	12	*Total*	*344*

4. THE COMMITTEE OF THE REGIONS

Member States	*Members*	*Member States*	*Members*
Germany	24	Bulgaria	12
United Kingdom	24	Austria	12
France	24	Slovakia	9
Italy	24	Denmark	9
Spain	21	Finland	9
Poland	21	Ireland	9
Romania	15	Lithuania	9
Netherlands	12	Latvia	7
Greece	12	Slovenia	7
Czech Republic	12	Estonia	7
Belgium	12	Cyprus	6
Hungary	12	Luxembourg	6
Portugal	12	Malta	5
Sweden	12	*Total*	*344*

21. Declaration on the qualified majority threshold and the number of votes for a blocking minority in an enlarged Union Insofar as all the candidate countries listed in the Declaration on the enlargement of the European Union have not yet acceded to the Union when the new vote weightings take effect (1 January 2005), the threshold for a qualified majority will move, according to the pace of accessions, from a percentage below the current one to a maximum of 73,4 %. When all the candidate countries mentioned above have acceded, the blocking minority, in a Union of 27, will be raised to 91 votes, and the qualified majority threshold resulting from the table given in the Declaration on enlargement of the European Union will be automatically adjusted accordingly.

22. Declaration on the venue for European Councils
As from 2002, one European Council meeting per Presidency will be held in Brussels. When the Union comprises 18 members, all European Council meetings will be held in Brussels.

23. Declaration on the future of the Union
1. Important reforms have been decided in Nice. The Conference welcomes the successful conclusion of the Conference of Representatives of the Governments of the Member States and commits the Member States to pursue the early ratification of the Treaty of Nice.

2. It agrees that the conclusion of the Conference of Representatives of the Governments of the Member States opens the way for enlargement of the European Union and underlines that, with ratification of the Treaty of Nice, the European Union will have completed the institutional changes necessary for the accession of new Member States.

3. Having thus opened the way to enlargement, the Conference calls for a deeper and wider debate about the future of the European Union. In 2001, the Swedish and Belgian Presidencies, in cooperation with the Commission and involving the European Parliament, will encourage wide-ranging discussions with all interested parties: representatives of national parliaments and all those reflecting public opinion, namely political, economic and university circles, representatives of civil society, etc.

The candidate States will be associated with this process in ways to be defined.

4. Following a report to be drawn up for the European Council in Göteborg in June 2001, the European Council, at its meeting in Laeken/Brussels in December 2001, will agree on a declaration containing appropriate initiatives for the continuation of this process.

5. The process should address, inter alia, the following questions:
– how to establish and monitor a more precise delimitation of powers between the European Union and the Member States, reflecting the principle of subsidiarity;
– the status of the Charter of Fundamental Rights of the European Union, proclaimed in Nice, in accordance with the conclusions of the European Council in Cologne;
– a simplification of the Treaties with a view to making them clearer and better understood without changing their meaning;
– the role of national parliaments in the European architecture.

6. Addressing the above-mentioned issues, the Conference recognises the need to improve and to monitor the democratic legitimacy and transparency of the Union and its institutions, in order to bring them closer to the citizens of the Member States.

7. After these preparatory steps, the Conference agrees that a new Conference of the Representatives of the Governments of the Member States will be convened in 2004, to address the above-mentioned items with a view to making corresponding changes to the Treaties.

8. The Conference of Member States shall not constitute any form of obstacle or pre-condition to the enlargement process. Moreover, those candidate States which have concluded accession negotiations with the Union will be invited to participate in the Conference. Those candidate States which have not concluded their accession negotiations will be invited as observers.

ANNEX VI

CHARTER OF FUNDAMENTAL RIGHTS OF THE EUROPEAN UNION
(OJ No. 364 of 18.12.2000)

PREAMBLE

The peoples of Europe, in creating an ever closer union among them, are resolved to share a peaceful future based on common values.

Conscious of its spiritual and moral heritage, the Union is founded on the indivisible, universal values of human dignity, freedom, equality and solidarity; it is based on the principles of democracy and the rule of law. It places the individual at the heart of its activities, by establishing the citizenship of the Union and by creating an area of freedom, security and justice.

The Union contributes to the preservation and to the development of these common values while respecting the diversity of the cultures and traditions of the peoples of Europe as well as the national identities of the Member States and the organisation of their public authorities at national, regional and local levels; it seeks to promote balanced and sustainable development and ensures free movement of persons, goods, services and capital, and the freedom of establishment.

To this end, it is necessary to strengthen the protection of fundamental rights in the light of changes in society, social progress and scientific and technological developments by making those rights more visible in a Charter. This Charter reaffirms, with due regard for the powers and tasks of the Community and the Union and the principle of subsidiarity, the rights as they result, in particular, from the constitutional traditions and international obligations common to the Member States, the Treaty on European Union, the Community Treaties, the European Convention for the Protection of Human Rights and Fundamental Freedoms, the Social Charters adopted by the Community and by the Council of Europe and the case-law of the Court of Justice of the European Communities and of the European Court of Human Rights.

Enjoyment of these rights entails responsibilities and duties with regard to other persons, to the human community and to future generations.

The Union therefore recognises the rights, freedoms and principles set out hereafter.

CHAPTER I

DIGNITY

Article 1
Human dignity

Human dignity is inviolable. It must be respected and protected.

Article 2
Right to life

1. Everyone has the right to life.
2. No one shall be condemned to the death penalty, or executed.

Article 3
Right to the integrity of the person

1. Everyone has the right to respect for his or her physical and mental integrity.
2. In the fields of medicine and biology, the following must be respected in particular:
   - The free and informed consent of the person concerned, according to the procedures laid down by law,
   - the prohibition of eugenic practices, in particular those aiming at the selection of persons,
   - the prohibition on making the human body and its parts as such a source of financial gain,
   - the prohibition of the reproductive cloning of human beings.

Article 4
Prohibition of torture and inhuman or degrading treatment or punishment

No one shall be subjected to torture or to inhuman or degrading treatment or punishment.

Article 5
Prohibition of slavery and forced labour

1. No one shall be held in slavery or servitude.
2. No one shall be required to perform forced or compulsory labour.
3. Trafficking in human beings is prohibited.

CHAPTER II

FREEDOMS

Article 6
Right to liberty and security

Everyone has the right to liberty and security of person.

Article 7
Respect for private and family life

Everyone has the right to respect for his or her private and family life, home and communications.

Article 8
Protection of personal data

1. Everyone has the right to the protection of personal data concerning him or her.
2. Such data must be processed fairly for specified purposes and on the basis of the consent of the person concerned or some other legitimate basis laid down by law. Everyone has the right of access to data which has been collected concerning him or her, and the right to have it rectified.
3. Compliance with these rules shall be subject to control by an independent authority.

Article 9
Right to marry and right to found a family

The right to marry and the right to found a family shall be guaranteed in accordance with the national laws governing the exercise of these rights.

Article 10
Freedom of thought, conscience and religion

1. Everyone has the right to freedom of thought, conscience and religion. This right includes freedom to change religion or belief and freedom, either alone or in community with others and in public or in private, to manifest religion or belief, in worship, teaching, practice and observance.
2. The right to conscientious objection is recognised, in accordance with the national laws governing the exercise of this right.

Article 11
Freedom of expression and information

1. Everyone has the right to freedom of expression. This right shall include freedom to hold opinions and to receive and impart information and ideas without interference by public authority and regardless of frontiers.
2. The freedom and pluralism of the media shall be respected.

Article 12
Freedom of assembly and of association

1. Everyone has the right to freedom of peaceful assembly and to freedom of association at all levels, in particular in political, trade union and civic matters, which implies the right of everyone to form and to join trade unions for the protection of his or her interests.
2. Political parties at Union level contribute to expressing the political will of the citizens of the Union.

Article 13
Freedom of the arts and sciences

The arts and scientific research shall be free of constraint. Academic freedom shall be respected.

Article 14
Right to education

1. Everyone has the right to education and to have access to vocational and continuing training.
2. This right includes the possibility to receive free compulsory education.
3. The freedom to found educational establishments with due respect for democratic principles and the right of parents to ensure the education and teaching of their children in conformity with their religious, philosophical and pedagogical convictions shall be respected, in accordance with the national laws governing the exercise of such freedom and right.

Article 15
Freedom to choose an occupation and right to engage in work

1. Everyone has the right to engage in work and to pursue a freely chosen or accepted occupation.
2. Every citizen of the Union has the freedom to seek employment, to work, to exercise the right of establishment and to provide services in any Member State.
3. Nationals of third countries who are authorised to work in the territories of the Member States are entitled to working conditions equivalent to those of citizens of the Union.

Article 16
Freedom to conduct a business

The freedom to conduct a business in accordance with Community law and national laws and practices is recognised.

Article 17
Right to property

1. Everyone has the right to own, use, dispose of and bequeath his or her lawfully acquired possessions. No one may be deprived of his or her possessions, except in the public interest and in the cases and under the conditions provided for by law, subject to fair compensation being paid in good time for their loss. The use of property may be regulated by law in so far as is necessary for the general interest.
2. Intellectual property shall be protected.

Article 18
Right to asylum

The right to asylum shall be guaranteed with due respect for the rules of the Geneva

Convention of 28 July 1951 and the Protocol of 31 January 1967 relating to the status of refugees and in accordance with the Treaty establishing the European Community.

Article 19
Protection in the event of removal, expulsion or extradition

1. Collective expulsions are prohibited.
2. No one may be removed, expelled or extradited to a State where there is a serious risk that he or she would be subjected to the death penalty, torture or other inhuman or degrading treatment or punishment.

CHAPTER III

EQUALITY

Article 20
Equality before the law

Everyone is equal before the law.

Article 21
Non-discrimination

1. Any discrimination based on any ground such as sex, race, colour, ethnic or social origin, genetic features, language, religion or belief, political or any other opinion, membership of a national minority, property, birth, disability, age or sexual orientation shall be prohibited.
2. Within the scope of application of the Treaty establishing the European Community and of the Treaty on European Union, and without prejudice to the special provisions of those Treaties, any discrimination on grounds of nationality shall be prohibited.

Article 22
Cultural, religious and linguistic diversity

The Union shall respect cultural, religious and linguistic diversity.

Article 23
Equality between men and women

Equality between men and women must be ensured in all areas, including employment, work and pay. The principle of equality shall not prevent the maintenance or adoption of measures providing for specific advantages in favour of the under-represented sex.

Article 24
The rights of the child

1. Children shall have the right to such protection and care as is necessary for their well-being. They may express their views freely. Such views shall be taken into consideration

on matters which concern them in accordance with their age and maturity.

2. In all actions relating to children, whether taken by public authorities or private institutions, the child's best interests must be a primary consideration.
3. Every child shall have the right to maintain on a regular basis a personal relationship and direct contact with both his or her parents, unless that is contrary to his or her interests.

Article 25
The rights of the elderly

The Union recognises and respects the rights of the elderly to lead a life of dignity and independence and to participate in social and cultural life.

Article 26
Integration of persons with disabilities

The Union recognises and respects the right of persons with disabilities to benefit from measures designed to ensure their independence, social and occupational integration and participation in the life of the community.

CHAPTER IV

SOLIDARITY

Article 27
Workers' right to information and consultation within the undertaking

Workers or their representatives must, at the appropriate levels, be guaranteed information and consultation in good time in the cases and under the conditions provided for by Community law and national laws and practices.

Article 28
Right of collective bargaining and action

Workers and employers, or their respective organisations, have, in accordance with Community law and national laws and practices, the right to negotiate and conclude collective agreements at the appropriate levels and, in cases of conflicts of interest, to take collective action to defend their interests, including strike action.

Article 29
Right of access to placement services

Everyone has the right of access to a free placement service.

Article 30
Protection in the event of unjustified dismissal

Every worker has the right to protection against unjustified dismissal, in accordance with Community law and national laws and practices.

Article 31
Fair and just working conditions

1. Every worker has the right to working conditions which respect his or her health, safety and dignity.
2. Every worker has the right to limitation of maximum working hours, to daily and weekly rest periods and to an annual period of paid leave.

Article 32
Prohibition of child labour and protection of young people at work

The employment of children is prohibited. The minimum age of admission to employment may not be lower than the minimum school-leaving age, without prejudice to such rules as may be more favourable to young people and except for limited derogations. Young people admitted to work must have working conditions appropriate to their age and be protected against economic exploitation and any work likely to harm their safety, health or physical, mental, moral or social development or to interfere with their education.

Article 33
Family and professional life

1. The family shall enjoy legal, economic and social protection.
2. To reconcile family and professional life, everyone shall have the right to protection from dismissal for a reason connected with maternity and the right to paid maternity leave and to parental leave following the birth or adoption of a child.

Article 34
Social security and social assistance

1. The Union recognises and respects the entitlement to social security benefits and social services providing protection in cases such as maternity, illness, industrial accidents, dependency or old age, and in the case of loss of employment, in accordance with the rules laid down by Community law and national laws and practices.
2. Everyone residing and moving legally within the European Union is entitled to social security benefits and social advantages in accordance with Community law and national laws and practices.
3. In order to combat social exclusion and poverty, the Union recognises and respects the right to social and housing assistance so as to ensure a decent existence for all those who lack sufficient resources, in accordance with the rules laid down by Community law and national laws and practices.

Article 35
Health care

Everyone has the right of access to preventive health care and the right to benefit from medical treatment under the conditions established by national laws and practices. A high level of human health protection shall be ensured in the definition and implementation of all Union policies and activities.

Article 36
Access to services of general economic interest

The Union recognises and respects access to services of general economic interest as provided for in national laws and practices, in accordance with the Treaty establishing the European Community, in order to promote the social and territorial cohesion of the Union.

Article 37
Environmental protection

A high level of environmental protection and the improvement of the quality of the environment must be integrated into the policies of the Union and ensured in accordance with the principle of sustainable development.

Article 38
Consumer protection

Union policies shall ensure a high level of consumer protection.

CHAPTER V

CITIZENS' RIGHTS

Article 39
Right to vote and to stand as a candidate at elections to the European Parliament

1. Every citizen of the Union has the right to vote and to stand as a candidate at elections to the European Parliament in the Member State in which he or she resides, under the same conditions as nationals of that State.
2. Members of the European Parliament shall be elected by direct universal suffrage in a free and secret ballot.

Article 40
Right to vote and to stand as a candidate at municipal elections

Every citizen of the Union has the right to vote and to stand as a candidate at municipal elections in the Member State in which he or she resides under the same conditions as nationals of that State.

Article 41
Right to good administration

1. Every person has the right to have his or her affairs handled impartially, fairly and within a reasonable time by the institutions and bodies of the Union.
2. This right includes:
   - the right of every person to be heard, before any individual measure which would affect him or her adversely is taken;

- the right of every person to have access to his or her file, while respecting the legitimate interests of confidentiality and of professional and business secrecy;
- the obligation of the administration to give reasons for its decisions.

3. Every person has the right to have the Community make good any damage caused by its institutions or by its servants in the performance of their duties, in accordance with the general principles common to the laws of the Member States.
4. Every person may write to the institutions of the Union in one of the languages of the Treaties and must have an answer in the same language.

Article 42
Right of access to documents

Any citizen of the Union, and any natural or legal person residing or having its registered office in a Member State, has a right of access to European Parliament, Council and Commission documents.

Article 43
Ombudsman

Any citizen of the Union and any natural or legal person residing or having its registered office in a Member State has the right to refer to the Ombudsman of the Union cases of maladministration in the activities of the Community institutions or bodies, with the exception of the Court of Justice and the Court of First Instance acting in their judicial role.

Article 44
Right to petition

Any citizen of the Union and any natural or legal person residing or having its registered office in a Member State has the right to petition the European Parliament.

Article 45
Freedom of movement and of residence

1. Every citizen of the Union has the right to move and reside freely within the territory of the Member States.
2. Freedom of movement and residence may be granted, in accordance with the Treaty establishing the European Community, to nationals of third countries legally resident in the territory of a Member State.

Article 46
Diplomatic and consular protection

Every citizen of the Union shall, in the territory of a third country in which the Member State of which he or she is a national is not represented, be entitled to protection by the diplomatic or consular authorities of any Member State, on the same conditions as the nationals of that Member State.

CHAPTER VI

JUSTICE

Article 47

Right to an effective remedy and to a fair trial

Everyone whose rights and freedoms guaranteed by the law of the Union are violated has the right to an effective remedy before a tribunal in compliance with the conditions laid down in this Article. Everyone is entitled to a fair and public hearing within a reasonable time by an independent and impartial tribunal previously established by law. Everyone shall have the possibility of being advised, defended and represented. Legal aid shall be made available to those who lack sufficient resources in so far as such aid is necessary to ensure effective access to justice.

Article 48

Presumption of innocence and right of defence

1. Everyone who has been charged shall be presumed innocent until proved guilty according to law.
2. Respect for the rights of the defence of anyone who has been charged shall be guaranteed.

Article 49

Principles of legality and proportionality of criminal offences and penalties

1. No one shall be held guilty of any criminal offence on account of any act or omission which did not constitute a criminal offence under national law or international law at the time when it was committed. Nor shall a heavier penalty be imposed than that which was applicable at the time the criminal offence was committed. If, subsequent to the commission of a criminal offence, the law provides for a lighter penalty, that penalty shall be applicable.
2. This Article shall not prejudice the trial and punishment of any person for any act or omission which, at the time when it was committed, was criminal according to the general principles recognised by the community of nations.
3. The severity of penalties must not be disproportionate to the criminal offence.

Article 50

Right not to be tried or punished twice in criminal proceedings for the same criminal offence

No one shall be liable to be tried or punished again in criminal proceedings for an offence for which he or she has already been finally acquitted or convicted within the Union in accordance with the law.

CHAPTER VII

GENERAL PROVISIONS

Article 51
Scope

1. The provisions of this Charter are addressed to the institutions and bodies of the Union with due regard for the principle of subsidiarity and to the Member States only when they are implementing Union law. They shall therefore respect the rights, observe the principles and promote the application thereof in accordance with their respective powers.
2. This Charter does not establish any new power or task for the Community or the Union, or modify powers and tasks defined by the Treaties.

Article 52
Scope of guaranteed rights

1. Any limitation on the exercise of the rights and freedoms recognised by this Charter must be provided for by law and respect the essence of those rights and freedoms. Subject to the principle of proportionality, limitations may be made only if they are necessary and genuinely meet objectives of general interest recognised by the Union or the need to protect the rights and freedoms of others.
2. Rights recognised by this Charter which are based on the Community Treaties or the Treaty on European Union shall be exercised under the conditions and within the limits defined by those Treaties.
3. In so far as this Charter contains rights which correspond to rights guaranteed by the Convention for the Protection of Human Rights and Fundamental Freedoms, the meaning and scope of those rights shall be the same as those laid down by the said Convention. This provision shall not prevent Union law providing more extensive protection.

Article 53
Level of protection

Nothing in this Charter shall be interpreted as restricting or adversely affecting human rights and fundamental freedoms as recognised, in their respective fields of application, by Union law and international law and by international agreements to which the Union, the Community or all the Member States are party, including the European Convention for the Protection of Human Rights and Fundamental Freedoms, and by the Member States' constitutions.

Article 54
Prohibition of abuse of rights

Nothing in this Charter shall be interpreted as implying any right to engage in any activity or to perform any act aimed at the destruction of any of the rights and freedoms recognised in this Charter or at their limitation to a greater extent than is provided for herein.

ANNEX VII

PROJECT PROPOSAL: THE CONSTITUTIONAL IMPACT OF ACCESSION AT THE NATIONAL LEVEL OF THE CANDIDATE COUNTRIES

1. Core Information:

Project name:	The Constitutional Impact of Accession at the national level of the candidate countries
Location:	The Hague, Budapest
Theme:	Preparing the national constitutions and national judiciary of the candidate countries for accession
Target group:	Expert scholars, civil servants, national judiciary, lawyers and members of Parliament of the candidate countries
Submitted by:	T.M.C. Asser Institute, The Hague
To be implemented by:	T.M.C. Asser Institute, The Hague, and European Law Academy, Budapest (Hungary)
Duration:	24 months (September 2001 – September 2003)
Total project budget:	....
Contribution requested:	....
Project Summary:	**summary**

The aim of the project is to raise the awareness of politicians, judges, experts and the general public in the candidate countries for the constitutional problems of accession, the rule of law and legal protection. The practice has shown that there is a growing need to adapt for example the national constitutions and constitutional laws. For some constitutions this adaptation is necessary in order to be able to ratify the Treaty of the European Union. In other constitutions the way in which the texts deal with the European integration process is rather poor. A comparative study will be made of the national constitutional provisions which are contrary to and contradicting to the acquis. In its comparative approach the project would support the efforts of the applicant countries in order to guarantee a more or less uniform legal language concerning EU topics and would stimulate the applicant countries to draft better constitutional texts.

The project would further by training of judges, prosecutors and lawyers in the candidate countries in the field of European law, improve the awareness of the national judiciary of their role as community courts. This is a necessity for the following reasons. The European Commission requires that the candidate countries being a Member should apply and give priority to Community law in the national legal order. For the European Commission it does in theory not matter what the Constitution looks alike, as long as Community law is applied in the national legal order with priority and as long as primacy, direct effect and direct applicability of Community law are recognized by the national courts. To reach such a result not only the texts of the national constitutions are relevant and important, but especially the interpretation ("living constitutions") given by the national judiciary. It is therefore necessary to train the national judiciary in the constitutional impact of accession and therefore in the concept of direct effect of community law.

In the pre-accession period a comparative analysis of the decisions of the national (constitutional) courts giving an interpretation of their constitutional provisions in relation to Europe Agreements would be a necessary element in the training.

2. Project Setting:

The objective of this multi-country project is to support the applicant countries through comparison of their efforts in adapting the *acquis communautaire* in their constitutional practice.

What are the advantages of this project?
The candidate countries may learn from the discussions in such a multi-country project from each other's experiences with adaptation of their national constitutions for EU accession and do not have to re-invent the wheel!

The practice has shown that there is a growing need to adapt the national constitutions or constitutional laws for example in order to be able to ratify the Accession Treaty to the European Union. The Copenhagen criteria for accession - the stability of institutions guaranteeing respect for the rule of law, democracy, protection of minorities and human rights - are topics which are generally laid down in the national constitutions or constitutional laws and practice. For an assessment of how these principles work in practice and to evaluate if the respective rights are also exercised in practice, an analysis of the national constitutional provisions and practice is necessary.

The adaptation or amendment of national constitutions could involve a long period taking into account the complicated amendment procedures. Sharing experiences with other candidate countries and with the Member States lawyers as well as with the European Commission is a need in order to guarantee a more or less uniform legal language concerning EU topics and would stimulate the applicant countries to draft better constitutional texts. The political support in the candidate countries for accession is changing sometimes negatively and could therefore form an obstacle for amendment of the constitution when the amendment procedure takes too much time because it is very rigid. Therefore, improving these procedures is necessary and important.

The target groups of the project will consist of scholars (Janusz Justynski, Nicolas Copernicus University, Torun, Poland, Prof Attila Harmathi, Eötvös Lörand University, Budapest, Hungary; Prof. Jiri Zemanek, Charles University, Prague, Czech Republic; Prof Vlasta Kunova, University of Mateja Bela, Banska Bystrica, Slovak Republic; Primoz Vehar, Slovenia; Evgeni Tanchev, Sofia University, Sofia, Bulgaria; Prof Tanel Kerikmae, Tartu University, Tartu, Estonia), Rodin Sinisa, University of Zagreb, Croatia), civil servants, lawyers and Parliamentarians (for example Anita Usacka, Constitutional Court, Latvia; Gunars Kusins, Head of Saeima Legal Bureau, Riga, Latvia, Vilenas Vadapalas, Vilnius, Lithuania) and also EU constitutional (Bruno de Witte) and legal experts from the EU member states.

The project is aimed to contribute to the current process of transformation in the applicant countries and to strenghten their European integration structures in a comparative and stimulating way.

According to the information received from the Netherlands Ministry of Foreign Affairs and the EU Delegations in some of the applicant countries, no such type of project is being currently implemented.

3. Objectives:

The long-term goal of the project is to contribute to the strenghtening of the **pre-accession process** in the applicant countries. A comparative study on the adaptation of national constitutions and national constitutional practice is necessary for the implementation and the application of Europe agreements, Accession Partnership, etc. in the national legal orders of the countries participating in this project. **The aim of the suggested project proposal** is to raise the awareness of politicians, judges, experts and the general public in the candidate countries for the constitutional problems of accession, legal protection and the rule of law. The Copenhagen accession criteria refer explicitly to democracy, the rule of law, human rights and protection of minorities, topics which are generally regulated by the national constitution or constitutional provisions.

The more specific objectives can be:

– ***Adaptation of the national constitutions***

Practice has shown further that for accession there is a growing need to adapt the national constitutions and constitutional laws for the following reasons.

For some constitutions this adaptation is necessary in order to be able **to ratify the Accession Treaty** to the European Union. The constitutions of the candidate countries may not form an obstacle for accession for the candidate countries to an international organization, as the EU for example is considered.

In some smaller candidate countries, who have regained their independence since 1991 there are political and psychological objections against for example the **transfer of sovereignty**.

In some national constitutions the way in which the texts deal with the European integration process is rather poor and not transparent ("European Deficit"). In its comparative approach, the project would support the efforts of the applicant countries in order to guarantee a more or less **uniform legal language and terminology** concerning EU topics and would stimulate the applicant countries to draft better constitutional texts.

There are many national constitutional provisions which are contrary to and contradicting to the acquis.

An example of the constitutional drafting problems is the wording of transfer of sovereignty in the English text of Article 90 (1) of the Polish Constitution which speaks about *delegation* of the competence of the organs of a State authority to an international organization, whereas it was observed at the conference that it should be *transfer* of the competence to an international organization. The meaning of *delegation* in constitutional law is limited to transfer of powers to a *lower* institution or organization. The transfer of sovereign or state powers to the European institutions is according to Community law, *permanent* and it is not possible, to draw these powers back, as is suggested by the term of delegation.

– ***Adaptation of the national constitutional practice by training the national judiciary*** in the constitutional principles of the EU (supremacy, direct effect, subsidiarity, proportionality etc.).

The project would further by training of judges, prosecutors and lawyers in the candidate countries in the field of European law, improve the awareness of the national judiciary of their role as Community courts. This is a necessity for the following reason.The European Commission requires that the candidate countries being a Member should apply and give priority to community law in the national legal order. For the European Commission it does in theory not matter what the Constitution looks alike, as long as Community law is applied in the national legal order of Member States with priority and as long as primacy, direct effect and direct applicability of Community law are applied by national courts.

– ***Comparative Analysis of national court decisions*** concerning the relationship between the national legal order and the community legal order (Constitutional courts, supreme courts etc)

4. Approach

The project will be executed under the administrative direction and financial supervision of the T.M.C. Asser Institute, The Hague. The Asser Institute will function as the accounting institution for the entire project and will act as the coordinating body, having overall responsibility for the quality of the delivery of the services, the planning timing and the management of the project.

Coordination partner of the Asser Institute will be the European Law Academy in Budapest (seat 1-3, Egytean Square, 1053, Budapest, Hungary). The Academy was established on 1st October 1999 by inter alia the President of the European Law Academy, Professor Lajos Ficzere, Dean of the Law Faculty of the Loránd Eötvös University, and by the Vice President of the European Law Academy, Professor Jenö Czuczai, visiting Professor at the College d' Europe, Brugge, Belgium.

The General Secretary of the T.M.C. Asser Institute, Alfred E. Kellermann, and the vice-president of the European Law Academy, Budapest, will be responsible for the project co-ordination and management of the project.

The English language shall serve as the official language project.

In the preparation of the project it is envisaged that the real execution of the project will commence in September 2001, after the publication of the Conference Proceedings "The Constitutional Impact of Enlargement at EU and National level".

In implementing the project **several study or working parties** have to be established in which all the countries are represented by at least three persons:

a scholar (for example University Professor) and two practitioners (for example judge from national court and civil servant from Ministry). The following sequencing and timing of activities is proposed:

This proposal has been devevoped in the first place only for the ten candidate countries of Central and Eastern Europe. For reasons of practicability and feasibility it has been limited to these ten countries but it could also be enlarged with Cyprus, Malta and Turkey and Croatia.

It is however also possible to implement this multi-country project with a smaller group of countries or even country by country if this would seem necessary for reasons to qualify for a subsidy or grant. However it is an advantage to have a large group of countries for reasons of comparative analysis and to benefit from each other's experiences as well as to lower the overhead costs when organizing the project and its seminars.

Preparatory Phase:
Period: May-September 2001

- Contacting relevant scholars
- Building of the network between Asser Institute and participants
- Establishing a Steering Committee for the project
- Preparing and sending a questionnaire concerning the abovementioned comparative study

First Phase:

Starting September 2001

- Preparing the answers and responses to the questionnaire
- Analysis of the relevance of the existing national constitutional provisions on supremacy of international law versus national law in the candidate countries, the status of implemented international law provisions within the national hierarchy of the legal acts.
- Drawing up of the specific national constitutional provisions which are contrary to and contradicting the *acquis*. They are different for each of the candidate countries – for example for Bulgaria – the ban on foreign physical and legal persons to acquire land property, ban on the formation of ethnic parties, requirements for holding of one and only Bulgarian citizenship to run in parliamentary and presidential elections, direct access of citizens to the Constitutional court etc.
- Adapting constitutional provisions implied for example by
  a) EU citizenship, participation in the local and European Parliament elections
  b) EMU and the Role of the European Central Banks
  c) Borders control and Schengen
  d) the Draft Charter for Fundamental Rights
  e) to the institutional reform of the EU before enlargement
  f) specific national provisions which contradict the acquis communauataire like the acquisition of land and real-estate by non-residents
- Organizing conferences and seminars on these topics for participants and national prosecutors, national judiciary, civil servants etc.

Second Phase: Starting March 2002 – September 2002

Implementing the results from the first Phase

- Drafting of a provisional report per candidate country
- Creating and supplying a common model and list of the constitutional requirements required for full membership. This has to be developed by regular meetings of expert working groups. The task of the team will be to draw the minimum content of the provisions, requirements for adapting the constitution at the moment of accession and to outline future trends in the adapting of the national constitutions.
- Raise the awaireness of politicians, judges, experts and general public in the candidate countries for the constitutional problems of accession, amendments of the constitutions as well as for the problems of harmonization and approximation of legislation as required for accession to the EU. This can be developed by lectures by experts, local conferences, discussion etc.
- Drafting the required constitutional amendments and parliamentary laws in the candidate countries

- Organizing conferences and seminars on these topics for national judiciary, prosecutors, civil servants etc.
- Publication of the results of the questionnaire

5. Relevance

The project is aimed to contribute to the current pre-accession process. In its comparative approach the project could support the efforts of the applicant countries in order to guarantee a more or less uniform legal language concerning EU topics and would stimulate the applicant countries to draft better constitutional texts. The project would raise the awareness of politicians, judges, experts and general public of the candidate countries of constitutional texts for accession.

The project components, the time-schedule foreseen and the definition of the project has resulted in a cost-efficient, feasible, comprehensive and well-defined set of activities with clearly determined operational objectives. The set of defined activities will lead to concrete results within the indicated time-schedule, therefore the output will be verifiable and of great practical use.

With respect to the importance and/or desirability of Dutch involvement, it seems appropriate to point at the results of subsequent discussions between the Ministry of Foreign Affairs and the T.M.C. Asser Institute.

The project will lead to an overview of the necessary amendments of the constitutions and constitutional practice of the applicant countries. As such, the project contributes to the pre-accession efforts of all Central and Eastern countries which apply for membership of the European Union.

The project could also contribute to an adaptation or revision of the national onstitutional texts , in which national constitutional legislators will fully reflect the true importance of the European integration process. Perhaps the development of such European models for national constitutions could also contribute to the development of an European Constitution.

6. Feasibility and Sustainability

The experience and knowledge of the members of the project team and the experience of the T.M.C. Asser Institute with similar projects, familiarity with local conditions and the good relations with the Central and Eastern European counterparts, is of paramount importance, which will guarantee an efficient and cost-effective execution of the project.

In the light of the experience of the T.M.C. Asser Institute with similar projects in several Central and Eastern European countries it can be concluded that the costs relating to the inputs and the actual long-term effects of the project and project-components are rather low. The fact, that the project as such has been initiated by the General Secretary of the T.M.C. Asser Institute together with various Professors coming from different Central Eastern European Countries is a further indication of the interest and sincerity for the Central and Eastern European recipients and a potential for success.

During and after the Asser Conference on the Constitutional Impact of Enlargement at EU and National level, held in The Hague, 20 – 23 September 2000 it was proposed to continue the network of participants of this conference. A proposal was published in the Conference Reader for a multi-country project for the development of some European models of constitutions. These European models of constitutions could be helpful for the candidate countries for the adaptation of their constitutions and a comparative study in a multi-country research project of their constitutions, could make the texts more transparant . At the Conference it was also stated that it matters how the Constitution looks alike for political and psychological reasons with reference to the "European deficit" of some national constitutions.

At the conference most candidate countries expressed their wish to participate in such a multi-country project. (See **Agence Europe 18/10/2000**). It was suggested that from every country three persons would participate. A representative of the judiciary (Constitutional court for example), a representative of Government or parliament and a representative of legal science (Professor of constitutional/or and European law). A side-effect of their participation would be that their skills and knowledge of European and comparative constitutional law would be enlarged.

On the Asser website (www.asser.nl) English texts of the national constitutions of the 13 candidate countries, and relevant documents and literature may be found.

In **May 2001 the Asser Institute will publish the Proceedings of the Conference on the Constitutional Impact of Enlargement** (20-23 September 2000) at EU and National level in bookform. This book will be an excellent manual for the support of the multi-country project.

7. Resources

The various components of the project will be implemented by a project team consisting of senior legal scholars and a project director from the T.M.C. Asser Institute. The project director heads the project management team and is responsible for the overall coordination; he must ensure that all services are delivered in a timely and professional manner.

The project requires also a part-time administrative assistant who is foreseen for the benefit of the preparation and coordination of the project and the comparative research in the Netherlands. This task can be fulfilled by the personnel of the Consultancy Department of the T.M.C. Asser Institute.

The Dutch members of the project-team, including the administrative assistant, will be based at the T.M.C. Asser Institute.

The Central and Eastern European project coordinator will be based at the European law Academy in Budapest.

8. Project Management

The Project Director will be directy involved in the implementation of the project. He will coordinate the activities of the study groups, determine the time-schedule and be responsible for the day-to-day-management.

9. Budget

The budget reflects the employment costs, conferences or semininars, meetings of the study groups and working groups, costs related to short study and research visits (DSA and travel), identification missions and communication, translation, editing, procurement costs and publication costs.

The Hague, 3 March 2001 Alfred E. Kellermann

LIST OF PARTICIPANTS

Fatos Acar, European Parliament, The Netherlands
Anneli Albi, European University Institute, Italy
Ivo Alehno, Riga Graduate School of Law, Latvia
F. Andriessen, ICRI, former member of the European Commission, Brussels, Belgium
Rinse van Arum, European Parliament, The Netherlands
V. Balas, University of West Bohemia, Pilzen, Czech Republic
Antonio Bar Cendón, European Institute of Public Administration, The Netherlands
K. Bard, COLPI, Budapest, Hungary
Bert Barnhoorn, T.M.C. Asser Instituut, The Netherlands
Marjolijn Bastiaans, T.M.C. Asser Press, The Netherlands
D. Belinová, Senate Czech Republic, Czech Republic
D. Benschop, Ministry of Foreign Affairs, The Netherlands
Leonard Besselink, Utrecht University, Instituut voor Staats en Bestuursrecht, The Netherlands
Lammy Betten, University of Exeter, The Netherlands
S. Bleekemolen, Free University Amsterdam, The Netherlands
A. Bloed, COLPI, Budapest, Hungary
Piotr Bodyl, The Netherlands
Lucian Bondoc, The Netherlands
Delfina Boni, University Milan-Bicocca, Italy
G. Bothe, Embassy of Slovenia, The Netherlands
M. Bothe, University of Frankfurt, Germany
Boudren, Office of the Attorney General, Ireland
T. van den Brink, Erasmus University Rotterdam, The Netherlands
T. de Bruin, Ministry of Foreign Affairs, The Netherlands
J.M. Bruno, Embassy of France, The Netherlands
Arnout Brussaard, Ministry of Justice, The Netherlands
A. Brydolf-Berg, NNR Service AB, Sweden
A. Bultena, Erasmus University Rotterdam, The Netherlands
Jadranka Cabric, Ministry for European Integration, Croatia
Tamara Capeta, University of Zagreb, Faculty of Economics, Croatia
Helene Charpenteau, T.M.C. Asser Instituut, The Netherlands
C. Chrysogonos, Thessaloniki, Greece
Inese Cimmermane, The State Chancellery of Latvia, The Netherlands
A. Ciobanu-Dordea, Ministry of Foreign Affairs, Bucharest, Romania
Patricia Conlan, University of Limerick, Ireland
Alison Connolly, Kluwer Law International, The Netherlands
R. Corbett, European Parliament, Strasbourg
F. Cottafavi, Embassy of Italy, The Netherlands
M. Culot, Institute for Legal Science B, Denmark
G. Cumes, Germany
D. Curtin, University of Utrecht, The Netherlands
J. Czuczai, Eotvos Lorand University Budapest, Hungary
A. Dashwood, University of Cambridge, United Kingdom
Gareth Davies, University of Groningen, The Netherlands
Francky Demeester, Berenschot EuroManagement, The Netherlands
J. Demmink, Ministry of Justice, The Netherlands
T. Dolcic, Govt. Office for Legislation, Slovenia
A. Dolezalová, Senate Czech Republic, Czech Republic
Jan Donner, Free University of Amsterdam, The Netherlands
Wybe Douma, T.M.C. Asser Instituut, The Netherlands
M. Eberle, Senate Czech Republic, Czech Republic
Karlis Eihenbaums, Embassy of Latvia, The Netherlands
W.T. Eijsbouts, University of Amsterdam, Hogendorp Centrum, The Netherlands
Elita Ektermane, The State Chancellery of Latvia, The Netherlands
F. Elderson, De Nederlandsche Bank, The Netherlands
N. Emiliou, Ambassador of the Republic of Cyprus, Dublin, Ireland
R. Errera, Council of State, Paris, France
R. Evers, European Parliament, Information Office, The Netherlands
Euripides Evriviades, Embassy of the Republic of Cyprus, The Netherlands
Erik Evtimov, University of Berne, Switzerland
B. Feiertag, Free University Amsterdam, The Netherlands
Erirs Flaumanis, Mission of the Rep. of Latvia, The Netherlands
Simone Folcherts, The Netherlands
Marco Formisano, Italy
G. Garzon Clariana, European Parliament, Luxembourg
W. van Gerven, Catholic University of Leuven, Belgium
Nevenka Gorec, Slovene National Assembly, Legislation and Legal Affairs, Slovenia

L.W. Gormley, Professor, University of Groningen, The Netherlands
G. Grancharova, The Netherlands
S. Griller, Economic University, Vienna, Austria
Pan Guoping, Peking University, Law School, China
A. Halbertsma-Wallemaco, Ministry Social Affairs and Employment, The Netherlands
Heikki Hämäläinen, Bank of Finland, Finland
A.G. van Hamme, European Commission, The Netherlands
S. Harbacevica, Riga Graduate School of Law, Latvia
A. Harmathy, Eotvos Lorand University, Constitutional Court Budapest, Hungary
Ingvill Helland, Norway
W. Henning-Roth, Institute for International Private Law, Germany
Christoph Herrmann, University Bayreuth, Germany
C. Hillion, Centre for European Legal Studies, Cambridge, United Kingdom
E. Hirsch Ballin, Tilburg University, The Netherlands
Michael Hofstotter, T.M.C. Asser Instituut, The Netherlands
G. Hogan, Dublin, Ireland
Fré Hogenbirk, Berenschot EuroManagement, The Netherlands
Félice van Hooff, The Clingendael Institute, The Netherlands
Nicole Hoornweg, European Parliament, The Netherlands
F.G. Jacobs, European Court of Justice, Luxembourg
G. Jambrink, The Netherlands
J. Jans, University Amsterdam, The Netherlands
Eppo Jansen, Information Office European Parliament, The Netherlands
E. Jansen, Ministry of Finance, The Netherlands
Irmantas Jarukaitis, Vilnius University, Faculty of Law, Lithuania
J. Justynski, Nicolas Copernicus University, Torun, Poland
Jongbloed, Jongbloed Juridische Boekhandel, The Netherlands
Sofie Joosse, Wageningen University, The Netherlands
A.E. Kellermann, T.M.C. Asser Instituut, The Netherlands
T. Kerikmae, Tartu University, Tartu, Estonia
Magdalena Klimova, Slovak Republic
H. Koch, Copenhagen, Denmark
Jan Klucka, Constitutional Court, Slovak Republic
Thomas Kolly, Embassy of Switzerland, The Netherlands
M. Koning, The Netherlands
Panos Koutrakos, University of Durham, United Kingdom
Katarina Kraij, Slovene National Assembly, Legislation and Legal Affairs, Slovenia
G. van de Kreeke, De Telegraaf, The Netherlands
Peter van Krieken, Ministry of Justice, IND, The Netherlands
V. Kronenberger, T.M.C. Asser Instituut, The Netherlands
Helle Krunke, University of Copenhagen, Inst. For Legal Sciences, Section B, Denmark
J. Kuderjavy, Embassy of Slovakia, The Netherlands
A.M. Kuijpers, University of Nijmegen, The Netherlands
A.S. Kuipers, Ministry of Justice, The Netherlands
V. Kunova, University of Mateja Bela, Slovak Republic
Eliska Kutenicova, Slovak Republic
R. de Lange, Erasmus University Rotterdam, Faculty of Law, The Netherlands
K. Lenaerts, Court of First Instance, Luxembourg
Atho Lobjakas, Radio Free Europe, Belgium
Anne Looijestijn-Clearie, Catholic University of Nijmegen, The Netherlands
John Louth, Oxford University Press, Academic Division, United Kingdom
Sacha Lüder, Ruhr University Bochum IFHV, Germany
C. Lui, Free University of Amsterdam, The Netherlands
Tamara Maan, T.M.C. Asser Instituut, The Netherlands
P. Maciak, The Netherlands
S. Majovská, Senate Czech Republic, Czech Republic
N. Mansourian, T.M.C. Asser Instituut, The Netherlands
Valentina Marolt, Slovene National Assembly, Legislation and Legal Affairs, Slovenia
M. Mataczynski, University of Poznan, Faculty of Law, Poland
Alison McDonnell, Common Market Law Review, The Netherlands
Bastiaan Meerburg, Wageningen University, The Netherlands
Hans van Meerten, Erasmus University Rotterdam, The Netherlands
Eduardo Menez, MAELP, The Netherlands
Susanne van der Meulen, T.M.C. Asser Instituut, The Netherlands
N.W. Meuter-Dikkers, European Movement, The Netherlands
E. Molier, Ministry of Foreign Affairs, The Netherlands
S. Molnar, Embassy of Hungary, The Netherlands
F. Monasso, Higher Institute for European Studies, The Netherlands
Gaston Moonen, European Court of Auditors, Luxembourg
M. Motoc, Embassy of Romania, The Netherlands
M. Moura Ramos, Court of First Instance, Luxembourg
S.M. Munnikendam, Free University of Amsterdam, The Netherlands

Deirbule Murphy, Office of the Attorney General, Ireland
Frans Nelissen, T.M.C. Asser Instituut, The Netherlands
T.B.H. Nguyen, HEBO, The Netherlands
L. Nieminen, Academy of Finland, Finland
Andras Nikodem, Istvan Bibo College of Law, Hungary
Suzanne Nollen, The Clingendael Institute, The Netherlands
T. Novotny, Senate Czech Republic, Czech Republic
P. van Nuffel, European Commission, Brussels, Belgium
Patricia O'Brien, Permanent Representation of Ireland, Belgium
Van Olst, Reformatorisch Dagblad, The Netherlands
Peter Paczolay, Constitutional Court of Hungary, Hungary
Mira Palhartinger, Slovene National Assembly, Legislation and Legal Affairs, Slovenia
Tanja Pandev, Slovene National Assembly, Legislation and Legal Affairs, Slovenia
M. Patijn, Member of the Dutch Parliament, The Netherlands
P. Pauser, Austria
W. Pedreli, Min. of Int. and Kingdom Relations, The Netherlands
J. Pelle, Erasmus University Rotterdam, Political Science, The Netherlands
G.Chr. Penders, Ministry of Economic Affairs, The Netherlands
L. van der Perk, University of Utrecht, The Netherlands
J. Peters, Ministry of the Interior and Kingdom relations of the Netherlands
J. Petrova Peteva, University of Utrecht, The Netherlands
M.-P. Piriou, European Commission, Batiment DM 24 41150, Belgium
Ramona Piscopo, University of Malta, Malta
Matjaz Pleveij, Slovene National Assembly, Slovenia
L. van Poelgeest, Ministry of Foreign Affairs, DIE, The Netherlands
A. Pohlová, Senate Czech Republic, Czech Republic
Miro Prek, Government Office for European Affairs, Slovenia
E.U.B.J. von Puttkamer, Embassy of Germany, The Netherlands
Agata Racan, Ministry for European Integration, Croatia
E. Rakhou, Leiden University, The Netherlands
Daria Ratsiborinskaya, MGIMO, Moscow, Russian Federation
Bert-Jan Rip, The Netherlands
S. Rodin, University of Zagreb, Faculty of Law, Croatia
Anton Rogelj, Slovene National Assembly, Legislation and Legal Affairs, Slovenia
Maija Sakslin, Social Insurance Institute, Finland
S. Salvina, The State Chancellery of Latvia, The Netherlands
R. Sánchez-Puerta, Embassy of Spain, The Netherlands
A.C. van der Schans, Ressortsparket, The Netherlands
M. Scheltema, WRR, The Netherlands
H.G. Schermers, University of Leiden, The Netherlands
A.H.J.W. van Schijndel, The Netherlands
Marleen Schouten, The Netherlands
A.A.M. Schrauwen, University of Amsterdam, Europa Institute, The Netherlands
Senk, Slovene National Assembly, Legislation and Legal Affairs, Slovenia
B. Sinkovec, Govt. Office for Legislation, Slovenia
Josef Skala, Swiss Institute of Comparative Law, Switzerland
Alja Skebin, Slovene National Assembly, Legislation and Legal Affairs, Slovenia
K. Skoupá, Senate Czech Republic, Czech Republic
Slynn, United Kingdom
Anne-Marie Smits, Utrecht University, The Netherlands
M. Soysal, University of Ankara, Turkey
J. Standera, Senate Czech Republic, Czech Republic
L. Steffková, Senate Czech Republic, Czech Republic
Lena Stenwall, Ministry of Foreign Affairs, Sweden
E. Steyger, Pels Rijcken & Droogleever Fortuijn, The Netherlands
Susanne Suppan, Utrecht University, The Netherlands
Johan Swinnen, Embassy of Belgium, The Netherlands
E. Tanchev, Sofia University, Sofia, Bulgaria
Angelina Tchorbadjiyska, Belgium
Yiannos Tolias, University of Edinburgh, United Kingdom
P. van Tongeren, T.M.C. Asser Press, The Netherlands
P. Tresselt, EFTA Court, Luxembourg
R.J.M. van den Tweel, Pels Rijcken & Drooglever Fortuijn, The Netherlands
A. Usacka, Constitutional Court of Latvia, Latvia
V. Vadapalas, Vilnius, Government of Lithuania, Lithuania
Jean Vandeveld, Bruylant, Belgium
S. Varouxakis, Embassy of Greece, The Netherlands
P. Vehar, Government Office for Legislation, Ljubljana, Slovenia
Kamen Velichkov, Embassy of Bulgaria, The Netherlands
G. Verheugen, EU Commissioner for Enlargement, Brussels, Belgium
Dewi de Veth, HEBO, The Netherlands
F. Vibert, ICRI, London, United Kingdom
Thor Vilhjalmsson, EFTA Court, Luxembourg
D. de Vlieger, University of Regina, Canada
Natasa Vorsic, Slovene National Assembly, Legislation and Legal Affairs, Slovenia

J.S. Watson, Ministry of Economic Affairs, The Netherlands
F. Weiss, University of Amsterdam, The Netherlands
Aleksandra Wentkowska, Poland
J.H.H. Weiler, Harvard Law School, USA, European University Institute (EUI), Florence, Italy
G.R.J. van Wesel, Ministry of Int. and Kingdom Relations, The Netherlands
Ramses Wessel, University of Twente, Center for European Studies, The Netherlands
A. Wessels-Voorbij, T.M.C. Asser Press, The Netherlands
A.J.B. de Wilde, The Netherlands
B. de Witte, European University Institute (EUI), Florence, Italy
J. Wouters, Catholic University of Leuven, Belgium
P.G. Xuereb, University of Malta, Malta
Esther van Zimmeren, Catholic University of Brabant, The Netherlands
J.W. de Zwaan, Erasmus University Rotterdam, The Netherlands
M. de Zwart, European Parliament, The Netherlands

The first session of the Asser Colloquium on European Law was held in 1972. The following is a list of sessions held since 1972:

23 March 1972	Uitvoering Gemeenschapsrecht in de Nederlandse rechtsorde
7 July 1972	Colloquium of law teachers
7 June 1973	Het onderwijs in het Recht van de Europese Gemeenschappen aan de Nederlandse Universiteiten en Hogescholen
6 September 1974	De verhouding tussen het onderwijs in het Europees Recht en het onderwijs in andere juridische vakken
11 September 1975	Rechten van de mens
9 September 1976	Plaats en taak van een Europees Parlement bij een verdere beleidsintegratie op sociaal-economisch gebied in Europa
9 September 1977	Externe betrekkingen van de Europese Gemeenschappen
7 September 1978	De Europese politieke samenwerking
6 September 1979	EEC-Comecon relations
5 September 1980	Uitvoering van het Gemeenschapsrecht in Nederland
4 September 1981	Europeesrechtelijke aspecten van consumentenbescherming
3 September 1982	De rol van de Europese Gemeenschappen in een Nieuwe Internationale Economische Orde
9 September 1983	EEG-Handelspolitiek en beschermende maatregelen tegen de invoer uit derde landen
7 September 1984	Gedifferentieerde integratie in de Europese Gemeenschappen
5/6 September 1985	Experiences and problems in applying the preliminary procedure of Article 177 EEC
5 September 1986	Legal aspects of technological development and cooperation in Europe
4 September 1987	Europees milieurecht: praktische problemen bij de totstandkoming en uitvoering
9 September 1988	Fraude in de Europese Gemeenschappen
8 September 1989	De economische en sociale samenhang in de EG de Europese structuurfondsen
7 September 1990	Een Economische en Monetaire Unie (EMU) in Europa juridische en constitutionele consequenties
12/13 September 1991	Free movement of persons in Europe legal problems and experiences
4 September 1992	Onderwijs Europees Recht in Nederland
3 November 1992	(Extraordinary Session) De BV Nederland op de interne markt
10 September 1993	Externe bevoegdheden van de Europese Unie
9 September 1994	Diversiteit van de besluitvorming van de Europese Unie
14/16 September 1995	The Treaty on European Union Suggestions for revision
13 September 1996	Recente ontwikkelingen op het gebied van de rechtsbescherming in de Europese Gemeenschap
5 September 1997	Ontwikkelingen met betrekking tot art. 90 EG, mede in verband met de privatisering van Nederlandse publieke ondernemingen
4 September 1998	Het begrip flexibiliteit in het Verdrag van Amsterdam
10 September 1999	Recente ontwikkelingen op het gebied van de toepassing van het Europees Kartelrecht
20/23 September 2000	The Constitutional Impact of Enlargement at EU and National Level